AMERICAN EDUCATION

Its Men

Ideas

and

Institutions

Advisory Editor

Lawrence A. Cremin
Frederick A. P. Barnard Professor of Education
Teachers College, Columbia University

Universal Education in the South

Volume II

Charles William Dabney

ARNO PRESS & THE NEW YORK TIMES

*New York * 1969*

Reprint edition 1969 by Arno Press, Inc.

*

Library of Congress Catalog Card No. 70-89170

*

Reprinted from a copy in
The New York State Library

*

Manufactured in the United States of America

Universal Education
in the South

Volume II

ROBERT CURTIS OGDEN

Founder of the Southern Education Conference and its president for thirteen years, chairman of the Southern Education Board, and member of
the General Education Board

Universal Education in the South

BY

CHARLES WILLIAM DABNEY

IN TWO VOLUMES

VOLUME II

THE SOUTHERN EDUCATION MOVEMENT

CHAPEL HILL

The University of North Carolina Press

INTRODUCTION

WELL did Dr. J. L. M. Curry exclaim at the conclusion of the Conference for Education in the South at Winston-Salem in 1901, "Now lettest Thou Thy servant depart in peace, according to Thy word ; for mine eyes have seen Thy salvation!" Obedient to the command of Jefferson to "preach a crusade against ignorance," Curry had for thirty years, as legislator, congressman, and agent for the Peabody Board, been preaching with splendid courage the doctrine of universal education in the southern states. The Conference had just taken steps to organize a "crusade against ignorance," which, he foresaw, would ultimately carry education to all the people of the South.

This volume tells of the origin and development of the Conference, of the Southern Education Board, of its campaign agent, and of the origin of the General Education Board and the various commissions which grew out of it to put a great educational crusade into effect.

The Southern Conference and its Board were propaganda agencies, designed to educate the people about the conditions in the schools and to arouse them to do their duty to the children of the South. The creed of their crusade was universal education: equality of opportunity for all—an idea which, through the influence of the Conference for Education, the Southern Education Board, and the General Education Board, was to conquer the South in the next decade.

It is the purpose of this volume to tell also the story of how the idea of universal education was implanted in the minds of the people—to explain the principles behind it, the conditions and influences which long delayed its general acceptance, and the changes which ultimately made its success possible.

Finally it will show how the example of these Boards led to the projection of other philanthropic movements for the improvement of the health, sanitation, and general educational, economic, and social conditions of the people of the country generally.

Like the previous volume, it is chiefly a biographical history. It tells the story of the Southern Education Movement in terms of the men who by their lives, their words, and their deeds, led a "crusade against ignorance."

CONTENTS

ILLUSTRATIONS

THE SOUTHERN EDUCATION MOVEMENT

"Preach a crusade against ignorance; establish and improve the law for educating the common people."

—THOMAS JEFFERSON

CHAPTER I

THE CONFERENCE FOR EDUCATION IN THE SOUTH

THE ORIGIN OF THE CONFERENCE

THE Conference for Education in the South had its origin in a small meeting of interested persons in the summer of 1898, which was suggested by Dr. Edward Abbott,[1] an Episcopal clergyman of Cambridge, Massachusetts, brother of Dr. Lyman Abbott of New York. Dr. Abbott had attended the conferences on Indian Affairs and on International Arbitration, which had been held at Lake Mohonk, New York, for several years at the invitation of the hospitable Smiley brothers. After traveling through the South, visiting the schools, and learning their needs, Dr. Abbott stopped at Capon Springs, Hampshire County, West Virginia, just across the Virginia line, and proposed to Captain William H. Sale, the proprietor, a former Confederate soldier, that he should invite a conference on southern education to be held at his hotel. After the success of the conferences at Mohonk had been explained to Captain Sale, he took up the matter with great interest and later authorized Dr. Abbott to form a committee to select the persons to be invited and to arrange a program. Thus it was that a Massachusetts minister of the Gospel and a Virginia follower of Lee united to start a great movement for the advancement of education, which, beginning in Virginia, was to be extended to the whole country and finally to be felt in many other parts of the world.[2]

Abbott appointed a committee, consisting of Bishop Thomas U. Dudley of Kentucky, Dr. Hollis B. Frissell of Hampton

---

[1] See letter of Dr. Abbott, quoted by Wickliffe Rose in *The Educational Movement in the South, Report of the United States Commissioner of Education, 1903*, I, 360-61.

[2] In a letter of July 8, 1931, A. B. Hunter writes: "Dr. Edward Abbott and I drew up the program for the First Conference. The project was his. He hoped to get the heads of Negro and Mountain schools together for mutual help. Mr. Ogden lifted the scheme from a provincial project and made it a national one."

3

Institute, the Reverend A. B. Hunter of the St. Augustine School of Raleigh, North Carolina, Dr. Julius D. Dreher, president of Roanoke College, Virginia, and the Reverend George E. Benedict of Cedartown, Georgia. On January 18, 1898, he wrote a letter to each of these gentlemen in which he proposed a conference of four days in June following, to be called "The First Capon Springs Conference on Christian Education at the South." "The plan," he wrote, "of Mr. Sale is to bring together for conference in the neighborhood of sixty leaders in the work of Christian Education among both whites and blacks at the South for the discussion of any matters of common interest.... It is Mr. Sale's purpose to entertain the entire body of invited guests for the whole time designated.... He will expect the conference to cover not less than three days."

Abbott asked for advice as to dates for the meeting, the topics to be discussed, and the list of guests to be invited. The gentlemen were expected to bring their wives. Frissell in replying wrote : "As to the topics, I should think it might be well to discuss the questions of how far the public school system in the South can be improved and made effective, how far it is feasible to introduce industrial education, what the relation of the higher schools and the church schools should be to the public schools, how criminality among Negroes can be decreased, the relation of the churches to the Negro, and in what ways the getting of land and homes by the blacks can be encouraged." Abbott adopted his suggestions in part and announced the first topics to be : How far can the public school system in the South be improved and made effective? and How far is it feasible to introduce industrial education? The subjects thus proposed were to engage the thought of the Conference and the many cooperating associations throughout the southern states for the next fifteen years with the result that these states have had a renaissance of education.

Sale's invitation was sent to about a hundred men and women of insight who had already done notable work for the cause of education in the South, including also General John Eaton, United States commissioner of education, and Dr. Amory D. Mayo, for many years agent of the National Bureau of Education in the South. Evidently feeling that they were starting an important movement, the members signed their names on a page of the minute book which has been preserved.[3]

Among the thirty-six persons in attendance there were fourteen ministers, representing seven religious denominations, and nine presidents and representatives of colleges and schools for both races in the South. Twelve states and the District of Columbia were represented.

THE FIRST CONFERENCE AT CAPON SPRINGS

The conferences met in the little chapel on the grounds of the Capon Springs hotel on Wednesday, June 29, 1898, at 8:30 P.M., and continued in regular session until Saturday night, July 2. This was no mere summer vacation party but a body of serious-minded men, earnestly seeking a way to solve a great national problem.

A committee on permanent organization, of which Dr. Dreher was chairman, reported a plan for the permanent organization of the Conference, which was to hold an annual meeting at Capon Springs in June of each year. The officers elected were: president, Right Reverend Thomas U. Dudley; vice president, Honorable J. L. M. Curry; secretary and treasurer, Reverend A. B. Hunter; and an executive committee of which Frissell was chairman.

Because of the pressing needs of Negro education and because of the presence of a number of educators of Negroes, the discussions of the first Conference gave prominence to the question of Negro education. Frissell read a paper entitled "A Survey of the Field," summarizing the situation with regard to the education of the Negro race in the South. With breadth and fairness he stated the difficult problem of Negro education.[3a]

The Conference was held on the eve of the dawning of a new era for America. It was a grave moment in the history of the nation and a time for solemn thought. While its members were deliberating on educational subjects, Sampson and Schley were watching for the exit of the Spanish fleet at Santiago. Mindful of this, prayer was offered for the soldiers before Santiago. The Conference adjourned on July 3, the day that the

[3] This list is given in Appendix I.

[3a] *Proceedings of the First Capon Springs Conference for Education in the South, Capon Springs, W. Va., 1898*, pp. 3-7.

Spanish fleet was destroyed and Spain was driven from the western hemisphere, yielding to the United States the responsibility for the direction of the life of large bodies of primitive and neglected people to whom our institutions were utterly new. Our nation had become suddenly a world power. The moral and spiritual effect of this stupendous event was felt probably in the South more intensely than in any other section. The South had sent its sons once more to wear the uniform and to follow the flag of the Union. Ex-Confederate soldiers commanded men in blue, and southern boys fought side by side with those of the North. This little war caused a great revival of national consciousness.

A revival of education was to come with the expansion of the influence of the United States throughout the world. As the events of the war opened our minds to the recognition of our obligation to the benighted folk of the other lands, so it deepened our sense of duty to our own people remaining in darkness. As the people of the Philippines, of Cuba, and of Porto Rico, to whom we had now given liberty, were to be prepared for self-government through education, so were the "forgotten men" of the South to be trained in the schools for a richer life and a more perfect citizenship. The teacher, the sanitarian, the scientist, and the agriculturist entered upon a new movement in the South, as well as in these foreign lands, and in time won a victory for civilization far greater than that of the army and the navy. It was a victory over ignorance, setting the minds and hearts of millions free to work out their own destinies in the lands of their fathers.

The Conference made a deep impression upon all its members, as is shown by their correspondence in the interval between it and the next meeting. They were all thinking about making it broader and more effective. At the suggestion of Mr. A. D. Mayo, the name of the Conference was changed from Conference on Christian Education to Conference for Education in the South.

The Second Conference at Capon Springs

As it happened, the majority of the speakers of the first Conference were interested in schools for Negroes, most of them church schools. Commenting on this Mayo wrote to the committee : "I observed in the meeting last year that the majority were interested in one phase of education only and that the one most foreign to the interests of the Southern people ;— the Northern schools for Southern Negroes. It seems to me that by proper representations a convention could be gathered next June that will really be a fair representation of Southern education and that great good will result simply from a hundred people of this sort living together for three days and talking themselves into an understanding of each other's position." The list of persons invited and the discussions of the second Conference show that the committee concurred in these views.

In a letter to Bishop Dudley, Frissell proposed to make the Conference more representative of the South : "If we can get together the leading superintendents of public schools in the Southern States, I think it would be wise." The Conference was being shaped up and finding its mission, which was to be the promotion of universal education in the South. Captain Sale issued invitations to the second Conference to over a hundred ladies and gentlemen, seventy-five of whom attended the meeting in June, 1899. The most notable man in a distinguished list of new members at the Conference was Robert Curtis Ogden of New York, who was destined to become the leader of the movement.

Ogden, who was president of the board of trustees of Hampton Institute, had been in the habit of taking a number of gentlemen to the commencements at Hampton as his guests. A believer in the effectiveness of social contact, he thought nothing promoted friendly understanding so much as the informal conversations of men and women when thrown together on excursions. Following his custom, Mr. Ogden brought to this Conference in his private car some twenty-five ladies and gentlemen from the North. This was the first of a series of excursions into the South, organized and conducted by him, which were described by Walter Hines Page as "excursions into ennobling experiences." Ogden's guests on this occasion included among others Mr. George McAneny of New York, President James MacAlister, Dr. J. L. M. Curry and Mr. A. D. Mayo of Washington, General Guy V. Henry, former governor of Porto Rico, Dr. George S. Dickerman of New Haven, Mr. William J. Schieffelin of New York, and a number of professors from Teachers College, Columbia University, and Hampton Institute.

Another notable addition was Mr. George Foster Peabody, the philanthropist and publicist of New York, who brought in his private car a company including among others the Reverend S. D. McConnell of Brooklyn, Dr. Edwin Knox Mitchell of Hartford, Dr. Albert Shaw of the *Review of Reviews,* Mr. St. Clair McKelway of the *Brooklyn Eagle,* Mr. Clark B. Firestone of the *Evening Mail* of New York, and Stanhope Sams of the *New York Times.* The eastern papers carried good reports of the proceedings of these conferences. It was significant that the southern papers scarcely noticed the first three meetings at all.

In addition to gentlemen present at the first meeting, the South was represented by President William L. Wilson and Honorable Henry St. George Tucker, of Washington and Lee University, Professors Ormond Stone and Charles W. Kent of the University of Virginia. Mr. William H. Baldwin, Jr., president of the Long Island Railway, who, as president of the Southern Railway, had become deeply interested in southern educational problems, and Mr. Alexander Purves, treasurer of Hampton Institute, were to become powerful factors in the Conference. Dr. Curry was unanimously elected president, Mr. Ogden vice president, and Dr. Hunter secretary-treasurer.

Curry's address on "Education in the Southern States" was a forcible presentation of the great difficulties in the way of progress in public education in the southern states and of the ways to overcome them. As this address furnished the basis of all the discussions in the Conference for sixteen years, and was the starting point of the campaign, it is printed as Appendix II.[4]

Coming as it did from a former member of the Confederate Congress and soldier in the Confederate army who had already been campaigning for years for schools for all the people, this address now became in a sense the charter of the Conference. Universal education—the training of both races in the South, beginning with the neglected whites and the development of Negro leaders—was henceforth its aim. The Conference, which at its first meeting devoted much of its time to the discussion of church and private schools for the Negroes, was now broadened into a movement for the training of citizens of all classes through the public schools.

[4] See p. 531, below.

Dr. Curry named the committee on resolutions as follows : Dr. MacAlister as chairman, and Dr. Albert Shaw, Professor Kent, and Messrs. Tucker, Bigelow, Woodworth, and Purves. The report of this committee, which was written by Shaw, was the first declaration of the Conference. After congratulating the Conference on the breadth of the discussions and calling attention to its value as a means for the exchange of opinion and the stimulation of thought and effort, and as a clearinghouse of information, the report affirms :

That the education of the white race in the South is the pressing and imperative need, and the noble achievements of the Southern Commonwealths in the creation of common-school systems for both races deserve the sympathetic recognition of the country. . . .

That the Conference recognizes the discernment and wisdom of the pleas that have been made in its sessions for the encouragement of secondary schools in the South, as a necessary link between the common schools and the colleges. . . .

That in the development of industrial education upon lines now well established by noteworthy models, the Conference recognizes a basis for hearty and united coöperation on the part of all friends of Southern education, and further recognizes it as a hopeful means towards the better working out of existing social, economic, and racial problems. . . .

That the Conference gives its grateful endorsement to the wise and helpful administration of the Slater and Peabody funds ; that it pays tribute to the rare comprehension and high devotion with which Dr. Curry performs the duties . . . devolving upon him under those trusts ; . . . that we commend the work of teachers' institutes at the South as promoted by Dr. Curry, and appeal for the improvement, by all possible means, of the lot of the young women teachers of the common schools.[5]

The committee proposed finally that the executive committee be authorized to employ an agent to work under its president, Dr. Curry, "whose duty it will be to study conditions in detail, and to ascertain such facts with respect to Southern education, both public and private, as will make more clear what methods and agencies are to be encouraged, . . . and will secure better harmony and a more efficient concentration of effort in all educational work carried on in the South." Dr.

[5] *Proceedings of the Second Capon Springs Conference for Education in the South, Capon Springs, W. Va., 1899,* pp. 7-8.

George S. Dickerman, of New Haven, Connecticut, served very effectively in this capacity for several years.

His membership on the committee on resolutions was the beginning of Albert Shaw's active service to the Conference, the Southern Education Board, and the General Education Board. A profound student of history and political science, with a great store of knowledge, Shaw has a breadth of view and an enthusiasm for service that has made him a leader in many causes. A friend once described him happily as a "practical fanatic." [6]

Shaw had always been deeply interested in southern affairs, had many friends among southern men, and had been greatly helpful in promoting many movements for southern advancement. From this time forward, he became an enthusiastic worker for the cause of education. A wise and faithful counselor in both the Southern and the General Education Board from the beginning, he had a large part in formulating their policies and in directing their work. Because of his literary ability, he was usually called upon to write the announcements for publication. By giving his time generously for visitations and conferences, and by public speech on many platforms, by reporting the progress and advocating the methods in his magazine, Shaw contributed greatly to the success of the enterprise.

THE THIRD CONFERENCE AT CAPON SPRINGS

The Third Conference for Education in the South met on the renewed invitation of Captain Sale at Capon Springs on June 27, 1900. Curry, the president, made an address on the objects of the Conference and surveyed the field of southern education. The address was unfortunately not reported.

The majority of the persons attending the third Conference, like those attending the preceding ones, were interested primarily in Negro education, with the result that the discussions were chiefly devoted to that subject.

Captain Charles E. Vawter, who had been one of Stonewall Jackson's "foot cavalry," a principal of the Miller School of Albemarle County, Virginia, a pioneer industrial school for white orphans, introduced his address with a humorous reference to this matter: "I count myself most happy, after the

[6] Edward Cary, in the *New York Times*, May 4, 1902.

great flood of eloquence that we have had here today in behalf
of Negro education, to have the opportunity of calling your
attention to the needs of the white race in the South and to the
rich results that can be secured by work in this field. I rejoice
in the favorable reports that have been made of your great
work in uplifting the Negro. You have before you in that field
a most difficult and intricate problem. For four long years, first
under Jackson and then under Lee, I did my best to relieve
you good people of the North of this great problem, and I
have never apologized for my earnest efforts in your behalf.
But we failed. You won, and thereby fell heir to this difficult
task. My sympathies are with you in this great work. You are
learning most useful lessons. You are doing great good, and
notwithstanding the forebodings of some who look only upon
the dark side, you will ultimately win, through the power of
Him who 'maketh even the wrath of man to praise him.' "

It was now agreed by all the members that the best way to
provide training for the Negroes was first to provide adequate
schools and training for the neglected whites. The educational
problem of the South was one problem, not two, and could not
be treated by separate measures. Separate schools there must
be, but these schools would have to be provided in one body
of laws and the system supported by taxes by all the people.
As the whites must inevitably pay the greater part of these
taxes, they must first be convinced that the only way to make
good and useful citizens of the Negroes was through proper
training in the schools. The discussions in all the meetings which
followed were therefore devoted to the needs of the schools
for both races.

Robert Curtis Ogden of New York, who had attended the
previous meeting as a listener, was unfortunately detained, and
therefore sent his paper on "The Objects of the Conference as
Seen by a Northern Business Man," which was most effective in
shaping the future work of the Conference. He began by
pleading for frankness in all discussions by men of the South
and those of the North. Northern men, he said, desire to help
in solving the problems of the South, and southern men must tell
them how they can do this :

In my judgment as a business man, this Conference can find a
wide sphere of salutary influence by bringing the subject of popu-

lar education urgently before the business men of the South as a business proposition, touching very closely their individual and collective interest.... Make the business man see that ... the common school, through the power of popular education, evokes forces that make for progress—progress that radiates wealth, refinement, intellectual power; progress that makes life happier by lessening the strain of anxiety and care; progress that gives intelligence to the State, and commands respect for the town....

The moment is opportune for such an appeal to the intelligent self-interest of the practical men of affairs in the education of all the people of the South.... As a class they have much to learn, and most especially should they realize that to them is committed, more than to any other class, the responsibility for the solution of the grave social and economic questions peculiar to their section.[7]

This frank suggestion impressed the members favorably. When Curry declined reëlection as president on account of the condition of his health the members immediately recognized that they had found their new leader. The Conference unanimously elected Ogden president, a position he was to hold for thirteen years. From this time on, the cause was more and more incarnated in his personality. He became the leader of the campaign, the Richard Coeur de Lion of the crusade for universal education in the South.

The Conference had now found itself, and future discussions and the work of the agencies it established were henceforth devoted to the two great problems of universal education—the training of all the people, both whites and blacks, for citizenship and service—and, as a means to this end, the development of agricultural and industrial education in accordance with the requirements of the states. The idea that was to conquer the South was now defined and accepted by all.

THE QUESTION OF FEDERAL AID

The question of aid from the national treasury for the public schools of the country had been before Congress since 1871, when Senator Hoar of Massachusetts presented the first bill for this purpose. While written so as to apply to the entire United States, this bill, and the others which followed it, were

[7] *Proceedings of the Third Capon Springs Conference for Education in the South, Capon Springs, W. Va., 1900*, pp. 24-28.

designed specifically to help the southern states establish efficient systems of education. Senator Hoar's bill provided that, in case any of these states did not have a system of schools for elementary education, the president was to appoint for each of them a superintendent of national schools, who should establish and conduct such a system. There were to be inspectors appointed by the secretary of the interior for each congressional district and local superintendents in the school districts. The financial support was to be derived from a direct tax and $50,-000,000 was to be levied annually in the several states, to be assessed and collected by national agents. The southern people objected strenuously to this movement because it tended to establish federal control of education in the states. After what they had seen of the schools for Negroes conducted by the Freedmen's Bureau they were thoroughly justified in opposing any such measures. The Hoar bill was also opposed by the National Educational Association and finally failed.

Realizing the great error of enfranchising the Negroes before preparing them for citizenship and the moral responsibility of the country for training them, realizing also the needs of the southern people themselves, who through war and Reconstruction had been stripped of most of their property, patriotic citizens sought to find some way in which the nation as a whole could help the southern states to solve this problem. Various proposals were made to find the money and to overcome the objections made. The most feasible one seemed to be the appropriation of the proceeds from the sale of public lands, which had always been considered the property of the states. The United States commissioner of education, General John Eaton, regularly in his reports between 1870 and 1886 recommended: "That the whole or a portion of the net proceeds arising from the sale of public lands shall be set aside as a special fund, and its interest be divided annually, pro rata between the people of the several states and territories and the District of Columbia, under such provisions in regard to amount, allotment, expenditure, and supervision as Congress in its wisdom may deem fit and proper."

In 1883 a bill was proposed by Senator Henry W. Blair, of New Hampshire, appropriating from the federal treasury $77,-000,000 for the promotion of education in the various states, the distribution to be in proportion to the percentages of the illiterates in the population. The bill thus contemplated larger grants proportionately to the southern states than to the other states, and was a frank effort to aid the South to educate its people, both black and white. The objectionable features of the Hoar bill, providing for the centralization of control, were eliminated from this bill, but it was still opposed by many of the strongest men in Congress. Three times, bills similar to this one were passed with good majorities in the Senate, but in each case they failed to receive favorable action in the House of Representatives. The division of the votes on these bills was never on sectional or party lines.

The discussion was long and in the end did good in enlightening the country on the subject. Some members feared that national aid to schools would demoralize the people of the whole country in the performance of their duty. Some leading southerners continued to oppose the Blair bills on constitutional grounds.[8] Since the foundation of the government, they maintained, schools had been a local matter with the states, and the nation should not interfere with them in any way. It must be realized that the nation could not support all of the schools of the country continuously and had best leave the whole business of schools to the people of the different states and localities. They believed that it was wiser to wait for a generation in the hope that the southern people would recover their fortunes than to make this beginning with national aid, which would certainly increase and would inevitably lead to the centralization of the administration of the schools.

On the other hand, many southerners argued that appropriations from the public land fund might be made by straight-out gifts from the national treasury, to be disbursed by the state authorities, who would administer the schools. Such national aid to education was no new thing. Since the beginning, the government had been distributing the proceeds of the sales of public lands to the states, which had usually been devoted by them to purposes of education. The government had in 1862 given land scrip to establish agricultural and mechanical colleges. In 1887 it had appropriated money directly from the treasury to establish agricultural experiment stations in connection with these colleges and had supplemented the funds of both the colleges and the stations by several acts providing for instruction

[8] See letter of J. B. Minor, p. 16, below.

in agriculture and mechanic arts. The school men of the South generally adopted the latter views, which did not interfere with their theories of states' rights.[9]

After the failure of the Blair bill in 1888, the matter was dropped for some years. In 1896 a committee of college presidents, including Presidents James B. Angell of the University of Michigan, William O. Thompson of Miami University, Ohio, Robert B. Fulton of Mississippi, and A. S. Draper of Illinois, presented a memorial from the National Association of State Universities petitioning Congress to make an equitable adjustment of the grants of lands to the several states as a means of providing funds for the public schools and the universities; but nothing was done.

Dr. Edward Abbott had asked at the second Conference for time to be set aside for the discussion of national aid for the schools, but the Conference did not reach the subject until the third meeting. Welsh, of Philadelphia, introduced a resolution favoring national aid, which after some discussion was adopted without revision on Thursday evening, June 28, and the executive committee was directed to get the people of all sections of the country to petition Congress for such appropriations. The next morning, President W. L. Wilson, of Washington and Lee, who had been detained by illness from the meeting the evening before, expressed his earnest dissent as a member of the committee on resolutions, and asked permission to present his views. After reconsideration was agreed to, he made a forcible and eloquent address opposing the whole theory of national aid. He opposed the proposal on constitutional grounds and pleaded that the southern people be given time to work out their own salvation and that of their former slaves through their own efforts. He had been a member of Congress when the matter was before it and was convinced that funds could not be given from the national treasury without following them up by the control of the schools, and that this was dangerous to the local governments. After hearing him, the resolution was referred back to the committee for reconsideration. There it slept forever afterwards. Unfortunately there is no record of

[9] See article on "National Aid to Education a Continuation of a Policy Already Begun," by Professor E. J. Jones of the University of Pennsylvania, *Andover Review*, V, 250. Extract quoted in Senator Blair's speech, Feb. 19, 1890, published in the *Congressional Record* of Feb. 3-March 7, 1890, p. 1494.

President W. L. Wilson's address. National aid was never taken up again by the Conference.

A proposal to petition Congress for federal aid for the schools having been presented to the legislature of Virginia of 1870, Dr. John B. Minor, the great professor of law at the University, in a letter to Dr. W. H. Ruffner, superintendent of schools of Virginia, of May 28, 1870, presented forcibly the views and feelings of the leading southerners of this period and doubtless reflected the view held by President W. L. Wilson.

You must not suppose me so "scholastic," as to regulate my political principles by my "hates." My objection to taking money from Congress for school purposes lies much deeper than the indignant resentment with which I regard the radical wrongs heaped upon me. It rests upon the conviction that, bad as the dependence is, yet the despised and isolated limitations of the Constitution, constitute the only compact which protects us, the weaker party, against the as yet untried outrages of a wicked, malignant and greedy majority, and that for us to solicit, or even to acquiesce in, the exercise of powers plainly not warranted by the Constitution, and subversive of all its safeguards, is to sell our birthright for less than a mess of pottage ; ... it is to surrender the citadel of freedom for a paltry bribe ; it is to unite with the worst men in this country, ... to pull down that structure which Virginia did so much to rear ; under whose shelter, if we are as true and steadfast as our fathers were, and as it becomes men descended from Saxon lines to be, our children may and will rejoice as the heirs of a rational freedom, founded on Constitutional guarantees and protected by the acknowledged rights and powers of the States.

As one of the oldest and not the least devoted of the friends of popular education in the State, I entreat you to beware how you muddle with this fatally edged, and *poisoned* tool! The very men who would persuade you to essay approaches to the powers at Washington, will not be there, on one pretext or other, to disown the proceeding when they feel the ground-swell of popular sentiment rising against it.

If indeed Congress shall be just enough to inaugurate the policy which ought to have been adopted long ago, of dividing amongst all the States, according to population, the proceeds of the public lands, I would not refuse our share and would not vex myself that the condition was annexed that the fund should be employed in education—whilst I might regard it as impertinent. But that proposition is very different from a humiliating dole of Pecksniffian charity from the Federal treasury, which would be the precedent and the excuse for ultimately assuming jurisdiction over the subject.[10]

THE SOUTHERN EDUCATIONAL ASSOCIATION

The friends of the southern schools had not been oblivious to their condition and for some years had been trying to start a movement for their improvement. Previous to these conferences they had made efforts to start a campaign to educate the people about the schools and to arouse them to pass the necessary laws and to appropriate the needed funds to make them what they should be, but they had not found the right organization to carry on such a campaign. It was first thought that this might be done through the Southern Educational Association.

The Southern Educational Association, an organization made up of the superintendents and principals of schools, teachers in the high schools and normal schools, college men, and such friends of education as chose to join, had been in existence for some years and had departments of superintendence, higher education, secondary education, elementary education, normal education, industrial education, and kindergarten, similar to the National Education Association. Several efforts had been made to get this association organized for a campaign for better public schools, but without success. At the New Orleans meeting, under the presidency of George J. Ramsey, a move was made to inform the people of the South about the real condition of their schools and to inaugurate measures for their betterment. But the members did not take hold. The association was useful for discussion, but not competent for the kind of propaganda that was needed. First of all, it was necessary that the people be informed fully about the wretched condition of the schools.

About this the university and college men, who for many years had been having a hard struggle to keep up their own institutions, were either uninformed or indifferent. Many of the men in the church colleges were still doubtful about the public schools. The state superintendents, generally political

[10] This was written in 1870 and is in the collection of papers of William H. Ruffner in the Historical Foundation of the Presbyterian and Reformed Churches at Montreat, N. C.

appointees, were afraid to discuss the question of Negro schools and to tell the truth about the illiteracy of the population and the condition of the rural schools.

The fact of it was that the Southern Educational Association was too much under the influence of the politicians and their friends, the school book and school supply agents, to be used as the basis of a campaign. It was necessary that some independent, outside force should create an opportunity for the friends of the schools to get together and make the fight for better laws and larger appropriations. This opportunity was provided by the Southern Education Conference and its executive agent, the Southern Education Board, the story of which is told next.

CHAPTER II

ROBERT CURTIS OGDEN

THE NEED FOR A LEADER

A NEW day was now dawning for schools in the South. The people were waking up and learning coöperation in the newly established democracy. The seed sown by the fathers was springing up, and the fields in many places were already ripening. Workers were ready to go into the harvest, but they needed to be united. The Conference for Education had found its task and defined its purpose—to help establish in all the southern states free public schools for both blacks and whites, which should show them how to live and how to make a living. The first thing to be done was to bring together the scattered workers in the different states, organize them under leaders, and provision them for their task.

The gallant Curry, who for forty years had been pleading the cause of the children, encouraging the lone workers for education, and helping schools wherever they started, had now nearly spent his powers and was about to pass from the scene. For organizing a new campaign as wide as the whole South, raising funds for it, and directing it, a new type of leader was needed. So far the movement had been supported chiefly by the impoverished people of the South, and the work had been done by southern men. Federal aid had not been granted. George Peabody and John F. Slater, recognizing the need and the opportunity, had sent first Sears and then Curry into the field. The government Bureau of Education under Commissioner William T. Harris had sent Mayo to investigate, to advise, and to encourage. These men had been of great assistance, but a dispersed army, composed mostly of school teachers, was making slow progress. Now, at last, universal education for the South had come to be recognized as a matter of wide national interest, one calling for the help of all the people, business and professional men as well as teachers, the North as well as the South. Since it was finally settled that the government was not to help, it was necessary for citizens to make the fight in their private capacity. A great volunteer army was gathering, and it needed a volunteer commander.

The people of the South must establish, and in the end support, their own schools, but citizens from other parts of the country could help. The purpose of the Conference for Education in the South was to encourage and to aid the southern people to build their own schools and provide for their administration and support. It was to be primarily a campaign of southern men and women for southern schools.

THE MAN FOR THE TASK

Seeing this opportunity for a great service, a few northern men, inspired by the example of Peabody and Slater, had already offered their assistance. Chief among those who came forward at this important juncture was Robert Curtis Ogden of New York. Having been interested in education in the South for many years, he was prompt to respond when his friend, Frissell, showed him the opportunity offered by the Conference. No sooner had his address been read at the second Conference than it was unanimously agreed that the new leader was found. In response to earnest solicitation and after careful investigation and consideration of the situation, Ogden took up the task with superb energy and devotion, and for thirteen years gave it freely of his thought, his time, and his means. The complete story of his life and activities in the cause of education cannot be told here ; but Ogden's personality became such a great factor in the movement that a description of the man, of his preparation for the work, and of his methods is advisable before taking up in detail, in later chapters, his work for southern education.[1]

Robert Curtis Ogden was the product of two of the strongest stocks forming our early American population. His father was of sturdy English, Puritan blood, and his mother was Scotch-Irish. An able business man and useful citizen, commissioner to the General Assembly of the Presbyterian Church, president of an insurance company, and a member for two terms of the legislature of New York, the father lived until 1893 to see his son take a high position in the business world and the church. His mother is described as "a large, handsome, far-

---

[1] P. W. Wilson has written his life, *An Unofficial Statesman—Robert C. Ogden,* published in 1924.

sighted lady who knew her son for the man he was to be,"
and trained him to strict and prompt attention to every duty.

In one of those simple brick houses with green shutters and
white marble steps, so characteristic of old Philadelphia, Robert
Curtis Ogden was born on June 20, 1836, and delivered into the
kind arms of an old Negro nurse. Did the love bestowed by
the black mammy upon her white child have any influence in
implanting in him that interest in her race which made him
one of the truest friends it ever had?

The boy's early schooling was brief, but excellent. He was
sent to the James Academy, a typical classical school, the best
in Philadelphia at the time. Although he did not finish the
course, the thorough training in the literary branches, which he
there received, laid the foundation for the boy's future self-
education.

Where did Ogden get that remarkable culture, that clear-
ness of thought, that penetrating insight into all kinds of situations, that command of strong English in both writing and
speaking, that made him such a fine advocate and leader? Much
was due to his excellent natural endowments. These were improved by constant study of both men and books. He read
books but he also read men. Life was his school, the life of the
home, the life of the store, and especially, as we shall see, the
life of the Sunday school and of the church. In a letter to his
granddaughter he says : "This matter of education is hard and
it is well that it is so. The people that must work the hardest
for an education are the ones that appreciate it most thoroughly."

When twenty years of age he commenced teaching in a
Sunday school in Brooklyn. Upon his removal to Philadelphia,
he immediately took up this work again and was made superintendent in The Holland Memorial Chapel, where he served
for eighteen years. He was a popular teacher and his room was
always crowded with visitors. When Holland Church was
organized in 1882 he was elected president of its board and
continued in the office until his removal to New York. In this
church, which is regarded as his monument, a stained-glass
window, with the figure of Joshua clad in armor with sword and
helmet, and the motto "Be strong and of good courage," was
dedicated to his memory in 1915.

In the Sunday school Ogden got much of the preparation

for his future social service. He read widely, but he said, "The Bible, especially the New Testament, is the greatest sociological treatise in existence." "No code of laws and ethics is so complete, satisfactory, and conclusive in the decision of all questions of duty between man and man." He also constantly mentioned Emerson, Browning, Matthew Arnold, and William Morris. Ogden was at times critical of the differences, the contentions, and the methods of the churches. In a letter he says, "By Christianity I do not mean the slow coach, the Church. The Protestant Church of America is a failure very largely. Its failure is giving socialism a chance.... The religion of Jesus Christ is pure democracy." In scientific theology he had little interest. Applied Christianity was his specialty. "My whole thought," he says in another place, "is of those who are not friends of God." "Jesus is a living fact—not an awful dogma." "I have no science of God, no theology. All I know—how little it is!—is out of limited personal experience." "Theological controversies die, love lives."

The church gave Ogden intellectual training, a knowledge of the Bible, "the best library in the world," a command of language, experience in teaching and speaking, a fine literary style, a knowledge of human nature, and training and experience in organizing men. From it he got his preparation for his successful leadership in public service. It rescued the business man from materialism and made him a practical philanthropist.

Meanwhile Ogden was going to another great school, the school of business. Having in 1854 followed his father to New York, he entered with him into the employment of a firm of clothing merchants. With this firm he continued for twenty-four years, rising from a clerkship to the position of a partner and general manager. The period Ogden spent with the company was rich in experience but also full of severe trials. It was while there that the young man had his first contact with southern people. In February, 1861, he was sent by his firm on a trip through North Carolina and Virginia to collect some bad debts and was there when the feeling against the North was very hot. Meeting some difficulty in getting home, he appealed to a friend who was the secretary of Governor John W. Ellis of North Carolina, himself a leader in the secession movement. Governor Ellis gave him an official pass, which said that "Robert C. Ogden of the City of New York is a merchant of good standing and his relations to us are such as to entitle him to our respect and patronage." This note gave him safe conduct to his home. Forty years later he returned to North Carolina as head of a great educational movement to help the South. He needed no pass.

During the business depression following the panic of 1873, Ogden was severely tried by the unreasonableness of his chief, who was disposed to hold him responsible for conditions which he had not given him the power to control. A man of masterful nature and sensitive honor, he continued to struggle with the situation until 1877, when he asked the dissolution of the partnership. Receiving an offer from John Wanamaker, he went to Philadelphia to take the management of a large establishment.

"Business Idealism"

Ogden was now forty-three years of age. He had had rich experience and hard training for thirty years and was much more matured than most men of his age. He entered now upon a period which was to be congenial, happy, and successful. When, therefore, in 1896 John Wanamaker took over the old A. T. Stewart store in New York, he asked Ogden to take charge of it.

In an article on "Business Idealism," published in *The Business World* of New York, Ogden gives his business code:

What do we mean by business? Business includes all money-gaining occupations, individual or corporate, industrial or commercial, that produce the means to meet our personal needs, the support of our dependents, the cause of education, the gratification of tastes, the claims of philanthropy, the exactions of taxation, and the other manifold demands for money.

What do we mean by idealism in business? ... It is made up of the highest ethical principles the mind can conceive controlling character and conduct....

In making these definitions of business and idealism, we stand, as did the Israelites of old, "between the mountains of the blessing and the mountains of the cursing"; that is, between the command, "Thou must," and the demand, "Thou shalt not." ... Is there, or is there not, an impassable gulf fixed? Can we maintain the activities, ambitions, competitions of business according to the Golden Rule?

There are many answers.... The world of business asserts that the acquisition of money is the only standard of business success.

The corollary is that money-getting by all selfish means is perfectly justifiable. Here is a straight issue. It demands a square answer.

Another voice declares that all governments—national, state, and municipal—are under the control of political parties or favored corporations,—that commercialism has dealt the death-blow to all spirituality in American life.

Then there is the voice of the pessimist, who declares that this must be so. He finds no answer to it, awakens no hope. In human society, the selfish motive must rule, and so on.

Finally, there is the voice of idealism. It gives the lie direct to the material doctrine that only money defines the measure of true success. The teachings of reason, of human experience, of the prophets through all the ages unite in testifying to the truth of the ideal, "As ye would that men should do to you, do ye even so to men." The idealist in business is the only true man of affairs. He is the only really practical man. The only really good bargains are such as benefit both buyer and seller.... Money made by the exercise of power, of combinations that compel one man to lose each time for another's gain, is money dishonestly made. The business man of ideals finds in social service a joy, in working for the public a privilege. The saving of society is the problem of our life. The business man of ideals strives to help do this.[2]

Ogden recognized fully that it was hard to live up to these ideals. In a letter to his friend, Armstrong, he says : "The struggle after a life guided by the higher motives among all the competitions of business is a desperate one, and one slips and falls. Fits of impatience, over-hasty judgments, indignation against wrong, often disturb the inward peace ; which, added to the outward struggles against the selfishness of the world, sometimes makes me feel like throwing up the sponge. ... Therefore a world like yours [the educational field], which brings the higher motives to the front and throws meanness into true perspective is a healthful tonic."

In a letter to William H. Baldwin, Jr., he says : "We need work in order to fulfill the obligations we have to friends, families, and parents, but we must regard money-getting not as the primary object of life but simply as the means to an end."

From these quotations we see that business was with Ogden the highest form of endeavor and in it he was being prepared for a still nobler service to the nation and the church.

[2] *The Business World*, Vol. XXV (June, 1905), No. 6.

His religious, philanthropic, and civic interests were many and varied. Ogden never held public office, but he never failed to serve the public when he could. His conscience was ever quick to answer the call of humanity. Disinterestedness, kindness, courage, and deep concern for the general good characterized the man in his public acts.

It is impossible to enumerate here all of Ogden's services to the public. When President Taft in 1911 negotiated a general arbitration treaty, Ogden stood strongly for it and organized meetings in its support throughout the country. He was the leading director of the Mount McGregor Fund, which purchased the estate in the Adirondacks where General Grant spent his last days. At the request of Mrs. Sage, he became a member of the Russell Sage Foundation for Social Betterment.

When the Conemaugh Valley and the city of Johnstown in Pennsylvania were overwhelmed on May 31, 1889, by the breaking of the dam of the vast reservoir in the mountains above, and more than two thousand people were swept to destruction and thirty thousand left destitute, everyone in Philadelphia pointed to Ogden as the man to lead in the relief and restoration, and he was made chairman of the Relief Commission. After making a hasty visit to the scene of disaster, he got to work immediately, sent out appeals to the various states and many foreign lands, raised over $4,000,000, organized sanitation, health and relief work, temporary housing, the distribution of food, clothing, and medicine, and took every step necessary to restore ordinary life to the stricken community. In connection with the suffering caused by the panic of 1893, the citizens of Philadelphia formed a permanent relief committee, of which Ogden was made chairman again. This work engrossed his energies through the remainder of his residence in that city. He studied not only the cure but the cause of poverty, making careful studies of the ways in which loan sharks, storage companies, and companies selling on the installment plan preyed on the poor ; and then he worked out plans for employment bureaus, loan societies, and other helpful agencies.

During the same period, Ogden was organizing relief for the Armenians at Erzerum, following the massacre there, and for the sufferers from the famine in Russia in 1892. His philanthropic activities, of which these are only a few illustrations, would have absorbed all the energies of an ordinary man, but he was always ready and able to take up a new problem. He had remarkable ability in organization and knew how to make all different interests and agencies work together; and such was the influence of his example and enthusiasm that he never failed to find efficient helpers and the money for all worthy causes.

Ogden was sixty years of age when in 1896 he took charge as managing partner of the vast new business of John Wanamaker in New York. At this age most men would have thought it time to retire, but he was beginning the most difficult business enterprise and the most important social service of his wonderful career. The trained man was able to handle the complicated organization and still to have time and energy for public service.

First of all, the civic affairs of New York interested him. He took the leadership in forming a committee of one hundred citizens to direct a campaign for better city government. Still deeply interested in religious education, he extended his efforts from the Sunday school to the theological seminary. Elected a director of Union Theological Seminary in New York, he was placed on a committee to make plans for removing the institution from Park Avenue to the vicinity of Columbia University, where it could share in the activities of the great educational center. The task required fifteen years in planning, raising money, and managing construction. Ogden became vice president in 1907 and the next year was made president of the board of directors of Union Theological Seminary.

OGDEN AND ARMSTRONG

The man who, above all others, had the greatest influence in shaping Ogden's life was Samuel Chapman Armstrong. Ogden was twenty-five and Armstrong was twenty-three when these young men met, to become fast friends for life. For years they spent their vacations together, and whenever Armstrong had a furlough from the Army, he visited Ogden. It was in the parlor of Ogden's residence in Brooklyn that a few interested men met to consider Armstrong's dream of an industrial institute for Negro "contrabands." Hampton Institute was there born and Ogden was associated with it for forty-five years as trustee, financial supporter, and finally as president of its board.

Ogden tells of Armstrong's influence in his address before the Southern Industrial Association in Philadelphia in June, 1901 :

For many years past I have been accustomed in some sort of fashion to plead for Negro education. My leader in this cause was General Armstrong, the one man, so far as I know, that brought the consecrated genius of common sense, extraordinary capacity, indomitable industry, true statesmanship, and prophetic vision to bear upon the race problem at its beginning. . . .

A generation has passed, and the world recognizes his methods and principles as the ones that fit the case ; and, more than this, high critical authority claims for him the honor of contributing more to American popular education than any other one person since Horace Mann. I rank myself with hundreds of Negro men and women as his pupil. Booker T. Washington was his spiritual child ; the Hampton School is his monument. The breadth of view which General Armstrong inspired has brought a large company of people through the influence of Negro education to the consideration of white education, and thus to see the Southern educational question as a unit.

The business of raising money for Hampton had always concerned Ogden greatly. After Armstrong's death, this became more and more his task and to it he gave much of his time and thought. The educational affairs of the school were directed by Frissell, and the two men became closely united and worked together as brothers. The long years of service in the Sunday school, church, Union Theological Seminary, and Hampton Institute prepared Ogden's mind for the educational work he was to do for the people of the South. For one thing, he had learned through studying the conditions of Negro education that an important factor in the solution of the problem was how first to educate the neglected white people of the South. "I have often argued for Negro education," he said. "For that I have no apologies to make. I shall still continue to do it. But strong as that appeal may be I think that I could make an argument more convincing and more deeply pathetic for the poor whites of the South."

OGDEN'S METHODS OF WORKING FOR EDUCATION IN THE SOUTH

With a keen mind, highly trained by private study, with a great heart that took in all mankind, and with a wide experience in organization, Ogden was an unsurpassed campaigner. Had he cared for such things he would have made a politician of the highest type. As governor or senator he would have been a great public servant, but he preferred for himself only the privilege of serving his fellow men. Friends called him an "unofficial statesman" and this he was—a great thinker and leader in building institutions for the good of men.

Ogden was a practical psychologist. Without formal training, he studied men in the laboratories of society, of church, of the world, and of business. He read men's minds and souls as few men could, not to criticize but to sympathize, to lead and to encourage them. He believed that the best way to remove misunderstandings and hate was to make people acquainted. He liked to tell this story :—When friends protested to Mr. Dana of "The Sun" that his vituperation of a certain gentleman, Mr. S., was entirely uncalled for and proposed that he first get acquainted with him, Dana said, "Mr. S. is the only man living that I abominate, the only man, therefore, upon whom I can unload my venom. If I met him, I might like him and then there would be closed the last safety valve of my suppressed exasperation." Bringing people together who needed to understand each other was Ogden's method of preventing trouble.

Ogden was an accomplished organizer of social functions, which he used for making people acquainted and promoting religious, social, and educational causes. He employed two methods of winning followers and getting them to support the causes he loved. He believed in bringing people together in conferences, either at dinners or more formal meetings, so that they might learn to know each other, discuss things together, and then work together. He was a social artist, a skillful planner of entertainments, a generous provider, a tactful, genial, and charming host. His conferences in the South and dinner meetings in the North were equally delightful and productive of results. His most original method of winning followers and getting them to support his causes was the excursion. In the early days he took numbers of his friends to visit Hampton Institute and showed them the students at work, in their classes and shops, in their laboratories or on the farm, and then to attend Hampton's wonderful family assembly of teachers and students. When you had heard him talk to them in his fatherly way, and had heard them sing their stirring spirituals, you caught the spirit of Hampton and became a convert to its ideals and its friend forever.

The success of these early excursions led him to extend them to institutions throughout the South. With extraordinary skill he selected members of his party from the North and added new ones as he travelled in the South, bringing his guests together on his fine trains in delightful intercourse. He thus not only made his northern guests acquainted with each other, but by introducing them to men and women of the South gave them the opportunity of establishing new friendships which proved helpful and delightful for all. Between 1901 and 1912 he conducted ten excursions of this kind through all sections of the South, taking hundreds of people to see the homes, farms, schools, churches, shops, and factories where the people, both whites and blacks, lived and worked. One saw for oneself and drew one's own conclusions. These excursions and conferences between the men and women of the North and the South did much to remove misunderstandings between the sections.

As Mr. Frank R. Chambers said : "On these excursions Mr. Ogden was at his best, . . . bringing together people of kindred minds . . . to appreciate the needs of a great cause, acquainting the best type of Northern men and women with the best type of Southern people and, through unity of purpose and sympathy, arousing enthusiasm for his propaganda for education in the South. . . . His powers of coördinating the views of other men and bringing harmony of action was one of his most remarkable traits."

"Excursions into Ennobling Experiences"

On Mr. Ogden's seventieth birthday on June 20, 1906, his friends sent him an address on vellum, engrossed, illuminated and appropriately bound, which was signed by two hundred and eighty-six of his friends, including William H. Taft. On the evening of December 3, 1906, a company of two hundred of Mr. Ogden's friends, including many members of the Southern Conference for Education and the Southern Education Board, met to honor him. Walter Hines Page, who presided, described the gathering as a company on an excursion for Mr. Ogden, but one which they were going to run themselves. Dr. Francis G. Peabody, in response to the toast, "Excursions into Ennobling Experiences," said : "We have all been exalted by these excursions. . . . Yet it is not easy to define that exaltation. We saw new things, we made new friends, yet these alone could not explain the uplift. For Mr. Ogden showed the way not only into new lands, but into new faith. He showed the charm of nobler living—the way out of sordidness and commercialism into a higher plane of thought and existence. This excursion is to show him how we love and honor him."

Mr. Ogden's friends had prepared a tablet three feet in diameter, the work of the artist, Karl Bitter, designed to express the idea in the work of the Southern Board. A graceful female figure, seated upon a plinth, holds the lighted lamp of knowledge before an awakening sphinx. Page made the speech of presentation and unveiled the tablet, which had been hung behind Mr. Ogden. Taken completely by surprise, Mr. Ogden's eyes filled with tears as he responded : "Dear, Good Friends : I came here tonight with mingled feelings. Perhaps the largest feeling of all was one of gratitude to be among you. . . . I am grateful to Dr. Peabody for lifting this occasion out of mere personality into the sphere of a higher thought that . . . makes enduring all our friendships. By this greeting tonight I know that I have a personal wealth untaxable, a wealth of friendships that grows richer by distribution. . . . There is a singular geographical unity of the States here. From Maine to Texas, every State is represented. . . . That you represent many types and convictions but only one purpose is the most hopeful sign of our progress in the work to which we are all devoted."

Such was the all-around education of the man who now took the direction of the Conference for Education in the South and afterwards of the Southern Education Board and, for a time, of its child, the General Education Board. To this great service he devoted his trained energies and ripened experience for the remainder of his days. After long training in business, in religious work, and in institutional management he was ready when duty called. In all relations of life Ogden was an idealist. His idealism in business, his idealism in education, and his idealism in service were the secret of his great usefulness in these earlier positions. The same idealism made him the great leader in this new movement. The campaign for universal education in the South—the education which was to bring this people both blacks and whites a "more abundant life"—had found the leader it needed. Ogden was the ideal man to lead this crusade for an idea. Who can doubt that he was "the man sent of God"?

CHAPTER III

THE FOURTH SESSION OF THE CONFERENCE

THE MORAVIAN BACKGROUND AT WINSTON-SALEM

THE Conference had now broadened out and taken in the interests of the whole South. It was desirable, therefore, that future meetings should be held in more central places where they would be accessible to more people and be more influential. An invitation to the Conference to meet at Winston-Salem, North Carolina, an active city formed by the union of an old religious and educational center with a modern commercial and manufacturing town, was extended by Mr. Henry E. Fries and Mr. William A. Blair, and accepted by the committee of arrangements. Bishop Edward Rondthaler, of the Moravian Church, and Dr. J. H. Clewell, president of Salem College, tendered the Conference the use of the buildings of these institutions. This proved a most happy and fortunate location.

Mr. Ogden organized a company of over a hundred persons for an excursion through the South, with the meeting at Winston-Salem as its chief point of visitation. He engaged a train of Pullman cars, with all the facilities for entertaining his guests on a trip of ten days. Leaving New York on April 15, 1901, with some seventy guests,[1] he had ladies and gentlemen from different points join them at Philadelphia, Hampton, Greensboro, and Atlanta.

It was a distinguished company which met at Winston-Salem on the afternoon of April 18 and continued in session until the evening of the 20th.

The people of Winston-Salem entertained the visitors in their homes, thus adding greatly to the pleasure and effectiveness of the Conference. Mr. John D. Rockefeller, Jr., who was to render such great service to this movement, was one of Ogden's guests. His name was not on the printed list of guests given to the press but was added in writing for the minutes of the proceedings. Mr. Rockefeller was the guest of Mr. John

[1] See Appendix III, pp. 536-37.

Fries, whose daughter, Miss Adelaide Fries, the historian of the Moravian Church, was Mr. Rockefeller's hostess and guide in Salem. Dr. Charles H. Parkhurst, who had never visited the South before, was present, and the writer recalls that he was appointed escort for the distinguished visitor. As he took Dr. Parkhurst through the section of the town inhabited by the Negroes, through some of their homes and the Negro schools, and finally through the great tobacco factories where he heard them singing their spirituals, the good man, with tears in his eyes, in a trembling voice expressed his interest and amazement, saying, "I never had a right conception of the southern Negroes before. This visit changes my whole view of the question and of what must be done for them. Now I see that the southern people know far better than I how to train and prepare them for American citizenship. I understand now why they should never have been made full citizens before they were trained."

No happier location could have been found for the meeting of the Conference than in this Twin-City, representing the best of the old and the new in southern life. From this time on, we shall witness a wide enlargement of the vision of the Conference, a deepened interest among its members, and a quickened feeling of fellowship between the northern and the southern people.

Salem was founded by Moravian pioneers who, seeking freedom of conscience and wider opportunities for service, settled on this site in the deep woods of piedmont North Carolina, in 1755, and named it Wachovia for their old home in Bohemia. This most ancient of Protestant churches, founded in 1450 on the teachings of the martyred John Huss, has through five centuries of persecutions maintained the simplicity of its early faith. Among the first to make the battle for religious freedom, its people lit the fires of the Reformation sixty years before Luther. Following the teachings of their great leader Comenius, the Moravians have been builders of schools wherever they have settled. They were among the first to open schools in North Carolina, and the pupils of these schools carried education throughout the South. The history of this church is thus a part of the educational history of the South. Its schools, churches and missions encircle the globe.

Calling themselves "Unitas Fratrum," Moravians strove first to purify the old Catholic Church by working within it. Failing in that, they organized an independent church in 1467 and devoted themselves to education and missions. In the work of foreign missions the Moravian Church was the pioneer of all the Protestant bodies. Their first missionaries began their labors in 1732 and have since extended their institutions to all the continents. Though existing in fifteen independent provinces and four missionary provinces, reaching to the ends of the earth, the Moravian Church is one throughout the world. It is the one international Protestant Church, witnessing to the possibility of world-wide Christian unity.

Crushed out by the Thirty Years' War the "Unitas Fratrum" were scattered into Poland and Germany. For almost a hundred years the few remaining in Bohemia carried on their services in secret until, the war having passed, they were gathered together and reorganized their Christian Brotherhood under Bishop Johann Amos Comenius (1592-1670) a founder of modern education. He was the first man to work out a practicable school method of teaching things as well as words—a method which was to reform the mediaeval system of education. He advocated including music, geography, history, and the arts and handicrafts, as well as Latin and Greek, in the school curriculum. The system of schools which he laid out is almost the exact counterpart of our American system as developed today, including kindergarten, primary, elementary, and secondary schools and the college and university. He was the first man also to teach effectively the importance of training children to observe nature, and to urge the duty of universal education as the basis of human development everywhere and among all races.

Forty years before the signing of the Declaration of Independence, the Moravians began their labors on the American continent among the red men and the early settlers all the way from New England to Georgia. Though taking its origin in the old country, like the other Protestant denominations, the "Unitas Fratrum" has become thoroughly Americanized in its methods and coöperates with the other Protestant churches in striving to build up the intellectual, moral, and religious life of all races and all peoples in the United States.

The Church of the Moravians in Salem, having this history and representing these principles, now became the place where a new campaign devoted to universal education was to

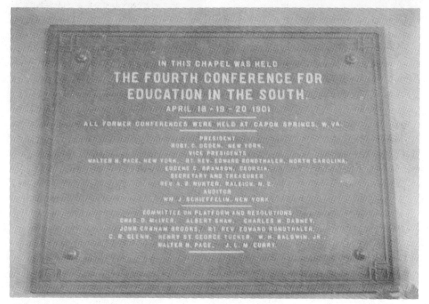

Upper left, the Right Reverend Edward Rondthaler, D.D., LL.D. (1842-1931), Bishop of the Southern Province of the Moravian Church, host of the Conference for Education in the South at Winston-Salem. Upper right, Albert Shaw, one of the originators of the Southern Education Board and a member of the General Education Board. Lower, Tablet in Salem College Chapel Commemorating the Fourth Conference, held in Winston-Salem in 1901

Upper left, Walter Hines Page, one of the originators of the Southern Education Board and member of the General Education Board (photo Paul Thompson, N. Y.). Upper right, Wallace Buttrick, member of the Southern Education Board and president of the General Education Board (Underwood & Underwood Studios). Lower left, Charles W. Stiles, scientific secretary of the Rockefeller Sanitary Commission. Lower right, Wickliffe Rose, member of the Southern Education Board, administrative secretary of the Rockefeller Sanitary Commission, president of the General Education Board, and president of the International Education Board

be started. It was significant and inspiring that on the platform of the chapel was a bust of Comenius. Everyone recognized at once that the Conference had been providentially led to this sacred shrine. Under the spiritual inheritance from Comenius it found itself at once in a congenial environment, made holy by long traditions of faithful service and bearing gracious marks of Christian sincerity and fellowship. In this ancient school and in the Moravian Church near by, the members of the Conference found joy in expressing to each other their message of freedom from sectional and racial hate and of earnest desire to coöperate in advancing the welfare of all the people. The men and women from different parts of the country and different educational associations discovered at once a common ground and a common goal. Here was started a great new campaign for universal education as taught by the Moravians three hundred years ago.

The Right Reverend Edward Rondthaler

Bishop Edward Rondthaler was an important influence in the Conference at Winston-Salem. He was the one hundred and eighty-fourth bishop of the Unitas Fratrum, or Moravian Church, counting from 1467, the date of its founding. He was descended from a long line of ministers and missionaries, many of whom had suffered for the faith's sake and removed to other lands where they might enjoy religious liberty. One such emigrant was his great-grandfather, Emmanuel Rondthaler, who removed to America and became pastor of the church at York, Pennsylvania.

Bishop Rondthaler was born in Schoeneck, Pennsylvania, where his father was pastor for five years. He attended the Moravian school at Nazareth, Pennsylvania, while his father was principal there. In 1859 he entered the Moravian college at Bethlehem, of which his father had become president, to prepare for the ministry. The youth was from the beginning an earnest student of the classics and became noted for his attainments in the languages of the Scriptures and the history and doctrines of the Christian faith, of which he was later such an able exponent. Following his graduation from the Theological Department, he studied at the University of Erlangen, where he came under some of the greatest teachers and theologians of the day. During his years abroad, he made many journeys afoot through Central Europe, familiarizing himself with the people, their history, and their national aspirations. This experience gave him that far perspective of international affairs and almost prophetic insight into world events which marked his writings of later years.

After serving for a year as a teacher in the Nazareth school, he was ordained deacon in 1865 and assigned to a church in Brooklyn and then to the First Moravian Church of Philadelphia. There he labored with great success until called in 1877 to the Salem congregation, the Home Church of the Southern Province. Three years later he was elected a member of the Elders' Conference, of which he was president for forty years. Between 1884 and 1888, he was principal of the Salem Academy and saw it grow into Salem College. In 1891 Edward Rondthaler was consecrated as Bishop of the Unitas Fratrum and put in charge of the Southern Province. Five times he represented this province in the General Synod of the church in Herrnhut; and once in London and another time at Berthelsdorf he was deputy to the Unitas Conference.

Bishop Rondthaler was a prolific writer and editor. During his pastorate in Brooklyn, he was on the staff of *The Independent* and was for forty years editor of the *Wachovia Moravian*. A great classical scholar, a great teacher, and a profound theologian, he was an eloquent preacher. Like his great Master, he was a lover of children, paying them especial attention wherever he went, and deeply interested in their education and training. He did not limit his interest in education to the schools of his own church, but was a friend and supporter of schools and institutions of all kinds. He died on January 31, 1931.

The University of North Carolina conferred on Bishop Rondthaler the degrees of D.D. and LL.D. As the Honorable James Y. Joyner wrote of him at the time of his death, "He was indeed and in truth the Bishop not of the Moravian Church, but of all the people of North Carolina." It was this man who welcomed the Conference to Winston-Salem.

THE MEETING OF THE CONFERENCE

The Conference was opened with music by the church band and singing by the choir. A hearty welcome was given the members by Governor Charles B. Aycock, who had made public schools the chief plank in•his platform and had earned the title of "Educational Governor" of North Carolina. "This is our Union, our own country," he said ; "we are one people, one in purpose, in high aim and in noble aspiration. So I welcome you to this state, now the more gladly because we have here entered upon a new educational era. North Carolina now recognizes her duty in the education of her children. . . . Three-sevenths of all the taxes levied by the state are set apart for . . . the schools. We have resolved to put a public schoolhouse in every district in North Carolina and to guarantee that no child, white or black, ten years from now, shall reach the age of twelve without being able to read and write. This is the problem we have set before us."

Bishop Edward Rondthaler, after cordially welcoming the Conference on behalf of the Moravian Church and the College, said, "We are not met on an occasion which calls merely for sweet words and soft speeches. What we want from one another is the truth. We want to have the great educational problems of the South stated fearlessly and truthfully, howsoever serious they may be. This is one of the most important occasions which can occur in a lifetime for strictly following the Scripture injunction 'to speak the truth in love.' . . .

"Nowhere has the fact been more deeply felt than here in Salem, under this old College roof, that the times require new methods of education. The Southern people are everywhere responding more and more to the needs of the New South and they deserve the fullest sympathy and support. Industrial education is not merely a need of the black race, but also of the white. The better the equipment of the white youth, the more will be done in the end for the blacks. Thus only can the entire population be reached and blessed. The bust which looks down upon us in this conference hall is that of the pioneer of modern education, our beloved Moravian Bishop, Comenius. He revolutionized the traditional methods of education for the benefit of the modern child. Let us not merely look into his face but follow his spirit in all our sessions and learn all the truth which must underlie a solution of our Southern educational problem." [2]

The Bishop's words of counsel made a profound impression.

[2] The *Winston-Salem Daily Sentinel*, April 19, 1901.

Educational plans proposed by Comenius two hundred and fifty years before were now about to be carried out in the South through the influence of this meeting. The effect of coming together as the guests of this ancient community, devoted to education, and in this hall, over which their prophet presided, impressed all present with the conviction that a great new educational movement was beginning.

The president, Mr. Ogden, responded, voicing this feeling : "It is especially impressive and fitting," said he, "that here in this place—honored by long history in the cause of religion and education—this Conference should convene.... I know that we shall be inspired not only by the graciousness of this welcome but by the presence in which we are assembled.... This company from the North, including men and women of force, thought, and experience, while originally interested in the South through negro education, ... have risen from that to the question of the entire burden of educational responsibility ... in this section of the country. We hope to share it with you ... as a national question, having to do with the North and with the South, with the prosperity and progress ... of the whole country." [3]

While waiting for the nominating committee to recommend officers, Dr. George S. Dickerman, the agent of the Conference, presented a paper, comparing the school facilities of the rural and urban population, North and South, and showing how sadly the country people of the South had been neglected.

Acting for himself and as a representative of other gentlemen desiring to help improve the conditions of the schools, Dr. Dickerman had for several years been exploring the educational needs of the southern people and advising and helping them wherever opportunity offered. As an investigator in the field, by his studies and reports he did much to promote the campaign which followed. His careful observations contributed greatly to the knowledge of the situation and his wise counsels, as associate secretary and field agent of the Southern Board, to the direction of the movement. By tactful kindness and helpfulness, he aided in opening the way for the mutual understanding of the men of the North and of the South and for the fra-

[3] *Proceedings of the Fourth Conference for Education in the South, Winston-Salem, N. C., 1901*, pp. 5-6.

ternal coöperation in the service of the schools, which from now on became so effective.

The committee reported the nominations, and Robert Curtis Ogden was reëlected president ; Walter Hines Page of New York, Bishop Rondthaler of North Carolina, and Eugene C. Branson of Georgia were elected vice presidents ; A. B. Hunter of Raleigh was reëlected secretary and treasurer.

Dr. Curry was then called to the platform, and he congratulated the men and women of the North on "coming here to consult about the 'common good of all.' " "The curse of our schools," he said, "is the infusion of sectarianism and partizanship in their conduct. The high test of statesmanship is the conscientious devotion of the citizen to the education of the people. I rejoice that in this day we are returning to the principles of Thomas Jefferson.

"I hope that out of this meeting will grow unity of effort and coöperation of forces, both material and moral, to uplift and educate both black and white. The State schools must do this work. We must proceed first to provide adequate opportunities for the whites. One properly educated white man will help to educate a dozen Negroes, while an illiterate white man will hold many more Negroes in the bondage of ignorance and degradation.... The education of the white youth of the South is the shortest road to the education of the Negro." [4]

This statesmanlike utterance from the great southern leader caused the Conference to take a broader view of its duty. Heretofore its thought had been occupied chiefly with Negro education ; from now on its thought was occupied with universal education, with adequate schools for the whites as the first thing to be provided.

In his report of the meeting in the *Review of Reviews*, Albert Shaw said : "The keynote of the conference was the urgent need for better public schools at any sacrifice. Along this line the most powerful presentation of the entire conference was made by President Dabney, of the University of Tennessee, who made an exhaustive statistical review of the condition of common-school education in the South during recent years, and who set forth the most painful facts without disguise and with absolute frankness. Dr. Dabney's position was not pessimistic ; it was simply business-like. Like the skillful

[4] The *Winston-Salem Daily Sentinel*, April 19, 1901.

surgeon, he laid bare the difficult and distressing situation, not to pronounce it hopeless, but as the necessary preliminary to remedial measures." [5]

Dabney declared that "Everything in the South waits upon the better and more general education of the people—good government, agricultural and industrial development, higher education, and even intelligent religion."

Using a series of charts to present statistics taken from official reports,[6] Dabney showed the wretched condition of the public schools—shacks for schoolhouses ; young, untrained, and indifferent teachers, with salaries of from $25 to $30 a month ; school terms of from three to five months ; only from 50 to 60 per cent of the school population enrolled, from 30 to 40 per cent in attendance ; total expenditures per capita of population from fifty to ninety cents, expenditures per pupil from $3.10 to $6.64, varying with the states. Opposition to local taxation prevailed everywhere and state or general funds were small. "The schools are poor because the people are poor and the people are poor because the schools are poor." Enough money was spent, he said, for prosecuting illiterates of school age to educate them and many others. Supervision was almost entirely lacking and political administration was the curse.

He pleaded for "justice and common sense in the education of the negro. . . ." "We must adapt our instruction to his needs, and, above all, give him that agricultural and industrial training which will prepare him to be a self-supporting citizen. He is in the South to stay—he is a necessity for Southern agriculture and industry—and the Southern people must educate him and so elevate him or he will drag them down. The Southern people are now prepared to undertake these problems. In fact the work is already going forward encouragingly in most of the States."

Concluding, the speaker said : "The immediate need of our people is information and guidance. They need leaders to show them the way. We need a central propaganda or agency which shall conduct a campaign of education for free public education and which, while it educates the people on this subject, shall use every opportunity to instruct them as to the best forms of legislation for their conditions and the best methods of

[5] XXIII (June, 1901), 646.

[6] The writer still recalls with gratitude that his friends W. J. Schieffelin and Henry E. Fries held up his charts during the entire talk.

organization for their schools. This is, then, the definite proposal that I would make to this Conference. Shall we not at this meeting take steps to establish such a propaganda for free public schools in the South?" [7]

It was moved by Curry to ask the commissioner of education of the United States and the state superintendents to publish Dabney's paper.[8] It was further resolved by the Conference that the president appoint a committee to draw up a platform and resolutions and to report to this meeting a plan of action as suggested by Dabney in his address.

Dr. G. R. Glenn, superintendent of schools of Georgia, expressed his gratification that "We have at last decided to get together as people who are genuinely interested in education. This is the first body of men, outside of professional teachers associations, I have ever known to assemble to study earnestly this great problem. What we need to do is to study the facts, as Dr. Dabney has presented them here, and resolve thereupon what is best to be done. We must do this work largely for ourselves. First of all we must provide proper facilities for the education of the country people both whites and blacks." [9]

The Committee on Platform and Resolutions, composed of McIver, chairman, Curry, Shaw, Dabney, Rondthaler, Glenn, Page, Brooks, Tucker, and Baldwin, met in Bishop Rondthaler's study following the evening session. The chairman, McIver, had requested Dabney to prepare resolutions embodying the plan for such a campaign as he had proposed. Dabney's plan was presented and adopted as written. After the committee had discussed at length the purposes of the Conference, Albert Shaw was requested to write a brief statement introductory to the resolutions. After some discussion the statement and resolutions were adopted without amendment as follows:

The Conference for Education in the South, on occasion of its fourth annual meeting, held at Winston-Salem, April 18, 19, and 20, 1901, reaffirmed its conviction that the overshadowing and supreme public need of our time, as we pass the threshold of a new century, is the education of the children of all the people.

[7] *Proceedings of Fourth Conference for Education in the South, Winston-Salem, N. C., 1901*, pp. 60-61.

[8] This was done in the *Report of the United States Commissioner of Education, 1900-1901*, I, 1009-1022. It is printed also in the *Proceedings of the Fourth Conference for Education in the South*, pp. 39-64.

[9] Report of Glenn's speech in the *Winston-Salem Sentinel*, April 20, 1901.

We declare such education to be the foremost task of our states-manship, and the most worthy object of philanthropy. With the expansion of our population and the growth of industry and eco-nomic resources, we recognize in a fitting and universal education and training for the home, for the farm and the workshop, and for the exercise of the duties of citizenship, the only salvation for our American standards of family and social life and the only hope for the perpetuity of our institutions, founded by our forefathers on the four corner-stones of intelligence, virtue, economic effi-ciency and capacity for political self-control. We recognize the value of efforts hitherto made to solve our educational problems, both as respects the methods to be used, and also as regards the sheer quantity of the work to be done. But we also find in the facts as presented at the sessions of this Conference the imperative need of renewed efforts on a larger scale ; and we also find in the improved financial outlook of the country and in the advancing state of public opinion better hopes than ever before of a larger response to this greater need. As the first great need of our people is adequate elementary instruction, and as this instruction must come to children so largely through mothers and women teachers in their homes and primary schools, we desire to emphasize our belief in the wisdom of making the most liberal investments possible in the education of girls and women.

Whereas, therefore, the conditions existing in the Southern States seem now fully ripe for the large development as well as further improvement of the schools ; and

Whereas, This Conference desires to associate itself actively with the work of organizing better school systems and extending their advantages to all the people,

Resolved, That this Conference proceed to organize by the appointment of an Executive Board of seven, who shall be fully authorized and empowered to conduct :

1. A campaign of education for free schools for all the people, by supplying literature to the newspaper and periodical press, by participation in educational meetings and by general correspond-ence ; and,

2. To conduct a Bureau of Information and Advice on Legisla-tion and School Organization.

For these purposes this board is authorized to raise funds and disburse them, to employ a secretary or agent, and to do whatever may be necessary to carry out effectively these measures and others that may from time to time be found feasible and desirable.[10]

[10] *Proceedings of Fourth Conference for Education in the South, Winston-Salem, N. C., 1901,* pp. 11-12.

The motion was made and unanimously carried that the president of the meeting should be made the eighth member of the executive board, named in the resolutions. These resolutions started the Southern Education Board, which in turn gave rise to the General Education Board and all its commissions and related foundations which followed.

The Conference was closed as it was opened by an address by Dr. Curry, reviewing the action taken and giving his impressions. Concluding an impassioned address, he said he beheld now "the rising of a new sun with healing in his wings to flood the Southland with rays of glory and happiness." Evidently realizing that his labors of fifty years for southern schools were about to close with success he added with deep feeling, "This is my *Nunc Dimittis*. Like the prophet of old I can say, 'Now lettest Thou Thy servant depart in peace, according to Thy word; for mine eyes have seen Thy salvation, which Thou hast prepared before the face of all people.' " [11]

THE CONFERENCE FINDS ITSELF

This was Dr. Curry's last Conference, but he continued a power in counsel and helped to direct the campaign for two years longer. At the conclusion of his address the Conference adjourned. Its members were all ready now to exclaim as the Greeks did at the conclusion of Demosthenes' celebrated oration, "Now let us go and fight Philip." The Conference had found itself and was ready for action.

In the beginning, the Conference for Education in the South was not a conspicuous force in southern life. Not until the Winston-Salem meeting did it command any public attention. Dreher says no secular southern papers took any notice of the first three meetings. At the third Conference only one religious paper had a representative present, but from the time Ogden took charge, the whole country awoke to the fact that a great movement was starting.[12]

The men who started the movement at Capon Springs were men of force and highly capable of leadership, but they were few in numbers and interested primarily in only two phases of

[11] In MS Minutes and repeated in letter to Ogden, Aug. 26, 1901, and in *Report of the United States Commissioner of Education, 1903*, I, 545.

[12] Memorandum by Julius D. Dreher, written for the author.

the southern problem—the education of the Negroes and of the mountain whites. They had no thought in the beginning of starting a general educational campaign and appealing to the whole body of southern people. But the movement, once started, was forced by the logic of the situation into the larger field of endeavor. Curry, Ogden, and Frissell had pointed out with rare vision that, if the Negro was to be trained for work, the white men of the South would have to do it. The neglected whites must be educated first. Not only must the whites of the South be converted to the idea of universal education, but they must be induced to tax themselves and taught how to make the money to pay the taxes. The whites owned nearly all the land and other facilities for production and they would have to pay nearly all the taxes. Every system of schools must have an economic as well as an intellectual and spiritual basis. Recognizing that all the wealth of the Peabodys, Slaters, Rockefellers, Carnegies, and other benevolent persons and societies in the North could not educate all of the people of the South of even a single generation, and having decided that national aid would never be given to help southern schools, there was no other method except to show the whites of the South how to develop their own resources and so provide the means to educate their own children and those of their former slaves. As soon as the Conference adopted this broader view of its duty, it had a new vision and took on a new life.

MISUNDERSTANDINGS

The southern education movement was naturally received in a different manner by different people. There were two classes of misunderstandings about it—the misunderstandings of the optimists, who expected too much ; and the misunderstandings of the pessimists, who thought that nothing good could come of it. The optimists hailed it with great enthusiasm as a movement which would immediately advance the whole school system. They dreamed of northern benefactors coming with large funds to pay the expenses of campaigns for increased taxation for the support of the public schools and to endow the private schools and colleges. Those who had these views were more dangerous to the movement than those who opposed it actively, for they were doomed to disappointment, and then became either indifferent or antagonistic.

A state superintendent of schools, who had attended one of the Conferences, wrote as follows to the agent of the Board : "To me the meeting was sublime in its sentiment, but I was distressed at the sordid public references or still more patently self-seeking private enquiries of those whose sole interest in the movement ... was ... to 'get hold of some money.' They were oblivious to the higher things, the spiritual wave, of the meeting, and were conscious only of 'the smell of money.' ... I found myself wishing that such a meeting had been possible with no prospect or chance of money to come from it."

This was too severe an arraignment of most of the good people attending the conference, but it warned the managers of a serious misunderstanding, which they thenceforward took pains to prevent.

Ogden and his colleagues strove constantly to remove such false impressions. The Southern Board had no money to give away. After the first two years even its current expenses were paid and its campaigns were financed by a few friends and by the General Board. The Conference was made up almost wholly of southern men and women, and the Board also contained a majority of southern men. The northern members simply asked the privilege of helping.

The misunderstandings of the pessimists were varied. Some people who looked upon the movement as the work of northerners resented the offer of direction, counsel, or even assistance, in the conduct of their domestic institutions. After what the southern people had seen of the educational work of the Freedmen's Bureau and of the Reconstruction legislatures and administrations, it was natural for them to be sensitive on this subject. Among some conservative-minded people there was a disposition at first to attribute to the promoters of the movement an ulterior motive. The fact that a few of its supporters were actively interested in Negro institutions suggested that the movement was designed to educate the Negro for the purpose of putting "the bottom rail on top,"—as the common saying was in Reconstruction days. Back of this antagonism was, of course, the old race prejudice and opposition to educating the Negro at all.

When a reporter asked Walter Hines Page if there was not

"a nigger in the woodpile," he said : "You will find when the woodpile is turned over not a 'nigger,' but an uneducated white boy. He is the fellow we are after. We want to train both the white boy and the black boy, but we must train the white boy first, because we cannot do anything for the Negro boy until his white friend is convinced of his responsibility to him." [13]

Referring to this prejudice, Ogden wrote to Page : "The sectional issue has ceased to be a factor of value to the northern politician. He used it just so long as it was useful, but it appears to me quite clear that the southern Democratic politician still has use for the sectional issue, and that fact constitutes one of the difficulties to be overcome. It is our task to show the southern people the simplicity and honesty of our efforts."

After the Winston-Salem Conference the governor of Georgia was reported in the newspapers to have said, "We can attend to the education of the darkey in the South without the aid of these Yankees and give them the education that they most need. I do not believe in the higher education of the darkey. He must be taught the trades. When he is taught the fine arts, he is educated above his caste, and it makes him unhappy." [14] This and the similar utterances in the papers in North and South Carolina caused the editors of some papers in the North to ask the other southern governors to express their opinions. As far as heard from, every one of them dissented from this view. Governor Aycock of North Carolina expressed in his reply the general opinion of the people of the South : "The Conference for Education in the South was a great pleasure to us and will be of incalculable benefit. We get more of the Northern view, and the visitors learn more of us. We do not entirely agree, but we respect more than ever the opinions of each other. If the Negro is ever educated it will be by the aid of the Southern white men. The North cannot do it. The education of the whites will precede the education of the Negroes." Speaking for North Carolina, he said : "Our purpose is to do our full duty by the Negro. We are willing to receive aid for his education, but without aid we shall in the long run teach him. He is with us to stay. His destiny and ours is so interwoven that we cannot help ourselves up without at the same time lifting him. What we want of the Northern people more than all their money is

[13] *Columbia State*, April 24, 1903.
[14] *Atlanta Journal*, April 24, 1901.

a frank recognition of this undeniable fact and we will do the rest." [15]

Some persons could not at first understand why northern men and women could be so much concerned about the white schools in the South. Politicians, who for years had been appealing to race feeling to maintain their party lines, found this movement a convenient subject for discussion and charged that it was nothing but another effort of the northern negrophilists to meddle with southern affairs.

In a letter to Dabney of May 21, 1904, Ogden wrote: "The Southern press charges us with being simply friends of the Negroes in disguise and the Negro press, on the other hand, is charging us with surrendering to the South. It is amusing." Toward opposition Ogden assumed an air of philosophical indifference and met all attacks made on him and the Board with calmness and good humor. He said: "A touch of heat was what we wanted. It kept the pot boiling. A little healthy opposition will do our cause much good."

Replying to the *Charleston News and Courier*, the *Columbia State* recalled that the movement originated in the South with southern men, who sought through the Conference to get together for mutual aid in a general effort to improve their schools: "For the beloved J. L. M. Curry, whose heart bled for, while he gave the rich labors of his life to, the south—a southern patriot deserving canonization by the enlightened people of his country—was the great inspiring soul of the movement. Mr. Ogden is in it because, as he said in his address . . . , he was 'recruited' for this work by Dr. Curry; and by southern men he has been advanced to, and maintained in, official rank. . . . For the sake of honesty, our contemporary must condemn Dr. Curry's labors. Dare it be consistent?

"None denies, on the contrary all applaud, the work of South Carolina and the south in educational matters, but the citizen who contentedly rests upon those laurels is dead to ambition and the spirit of progress. We may boast of what has been done; but so long as there are schools open but three months of the year, so long as there are schools open but eight months of the year; so long as there are children in South Carolina neglecting to take advantage of the educational oppor-

[15] *New York Herald*, April 27, 1901.

tunities offered by the State, there is work for educational conferences." [16]

The political superintendents were inclined to interpret the movement in the same way, and the state boards to be suspicious or indifferent. The agents of the Southern Board adopted the policy of frankly telling the people about the wretched condition of their schools. This nettled some of these gentlemen, who always claimed progress in their work. In many rural counties in the South, where there was very little wealth, there were no public schools whatever. The people were too poor to support schools by themselves and the state aid was too small to accomplish anything. Efforts to raise larger sums by a state tax to aid these schools were resisted by the large corporations and the people of the rich counties. In one case where a president of a university described these people as ignorant because they were poor and destined to remain poor because they were ignorant, he was sharply attacked by the governor and the state superintendent of public instruction and was invited to leave the state "whose people he defamed in this way." The superintendent declared that the president of the university had nothing to do with the public schools, which belonged exclusively in the domain of the state superintendent—this in the face of the fact that there were less than half a dozen high schools in the state at the time competent to prepare students for the university. This kind of opposition was soon overcome by the votes of the people, who wanted better schools.

In opposition to all of these misunderstandings, Ogden took every opportunity to explain the purposes of the movement and to emphasize the fact that the active work was entirely in the hands of southern men and that the men of the North only asked the privilege of aiding them to induce the people to build their own schools. Neither the Conference nor the Southern Education Board had any money to give for schools. The enterprise was too vast to be supported from the outside. Through improving their agriculture and other industries, the people of the South had first to make the money to build and support their own schools. To point the way and to teach the people to do this was the purpose of the movement. These ideas and plans, when finally understood, were cordially accepted by the vast majority of the southern people.

[16] *Columbia State*, April 28, 1905.

The misunderstandings and the opposition attending the movement were convincingly met by Dr. George W. Denny, president of Washington and Lee University, in an address at the opening of the Conference at Columbia, South Carolina, in 1905, the original old Confederate state which seemed to be at first the center of this feeling of doubt. Coming as he did from the university of Robert E. Lee, the mecca of southern faith and tradition, and being the successor of President William L. Wilson, one of the founders of the Conference, his testimony to the purposes of the Conference and his explanation of its plans were calculated to bring understanding to every southern mind and win the coöperation of every southern patriot in the prosecution of the noble work undertaken.

Some, he said, "have interpreted the conferences as nothing more than junketing expeditions ... without definite aim. ... Others ... characterized them as a well intended, but misdirected, effort on the part of certain gentlemen in other sections of the country to impose upon the people of the South certain peculiar views ... alien to what is best in ... Southern thought" and therefore the movement imperiled "the integrity of long-cherished ideals and fundamental convictions in society, in politics and in education." Others, he continued, were blunt in stating their opposition by declaring that the Conference presented merely a plan to promote a type of Negro education and Negro social and political life to which the southern people would never accede.

The Conference, he again pointed out, was made up almost exclusively of southern people. Its primary doctrine of universal education was that of all great southerners from the time of Jefferson down. The man who started the movement was that great Confederate, Colonel Curry, and its membership was almost totally composed of southern men interested in education, with only a few northern gentlemen who had been drawn into the movement through their interest in the development of the southern people. He described the doubters as men who still "nurse the scars of the conflict that has vanished, ... who would stir the ashes of an ancient feud, who would dig up the bones of the dead past," and he characterized the men of the movement as men who had faith in their fellow men, who desired to exemplify the ideals of social service, and, who, believing in the absolute necessity of public education and democracy, would aid in organizing "a campaign for education," such as Jefferson had pleaded for a hundred years before.

The Conference, he said, must be judged by its works and there was nothing in its work or influence that a southern man could reasonably refuse to endorse. It was evident that the Conference had, in the eight years of its existence, a large part in stimulating the remarkable growth of public opinion in favor of universal education and of taxation to support it. It had a large part "in readjusting old view-points and in reconstructing new theories," and incidentally in helping people to shed old prejudices and purge their memory of soul-destroying bitterness and long-spent quarrels. It had added energy, enthusiasm, fervor, fullness, faith, and hope, to new duties and new obligations of those called upon to fulfill a mission in the new time, "not amid the dead issues of the past, but in the presence of the living problems of today and tomorrow." It had taught that all individuals and institutions born of the same devotion and cherishing the same ideals should unite in their endeavor to hasten the coming of that day of universal knowledge and righteousness, "foreseen by seers and divinely promised," toward which our age is marching. The Conference thus stood "approved and justified by the logic of the three tests by which we judge ... all human agencies and human institutions"—the character of the people who are carrying it on, and by its purposes, and by its results.

THE PURPOSES OF THE CONFERENCE

What, then, was the *raison d'être* and what were the purposes of the Conference? Let us sum them up. The southern states were not chosen as the immediate objective of the efforts of the Conference because of any doubt as to the ability of the South to build in time its own institutions in completeness and efficiency, and so take its place in the nation as equal to any other section of the country. The Board came not to dictate to the people of the South, but only to awaken, encourage, and help them. Neither were the measures to interfere with the professional or executive work belonging to any officials or associations of teachers in the South. Rather, the Board offered to coöperate in a national enterprise of vast and vital importance. One misses the central idea of the movement if he thinks it was not truly a national one, having a national objective as well as a sectional one. The choice of the southern states as the theatre of effort was made for these reasons : First, because of their isolation ; second, because of their submergence for long years in a land in which the family organization, burdened with slaves, was the only unit of community life.

A land sparsely settled presented the most difficult social conditions for public schools. A land inhabited by two races, one having nearly all the education and wealth, and the other ignorant and poor—a separate people—involved a duplication of schools which must be supported almost exclusively by the superior race, which at first had to be taught to see its duty to its inferior fellow citizens. Sympathetic relations had to be established which would lead the superior race to recognize not only its duty but its economic interests as well. Because of the long and angry discussion over the question which had led finally to war, this process of understanding was to be most difficult.

Probably no other country, unless it was central Europe after the Thirty Years' War, had ever known in its direst and completest form such results from war and defeat. No other country among the civilized nations of the time ever lost in five years one-tenth of its male population and nearly four billions of its wealth. Only their unconquerable courage, self-reliance, and steadfastness supported these people.

Further, the South was just passing with great rapidity and vigor from a purely agricultural to an industrial state, in which it was striving to regain its wealth through the utilization of its natural resources and thus to reëstablish itself as an influential part of the nation and to attain a sense of national solidarity which it had not known for a century. Though decimated in numbers, the citizenship of the South, both the sturdy old stock of the hills and mountains and the sons of the eastern aristocratic planters, sobered now by bitter trial, promised rich results in character and efficiency to the united nation. Added to these stocks was a still primitive, backward, untaught race that had just been projected from a state of servitude into full citizenship in the great American republic, and had been thrown upon its own economic responsibility. Always guided as children heretofore, they were without the preparation, without the land or tools, which were required in order that they might at once begin to earn their own living. In their ignorance they were made, by the unscrupulous, to consider themselves the enemies of their previous masters, and to support with their votes evil political measures.

After some years of misdirected but well-intentioned effort by the people from the North and of opposition from the people of the South, the time had come to make a thorough and dispassionate study of these serious problems. The welfare of the whole nation was at stake in this proposal, and patriotic men and women from both the North and the South proposed that they get together, look each other in the face, and learn to know each other, so that they might understand the conditions better, appreciate each other's ideals and feelings, and prepare a program for the solution of the great problem.

Surely there never was, in modern times, a movement grounded in a higher purpose, or, as it turned out, conducted on a better plan, and carried forward with nobler zeal than the movement aimed to make this people, so stricken, so impoverished, and so burdened, an integral, prosperous, and happy part of the nation their fathers had helped to build.

The members of the Conference recognized from the beginning that there was only one way to do this and that was through the education of all the people of these states ; and in doing this, it was frankly agreed that the superior, the dominant part of this society, must be educated first before they could possibly be induced and made able to do their duty to the less fortunate race.

It was not yet determined how much coöperation should be given by the white men in the training of the Negro in this free country, but a vast amount of earnest sympathy in his training had already been shown, as had been splendidly illustrated at Hampton and Tuskegee. It had not been determined just exactly in what spirit the Negro would accept this interest in education and to what extent he would respond to its purposes. There were still Negroes as well as white people who were prejudiced and even rebellious against the new conditions. Education and training are a soul process. It was realized that the training of the Negro to take his place and do his duty in a new and difficult relation and the training of the white man to give the Negro his dues was a matter in the hands of God. Undoubtedly a fuller development of the spirit of Christian brotherhood in both races was the only solution.

It is no use denying the great difficulties involved in the relations of two peoples of such widely 'different racial types, who must now live together in a land where all their past experiences had tended to separate them. But as Dr. Curry always said : "There is but one thing to do for the human being and that is to give him a chance." And it was hoped that at last his white fellow citizens were resolved to give the Negro a chance.

The crucial question now was .not, Shall the Negro be educated, but How shall he be trained? On the old plantation where he was trained in contact with the white families in the condition of simple domestic service he learned all the arts of the farm and many of those of the shop. General Armstrong at Hampton and Booker T. Washington at Tuskegee had taught that his training should be primarily agricultural and industrial.

To carry out a general plan of education southern leaders believed that it was a matter of state duty to raise the money for the support of schools by a fair, general system of taxation. Every state must provide for the education of all its people, the wealthy communities helping the poor, and every local community doing all it can to improve its home schools. The power of taxation is a sovereign power, to be exercised by Congress and state legislatures, but local groups of people should be permitted to levy special taxes for their own benefit. This meant that in the South the public funds of the states and the people must be distributed fairly for the education of all the people, to the Negroes on the basis of their needs, as well as to the whites. Control, it was thought, should be exercised by the state and the local people—chiefly in the hands of the home people—and should not be in the nation. It might be necessary, during this period of transition from weakness to strength, that the state have certain executive and supervisory control, but the local interest in the schools should grow stronger and stronger until the legislative power should touch only the general and vital principles, while the detailed organizing and directing power should become local. Already many helpful changes were seen in the direction of local support and management of the schools. This was the most encouraging sign of the time.

CHAPTER IV

THE ORGANIZATION OF THE SOUTHERN EDUCATION BOARD

PRELIMINARY CONFERENCES

THE removal of the Conference from the quiet mountain resort of Capon Springs to the bustling modern town of Winston-Salem, and the coming together of the visitors from the North and the public school and college men of the South, changed the whole character of the Conference. The spirit of academic meditation, which had characterized the meetings at Capon Springs, became now an earnest endeavor to accomplish results.

The resolutions of the Conference had authorized the president to appoint an "Executive Board" of seven, of which he should be the eighth member and chairman, to conduct a campaign of education and to establish a bureau of investigation and information. Ogden immediately announced that he would take the necessary time to select this "Executive Board." As a matter of fact, he took the whole of the following summer and held conferences with many friends before he decided upon a plan of organization.

To his first conference Ogden invited Peabody, Page, Shaw, and Dabney. He was in the habit of holding important meetings in his private office on the upper floor of the old Wanamaker store, and here these men met him around a lunch table on a day in June, 1901. This office became the regular place for these meetings. Many important conferences were to be held in this room in the next ten years, but probably no meeting fraught with such great results was ever held there as this one, called to form the Southern Education Board.

In his memorial address for Mr. Ogden, Dr. Francis G. Peabody has described these meetings. "There, above the noises of trade, a dozen of the busiest of business men sat in quiet deliberation concerning great projects of national welfare, and interchanged their dreams of the better America, which they saw, not by sight, but by faith. It was a symbol of religion in the twentieth century, of a faith known by its works, of a service which was perfect freedom, of the spiritualization which is still possible for men of the world." [1]

Ogden had asked Dabney to come a day in advance of the meeting for a personal conference and requested him to prepare a memorandum for the organization and work of the board which Ogden had been authorized to appoint.[2]

The first question that came up was the form the association should take. It was thought necessary at first to form an incorporated society with a regular membership to support it. The Conference so far had been an open one. Now a more permanent organization seemed called for as a basis for real business. With these conditions in mind, Dabney, at Ogden's request, submitted to the gentlemen at the luncheon a brief plan providing for a "Society for Education in the South," the object of which should be the promotion of public education, especially "free public schools for all the people black and white alike," [3] the members to consist of the persons enrolled at Salem and elected thereafter. The Executive Board would consist of the president and seven members appointed by him to have charge of a "Campaign of Education in the South, to be carried on for at least five years" by a staff consisting of an executive secretary and field agents, and a "Literary Bureau and Bureau of Information," to investigate and publish information on school legislation, etc. To pay the expenses it was proposed to raise $25,000 for each of the first five years.

After considering the advantages of open conferences in which everyone could participate, as had been so happily illustrated at the Capon Springs and Winston-Salem meetings, it was decided not to form a corporation, but to continue the Conferences as open meetings for discussion and propaganda. A board was formed to conduct all the business. This plan worked so admirably that it was continued to the end of the campaign, the meetings growing in size, interest, and power from year to year, until the second Richmond meeting in 1913 was attended by over two thousand persons, composed of

---

[1] Francis G. Peabody, "Robert Curtis Ogden," Address at the Ogden Memorial Service at the Central Presbyterian Church, New York, Oct. 26, 1913. Published in *A Life Well Lived*, 1914: *In Memory of Robert Curtis Ogden*, 1916; and in *The Southern Workman*, Vol. XLII (December, 1913), No. 12.

[2] Wilson, *op. cit.*, p. 230.

[3] See copy of the original in Appendix IV.

school officials, publicists, and citizens generally, representing the entire South.

The first problem was naturally that of finances. Where was the money to come from to carry on the proposed campaign? A number of gentlemen familiar with such problems met in Bar Harbor, Maine, on August 14, 1901, at the home of Mr. Morris K. Jesup. A memorandum made at that meeting reads in part:

[Mr. Ogden and the gentlemen] reached the conclusion that if the facts made known to them were made known to the public in an authoritative form, through a suitable agency,... generous gifts would be offered and channels of usefulness would be opened to those who could give large or small amounts. It was made clear that, at the present time, much force and much money are wasted by unorganized and unfruitful efforts to promote the welfare of that part of the country. Information was brought forward, from trustworthy sources, indicating that large sums of money will be given in the course of the next few years, if wise plans for the distribution and administration of such funds can be presented. Under these circumstances, the gentlemen assembled determined to ask the Trustees of the Peabody Education Fund, the Trustees of the John F. Slater Fund, and the Committee of the Southern Education Conference, each of them, to appoint a committee of two or three persons to meet and consider this subject, and devise some plan of coöperative action....

Dr. J. L. M. Curry ... was requested to present this statement, with such additional facts as may be within his knowledge, to the several Boards, at the earliest opportunity.

On August 2 Ogden announced the appointment of the "Executive Board" in a letter to the members: "After much consideration the Committee on Southern Education, ordered by the Conference at its Winston Meeting, is made up and announced as follows:

> Hon. J. L. M. Curry
> Dr. C. W. Dabney
> Dr. E. A. Alderman
> Dr. Charles D. McIver
> Dr. H. B. Frissell
> George Foster Peabody
> Rev. Wallace Buttrick, D.D., Albany, N. Y.

By action of the Conference I am added ex officio."

As Dr. Curry had not been able to come to the conference in New York in June, Mr. Ogden requested Frissell, McIver, and Dabney to go to North Carolina to confer with him. They met Dr. Curry at Asheville on September 14. Alderman, happening to be in Asheville, joined in the conference. Frissell gave an account of a meeting at Bar Harbor and presented the paper agreed upon there. This conference recommended:

The Board should be incorporated under the name of the Southern Education Commission.

We agree heartily to the proposal to coöperate with the Peabody and Slater boards; ... our Commission should meet in New York on the 2nd of November and continue in session as long as may be necessary to confer with the said boards and to complete its own organization.

The work proposed for this board divides itself into two departments:

(1) The campaign for education in the South as outlined in the resolution of the Winston-Salem conference;

(2) The work in the North to create interest in Southern education and draw out support for it.

An organization should be formed to carry out, as far as possible, these two lines of effort. To this end the following organization is suggested for the Commission:

A President,
A Recording Secretary,
A Treasurer,

forming the general organization of the Commission.

The Commission should have the following executive officers corresponding to the two great lines of work:

(1) A General Secretary, ... who shall be the executive officer of the Commission, and who shall have a general supervision over the work undertaken by the Commission for the advancement of education in the South. This work shall include investigations of educational conditions and the raising and distribution of funds, both for the current expenses of the Commission and for the aid and endowment of educational institutions.

(2) The General Agent of the Peabody and Slater boards should be the General Southern Agent of the Commission, and should advise and direct the following subordinate agencies:

(a) A Literary Bureau, to investigate and report upon state public school systems ... and prepare statistical and other reports and papers, recommending improvements and reforms ; to conduct the campaign for education by publishing and distributing literature to state officers, newspapers and the people ; to conduct a bureau of information and advice on legislation, school organization, etc.

(b) A Field Agency, to direct the work before legislatures, conventions, and in public meetings ; to conduct a general campaign for local taxation for public schools and for increased public interest in, and support of, . . . the education of teachers.

(c) An Agency for the promotion of the industrial and general education of the colored people. It shall be the duty of this agency to strengthen the growing interest and sympathy in educational matters between the races, and to induce the white people to share in the active work, not only of aiding but of directing the development of colored schools.

THE SOUTHERN EDUCATION BOARD ORGANIZED

Having through this series of conferences—first in New York in Mr. Ogden's little "upper chamber," at Mr. Jesup's in Bar Harbor, and finally at Asheville—arrived at certain tentative plans and having appointed the members, Ogden on October 11 called the Board to meet in New York City on Monday, November 4, for the purpose of organization.

The minutes [4] say, "The Executive Board of the Conference for Education in the South convened pursuant to notice in the office of Robert C. Ogden in New York at two o'clock P.M. November 4, 1901. Present were : J. L. M. Curry, C. W. Dabney, E. A. Alderman, H. B. Frissell, Wallace Buttrick, George Foster Peabody, Robert C. Ogden, and C. D. McIver."

The meeting was opened with prayer by Dr. Buttrick. The platform and resolutions adopted at the Southern Education Conference, Winston, N. C., April 20, 1901, as the authority by which the Southern Education Board was created, were read for information and ordered spread on the minutes. The Board was organized for business by the election of Robert C. Ogden, President, C. D. McIver, Secretary, and George Foster Peabody, Treasurer.

[4] The minute book is preserved in the Library of the University of North Carolina.

Mr. Dabney presented for the consideration of the Board certain expressions of opinion concerning the organization for practical work which had resulted from informal conferences held in New York, Bar Harbor and Asheville. These suggestions referred to the executive officers, objects to be attained, and various possibilities of usefulness. [This memorandum was inserted in the minutes.]

The Board met every day at 10:30 A.M. in Ogden's office, adjourning on November 9. The conclusions of this meeting may be summarized as follows:

The first thing done was to elect William H. Baldwin, Jr., Albert Shaw, Walter Hines Page, and H. H. Hanna members of the Board. Baldwin, Shaw, and Page were immediately received and greeted. Peabody was requested to communicate with Hanna, who joined the Board at the next meeting.

As first conceived, the Southern Education Board, as it was now called, was to have two functions:

First. It was to be the agent for creating public opinion in behalf of the public schools.

Second. It was to be an agency to handle gifts from private persons, boards, and foundations to promote public education.

It was promptly decided, however, that these functions should be separated and placed in the hands of different agencies. The Southern Education Board was, therefore, organized to discharge the first function; namely, the creation of public opinion for schools. The first record of this is in a resolution appointing the president of the Board and Dabney a committee "to investigate the question of incorporation of this Board and of a Board of Trustees to be nominated by this Board to whom shall be committed the custody of any capital funds that may come to this Board for administration." Here is the first suggestion of the General Education Board. "The Board of Trustees" became the General Education Board and was incorporated and charged with all the financial operations. The Southern Education Board devoted itself exclusively to the propaganda work to create public opinion in behalf of the public schools.

After discussions, extending through several meetings, a definite organization was formed under the name of "Southern Education Board," with the sub-title, "The Executive Board of the Conference for Education in the South" (afterwards dropped).

A budget, to pay the expenses of the proposed propaganda, was adopted, which called for a sum of $40,000 for each year for two years beginning January 1, 1902. Mr. Ogden had borne all the expenses so far, and he continued to carry those of the excursions and the social meetings arranged by him for the next eleven years.

At this critical juncture, when everything depended upon the prompt solution of the financial problem, a patriotic son of the South, George Foster Peabody, came forward and underwrote the amount of $40,000, which made it possible to begin the work immediately.[5]

As one of the organizers and the first financial guarantor of the Southern Board, George Foster Peabody ranks alongside Ogden. From this time forward they worked together like brothers; Peabody, the social philosopher, counseling and helping everywhere; and Ogden, the organizer and man of action, commanding and leading the forces in the field. Their record of personal service to philanthropic and educational institutions has never been surpassed. As Edgar Gardner Murphy said: "If personal devotion to noble and fundamental causes be a test of patriotism, ... it may be said, both of Mr. Peabody and of Mr. Ogden, that they have left business and have retired into public life." [6]

To raise funds for future expenses, a finance committee was appointed, consisting of Ogden, Baldwin, Page, Shaw, and Peabody. This committee conferred with, among others, Dr. Frederick T. Gates, the representative of Mr. John D. Rockefeller, and out of their thought and Mr. Rockefeller's munificence grew the General Education Board. Baldwin became the first chairman of the General Board; and Peabody, treasurer, as well as treasurer of the Southern Board. Ogden, Curry, Page, and Shaw were also members of the General Board from its beginning in 1902.

The Conference was Ogden's distinctive personal interest and contribution to the cause. By his excursions, dinners, and private conferences and by the great conventions in different centers in the South, which he organized and conducted, he

---

[5] It was not known even by members of the Board who provided these funds until long afterwards. Ten thousand dollars having been raised from other sources, Mr. Peabody supplied $30,000 for the first year.

[6] *Proceedings of the Tenth Conference for Education in the South, Pinehurst, N. C., 1907*, p. 35.

made this a powerful agency for awakening the southern people to a sense of their duty. Of the army of workers in this crusade, he was the commander-in-chief, as he was also for the remainder of his life the moving spirit of the Southern Education Board.

Among the social gatherings held during the week of the organization of the Southern Education Board was a meeting at the Century Club of the members of the Board with the president of the United States. President Roosevelt expressed deep interest in the plans of the Board and gave its members encouragement. Other informal conferences were held during the week at the luncheons and dinners given to the members of the Board. These conferences resulted in greatly deepening the interest in the objects aimed at and in clearing the minds of the members as to the methods to attain these objects.

THE MEETING AT THE WALDORF-ASTORIA

Finally, on the evening of November 8, Mr. Ogden invited a large company of gentlemen to meet the members of the Board at dinner at the Waldorf-Astoria. From his extensive acquaintance in business, educational, and church circles, the chairman assembled a distinguished company.[7] The object of the dinner, as stated by Mr. Ogden in his opening remarks, was to inform the makers of public opinion in the country as to the real condition of public education in the South and to enlist their interest. He explained the purpose and the methods of the Board and introduced the members to his friends. The sum of $40,000 annually for two years had been guaranteed for the work. The money raised was to be spent in stimulating the

[7] Besides the members of the Southern Board, headed by Dr. Curry, and many gentlemen from the South, belonging to the Conference, there were present at this dinner, among others, Dr. Daniel C. Gilman, president of Johns Hopkins University, Professor Woodrow Wilson of Princeton University, John Crosby Brown, Morris K. Jesup, R. Fulton Cutting, Isaac N. Seligman, Dr. James MacAlister, Dr. Lyman Abbott, John D. Rockefeller, Jr., Mr. A. S. Frissell, Bishop William Croswell Doane, Reverend Francis G. Peabody, Reverend Charles H. Parkhurst, F. N. Doubleday, Dean James E. Russell, William J. Schieffelin, St. Clair McKelway, George McAneny, S. M. Lindsay, Leslie M. Miller, Adolph S. Ochs, President Nicholas Murray Butler, Oswald G. Villard, Edward Cary, E. R. L. Gould, Reverend S. D. McConnell, George A. Plimpton, Reverend William Adams Brown, D.D., William R. Moody, Professor Paul H. Hanus of Harvard, General T. J. Morgan, Felix Adler, Henry L. Stoddard, Reverend Charles L. Thompson, Henry W. Farnam of Yale, and Hamilton W. Mabie.

southern people to build better systems of public schools; that is, for educational propaganda and not for education itself. It was hoped that the people of the South could be so interested in the ideas presented that they would tax themselves and take measures of their own for the educational work itself.

The *Times* said the next morning: "The keynote of the discussion which followed the dinner was sounded in an earnest plea by Charles W. Dabney, director of the Bureau of Investigation, for the education of the whites of the mountains and rural districts which had few school advantages and of the Negroes." " 'The time will come,' he said, 'when the nation will also want the help of the blacks in the South.' ... He advanced three reasons for the deplorable neglect of Southern education,—paucity of population, poverty of the people, and the baneful influence of local politicians who control the school affairs. He summed up the present conditions by saying that 'the people are poor because they are ignorant and they are ignorant because they are poor.' " [8]

President Alderman of Tulane University argued that "the most effective way of helping the Negro is to help the white man. The education of one white man to the point where it is clear to him that knowledge and not prejudice must guide his conduct and that for the honor of his name, his country, and his posterity, he must deal with these people in justice, kindness, and Christian forethought, is worth more to the black man himself than the education of ten men of his own race." [9]

Charles D. McIver, president of the North Carolina State Normal and Industrial College, pleaded for the education of the women as the surest means of educating all the people of the South. Other speakers were Dr. Curry, Dr. H. B. Frissell, and Dr. Edward Abbott of Cambridge, the originator of the Capon Springs Conference.

MEMBERSHIP AND MOTIVES

In a four-page circular entitled "A Brief Statement Concerning the Origin and Organization of the Southern Education Board, the Executive Board of the Conference for Education in the South," Ogden now announced the organization of the

[8] Report in the *New York Times*, November 9, 1901.
[9] *New York Tribune*, November 12, 1901.

Board. This circular, which was the first publication of the Board, is given in the Appendix in full.[10] It contains the resolutions of the Fourth Conference at Winston-Salem, authorizing the plan of organization of the Board, and the list of members and officers. In announcing the membership the president said it would be increased and the staff changed as the work required. This was done but it always remained a compact body of persons and never became a mechanical corporation. The circular concluded with this statement : "The Board has decided that no portion of the fixed sum of money it hopes to secure for current expenses shall be applied 'to the assistance of any institution or school, but that it shall be expended exclusively for the purpose of stimulating public sentiment in favor of more liberal provision for universal education in the public schools.' The practical work of the Board is in the form of a popular propaganda, through its own printed issues, the public press, and more especially public speech—the living epistle."

The objective points of the work of the Board, formulated later, were to be :

Stimulation of interest in universal education ;

Voluntary local taxation for the increase of school facilities ;

Compulsory education ;

Lengthening of school terms ;

Consolidation of weak schools ;

Education of teachers ;

Industrial and agricultural instruction ;

Conferences of the county superintendents of education by States ;

Improvement of schoolhouses and their equipment ;

Establishment of high schools and their co-relation with elementary schools and colleges.[11]

The following is the list of the first members of the Board as published by Mr. Ogden in his circular of November, 1901 :

Honorable J. L. M. Curry, Agent of the Peabody and Slater Boards, Washington, D. C. ;

Dr. Charles W. Dabney, President of the University of Tennessee ;

[10] See Appendix V.
[11] Robert C. Ogden, in *Proceedings of the Ninth Conference for Education in the South, Lexington, Ky., 1906*, p. 12.

Dr. Edwin A. Alderman, President of Tulane University of New Orleans;

Dr. Charles D. McIver, President of the North Carolina State Normal and Industrial College for Women, Greensboro, N. C.;

Dr. Hollis B. Frissell, Principal of Hampton Institute, Hampton, Va.;

George Foster Peabody, New York;

Reverend Wallace Buttrick, D.D., Albany, N. Y.

The Board held its first meeting in New York City in the week beginning November 3, 1901, and added to its membership:

William H. Baldwin, Jr., New York

Dr. Albert Shaw, New York

Dr. Walter H. Page, New York

Honorable H. H. Hanna, Indianapolis, Ind.

Mr. Ogden announced that, as its plans developed, the Board would call into service other men in the South. Edgar Gardner Murphy was executive secretary, associated with the president, from the beginning, and became a member of the Board in 1902. Chancellor Walter B. Hill, of the University of Georgia, was elected in 1904, and Mr. Frank R. Chambers, of New York, a native of Alabama and for many years interested in the education of southern youth, was elected in 1905. Chambers succeeded Mr. Ogden as chairman of the Board. David F. Houston, president of the University of Texas, and George S. Dickerman, of New Haven, Connecticut, who had been for many years studying the condition of southern schools and was the first agent of the Conference, were both elected members in 1906. In December of the same year, Professor Samuel C. Mitchell, of Richmond College, Henry E. Fries, of Winston-Salem, North Carolina, Sidney J. Bowie, of Alabama, and Philander P. Claxton, of the University of Tennessee, were elected members. Subsequently were added, Dr. James H. Dillard, dean of Tulane University, Dr. John M. Glenn, of the Sage Foundation, Chancellor James H. Kirkland, of Vanderbilt University, Dr. Wickliffe Rose, professor in the Peabody College and in the University of Tennessee, and a member and president of the General Education Board. Bruce R. Payne, and A. P. Bourland, the last executive secretary of the Southern Conference, were elected to the Board after Mr. Ogden's death.

When the Board dissolved in 1914, Ogden, Curry, Baldwin,

McIver, Hill, and Murphy were dead. Only H. H. Hanna resigned on account of his health.

Such was the Southern Education Board. It had no formal charter, constitution, or bylaws. Its agencies were changed from time to time to suit the work to be done. The Board was a voluntary association of men, devoted to the common cause of educating the people in the South. It was a composite of personalities rather than a corporation, a band of brothers who found a bond of union under the leadership of Robert Curtis Ogden.

THE RELATION OF THE BOARD TO THE CONFERENCE

Such, too, were the objectives of the Conference for Education in the South, which was the public assembly of the Board and its co-workers and friends. Like the Southern Education Board, this Conference was a purely voluntary association. The only qualification for membership in it was sympathetic accord with its purpose and the desire to promote it. This purpose was the saving of society by saving the child. Believing in the moral progress of the world, it began with the child—"A little child shall lead them." It was an assembly of men and women from all sections, citizens and officials, professional men and business men, all united in the one interest of serving the country through the education of its children. Like the Board, the Conference had no constitution or bylaws. Its meetings were open forums led by Mr. Ogden or by gentlemen elected by those present. It elected executive officers and committees and pressed into service all whose assistance it required. This absence of definite organization tended to emphasize the inner life and spirit of the Conference and kept it plastic for adaptation and expansion.

Never before was there such an organization as this. There had been many associations of school officers and teachers from the different states and cities and the nation at large, and many societies representing different types of schools and colleges and different professions and specialties; but never had there been an educational association in which non-professional and unofficial men and women led in working for schools. In this respect the Conference for Education in the South was a unique organization—without counterpart in the world.

The Board and the Conference Primarily Southern

The Conference was not, as was charged at first, a northern missionary society to educate southern people. It was from the very beginning a southern organization—a forum in which southern men and women discussed their own problems. The movement began in the South and had been carried on by Curry and his disciples for twenty years before the men of the North joined the men of the South to give it form and to provide it with resources. The Southern Education Board as first organized contained five southern-born men and three northern. In the whole life of the Board, from 1901 to 1914, twenty-seven men sat in its councils and shared in the fellowship of its work, and of this number twenty were southern-born and seven northern. With one exception, Dr. Dickerman, the zealous pioneer of the Conference, all of the agents of the Board through its whole life were southern men. The Board associated itself in all its work with state officers, schools, colleges, and universities and helped them start summer schools for teachers, always under local or state control. It encouraged the state superintendents of the South to form an association for mutual help and paid their expenses on tours of visitation. It aided state coöperative educational associations and women's school improvement leagues and paid their agents. It never sought to do anything independently of the southern people.

The aim of the association was definite. It was universal education, the education of every child in the South, rich or poor, native or foreign born, white or black. Ever since the days of Thomas Jefferson, patriotic men had been struggling to make this ideal an actuality, but it had not been possible to do so. Now, however, the southern people were awakening to the realization that the training of all the people furnished the only hope of the restoration of their land. It was the psychological moment. In the beginning of the century, Jefferson had commanded, "Preach a crusade against ignorance." Now, at the beginning of the new century, this association answered him, "We preach a crusade for education." Jefferson had taught the necessity of an enlightened citizenship for the democracy of his day ; the Conference proposed to educate all the people for complete living. With this mixed citizenship of ignorant black and neglected white people, facing political, economic, social, and moral problems such as no people ever faced before, the members of this association were impelled by a feeling that would have been akin to desperation, if they had not had faith in a Supreme Ruler of the world.

The spirit of the association was altruistic, patriotic, and religious. Its appeal was to the civic consciousness. Its hope was in the creation of a public mind with a sense of responsibility for general education. Its method was the promotion of taxation for the support of adequate school systems, but with an ideal far higher than that of mere material results. The ultimate aim of the movement was the inspiration of the people to a higher and fuller realization of their duty to all their fellow men and to their nation. Not intelligence alone, but a higher ethical standard of citizenship, was the ultimate aim of this Conference for Education.

GEORGE FOSTER PEABODY, TREASURER

The first man to finance the Board, George Foster Peabody, was also its unfailing supporter. Born in Columbus, Georgia, in the decade preceding the outbreak of the War between the States, George Foster Peabody, like many another boy of that period, had to assume early in his youth the cares and responsibilities of manhood. In 1865 with his impoverished family he left the southern homeland in desolation to begin life anew in Brooklyn, New York. After six months of schooling it became necessary for the boy, then only thirteen years of age, to get employment in a wholesale drygoods house in order to add to the family income. He worked as a clerk in this and similar houses until 1881, when with his friend, Spencer Trask, with whom he had been associated for some years, he formed the banking house of Spencer Trask and Company.

During his banking activity Peabody was prominent in the corporate development of railroads, in the Edison Electric Companies, and in enterprises in Mexico, including the Mexican National Railroad, of which he was vice president. He was also chairman of the Board of the Rio Grande Western Railway, and the St. Louis Alton, and was connected with many other railroads in the United States and Canada. He was active in the Chamber of Commerce of New York and in the Morton Trust Company, the General Electric Company, the Cleveland Electric Companies, and the Broadway Realty Company of New York.

From 1880 on he was associated with the Democratic party on the Independent side. In 1897 he helped to organize the Indianapolis Monetary Conference and the Monetary Commission which drew the bill establishing a plan for currency reform and did much to shape the public opinion which prepared the way for the present Federal Reserve System. When the Federal Reserve Bank of New York was organized, he was appointed by President Wilson a director of it. He was for six years deputy chairman of the Board, retiring by his own wish at the end of his third term.

Believing that it was desirable that the members of the Southern and General Education boards should confer easily and fully with each other and with the friends of the cause, Mr. Peabody invited them several times to visit him for a week in the summer at his home, Abenia, on Lake George, New York. The meetings were most delightful and refreshing for these busy workers, and proved even more fruitful of results than the formal sessions. Living together quietly in this beautiful place for a week, apart from current affairs, concentrated the minds and moved the hearts of all to new efforts for clear understanding and right planning. Here were formed most of the new plans for developing the schools. Here on the lawn among the flowers, on the verandahs looking out over the lake, around the hospitable table or over the coffee cups in the spacious library, were discussed and decided many of the serious questions which later came before the executive boards. It was here that the plans were made for establishing high schools, for encouraging larger taxation for elementary schools, and for establishing more normal schools and departments of education for the training of teachers. It was here that such great new undertakings as the eradication of the hookworm, proposed by Dr. Stiles, and the demonstration of practical agricultural methods as developed by Dr. Knapp, were first planned.

Of these meetings at Abenia, Walter Hines Page wrote Dr. James H. Kirkland on August 13, 1908: "Not the least important part of this Board's work is, what for the lack of a better name, I shall call its spiritual communion and uplift,... One of these days, if I ever have time and I can get my pencil sharpened at the right angle, I am going to try to tell what that

George Foster Peabody, one of the founders and treasurer of the Southern Education Board and member of the General Education Board

THE FIRST SOUTHERN EDUCATION BOARD

Seated, left to right, William H. Baldwin, H. H. Hanna, Robert C. Ogden, George Foster Peabody. Standing, left to right, Charles Wm. Dabney, Wallace Buttrick, Charles D. McIver, Albert Shaw, Edwin A. Alderman, Walter H. Page, Edgar Gardner Murphy

Board has meant to me (and I am sure it has meant a corresponding thing to all the other members) by giving me a continual encouragement in trying to be of some little help to further right ideas and in drawing me out of my own more or less personal affairs into a clearer and wider atmosphere. It is an experience such as a man cannot have many times or by many kinds of associations in one's life."

Mr. Peabody has been active throughout his whole career in liberal movements in politics, economics, religion, and education. Better·schools for both races in the South have, however, been his special interest. By his labors as well as his means he has contributed greatly to their growth. He is, by special act of the legislature, a life trustee of the University of Georgia, a trustee of Colorado College, of Skidmore College, of Hampton Institute, of Howard University in Washington, of St. Paul's School in Virginia, of Penn School on St. Helena Island, South Carolina, of the Fort Valley Industrial School in Georgia, of the Mount Meigs' School in Alabama and the Voorhees Normal and Agricultural Institute in South Carolina, of the American Church Institute for Negroes of the Protestant Episcopal Church, of the Lake Placid Educational Foundation, and of the Warm Springs, Georgia, Health Foundation.

It is a matter of great gratification to Mr. Peabody's many friends that he still continues deeply interested in the education of his fellow citizens. He is now striving to aid plans for adult education in the South. In a statement sent out recently to his friends he wrote : "In the past winter (1933-4) I have spent six months traveling in Georgia, my native State, and in Alabama, Mississippi, the Carolinas and Virginia. I have come to a personal realization of the very desperate conditions resulting in that section from the wide spread influence of the economic debâcle of these past years. . . . Twenty-five per cent of our people live in our Southern States. . . . They are desperately poor as regards per capita wealth but rich as regards natural resources, and also as regards native talent. My lifelong relationship to political activities from the point of view of my economic principles has caused me . . . to keenly apprehend the danger which confronts us during the coming ten years, if the level of knowledge and understanding shall not be raised and broadened. The voters will need to know more. . . . It is therefore of greater importance than ever before in the history of the world that these twenty-five per cent of Anglo-Saxons be taught to think straight and deeply. This means adult education. There is not time to wait for the younger generation."

EDGAR GARDNER MURPHY, SECRETARY

The first executive secretary of the Southern Education Board was Edgar Gardner Murphy. As Alderman was the eloquent voice, so Murphy was the facile pen of this movement at its beginning. Born in Texas, he received his early education in the South and then attended Columbia University and the General Theological Seminary in New York. While rector of a church in Montgomery, Alabama, he took great interest in the civic life of the city and helped to found the public library and the Young Women's Christian Association.

Realizing that one of the handicaps of childhood in the South was the working of young children in the cotton mills, he threw himself into the efforts for the betterment of the conditions with regard to child labor in Alabama. He was distressed to find that the humane laws enforced in the cotton mills in the state as early as 1888 had been so changed at the behest of their Massachusetts owners as to make them among the worst in the country. Like the true crusader, he took the matter to Boston and with the support of the *Transcript* carried on in the newspapers one of the hottest contests ever waged concerning child labor.[12] Murphy's letters when published in the Alabama papers awakened wide interest and were largely responsible for the reform in legislation in that state concerning the labor of children in the mills. He organized and became chairman of the Alabama Child Labor Committee and founded the National Child Labor Committee, which stimulated interest in all the industrial states.

When, in the midst of the excellent advance being made along this line in every state, it was proposed to ask Congress to pass a law regulating child labor, Murphy opposed the measure with great earnestness on the ground that it was a matter for the states and not for the national government. In an open letter to the author of the National Child Labor bill, Honorable A. J. Beveridge, he marshaled his arguments with such power that the bill was defeated. Later decisions of the United

[12] Edgar Gardner Murphy, *The Present South*, Appendix B.

States Supreme Court have confirmed his reasoning that such statutes are unconstitutional, and subsequent legislation in the states has completely vindicated his judgment that such conditions can be best remedied through the forces of local initiative. Because of his inflexible opposition to its program in this case, Murphy withdrew from the National Child Labor Committee. But he never relaxed his interest in its labors, and on the twenty-fifth anniversary of its founding, handsome recognition of the constructive character of the service he had rendered it as its founder and the inspirer of much of its early labors was made by the Committee.

Murphy had always been deeply interested in the Negro problem of the South, and he was chiefly instrumental in organizing the committee in Montgomery which called the great Conference on the Race Problem, held there in 1900. His addresses on this subject show a rare insight into the special problems of the race issue. He had a keen interest in all the problems resulting from the existence of the black and the white race side by side, which raised such acute social and economic issues. Unlike many other students of the subject, while bold in advocating the educational and political rights of the Negro, he exhibited a thorough understanding of the southern aspects of the problem. Still he was never sidetracked from his search for the fundamental causes of the existing evils and was fearless in the exposure of their roots. He was deeply concerned, for example, by the injustice done the Negro in the allotment of school funds. His skillful diagnosis of social diseases and his intense interest in their origin always saved him from being called a mere "reformer."

A letter of Murphy to Walter Hines Page states his views on race relations. He is advising with regard to a program for a conference :

"Let us make the central idea the rightness, wisdom, and necessity of *Universal Education*—Education not as a badge of social distinction, but as the universal condition of fruitful industry and of wholesome and effective political reformation. I have never seen any .racial friction between two representatives of different races when *both* the individuals considered were really educated. Wherever there is a race problem— whether in the South or in the Philippines, our schools will do more than our armies.

"Nor should I limit the form of the appeal for education. . . . The misfortune and the degradation of the lowliest of its people is not only a moral peril, but an economic embarrassment to the noblest and the strongest. The solidarity of the people is not only a political result of our national experience in the past, but a vital economic and social condition of our progress in the future. . . . Industrial education should hold the first place with all peoples who possess a small degree of economic efficiency, but no limitation to the development of capacity should be imposed by restraint from without. *Repression,* as a policy, has never accomplished anything.

"We should insist for all races upon the priority of industrial and economic efficiency in relation to political privilege. We should strenuously oppose any suffrage regulation anywhere that was based upon purely racial discrimination. . . . It is increasingly necessary for white men, as well as Negroes, for Filipinos as well as for Americans, that there should be a clearer understanding of the relation between social efficiency and political power. Political power is . . . an instrument of damage save as it is wielded by trained citizens. Lowell's argument that the ballot would be in itself an education, and would develop the civic faculties which it implies, has largely broken down, not only at the South among both races, but under such conditions as those presented among immigrants in the State of Pennsylvania and in the City of New York." [13]

The appalling illiteracy among the whites, as well as among Negroes, of the South stirred Murphy deeply, and his study of the conditions in the public schools inspired the address delivered before the National Educational Association in Boston in 1903, which aroused great interest throughout the country.[14] Becoming absorbed in these educational and social causes, Murphy withdrew from the ministry in 1903 to become associated with Robert C. Ogden, president of the Southern Conference and Southern Education Board. In this capacity he rendered brilliant service to the cause, writing and speaking effectively wherever opportunity offered until invalided in 1910.

Murphy was vice president of the Conference for Education

---

[13] A statement accompanying a letter from Murphy of February 22, 1901, to Walter Hines Page.
[14] See Murphy, *op. cit.,* p. 31.

in the South and a member of the Southern Education Board up to the time of his death on June 23, 1913.

In addition to his book, *The Present South*, an account of the educational conditions, published in 1904, he published in 1909 *The Basis of Ascendency*, a discussion of the race problem. His books, articles, and speeches contributed greatly to the enlightenment of the American public on these questions.[15]

[15] For his life see *Dictionary of American Biography*.

CHAPTER V

FACTS AND FIGURES ABOUT SOUTHERN SCHOOLS

THE BUREAU OF THE SOUTHERN EDUCATION BOARD

AT Knoxville, Tennessee, on February 1, 1902, the Southern Education Board established a "Bureau of Information and Advice on Legislation and School Organization" to aid in carrying on a "campaign of education for free schools for all the people by supplying literature to the newspapers and periodical press, by participating in educational meetings, and by general correspondence." The Bureau was placed under the direction of Charles W. Dabney. P. P. Claxton was chief and Joseph D. Eggleston, Jr., was secretary and editor. Charles L. Coon became secretary and editor in February, 1903, succeeding Eggleston. George S. Dickerman rendered invaluable help in the statistical work. Wickliffe Rose had charge of the study of schools for teachers; Lilian W. Johnson assisted for a time in the women's work; and Edgar Gardner Murphy, executive secretary of the Board, contributed articles and bulletins. After a few months, the Bureau was given quarters in the buildings of the University of Tennessee.

Of the function of the Bureau, Dr. Rose wrote:

This is among the most important tasks undertaken by the board. It is not a difficult task to arouse a popular momentary enthusiasm on vital subjects. The campaign of education, as being conducted, has already awakened in many communities educational enthusiasm amounting to religious fervor. But unless this emotion be transformed into quiet intelligent interest it can not last, neither can it construct efficient schools unless it be guided by sane educational statesmanship. This statesmanship can not be adequately supplied by a few minds capable of taking the larger view, for in a democratic community schools and school systems must, in the last resort, be constructed by the people. It is of the highest importance, therefore, that while the campaign orator is kindling a popular enthusiasm the people be given a broad perspective of the real problems before them. They should be given the facts which portray the schools and school systems as they are in the Southern States. They should be led to view the situation in the light of the larger educational experience of other sections of our country and of other countries, and to use this comparison for constructive criticism in harmony with the genius of their own civilization. This should constitute the objective of the whole campaign, and the bureau calling into its service the educational leadership of the South should be, in President Ogden's happy phrase, the "ordnance department." This is the theory of the bureau.[1]

As indicated in the order establishing it, the activities of the Bureau were of three kinds :

1. The investigation of the conditions of the elementary schools, high schools, normal schools, industrial schools, and other institutions forming the educational systems of the southern states. The county systems of education were systematically studied as regards their schoolhouses, equipment, teachers, enrollment and attendance, supervision, expenditures, and especially their methods of local taxation. Special studies were made of illiteracy in the southern population ; of organization and supervision ; and of methods of consolidating schools and transporting pupils. These inquiries required much field work, some of which was done by volunteer teachers and students.

2. Dissemination of information. The Bureau undertook to supply information on these subjects in the form of circulars, bulletins, and newspaper notes, with illustrations from the experiences of other states and foreign countries.

3. Correspondence and meetings. In addition to the correspondence necessary to collect the data and material for these investigations, extensive correspondence with superintendents and principals seeking information with regard to supervision, courses of study, coördination, manual training, nature study, and a great variety of subjects touching school work was carried on. Frequently such inquiries could be answered by printed documents, issued by the Bureau, or the Bureau of Education in Washington, or some other office ; often a letter would have to be referred to several persons to supply the information asked for.

The officers of the Bureau attended many educational meetings and visited many schools. They took part in the state campaigns whenever possible.

[1] *Report of the United States Commissioner of Education, 1903,* I, 382.

The Southern Education Board made appropriations for the support of the Bureau, amounting to something less than $20,000 for the nearly two years of its existence. This work could never have been carried through had not the salaries in the Bureau been supplemented from money raised specially for the purpose by the Director of the Bureau. The University of Tennessee gave the Bureau quarters, heat, light, and water free. The Director served without compensation. The chief items of expense were salaries, travel, printing, and postage. The Bureau was discontinued after two years for want of support.

The serial publications of the Bureau, corresponding to the lines of work, consisted of :

1. Circulars, giving brief statements and arguments for use by the workers as campaign documents. Editions of these, numbering from 15,000 to 25,000, were printed.

2. Bulletins, carrying the more important reports on the investigations made. The bulletins were continued as a series under the title of *Southern Education*. The twenty numbers of *Southern Education* contained 420 pages.

3. *Southern Education Notes*, a bi-weekly series of slips, designed for the newspaper editors' hooks. They supplied facts, news, and discussions for the promotion of the campaign through the public press. Twenty-six numbers were issued. Starting with 1,400, the edition of these slips increased to 2,000.

Of these different pieces 113,200 copies were printed and distributed by the Bureau during the two years of its existence.[2]

For two years the Bureau edited the proceedings of the Southern Education Conference and Board. It published a number of non-serial circulars and pamphlets for use in the different states. The first circular contained a statement of the origin and purpose of the Southern Education Board. The second gave a brief summary of the teachings of Thomas Jefferson with regard to the necessity for public schools in a republic. The third was a statement concerning the Southern Board, and the fourth described the progress of the campaign during the first year.

The first Bulletin discussed the educational conditions in the southern Appalachian region. This region is the home and training ground of most of the southern whites who have gone out for a hundred years to fill the western portion of our country all the way from southern Indiana to Texas. They are the

---

[2] See list of publications in Appendix VI.

people whose fathers fought the battles of King's Mountain and Guilford Court House in the Revolution ; who won the day under Jackson in New Orleans ; who furnished a large proportion of the American soldiers in the War of 1812 and the Mexican War ; who sent out more soldiers in the Civil War on the two sides than any other section of the country ; and who in the Spanish-American War furnished more volunteers than any other section except Massachusetts. The report described the physical features of the country, the origin of these people, and their educational conditions in 1900. As the Appalachian range is the backbone of the eastern American continent, so these people may be justly described as the backbone of the southern states.

In the counties of the Appalachian region in the states of West Virginia, Virginia, Kentucky, North Carolina, Tennessee, South Carolina, and Georgia, in 1900, out of a population of 870,000 there were 142,000 illiterates, or 16 per cent.

This region had long been treated as the backyard of these states, and the people had never received the help to which they were entitled. They had long clamored for schools, but with the exception of Dr. Wiley's efforts in North Carolina, no adequate steps had ever been taken to give them proper schools.

Another bulletin discussed the "Educational Conditions in Tennessee." It gave the school population, white and colored, the number of schools for each race, the value of the schoolhouses and equipment, the number of teachers, salaries, enrollment, attendance, length of school term, and other pertinent facts.

The *Southern Education Notes* were intended to furnish a clearing house of educational information for the convenience of the newspapers and were issued every two weeks. With the first number of the *Notes* a letter was sent out to fourteen hundred newspapers of the South asking them to use the matter freely, without acknowledgment of its source, if they so wished. The results were gratifying. Never before had public education received so much attention from southern newspapers. The articles traveled around from newspaper to newspaper until they covered practically the entire section. Some of them were discussed pro and con, which helped the cause. These *Notes* and other publications of the Bureau awakened interest in the schools among people who had never given them serious thought before.

The policy of the Bureau was to give the facts about the conditions in the schools in the hope that the people of the South might be awakened to do their duty. With the purpose of informing the citizens at large, the Bureau published the actual conditions of the schools as shown by the reports of their superintendents.

The pamphlet entitled, *Facts about Southern Educational Progress, A Study in Public School Maintenance*,[3] was prepared by Charles L. Coon for the use of the workers in the field. It was based on the census of 1900 and the state school reports of eleven southern states (Virginia, North Carolina, South Carolina, Georgia, Florida, Alabama, Mississippi, Louisiana, Texas, Arkansas, and Tennessee) for 1903-1904.

It discussed the population; in 1900, 40 per cent of the people were Negroes; concerning illiteracy it pointed out that 27.7 of the male population of voting age were illiterate and of these 12.3 per cent were whites. It also gave the white and colored school population, the enrollment, attendance, and length of the school term, which for 1903-1904 was only 170 days for both white and colored schools. The average amount of property behind each child of school age in these eleven states was only $1,837 as compared with $4,236 on the average for the whole United States. The average funds expended for each child in the South, including town schools, was in 1903-1904 only $3.89 as against an average for the whole United States of $11.20. Florida and Texas were the only states expending half the latter amount.

The average annual salary of rural school teachers in these eleven southern states was $150, and the average salary of county superintendents was $900; the average value of rural schoolhouses was $285.

This publication also gave the constitutional provisions and the state school laws for taxation and administration in the eleven states at this time.

One circular discussed the relations of production and education:

[3] *Facts about Southern Educational Progress: A Study in Public School Maintenance*, by Charles L. Coon, Bureau of Investigation and Information, Southern Education Board, and the North Carolina Department of Education, June, 1905.

The relations between the opportunities for education and the production of wealth are now so well understood that we can measure the wealth-earning power of a people by the school privileges which they enjoy. Statistics show that the power of a people to earn money is in direct proportion to the length of the period the average citizen has attended school.

To illustrate, the average school period in 1898-99 of each inhabitant of the United States was 4.4 years ; of Massachusetts 7 years ; of Tennessee a little less than 3 years. The annual production per capita of the people in the United States in 1899 was $170 a year, or 55 cents a day. The production in Massachusetts in 1899 was $260 for each man, woman and child, or 85 cents a day. The most favorable figures make the total annual production of the people of Tennessee in 1899 less than $116 a year or 38 cents a day for each inhabitant....

Putting these facts together we get this comparison :

Education is as 14 in Massachusetts to 8.8 in United States to 6 in Tennessee.

Production is as 13 in Massachusetts to 8.5 in United States to 5.8 in Tennessee.

This is not a mere coincidence in the case of Massachusetts, the United States, and Tennessee ; it is the law the world over. The productivity of a people is everywhere proportional to their education—to their intellectual, physical, and moral training. It is not the natural resources, the climate, the soils, and the minerals ; it is not altogether the race, much as these things count ; but it is education which above everything else determines the wealth-earning power of a people....

Massachusetts expended for all purposes on her public schools in 1898-99, $13,889,838, which was $38.55 per pupil and $5.07 per capita of her population. Tennessee expended for her public schools in the same year $1,628,313, which is $4.62 per pupil and only 83 cents per capita of population. The average expenditure for all the states of the Union is $19 per pupil and $2.67 per capita of the population....

If the people of the South would compete in production with those of other States and of the world—and they must do so whether they will or not—they must educate all their children, not only their white children, but their black ; and they must educate them all, not poorly for a few months in the year and a few years in their lives, but thoroughly through a long series of years. If history teaches us anything it is the solidarity of all mankind, that "no man liveth unto himself," and "no man dieth unto himself," but that each is his "brother's keeper."

Our great resources in the South, climate, soils, and minerals, are useless in the hands of an untrained people. Moreover, if we do not educate our own people to use these resources intelligently, the trained men of other States will come in and do so, and make us "the hewers of wood and drawers of water" in their industries.[4]

To paraphrase Dr. Curry, a people's poverty is the most unanswerable argument for the expenditure of any amount of money necessary to give them good schools, for the right kind of school is the only remedy for poverty, as well as for crime. The southern people are too poor to afford the wastes of ignorance. If they spent more money for education they would not only save much in criminal prosecutions but would increase enormously their earning power.

These and similar statistics were widely published and commented on by northern papers.

But the Bureau did not stop with telling this sad story of the condition of the schools. Every such paper or address concluded the analysis of the situation with a plan for improving it. One of the reports of the Director concludes with definite recommendations for improvement of the conditions :

What is needed is :
1. Men and money to do more missionary work among the... more isolated populations. The people in one-half of the counties of the South are not able to support any kind of a decent school.... They must first be taught...how to cultivate the soil properly, how to utilize their forest and other resources and so to make money with which to maintain their schools....
2. Model consolidated schools should be established in every county.... If there were even three or four such schools in each State, properly located,...they would, we believe, multiply themselves very rapidly....
3. We must have normal schools for elementary teachers... in each State to train the country boys and girls to be teachers in the rural schools.
4. Superintendents, men competent to direct educational work, to organize and administer schools—educational engineers of all grades and classes—are greatly needed as well as principals of schools and supervisors of agricultural and industrial education,

[4] From leaflet by Charles Wm. Dabney entitled, *A World Wide Law : Ratio of Education to Production. University of Tennessee Index*, Series II, No. 10, Jan., 1901.

manual training, domestic science and art and the other newer branches.[5]

School Laws and Finances in the South, 1903-1904

Among southern people in 1903 there was still great need for clear thinking concerning the fundamental importance of public education. Some continued to believe that schools were in the nature of a luxury; that what was spent on them was economic loss; that the effect of expenditures for schools was to reduce the total income which might be saved for other purposes.

It was necessary to convince these people that instead of constituting an economic loss, money spent for schools is in the nature of an investment and of protection for the national government, the state, and the individual. Expenses for schools are an investment in that they create intelligence which makes an efficient economic system possible. Ignorant untrained citizens are neither good producers nor good consumers. Therefore, the people of the South had to be brought to realize that the money spent for education was an investment of the highest order.

In the second place, they still needed to be taught that education constitutes a protection necessary to preserve our institutions. The right kind of education is necessary to make a good citizen. Were it not for education, our whole civilization might gradually disappear and we would start on the way back to savagery. Some think that we might return to our level of education and efficiency of thirty or forty years ago and still be safe. But would we be in these new times? Shall we not preserve our recent gains and try to advance still further? To do this we must constantly improve our schools. It is important, therefore, that our schools be not only good schools, but very good schools, that they give vocational instruction and civic instruction as well as literary training.

The variation in the amount of wealth produced by different people in different places is still to be expected. The rich communities must, therefore, continue to aid the poor in maintaining their schools. This is as much an investment and protection for them as it is for the local people.

[5] Proceedings of the Sixth Conference for Education in the South, Richmond, Virginia, 1903, pp. 45-46.

Before any rational plan could be projected by the Southern Board in any particular state looking to the improvement of its schools it was necessary to know what the state was already doing—that is, what the school laws were and what the resources were for the use of the schools. Therefore one of the first things undertaken by the Bureau of Information was a study of the laws of each of the different states and an investigation of the educational funds available. This study was started and prosecuted in the Bureau under the direction of Dr. Rose while he was connected with it. When he became agent of the Peabody Board, the investigation was continued under his direction in the office of that Board. The results of this study were published in 1909 in a book entitled *School Funds in Ten Southern States.*[6]

This report showed the relative ability of the ten states to raise revenues for the support of their schools, the methods used by them in raising such revenues, and what each of them was doing at the time for the support of schools, with suggestions looking towards the improvement of their methods for raising school revenues. This was followed by a critical interpretation of the use which these states were making of the revenues then available. The report thus illuminated the subject of school finances from every point of view.

The South's frightful handicap owing to the great loss during the Civil War and Reconstruction period had first to be stated, in order to make plain the financial conditions facing those who worked for increased revenues for schools.

The poverty of the South in 1870 when she commenced to try to build up public schools was terrible. Her losses between 1860 and 1870 had been tremendous. In 1860 the southern states ranked up very well as compared with other states in their average wealth per capita. In some of them the per capita wealth was even greater than that of the rest of the country. The total wealth of the whole country, North and South, was in round numbers sixteen billions in 1860 ; these ten southern states had five billions, or approximately 30 per cent of it. By 1870 the total wealth of the whole United States had increased to thirty billions while that of the ten southern states

---

[6] *School Funds in Ten Southern States,* 1909, by Wickliffe Rose, of the Bureau of Investigation and Information, Southern Education Board ; General Agent, The Peabody Education Fund.

had dropped to a little more than two and a half billions, or about 8.3 per cent of the total. And this is not all. While the South had lost practically half of its property, its public debt had been increased greatly. Partly through the war and partly through the infamy of Reconstruction the debt of these southern states had more than quadrupled (from forty-eight and a half millions in 1850 to two hundred millions in 1870). The state debt of North Carolina, for example, was increased thirty-two fold and in 1870 it was equal to about a quarter of the total assessed value of all property in the state. In Virginia the public debt was about one-sixth, in Tennessee about one-fifth, of the total assessed wealth in 1870. And so for the other states.

But greater infinitely than the loss of money was the loss of men. This we cannot reduce to a statistical statement but we know that the South lost one-tenth of its male population from about sixteen years of age up. And that was not all. The severe conditions following the war and Reconstruction caused two and a half millions of its people to leave the South and seek homes in the West or in foreign countries (some went to Brazil) where conditions were more favorable. Worst of all was the loss of leaders of thought and action.

The South suffered the total destruction of its economic system and had to adjust itself immediately to a new one. The passing of slavery was in the end, of course, an economic gain, but the immediate effect was disastrous to the South's productive power. The subversion of the South's social and political systems set up a great barrier against economic progress. In the total lack of economic order, efforts at readjustments, including disastrous repudiations and political fights over the readjustments of debts, consumed the energy of strong men which ought to have been devoted to constructive work. For thirty-five years, from 1865 to at least 1900, immigration and capital both shunned the South. The opening up of the great new states of the West at this time invited men of energy and money to go there. The trend of the country's economic development was now for many years away from the poor southern states. The South also lost many of the markets for its products in the eastern states and in foreign countries.

The loss of property and of men, the burden of debt, the destruction of institutions, economic, social and political, the destruction of credit and the drift of money and men away from the South, the loss of markets—all these things combined to impoverish the South and to prevent its getting a new start.

In the thirty years from 1870 to 1900 the wealth of the whole United States increased 194 per cent, while through the strenuous efforts of the brave southern people the ten southern states gained 178 per cent. By 1900, after a hard struggle, just three of the ten states had regained a good portion of their per capita wealth of 1860. For example, the higher price of cotton had enabled Mississippi and South Carolina by 1900 to win back one-half of the per capita wealth that they had in 1860. The other southern states were dragging far behind. It is notable that during this period the total wealth of the United States increased from sixteen billions in 1860 to eighty-eight and a half billions in 1900, or an average per capita for every man in the country of $1,165, a gain of over 100 per cent. There was one note of encouragement for the South ; by 1900 these ten states had reduced their public debt to a manageable amount.[7] The South had, at last, begun to accumulate a small surplus of working capital to be used in the production of more wealth.

After making clear the financial condition of the South in the decades immediately preceding, Dr. Rose next discussed the ability of the South to support schools in 1904. His tables show the per capita wealth of these states on the basis of the true value and the relations of the wealth to the school population as compared with other states. His statistics show, for example, that, while the ten southern states had one-fifth of the population, they had in 1904 a little more than one-twelfth of the wealth. One state, Illinois, with less than one-third as many people, had nearly as much wealth as the whole ten southern states. The combined population of Massachusetts, New York, and Pennsylvania, which was about equal to that of the ten southern states, had four times as much wealth as all of these ten southern states.

The per capita wealth of the South in 1904 was only $527 ; for the whole United States, it was $1,318, or two and a half times as great. The percentage of adult males in the population,

[7] The statistics are from the census and are for the ten southern states, Alabama, Arkansas, Florida, Georgia, Louisiana, Mississippi, North Carolina, South Carolina, Tennessee, and Virginia. Texas was omitted because, lying across the Mississippi, it did not suffer the ravages of the war as the other states did and, having vast untouched resources, recovered more rapidly than the other states.

who have to support the schools, was less in the South than in
the rest of the country. The average wealth for each adult male
in the South in 1904 was $2,280 ; for the whole United States,
the average was $4,738. In order to raise $12 a year for each
child of school age in 1904, the average for each child of school
age in the United States, each mature male had to raise only
$12, while in the South where there are fewer males each one
had to produce $16.80. In Alabama, to raise this amount, the
tax on each male would have been $18 ; in North Carolina,
$19.20, whereas in Connecticut and Massachusetts each male
would have had to pay only $8.90.

In addition to this, Dr. Rose showed that the school population in the southern states is relatively large. There are more
children to the family. Of the total population of the United
States the ten southern states have about one-fifth, but of the
school population they have one-fourth. The total amount of
wealth given each child of school age in South Carolina in 1904
was only $1,190 while in New York it was $7,940. To express
it in another way : for every $1.60 for each child of school age
in the South, the whole United States had $4.65 ; Connecticut
had $6.30 ; and Massachusetts, $7.35.

Next Dr. Rose compared the ability as represented by the
wealth with the burden upon these different sections. In 1904
the United States raised, as we above found, about $12 for each
child of school age. What tax would have been required to
raise this amount in each southern state? In South Carolina a
tax on $100 of property would have to have been $1, while in
New York it would have been only fifteen cents ; in Massachusetts, sixteen cents ; in Illinois and New Jersey, nineteen
cents. An average tax for the whole United States would have
been less than twenty-six cents, while that of the southern states
would have to have been seventy-five cents in order to raise
this $12 for each child.

To sum it all up, these figures show that to raise a certain
amount of revenue for each child of school age, the burden on
these ten southern states in 1903-1904 would have been three
times as heavy as for the whole United States. In addition to
this two other serious considerations must be added—the necessity for a duplicate set of schools and the fact that the South
is so largely a rural, agricultural section, a land where the school
population is scattered over large areas, necessitating the main-

tenance of a large number of schools, where the tariff is always against it.

The school expenditures on the basis of average daily attendance, shown in the report, give us more light. For the whole United States in 1906 the average daily attendance on schools was nearly 50 per cent; for the South, 41 per cent. This, of course, tended to increase for the South the relative expenditure for each pupil. The United States spent in 1906 for each pupil in average daily attendance $25.40 while the South spent $8.90. From this point of view South Carolina ranked lowest of the southern states with an expenditure of $6.51, Louisiana highest with an expenditure of $14.83, while the average for the United States was nearly four times as much as the expenditure of South Carolina. To put it in another way—for every dollar spent in the South for each pupil in daily attendance the United States spent nearly three dollars. In other words, in 1905-1906, the school revenues were absolutely inadequate.

The report next compared the actual support given the schools with the financial ability of these states. Referring now to the compilation of the total wealth for 1902, in the first place we find that the total taxes levied for all purposes in these southern states for the year 1902 represented an average rate of 68 cents on each $100 of true value of property, while the general average for the United States the same year was 74 cents. For example, in North Carolina every $100 of wealth had to produce 52 cents of revenue, while in Massachusetts every $100 of wealth had to produce $1.06 of revenue. In Tennessee the tax rate equaled that of the United States; in Georgia and Louisiana it was greater than the United States on each $100 of value. In the other seven states of this group the average was lower than the United States, being for Alabama 56 cents, for Virginia 58 cents. From this it appears that in raising public revenue by taxation, if we take the average of the United States as a standard, only three of the southern states were living up to their ability in 1902-1903. In the southern states, however, as already stated, a much larger share of the revenues than in the rest of the country comes from sources other than the general property tax. Another compilation in this report showed that for the general average for the ten southern states, $100 of wealth produced a revenue from all sources of $1.12 as against the general average for the United States of $1.13. From all this it appears that in 1902 the southern states raised for all purposes—state, county and town—practically as much revenue according to their financial ability as did the rest of the country. But for public schools, their most important item of expenditure, the southern people were doing less according to their financial ability than the rest of the country. In this connection we should recall that, of the country's population in 1904, the South had about one-fifth, while of its wealth it had only about one-twelfth.

The report next considered the relation of wealth to the actual expenditures for schools in the year 1904. For the United States the total expenditures for public schools for each $100 true value of all property was over 25 cents; in the western division it was 24 cents; in the north central division, 26 cents; in the north Atlantic division, 27 cents; but for the south Atlantic, only 20 cents. For the south central division, it was less than 20 cents. For each $100 of its wealth Georgia spent for public schools in 1904 just 19 cents; Virginia, 17 cents; Louisiana, 15 cents; Alabama, 13 cents, which was little more than half the general average for the United States. The wealthy states were not only spending a larger amount of money for schools but they were spending more for each $100 of their wealth. For example, Connecticut was spending 27 cents per $100 of wealth; Indiana, 30 cents; and Massachusetts, 33 cents. The great northwestern states were doing the best for education. The state of Washington, for example, was spending for every $100 of her wealth over 30 cents, or two and a half times as much as Alabama. These figures are sufficient to show that in the support given to the schools, the southern states were not, by any means, living up to their financial ability in 1904.

Reviewing now the facts about the sources of funds and the totals collected in the different states given in this report, we found in 1904 that in some states, like Alabama, the public school fund derived from local sources was extremely small.[8] From this followed two fundamental serious defects. The elementary schools there became too great a burden upon the state. The state money also inhibited local interest and prevented local initiative. The experience everywhere shows that the elementary schools cannot be wholly given the people from

[8] The details of state funds will be found in the report previously referred to, *School Funds in Ten Southern States*.

above ; they must be locally supported in large part. The schools should be born out of the home, grow out of the community which they are intended to serve, and be the result of local effort and local work. The plan of supporting the local schools entirely from the state treasury has a very bad effect also upon the higher institutions. After the large appropriations to public schools are made, the lawmakers are apt to feel they have done their share, and therefore they give the higher institutions very little. As a matter of fact, there is usually very little left for the higher institutions. The plan of supporting the town schools entirely from the state is thus the worst conceivable one for maintaining schools. The educational system of a state ought to be supported by local districts, counties, and the state all together.

CHAPTER VI

THE ATHENS CONFERENCE, 1902

BROADENING CONCEPTS

D R. CURRY'S declaration in his memorable address at Capon Springs that "the white people are to be the leaders, to take the initiative, to have the directive control in all matters pertaining to the civilization and the highest interests of our beloved land," was accepted fully thenceforward, by the northern as well as by the southern friends of the Negro, as a fundamental proposition. At the Winston-Salem Conference, therefore, the education of the whites had been the chief subject of discussion, and the organization of a campaign for universal education was its practical outcome.

The next line of advance of the Conference in the definition of its purpose was from the education of the individual to the education of the community. The first practical problem was how to provide more school funds ; better school buildings and equipment ; longer school terms and better teachers. To get these it was necessary to enlighten the people and arouse their social conscience. Before the schools could be made what they should be, the people had to be given a new conception of public education, a new interest, and a new spirit. From now on, the task of the Conference was to awaken the people to their duty to the children, to instruct them as to what constituted good schools, and how to get the legislation to build and support them. This plan, as has been shown, found expression in the organization of the Southern Education Board, with its bureau and its field agents in the different states. Through these agencies and through the many local associations which now sprang up, the spirit of the Conference, with its gospel of universal education, was to be carried in the next ten years into every community in the South.

At the meeting in Athens, Georgia, in 1902, the Conference reached another stage in liberalizing its spirit and enlarging its purpose in terms of the national life and the large movements of civilization. This followed logically from the consideration of educational reform as the primary phase of the general movement. As from the individual to the community was the first step, so from the community to the nation was the next step. So it was that education and democracy, the solidarity of the common duties and privileges involved in the ideal of American citizenship, became the dominant note of the Athens meeting. This note, sounded by several speakers, met with hearty sympathy and aroused great expectations in the minds of all there present.

Mr. Ogden again brought a large company from the North, which was joined by a number of his friends along his way through the South.[1]

A Cosmopolitan Gathering

The Winston-Salem Conference had made a great impression on the people of the South, and there was now a large attendance of state officers, state superintendents, superintendents and principals of schools, presidents, trustees, and professors of colleges, teachers, and representatives of women's clubs and other societies from that section.

The people of Athens entertained the members of the Conference in their homes with a gracious hospitality that added much to the spiritual influence of the meeting. Chancellor Walter B. Hill of the University, soon to become a member of the Southern Education Board and an influential worker for the cause, and Eugene C. Branson, president of the State Normal School and the South's chief authority on economic and social conditions, were the hosts. At the invitation of the governor and the legislature of Georgia the Conference assembled in the ancient chapel of the University where J. L. M. Curry, Ben

[1] Among those who had not attended previous meetings were : Professor Paul H. Hanus of Harvard, Professor H. W. Farnam of Yale, Edward Cary of the *New York Times*, Dr. William Adams Brown of Union Theological Seminary, New York, Dr. William T. Harris, United States commissioner of education, Oswald Garrison Villard of the *New York Evening Post*, Lilian D. Wald, Hamilton W. Mabie, Reverend S. D. McConnell of Brooklyn, James M. Taylor of Vassar College, L. H. Bailey of Cornell, Felix Adler, leader of the Institute of Ethical Culture, Talcott Williams, editor of the *Philadelphia Press*, Arthur Curtis James of New York, and St. Clair McKelway of the *Brooklyn Eagle*. Among the governors of the southern states present were Montague of Virginia, Aycock of North Carolina, Frazier of Tennessee, Jelks of Alabama, Longino of Mississippi, and ex-Governor Northern of Georgia.

Hill, Robert Toombs, Alexander Stephens, and Henry Grady were educated.

Mr. Ogden in his annual address as president explained again the character of the Conference and its purposes, organization, plans, and agencies as developed in accordance with the resolutions of the Winston-Salem meeting.

It was the mission of the Conference, he said, to bring together and unite in common service the many workers for public education in the South. Northern people interested in the cause came each year in response to invitation to see how they might help carry the load that seemed too heavy to be borne in localities where sparse population and small means gave insufficient public revenue and made private support impossible. "With no pride of opinion or dictation as to method, working through men born on the soil and using local machinery, they come in fraternal spirit with such means as they can command and such experience as they can contribute."

The personnel of the meeting was thus most cosmopolitan. There were governors of states, officers of railroads and other great corporations in the South, educators of every degree, clergymen of many communions, editors, authors, bankers, merchants, lawyers, all of whom set aside for the time their several cares to confer together about the educational interests of their common country.

FELIX ADLER'S ADDRESS

The Conference was notable for its many addresses and for its harmony and enthusiasm. Dr. Felix Adler argued that the purpose of the Conference should be to introduce true democracy through the education of a competent citizenship. He said it was not enough that education should foster economic welfare, wipe out the blot of illiteracy—those things must be done; but in addition, beyond them, the American ideal must be subserved; that ideal was the yet unsolved problem of a true democracy, and the first condition of that democracy was to make the best life possible for every citizen. "The best life . . . is that which will make possible for every man to do that sort of work for which he is best fitted, to earn for himself maximum power and usefulness." The second condition, he argued, was that everyone shall actually do the work for which he is best fitted, which means that the best shall rule, not an aristocracy of race or wealth. "What we need in this country is a democratic aristocracy, one that shall be founded ... on merit, not on family or wealth, ... a house of aristocracy, the gates of which shall be ever open, both ways, to let the unworthy out and to let the best and noblest in." And here is what the South can contribute to the nation's greatness. "I have in mind not only the graces of manner and social charms, ... not only the splendid oratory, ... of which we have had such admirable examples, not only the absence of commercialism, which I think is still a ... conspicuous trait in the Southern attitude toward life, but I have in mind especially the tradition of a democratic aristocracy which lingers amongst your people and which ... may form a most valuable aid in developing the idea of a democratic aristocracy throughout our land. What I have in mind is that the New South ... shall not merely be a late learner and imitator of models set up elsewhere ; but that the best traits of the Old South after taking on a new form shall be incorporated as a priceless and lasting constituent in our national ideal."

HOKE SMITH'S ADDRESS

Governor Hoke Smith, formerly secretary of the interior and senator from Georgia, emphasized the necessity of the improvement of the rural school as the greatest problem of the South. He said, "Eight-tenths of our people live in the country, and yet not one-third of our lands are being tilled, and that which is being cultivated is not tilled as it should be." The sparsity of the population and the tenant system, he pointed out, are great obstacles. He made use of statistics, saying that Massachusetts had 8,000 square miles and Georgia 58,000 square miles ; that the people of Massachusetts were worth five times as much per capita as the people of Georgia ; that the population of Massachusetts was 400,000 larger than Georgia and yet Georgia had 200,000 more children. Massachusetts could build a school to every square mile and have sixty-five children to put in it ; Georgia had only eleven children to every square mile, and five of these were black, requiring separate schools. Of the taxes in the South, 95 per cent were paid by whites ; still over $100,000,000 had been spent by the South since the war for the education of Negroes. "The Negroes are free, independent men and women, and unless their minds and characters are lifted upward, the danger is that they may rapidly go backwards.... As intelligent and Christian character pervades our people ... they will become more in favor of educating ... the Negro as well as ... the white children."

CHARLES B. AYCOCK SPEAKS

Governor Aycock of North Carolina seconded Governor Smith's address and then urged the members of the Conference to remember that the real work had to be carried into the rural districts ; the people would not come to them. "When a man is hungry he will come to you for bread, but the ignorant man will not come. We have to go to him and insist that he educate his children." He stated that 82 per cent of the population of North Carolina lived in the country, and to that field the workers must go and urge the people to vote for local taxes for the public schools.

ALBERT SHAW'S ADDRESS

Albert Shaw called attention to the fact that the South had never had its reasonable share of the funds given for education out of the surplus wealth, to which the resources of the whole country had contributed. Of the $19,000,000 contributed in this country for educational institutions during the single year of 1900 only a little more than $1,000,000 came into the southern states for the education of both races. In other words, only 5 per cent came to the portion of the country containing 25 per cent of the population, where undoubtedly the needs were the greatest. The civilized world thought it very severe when the Germans exacted an indemnity of milliards from the French after conquering them and destroying a great part of their country in 1871. We forget that in a different way the North has exacted much more from the impoverished South since the Civil War. The southern states were much more nearly ruined by the war than France was; the debts to their own people were all repudiated; for years, as they have painfully worked their way back to solvency, they paid their part of the debt which the North created to defeat them. For one item, the South has been paying from fifty to sixty million dollars a year to the national pension fund, very little of which is returned to its people. Meanwhile, high tariffs favoring the eastern manufacturers added to this burden upon the agricultural people of the South. This great tax upon its resources the South has borne with amazing patience and avoidance of open complaint. This fact furnished an additional reason why the South should be generously supported in its educational work with whatever resources, public or private, were available for the promotion of education in America.[1]

William T. Harris's Estimate of the Conference

Dr. William T. Harris, United States commissioner of education, expressed his hearty approval of the purposes of the Conference in its effort to put the means of education within the reach of every child, white and black. The Conference was doing more for the United States as a whole than any other one agency in the country. The most important business in the United States for the North as well as for the South was the movement this Conference was leading.

Reports from the Field

The business proceedings consisted of reports from the Bureau of Investigation and Information, and upon the work of the different directors in the states in organizing community effort, addressing meetings of citizens, securing and increasing taxes, longer terms for schools, efficient teachers, and improvements in the school buildings and equipments. The whole situation of southern education was reviewed. The South was awakening to a realization of the condition and to a sense of its duty. New social forces were organizing and new leaders coming forward. The sentiment for schools, which had so long been held back by prejudice, was gathering strength for the support of this movement for universal education. The southern people were realizing that politicians had been keeping up the race feeling for selfish reasons. The Negro was to be made a friend and a fellow citizen. All the forces of southern life were bursting forth like vegetation in the springtime.

[1] *Proceedings of the Fifth Conference for Education in the South, Athens, Georgia, 1902*, pp. 99-100.

The Conference adjourned for the services of the regular Confederate Memorial Day and its members attended them in a body. In a gracious way the General Education Board announced a gift to the Georgia State Normal School to complete the Winnie Davis Memorial Hall and also the gift to the school of fifty additional scholarships. It was evident that the Conference had now become national in its character, and, as Hamilton Wright Mabie said, "had taken hold of the people of the South as nothing had taken hold of them since the Civil War. It is a movement not only for the betterment of a great section but for the knitting of closer ties between all sections." It was helping to complete the re-nationalization of the southern states.

The announcement of the gift of Mr. George Foster Peabody, the loyal son of Georgia and supporter of the Board, of a library building for the University was also made at this time.

CHAPTER VII

THE RICHMOND CONFERENCE, 1903

THE GROWTH OF THE EDUCATIONAL MOVEMENT

THE year following the Conference at Athens was one of rapidly increasing activity in the southern educational field. The district directors of the Board were at work forming additional state, district, and local organizations of different kinds to carry on the program. Meetings of school superintendents were held in eight different states to promote acquaintance and the discussion of local problems. Permanent organizations were formed for annual or quarterly meetings. The people gathered in courthouses, public halls, and churches to hear the leaders talk on education. Questions of improved legislation, local taxation, state appropriations, efficient superintendence, and administration of educational systems of the states were discussed. Everywhere the interest was increasing.

The politicians soon found that the people took more interest in school matters than in hackneyed political themes. Governor Aycock of North Carolina, who had led in these discussions from the beginning, testified that he had far larger and more interested audiences at educational meetings than had ever attended his political gatherings. College professors, ministers, doctors, business men, and citizens generally joined in the campaign with enthusiasm.

The increasing power of the movement appeared in the sixth Conference, held in Richmond in 1903. The governor, the legislature, the state department of education, the Richmond chamber of commerce, the University of Virginia, the University of Richmond, Washington and Lee University, and other representative institutions had invited the Conference to meet in Virginia.

THE GATHERING IN RICHMOND

The Richmond Educational Association took charge of all local arrangements. The railroads gave a liberal rate for transportation. The press of Richmond and Virginia joined in the generous welcome and did much to help the cause. The *Times-Dispatch*, after declaring its faith in the purposes of the meeting, invited all who were still suspicious of the purposes of the Conference to "come and see" for themselves. Dr. Hollis B. Frissell, field director in Virginia, said : "One of the most helpful agencies for the creation of public sentiment favorable to free schools is the state press. Almost without exception, the religious and secular papers have opened their columns to educational news and have published editorials bearing upon the needs of the schools."

There was a more representative attendance from the North than at any previous Conference. Mr. Ogden brought a distinguished company of one hundred and twelve persons on his private train.[1]

Many others came from all parts of the country. Included among the members of the Conference were thirty-seven college and university presidents, thirty-nine college professors, twenty-six principals and teachers of academies, institutes, and other similar schools, ten state superintendents, eleven city and county superintendents, and fifteen representatives of newspapers. The total attendance was over two thousand.

The meetings were held in the Academy of Music from April 22 to 24 and then continued at the University of Virginia on the twenty-fifth. On the twenty-sixth, which was Sunday, an impressive memorial service was held in Richmond for Dr. Jabez Lamar Monroe Curry, the founder and great leader of the crusade, who had died on February 12.

The governor of Virginia, Andrew Jackson Montague, welcomed the Conference, before a large audience, in an address

[1] Among his guests who had not attended previous meetings were : Mr. and Mrs. Edward Bok, Mr. and Mrs. Frank R. Chambers of New York, Reverend Hugh Chapman of London, Mrs. F. N. Doubleday of New York, Professor and Mrs. Richard E. Dodge of Teachers College, Dr. and Mrs. Paul R. Frothingham of Boston, Miss Laura Drake Gill, President of Barnard College, Mr. and Mrs. Richard Watson Gilder of New York, Reverend Teunis S. Hamlin of Washington, Honorable Hilary A. Herbert of Washington, ex-Governor and Mrs. Thomas J. Jarvis of North Carolina, Mr. and Mrs. William R. Moody of Northfield, Massachusetts, Reverend Leighton Parks of Boston, President Ira Remsen of Johns Hopkins University, Baltimore, W. W. Stetson, state superintendent of public instruction, Augusta, Maine, Mr. and Mrs. J. G. Thorpe of Cambridge, President M. Cary Thomas of Bryn Mawr College, J. H. VanSickle, superintendent of public schools of Baltimore, Everett P. Wheeler of New York, and President Mary E. Woolley of Mount Holyoke College, Massachusetts.

in which he stressed the necessity of the education of all the people in a democracy. Recalling how the ruling class of Old Virginia opposed for years free public schools for all the people, Governor Montague's address marked a new epoch in education.

Delighted with the splendid welcome given the Conference, the president, Mr. Ogden, after thanking the governor, the legislature, and the various institutions which extended the invitation, made an address in which he explained the plans and purposes of the Conference.[1a]

Following this meeting, a reception, given to the members by the citizens at Richmond College, did much to develop that fellowship between the members from the North and the South, which had been growing since the Winston-Salem meeting and which was to continue to grow and to become a most powerful factor in advancing the cause.

Professor Wickliffe Rose of the University of Tennessee discussed "The Place of the University in Modern Life." He was followed by Chancellor Kirkland of Vanderbilt University on "The Teacher and the State," President Venable of the University of North Carolina on "The Work of the University in the Southern States," and Professor Edwin Mims of Trinity College on "The University in the South."

Josephus Daniels of North Carolina discussed the difficulties which had prevented the development of the public schools in his state—the Negro question, poverty, lack of qualified teachers, the sparsity of the population. President David F. Houston, of the Agricultural and Mechanical College of Texas, discussed "The Education of the Farmers," and Dr. L. H. Bailey, of Cornell University, spoke on "Education through Agriculture." He said, in part :

The history of education for the past two hundred years has been a constant encroachment of those subjects that have relation to the daily life upon the school courses.... Little by little the schools have come to the people. The steps by which they are beginning to touch the life of the people are six :

1. The ... fulfillment of the idea that it is the duty of the state to provide for education for all the people....

2. The rise of equal opportunity for women....

3. The ... idea that the State ... must compel its children to attend school....

[1a] See Appendix VIII for extracts from this address.

4. The ... development of the scientific spirit in education. ...
Every subject is studied by the scientific method. ...

5. The ... idea that education should be related ... to the daily
life. ...

6. The missionary and altruistic spirit has seized us. We would
bring the schools to all the people everywhere.[2]

Professor Bailey then explained the modern methods of
teaching agriculture through the schools, the normal schools,
and the agricultural colleges. He declared that, agriculture being
the chief industry of the South, agricultural education should
receive first attention in the schools.

When our agricultural teaching is renewed and revitalized,
when it shakes off academic methods, ... when it puts itself in line
with the best ... thought of the time, when it teaches more with
objects than with books, then the young people will fill our agricultural schools, whether they desire education for living or for
culture. ... Begin with the young children in the elementary
schools. ... Build schoolhouses. Equip them well. Employ soulful
and inspiring teachers. ... Tax the property to pay for it; it will
be an investment. Then relate the school to the daily life of its own
community. Then every schoolhouse will have a voice, and it will
say, "I teach!"

> I teach!!
> The earth and soil
> To them that toil,
> The hill and fen
> To common men,
>   That live just here ;—
>
> The plants that grow,
> The winds that blow,
> The streams that run
> In rain and sun,
>   Throughout the year ;—
>
> And then I lead
> Thro' wood and mead,
> Thro' mould and sod
> Out unto God,
>   With love and cheer.
> I teach! [3]

[2] *Proceedings of the Sixth Conference for Education in the South, Richmond, Virginia, 1903*, pp. 112-15.

[3] L. H. Bailey, from original poem entitled, "The Ideal of the Rural
School." *Proceedings of the Sixth Conference for Education in the South,
Richmond, Virginia, 1903*, p. 123.

WALTER B. HILL ON "UNCLE TOM IN HIS OWN CABIN"

A significant address was that of Chancellor Hill of Georgia, entitled "Uncle Tom in His Own Cabin." Walter Barnard Hill was a fine scholar, a magnetic personality, and a wise patriot with broad vision of the southern problem, and his paper on the Negro was a classic discussion. There are three periods, he said, in the history of Negro education. The period of slavery Hill described as "Uncle Tom in His Owner's Cabin." The second period, the period of Reconstruction, he called "Uncle Tom Without a Cabin." He was promised forty acres and a mule in the new era, but he got neither of these things. The third period was "Uncle Tom in His Own Cabin" when he became a home-maker on the soil.

In the period which he called "Uncle Tom in His Owner's Cabin" Hill discussed the Negro's tutelage as a slave. "The tutelage of the slave developed the Negro in a century and a half from the condition of the savage to a status where, in the judgment of those hostile to slavery, the Negro was fitted for the privileges of American citizenship. No free civilized race ever made equal progress from barbarism in so short a time. The education of slavery was not in books ; books were not needed in the beginning. It was an education and discipline in practical ethics ; in the virtues of order, fidelity, temperance and obedience."

The second period, "Uncle Tom Without a Cabin," began shortly after emancipation and included the blunders of the Reconstruction period :

As the teaching of books had been denied to the Negro in slavery, so now it was assumed that the only education needed was to supply this omission, and accordingly an effort was made in schools and colleges to insert into the mind of the Negro race, as by a surgical operation, the culture for which the Anglo-Saxon race had been preparing through long centuries of growth.... The result of this error was to create a body of opinion in the South that education so-called was spoiling the Negro as a laborer and not fitting him for anything else. Both the mistakes abounded until it was seen that the need of the Negro race was not so much a reversal of that education which began under slavery as a system that would supplement and develop it.... It is embodied in Hamp-

ton and Tuskegee as concrete examples. They are the pioneers
blazing the path and pointing the way.

The third period, "Uncle Tom in His Own Cabin," is discussed at greater length. It is the era ushered in under the
leadership of General Armstrong and Principal Washington,
when the Negro is becoming a home-maker, a farmer, a mechanic, and a good citizen. "There is no race problem as between
the good citizens of the South among the whites, and the good
citizens of the South among the blacks. The solution of the
Negro problem . . . is Uncle Tom in His Own Cabin, or as I
should prefer to say, in his own home on the soil of the South
where he has grown up."

The Nation has remanded the solution of the Negro problem,
including his education, to the South. . . . There are some to be
found who say, or at least imply, that the South cannot afford
to do full justice to the Negro in the matter of education. They
affect to fear that the result of such a policy will be to bring the
Negro into dangerous competition with the white race. There is
no surer way in which a member of the white race can exhibit his
unworthiness of the blood in his veins than to entertain an appre-
hension that the Negro can so overcome racial characteristics and
the advantage of a start of at least two thousand years as to
endanger the supremacy of the race. . . . The only thing which the
South cannot afford in its relation to the Negro race, is injustice. . . .
Injustice injures and deteriorates the individual or nation that practices it, while on the other hand, it develops patience . . . —tenacity
and strength—in the people upon whom it is inflicted. . . . Plato said :
"Better is the case of him who suffers injustice than the case of
him who does it." [4]

Hill taught that injustice alone would endanger the supremacy of the white race. This will not happen, he said, for the
South is ready to bring to this problem not only the spirit of
justice but the spirit of kindness. "There is a kindness born of
old Southern traditions drawn in with the mother's milk, a feeling which survived the unspeakable indignities of reconstruction and will outlive all the irritations of the present and the
future." Concluding, Hill said :

The South has done much for the education of the Negro
already and will take no backward step. . . . The United States com-

[4] *Ibid.,* pp. 209-11.

missioner of education has said that since 1870 the South has disbursed for Negro education $109,000,000 (Report of 1899-1900, Vol. 2, p. 2501). For every dollar contributed by the philanthropy of the North for this purpose, the South, out of her poverty, has contributed four dollars. It cannot be truthfully claimed that all the people of the Southern states are pleased with this situation. It must be frankly admitted that a very considerable number, though a minority, are restive under it. It can be asserted, however, that the leaders of thought among the people are the friends of Negro education. . . .

The South will take no backward step in this matter. Negro education will share in all the increase of public taxation from the rapidly developing wealth of the section. The policy of separate schools will, of course, be maintained ; and it is gratifying that this is not only the settled purpose of the whites, but that the intelligent Negroes are coming to see . . . that co-education of the races or any other intermingling is not to be desired from the point of view of the best interests of the Negro race.[5]

The meeting on the last day of the Conference was a most enthusiastic one. The visitors taxed the capacity of the great Academy of Music. It was said to have been one of the greatest audiences ever assembled in Richmond at such a Convention. From ten o'clock in the morning until eleven o'clock at night there was practically a continuous session.[6] The first wave of enthusiasm of the day was evoked by the announcement of the reëlection of Robert C. Ogden to the presidency of the Conference.[7]

AT THE UNIVERSITY OF VIRGINIA

The entire Conference went to the University of Virginia on Saturday, April 25th. Dr. Paul B. Barringer, chairman of the Faculty, welcomed the meeting and extended to the members the freedom of the University founded by Jefferson. He gave Mr. Ogden the cue by referring to Jefferson as the first

[5] *Ibid.*, pp. 211-12.

[6] The chief speeches of this meeting were published, as a contribution to the study of social conditions in the South, in the *Annals of the American Academy of Political and Social Science*, XXII (July, 1903, to December, 1903), 245-329.

[7] The others chosen were : vice president, Edgar Gardner Murphy, Montgomery, Alabama ; secretary, B. J. Baldwin, Montgomery, Alabama ; treasurer, W. A. Blair, Winston-Salem, North Carolina ; chairman of the executive committee, B. B. Valentine, Richmond, Virginia.

champion of free public schools and the author of the first plan for a public school system in America.

After thanking the University, Mr. Ogden said: "We are here today observing the genius of a single man as applied to the problem of our civilization. Most of the institutions of learning throughout this land have some personal association with some great man. The University of Virginia owes its creation to the genius of Thomas Jefferson.... All of these influences come rolling back upon us ... in this period, bringing to us the responsibility of fulfilling their ideals." [8]

Professor Charles W. Kent, of the University, said that Jefferson "left as his written opinion that if there should be any choice between the education of the few in the university and the education of the many in the primary schools, the primary schools should be taken care of first ...; that it is indeed a matter of necessity to us in a democratic government, trusting as it does to the intelligent support of individual citizens, a matter of more vital consequence that all men should be educated in ... the fundamental principles than that a few should have the higher education." [9]

Charles W. Dabney spoke of "Jefferson the Seer," or prophet of education in America, whose dream was at last to come true.[10]

Professor Richard Heath Dabney, of the University, reminded the company that this man, Jefferson, governor of Virginia, minister to France, secretary of state, vice-president and twice president of the United States, founder of a great party, purchaser of a vast territory to be added to his country—this man, the greatest scientist and philosopher of his day, and yet preëminently a man of affairs, a practical man, this man said that the first and last, the earliest and latest, the alpha and omega, of his thoughts was education.[11]

In summarizing his impressions of the Richmond Conference, Dr. Lyman Abbott said that the revival of education in the South meant "a revival of industry, a humanizing ... ennobling of all vocations." It meant also a "revival of political

---

[8] *Proceedings of the Sixth Conference for Education in the South, Richmond, Virginia, 1903*, p. 233.

[9] *Ibid.*, p. 235.

[10] *Ibid.*, pp. 244-47; and *Jefferson the Seer*, by Charles Wm. Dabney.

[11] *Proceedings of the Sixth Conference for Education in the South, Richmond, Virginia, 1903*, pp. 240-43.

liberty," because in universal education it lays the only enduring foundation for universal freedom. The revival of education was also a revival of the home, since everything done to educate the child and to protect him from exploitation was a recognition of the value of the individual to the state and of the value of the home "as the beginning and the end, the foundation and the capstone, of American civilization." The educational revival was also a revival of religion, since "the schoolhouse and the church are partners in a common enterprise," "the making of men and women."

"We may well hope," he said, "that the present Southern educational enthusiasm may spread to the Northern States, where education is in danger of becoming somewhat perfunctory, may inspire it with new and deeper life, and may end by creating throughout the Nation an educational revival, the modern analogue of the evangelistic revivals of a past epoch, and carrying with it the promise and potency of a revival of industry, freedom, domestic life, and a purified religious spirit." [12]

Dr. Shaw said in the *New York Times*, May 1, 1903, "This year's conference has confirmed my belief that the Constitutional amendments recently enacted in the various Southern States respecting Negro disfranchisement were timely and necessary. It really gives him a vote, for heretofore he has never had a vote. Before this time the South has taken the stand that Negro suffrage was forced upon her. Now she has given the Negro a chance to place himself upon a footing with any citizen of Massachusetts."

[12] *Ibid.*, pp. 221-30. Given in full in *The Outlook*, May 9, 1903, p. 106.

CHAPTER VIII

THE TRAINING OF TEACHERS

THE SUMMER SCHOOL OF THE SOUTH AT KNOXVILLE

THE Conferences held in the South each year under the leadership of Mr. Ogden had been very successful in bringing together the superintendents and principals of the schools and citizens interested in the advancement of southern education. In the discussions at these meetings the sparse population and the poverty of the people, the poor school buildings and inadequate equipment, the pitiful salaries of the teachers, the short terms of the schools, and the resulting illiteracy, all had been emphasized. The worthlessness of the schools, however, could not be adequately expressed in these terms alone. Between the educational machinery and the money to operate it, on the one side, and the children, on the other side, stands the living teacher to transform the mechanical into the vital, to translate the material into the life of power and efficiency. Buildings and money constitute only the material instruments of education, which wait upon the teacher for their vitalizing. The time had come when the teacher must be made the center of interest. So from now on attention was directed to the improvement of the teachers and their enlistment in the movement. They were to be the real builders of the future systems of schools in the South, and it was necessary that the campaign should reach them. The Conferences had engaged the great body of school officials, the captains and generals of the school army. It was necessary next to reach the rank and file of the teachers in the southern schools.

A few summer schools had been held in connection with some southern universities, and normal institutes of elementary methods had been conducted in North Carolina and other states ; but there had never been in the South a summer school for the higher professional training in teaching corresponding to those in the North. Many of the better teachers in the South had been attending summer schools in the North and the West, but the vast majority were unable to do so on their very small salaries. It was deemed most important, therefore, to establish a summer school of the highest grade within reach of all these teachers. With this end in view it was decided to establish in the heart of the South a summer school of the highest grade, which should answer the purpose of a conference, a campaign, and a school of solid academic and professional instruction.

The University of Tennessee located at Knoxville, near the geographical center of the territory south of the Potomac and the Ohio and east of the Mississippi, was selected as the place for the first summer school, in 1902. The General Education Board, the Peabody Board, George Foster Peabody, Robert C. Ogden, Albert Shaw, and other friends, and the people of Knoxville, assisted in providing the necessary funds. The school had no organic connection with the University of Tennessee but at the request of its president the University gave the use of its whole plant, grounds, lecture halls, dormitories, library, and laboratories, with gas, light, and care of the buildings for a period of six weeks free of charge. Shelters with seats were put up under the trees for additional lecture halls, and a large pavilion, seating three thousand persons, was erected for the general assemblies. This pavilion was named Jefferson Hall and the other lecture halls were designated by the names of Peabody, Curry, and Ogden. In addition to the dining-rooms provided by the University, two large halls, accommodating eight hundred persons at a time, were erected and equipped the following year. The University dormitories and all available space in the other buildings, not used for the school, were furnished in a simple manner for the accommodation of the students. Special arrangements were made with the hotels and boarding houses throughout the city for cheap board.

The school was organized by President Charles W. Dabney, as manager and treasurer, independently of the University management. The University of Tennessee assumed none of the expense of the organization and the president carried this responsibility personally for three years, making his reports to the General Education Board and other subscribers. Philander P. Claxton was superintendent in charge of the instruction, and Edgar Gardner Murphy, executive secretary of the Board, was director of the platform exercises and conferences the first year. The second session Wickliffe Rose was secretary, and Burtis B. Breese was registrar.

The instruction was organized in four departments :

I. Common school subjects and methods. Kindergarten, elementary, and rural schools, including physical education, music, manual training, nature study, agriculture, and gardening, with lectures and discussions on organization, classification, and management.

II. Psychology and pedagogy, including the history of education.

III. High school and college subjects. The English language and its literature, ancient and modern languages, mathematics, the sciences, history, government and economics, the literature of the Bible.

IV. General lectures and conferences. A series of lectures, two a day, (1) on the history, condition, and needs of southern schools and (2) popular lectures on science, art, and the philosophy of education.

For the first session a faculty of forty-five instructors, chosen from all parts of the country, was engaged to give the instruction in the first three departments. Some of the best known professors and instructors in the country were selected. They gave one hundred and forty-nine courses. The lecturers before the general assemblies included members of the Southern Board, the governors of several states, superintendents of schools, and other citizens interested in the movement. These professors and lecturers constituted the largest body of eminent men and women, specialists in their respective fields, ever brought together at one time in a summer school. Daily meetings of school officers and institute conductors in the southern states were held for discussion of their peculiar problems.

The exercises extended through six days a week for six weeks from the middle of June to the end of July. On Sundays meetings were held for Sunday school teachers, addressed by experienced Sunday school workers, and round table discussions followed. On Sunday mornings the president gave lectures on "The Social Teachings of Jesus." The general lectures were given at noon and at five P.M. The evenings were devoted to music and entertainment.

An exhibit of school work, including drawing, manual training, written work, reports, programs, etc., from some of the best city schools in the country, served as concrete illustration of good work and as standards for the teachers. Two model school libraries, one for towns, the other for rural schools, and a library for teachers, with printed lists, were shown. There was an exhibit of model school apparatus, of school supplies, and of textbooks. For many teachers who had never had the opportunity to see such collections these exhibits proved very helpful.

Tuition was free. The only charge to the students was a registration fee of $5. The expenses were made as low as possible. A round trip rate of one fare was secured on all southern railways with the limit of September 30, which permitted the students to take a vacation in the mountains after the close of the school. Rooms for four hundred were provided in the dormitory buildings of the University. The rate for lodging and board in these was $30 for a term of six weeks, or $6 a week by the week. In addition to the railroad fare, the total necessary expenses of a student for six weeks were from $40 to $50.

The first summer school was well advertised through the South. In the following years only announcements needed to be sent out. Eighty thousand copies of the announcements were mailed to the addresses of teachers sent in by school officers. The superintendent of the school made a trip through several southern states, addressing teachers' associations. State superintendents and principals organized parties of teachers to come to the school. One party from Georgia the first year contained one hundred and fifty.

The Fourth of July celebration took the form of a school campaigners' convention. Leading educators from all parts of the South joined in the discussion of the needs of the rural schools. Such was the interest that this discussion was continued at a great open meeting held on the last night of the school. The celebration opened with a procession of the students, who marched in columns by states in alphabetical order with state badges, flags, and banners with mottoes. The company then gathered in Jefferson Hall, where a representative of each state made a statement about its progress in public education and future plans. This was followed by the singing of the state songs and the bringing of the state flags to the platform, where they were massed around the national flag. The exercises closed with the adoption of a "Declaration of Principles," for the educational policy of the South, prepared by a committee from the school body.[1] The assembly sang the national hymn and adjourned. Describing the celebration, William E. Curtis said in the *Chicago Record-Herald* :

The whole incident from start to finish was unique and remarkable. It was manifest that every person present was hungry for coöperative sympathy and felt the gratification of exchanging experiences with others surrounded by the same difficulties and subjected to the same trials that ... Southern teachers have been compelled to endure. The declaration, published in nearly every newspaper in the South, was effective in arousing interest in educational work among people who had never given it any attention before.

The interest in the problem of the southern schools grew every day to the end, when a great mass meeting was held on the last night for the discussion of a solution.

At the first session of the Summer School of the South there were 2,019 registered students, of whom 687 were men and 1,332 women. Two-thirds were graduates of the colleges and normal schools ; 1,500 were teachers of the common schools of the South.

Taking the second session, in 1903, as representative, there were ninety-one members of the faculty who gave 151 courses ; sixty-four taught the entire six weeks ; the others were arranged so as to make the courses consecutive. The students registered numbered 2,150 ; 1,488 were women and 662 men, a much larger percentage of men than in any summer school up to that time. Of these students 827 were graduates of colleges or normal schools and 1,246 were engaged to teach the following year. They came from thirty-one states and territories, Canada, Porto Rico, India, and Japan. From Tennessee there were 1,172 students ; 823 from Knox County and 349 from the other counties. From the other southern states there were : from Alabama, 204 ; Arkansas, 21 ; Florida, 33 ; Georgia, 160 ; Kentucky, 62 ; Louisiana, 41 ; Maryland, 7 ; Mississippi, 52 ; North Carolina, 103 ; South Carolina, 99 ; Texas, 73 ; and Virginia, 26. From the other states, territories, and foreign countries there were ninety-seven. In addition to the registered students, 703 visitors attended the lectures, conferences, and conventions more or less regularly. It was the largest summer school for teachers in America up to that time.

[1] See Appendix VII.

The total attendance during the first six years of the school, 1902 to 1907 inclusive, was 11,016 from forty-three states and foreign countries. The school thus became national in character and influence. During these six years the students from Alabama numbered 638 ; Arkansas, 114 ; Florida, 175 ; Georgia, 802 ; Kentucky, 312 ; Louisiana, 193 ; Mississippi, 412 ; North Carolina, 494 ; South Carolina, 336 ; Texas, 278 ; Virginia, 126 ; and Tennessee, 6,484. These men and women represented the most wide-awake progressive teachers in these states and their influence in advancing the schools was great.

The expenses of the school for 1902 totaled $14,795.75. The total expenditures of the second year (1903), when additional buildings had to be erected, were $30,398.15. Of the third year (1904), they were $23,419.55. For each of these two years the General Board contributed $10,000, the remainder coming from the people of Knoxville and Knox County and the student registration fees.

RESULTS OF THE MOVEMENT

This summer school had a breadth of view never attained in any school in the South before. It aimed to give all teachers, on whatever level they worked, the very best instruction that could be had. It was the first school to get away from the limits of elementary and high school subjects and to teach such subjects as music, school gardening, agriculture, and soil physics.

The school stimulated a great many struggling interests and originated a number of new movements. The kindergarten work in southern schools was greatly promoted through its courses and its model school. The National Story Tellers League and the National Playground Association, afterwards the Association for Physical Education, were organized here. A course in rural life for country preachers was given here for the first time. With the coöperation of the Jewish Chautauqua Society courses were given in Hebrew history and literature, in addition to those in the New Testament and in the King James version of the Bible as a whole.

This summer school proved an important factor in raising the educational standards of the schools of the section. The South had been too long hampered by provincialism and sectionalism. This school gave the teacher a wider horizon, a clearer

vision, and a higher conception of his work. It brought him
into touch with the best educational thought of the country and
enabled him to know and to appreciate his fellow workers.

The chief teaching of the school was the need of a great
central college for teachers. The eagerness of those who came
by thousands during these years proved that they felt the need.
They represented the best teachers and voiced the longing of
the other thousands left at home, eager for better professional
training, who were too poor to come. The school demonstrated
more clearly than had ever been done before the need of
teachers and of leaders for southern school systems.

Edgar Gardner Murphy, the executive secretary, said in his
report :

A gathering of more than two thousand men and women, fairly
representative of the potential and actual teaching force of such
a section, was therefore both an achievement and an inspiration.
It was also of far-reaching social significance. . . .

The quality of the personnel of the student body was the subject of much comment on the part of visitors from other sections.
The relative poverty of the South has its compensations. It places
at the command of the public school system of the Southern States,
at remuneration which would seem absurdly small elsewhere, a
teaching force of real culture and the truest refinement. This high
social average of the Southern teachers means that the training of
the children of the South is in the hands of worthy representatives
of its thought and feeling. It means that in its public school system
the South today is touching through its *best* the life of the
future. . . .

Here were throngs of men and women giving their precious
vacation weeks to better preparation for the service of their profession. Many of them had never known salaries larger than thirty
or thirty-five dollars per month, many of them were expending
practically the whole of their slender savings in meeting the expense
for railway travel, for board, for the few necessary books (there
was no charge for tuition save the registration fee of $5), and yet
every sacrifice was made, and the serious work of the School was
continued until the end—all in an atmosphere of pervasive cheer-
fulness and amid every evidence of buoyant and hopeful courage.

Upon the part of all present there was, for the serious instruction, the response of genuine intellectual enthusiasm—not only the
hunger for light, but the joy of a coöperative sympathy—a desire
for the best and a desire to put it at once to work. There was not
merely a zeal for admiring things, but a zeal for using them. The

dominant note, the constant and heroic note, was, therefore, practical. All in all, I have never witnessed anything finer in American life.

At the Fourth of July celebration of the first session of the Summer School of the South in 1902, when the superintendent announced that just 1902 students had registered up to that day, Dr. G. Stanley Hall issued a statement to the press in which he said :

It is the biggest one [summer school] in the world. In numbers and interest it has never been surpassed. From what observation I have been able to give the class work, the character of the work being done is of the best. I think that the greatest impression made upon me, next to the number, is the social quality of the students. You have the advantage over us in the North by far, in the high character, socially, of the ladies especially, who are teachers in the schools. Most of our teachers are from the lower walks of life while yours are from the best. This means more than you can possibly appreciate. The school is sure to have a tremendous influence upon Southern civilization.

P. P. Claxton had been the zealous and efficient superintendent of the school from the beginning and to his labors its success was chiefly due. He continued in charge of the school for seven years after Dabney resigned to go to the University of Cincinnati, carrying it on largely on his own responsibility with great success until 1911, when he became commissioner of education of the United States. The enrollment in some of those years was as high as two thousand five hundred. The University of Tennessee continued the school for three years after Claxton left.

E. C. Branson, president of the Georgia State Normal School at Athens, Georgia, wrote in 1902 : "Our little city has raised $2200 for our summer school next summer, and we are planning a session that will not conflict with yours, if possible. We are expecting to relieve you of some of the teachers that your success last year would overwhelm you with next summer. . . . Imitation is very sincere flattery, and you must expect to see summer schools spring up everywhere in the South now that you have stood the egg on end." [2]

Branson's prophecy came generally true. The success of this

[2] Letter from E. C. Branson to Charles Wm. Dabney, Oct. 27, 1902.

effort led to the establishment of schools, beginning in 1903, in connection with the state universities in all the southern states. The normal school previously conducted by Superintendent E. C. Glass of Lynchburg, Virginia, was transferred to the University at Charlottesville and became an influential institution. The summer normal at the University of North Carolina has developed into an institution of great influence. Similar schools were established in Georgia, South Carolina, Alabama, and other southern states.

The number of college and university men who joined in the conferences at these summer schools increased from year to year. The example of Alderman, at this time in Louisiana, McIver of North Carolina, Johnson of South Carolina, and Branson of Georgia, stimulated others and after the first few years practically all the southern colleges came to the support of the movement and started some kind of work for helping teachers. The reaction upon these institutions was soon apparent, and the colleges which put themselves into vital relations with the public schools entered upon a new life for themselves and a larger service to their communities.

But mere summer schools for teachers could not meet all the requirements. Summer schools stimulate teachers already partly trained, who through experience have learned their deficiencies and seek to remedy them. They cannot give the complete general education it takes to make a good teacher. A teacher is not educated and trained in a few summers; high schools, colleges, and universities are necessary to give fundamental education and special professional training. This subject Dabney discussed in his report to the Boards on the first session of the Summer School of the South in 1902, as follows (in part) :

In response to our invitation some 2,500 different teachers have come from the Southern states to this Summer School. They probably represent the most advanced teachers we have.... Their presence indicates our greatest need. There is not now an institution in the whole Southland prepared to meet the demands of these teachers and those like them in these states. This school, with its liberal provisions—the most liberal ever provided in the South—was completely overwhelmed. The classes were too large for the best work. ... Probably 2,500 other teachers went from the South this year to Northern and Western schools. They go to them because they have not found at home what they wanted. The truth is that with all our so-called normal schools, colleges, and universities, we have no institution equipped for giving these men and women the training they need. The ordinary normal school does not give either the fundamental education or the higher professional training. . . .

What is needed, therefore, is a great university planned and equipped to be the center for the promotion of education in the South. Such an institution should be planned on the most liberal scale. It should be free from both church and state influence, and stand for the highest culture and the freest teaching and study. It should have departments for training teachers for every line of professional service, from the kindergarten to the college and the university itself. . . .

Such are the opinions of the members of the Faculty, the more mature students, and the interested observers of this school. It was a great new development in this movement. From its success we should take courage, but we should recognize that it puts upon us a great new responsibility. It should be continued but a mere Summer School cannot meet all the demands of the situation. We must go to work at once to build an institution which shall permanently supply the demands of the situation, as this school has discovered them.

The Southern Board has been striving so far to create a public sentiment in behalf of the local support of schools for all the people. . . . But our education cannot be built up on sentiment alone, or even upon money. We may arouse enthusiasm among the people and awaken them to give millions to the support of the schools, but this is not enough. Enthusiasm and money alone will not build the schools we need. We need educated leaders, public-minded citizens, as well as teachers, who know how to construct, direct, and maintain good schools ; and such citizens are only to be trained in the university.[3]

This plan, which had been in the minds of many southern educators for years, was finally realized in the George Peabody College for Teachers, established in 1909 on the basis of the University of Nashville and its Peabody Normal School, which was then endowed with $1,000,000 of the principal of the George Peabody Fund.

[3] From the manuscript report of President Dabney of the First Summer School of the South, June 19 to July 31, 1902, to the Peabody Education Board and the Southern Board.

George Peabody College for Teachers

Mr. Peabody had provided that after thirty years the principal of the fund might be located at one institution or it might be distributed and the business of the Board wound up. By the end of the appointed thirty years, every state in the South had become thoroughly committed to an adequate public school system and some states had one or more normal schools to train teachers. The fund had expended $1,148,183 in small amounts to help the poorer communities to get their school systems and normal schools started. The time had come for the fund to be used in some central institution of more definite scope for the higher training of teachers. The rapidly growing public school systems required officers to direct their operations, trained superintendents and principals. For the increasingly numerous normal schools, professors and instructors were needed to train public school teachers. Many questions in regard to curricula, methods, and organization needed to be studied. It was necessary to establish a higher school than any in existence. The Board therefore sought coöperation in establishing a college where these teachers of teachers and educational experts could be trained. Nashville, Tennessee, appeared to be a suitable place, as the arts college of the venerable University of Nashville, which had some buildings and an endowment too small to accomplish much as a separate institution, offered to place these assets at the disposal of the Peabody Education Fund.

Dr. J. Berrien Lindsley, chancellor of the University of Nashville, had made the first proposal for a normal school in connection with the University of Nashville in June, 1867. He had tried for several years to get the state to establish a normal department in it, but the state had refused. He had then obtained authority from the trustees to request the Peabody Board to establish a normal school in connection with the University. His agitation of the subject created public interest which would not be downed, so that finally the legislature, at the session of 1875, created a state board of education of six members, which was empowered to establish a normal school. The educational institutions of the state were granted power to give the use of their property for this purpose; but the state refused to do anything itself. When, after several years of effort, it was realized that the state would not make an appropriation for the school, Lindsley, encouraged by Dr. Sears, succeeded in getting it to pass a bill amending the charter of the University of Nashville so as to substitute for the literary department of that institution a normal school under the chief direction of the Peabody Education Fund. The Peabody trustees offered to give $6,000 annually for such a school if the state would give a like amount. But the legislature adjourned without taking action. Finally, in May, 1875, Dr. Sears made a proposal to the trustees of the University of Nashville that, if they would give the use of their grounds, buildings, and a certain income from their small endowment, the Peabody trustees would give $6,000 annually. This proposal was promptly accepted and this was the actual beginning of the State Normal School, renamed The Peabody Normal College in 1887. The story of Dr. Sears's initial attempt to interest the people of Tennessee is that he walked into the office of Governor Porter of Tennessee in 1875 and said to him : "I have just returned from a visit to every capital in the South and have decided to establish the Peabody Normal College in Tennessee. I have reported to the Board that Nashville is the best place. . . . The purpose of the Board is to make it a great teachers college for the whole South and I want your active coöperation." This coöperation Governor Porter gave whole-heartedly, serving as president of the College at a critical juncture (1901-1909) and working for it as long as it was connected with the University of Nashville. The normal school thus established was thus the joint work of three bodies : The Board of Trustees of the University of Nashville, the Tennessee State Board of Education and the Trustees of the Peabody Education Fund. The University of Nashville had been a quasi-state institution. Hoping that the school would be supported by the state at some future time, this school was called, by a stretch of the imagination, the "State Normal School." In accordance with the purpose of the Peabody Board, it was, however, to be "a normal school for the whole South ; . . . to do a higher order of work than the ordinary normal school ; to train teachers for the most responsible positions in the public-school service, and to be a center whence should be diffused the most advanced thought on the subject of education." [4]

In September, 1875, Dr. Eben S. Stearns was appointed

[4] Lucius S. Merriam, *Higher Education in Tennessee*, p. 55.

chancellor of the University of Nashville and president of the Peabody Normal School. Stearns had been president of the State Normal School of Massachusetts and had been associated with Dr. Sears, then secretary of the Massachusetts Board of Education. In the face of the indifference of the state authorities in Tennessee, Stearns inaugurated the Normal School on the first day of December, 1875. Thirteen young women matriculated. Besides Dr. Stearns, there were only two other members of the faculty, Miss Julia A. Sears and Miss Emma M. Cutter. They commenced work without much apparatus, books, or equipment of any kind. Notwithstanding all these disadvantages, the school grew, and at the end of the first year had an enrollment of sixty. A three-year course of study, based upon scant high school preparation, led to the diploma of Licentiate of Instruction. The course was described as "a rapid review of the more elementary studies with reference to the best methods of teaching them, a review of the higher branches of knowledge with the same object, and a careful study of such other branches as time and circumstances would permit." [5]

The most important thing the Peabody Board did was to establish in 1879 twenty-five Peabody scholarships at $200 a year, distributed among all the different southern states, excepting Mississippi, Florida, and Tennessee. Mississippi and Florida had repudiated their bonds belonging to the Fund. In view of the location of the school in Tennessee, it was thought that this was fair for that state. They were awarded in the several states on competitive examinations held under the direction of the state superintendents, the questions being sent out from the Normal School. The applicants had to declare their intention of making teaching their profession, of continuing in college for two years, and of working in their states for at least two years after completing their courses. Nineteen of these scholarships were filled by selected men and women the first year, and their number was steadily increased until in 1892 there were 184. The scholarships were good for two consecutive years above the freshman class or for post-graduate work. In 1878 Dr. Sears secured the consent of the trustees to extend the curriculum to include a fourth year, which led to a bachelor's degree.

In view of the continued indifference of the Tennessee legislature, Dr. Sears opened negotiations in 1878 with Dr.

[5] Quoted in *ibid.*, p. 56.

Gustavus J. Orr, state commissioner of education of Georgia, and the Georgia legislature passed a bill creating the Georgia State Normal School and appropriating $6,000 annually to its support, provided the Peabody Board would do the same. Atlanta and other towns made liberal offers of sites. This aroused the people of Nashville at last, who now pledged individually $4,000 annually, until they should be relieved by the legislature, on condition that the Normal School should remain in Nashville ; and the trustees of the University of Nashville agreed to appropriate to the school the interest on an endowment of $50,000 in Tennessee bonds. In 1881 the Tennessee legislature finally made its first appropriation of $10,000 annually to the school for two years, $2,500 of which was to go for the education of Negro teachers in separate schools ; and in 1883 it appropriated $10,000 annually to the Normal School on condition that the Peabody Board would give Tennesseeans scholarships, as they had been given to other southern states. Tennessee received, at first, fourteen scholarships. When the legislature increased its appropriation to $15,000 on condition that each of the thirty-three senatorial districts in the state would be allowed a scholarship of $100 with railroad fare, the Peabody Board increased its appropriation to $15,000 a year. In spite of this niggardly, trading policy, the school continued to grow in numbers and influence ; and by 1887 the number of students had increased to 178.

When Dr. Stearns died in April, 1887, Alexander J. Porter, president of the Board of Trustees, was made chancellor of the University pro tempore, and when he died a year later, James D. Porter, ex-Governor of Tennessee, was elected chancellor. There was some difference of opinion as to which of the boards should select the successor to Dr. Stearns as president of Peabody Normal College, but it was fortunately settled by permitting the Peabody trustees, who were chiefly responsible for the existence of the college, to do this. Dr. William H. Payne, professor of pedagogy in the University of Michigan, was then selected, and the choice was ratified by the State Board of Education and by the board of the University of Nashville. Dr. Payne was a fine scholar and teacher and had been a successful administrator of the Michigan department. The influence of the college now grew, and the attendance increased to 422 by 1890-91. The school, which had started with three teachers, now had eighteen on its faculty. Its courses of liberal studies were greatly enlarged, and it was converted into a strictly professional training school for teachers, the first one in the South. There were other normal schools, but this was the first institution to educate teachers of teachers, leaders and investigators and educational experts who purposed to devote themselves to the cause of public education.

The Peabody Normal College at Nashville, Tennessee, built thus on the foundation of the old University of Nashville, was the first college aided by the Peabody Board. In 1903, J. L. M. Curry, Dr. Sears's successor, dictated, on his death bed, a communication to the Peabody Board urging them to endow the college with the residue or principal of the Peabody Education Fund.

The friends of the institution at Nashville began a movement immediately to endow and enlarge that institution. Dr. Wallace Buttrick, the agent of the Board at the time, presented to the Trustees of the Peabody Education Fund, with his approval, the petitions of the friends at Nashville and of many influential educators through the South, requesting them to donate the residue of the fund for the endowment of a greater Peabody College as a worthy memorial of its beneficent founder. On January 24, 1905, the Trustees of the Peabody Education Fund adopted these resolutions:

This Board recognizes that the establishment of a college for the higher education of teachers for the Southern States is essential to the completion of an efficient educational system for said States, and would be the noblest memorial to George Peabody;

The Board is of the opinion that said College should be located at Nashville, Tennessee, and should be established ... by this Board in said city, and for the purpose of continuing on broader and higher lines the great work which has been done by said Normal College for the cause of Southern education.

They then appropriated $1,000,000 of its principal to endow George Peabody College for Teachers.[6] A committee was appointed to report on a plan for its organization. This committee consisted of Daniel C. Gilman, president of the Johns Hopkins University; Morris K. Jesup, of New York; and Charles E. Fenner, of New Orleans.[7] Dr. Gilman, for the special Commit-

[6] *Peabody Proceedings*, VI, 260.   [7] *Ibid.*, p. 285.

tee of Three, made the report on October 3, 1906, prepared with the coöperation of Dr. Buttrick, who was also secretary of the General Education Board.[8] This report declared that the South needed :

A. An institution to organize and direct the forces at work in the field of elementary education. . . . Its prime need is for trained educational leaders in this field. [The College would render efficient service] :

1. By educating men who can go into rural communities and create schools that will meet the demands of modern life under rural conditions.

2. By training men for county and city superintendents.

B. For the training of principals and teachers for the public high schools. The most important constructive work going on in the public school system of the Southern States is the organizing of public high schools.

C. The Teachers' College is needed to reinforce the work of the State normal schools.

1. By training their principals and teachers.

2. By supplying a graduate school for those who, after completing the normal school course, desire more advanced work.

D. Finally, The importance of this Teachers' College may be seen in the peculiar advantages which the South offers to an institution centrally located and serving the South as a whole. . . . Southern teachers under present conditions must seek advanced training in institutions outside the Southern States. It will be a decided gain both in economy and efficiency, if these teachers could be educated in a college on their own soil in intimate touch with Southern life and in direct response to Southern educational conditions and needs.

The report concludes :

The George Peabody College for Teachers, to be located at Nashville, will occupy the point of highest strategic importance in Southern education. The fund invested in it will touch every aspect of the educational system from the kindergarten to the college and will reach every city, town, village, and rural community throughout the Southern States. It is our firm conviction, therefore, that the founding of this college is the most important work which this Board has undertaken or can undertake for Southern education.[9]

[8] *Ibid.*, p. 459.
[9] *Ibid.*, pp. 467-73 ; see also *The South's Great Need* (small pamphlet).

This report, which was adopted as the basis for the organization of the College under its new name, is a masterly review of the educational needs of the South at the time and should be read by every student of Southern educational history.[10]

In order that the College might have the advantages of Vanderbilt University, the buildings and grounds of the University of Nashville were sold and the new College was located in Nashville on grounds adjacent to Vanderbilt. The idea was that this institution would supply the general classical, literary, and scientific training for the students, and Peabody, the professional and technical training, the students of either institution having access to the courses offered in the other ; and that through the exchange of facilities on a definite unit basis of cost, much expense for equipment and instruction would be saved in both institutions.

The Peabody Normal College was chartered as George Peabody College for Teachers in 1909. Its new funds (at the beginning, $1,700,000) became available in 1910. The Normal College continued its work on the old campus until June, 1911. The new institution was liberally aided by other foundations. The Carnegie Foundation gave $185,000 for a library and $75,000 for the endowment of art. The estate of J. P. Morgan gave $250,000. The General Education Board has given $1,150,000 for buildings and $1,550,000 for endowment, besides contributing largely for the annual support of the college. John D. Rockefeller, Sr., gave $300,000 for the central Social Religious Building. From other sources, $4,865,000 has been received towards buildings and endowment. When three new buildings became available, teaching was resumed in them, beginning with the summer session in June, 1914.

Dr. Bruce Ryburn Payne, head of the department of education at the University of Virginia, was elected president of the new college in 1911 and became its organizer and efficient executive. Having come under the influence of McIver and Alderman in their campaign for schools in North Carolina, Payne decided early to devote himself to the cause of public education. From the time he was graduated from Trinity College, now Duke University, in North Carolina in 1896, he has been continuously in the service of the schools and their teachers. He decided that the greatest need of the schools was better

[10] *Peabody Proceedings*, VI, 467-80.

trained teachers, and, therefore, has given his life chiefly to this cause. While principal of the Morganton Academy, Burke County, North Carolina, and superintendent of the county schools (1896-99) and instructor in the Durham High School (1899-1902), he devoted his spare time to teacher training and his vacations to working in normal schools and institutes. After taking his Ph.D. at Columbia in 1904, he was elected professor of philosophy and education at the College of William and Mary. When the department of education was established at the University of Virginia, he was called there to be professor of secondary education and director of the summer school. Here he continued for seven years, holding institutes and aiding in the campaign for schools. He was an active participant and director of publicity in the "May Campaign" for schools in Virginia in 1905.

When the George Peabody College for Teachers opened in 1914 on the new site, the great constructive service of the Peabody Board was concluded, and a magnificent monument to the South's noble benefactor was permanently established. The Peabody Board had completed its work in a wise and statesmanlike manner. Following Dr. Curry, the chief men aiding the Board in bringing about this admirable conclusion were Wickliffe Rose and Wallace Buttrick. Though smaller than many other funds since given for southern education, George Peabody's noble gift was so timely and was administered in so wise a fashion that it may fairly be said to have laid the foundation for the present improved public school systems of the South.

It has been justly said that "no two million dollars in the world has ever done so much good as this Trust Fund created by Mr. Peabody."

CHAPTER IX

THE GENERAL EDUCATION BOARD

THE FORMATION OF THE BOARD

EVENTS arising out of the movement for southern education led directly to the inauguration of a series of the greatest philanthropic enterprises the world has ever known. Out of the Southern Education Board was born a number of foundations which, beginning by promoting public elementary, high school, industrial, and agricultural education for both races in the South, extended aid to colleges and universities, and later engaged in the development of sanitation, public health, and medical education throughout the United States, in China, and in many other foreign countries. These great enterprises were all founded on the munificent gifts of one man, Mr. John D. Rockefeller. The story of their origin will here be told.

As the result of the visit of Mr. John D. Rockefeller, Jr., as Mr. Ogden's guest, to the Winston-Salem meeting in April, 1901, and the conferences held in New York in November, Mr. Rockefeller, the senior, invited a group of gentlemen to meet him to consider forming a board to hold and disburse funds for the benefit of education. Mr. Rockefeller had for years been coöperating with Mr. Frederick T. Gates of Minneapolis, secretary of the American Baptist Education Society, in aiding schools and colleges. Gates had been one of Rockefeller's advisers in the founding of the University of Chicago, and to him Mr. Rockefeller appealed first for counsel as to the needs of the southern schools. Dr. Wallace Buttrick, who was associated with Gates in the same Church Education Society as chairman of the Board for Negro Schools, was a friend of Mr. Ogden. In response to Mr. Rockefeller's invitation, a group of gentlemen met on January 15, 1902, at the residence of Mr. Morris K. Jesup in New York City, to form the provisional organization of a "General Education Board," which should be a holding board for funds to be used in the cause of education. These men were all either members of the Southern

Education Board or actively interested in it. An organization was formed, a statement of principles was drawn up, and steps were taken immediately to secure its incorporation by Congress. This was accomplished a year later, and offices were first established in Washington.

In the history of the General Education Board from 1902 to 1914 we read, "The propaganda in behalf of popular education in the South carried on by" the Conference for Education in the South and the Southern Education Board "was a factor in crystallizing Mr. Rockefeller's already profound interest in this particular problem." [1] From the history of the Peabody and Slater funds, he had also learned "that there was room for still another type of institution—an institution permanent in character, and with an assured income, devoted in part, at least, to coöperation with the southern people in the development of a comprehensive educational policy. For some years previous to the organization of the General Education Board, Mr. Rockefeller's attention had been directed to the needs of the people of the South, both white and colored, and particularly to the existing conditions in respect to elementary education. Its charter was so drawn as to enable the General Education Board to enter this field. While the precise part to be undertaken was not defined in advance, Mr. Rockefeller, in making his first gift to the Board, called attention to the educational needs of the people of the Southern states and indicated his special interest therein." [2]

The new organization was called the General Education Board to distinguish it from the Southern Education Board, and to indicate its purpose to extend aid to the schools and colleges of the whole country. Mr. William H. Baldwin, Jr., a member of the Southern Education Board and of its finance committee, was elected temporary chairman of the new Board.

John D. Rockefeller's Gifts

The General Education Board having completed its organization on March 1, 1902, Mr. John D. Rockefeller, Jr., addressed a letter to Mr. Baldwin, the chairman, endorsing its plans and announcing his father's gift. This letter reads in part as follows:

[1] *The General Education Board, 1902-1914*, p. 11.
[2] *Ibid.*, p. 12.

John D. Rockefeller and his son, John D. Rockefeller, Jr.

Above, the Social-Religious Building at the George Peabody College for Teachers, Nashville, Tennessee. Below, a temporary building of the Summer School of the South, the University of Tennessee, Knoxville, Tennessee, 1902

Understanding that the object of this corporation is to promote education in the United States of America without distinction of sex, race, or creed ;

That the immediate intention of the Board is to devote itself to studying and aiding to promote the educational needs of the people of our Southern States.

Upon this understanding my father hereby pledges to the Board the sum of One Million Dollars ($1,000,000.) to be expended at its discretion during a period of ten years, and will make payments under such pledges from time to time as requested by the Board or its Executive Committee through its duly authorized officers.[3]

Thus was started a series of gifts to this and related foundations and commissions which in time were rapidly enlarged and extended to include elementary, liberal, industrial, and professional education, sanitation, public health, medical education, and social service. The initial donation was to be used for educational work in the South.

To the letter Baldwin, as chairman, replied to Mr. Rockefeller confirming his understanding and thanking him for his munificent gift. In conclusion, he added :

I believe that no set of men could have been selected to represent more fully the advanced movement of the education of the Southern people. It is our belief that never in the past has the time been so opportune as this moment for an active and aggressive movement in the Southern States, and especially it is to be noted that the educational point of view of the Trustees of the General Education Board is in perfect harmony with that of the Southern men who represent the intelligent opinion of the South.

In return for your generous offer, we pledge our devoted support to the principles which have been laid down in our Statement of Policy, and it will be our chief aim to prove ourselves worthy of the great responsibility which you have placed upon us.[4]

By an Act of Congress on January 12, 1903, William H. Baldwin, Jr., Jabez L. M. Curry, Frederick T. Gates, Daniel C. Gilman, Morris K. Jesup, Robert C. Ogden, Walter H. Page, George Foster Peabody, and Albert Shaw, and their successors, were incorporated as the General Education Board. The men named in this charter were all members of the Southern Education Board except Gates, Gilman, and Jesup, who

[3] *Ibid.*, Appendix II, p. 216.   [4] *Ibid.*, p. 218.

however had been in its counsels from the beginning. The charter which embodied the "Statement of Principles" declared the purpose of the Board to be :

The promotion of education within the United States of America, without distinction of race, sex, or creed.

That for the promotion of such object the said corporation shall have power to build, improve, enlarge, or equip, or to aid others to build, improve, enlarge, or equip, buildings for elementary or primary schools, industrial schools, technical schools, normal schools, training schools for teachers, or schools of any grade, or for higher institutions of learning, or, in connection therewith, libraries, workshops, gardens, kitchens, or other educational accessories ; to establish, maintain, or endow, or aid others to establish, maintain, or endow elementary or primary schools, industrial schools, technical schools, normal schools, training schools for teachers, or schools of any grade, or higher institutions of learning ; to employ or aid others to employ teachers and lecturers ; to aid, cooperate with, or endow associations or other corporations engaged in educational work within the United States of America, or to donate to any such association or corporation any property or moneys which shall at any time be held by the said corporation hereby constituted ; to collect educational statistics and information, and to publish and distribute documents and reports containing the same, and in general to do and perform all things necessary or convenient for the promotion of the object of the corporation [and all the usual powers of the corporation not for profit].[5]

William H. Baldwin, Jr., was elected president, George Foster Peabody, treasurer, and Wallace Buttrick, secretary of the General Education Board. Thus was formed the greatest of the funds established by Mr. Rockefeller for educational purposes.

The plan of using groups of experts to investigate and recommend to him where and how to use his resources for the advancement of mankind was largely original with Mr. Rockefeller. The success of this method has caused it to be followed in the formation of many other foundations in this and other countries.[6]

Dr. Buttrick's Statement

In an address before the National Education Association at Boston on July 10, 1903, Dr. Buttrick made a statement with

[5] *Ibid.*, Appendix I, pp. 212-13.   [6] See below, pp. 135-43.

regard to the conditions and hindrances to universal education in the southern states and of the policy to be pursued in overcoming them. This statement is so fair, sympathetic, and statesmanlike that it commanded at once the interest and hearty cooperation of the people of both the North and the South. After referring to the work that the Southern Education Conference and its Board had been doing during the last two years to arouse the people of the South to make greater efforts to improve their schools he said :

The Northern members of the Board became convinced that something more than an educational propaganda was needed. They came to appreciate the heroic earnestness of their Southern brethren in their effort to promote universal education. They saw also the peculiar difficulties which hinder and limit the development and support of free schools for the people in the Southern States.

Let us for a few minutes consider some of these conditions and hindrances peculiar to the South Central and South Atlantic States at this time (1903).

I. THE SERIOUS RESULTS OF THE WAR BETWEEN THE STATES

It is not easy for us to realize the condition of the Southern people after the surrender at Appomattox. Some of us recall the rejoicing at the North as our boys came marching home singing the songs of victory. We recall the tremendous wave of business prosperity that set in at the North even before war had ceased. Not so was it at the South. I have sat in the homes of these Southern heroes and listened to their stories of the desolation and almost despair of the people as the returning soldiers began anew the works of peace. One-tenth of the white male population had been lost on the field of battle ; the entire accumulated capital of the South had been swept away ; in many places their houses had been burned and their fields were wasted ; the very institutions of their civilization had been uprooted and destroyed. Then followed the period of reconstruction when good men made mistakes and bad men ran riot. During this unhappy period the already impoverished States were loaded with added burdens of bonded debt, amounting, in some cases, to practical confiscation. And what was even worse, prejudices were formed and animosities aroused that have lasted to the present day, and still stand in the way of progress. The war, with the awful aftermath of reconstruction, involved the building anew of an entire civilization.

II. EIGHTY-FIVE PER CENT OF THE POPULATION OF THE SOUTH IS RURAL

The North Atlantic States average 130 people to the square mile ; the South Central and South Atlantic States average but 31 to the square mile. The former Confederate States have but 26 cities with a population of 25,000 or over ; the single state of Massachusetts has 23 such such cities. The sparse population of the South necessitates small schools, widely separated and with inadequate support. This difficulty is further seriously aggravated by the poor roads which are always found in sparsely settled regions. The cities and larger towns of the South have excellent school systems, in the development of which the Trustees of the Peabody Education Fund have borne a large and honorable part. But the average term of the rural schools is less than 80 days, and the entire school life of the average child but three of these short years—or 240 days in all.

III. THE NECESSITY OF SUPPORTING TWO SYSTEMS OF SCHOOLS

The South with its limited wealth, its inheritance of debt and its sparse population, has the added burden of supporting two distinct systems of schools—one for the white and another for the colored children. The decision of the people of the South regarding this matter of separate schools is final and admits of no challenge. Experience shows that it works to the advantage of the colored race as well as the white. Without separate schools the Negro would have little, if indeed, any opportunity for the development of that race leadership which is the great necessity of race progress. It is the sphere of the teacher that has furnished the Negro his largest opportunity for demonstrating his power of leadership. This necessity for a dual system of schools involves an expense nearly twice as large as would be necessary for the education of one race.

IV. LACK OF BELIEF IN THE DUTY OF THE STATE TO EDUCATE

Before the period of the civil war education was looked upon as the privilege of the favored few rather than as the right of all. The people of the South regarded the obligation to educate as belonging to the parent and not the State. Private schools educated sons and daughters of a select class, while the great mass of the people had little schooling and many of them none at all.

A great change in sentiment and conviction has taken place in recent years, and "universal education at public expense" has become a political shibboleth ; but any careful observer of conditions at the South will quickly see that the old aristocratic ideal of society still mightily retards the progress of "Free schools for all the people" which was the watch-cry of our beloved Dr. Curry.

V. INDIFFERENCE TO EDUCATION IN THE RURAL REGIONS

This is far from being universal, yet it is certainly a serious hindrance in many sections of the country. In a recent article (*South Atlantic Quarterly*, April 1903), "Some Phases of Southern Education," President Kilgo says : "It may sound a bit rude, even unkind, to say that the South has as much education as it wants, but unfortunately this is the truth. Not all are satisfied, for there are many chafing spirits, but they are in the minority. Ignorance in any part of America at this time is voluntary. It is, therefore, no malicious criticism to say that the South has all the education it wants. The growth of wealth in the South has been marvelous, while the growth of education has been slow and tedious. What has been accomplished is the result of persistent struggle on the part of a few leaders. There has been no general and enthusiastic spirit behind these efforts." I am sure that President Kilgo is somewhat extreme in this statement, doubtless he makes a deliberate attempt to awaken serious thought by being "a bit rude" ; but I am equally sure that indifference to education on the part of parents is one of the most serious obstacles in the way of universal education in the South.

VI. AN EXAGGERATED INDIVIDUALISM WHICH LOOKS WITH DISFAVOR ON SCHOOL SUPERVISION AND A CENTRAL BOARD OF DIRECTION AND CONTROL

State and County School Superintendents in the Southern States have very little authority.... They do not appoint teachers and rarely have they power of removal. In fact these officers in most cases do little more than counsel the teachers and see that certain laws and traditions are observed.... In some instances men of intelligence and moral force do control school affairs, and exercise a real supervision, but this is the result of personal force and not of the exercise of any recognized authority. This exaggerated individualism hinders and often makes impossible the development of State or County *systems* of schools.

VII. A DISLIKE OF DIRECT OR LOCAL TAXATION

This may have had its origin in Revolutionary times, but it was greatly intensified by the unhappy experiences of the reconstruction period. Nearly all of the rural schools of the South are maintained by State funds, as distinguished from funds raised by County or District taxation. School "holds" as long as the State apportionment holds out. Furthermore, a large part of this State School fund is raised by indirect taxation. There is very little local taxation for schools. This state of things results in poor schools and short terms, from the lack of money indeed, but still more because "What we don't pay for we don't care for."

These are some of the hindrances that have come under my personal observation as I have met State and County Superintendents in nine of the Southern States during the past year. They are not all peculiar to the South; most of them are, and all are conspicuous and serious. Taken together they constitute a peculiar problem inviting interest, sympathy and help.

WHAT THE SOUTH HAS DONE

Let us now see and consider what the South has done in the face of these difficulties.

Soon after the war the different State Legislatures undertook the development of free public schools, in the belief that the education of all the people would be the greatest means of reconstructing their shattered fortunes and of rehabilitating their broken civilization. The aristocratic view of education is slowly yet surely yielding to the democratic, until now every State has a well defined system of public free schools, and a sentiment favoring "Free Schools for all the People," pervades the social and political life of the South.

This change in public sentiment is traceable to several causes:

1. The influence of denominational schools, i.e., schools founded and maintained by the several Christian denominations.... Established for public rather than for sectarian ends; supported by personal and financial sacrifices; they have been one of the great forces in the educational advancement of the South, supplying teachers of the free schools and leaders of public thought....

2. The work of the Peabody and Slater Education Funds: the former in promoting school systems in cities and towns, and schools for the training of teachers; the latter in promoting schools for Negroes....

3. Appreciative mention, also, should be made of the wide influence on public education of such great schools as Hampton and Tuskegee, and likewise of many schools for Negroes that have been founded and maintained by Northern philanthropy....

4. The enthusiastic leadership of a company of young men, who, often at personal sacrifice and always with genuine heroism, have campaigned the South,—their war-cry being

"Free Schools for all the people." ... I wish you could appreciate the amount of devoted heroism and personal self-sacrifice implied in the 10,000 teachers hard at work during their vacations. They are giving their time, indeed, and in many cases expending their entire savings. ...

A BRIEF SUMMARY OF PRACTICAL RESULTS

Since 1870 $690,000,000 raised by taxation have been spent for public schools, of which amount $130,000,000 have been devoted to the education of the Negroes. The public expenditure for both races is now nearing $40,000,000 a year.

Enthusiasm for common schools is seen in public, private and denominational conferences called for the discussion of these problems. ... This enthusiasm is also seen in : the speeches and messages of Governors ; the emphasis of the press, the platform, and the legislatures ; the rapid spread of local taxation and the consolidation of schools ; the general advocacy of manual and industrial training ; the increase of high school studies in the public schools (heretofore secondary education has been almost exclusively under private or denominational auspices) ; the development of agricultural and mechanical colleges ; the growth of public and private normal schools, teachers' training classes, summer institutes, and summer schools for teachers. In a word, the paramount question in the Southern States is that of the promotion of public education. It is the chief plank in all political platforms ; the shibboleth of men and women of light and leading.

The knowledge of such facts as these led to the formation of the General Education Board. In a Nation such as ours, where all initiative is with the people, no problem is ever strictly local. No locality in our country ever "liveth unto itself." "When one member suffers then all members suffer" is involved in the very idea of our peculiar National life.

A STATEMENT OF POLICY

The underlying principle of the association is the recognition of the fact that the people of the Southern States are earnestly engaged in the promotion of public education, and that in this effort they should receive generous aid ; and to this end, and in pursuance of the following named and kindred objects, the Board will seek gifts, large and small, from those in sympathy with its plans.

It is the purpose of the Board :

1. To promote education within the United States of America, without distinction of race, sex or creed.

2. To develop the public school system, especially in rural districts.

3. To develop the principle of self-help by urging increased local taxation, local contributions, or by other means.

4. To further the establishment of training schools for teachers, especially those designed to educate teachers of industrial and manual training.

5. To coöperate with other organizations interested in educational work, and to simplify and make effective the general work of education, avoiding unnecessary duplication.

6. To aid in the maintenance and improvement of educational institutions already established.

7. To collect full information and statistics in respect to educational matters in the districts covered by the operation of the Board, which shall be kept at a general office.

8. To furnish the public with information, suggestions and counsel, and for this purpose to act somewhat as a clearing-house for educational statistics and data to be collated by the Board.

9. To educate public opinion in all matters pertaining to the general cause of education by publication of reports through the daily press and by other means.

10. To promote by all suitable means every form of valuable educational work.[7]

FURTHER GIFTS TO THE BOARD

One object of the General Education Board was to relieve the officers and representatives in the field of the Southern Board of the embarrassment caused by the many applications for financial aid which came to them from private, and also from some public, institutions in the South. As soon as it was announced that Mr. Rockefeller had given the Southern Board funds, requests for money poured in upon it.

The Southern Education Board was, as explained above, intended from the beginning to be merely an agency of propaganda to develop public opinion in favor of legislation providing for local taxation, and to supply information and guidance in the better organization and improvement of the schools. The resources of the Southern Board, which were always very limited, were devoted exclusively to the expenses of the cam-

[7] Wallace Buttrick, "The Beginning and Aims of the General Education Board," *Journal of Proceedings and Addresses of the Forty-second Annual Meeting of the National Educational Association, Boston, Mass., 1903*, pp. 116-23.

paign for these causes. It never proposed to give money to schools. It had none to give. To have undertaken to distribute money would have completely destroyed its usefulness. The consideration of such matters was left to the General Education Board. The first purpose of the General Education Board was to provide support for activities that had been promoted by the Southern Education Board, but its aid was also extended to many schools in other states of the Union.

On June 30, 1905, Mr. Rockefeller authorized Dr. Gates to announce to the General Education Board an additional donation of ten million dollars ($10,000,000) "to be held in perpetuity as a foundation for education, the income above the expenses of administration to be distributed to, or used for the benefit of, such institutions of learning, at such times, in such amounts, for such purposes and under such conditions, or employed in such other ways, as the Board may deem best adapted to promote a comprehensive system of higher education in the United States." [8]

And again on February 5, 1907, Mr. John D. Rockefeller, Jr., announced another gift of his father to the General Education Board of thirty-two million dollars ($32,000,000), "one-third to be added to the permanent endowment of the Board, two-thirds to be applied to such specific objects within the corporate purposes of the Board as he or I may from time to time direct, any remainder, not so designated at the death of the survivor, to be added to the permanent endowment of the Board." [9]

To this the Board replied :

This is the largest sum ever given by a man in the history of the race for any social or philanthropic purposes. The Board congratulates you upon the high and wise impulse which has moved you to this deed, and desires to thank you, in behalf of all educational interests whose development it will advance, in behalf of our country whose civilization for all time it should be made to strengthen and elevate, and in behalf of mankind everywhere in whose interest it has been given and for whose use it is dedicated. The administration of this fund entails upon the General Education Board the most far-reaching responsibility ever placed upon any educational organization in the world. As members of the Board we accept

[8] *The General Education Board, 1902-14*, Appendix II, p. 219.
[9] *Ibid.*

this responsibility, conscious alike of its difficulties and opportunities. We will use our best wisdom to transmute your gift into intellectual and moral power, counting it a supreme privilege to dedicate whatever strength we have to its just use in the service of men.[10]

On June 29, 1909, Mr. John D. Rockefeller, Jr., announced still another gift of ten million dollars ($10,000,000) to the General Education Board. In a letter, also of June 29, Mr. John D. Rockefeller, Sr., authorized the Board to distribute, by a two-thirds vote, the principal of this and the previous ten millions or any part thereof. The Board replied to these communications on July 9 :

The Board accepts with gratitude this new proof of your generosity, your zeal for an educated citizenship in this democracy, and your confidence, and will endeavor to use the gift with large-mindedness and good sense, to the end that the interests of society in the Republic may be increasingly benefited by this great foundation.

The Board begs to acknowledge also the receipt of your personal communication of June 29, 1909, wherein you authorize and empower the Board and its successors, under wise and proper regulations, whenever in their discretion it shall seem wise, to distribute the principal of this fund and all other endowment funds hitherto contributed by you to this Board.

The Board accepts this release from the obligation to hold these funds in perpetuity as an endowment, with a very clear appreciation of the wisdom, the long look ahead, and the faith in the future manifested in the authorization.[11]

Including the first million dollars ($1,000,000) given the General Education Board, Mr. Rockefeller gave to this Board up to and including March, 1932, the sum of one hundred and twenty-nine million, two hundred and nine thousand, and one hundred and sixty-seven dollars and ten cents ($129,209,167.10). Many of these gifts were the result of the work of the Southern Conference and Southern Education Board and its members. The story of the Rockefeller Foundation and its service is another one of profound interest, which will be noticed later.

At the instance of Dr. Frissell, whom she called in conference, Miss Anna T. Jeanes of Philadelphia in 1905 gave the

[10] *Ibid.*, p. 220.   [11] *Ibid.*, pp. 221-23.

General Board two hundred thousand dollars ($200,000), the income to be used in the improvement of the rural schools for Negroes in the South.[12]

JOHN D. ROCKEFELLER'S PRINCIPLES AND PLANS OF PHILANTHROPY

Mr. John D. Rockefeller, Sr., is the greatest donator of money for the good of mankind that the world has known ; but he is more than a mere giver of gifts. As a careful and sagacious business man, he has striven to help his fellow men wherever he could in the most effectual manner. In doing this he has developed certain definite principles and plans which constitute a valuable contribution to the science of philanthropy. What his ideals and principles, his purposes and plans were in his vast and varied philanthropies can best be learned from his words and acts.

Up to 1902 Mr. Rockefeller had made his donations to education chiefly through the American Baptist Education Society, an organization of his denomination designed to aid institutions affiliated with it in the United States and Canada. This society had planned a system of colleges and academies which should form a substantial part of the educational resources of the nation, and Mr. Rockefeller had for a decade been its chief benefactor. The University of Chicago, projected in this spirit, had recently been founded by him as the capstone of this system. As his fortune grew, his interest in education deepened and broadened, and his sense of responsibility and public duty passed beyond all denominational and sectional lines. When at this time, the plans of the Southern Education Board were made known to him, they appealed to him so favorably that he promptly offered his financial assistance in carrying them out.

After watching the work of this Board in the South for a time, he decided in 1902 that he would establish a board to extend its methods to the whole country, and the General Education Board, as we have seen, was the result.

Always reticent about his philanthropic work, Mr. Rockefeller up to this time had made no statements about his ideals and plans. His methods had been steadily developing, however, for some years and now became more definitely organized.

[12] *Ibid.*, p. 224.

They are revealed best in the things he did and the way in which he did them, but his "Reminiscences," which Walter Hines Page induced him to publish in his magazine in 1908-1909, give us a starting point for the study of the principles underlying the vast scheme which now begins to unroll before us.[13]

In a chapter on "The Difficult Art of Giving," he says:

In this country we have come to the period when we can well afford to ask the ablest men to devote more of their time, thought, and money to the public well-being. I am not so presumptuous as to attempt to define exactly what this betterment work should consist of. Every man will do that for himself.... It is well, I think, that no narrow or preconceived plan should be set down as the best.... Every right-minded man has a philosophy of life, whether he knows it or not. Hidden away in his mind are certain governing principles, whether he formulates them in words or not, which govern his life. Surely his ideal ought to be to contribute all that he can, however little it may be, whether of money or of service, to human progress.... I have always indulged the hope that during my life I should be able to establish efficiency in giving so that wealth may be of greater use to the present and future generations. ... The man who plans to do all his giving on Sunday is a poor prop for the institutions of the country....

One's ideal should be to use one's means, both in one's investments and in benefactions, for the advancement of civilization. But the questions as to what civilization is and what are the great laws which govern its advance have been seriously studied. Our investments ... have been directed to such ends as we have thought would tend to produce these results. If you were to ... ask our committee on benevolence ... in what they consider civilization to consist, they would say that they have found in their study that the most convenient analysis of the elements which go to make up civilization runs about as follows:

1st. Progress in the means of subsistence, that is to say, progress in abundance and variety of food-supply, clothing, shelter, sanitation, public health, commerce, manufacture, the growth of public wealth, etc.

2nd. Progress in government and law, that is to say, in the enactment of laws securing justice and equity to every man, consistent with the largest individual liberty, and the due and orderly enforcement of the same upon all.

[13] *World's Work*, Vols. XVI and XVII (1908-1909). Published afterwards in a book, *Random Reminiscences of Men and Events*, by John D. Rockefeller, New York, Doubleday, Page & Company, 1909.

3rd. Progress in literature and language.
4th. Progress in science and philosophy.
5th. Progress in art and refinement.
6th. Progress in morality and religion.

If you were to ask ... which of these we regard as fundamental, we would reply that we would not attempt to answer, that the question is purely an academic one, that all these go hand in hand, but that historically the first of them—namely, progress in means of subsistence, health and wealth—had generally preceded progress in government, in literature, in knowledge, in refinement, and in religion. Though not itself of the highest importance, it is the foundation upon which the whole superstructure of civilization is built, and without which it could not exist.

Accordingly, we have sought, so far as we could, to make investments in such a way as will tend to multiply, to cheapen, and to diffuse as universally as possible the comforts of life. We claim no credit for preferring these lines of investment. We make no sacrifices. These are the lines of largest and surest return....

The giver of money, if his contribution is to be valuable, must add service in the way of study, and he must help to ... improve underlying conditions.

In all his giving Mr. Rockefeller's first aim was to do the most permanent good to the most people. With this purpose he was particularly concerned not to destroy their initiative. He would do all he could to develop initiative among the people helped and then withdraw. "The best philanthropy," he said, "the help that does the most good and the least harm, the help that nourishes civilization at its very root, that most widely disseminates health, righteousness, and happiness, is not what is usually called charity. It is, in my judgment, the investment of effort or time or money, carefully considered with relation to the power of employing people at a remunerative wage, to expand and develop the resources at hand, and to give opportunity for progress and healthful labour where it did not exist before. No mere money-giving is comparable to this in its lasting and beneficial results.... Money which comes to a man without effort on his part is seldom a benefit and often a curse. ... But, if we can help people to help themselves, then there is a permanent blessing conferred."

Following out this idea, Mr. Rockefeller usually made his gifts conditional. This plan was an essential part of his system. His reason for making contributions in this form he states as follows : "It is easy to do harm in giving money. To give to institutions which should be supported by others is not the best philanthropy. Such giving only serves to dry up the natural springs of charity. It is highly important that every charitable institution shall have at all times the largest possible number of current contributors. This means that the institution shall constantly be making its appeals ; but, if these constant appeals are to be successful, the institution is forced to do excellent work and meet real needs. . . . We frequently make our gifts conditional on the giving of others, not because we wish to force people to do their duty, but because we wish in this way to root the institution in the affections of as many people as possible who, as contributors, become personally concerned, and thereafter may be counted on to give to the institution their watchful interest and coöperation."

The distinguishing characteristic of Mr. Rockefeller's system of philanthropy is his investigating board. "Down to the year 1890," he says, "I was still following the haphazard fashion of giving here and there as appeals presented themselves, . . . and worked myself almost to a nervous break-down in groping my way, without sufficient guide or chart, through this ever-widening field of philanthropic endeavor. There was then forced upon me the necessity to organize and plan this department of our daily tasks on as distinct lines of progress as we did our business affairs."

This part of his business he organized as he did his other affairs by selecting experts and forming them into committees of investigation. Among them were legal and financial, as well as educational, scientific, and medical authorities.

Before entering upon any new line of benevolence, he would have a committee investigate every point bearing on its worth and the methods to be pursued in executing it. When a particular enterprise had been studied and approved, he proceeded to take it up with great liberality and to support it until it was carried through to a finish. He "was never content," he said, "to let the benevolences drift into the channels of mere convenience—to give to the institutions which have sought aid and to neglect others. This department studied the field of human progress, and sought to contribute to each of those elements which we believe tend most to promote it. Where it did not find organizations ready to hand for such purpose, ... it sought to create them."

The great value of dealing with an organization which knows all the facts, and can best decide just where the help can be applied to the best advantage, has impressed itself upon me through the results of long experience. ... It is wise to be careful not to duplicate effort and not to inaugurate new charities in fields already covered, but rather to strengthen and perfect those already at work. There is a great deal of rivalry and a vast amount of duplication, and one of the most difficult things in giving is to ascertain when the field is fully covered. Many people simply consider whether the institution to which they are giving is thoughtfully and well managed, without stopping to discover whether the field is not already occupied by others. ... It may be urged that doing the work in this systematic and apparently cold-blooded way leaves out of consideration, to a large extent, the merits of individual cases. My contention is that the organization of work in combination should not and does not stifle the work of individuals, but strengthens and stimulates it.

To aid in carrying out this plan on a large scale liberal donations were made outright to the Southern Board, to the General Education Board, and to the Rockefeller Foundation, to be used for the purposes for which they were organized, as their members should decide.

As one method of doing the most permanent good to humanity, Mr. Rockefeller has always been deeply interested in scientific research in medicine and surgery. He says :

Great hospitals conducted by noble and unselfish men and women are doing wonderful work ; but no less important are the achievements in research that reveal hitherto unknown facts about diseases and provide the remedies by which many of them can be relieved or even stamped out.

To help the sick and distressed appeals to the kind-hearted always, but to help the investigator who is striving successfully to attack the causes which bring about sickness and distress does not so strongly attract the giver of money. ... Yet I am sure we are making wonderful advances in this field of scientific giving. All over the world the need of dealing with the questions of philanthropy with something beyond the impulses of emotion is evident, and everywhere help is being given to those heroic men and women who are devoting themselves to the practical and essentially scientific tasks. It is ... an inspiring thing to recall occasionally the heroism, for example, of the men who risked and sacrificed their lives to discover the facts about yellow fever, a sacrifice for which untold generations will bless them.

Research he considered far more important than the mere dissemination of that which is already known.

An individual institution of learning can have only a narrow sphere. It can reach only a limited number of people. But every new fact discovered, every widening of the boundaries of human knowledge by research, becomes universally known to all institutions of learning, and becomes a benefaction at once to the whole race.

With these ends in view he established the great Institute for Medical Research in New York, the Sanitary Commission for the South, the International Health Board, and the China Medical College ; and he aided many scientific and medical institutions in America, Europe, and other countries.

Mr. Rockefeller has great hope of these Benevolent Trusts or Foundations for administering funds given for public services. He writes :

The Benevolent Trusts is a name for corporations to manage the business side of benefactions. The idea needs, and to be successful must have, the help of men who have been trained along practical lines. The best men of business should be attracted by its possibilities for good. ...

Today the whole machinery of benevolence is conducted upon more or less haphazard principles. Good men and women are wearing out their lives to raise money to sustain institutions which are conducted by more or less unskilled methods. This is a tremendous waste of our best material.

We cannot afford to have great souls who are capable of doing the most effective work slaving to raise the money. That should be a business man's task, and he should be supreme in managing the machinery. ...

When these Benevolent Trusts come into active being, such organizations ... will be sure to attract the brains of the best men we have in our commercial affairs, as great business opportunities attract them now. ... The good people who bestow their beneficence on education may well give more thought to investigating the character of the enterprises that they are importuned to help, and this study ought to take into account the kind of people who are responsible for their management, their location, and the facilities supplied by other institutions round about. A thorough examination such as this is generally quite impossible for an individual, and he either declines to give from lack of accurate knowledge, or he may give without due consideration.... This work of inquiry is done, and well done, by the General Education Board, through officers of intelligence, skill, and sympathy, trained to the work.

Speaking to a meeting of business men on this subject Mr. Rockefeller once said :

You men are always looking forward to do something for good causes. I know how very busy you are. You work in a treadmill from which you see no escape. I can easily understand that you feel, that it is beyond your present power carefully to study the needs of humanity.... Why not do with what you can give to others as you do with what you want to keep for yourself and your children : Put it into a Trust? You would not place a fortune for your children in the hands of an inexperienced person, no matter how good he might be. Let us be as careful with the money we would spend for the benefit of others.... Let us erect a foundation, a Trust, and engage directors who will make it a life work to manage, with our personal coöperation, this business of benevolence properly and effectively. And I beg of you, attend to it *now*, don't wait.

With these statements and the records of his boards during the past thirty years before us we may now analyze and summarize Mr. Rockefeller's principles and plans. Primarily, he did not believe in creating new institutions. He established but one Rockefeller institute, The Rockefeller Institute for Medical Research in New York. This was founded before the General Board or the Foundation was formed to systematize his benevolences. He preferred to coöperate with the existing institutions of the people and sought to promote their initiative. Spontaneous movements, when properly planned to promote needed betterments, offered, in his opinion, ample opportunities for effective service. As in the case of the southern education movement, after satisfying himself of the need and the usefulness of an organization, he would ask to be permitted to help it. Seeking to develop institutions which would live, he would plant them where they would grow up in their natural environment and be nourished from their own soil. Only by such measures could there be created a unity of all the agencies for public good in harmony with the feelings and customs of the people. He recognized, moreover, that money was not the only factor in building useful institutions. Wise and faithful men to administer them, community coöperation, and local support he regarded as more important.

In accordance with these principles, it was the policy of his boards to coöperate with the existing agencies of the people, whether public or private, in initiating all new enterprises. They would first investigate the field carefully to ascertain the need of the institution, the suitability of the locality, and the prospects of local support. If there was any hope of an existing agency's doing the work, they would never encourage the establishment of a new one. They would frequently assist in consolidating several old institutions and then strengthen and enlarge the new one thus created. When called on to found a new department in a university, they saw to it that it was thoroughly integrated with the existing departments and adjusted to grow into the institution. Nothing was ever promised until the proper authorities or representatives of the people concerned had given reasonable assurance of their intelligent and faithful coöperation.

Mr. Rockefeller's plan of philanthropy may thus be summed up in these three points : first, the development of initiative ; second, coöperation with existing agencies ; and third, the integration that would produce the most complete unity possible of all the social institutions of the democracy. To accomplish these ends fully, he would give liberally and continuously until the purpose was accomplished. "Finish the job!"—was his dictum.

The methods of Mr. Rockefeller's boards were always strictly democratic. As Dr. Buttrick explained before the Georgia legislature in 1902, they never went in unless invited and then only to coöperate, never to dictate or control. After investigating thoroughly, they gave unreservedly.[14] Mr. Rockefeller's gifts had "no strings tied to them."

The example of Mr. Rockefeller has already had a great influence on philanthropists interested in education and human betterment. At a time when men of good will everywhere were

[14] Wallace Buttrick's Atlanta address, p. 157 in this book.

seeking to find ways to use their means for the greatest benefit to mankind, Mr. Rockefeller made a most valuable and practical contribution to the solution of the problem of wise philanthropy.

FREDERICK T. GATES

Mr. Rockefeller's chief aid and counselor for over thirty years was Dr. F. T. Gates, who was chairman of his office committee and his chief almoner. He was also chairman of the Board of the Rockefeller Institute for Medical Research, chairman from 1907 of the General Education Board, a trustee of the Rockefeller Foundation, chairman of the Sanitary Commission, and a member of the International Health Board and the China Medical Board.

Frederick T. Gates was born in Maine, the son of a Baptist missionary who was a pioneer in Kansas, where the boy grew up. He was educated at the University of Rochester and the Rochester Theological Seminary. While pastor of the Central Baptist Church of Minneapolis, he was chosen secretary of the American Baptist Education Society, through which he came into contact with Mr. Rockefeller. Impressed with Gates's energy and sagacity, as well as his high character and public spirit, Mr. Rockefeller had him investigate some business enterprises. His reports showed such keen insight and sound judgment that Mr. Rockefeller asked him to become his personal assistant in his philanthropic work. In his "Reminiscences" he says of him :

I give credit to Mr. Gates for possessing a combination of rare business ability, very highly developed and very honorably exercised, over-shadowed by a passion to accomplish great and far-reaching benefits to mankind, the influence of which will last.... His efforts in the investigations in connection with our educational contributions, our medical research, and other kindred works have been very successful.

The General Education Board made this minute about Dr. Gates :

The services rendered by Mr. Gates in connection with the several foundations established through the munificence of Mr. John D. Rockefeller cannot be adequately understood unless these foundations are recognized as parts of a well ordered whole, in the planning of which his thought, his imagination and his powers of vigorous and persuasive utterance were dominating factors. As he himself once said, the objects for which the several Boards were set up represented not an accidental succession of ideas but one logically developed scheme through which he and his associates sought to make effective the vision and benevolence of the founder. It is hardly too much to say that the great problem of philanthropy —how to do the greatest amount of good and the least amount of harm with private wealth dedicated to the welfare of mankind— had never before been envisaged with the breadth of view and the thorough analysis that Mr. Gates brought to this task. He planned the attack on human wants, individual and social, whether in the domain of health, of education or of economic need, along lines of what can fittingly be called *major strategy* ; and like all great strategists he thought in simple terms. . . . He saw the dependence of both education and economic progress on health and guided the pioneering labors of the Rockefeller Sanitary Commission, which later, as the International Health Division of the Rockefeller Foundation, extended to other countries a technique worked out in the southern states. Thus he saw the dependence of public health upon the coördinated services of medical research and medical education. In all this large and unprecedented undertaking Mr. Gates effectively interpreted the fundamental principle actuating the founder, namely, that private means applied to the public good could in the long run accomplish that good only if it helped to call out from the communities to be benefited the permanent support of their own resources. Temporary aid that left a community or an individual less rather than more self-reliant by the time the aid was withdrawn he recognized as an injury rather than a service.[15]

As an investigator Gates's methods were those of the scientific man ; as a social philosopher his plans were constructive and practical. On the walls of the General Education Board office hung a great map of the United States upon which Gates "would mark the fortresses and outposts of education with reference to the distribution and concentration of population and the available sources of public and (or) private wealth for their support." [16] To a friend who visited him he described his office at the top of the huge building on Broadway, overlooking the great harbor bearing ships of all nations,

[15] *Annual Report of the General Education Board, 1928-1929,* pp. xi-xiii.
[16] *Ibid.,* p. xii.

as "a mental observatory," from which he looked out upon the whole world, seeking to find places where the most permanent good could be done for mankind.

WILLIAM HENRY BALDWIN, JR.

William Henry Baldwin, Jr., the first president of the General Education Board, lived to serve it only six scant years. But between the second Capon Springs Conference in June, 1899, where he had an influential part and made a notable address on the problem of Negro education, and 1904, when he became invalided, he was a most earnest and effective worker for it. One of the first members of the Southern Education Board, he took hold of its problems with fine intelligence and zeal. He was a member with Mr. George Foster Peabody and Mr. Ogden of the first finance committee of the Southern Board, and with Dr. Gates he planned the General Education Board.

We are interested to learn what influences or training made this comparatively young man, dying at forty-two, so effective in shaping this campaign for southern education.[17] The answer is that Baldwin was prepared in mind and heart when he joined the movement. He already had a deep interest in the southern problem, a clear knowledge of its conditions, and experience in handling such causes.

Both heredity and training contributed to the making of Baldwin. He came of a New England family of pure English origin, noted for its ability and integrity. His father, William Henry Baldwin, after acquiring in business a modest competency for his family, gave his whole life to the service of the Young Men's Christian Union of Boston. This institution filled a high place in the larger civic and religious movements of the time. Baldwin was its president and its soul for twenty years. That a man with a large family should give up a successful business and devote himself exclusively to social work and should persist in it in the face of all offers to go into business, was considered remarkable and made Baldwin an outstanding character in Boston. The father's example made a deep impression on the boy.

William Henry Baldwin, Jr., was born on February 5, 1863,

[17] John Graham Brooks, *An American Citizen: Life of William H. Baldwin, Jr.*, is the source of information about Baldwin's early life.

the sixth of nine children. He was a very real boy, not remarkably studious at first, but intensely active and a leader among his schoolmates. When a small lad he would get up at half past four o'clock in the morning to sell newspapers to earn money to help his mother. This eagerness for work and the desire to be helpful were characteristic of the boy in school, in college and throughout his whole career.

After a course in the Roxbury Latin School, where he was a fair student and a leader in all the games, he entered Harvard College, being graduated with good standing in 1885. He was a member of the glee club, an actor on the college stage, and an editor of the students' journal; and he took part in the athletic sports both in the field and on the river. He early showed remarkable talent for organization and administration. Taking hold, for example, of the Harvard Dining Association at a time when its affairs were in a bad way, he straightened it out. He was treasurer of the Coöperative Society and chairman of his class committee as long as he lived. His biographer says that he was "athletic without excess of over-concentration upon any sport. None of his popularity was owing to the noisy idolatry of mere athletic prowess, and ... he had none of its dizzying distinctions."

One of his professors, writing of him at this time, said: "Sincere and straightforward by nature, he has a rough and sweeping contempt for shams and empty forms. ... He can be discovered in no position more frequently or more characteristically than in that of stepping out of his way to exert himself for some one else—as often as not, a perfect stranger." [18]

When it came to planning his life work, the dominating thought in the young man's mind was how he could render the best service to his fellow men. The question of choosing a profession was a serious one upon which he sought counsel from his father and friends. One of the latter says: "He came to me with questions about some 'social work,' with which he expressed strong sympathy. It was clear ... that the long and splendid service of his father ... was in his mind ... but that the work at the Union did not wholly satisfy the son's ambition." [19] He sought something broader in which he could use his organizing and administrative talents. He first thought seri-

[18] *Ibid.*, pp. 44-46.   [19] *Ibid.*, pp. 47-48.

ously of the ministry. He said: "I have naturally a strong interest in the doing good part of the ministry." Much interested in the question of "capital and labor," which was prominent at the time, he doubted whether a clergyman could in time of trouble between employers and employed exercise real influence.

He finally concluded that the ministry would not give him an outlet for his special talents. His desires and capacities seemed at first to lead him to go into the law, but when he consulted his lawyer friends, he says he got scant encouragement with regard to the possibilities of the profession for social service. His interest in the natural sciences led him next to think of medicine, but he turned from it when its specific duties were faced. They appeared to him too technical. "I am sure of one thing," he says, "I want to work for humanity. When and how can one do most for his fellows?" Finally he came to recognize that his capacities and interests fitted him for business. "I feared the tendency to a lack of a broad life in business," he said. "I have heard so much of the bad side of it. Still, I have always had the feeling that my natural tastes led me towards business, that is as far as experience has shown any capacity." [20]

The problem was solved for him when, upon the request of Mr. Charles Francis Adams, president of the Union Pacific Railroad, for an able young man, President Eliot recommended young Baldwin for his service. So in February, 1886, he went to Omaha, Nebraska, to take a small position in the auditor's office of the railroad. A grum old officer evidently took pleasure in giving the young Harvard graduate, who came as a friend of the president, a very difficult piece of work—it was a batch of monthly reports and accounts in great confusion—saying: "Go to it. No one but the Almighty can understand them." The young man took hold of them and brought order out of the chaos. Given many other hard jobs he soon made a reputation for ability and energy. He made a reputation also for doing unimportant things thoroughly and was promoted rapidly from one position to another, until in May, 1887, he was made a division freight agent of the Union Pacific.[21] Now he was advanced rapidly through various positions which gave him experience. Omitting various minor appointments, we find he was made in 1889 general manager of the Montana Union

[20] *Ibid.*, p. 52.   [21] *Ibid.*, pp. 54-56.

Railroad ; in 1890 he was assistant vice president of the Union Pacific ; and in 1891 he was general manager of the Flint and Père Marquette Railroad. In July, 1894, he was promoted to be a vice president of the Southern Railway with headquarters in Washington, and commenced the study of the South. In 1896, when the Pennsylvania undertook the job of building its great new station in New York, he was made president of the Long Island Railroad and given charge of that great task. Rarely did any man rise so rapidly in the railroad business. In ten years he advanced from a clerkship in an auditor's office to the presidency of a great railroad.

A citizen of New York now, he took up with zeal the study of the political and social problems of the city. Among other things he became chairman of the Committee of Fifteen to investigate the social evil in New York City and directed the investigation which produced the well known report. To this and many other civic tasks he gave all the abilities of a trained mind and the zeal of an ardent heart.

It was during the New York period, when he was putting through tremendous railroad enterprises and doing a difficult piece of social work, that he helped to organize the General Education Board. The intense work he did during these last ten years shortened his life. Even after giving up active work, he followed, with the deepest interest, the growth of the great institutions he had helped to found, receiving reports and advising about their business to his last days.

Though deeply interested in these subjects all his life, social service was not his chief work. He was proud of his profession as a railroad man. He said : "It opens up more chances than any man can meet, and nothing shall induce me to switch off." The first problem he faced was the one of business ethics. "I was told that I would have to be a champion liar . . . to secure any business. I gave orders, however, that all business from my office must be done on an honorable basis, and that any statement made must be the truth. I decided to work the opposite of the game played by many of my competitors." He wrote later that his methods "worked."

He took keen interest in the welfare of his men, in their wages, hours, and living conditions. He helped establish Y.M.C.A.'s, clubs, and libraries for those who could not reach the existing ones. He himself prepared lists of books for these.

Though he believed in sincere "welfare work," which brought employers and men together for their mutual education and broadening, he had only condemnation for those employers who, as he said, only "played with these philanthropies." "If they want to fight trade-unions," he said, "let them do it openly and not in the guise of baths, gymnasiums, cheap lunches, and entertainments." He believed in the labor unions and dealt with their various orders. When called to be president of the Long Island Railroad he said to the directors : "I hardly think you wish me to become president of your road. You know my attitude toward the organization of labor is that every manager should treat with the representatives of the organization. ... They know their needs better than I can know them, and ... upon them I must depend in order ... not to do them injustice." No one has ever put the case for the Union better than this. He had his difficulties in his time, but he settled them on this principle.

In a paper which Baldwin wrote on "Industrial Arbitration," he objects to compulsion in every form, because it puts the responsibility on the party that cannot understand the conditions. "The essence of industrial peace is so to organize between both camps that there shall be the freest possible play in personal relations between capital and labor." Carroll D. Wright of the Labor Department said : "If you could get Baldwin's capacity, sympathy, and moral insight into all our big employers, there would be an end to all serious labor trouble within two years." [22]

This much has been told of Baldwin's views on the labor problem to show the spirit of the man. But, greatly as he was interested in these questions, they were not his chief interest. His chief interest was in the education and training of neglected men. From the time he took service with the Southern Railway this interest centered on the training of the Negroes of the South. All his early work was a preparation for this.

Baldwin, though descended from a line of abolitionists, was too young to carry with him any of the prejudices of that old party. He went South as a business man whose responsibilities compelled him to take account of the question of Negro labor. Negro labor was necessary for the constructive service of his railroad. He needed the coöperation of thousands of trained

[22] *Ibid.*, pp. 148-49, 161.

Negroes. More than this he realized that the prosperity of the South, and therefore of the railroads, depended upon the productive ability of the population, and that was now and would always be partly a black population. He believed the Negro was in the South to stay. For these as well as for humanitarian reasons he became at once intensely interested in the question of Negro education.

Dr. Booker T. Washington in his address at the unveiling of the tablet to Baldwin at Tuskegee tells how he visited him and finding him much interested in the subject, asked him to become a trustee at Tuskegee. "After looking me over, up and down," he said : " 'No, I cannot become a trustee ; I will not say I will become a trustee because when I give my word to become a trustee it must mean something. But I will study the institution at Tuskegee, I will go there and look it over and after I have found out what your methods are, what you are driving at—if your methods and objects commend themselves to me, then I will consent to become a trustee.' And I remember how," continues Washington, "... that upon one day when we were least expecting it, he stopped his private car off here and appeared upon our grounds, and ... went into every department of the institution, ... into the class rooms ... through the shops, ... through the farm, ... through the dining room. Then ... after he had studied our financial condition, after a number of months had passed, he consented ... to be one of our trustees, and from the beginning to the end we never had such a trustee. He ... devoted himself ..., in season and out of season, to the interests of this institution." [23]

It was thus that Baldwin became actively interested in southern education. He was first interested in the proper training of the Negroes, which he called "our greatest problem," [24] but he was also earnestly concerned about all the neglected peoples of the South and of the whole country.

Like the scholar and philosopher he was, Baldwin now took up a careful study of the Negro problem. In a paper entitled "The Negro in the United States of America," which he says he wrote for his own self-instruction, he gives the re-

[23] *Unveiling of the Memorial Tablet to William H. Baldwin, Jr., Tuskegee Institute, Ala., April 4, 1909*, pp. 6-7.
[24] See Baldwin's address on "Negro Education" at the Second Capon Springs Conference, *Proceedings of the Second Capon Springs Conference*, pp. 67-77.

sults of his investigation and thought on this subject. It is an excellent study of a most difficult problem—the problem of race understanding and sympathy as well as of education.

He attempted first to get a mental picture of the slave in America—How did he come here?—By what agencies?—What governments were responsible for his coming?—In what respect was the commerce in Africans different from that in other races?—How did the traffic gets its legal sanction?—The origin of the emancipation movement.—The fate of the American Colonization Society in Liberia.—The development of the Negro in America ; his training and progress under slavery ; his present condition and his future, etc. These were some of the broad questions to which he sought answers.

Here are a few of the things he learned. Whites were sold in the seventeenth century just as the Negroes were sold ; the people of the North were for generations as unconscious of the evils of slavery as those of the South and were engaged in the business of importing them. He was shocked to learn that some Negroes were imported from Africa by northern agencies down to a few months before the Civil War.

He made a study of the growth of the Negro population ; the proportion of Negroes in the entire population of the country had sunk since 1790 from 19 per cent to 11 per cent in 1900. From 1860 to 1900, the whites had increased 150 per cent ; the Negroes, only 100 per cent. The difference was due chiefly to immigration. He thought that the problem, therefore, should grow easier for the future.

A study of the occupations among the whites and the Negroes interested him greatly. The industrial chances, he found, were diminishing rapidly for the Negro. The farm seemed to be the only place for him.

He defended the Negro against the ugly conclusions drawn from his criminal record. The colored man was turned out of domestic slavery without training, and equal justice has been withheld from him. With all its evils, domestic slavery was an admirable system of discipline and constraint for a savage people. It made them remarkably peaceable and docile as long as they were slaves. The Negroes left in charge of the homes of the whites labored faithfully for their masters in the war and took care of the wives and children of the white men. This fidelity lingers and deserves all the tributes it has inspired.

Monuments have been erected by the former masters to faithful slaves. The wicked policies of Reconstruction filled the Negro mind with ideas of freedom and threw upon him economic responsibilities for which he was not prepared.

Baldwin concluded that, when looked at from the point of view of his African origin, the Negro is a steadily improving race. Slavery lifted him, and Baldwin believed that freedom would lift him further, if he is properly trained. In spite of all the dark and ugly results of sudden emancipation, he thought that "the negro under freedom has proved his case. Not that the mass has yet given this proof, but that a steadily growing minority has met the tests of civilization by property ownership, better morals, and by so much educational acquirement as to show that further opportunity will lift him higher still." [25]

Basing his conclusions on this study, Baldwin argued that industrial and agricultural education was the proper training for the majority of the Negroes.

"Baldwin was not only interested in education." His passion for service brought him to support all causes through which the South was attempting to develop her backward elements. He did not believe in superimposed schemes, but always said that he desired "to work, not against southern influences, but *with* them." He saw clearly that the southern conditions of the time presented the supreme test of modern democracy. Because the dangers were so great and the opportunities and rewards seemed so abundant, he wished during this creative period to stand and work side by side with southern people. Appreciating thoroughly the difficulties and privileges of his southern associates, he frequently said with deep earnestness : "What would I not give to be a southern man?"

[25] Brooks, *op. cit.*, p. 187.

CHAPTER X

WALLACE BUTTRICK: HIS METHODS AND WORK

A Great Worker in the Southern Campaign

D R. WALLACE BUTTRICK was in the habit of saying that he commenced work as secretary and executive officer of the General Education Board in a single room with only a messenger on All Fools' Day, 1902. Mr. Rockefeller had just given this Board a million dollars to be used at its discretion over ten years, in work for southern education. Thus was started the active work of this great educational agency, which disbursed over a hundred million dollars for education in the United States during the twenty-four years of Buttrick's service.

From this time on, the functions of the two boards, the Southern Education Board and the General Board, were to be more definitely defined and discriminated (the former, under the direction of Mr. Ogden, continuing its propaganda work through conventions, summer schools, local associations and district agents, and the latter taking over the financial end of the business and the actual promotion of schools, colleges, and universities) ; but nevertheless we claim Dr. Buttrick as one of the greatest workers in the southern campaign. He was a member of the Southern Board and acted as its representative through the whole of his career in the South and did a tremendous work there. The fact that he was also an officer of the General Board and paid by them does not take him out of this story. His great heart was in the South and his chief work was in the South, where the people respected and loved him. We claim, therefore, that the story of his work in the South belongs in this book.

Preparatory Years

Wallace Buttrick was born on October 23, 1853, at Madrid, New York. His father was a farmer, the village merchant, and a devoted member of the Baptist Church. The son obtained his general education at the Ogdensburg Academy and the Potsdam Normal School, which he attended between 1868 and 1872. As a youth he was a messenger in the state legislature at Albany where, being a good reader, he was frequently called upon to read bills in the House. He next served for five years as a railway mail clerk between Rome and Ogdensburg. These experiences gave him a good knowledge of men and of the methods of public business. Buttrick then studied at the Rochester Theological Seminary where he met Dr. Frederick T. Gates, who later became his closest friend and associate in church and educational work. He was graduated in 1883 and was immediately elected pastor of the First Baptist Church at New Haven, Connecticut. In 1889 he became pastor of a church in Saint Paul, Minnesota, where he formed a strong friendship with Archbishop Ireland, whose humanitarian spirit and broad Americanism he greatly admired. He served the Immanuel Church in Albany, New York, from 1892 to 1902.

For many years Buttrick was associated with Gates as a member of the Baptist Educational Board. As the agent of the Board, he was sent South to study the educational work for Negroes which was being conducted by it. After spending several years in the investigation, he submitted a report to the Baptist Association of Boston with recommendations as to future procedure. He said that when he presented his report to a thin meeting on a stormy night he did so with some trepidation. He feared he had wasted his work, for his proposal was that the Board should close its schools. Instead of trying to maintain separate denominational schools, as it and most other religious organizations had been doing for years, he recommended that it should coöperate with the existing educational interests in the South. No one had ever dared to make such a radical recommendation to the Baptist Educational Board before. It changed the whole working organization of the Church. Mr. Rockefeller had been supplying most of the money for this work. Gates, who was Mr. Rockefeller's representative and a member of the Board, came at once to Buttrick's support and said : "For the first time in my life I see some light with regard to the work this Church is doing." According perfectly with Mr. Rockefeller's principles, Buttrick's plan was accepted. Instead of building separate church schools, coöperation with the existing state and other public agencies was the plan followed thereafter. Incidentally this decision determined Buttrick's future life's work.

SECRETARY AND EXECUTIVE OFFICER OF THE GENERAL EDUCATION BOARD

This was the origin of the plan of the General Education Board for helping to develop better schools for both the whites and the blacks in the South, and all of the succeeding Rockefeller agencies in their service throughout the world. As soon as Buttrick was installed, he started his method of coöperation with the existing, educational agencies in the South, and it became the basis of his notable success. With wisdom, common sense, sympathy, and tact, he first established relations with state and municipal boards, normal schools, and colleges, which enabled him to find out how to help them effectively. He said that while he often won men to his view of things, he just as often got new views from them.

Buttrick's method of aiding educational systems and investigations was that of experiment. In a letter written shortly before his death, he gave the result of his lifelong experience in investigating existing educational situations: "The only way to study a situation is through an attempt to do something for it. Any academic study of a situation is not likely to be of much value except in connection with some program of real activity. I do not see how anyone can study Africa, or for that matter anywhere else, without a knowledge gained through active effort to promote the well-being of the people." "Learning by doing" was his method.

During the nearly twenty-five years that Dr. Buttrick was connected with the various boards, he rendered official service in the following positions: He was first a member of the Southern Education Board. He was one of the first members of the General Education Board and became its secretary and executive officer in 1902. In 1917, he became president of this Board. He was general agent of the Slater Board from 1904 to 1907 and a member of it until 1910; he was a trustee of the Rockefeller Foundation; he was a member of the International Health Board from 1917, a member of the China Medical Board, and a member and chairman of the International Education Board from the time these boards were established.

Buttrick's job, as he defined it, was "to find fields in which these organizations could be helpfully coöperative,"—that is, to find out what could be done to improve the existing schools and colleges, or locations where the needs and conditions justified new ones. His first task, therefore, was to survey the field. In this he spent many months in traveling ; visiting the schools, colleges, and universities ; interviewing the trustees and faculties ; and observing the economic, educational, and social conditions of the people. In this way he got first-hand information as to their constituencies, areas of influence, resources, and other pertinent facts. With these data in hand, he was able to decide which schools were needed in each area and how best to help them to meet the requirements of the population. His method was to find the men who were trying to do the right work and help them ; to discover institutions that promised to be useful and aid them. When he needed agents, he employed local men connected with the schools or universities to make surveys for him.

By these methods Buttrick accumulated a vast amount of valuable information about the schools, colleges, and universities of the country. He knew the people responsible for their development and support, the places they filled in their respective communities, the kind of work they did, and its value, economically, educationally, and socially. So thorough was his knowledge and so accurate his judgment that presidents and trustees of colleges frequently sought advice from him about their own problems. Boards of trustees consulted him about men for their faculties, and people who had money to give for education asked his advice as to where and how to give it to the best advantage.

From his studies emerged in time a comprehensive plan, which included the development of the elementary and secondary schools in the southern states ; a system of farm demonstrations in connection with the rural schools throughout the country ; a plan of aid for Negro education ; of contingent gifts towards the endowment of colleges and universities ; and public health institutions in our own and many foreign lands.

Although a northern man and an outsider, Buttrick quickly made friends with southern leaders, both white and black, wherever he went, and won their confidence and coöperation in the solution of their problems. One of the best things he taught the southern people was how to coöperate with each other and with the state and national boards in educational improvement.

Address Before the Georgia Legislature

The best way to explain Dr. Buttrick's methods and those of the General Education Board in its work in the South is to quote him. In a letter to his friend Gates he tells how he was called upon to address the Georgia legislature on November 4, 1902 : "By a joint resolution of the Senate and House of Representatives of Georgia I was invited to address them at noon today. I am sending you by this mail a copy of the speech. ... It seems to me that this was a rare opportunity for presenting our work to the law making power of the state."

This able address was published in the Atlanta papers and was widely read and discussed. It had great influence in clarifying the subject in the minds of the southern people. The following passages are recorded as a part of the history of the movement :

Our first duty was the study of the situation. We were convinced, ... that before proceeding with a work of such importance there should be accurate and comprehensive knowledge of educational conditions in the south. We had not proceeded far in this study before we became convinced that our energies should be directed chiefly to the promotion of education in the rural districts. ... We also saw that a great need was of the preparation of teachers for these rural schools, and we therefore resolved that a considerable part of our work should be that of coöperating with normal schools and with other schools prepared to train teachers. Now then, our problem was defined and we were in a measure prepared to grapple with it. We decided that the only proper avenue of approach to the public schools of a state was through its state department of public instruction. We do not for a moment contemplate an independent campaign for education. We have no thought of colonizing northern teachers at the south, or of propagating northern ideas at the south ; quite the contrary, we believe that the teachers of the south must be the people of the south, and that your schools must be organized and maintained by you in harmony with your institutions and traditions ; in fact, we have conceived of ourselves simply as silent partners in the great and important movement. ...

Let me now refer to one of the most important features of our work, namely, that of conferences with state and county superintendents. We do not presume to call such conferences ourselves; quite the contrary, we confer with state superintendents and the conferences are called by these officials and we meet them as invited guests. I am proud to say that the first of these conferences was held in the state of Georgia. . . .

At this point . . . I ought to say that we are especially interested in promoting what is known . . . as "the new education." We have accepted the principle that, "given a thousand facts for purposes of culture, a thousand facts from your own door yard are worth more than a thousand facts from classical antiquity."

I am happy to say that conferences such as was held at Athens have been arranged for in the following states: Virginia, North Carolina, South Carolina, Alabama and Louisiana, and we are already in correspondence with the remaining state superintendents of the south. I think you can at once see the great value of these conferences. The meeting together and the discussion of practical questions by the county commissioners of the state is of itself sufficient reward for the pains and labor involved, but in addition to this the board which I represent is made acquainted with the facts in a state, with the men who are charged with the responsibility of educating the young, and we are able to select certain favorable places in a state where . . . practical work for rural schools can be done.

Here Dr. Buttrick gave a number of illustrations of the manner in which his board was helping counties which had raised additional money to improve their schools, and then continued :

The only hope of general and universal education rests with the taxpayer. Permanent schools cannot be established on a private foundation and under private direction and support, whether it be by a local board of trustees or a church organization. We are convinced that upon the state rests the responsibility for education and that the smaller the political unit charged with that responsibility the surer and prompter will be the establishment of adequate school facilities. . . .

Let me say that we believe our board is established on a permanent moral and financial foundation. We crave the high privilege of bearing a part with you in the education of the youth of the land. . . . We seek your counsel and your advice ; we seek to coöperate with you in this work of education and I am quite sure that before your eyes, as before mine, there is a vision of an onward marching column of ... youth who within a few short years will take our places in the world, and we hope and pray that they will be better prepared than we to assume the solemn obligations and enjoy the high privileges of American citizenship.[1]

"FIVE POINTS OF EDUCATION"

As a man Wallace Buttrick was wise, modest, courageous, liberal-minded, and generous. He was ever genial, gracious, and sympathetic, and he had a quaint humor which never failed and which made him most attractive. Writing to one of his field agents he said : "I find that it is becoming perilous for us to visit schools. . . . The people at once infer that money is to be given them. . . . Really, my dear sir, we are greatly embarrassed by the expectations that have been created in the South. Our whistle is altogether too large for the size of our boiler." [2]

Buttrick had an acute intellect which took in situations quickly, great directness of thought, and sound judgment. He was a very direct, succinct writer and speaker. Unfortunately most of his speeches were extempore and not reported. His letters were always clear and frequently sparkling with humor. He was an attractive and entertaining talker, but steadily refused to write down any of the fine things which he said in informal conversations. President Payne of Peabody College tells how he finally induced him to formulate his views on what constitutes an education as he had heard him frequently express them. He cornered him in his office and told him he would not leave him until he wrote out an outline of what he had just heard him say. Buttrick took a sheet of note paper and jotted down on two small pages his "Five Points of Education." Payne afterwards got him to expand them into a paper which was published in the *Peabody Journal of Education.*

It is interesting to learn what were the ideas of this self-educated man who never attended a college or university and never taught in school. Here are his Five Points :

I. *All Education is Self-Education*

No person or institution can educate anybody. Education is a voluntary process. In the very nature of the idea, one must educate

[1] *Atlanta Journal,* Nov. 4, 1902.
[2] To George S. Dickerman, Jan. 21, 1903.

himself. Schools and colleges may be helpful ; they often are ; so
with libraries, laboratories, and the association of fellow-students.
Possibly, but doubtfully, textbooks are useful. We are greatly
helped by wise and knowing teachers. But all these are not absolutely necessary to education. Pasteur did his greatest work in a
dark room under a stairway.... Great collections of books, often
of a miscellaneous character, bewilder us. Textbooks create the
impression, unconsciously be it said, that when one has learned the
contents of the textbook he knows something—such as history, or
science, or mathematics. Assigned fragments of subjects reported
back to teachers in what we call "recitations," duly marked and
graded, fool us with the notion that they are educative. These are
generally but "re-citations," properly so called. The room where
the performance takes place is a recitation room. How foolish it all
sounds when we state it plainly! [3]

Education is the determined and long-continued effort of a
serious-minded person to train his powers of observation, thinking,
and reflection through gain in knowledge. A "student," rightly so
called, is a person who comes to college to avail himself of assembled opportunities for self-education.

We do not think straight about these things. We seldom think
of the college as a place of high opportunity for serious men....
We seldom say to a young man : "Here is opportunity to gain
high spiritual satisfaction for yourself and to make yourself worth
while in promoting the well-being of mankind." Education means
the abundant life, and a few of you who have studied Latin know
that "abundant" in that language means overflowing, a fountain of
life springing up within you....

II. *Capacity for Intelligent Self-Direction*

Self-directed intellectual inquiry—that's the thing. We think of
such capacity for self-direction as the goal of the training got in the
schools. And in a real sense it is, for the time comes when we
must launch out on life's ocean and steer our own ships. But
capacity for self-directed education should be gained very early in
life....

A fault with education in America is too much teaching, too
much prescribing of what shall be learned and how it shall be
learned. Freedom is what is needed in education. Start a boy right
in any subject ; better, help a boy start himself right in any sub-

[3] *Peabody Journal of Education*, Vol. III (November, 1925), No. 3.
In the notes for the address he was to make at Colorado College in June,
1926, he says, speaking to teachers : "Don't give them stuff they are to
regurgitate in examinations."

ject, and then say to him : "Come to me when you get stuck, and we will talk it over that we may help each other ; but, son, if you are going to be an educated man, you must have large liberty in directing yourself."

III. *Trained Capacity for Sustained Attention*

We need to get the mastery of our brains and of our minds so that they become working instruments which we control. In education, will must master mind. . . . Many people who are supposed to have trained intelligence are the slaves of moods. They can only do serious, intellectual work when they "feel like it." Now, I have noticed, in the observations of a long life, that the men and women who succeed in law, in medicine, in business, in preaching, in teaching, in authorship, in research (and they are so few) are the men and women who make their minds serve their wills. . . . What we call "moods," alleged inability to work because of humidity without or dyspepsia within, when reduced to simplest terms, is only laziness. If you would be numbered among the educated, you must be able to say to your minds : "Come now, let us work. Mind, I am your master ; go to work."

IV. *Education is Never Finished ; It is as Long as Life*

There is no such thing as a completed course of education. "Commencement" is an unfortunate word, for it has lost its meaning. It has come to mean : "The job is done, I have my diploma, I am an educated man." Wouldn't it be fine if we could substitute that great Saxon word "beginning"? I hail the college that dare do it. When one gets a diploma certifying that he has completed certain prescribed things called "education," he really has only served an apprenticeship. . . .

You have learned a little chemistry, a little physics, a little biology, a little mathematics. What will they mean to you after today if you drop them now? You can at least read with fair regularity a good journal in these great scientific subjects and thus know what is going on in this age of science and keep yourself alive.

You have had some work in history, in economics, in English literature, and in modern languages, with a bit of their literature. I tell you that ninety per cent of you will probably stop right where you are. Or I might say that, because of the inevitable shrinkage of your mentality, you will know less than you do now. . . .

Education is for life, even down to old age, if one is educated at all. The person who cannot say at the end of any calendar year,

"I have learned more during these twelve months than during any previous year of my life," does not belong with the company of immortals called "educatéd persons."

V. The Object of Education is Character, not Efficiency

I mean character in the sense of high and serious purpose, of severe intellectual attainment, of the mastery of mind, of sound philosophy of life.·

I have little patience with vocational training in college, the taking of valuable time for the learning of a trade. Mastery of one's self prepares for mastery in any honorable career. Michael Pupin was first of all a classical scholar. He had the highest marks in Greek ever given at Columbia. Afterwards he became a master of science.... Two leading pathologists of my acquaintance were classically trained, with a little college science. One of them said to me : "I regard the classical training got in college without a squint toward the vocational as the best possible training for a scientific career." Efficiency is a fine by-product of education, but to make efficiency the object of education is to debase that fine thing which we call "character."

...It is a very serious tendency which we observe in college catalogues of the present time—this tendency to use the precious four years of college to enable a man to get a living. Those years should be devoted to making living worth while.

But you will ask : "How is education, the process of education, this lifelong process of education, to be assimilated to character?" Let biology answer us—by functioning. The generous use of knowledge and training in promoting the well-being of mankind will return to us in character, in ever-growing high manhood, in satisfactions that perish not, in those qualities of being which live on forever, because they are life....

In an address to students Buttrick said : "I have just begun my second seventy years, and I feel myself a boy again. Let us here and now make high resolve that we will continue this process of self-education until our eyes are closed in death ; that we will learn in order that we may serve, in order that we may find our highest joy in making this world of ours a better place in which to live."

THE MAN AND HIS WORK

Dr. Buttrick with all his geniality and consideration of others held positive opinions. He had a happy way of getting people to think and discuss things, but always avoided the appearance of dictation or patronage. When his Board gave funds to an institution, it never dictated its policies. Asked what his advice was, Buttrick would say : "We tie no strings to our gifts." The General Education Board held that the colleges should be entirely free to manage their own affairs. Speaking before the Harvard Teachers' Association on April 29, 1922, Buttrick said : "We have been avowedly, persistently, and aggressively interested in academic freedom, freedom to think and freedom to utter one's thoughts within the limits of public morals." The Board imposed no conditions with its gifts to colleges, except that the funds given for endowment should be "preserved inviolate, ... the income to be expended by the trustees in their own way," and that before any money was due and payable, the institution should be out of debt. There was only one limitation on its giving. Under the terms of its charter, the Board could not give anything for theological education.

As an executive, Buttrick combined high ideals and great seriousness with the most engaging informality, which manifested itself in a very human interest in the personal welfare of those who worked with him. He had the peculiar gift of stimulating his associates and putting them at ease, while he threw responsibility upon them and developed their initiative.[4] With this he had great ability in getting rapidly at the heart of new problems and of finding solutions for them. His remarkable insight, his common sense, and sympathy enabled him to grasp human situations and to handle the difficulties which arose with a firmness and kindness that won the admiration, confidence, and loyalty of all associated with him. These abilities and this spirit made Buttrick a most responsible, trusted, loved, and successful executive. In all the boards of which he became a member, his vast store of knowledge, ripe wisdom, and extensive experience were greatly valued and most influential.

In the field of southern education, Buttrick was both investigator and executive in all the various lines of work undertaken there. As Ogden was the leader of the propaganda, the Coeur de Lion of the crusades, so Buttrick was the strategist, the Napoleon, directing the war against ignorance in the South.

[4] Appreciation of his associates of the various boards of which he was a member, adopted Nov., 1926, *Review of Reviews*, LXXV (Jan., 1927), 86.

He directed the services of the field agents, investigating both the white and the Negro schools in the South, and supervised the corps of agents for rural schools in connection with the office of the state superintendents and of the high schools in connection with the universities.

After studying Dr. Knapp's methods of fighting the boll weevil and in the production of cotton, Dr. Buttrick induced the General Board to extend Knapp's methods of farm demonstrations to all farmers. After demonstrating the possibility of this in the South, the United States Department of Agriculture was induced to extend the farm demonstrations throughout the country. Buttrick investigated and advised the General Board as to the needs of the southern colleges and universities.[5] A description of some of these lines of work will follow in this book. Buttrick's services were interwoven, in fact, in all the enterprises of the several Rockefeller boards in sanitation, education, science, and medicine throughout the world. To a large extent the record of these boards throughout these years is the record of the labors of Buttrick.

Dr. Buttrick died suddenly on May 27, 1926, in Baltimore on his way to make an address at Colorado College. Everyone who knew him, and his friends numbered thousands, joined with Dr. Rose and the boards he served, in their appreciation of him :

"Dr. Buttrick," said they, "has not only held the affection of all his associates, but his balanced wisdom, his statesmanship, in all that pertains to the country's education and progress, his courage and his broad human sympathy have given him a foremost place among the leaders of his generation." [6]

The men and women of the South who worked with him will ever remember him as the intelligent, sympathetic friend and counsellor, always coöperating with them zealously wherever he could in building institutions for the education of their people. His monument is in these schools he helped to build and in the lives of the generations of men and women trained in them.

---

[5] See below, the account of Dr. Knapp's farm demonstration plan on pp. 177 ff.

[6] *Annual Report of the General Education Board, 1925-1926,* p. xii.

CHAPTER XI

MANUAL LABOR SCHOOLS

INDUSTRIAL AND TECHNICAL EDUCATION

THE older public schools of the South of all grades, especially the schools established under the churches, did not at first recognize the necessity of adapting their plans to the needs of the pupils and the community in which they lived. The literary course of the three R's was the rule through all the elementary and high schools. In the case of the church schools the idea of schools as centers of religious propaganda was made prominent.

Education to be effective in life work must be closely related to the actual life of those taught. It must take account not only of the resources of the country, but of the instincts, experiences, and interests of the people of the community. The aim should be to equip the children for the life which they will have to live in the community. The old school put too much emphasis upon a literary curriculum and did not give enough training in the necessities of real life, such as health, hygiene, the making and keeping of a home, and especially the earning of a livelihood on the farm and the proper training in civic knowledge and coöperation. The school should take account of the life not only of the pupil, but of his community; it must consider the child's relation to the larger life which it must serve.

The idea of the manual labor school after the plan of Fellenberg and Pestalozzi, where the boy could earn his way by labor, was taken up with much interest in this country during the 1830's and 1840's, and many schools—public, church, and private—were established on this plan. Such schools proposed to improve the health and strength of the boys and girls and to train them in habits of industry by requiring a certain amount of manual work as a part of the regular program, which would help to support them. It was hoped in this way to make all honest labor democratic, to destroy distinctions in society, and so to preserve republican institutions. The plan appealed especially to the churches as a means of building character and educating poor children who by their labor paid their expenses in part. A society was formed to promote these schools and they were started in various places in all of the older southern states, where they ran for three or four years. Of all places, however, the southern states were the least adapted to this plan of education. Such schools were bound to meet disfavor in the South, where manual labor was looked down upon by the upper classes and where the poor white boys had all the work they wanted on their fathers' farms, and so the system proved a complete failure there.

The matter of industrial education thus stood still until after the Civil War. Meanwhile, manual training schools, based on the Swedish system, had sprung up in various places in the North, and several new plans of industrial training were being tried out. The Mechanics Institute of Worcester, Massachusetts, for example, adopted the plan of having students manufacture real things for sale. Its theory was that in order that the student might learn what real work was he should make a real article which could be sold. Other schools developed the Swedish plan of manual training, which teaches the pupil to use different tools in making model parts. Plans for working students on farms were abandoned in most places until the Morrill act for the establishment of agricultural and mechanical colleges was passed in 1862 in the midst of the war. These institutions, which began to be established in the southern states soon after the Civil War, generally provided farms and shops, but were very slow in finding out how to teach practical agriculture and mechanic arts. Methods of industrial education were now developed chiefly through four classes of institutions :

1. Schools for orphans and poor children, which had the girls do the domestic work of the institutions, and the boys clean the grounds, work in the gardens and on the farms.

2. Elementary and secondary schools, in which manual training was introduced. Such schools usually trained the boys in carpentry and machine shop work, and the girls in sewing, cooking, and other simple domestic arts.

3. The so-called normal and industrial schools for girls, which usually gave courses in the domestic and industrial arts, but paid more attention to music and the so-called fine arts.

4. The agricultural and mechanical colleges, which soon abandoned the plan of making their students do ordinary labor

on farms and gradually developed plans for having them take charge of test plats, do "projects," or experimental work. Not until Dr. Knapp developed a system of farm demonstrations for the older men and clubs for the boys and girls, was an effective plan found for teaching practical agriculture and horticulture.

Representatives of these types of schools have existed in the South and they have all contributed something to the development of industrial and agricultural education.

The Miller Manual Labor School in Albemarle County, Virginia

The Miller Manual Labor School, for orphans, made a great contribution to the solution of the problem of industrial education. This institution was founded on the bequest of Samuel Miller of Lynchburg, Virginia, which provided a fund for farm buildings, shops, and about $1,250,000 for endowment. The instruction was to be limited to the elementary and secondary training of orphan boys and girls from Albemarle County, and Mr. Miller enjoined that manual labor was to be a part of the program of the school. Orphan asylums heretofore had usually provided simply for the sustenance and general education of their wards without giving them any special training for making a living. Miller directed that the school should make practical work of some specific kind a regular part of the training of all the pupils. Each child was to be trained first to make a good life and then to earn a good living. The endowment thus provided offered a rare opportunity for demonstrating what such institutions could and should do.

Fortunately the bequest fell into the hands of some of the wisest educators of Virginia. The county judge who was charged with organizing the board of trustees was the Honorable John L. Cochran, and he appointed as trustees Colonel Charles S. Venable, who had been an aide to General Lee throughout the war, and Professor Francis H. Smith, both distinguished members of the faculty of the University of Virginia. After canvassing the fitness of scores of candidates, the trustees selected for the builder and superintendent of the school Captain Charles E. Vawter, an experienced teacher, at the time professor in Emory and Henry College.

CHARLES E. VAWTER

Vawter was eminently qualified for the new task. His history is a large part of the story of this institution which was destined to do so much for the children of Albemarle County and to become the pioneer institution of industrial education in the South.

Charles E. Vawter (born, June 19, 1841 ; died, October 27, 1905) was the son of Captain John Henderson Vawter, a farmer, tax assessor and civil engineer of Monroe County, Virginia (since West Virginia), a highly honored citizen and a representative in the legislature for twenty years. Charles received his early education in a local school conducted by a minister ; and he had been a student at Emory and Henry College for two years when at nineteen he joined the Confederate Army with his father, then sixty years old, and three brothers. They all became captains. Young Vawter enlisted in the Monroe County Guards of the twenty-seventh regiment of the famous Stonewall Brigade. His power of clear seeing and clear thinking, his courage, self-reliance, and judgment were soon manifested, and he was appointed captain of a company of sharpshooters in 1862. He served in all the campaigns and battles of Jackson's, afterwards Early's, army, and was highly commended by his officers. Left on the field for dead in one battle, he recovered, and went immediately back into the line. Captured in the severe conflict at Waynesboro, he was imprisoned in Fort Delaware in March, 1865, and held there until late in June. He then returned to Emory and Henry to take up his course of study, and was graduated in 1866.

After teaching a year as master of a school for boys at Chattanooga, he entered the University of Virginia and was graduated with distinction in mathematics. He was elected professor of mathematics at Emory and Henry College in 1868 and did excellent work there for ten years.

Vawter had formed in his mind a theory and a plan of education which he now proceeded to carry out. Reared on a farm and trained in the army, he had very positive views with regard to the place of labor and discipline in schools. He was a confirmed believer in systematic manual labor, and believed it had great value in character building, making good citizens and preventing social disorders.

"Do not mistake what I mean by manual training," he said. "It is not learning a trade. It is not becoming a machinist or a mechanic. It is simply the training of the hands through the guidance of a trained brain. It means the unification of all our powers."

He believed that the universal education of all the people to use their hands and brains together would solve the problem of labor and capital. "Labor and Capital will one day be at peace. But that will not come by arbitration, which only smothers the fire ; nor by unions, which only lead the ignorant by a way that they know not ; nor by laws, for conquest by force is an eternal battle. It will only come when in the capitalist the humanities of life root out the greed, and in the laborer when intelligence and skill supplant ignorance and awkwardness. Industrial peace will come when in our States every child, white and black, rich and poor, must go to school ; and when our school officers, composed of both men and women, are selected solely with reference to their ability to guide in this most important work of the State ; and when our teachers are selected solely with reference to their special fitness for their work, and retained so long as they continue to grow, and when they are amply paid all that their services demand. When brain and brawn have made peace their united forces shall lift humanity heavenward."

Captain Vawter had definite views also on the particular needs of the southern people at this time. He believed that universal education was the first need, the first measure to be used, and that moral, manual, and mental training were the only means to power for this people. Schools were, therefore, the first things to be provided in the existing condition of the people of the South. They offered the only method of rebuilding the old commonwealths and restoring them to a position of influence in the nation. He believed in industrial education also as a means for developing the resources of the land and returning it to a position of economic prosperity. He came forward just at the right moment and with great wisdom and common sense directed the introduction of the new methods in the schools of Virginia.

Although in principle and sentiment Vawter was a strong southerner, he was neither prejudiced nor narrow, but genuinely national, and his patriotism included the best good of all the children. Interested in both races, he first considered the children of his old comrades and of the white men of the hills among whom he was reared, and then made sincere efforts towards schools for the Negroes. When in 1878 he was selected to be superintendent of the Miller Manual Labor School, he saw in it the opportunity to realize his vision of a school that would train mind and hand together. Under his leadership Miller School became a model elementary and secondary institution illustrating the use of manual work in education. Recognized as a leader, Captain Vawter was called upon to advise and help school boards throughout the South to develop new and better systems. In the formative period of Virginia's educational progress (1898-1904), his work was an outstanding feature and the service he rendered was acknowledged by a succession of official appointments. He was made a member of the State Board of Education to organize the schools of Virginia under the new constitution of 1902. He served as chairman of the board of trustees of the Normal and Industrial School at Farmville, since called the State College for Women, and of the board of the Normal and Industrial Institute for Negroes at Petersburg, and he was for many years the head of the State Board of Charities and Correction. For fourteen years he was rector of the Board of Trustees of the Agricultural and Mechanical College, now called the Virginia Polytechnic Institute, where he aided President McBryde in shaping the policies of that institution.

Vawter was one of the founders of the Conference for Education in the South. He was firm for school management entirely divorced from politics. A man of great moral courage, a good fighter, he was beloved by those who shared these views and feared and avoided by those who did not.

CARLETON BARTLETT GIBSON, OF COLUMBUS, GEORGIA

One of the chief leaders in education in the South during the period of which we are writing was Carleton Bartlett Gibson who at Columbus, Georgia, established the first schools for industrial education in that portion of the South. Gibson was the first man to plan and organize industrial courses in both the elementary schools and the high schools designed to prepare children for the work they were to do in the mills in Columbus, where there was a factory population of several thousand souls. When Gibson commenced his work there were at least a thousand children in the town who had never been brought into the public schools.

The town of Columbus had always been liberal in its support of the schools ; it had added to its already good academic course the usual studies, normal training, domestic science, art, and music, and had extended the high school course. Through the generous efforts of some of the good women of the town it had established three kindergartens. But there was still a large class of people in the factory quarter of the town who had not been reached when Gibson commenced his special work for them.

Through the generosity of Mr. George Foster Peabody, a native of Columbus, and the increased liberality of the city council, Gibson was enabled in 1900 to establish what he called a Primary Industrial School, a school that used few textbooks, had few rules, had no fixed course of study, no grades, and three sessions a day, which, however, extended over twelve months of the year. In this school he introduced some twenty lines of handicraft. Children from seven years up were taken in and kept as long as they could be kept, which unfortunately was not beyond the age of twelve or fourteen, as they were permitted at that time to go to work in the mills at these ages. The school was a novelty and at its opening the children crowded into it eagerly.

An old residence located in the largest factory square of the town was rented as a schoolhouse. It did not have the appearance of the traditional schoolhouse, so that Gibson was able to make it rather a school home and shop for the children than a formal school. Through the personal offices of the teachers, and considerable missionary work by them, he sought first to bring the children into the ordinary school grades. Not much was accomplished in this way, since there was no compulsory school law. The children from the hovels of the factory square found it impossible to keep their noses between the lids of books. So in lieu of textbooks, tools and benches were substituted where the children could work at manual training. The kitchen was equipped and furnished where little girls were taught cooking. All were taught pottery, working in clay taken from the hillside near by. The girls were taught sewing, beginning with simple stitching and leading up to garment making, and learned to make their own dresses. They were also taught regular weaving and the simplest form of loom-weaving. They made their own looms in the shops. They were taught basketry, raffia work, housekeeping, and gardening. Gibson had the teachers live in the schoolhouse where the children could see something of more decent living than in their own homes. Every teacher's room was open to the inspection of the pupils at all times. The result of all this was that the children assembled promptly in the mornings without compulsion and began their work with considerable zest. Gibson says :

When we first established this school, these little children were the most uncivilized barbarians I ever saw. They came to the school noisy and without any regard whatever for the teachers or the building. . . . Many of the boys came smoking cigarettes and some of the girls came barefooted with one frock, and that hardly fastened. They were a slovenly set, and did not know what it was to be prompt or to carry out any commands promptly. . . . After a few weeks, I found them the most orderly and quiet set of pupils in the schools of Columbus. . . .

Though they have no text-books, these children learn to read more rapidly than children of ordinary graded schools. They learn board work more rapidly. Whenever they have a bit of cloth to cut up in their sewing they have instruction in measurement, and calculate the number of yards of cloth for a certain number of articles.

In the rear of our lot one of the teachers, with the boys and some of the girls, has started a school garden . . . in a brick-covered yard. The boys dug up these bricks and the little fellows, with the greatest joy, piled up their bricks, sold them and used the money which they themselves had made. This backyard was in a short time turned from a most unsightly place into a place of beauty. . . .

The school reaches this class of children and interests and develops them as no other school I know of. . . . It will not only reach and interest and develop them, but it is preparing them for the life they are to lead hereafter. Our whole scheme of education ought to conform somewhat to our social ideal.[1]

[1] *Proceedings of the Fifth Conference for Education in the South,* Athens, Ga., *1902,* pp. 70-71.

As stated above, the school had three sessions a day and was carried on right through the summer months as long as the children could be interested. Many of the children had to carry dinner pails to the older people in the mills, so that the school which began at eight o'clock adjourned at ten-thirty. There was another session beginning at one o'clock and extending to three-thirty. Many who worked in the mills during the day would attend the night sessions of the school.

Here was a remarkable experiment in the adaptation of education to a particular class of neglected children. The school reached these children and developed them as no other school could possibly have done. It led many of them into the regular schools and prepared all, somewhat at least, for the life they were to lead.

Carleton Bartlett Gibson, pioneer in the new education, was born in Mobile, Alabama, September 18, 1863. He was graduated at the University of Alabama with an A.M. degree in 1885. Gibson served first as principal of a public school in Mulberry, Alabama, 1884-85 ; was then president of the State Normal School at Jacksonville, Alabama, 1885-91. He was principal of the University Military School, Mobile, Alabama, for one year and then became president of the Central Female College of Tuscaloosa, Alabama, for a year. He finally found his real place of work in Columbus, Georgia, as principal of the high school in 1894-95 and was made superintendent of schools there in 1896. Here he remained until 1909, doing the great work described, when he was called by Mr. Eastman to become the president of the Mechanics Institute at Rochester, New York. At the opening of the World War Gibson offered his services and was assigned to Red Cross work in northern Germany and Poland. Here he suffered serious illness and was operated on and never quite recovered his health. Returning to the South from Rochester in 1916, he became superintendent of public schools of Savannah, Georgia. He died in 1927.

LAWTON B. EVANS'S SCHOOL FOR MILL CHILDREN

Other factory towns followed Gibson's methods with great success. In Augusta, Georgia, for example, Lawton B. Evans, superintendent of schools, set up a school of much the same character in the mill quarter. The only building he could get for the school was a large room over a saloon. While lessons were going on, the clink of glasses and shouts of drinkers could be heard below. Sometimes there would be a great row downstairs. The teacher would "sit steady," however, and the school go on. At his first attempt he was able, by a house to house canvass, to bring only about fifty children into the school. He says: "It was a motley crowd, showing all the symptoms of neglect, which we collected in this remarkable place. Faces unwashed, hair uncombed, clothes coarse, rarely clean, and guiltless of any effort at adornment, they could with all conscience be called 'tough.' No wonder, when but few of their parents could read and write, when they lived huddled together in small unventilated rooms, when they arose at daybreak, ate an ill-cooked breakfast, put up a cold dinner, and ran on the streets."

After one year's operation the school had outgrown the room over the bar, and a schoolhouse with two rooms had been built nearby. Two teachers were needed now, and one hundred children were gathered in. By the third year the school had grown to one hundred and fifty, for the community was also growing. There were churches, stores, and houses to rent, and people were moving in rapidly. But it was not a school crowd—far otherwise. The fourth year the schoolhouse had four rooms and Evans sent the teachers out into the highways to seek for the lambs and to bring them in, and they brought them in, "poor little outcasts." After six years the eight-room schoolhouse grew to a handsome fourteen-room building, and the original fifty pupils over the bar-room had increased to six hundred. The bar was no larger than it was ten years before, but was doing the same evil work. Evans says of his work:

If there is one class of people that needs the influence of school more than another, it is the class that lives in the reek and wither of a cotton mill. If one child gets my sympathy more than another, it is the one with the pale and old-looking face and stoop shoulders, that indicates hard work in a hot mill, little food badly cooked, and insufficient sleep in a stuffy room. But of such there are many in the mill districts of the land, and they need our prayers.

It does not need an array of statistics to bring to your notice the rapid growth of the mill interests in the South.... The whir of the Southern mill is the first note of an awakened industry.... With it comes its problems, social, educational and industrial. The factory class is distinct and pronounced, and its peculiar conditions bring peculiar temptations and these demand peculiar powers of resistance.

If you ask me what the school has done for the children I will answer : It is not the purpose of the school to lift the children above work, but rather to supply ... that which the mill can never give them, mental recreation in books and papers, the joys and comforts of a decent home life with all that it involves in the way of sewing, cooking and decorating. So long as ignorance and stupidity and dullness stand at the loom, and eat and sleep in filth, so long will disease and crime, and dissension and discontent riot with the lives and property of the people. The lives of the mill people are cheerless and unimaginative, made so by the relentless click of the shuttle as it goes back and forth, beating down their brains and weaving into the cold, gray warp of their lives a filling of unutterable dullness. It is the mission of the school to introduce a thread of gold into the woof of their lives. And this is what the school has done for the children. It has worked a regeneration in the lives of the boys and girls who have gone through it. There is no longer any fight over clean hands.... The morning devotions have now more to do with music, poetry and the Bible than with soap, water and towels as at first. They have passed the physical and are well into the spiritual stage of their progress. They have learned to love learning, and they read books.... Their newly learned arts they use at home. They have learned how to make the most of the hard life that must necessarily forever environ most of them.[2]

THE BERRY SCHOOLS

By reason of both their origin and their work the Berry Schools at Mount Berry, Georgia, founded entirely through the efforts of Miss Martha Berry, are among the most interesting industrial schools in the country. The first school, the Mount Berry School for Boys, grew out of a Sunday school taught by Miss Berry in 1901 in a little log cabin on her plantation in Floyd County, which is still preserved. The opportunity to learn to read and write awakened so deep an interest among the neglected white children and their parents in the Southern Appalachians that their teacher was roused to consider this great need and the means to meet it. The place where the Sunday school was held was called Possum Trot, and the children

2 *Proceedings of the Fifth Conference for Education in the South, Athens, Georgia, 1902,* pp. 72-75.

named Miss Berry the Sunday Lady of Possum Trot. Here this remarkable young woman got the inspiration to establish her "Christian Industrial schools to help needy boys and girls from the mountains and rural districts of the South." [3] The school began with five boys on January 13, 1902, with Miss Berry, her sister Frances, and Miss Elizabeth Brewster as teachers. The Martha Berry School for Girls was started with five girls on Thanksgiving Day in 1909 in a log building erected by the boys. The Berry Junior College was started in 1926 with twenty students and the Senior College in 1929 with seventeen students, who were graduated with the bachelor's degree in 1932. The Berry Colleges are accredited to the Southern Association of Colleges and Secondary Schools. These schools and colleges had in 1935 over a thousand students. A model practice school with seven grades was started in 1933.

The property of the Schools consists of a 700-acre farm for vegetables and fruits, for sheep, goats, and poultry. There is a 500-acre dairy farm. The Schools' Forest includes twenty-five thousand acres rich in wild life and containing three lakes. The Schools have nearly a hundred permanent, well-equipped buildings of log, brick, and stone. These were erected for the most part by the boys, who cut the logs, made the bricks, and quarried the stone. The whole of this wonderful development is the result of the personal efforts during thirty years of Martha Berry. Within the past few years Mr. and Mrs. Henry Ford have erected a handsome stone building for the academic department and the administration offices of the institution.

The Schools maintain twenty different industries, and all the students, both girls and boys, are required to work two days a week. In this way they earn a part or all of their expenses. The remaining four days are devoted to study in the usual high school or college departments, which include commerce, education, home economics, music, government, and sociology. Conducted under the direction of experts, the educational and industrial systems of the Berry Schools have proved most successful in making earnest, industrious, and loyal citizens.

[3] Tracy Byers, *Martha Berry, The Sunday Lady of Possum Trot* (New York, G. P. Putnam's Sons, 1932), pp. 35-47.

CHAPTER XII

DR. KNAPP'S FARM DEMONSTRATION PLAN

The Status of Agricultural and Mechanical Education at the Close of the War

AS explained in the chapter on his views concerning education, General Lee was the first man to start the movement in southern colleges for the introduction of applied sciences and arts in those institutions. Considering the time and the circumstances, it is remarkable that General Armstrong at Hampton had the same prophetic insight in regard to the vital principles which must underlie all universal education as did General Lee. He also saw that through honest manual labor the mind must be trained and the character developed. "Didactic instruction and dogmatic work and discipline he held had little to do with the formation of character. This must be done by making the school a little world in itself. The school life should be like real life." The primary purpose, therefore, of industrial education is the formation of character through the activities of the field, the shop, and the home as well as the classroom. He saw also that in view of the wretched economic status of the people in the South, the only hope for improvement lay in training them to develop the natural resources of the country, beginning with the land.

The colleges of the South stuck to the old literary curriculum for twenty years longer. When the agricultural and mechanical colleges were established in the United States in 1862 in the midst of the Civil War, no one knew how they would be organized or what they would teach. Even after the states had received the land grant for agricultural and mechanical colleges and had established institutions or departments called by this name, the courses of instruction remained much the same. The law was vague and said only that the newly established institutions must teach "the sciences pertaining to agriculture and mechanic arts" and give "military training." We are concerned here only with their influence on the teaching of agriculture.

There were, of course, many excellent practical farmers and gardeners, but no professional teachers of agriculture in the country. Agricultural colleges or departments were immediately started in most of the northern and western states. By 1880 these colleges had been established also in nearly all of the southern states. In the absence of experienced organizers and teachers, funds derived from the land grants given in support of these institutions were used largely for giving instruction in the common literary subjects and in the elementary sciences. The typical agricultural college of the eighties and nineties, both in the North and in the South, was an ordinary college with a farm attached, upon which the boys were required to labor so many hours a day. They did chores about the institution; they hoed, plowed, shoveled manure, dug ditches, and, when no other work was at hand, chopped wood or raked the leaves on the campus. The small wages earned were generally credited to their board and tuition.

When Congress in 1887 appropriated funds for agricultural experiment stations in the states, the majority of them were established in connection with these colleges. There were few persons in the country who knew how to conduct agricultural experiment stations any more than agricultural colleges. At first these stations had little equipment for the study of agricultural sciences or for field experiments. The first stations devoted themselves chiefly to making analyses of fertilizers and fertilizer materials and of soils. Several experiment stations, not connected with colleges, had small farms for practice, and animals for use in making feeding and dairy experiments. Later they made experiments with various standard crops and with soil improving legumes and new plants sent them by the Department of Agriculture to be tested.

The information obtained from these analyses and experiments was distributed in reports and bulletins. These were not always written in the clearest style, and as few of the farmers read the bulletins little was accomplished in improving agricultural practice. The problems of how to get the information obtained at the colleges and stations to the farmers and how to get them to apply it still remained unsolved. The few demonstration farms which had been started by farmers needed to be multiplied and the results brought to the attention of their neighbors.

It was thus over thirty years after the establishment of the first agricultural colleges in the South and twenty years after that of the experiment stations that a real method of teaching practical agriculture through farm demonstrations was introduced in America. The originator of what it now known as the method of teaching agriculture by farm demonstrations was Seaman Asahel Knapp, the greatest teacher of agriculture our country ever had. His methods, first tried out in the South and approved there, are now used all over this country and in other countries as well.

DR. SEAMAN A. KNAPP

Seaman Asahel Knapp was born in 1833 in Essex County, New York, was prepared for college at the Troy Academy at Poultney, Vermont, and was graduated at Union College, Schenectady, in 1856. It was at college that he acquired his first interest in gardening and agriculture. At Schenectady he came under the influence of President Eliphalet Nott, one of the greatest and most liberal-minded educators of the time, who had introduced into Union College courses in gardening and agriculture. Young Knapp worked under Nott and apparently got here his first ideas about agriculture and horticulture. He taught next for several years at the Institute at Fort Edwards, New York, and was then associated for a time in the management of the Ripley Female College at Poultney, Vermont. His health, becoming impaired for life, as was feared, he retired, moved to Iowa, and in 1866 settled on a farm in Benton County. Inability to engage in active work caused him to take the position of superintendent of the State College for the Blind at Vinton. In 1874, while still unwell and living on a small farm, he undertook the raising of some livestock, principally a few Berkshire hogs and shorthorn cattle. Taking interest in all farm enterprises and trying to learn the methods of livestock raising, he became a member of the first Iowa Stock Breeders Association. Knapp always observed and thought as he worked. He at once became a leader in agricultural clubs and wrote for farm papers, advocating a mode of diversified agriculture in Iowa, where corn and hogs had hitherto been the rule. He became professor of agriculture in the Iowa State College of Agriculture in 1879 and president in 1884.

During this Iowa period, Knapp was active in all teachers' organizations and institutes, attending the meetings for the establishment of agricultural experiment stations in several states, and helped at Washington in 1887 to get passed what is known as the "Hatch Act" for experiment stations. He advocated the connection of these experiment stations with the agricultural colleges so that the students could have object lessons of practical value. He became acquainted with the leading agriculturists of Iowa and notably with James Wilson, known among his fellow farmers as "Tama Jim," afterwards professor of agriculture in the Iowa State College and the great secretary of agriculture of the United States for sixteen years. This was a fortunate conjunction of two wise, hard-headed men who were ever after devoted friends. It was under James Wilson's administration of the Department of Agriculture in Washington that Knapp's plan was first adopted by the national government and put into action throughout the country.

RICE GROWING IN SOUTHERN LOUISIANA

His health failing again, Dr. Knapp in 1886 went to Lake Charles, Louisiana, where he was placed in charge of the agricultural department of a large land company. He found it difficult to interest the native population and to secure their cooperation in developing the improved methods of agriculture he proposed. Farmers from the North refused to settle upon the government lands because the agricultural and social conditions seemed so unfavorable. Sugar cane was the only crop, and the price of the product was always uncertain. Finally some of Knapp's neighbor farmers were brought down from Iowa and other northern states to show what could be done by correct farming. Under his direction the plan was so successful that in a few years thousands of northern farmers settled in this region and carried on Knapp's improved methods.

Rice growing was the chief feature of this enterprise at the beginning. Formerly rice had to be planted by hand in the flooded land and then harvested by hand. Knapp taught the people how to sow the rice with machines, and then, after drawing off the water and letting the ground dry, to harvest the crop with machinery similar to that used for wheat. These

Upper left, J. A. Evans, Dr. Knapp's right-hand man, who directed the Farm Demonstration Movement from the Department of Agriculture in Washington. Upper right, Seaman A. Knapp, originator of the Farm Demonstration Plan of teaching agriculture. Lower left, Carleton B. Gibson, who inaugurated industrial education in the schools of Columbus, Georgia. Lower right, Charles E. Vawter, superintendent of the Miller Manual Training School in Albemarle County, Virginia

Above, a typical Negro cabin in Florida, with wooden shutters instead of glass windows. It is unusual in having a porch and a fine tree near. Below, the Jesup Agricultural Wagon carrying better methods of agriculture to colored farmers

methods became immediately so successful that they were rapidly extended into Texas and the other states along the Gulf.

Knapp organized the Rice Growers' Association of America and was its president for several years. Finding that new varieties of seed were desirable, Secretary Wilson in 1898 sent Knapp to China, Japan, and the Philippines to investigate all varieties of rice grown in those countries and to study their methods of production and milling. Japanese varieties were found which were better adapted to Louisiana and Texas than any others they had previously planted, and these were successfully introduced. Three years later he went again to the Orient as the official agent of the Department of Agriculture to study rice culture, and in 1902 he was appointed to investigate for the department the resources and proper methods of agriculture to be introduced into Porto Rico.

It was in southern Louisiana that Dr. Knapp worked out his scheme of farm demonstrations. Here, as he said later, he learned how to teach practical agriculture. At that time the farmers of Louisiana, as everywhere else in the country, in fact, were quite skeptical about the teachings and methods of "those scientific fellows," as they were called. Knapp realized that owing to this prejudice it was necessary to employ practical farmers to carry out his demonstrations. He followed this rule in the employment of the first county agents and did not engage college-trained men until after the farmers had been generally won to believe in his methods. He made his first demonstrations, therefore, of very simple character. He first showed the people new cultural methods and the importance of good seed. A little later he introduced soil improving and cover crops. Today every phase of agriculture is dealt with through these demonstrations so that agriculture has been practically reorganized and saved by the contribution of this man.

Farm Demonstrations Versus the Boll Weevil

Perhaps the most dramatic example of the application of Dr. Knapp's farm demonstration plan to the solving of serious agricultural problems is the story of his fight against the boll weevil. About 1902 Knapp, while working with Dr. Beverly T. Galloway, chief of the Bureau of Plant Industry, had established a number of demonstration farms in Louisiana, Mississippi, Alabama, and Texas to show how his favorite theory of teaching agriculture could be carried out in that region by using other crops besides cotton.

The boll weevil had entered Texas in 1892 from Mexico and had been marching steadily eastward about two hundred miles a year across the state. After Drs. L. O. Howard and Schwartz, of the Division of Entomology, had studied the habits of the insect and had found poisoning impossible, it was decided that the thing to do was to get the nation or the state to forbid the growing of cotton in a belt two hundred miles around the region in Texas infected with the weevil. Cotton was the weevil's only food plant, and it was thought this would halt its progress and give time to study the habits of the insect and devise some means of preventing its ravages. The writer, who was then assistant secretary of agriculture, went to Texas with Dr. Howard for the purpose of studying the situation. After securing the coöperation of the governor of Texas, Honorable Charles Culberson, a former fellow student at Virginia, he with these experts appeared before the committees of the state legislature and demonstrated the boll weevil, its habits and methods of operation, and explained to them the danger of its invasion of the whole South. In spite of frequent conferences with the committees, most of whose members were cotton farmers, some of them from the region already infected, the legislature refused absolutely to give any heed. A bill to establish a two-hundred-mile belt of no-cotton was introduced, but received little attention. The farmer members of the legislature declared that the weevil was nothing new to them, that they had known it as the "sap-sucker" for many years, that it appeared only occasionally. The recommendation was ignored, the bill turned down. The boll weevil now continued its march and proceeded northeastward across the cotton states at its regular pace of about two hundred miles a year. Many methods to poison the weevil were tried without results.

Dr. Knapp found that the only method of securing a cotton crop in an infested region was to plant an early variety, harvest the cotton before the boll weevil became too numerous, and burn all the bolls, leaves, and stalks. By such measures the ravages of the weevil were considerably reduced.

Now what has the boll weevil to do with the schools? We shall see. In many counties in Texas the situation soon became quite desperate. It was at this juncture that Dr. Knapp came to the front with his practical proposal for a new type of farming. He took up the matter in 1903 first with the farmers and business men at Terrell, Texas. Fifteen hundred dollars was raised and a committee formed to put into action on a limited scale his plan.

Mr. Walter C. Porter deserves to be mentioned as the first man to volunteer the use of his farm and to make a success of the demonstration to beat the boll weevil by the use of early varieties of cotton, of fertilizers, and of improved methods of planting and culture, under Dr. Knapp's direction. Mr. Porter's account of his first year's operation is worthy of record. "There was no money appropriated for the farm, but the Terrell business men put up $1,500 to guarantee the farmer against loss in the operation of the demonstration. . . . I devoted 100 acres to the first demonstration, one-third cotton, one-third corn, and one-third speckled peas. . . . My demonstrations aimed to find the best varieties, . . . to test fertilizers and to emphasize cultural methods. . . . Wider cotton rows, five feet apart, and plants eighteen inches apart were new among us for we had formerly planted cotton in rows three and a half feet apart with plants ten inches apart.

"Now some results. The farm showed a profit of $6 to $8 per acre above normal. We were convinced at once that the new practices were a success." Mr. Porter has since educated nine children on the proceeds of his farm and has sent five boys to the Texas Agricultural College. When asked what he thought of the demonstration, he said: "My opinion is that the only way to improve agriculture in this country is by farm demonstrations conducted at first under the direction of the county agents. It is the only means of building up agricultural prosperity." Asked how he succeeded in educating so many children from the products of his farm, he said: "I have a wife back of me, and we have brought up our children by farm demonstration methods."

In the fall of 1903 Secretary Wilson of the Department of Agriculture and Dr. Galloway, chief of the Bureau of Plant Industry, visited this region devastated by the boll weevil in Texas, and examined carefully the methods and results at Terrell. The result was a recommendation to Congress to provide an emergency appropriation of $250,000 to combat the boll weevil; half of this was given to the Division of Entomology and half to the Bureau of Plant Industry, $40,000 of which was assigned to Dr. Knapp to enable him to take to the farmer on his own farm the information that would enable him to grow cotton despite the presence of the weevil.

Establishing his headquarters now at Houston, Texas, in 1904, Knapp took counsel with the farmers, bankers, railroad presidents, and other business men, secured contributions of money and other aids, and, with Mr. W. D. Bentley to help him, started out to hold meetings throughout the state. Knapp advocated new methods of growing food crops and less cotton, pushing cotton forward early so as to get ahead of the boll weevil. Many farmers were unwilling at first to undertake demonstrations, but after a time demonstrations were secured in ten counties.

The Work of J. A. Evans

Mr. J. A. Evans, now associate chief and regional agent for the southern states of the Farmers' Coöperative Demonstration work, was one of Dr. Knapp's first assistants. When the work was first provided for by Congress in 1903 Evans was put in charge in Texas. From that time he has been continuously in this service. When the demonstration work spread to other states he was made state agent for Louisiana and Arkansas. In 1911 he was called to Washington to be assistant chief of the office of Extension Work in the South, and in January, 1920, was made chief.

When the offices directing the Extension Work in the North, South and West were combined, Evans was made the associate chief of the new office of Coöperative Extension Work for the whole country. A pioneer in this type of education, the teaching of agriculture by demonstration, Evans has had much to do in molding all the plans and policies of the government in connection with this movement.

The Spread of the Farm Demonstration Plan

The following year scores of agents were employed in Texas, Louisiana, and Arkansas. Over a thousand meetings were held in one year (1904), and seven thousand farmers were induced to try the demonstrations. Conventions of farmers were held and profits from the demonstrations reported. The benefits of pure cotton seed, of deep plowing, and of more frequent cultivation, and especially the growing of home supplies, were the chief topics discussed. The matter of getting ahead of the weevil with early planting of the cotton, early maturing varieties, and the treatment of the soil to promote rapid growth were the chief points emphasized.

The methods used in this new plan of teaching agriculture were original. The agents would visit the best and most intelligent farmers and obtain their assistance as demonstrators. These men were then furnished with working plans and instructed in keeping records and making reports. Each demonstrator was required to grow, according to his ability and facilities, from five to twenty acres of cotton, following the directions given. Agents visited these farmers at least once a month. The neighbor farmers came in flocks to see the demonstrations.

In 1906 Dr. Wallace Buttrick, secretary of the General Education Board, visited Dr. Knapp in Texas. The result was that he approved enthusiastically all that Knapp was doing and recommended to Mr. John D. Rockefeller that he support, in a tentative way at first, this method of farm demonstration as a means of securing larger farm profits. This was approved, with the result that the General Education Board proposed to the secretary of agriculture of the United States that the Board coöperate with his Department in combating the cotton boll weevil. A division of the work was arranged. The Department had at that time a fund it could use for combating the boll weevil, but nothing for strictly educational purposes, so that the government supplied the funds for demonstration work in the weevil-infested states, while the General Education Board supplied the funds for similar work in the states which the weevil had not yet reached. The campaign, however, was planned as one unit under the Bureau of Plant Industry with Dr. Knapp as special agent in charge. The money of the Board was used in paying the salaries and the expenses of agents, who then received commissions as collaborators of the government Department, which gave them official status with authority.

Under this plan in 1906 the total number of demonstration agents was twenty-four, four of whom were paid by the General Education Board and appointed by the government.

Unfortunately for the farmers, but fortunately for the plan of educating them, the ravages of the boll weevil became so severe that many men in Texas and Louisiana were giving up farming. The coöperation of the business men and the banks of the community was sought from the beginning, and business men came forward to pay a share of the expenses of the agents to introduce the plan of demonstration in counties where their customers were numerous. As an illustration, in three counties in Texas and two parishes in Louisiana, the chambers of commerce provided $750 to $1,000 to obtain the services of an agent to show their people how to combat the boll weevil and to grow the food crops necessary to keep the people alive. Many of the farmers thought the experiments would be a loss of time and money and were not disposed to undertake them. Therefore, in order to get the farmers to set aside a certain acreage for demonstrations, the business men agreed to supply the funds to buy the seeds and fertilizers as an encouragement to the farmers to follow instructions.

After the illustrations of the success of the work in 1906 and 1907, the demonstrations multiplied. Starting in 1907 with forty-nine agents, most of them in the states of Texas, Louisiana, Arkansas, Mississippi, and Alabama, the agents were increased as follows: In 1908, 153; in 1909, 317; in 1910, 464; and in 1911, when the women agents were added, 583. In 1912 women joined in large numbers taking charge of the domestic work, including poultry, dairying, gardening, etc., so that the total number that year was 851; in 1913, 878; in 1914, 1,138; and in 1915, 1,229. So the agents increased all over the country. The total amount contributed by the General Education Board to the farm demonstration work in the whole country was in round figures $1,180,000.

THE PLAN AMONG THE NEGROES

As great potential producers the Negro farmers were not forgotten. After some of them had observed the results of the demonstrations on the white farms, it was easy to persuade them to take part in similar work. Negro agents were found who could work sympathetically with their own people and adapt the demonstrations to their needs and habits. Having been trained in these methods, the men from Hampton and Tuskegee were particularly helpful. Two men from Hampton, J. B. Pierce and T. M. Campbell, who were employed by the General Education Board in 1906 in this work, were most successful and are still in this extension work (1933). Begun in Alabama, the work for the Negroes was extended two years later to South Carolina, Georgia, and Mississippi; and by 1912 thirty-three agents were at work among the farmers of their race in the South. These agents supervised demonstrations in growing cotton and corn and made a point of encouraging the planting of home gardens, the keeping of hogs, cows, and poultry, and the use of improved machinery. They also taught the sanitation and cleaning up of the premises, the whitewashing of houses and fences, and in general how to live, with the result that in two years a Negro demonstration farm could be told on sight.

By 1913 white and Negro agents were supervising 102,700 demonstrators, who made for 1912 definite reports on nearly 30,000 corn and cotton demonstrations covering 212,500 acres. The average yield of these demonstration farms was that year 1,055 pounds of seed cotton and 35½ bushels of corn per acre compared with a general average in these states of 579 pounds of seed cotton and 19 bushels of corn. In 1909 Dr. Knapp in his report had said: "The aim of the farmers' coöperative work is to place an object lesson before the farmer himself, illustrating the best and most profitable methods of producing the standard farm crops, and to secure such active participation in the demonstrations as to prove that farmers can make a much larger ... crop and secure a greater return for their toil."

"TEN COMMANDMENTS OF AGRICULTURE"

Dr. Knapp's "Ten Commandments of Agriculture" were:

1. Prepare a deep and thoroughly pulverized seed bed, well drained.

2. Use seed of the best variety, intelligently selected and carefully stored.

3. Give the plants in the rows a space suited to the plant, the soil and the climate.

4. Use intensive tillage during the growing period.

5. Secure high content of humus in the soil by the use of legumes, barnyard manure, farm refuse and commercial fertilizers.

6. Carry out a systematic crop rotation with a winter cover crop.

7. Accomplish more work by using more horse power and better implements.

8. Increase the farm stock to the extent of utilizing all the waste products and idle lands of the farm.

9. Produce all the food required for the men and animals on the farm.

10. Keep an account of each farm product, in order to know from which the gain or loss arises.[1]

THE DEMONSTRATION PLAN AS A METHOD OF AGRICULTURAL EDUCATION

The demonstration method developed by Dr. Knapp is essentially new. It is not "extension" as formerly carried out by the colleges. "Extension" means taking out from the college information or instruction to the people beyond. It presumes there is a reservoir of knowledge to be pumped out to distant fields, while "demonstration" assumes that the garden or plot is to be made the source of experiment, information, and training. All sources of knowledge and all forces of nature contribute to the success of the demonstration, and all who work or observe it will day by day get the benefits of the demonstrations. Demonstration will largely take the place of the old extension ; it will at least be made before the extension begins. The extension will be made from hundreds or thousands of points instead of from one in the state.

Dr. Knapp's demonstration work had many fruitful results. It led to the broadening of the scope of the farm work by using legumes and winter crops to enrich the soil ; by preventing soil erosion ; by teaching the rotation of crops and green manuring ; by showing the value and uses of barnyard manure which had been largely wasted ; by the proper preparation and use of commercial fertilizers ; by using simple methods of drainage ; by the improvement of natural pastures and meadows ; by showing the most economical crops for feeding work animals and livestock for meat production ; by the improvement of the homes and home grounds ; by the development of good roads ; and by the improvement of the school buildings and churches.

[1] Alfred Charles True, *A History of Agricultural Extension Work in the United States, 1785-1923*, p. 64.

All the social forces of the community were helped as the result of these demonstrations.[2]

As Dr. Knapp put it : "The farmers' coöperative demonstration work may be regarded . . . as the first step toward a true uplift, . . . or . . . as a system of rural education for boys and adults by which a readjustment of country life can be effected and placed upon a higher plane of profit, comfort, culture, influence, and power. The knowledge . . . helpful to husbandry that is annually worked out and made available by the scientists in the United States Department of Agriculture and the state experiment stations and by individual farmers . . . is sufficient to readjust agriculture and place it upon a basis of greater profit, to reconstruct the rural home, and to give to country life an attraction, a dignity, and a potential influence it has never received."

Seaman Asahel Knapp died April 1, 1911, all too soon, for he was in the midst of the greatest work for agricultural education ever undertaken in this or any other country. He lived, however, to develop a system that has done a vast deal of good and that will continue to do good as long as the country stands. The organization he developed had become fixed and legislation and appropriations had been made in the states and the nation to carry it on. His system was peculiarly adapted to conditions of southern agriculture at the time. No other method could have brought the facts of agricultural science to the farmers so effectively. He had practical experience of agriculture and a remarkable knowledge of the social and economic conditions in the South. In addition he had a big heart, full of sympathy for the poor burdened people on the farms of the South, both white and black, and the knack of getting hold of them as few men had. He was interesting and effective in conversation and eloquent in public speech. His practical plan appealed at once to both farmers and business men. When he started it, most of the southern farmers, both white and black, were still in the grip of the credit system in which the banker and the merchant "carried" the farmer, supplying him with all his needs through the year and insisting always upon his making cotton as the money crop, when he should, of course, have

[2] In an article in the *Yearbook* of the Department of Agriculture in 1909, Dr. Knapp tells of these and many other admirable results that followed from his work.

grown food crops first. Knapp dealt some severe blows to this system. His demonstration work proved in the end a true mission to the southern farm tenants. He was indeed a prophet of good news. He brought knowledge, hope, and prosperity to a stricken people at a time when they were almost hopeless. He will ever be remembered in the South as one of its truest friends.

Wallace Buttrick described Dr. Knapp as the greatest practical teacher of agriculture in our country and called the attention of the young to the fact that he had prepared himself for the splendid service he rendered through long years of study and training. As Dr. Buttrick put it : "He spent seventy years in preparation for seven years of service."

At the meeting of the Southern Education Conference at Jacksonville, Florida, a memorial service was held for Dr. Knapp. He was a prophet, said Frissell, "a man who saw visions, . . . who dreamed dreams, . . . and a man who had the power to translate those visions into the common, ordinary things of life. He walked with God and yet his feet were on the solid earth. . . . He brought the spiritual life into the common things of everyday life. Though a dreamer and a prophet, he had the strongest conviction as to the absolute necessity of proper economic living in the country. . . . Once he said to me, 'Whether this country is going to be a democracy or a plutocracy will be decided in the next ten years and . . . decided largely along these lines : As to whether or not the ordinary man makes the soil prosper, whether he wins the ownership of the land and then the proper understanding of how to cultivate it and get his share of the profits of the country.' " [3] How well these words fit present conditions! Never did we need to consider them so seriously as we do today.

[3] *Proceedings of the Fourteenth Conference for Education in the South, Jacksonville, Fla., 1911,* pp. 295-96.

CHAPTER XIII

BOYS' AND GIRLS' CLUBS

THE BEGINNING OF THE MOVEMENT

THE farm demonstration work had such fine results in interesting people in agricultural education, as well as increasing production, that work of a similar character for boys and girls was next started for the purpose of awakening them to new aspects of life, giving them some knowledge of nature, a training in agriculture and home industries, and a better conception of the objects of life and work. It is a common criticism, and a just one, to say that our schools, especially our country schools, deal too much in abstractions. Children are taught books and not things. "We educate children for 'white collar jobs' that do not and may never exist. This results in a generation of hobos who have to engage in some racketeering business for subsistence since they have been taught that to work with their hands is degrading." [1] This is one of the reasons why the people of the South have been so slow to tax themselves for the building of schoolhouses and the support of the schools. The schools did not prepare for any definite service. Since, however, the system of farm demonstrations and clubs has been introduced and instruction in the schools has been focused on the study of the soil, plants, and animals, excellent results have been accomplished in increasing popular support for the schools.

Mr. O. B. Martin, one of the earliest of the extension workers in the states and in the United States Department of Agriculture, now director of coöperative extension work in Texas, states the objects of the boys' and girls' demonstration work as follows :

1. To make good demonstrations in farming in thousands of communities.

2. To teach the principles of agriculture and horticulture in a practical manner.

[1] In a letter, April 5, 1935, J. S. Lambert, Alabama Department of Education.

3. To teach the love of plant life and the value of the soil.
4. To dignify labor and make it intelligent.
5. To give purpose and direction to youthful lives.
6. To teach earning, owning, and accounting.
7. To help the family.
8. To show the value of coöperation in the production and marketing of crops.
9. To vitalize school work.
10. To develop manhood and womanhood.[2]

This boys' and girls' movement is one of the most original and interesting methods of education ever tried in this or any other country. A few boys were enlisted as demonstrators first in Holmes County, Mississippi, in 1907. The experiment proved such a success and attracted so many observers that during 1908 boys' corn clubs were organized in several states with a total enrollment of two thousand. A special assistant was appointed by the United States Department of Agriculture in 1909 for this service and arrangements were made in several states for state club agents. Efforts were made to organize clubs in a few counties in every southern state, so that all the people might have an opportunity to observe them. The movement spread with astonishing rapidity, attracting attention throughout the whole country. The enrollment in 1913 was ninety-one thousand boys. In 1934, the enrollment in the boys' 4-H Clubs for the whole United States was 366,703, and for the southern states, 158,811. At first the work was done through the schools ; but, as most of the school officials did not have the time and some did not have the qualifications to give this new business proper supervision, it was found necessary to appoint special agents to direct the clubs. In many counties the boys' club programs could be directed by the same agents that had charge of the men's work. Though carried on under different persons, the work was usually associated with the schools and thus had a good influence upon the instruction in them.

If the homes were to be reached and better living conditions and ideals for community life were to be established, it was apparent that something of a similar kind must be done for the girls and women. There was great need, especially in the South, that the girls should be taught the care of the home, home

[2] *Proceedings of the Fifteenth Congress for Education in the South, Nashville, Tenn., 1912*, p. 206.

economics, gardening, care of poultry, dairying, and other industries belonging to the farm. As the boys were taught to make the farm a place of interest and profitable service, so the girls should be trained to make the home a place not only of eating and sleeping but of happiness and contentment.

When the law was first passed it was not permitted to give public money for home demonstration or club work for women and girls, but the General Education Board came forward and agreed to finance both lines of work, for girls as well as for boys, so that they could be established in a way to justify their permanent establishment on government appropriations.

The first organized demonstration work for girls under the direction of Dr. Seaman A. Knapp was begun in the early part of 1910, in Aiken County, South Carolina. Miss Marie Cromer, a county school teacher, started the work. Later in the same year a similar program was started in three counties in Virginia under the direction of Miss Ella G. Agnew, who had already been working with boys' and girls' clubs. The results in South Carolina and Virginia were so interesting and successful that other southern states promptly asked for similar work among boys and girls. In 1911 Mrs. Jane S. McKimmon in North Carolina and Miss Virginia P. Moore in Tennessee began the movement in two counties in each of these states. The movement received enthusiastic approval and was soon followed in the other southern states.

THE WORK OF THE CLUBS

When Jere H. Moore, of Winona, South Carolina, made, for example, 228¾ bushels of corn from one acre, the highest record for 1910 and next to the highest yield ever made in the world, it was published all over the country, and Jere became a hero for southern boys. His success stimulated enthusiasm for the methods of the clubs, and many other boys followed his example. People from all the surrounding country would visit the plots to see cornstalks taller than they had ever seen before and would attend the celebration after harvesting to see the piles of beautiful yellow ears measured up. Unusual amounts of fertilizer and elaborate systems of culture were of course used to produce these large crops. So it became necessary to restrain the boys somewhat from giving the impression that any farmer could grow on a large scale what they were doing on small plots. But the net result was excellent in promoting better cultural methods in the entire country.

There were heroines among the club girls also. Katherine Funkhauser, a 4-H Club member of Clarke County, Virginia, at the age of thirteen grew a pure-bred Shorthorn baby beef steer, "Billy," which she exhibited at the county show in Berryville (Virginia) in August, 1922. This animal was also shown by Katherine that year at the state fair and won the grand championship in his class. When exhibited at the fair, "Billy" was thirteen months old and weighed eleven hundred pounds. He was sold at auction on the fair grounds to the Old Dutch Market of Richmond at forty cents per pound and was exhibited on foot in the Market's show window for several days. Katherine received more publicity that year than any other farm girl in the United States. While she was devoting time to this 4-H Club project she led her classes in high school. The proceeds of the sale of "Billy" were used by Katherine in defraying her expenses at Hollins College in Virginia, from which institution she was graduated. She is now teaching in the Boyce High School, where she had joined the 4-H Club and started her career as a producer of baby beef.

The method of organizing these clubs was unique. Fifty or seventy-five boys would get together in a county and form a club and make plans for each of them to produce some crop or rear some animal. They would organize in the usual way, learn to conduct formal meetings, discuss their experiences, and so learned to coöperate. They wore badges and used trademarks on the products they sold, which emphasized the fact that there was a community purpose behind the project. The girls would organize in a similar manner.

The boys' clubs were usually called Corn Clubs and the girls' clubs Canning or Tomato Clubs, tomatoes being their first garden product and canning their first business. Both classes of clubs are now called 4-H Clubs—that is, clubs for the development of head, hand, heart, and health. They frequently had joint meetings for mutual assistance and encouragement. The county and district conventions of the 4-H Clubs are now doing much to develop coöperation, community spirit, and state pride.

By 1911 there were twenty-one agents in the field and three thousand girls enrolled in the southern states alone. The girls'

Above, Katherine Funkhauser, a 4-H Club member of Clark County, Virginia, showing her pure-bred shorthorn baby beef steer, "Billy," in August, 1922. He won the grand championship in his class at the state fair. The boy in the upper picture is Raymond Fishpaw, with his Angus baby beef, which took second place. Below, Jere H. Moore of Winona, South Carolina, who made 228¾ bushels of corn on one acre, the highest yield reported for 1910 and next to the highest ever reported

Above, a club member seven years old, with his pig. Through the boy's influence his father changed his herd from mixed to pure-bred. Below, county agent demonstrating to club members points in judging dairy cattle

movement grew rapidly, paralleling that of the boys, until in 1915 there were 387 home demonstration agents in fifteen southern states with a club enrollment of forty-five thousand six hundred girls. In 1934 the enrollment in the girls' 4-H Clubs in the United States was 549,359, and in the southern states, 238,672.

The girl club members were instructed the first year in the cultivation of a certain garden crop. Tomatoes seemed to furnish the best crop for instruction in both production and canning. The girls were, therefore, taught to select and prepare the soil, fertilize it, study the plants, cultivate and prune them, and finally to harvest the crop and can it according to the most scientific methods. Of these, eight thousand put up six million pounds of tomatoes and other vegetables in two million cans, jars, and other containers, of an estimated value of $300,000, at least $200,000 of which was clear profit. The average profit of each girl club member was about $25. Other products of the orchard and the farm, such as peaches, berries, figs, oranges, and other fruits peculiar to the South were put up in the same way. Some of the individual records of the girls were remarkable. Cora Brown, of Polk County, Georgia, for example, put up one year (1914) 5,290 pounds of fruit and vegetables at a profit of over $150. This created great interest in many farm homes in the South where there had been few gardens and where canned vegetables were not used except those bought at the store. The cold-pack canning of beans and other vegetables followed, causing a revolution in the diet of the people of the cotton country. The canning industry in the homes has become a large one, and it is evident that it will hereafter continue to be a chief measure for supplying healthful food for the inhabitants of the country.

A Poultry Club was organized next by the girls, and in two years some three thousand were engaged in this work. The agricultural colleges gave the assistance of experts, and in 1913, two hundred women were enlisted as home demonstration agents.

The girls' club work promoted the home demonstration work. When an agent was admitted to the homes, she found many opportunities to help the mothers with their problems. It was a process of educational evolution along lines of helpfulness and was carried out in a perfectly natural way. For example, following the work with garden and poultry products, the agent easily found access to the kitchen to give demonstrations in bread-making or cooking. Where there was no water supply or drainage, the agent would suggest means of introducing useful conveniences and helpful utensils. This program led naturally to home beautification and sanitation. It was easy to suggest that inexpensive water supply contrivances, fly screens, and other measures for health protection, be put in. Next would come lessons in sewing and embroidering, the making of clothing, and all the arts of the mother of the family. Many other opportunities were thus offered to practical teachers to give advice and make suggestions. The system now covers almost every kind of activity that belongs to the woman or the girl on the farm.

The leading livestock demonstrations consisted of what were called "Pig Clubs." They were made along three lines : Demonstrations of the mother sow and her litter ; growing pure-bred pigs for breeding purposes ; and fattening pigs for market. Cattle demonstrations were started in the later years and also proved very instructive. As with the pigs, the demonstrations were divided between growing young stock for breeding purposes and fattening them for the market. Thousands of boys have carried these demonstrations to completion under difficult circumstances.

Since the beginning of this work, many of the club boys have grown to be men. They make the best farmers and the very best demonstrators in the country.[3]

A writer in the General Education Board's report for 1902–1914 has interpreted the farm demonstration and youths' club movement from the educational point of view. He says : "This was, in effect, ... a trade continuation school for agriculturists. The demonstration movement embodied ... the idea that a man is a single organic thing ; that his education and environment are vitally related to each other ; that this relation does not arbitrarily stop until he stops ... ; that all his life a really live man ought to be gaining from his environment and reacting favorably on his environment ; that out of this shuttlecock movement come increasing economic security, widening of hori-

[3] See W. S. Newman, *The Earning Ability of Farmers Who Have Received Vocational Training, Bulletin No. 167, Federal Board for Vocational Education, Washington, D. C., 1933.*

zon, and spiritual awakening. The trade continuation school is valuable because it favors this sort of growth for the urban artisan ; the farm demonstration work has achieved precisely the same thing for the agriculturist. . . .

"The boys' corn clubs and the girls' canning clubs may be similarly interpreted. They were . . . unpretentious outgrowths of the demonstration idea. What more natural than that, after the father has been assisted to make more cotton and more corn and better cotton and better corn, the boy should be caught earlier, and the girl taught the domestic sides of improved agricultural processes? . . . The step was taken to meet a situation ; and like all sound steps similarly taken, it developed unsuspected significance.

"The Southern club movements may contain the solution of the vocational problem in the rural districts. They take up relevant, vital, fundamental activities and make them part of the normal process of growth. The activities involved are useful ; they are productive ; they make for intelligent living in the child's environment ; they increase his economic competency ; they do not tie him to the soil, if any sufficient reason exists for his leaving it ; they make him more contented and more efficient, however, if he stays there. They fit in with the more intellectual work in the schoolroom without overburdening the school by making it the sole custodian of the growing child, the sole sponsor for everything he gets—a tendency all too plainly evident in urban education ; finally, the clubs develop the capacity for united action and may thus prove the beginning of more effective coöperation in our future rural life. A serious problem would be solved if some form of vocational training could be found for the city boy that is equally simple, general, concrete, useful, profitable, broadening, and allied with other equally valuable concrete and social activities.

"There is, however, still another aspect to be pondered. Too often the school devitalizes material in order to adapt it to what are supposed to be schoolroom requirements. . . . Manual training, though of undoubted educational value as sense and muscle training, has fallen short of the hopes based upon it, to the extent that it has been formalized. Industrial and vocational training is clearly open to the same danger ; for the more or less mechanized imitation of industrial and vocational processes, apart from the exigencies and stimuli of real conditions, may prove to be only another kind of manual training. It is fortunate, indeed, that the rural situation is so far simple that it can be handled on the vocational side, without transferring everything to the school ; indeed, without subjecting the vocational subject matter to the processes of refinement and abstraction that are all too apt to result in sterilization. The Southern club work has wholly escaped this fate, because it has been carried on in normal ways in its natural habitat, and because its outcome has been subjected to the real tests of the market. The boys have cultivated a real acre apiece on the farm ; the girls have cultivated a real tenth of an acre in the family garden. The boys have measured their corn . . . and sold it at market price ; the girls have had to comply with the pure food law. The cash return has been larger or smaller, according to the quality and quantity of the result. The conditions have been precisely those prescribed by the task itself ; the incentives have been precisely those that operate upon mature men and women, and the reality of both process and result grips the growing boy and girl. For this reason the club work is likely to be a determining influence in life ; the activity is actual, the standards are actual, and the results—economic and moral—genuine." [4]

"Bug House Laboratory and Field Museum," Washington, North Carolina

Many interesting and valuable developments have grown up out of the boys' and girls' clubs. The young people trained in them frequently carry forward into their mature life the principles and methods learned. The reading and study clubs growing out of this movement are advancing the cause of education in their communities. Some of the clubs, begun in the schools, have grown into permanent local societies. A marked illustration of such a society is the "Bug House Laboratory and Field Museum," which grew out of a boys' club in the local school at Washington, Beaufort County, North Carolina.

In 1923 four boys of the school in Washington who wished to start a club were advised by their teacher to have a hobby, or to choose something special to do. After talking it over they decided to collect insects and went to work with zeal, making field trips on Saturdays and Sundays into the surrounding

[4] *The General Education Board, 1902-1914*, pp. 67-70.

Above, Bug House Laboratory and Field Museum, an outgrowth of boys' club work in the local high school in Washington, Beaufort County, North Carolina. Below, the first canning club organized in Anson County, North Carolina, in 1913. Mrs. Rosalind A. Redfern was the home demonstration agent

Above, a Kentucky log schoolhouse used until 1910. Below, a consolidated school at Mayslick, Kentucky, in 1919

country. A small tent made of tow sacks was their first club house. Needing a safe place in which to preserve their specimens, they took possession of a vacant house in the backyard of the home of one of the boys. Here they worked on the specimens and preserved them. The people of the neighborhood became interested in their work and helped them. The other children brought them specimens. One day a young lady went to see the collection and as she entered said : "What is this, a bug house?" The boys liked the name and so they decided to call their club the "Bug House Laboratory." As their collection grew they moved several times into larger quarters, and finally, after three years of work, they were given a vacant room in the city hall with free rent, light, and water.

The boys now took into their club girls, associate members from the interested school children, and honorary members from the grown people. The graduate members have continued very active. The club is composed at present (1935) of some twenty-five young men and women from sixteen to thirty years of age, with a junior associate group of about twenty younger boys and girls, ranging in age from twelve to sixteen. Qualifications for membership are based upon an interest in science and history and willingness to take part in the club activities. No person is taken in as a regular member until he has done something definite and worthwhile for the collection. This stimulates the associate members to work and increases the interest of their parents. The exhibits at the Beaufort County Fair and the State Fair increased the interest of the people of the town and county and encouraged the boys to ask for aid in erecting a building of their own. Friends gave them the logs ; and with the permission of the town government to locate the building in the city park and with the aid of grown-up members, the log house shown facing page 198 was erected. The building contains in one wing a laboratory, where the work is done, and a central hall and three wings for a museum of natural history. To meet the expenses of the museum, membership fees were established and admission is charged to see the collections.

The museum already has a large collection of insects, a department of marine life where some two hundred specimens are preserved, and a number of groups of fishes and small animals. One group shows the life on a coral reef, another some of the sea fish collected in the Caribbean. There are departments of reptiles, birds, and amphibians. There is a collection of minerals, fossils, and rocks from the state at large. In a department of "antiques" an effort is made to illustrate the history of the town by old furniture, tools, utensils, guns, coins, newspapers, and so on. An outdoor museum is now being developed in a beautiful little park where flowers, plants, and trees are cultivated.

The activities of the club, though primarily recreational, are also educational. From three hundred to six hundred persons visit the museum each month. All the active members at present are out of school and are employed in various business houses in the town. Therefore the major portion of the activities are carried on after business hours in the evenings and on holidays. Regular business meetings are held once each month ; and at least once each week some of the active members meet with the younger group, made up of high school students, to give them instructions. The objective of the active members is to train the junior associate group to become regular members. All the actual work is done by the members, active and associate. It consists of field trips for the collection of specimens, proper classification and preservation of the material, and arrangement of the specimens for exhibition.

The organization publishes a quarterly journal called the *Reporter of the Bug House Laboratory* which tells of the work done and the additions made to the museum. In the number for October, 1934, for example, we read : "The Washington Field Museum, the largest and oldest amateur museum in America, founded in 1923, is recognized now by the American Association of Museums and the North Carolina State Museum.... It is supported by the dues of members, financing memberships, and the contributions of visitors."

From the same number we quote the following characteristic note : "While fishing near Beaufort Inlet October, 1922, 'Doc' Kugler caught a beautiful cero commonly called king mackerel. It weighed thirty pounds and was approximately four and a half feet long. He gave it to the Bug House Laboratory where a plaster cast was immediately made. The reptile department received an order from other laboratories for seventy-five spade foot frogs. This species is found only when they come out of the ground, where they spend most of the time, to breed one night in the year, usually during March.

George W. Ross reports that one night following a heavy rain he caught between 8:15 and 11:30 on a tramp of a quarter of a mile forty-two spade foot frogs. Not one jumped from the time the light was shone on him. This was the luckiest night we ever had at frogging. He also caught several other rare species."

The spring number of the *Reporter* for 1935 tells how the building was financed and erected. It gives a list of accessions of mammals, birds, minerals, fossils, etc. There are articles on the "Nest and Eggs of the Logger-head Shrike," the "Carolina Short-tailed Shrew," the "Arrival of the Warblers," "Albino Frogs," and the method of catching frogs for university laboratories. It reports 1,280 visitors during the first three months of the year.

The Bug House Laboratory has become a permanent institution of which the community is very proud. It sends exhibits regularly to the State Fair, and, upon invitation, to the schools throughout the state. It has had already a decided influence in promoting the study of natural history in the schools of North Carolina.

The Work of I. W. Hill

Mr. I. W. Hill has been the field agent for the boys' and girls' clubs of the southern states ever since 1912. He was reared on a farm near Auburn, Alabama, educated at Emory College, Atlanta, and he has served as teacher, principal of high schools, superintendent of city schools, and finally superintendent of education for Alabama. As field agent in charge of boys' and girls' club work in the southern states he has presided every year with genial dignity and tact over the conventions of the boys and girls who assemble in Washington from all parts of the country and has made himself greatly loved by the young people. The work of the 4-H Clubs has been to him a vital and living thing, and he has made it the devoted task of thousands of boys and girls.

Significant Results of the Movement

The prizes awarded for club work are of various kinds. Ribbons, badges, and medals are distributed, but the greatest prize of all is the award of a trip to Washington for the best

club boys, or girls, from each state. In Washington they are received by officials of the Department of Agriculture, are
shown through the Capitol and the departments, and are frequently introduced to the President. Winners of contests at state
and national fairs are rewarded in various ways, thus producing
immense interest and enthusiasm.

An important result of the club work among boys in the
South has been that it does away with the idea in the minds
of many of them that they must be proprietors, gentleman
farmers, and that they should not work with their hands but
should leave all manual work to Negroes. When several hundred boys, however, of the best families in the country unite in
working on demonstration plots, it restores the dignity of labor
and introduces new ideals and new standards of action which
the others follow. The same is true of girls. The final decision
as to one's lifework is made during the period of adolescence,
and it is most important that some worthy purpose and valuable
work be undertaken by the youth at this time. By energy, intelligence, and hard labor for a few years a boy gains power
and judgment to direct him in the future. It is not meant by
this that all of the boys of the South should be farmers. The
agents do not preach "Back to the Farm," or "Stay on the
Farm," for all. But they try to show each boy the beauty,
the value, and the possibilities of farm life by demonstrating
what he can do on a plot of ground, and then leave his decision
to the future. A great many of the boys go to agricultural colleges and then become real "dirt farmers." These colleges,
which graduated before 1900 comparatively few young men
who became actual farmers, are now turning out thousands of
boys, eager and zealous to get back on the farms and to become
real farmers. Many have earned money with which to start
their own farms and homes. Some of the most interesting, happy,
and prosperous homes in the South are those of boys and girls
who became acquainted and got their start in life in these
clubs.

Similar clubs were organized later for Negro boys, who
received instruction adapted to their needs and conditions. They
performed their work under the same relations as those of the
white boys' clubs. These clubs have developed at good rate
and have resulted in special training schools in agriculture for
Negro youth in several southern states. There is a force of

Negro agents, men and women, who work exclusively with the Negro farmers and farm women. Clubs of farmers are organized on plans similar to those for the whites, and the members are formed into committees on the preparation of the land, its fertilization, planting, cultivation, on harvesting, and on marketing.

A significant economic development has been the establishment of the farm markets. The agents have taken advantage of the opportunities offered to train the people in their organization and conduct. Hundreds of farm and club markets have been conducted in the South in villages and towns. Chambers of commerce and boards of trade have provided storehouses, and in some places special buildings have been erected for this purpose. Here men and women, boys and girls, bring their selected and carefully graded products for sale. Rest and comfort rooms are provided so that the market places become centers. Fruits, vegetables, meats, butter, and eggs carefully prepared and standardized by specialists are here offered for sale at fair prices. One farmer boy may bring in the products for half a dozen neighbors. Sometimes they take turns in taking their products to market and the opportunity is eagerly sought as one for recreation and pleasure. A club girl will have a desk in the center of the market where she receives reports of sales and keeps a record of them, taking a small commission for the wrapping paper, bags, and incidental expenses. These markets have become very popular with the people and do much to promote coöperation and community spirit.

After this movement for farm demonstrations, the boys' and girls' clubs, and home demonstrations proved so very successful and received so much publicity, there was no difficulty in drafting legislation for making it all permanent throughout the country. This was accomplished in what was known as the Smith-Lever Act, which went into force in May, 1914. All of the demonstration work of the Department of Agriculture, including the farm demonstrations and the club work for boys and girls, was now included in one comprehensive system. Each state established in connection with its agricultural college an extension division alongside of its agricultural experiment station, which directed the whole business. There is a director of extension, as there is a director of the experiment station, who has charge of the entire demonstration and supervisory force in each state. He has an assistant for each leading line of work, men and women, and district agents, who have charge of the different lines in groups of counties. There are in most counties in addition, county men and women agents also. The men agents look after the boys' club work, and the home demonstration agents look after the girls' clubs. The county agent is the authoritative leader of all agricultural extension work in the county and covers all kinds of farm problems. Many community, county, and state organizations have been formed for the support of this movement and for the benefit of the farm interests. These associations have been most helpful in special campaigns, such as that for the improvement of livestock, prevention of hog cholera, tick eradication, better marketing of farm products, and farming in general.

The Smith-Lever Act was supported in an important way by the so-called Smith-Hughes Vocational Act appropriating funds for instruction in high schools in agriculture, home economics, trades, and industrial subjects. The high schools receiving such funds train teachers, agents, and supervisors for demonstration and club service.

CHAPTER XIV

VOCATIONAL EDUCATION

THE SMITH-HUGHES ACT

THE farm demonstration and boys' and girls' club system, originated by Dr. Knapp and initiated by the General Education Board, constituted together the most original and remarkable method of vocational education in agriculture ever projected in this country. The demonstrations and clubs were rapidly extended and greatly increased the interest in this form of practical education in the South. The demand for demonstrators, teachers, and leaders to carry on this system made it necessary to provide training schools for vocational education teachers. This led to the Vocational Educational Act, commonly called the Smith-Hughes Act, of February 23, 1917, providing for the coöperation of the government with the states in the promotion of vocational education in the high schools and the establishment of training schools for teachers in these subjects. As the Smith-Lever Act providing government support for farm demonstrators grew out of Dr. Knapp's work, so this Smith-Hughes Act for establishing vocational departments in high schools was made necessary by the Smith-Lever Act. Thus a great new national plan of agricultural, industrial, and home economics education was built up on the basis of the work of the Southern and General Education boards in the South.

The first Smith-Hughes Act authorized appropriations for only a limited number of years. Later acts of Congress provided for further development of vocational education in the several states and territories and finally made them permanent. Similar acts extended the benefits of these laws to the Territory of Hawaii, the Island of Porto Rico, and the District of Columbia.

Beginning with the Vocational Rehabilitation Act of June 2, 1920, special appropriations were made for the vocational rehabilitation of physically disabled persons and their restoration to economic self-sufficiency. These funds were placed under the direction of the same national office and state authorities

as those administering the Smith-Hughes Act, and this service
has recently taken a good deal of the time of the various supervisors to the injury of their other work. The persons to be re-
habilitated have been trained chiefly in the evening and in night
classes of the regular schools, though in some cases special
schools have been provided for them. Though important, this
service will not be included in the present study.

In accordance with the Smith-Hughes Act, allotments were
made to each state, first, for agriculture, a sum in the proportion
which the state's rural population bears to the total rural population of the nation ; second, for trades, home economics, and
industries, a sum in the proportion which the state's urban population bears to the nation ; third, for teacher training, a sum
in the proportion which the state's total population bears to
the total population of the nation. These appropriations were
made on condition that for each dollar of government money
expended for the salaries of teachers, supervisors, directors, etc.,
of agriculture, trades, or home economics, the state, or the
local community and state together, should expend at least
an equal amount. Grants were made in accordance with the
definite plans of work proposed by the Federal Vocational
Board which was organized for this purpose. The money did
not belong to any state as a right ; it was entitled to receive
this aid only when it agreed to conform to the Act and its plans
had been approved.

A due proportion of the amount allotted to each of the
southern states by the Smith-Hughes Act is expended for Negroes in accordance with the same plans. It has aided greatly in
preparing teachers to give instruction in agriculture and home
economics in Negro high schools and training schools, the kind
of instruction they need most.

This new system of vocational education was organized
under an assistant commissioner in the Office of Education of
the Department of the Interior. State boards for vocational
education were appointed by the governors. State superintendents are usually the executive officers of these boards. They are
assisted by a number of supervisors of the different types of
vocational education, such as supervisors of agricultural education, supervisors of trade and industrial education, supervisors of
home economic education. There are, in addition, training

Upper left, Miss Martha Berry, founder and director of Berry College and
Schools, Mount Berry, Georgia. Upper right, Philander P. Claxton, member
of the Southern Education board, secretary of the Conference for Education
in the South, member of the Rockefeller Sanitary Commission, and commis-
sioner of the United States Bureau of Education for ten years (Harris &
Ewing, Washington, D. C.). Lower left, Bruce R. Payne, president of the
George Peabody College for Teachers (photo Kay-Hart, N. Y.). Lower right,
Joseph D. Eggleston, active in the "May Campaign" of 1905, state superintendent of public instruction for eight years, now president of Hampden-
Sydney College (Foster Studio, Richmond, Va.)

The Dabney Consolidated School, at Dabney, Vance County, North Carolina

schools for agricultural teachers, home economics teachers, and trade and industrial teachers, with state supervisors for each of these systems of schools. The training departments for home economics and trade and industrial teachers are usually connected with the state colleges. The number of these supervisors varies with the extent of the work undertaken in the different states. Virginia, for example, has a chief supervisor for agricultural education with four district supervisors. Tennessee has four, Georgia three, and Florida one. All of these southern states have supervisors of agricultural education in Negro schools and in training schools for Negro teachers in both agriculture and home economics. Such training schools are usually connected with the state colleges for Negroes.

Some Results of the Smith-Hughes Act

These proposals of the national government for vocational education, to be given under plans approved by the Federal Vocational Board, met with some opposition at first from the old-fashioned literary teachers at the heads of the high schools who did not want vocational departments in their schools, and from some of the labor organizations and other working people who thought the new vocational schools would train too many skilled laborers to compete with them. These objectors were soon silenced, however, by the success of the vocational departments established in many of the high schools, and today practically all of the southern states are accepting all the money allotted them and matching it, as required, by their own funds for conducting the vocational courses. The laboring people have become thoroughly converted to vocational education since they have found that their children are so much benefited by it. About the only opposition remaining in the South to this type of education is from a small group of people with academic or literary training, who are still unable to adjust themselves to the new education. The admirable service of the new schools and their graduates during a period of depression has converted most of the doubters to the necessity of vocational education as a permanent feature of our educational program.

The federal funds for these different types of vocational education are derived from the original Smith-Hughes Act, which has now been made permanent, and from the George-Ellzey Act of 1934, which made additional appropriations for the years 1935 to 1937 inclusive to enable the states to give training to the unemployed and assist them to find work. The states have generally added from their own treasuries from two to three times the amounts received from the federal funds. Only the total expenditures for these different types of schools are reported here.

As the vocational education of all the youth is now one of the most important subjects before the people of the South, a brief review of the work done in agriculture, trade and industry, and home economics education in the twelve southern states from Virginia to Texas will be given.

The total expenditures of federal, state, and local money for vocational education for the states of Alabama, Arkansas, Florida, Georgia, Kentucky, Louisiana, Mississippi, North Carolina, South Carolina, Tennessee, Texas, and Virginia for the year ending June 30, 1934, were as follows : [1]

For agricultural education including all types of schools and classes	$2,970,878.79
For trade and industrial education, not including part-time continuation schools but including all other types of schools and classes.............	608,891.66
For home economics schools, all classes and types ..	1,284,718.80
For the training of vocational teachers of all classes. Of this amount $207,745.17 was expended for the training of agricultural teachers ; $135,733.34 for training trades and industrial teachers ; and $167,302.95 for the training of home economics teachers	510,781.46
Total expenditures of federal, state and local money	$5,375,270.71

The number of federal-aided schools of all classes in these states giving different types of vocational instruction were as follows :

[1] These statistics were assembled from the *Digest of Annual Reports of State Boards for Vocational Education to the Office of Education, U. S. Department of the Interior, for fiscal year ended June 30, 1934.*

Schools and classes giving instruction in agriculture......   5,589
Schools and classes giving instruction in trades and industries [1a]   812
Schools and classes giving instruction in home economics   1,939

Total number of federal-aided schools of all classes giving different types of vocational instruction...........   8,340

The enrollment in the federal-aided schools in these twelve southern states was :

In agricultural schools and classes of all types   147,915
In trade and industrial schools and classes of all types   71,992
In home economic schools and classes of all types   93,410

Total number of pupils in federal-aided vocational schools of all types   313,317

The states of Alabama, Georgia, Mississippi, South Carolina, Tennessee, Texas, and Virginia have, in addition, a number of schools and classes of agriculture, trades and industries, and home economics organized under state plans and supported by the states without federal aid. Their enrollments run from two to nine thousand each.

There are fifty vocational teacher-training institutions and other agencies in these states which were federally aided in the year ending June 30, 1934. In addition, Florida has five and Virginia six schools for training teachers for trade and industry. The total expenditures of federal, state, and local money for these vocational teacher-training institutions for the year ending June 30, 1934, was $510,781.46, or an average of about $10,000 for each school. The total enrollment in these vocational teacher-training institutions in the year ending June 30, 1934, was 4,200, or an average of eighty-four students to each school. The majority of the students are women preparing to teach home economics. Next in numbers are the men preparing to teach vocational agricultural courses. At the present time there appears to be an adequate supply of teachers for home economics. These institutions fall far short of meeting the demand for vocational

[1a] The number of trade and industrial schools and classes, including all-day, part-time trade, part-time continuation, and evening (often two or more in the same school) was supplied by J. C. Wright in letter of April 23, 1935.

teachers of agriculture. On account of the low salaries paid in many of the southern states for agricultural teachers, there is no surplus of such teachers at the present time, and many of them are leaving the schools to go into farming or other business.

Conditions and Prospects of Agricultural Education in the South

In consideration of the great importance of agricultural instruction for the youth of both races we shall direct our attention chiefly to the condition and prospects of agricultural vocational education in these southern states.

The aim of instruction in vocational agriculture is to train prospective farmers for proficiency in farming. It is recognized that this proficiency can be developed only as the individual acquires the separate abilities needed by him in the type of farming he intends to follow. While there is a wide difference in the type of abilities needed to be developed in different boys, there are certain abilities that are required to a greater or less degree by every boy. These have been termed contributory objectives of agricultural education and are enumerated by the American Vocational Association as follows :

1. To produce agricultural products and market them efficiently.

2. To be able to select suitable farm equipment and supplies and buy them wisely.

3. To coöperate intelligently with the neighbors in farm and home economic activities.

4. To manage the farm business intelligently and effectively.

5. To maintain a good farm home.

6. To be able to repair and keep in order farm machines and other properties.

7. To unite with neighbors in rural social activities and exercise constructive leadership.

8. To increase one's scientific knowledge and apply it to farming.

9. And finally, to have the ability to become a successful farmer who will constantly improve his business.[2]

It is evident that these types of training are adaptable to individuals in distinct periods in their lives : First, for farm boys

[2] Quoted in *Annual Report of the Superintendent of Public Instruction of Virginia for 1933-34*, pp. 72-73.

in the high schools and colleges who expect to enter farming after graduation. Such take all-day courses continuing three or four years. Second, for the farm boys who have already been graduated or have dropped out of high school and have begun to farm. For these courses should be offered in the winter months in the evenings or in part-time classes during the day. Third, adult farmers interested in improving their knowledge and conditions. They attend evening classes held through the year at their convenience. All three of these types of instruction are being given in the schools described. In connection with all these types of instruction, the students carry out on their home farms, with the aid and supervision of the teacher of vocational agriculture, a program of farm practice.[3]

The question is, to what extent are the existing agricultural schools reaching the farm boys and the farmers of the South? Robert D. Maltby, federal agent of the southern region, says : "As near as we are able to determine there are about as many boys out of school as there are boys in school. In communities in which vocational agricultural programs are now operating, we are reaching between 60 and 80 per cent of the farm boys in school. It would seem therefore that we should reach at least 30 to 40 per cent of the boys out of school, if we are to extend equal opportunities to this group.

"The best program we have carried on has been the one for the boys in . . . schools. . . . Here we have provided courses built around a system of farming and based on the activities and jobs of that system. We have provided for a balance between participation and instruction. . . . But the same degree of perfection does not characterize the adult program. There has been little evidence in this program of a planned system of adult instruction. While the quality of instruction given adults has been exceptionally high, the courses offered were based upon expediency rather than upon a long-time program. . . . We should organize our program with a view to retaining a given group of farmers over a given period of years.[4]

"But our greatest weakness has been with the out-of-school boy problem. I have in mind the group ranging in age from sixteen to twenty-five. Boys in this group are in the stage of late

[3] Ibid.
[4] Robert D. Maltby, Report of Federal Agent on Problems in the Southern Regional Program of Work, January 28, 1935.

adolescence and early maturity when they are trying to find themselves, the period just prior to assuming the responsibility of a home and a farm. We must accept the fact that part-time work with this group is possible and is of vital importance. It should therefore represent a much larger percentage of our activities than it does at present. . . . Our vocational program for a given community will not be complete until we have actually done something effective for this out-of-school farm youth and have given these lads equal opportunity with the other groups." [5]

At the present time, when agriculture is so depressed in the South and when white tenancy is increasing, it is very important to ascertain whether this instruction in vocational agriculture is going to be effective in increasing the earning power of the young men who take these courses. Are farm demonstrations, boys' clubs, agricultural instruction in high schools, producing better farmers? In short, does agricultural vocational education pay? Though few tests have been made to ascertain the economic results, as shown by the increased earning power of the persons so educated, the common experience is that the instruction given increases their wages from 50 to 100 per cent from the beginning.

Dr. Walter S. Newman of the Virginia Department has made an interesting study in Virginia of the earning ability of the young farmers who have received vocational training in agriculture as compared with an equivalent group who did not receive such vocational training. His results are interesting and encourage us to believe in this method of training.

A group of vocationally trained farmers was compared as to labor income with a vocationally untrained group of similar race, nationality, age, and physical condition working on soils of similar character, under conditions as nearly similar as possible as to location and size of farm, acreage cultivated, and capital used. All had been high school students and had had approximately the same farming experience since leaving high school. The following summarizations were given.[6]

One hundred and thirty-six vocationally trained farmers were selected from sixty-one different communities in the state for this study. It was necessary to survey eighty-seven communities to locate sixty-nine untrained independent farmers

[5] *Ibid.*   [6] Newman, *op. cit.*, pp. 38-39.

with the ordinary high school education who met the specifications. Of the trained group, 87.2 per cent went directly into farming from high school, while only 71.2 of the untrained high school graduates went directly into farming. There is a distinctly stronger tendency on the part of the trained group to enter farming immediately upon leaving school rather than to try other occupations before returning to the farm. It was distinctly notable also that the data returned by the trained group were more accurate than that secured from the untrained group. The trained men kept better farm records and accounts.

Dr. Newman reports : "Vocationally trained farmers realized greater average labor incomes than non-vocationally trained farmers for each type of farming. . . . The difference in weighted average labor incomes of all individuals of $311 in favor of the vocationally trained group, is a comparatively large difference considering the abnormal farming conditions during the years 1930 and 1931," when the study was made. "The average labor income of the vocationally trained group was 163 per cent of the average labor income of the untrained group. . . . Vocationally trained farmers show a better balance in their farming business as indicated by a better distribution of income from various sources and a better adjustment of expenses in operating the farm. The vocationally trained group participated in cooperative buying and selling of farm supplies and products to a greater extent, made greater use of approved sources of agricultural information, and were more active in farm organizations."

Dr. Newman estimates that there were some 1,300 farm operators in Virginia who had received vocational agricultural training and some 1,450 other high school graduates engaged in farming, though not as independent operators, who also received this vocational training. He found that the increase of earning power as a result of training for the 1,300 farm operators who had vocational training alone means an aggregate increase for this group in income of over $400,000 a year, Director J. C. Wright in the foreword to this report of Dr. Newman's says :

"On the assumption, which seems entirely warranted, that farmers generally in Virginia might have profited in some such measure by vocational training as is shown by this study to have been in fact realized by the group studied, one may estimate the potential profit to the State from a program which would extend training generally to the farming population. Leaving out of account other farm workers, it appears according to census returns that there were some 36,000 farm operators in Virginia in 1930. An increase of earning power such as the present study indicates is to be normally expected from adequate vocational training would accordingly add some millions of dollars annually to the aggregate income of farmers in this one State.

"It is to be noted that while the increase in earning during the first few years after graduation more than covers the cost of the training, the increased earning power continues effective during all succeeding years of life expectancy of the farmer," [7] and it may be added that his example and teachings are sure to improve the earning power of his neighbors and successors.

These facts show the progress of vocational schools, and their results have great significance for us at this time. For one thing, they mean that if all our independent farm operators had received agricultural vocational training, more of them would be subsistence farmers instead of speculators in cotton and tobacco—for that is what the one-crop farmer is—and that the southern farmers would not be on relief in such numbers as they are today. These facts have a very important lesson also for us in connection with the problem of what to do for our growing class of white tenants and of Negro croppers. They teach us that the training which will make them subsistence farmers first is the only way to keep them off relief ; that our next duty is to see that their children have the kind of vocational education in the elementary schools that will lift them out of the sad condition of their parents and make of them independent self-supporting producers and good citizens.

"FUTURE FARMERS OF AMERICA"

All principals, superintendents, and teachers engaged in rural education have recognized that the morale of the farm youth and of the farmer himself in many cases has been at a very low ebb recently in the South, and that the development of certain abilities essential to success cannot be achieved without group or coöperative effort. Effort has been made, therefore, within the

[7] *Ibid.*, p. vii.

last several years to add an additional group activity or club to the number already in operation in the various high schools. This new organization is one composed of students of vocational agriculture and is called "Future Farmers of America." The idea has spread throughout the nation and has been taken up with much enthusiasm by the boys who have had this training. The Future Farmers has become a national organization with branches in the different states and numerous chapters in the counties and districts. The objects of this organization are to promote vocational agriculture in the high schools and colleges of America by making the Future Farmers proud of their calling and by encouraging them to study and improve their work continuously ; to establish the confidence of the farmer youth in himself and his work ; to create a love of country life ; to develop more intelligence in the choice of farming occupations ; to promote thrift among the members through the establishment of savings accounts and investments in agricultural enterprises of mutual benefit ; to provide recreational and educational entertainment ; to provide a medium for coöperative buying and selling ; and to develop local leadership.[8]

The organization has taken a good hold already in some of the southern states, especially in Arkansas, Florida, Louisiana, and Tennessee, where there is a chapter in every district. There are numerous chapters in all the other southern states. Some of the more important activities of the Future Farmers of America in the South during the recent years have been relief work, farm fire prevention, farm home improvement, conservation of natural resources and prevention of soil erosion, coöperative buying and selling, thrift banks, and parliamentary training and public speaking.

Each local program of work for these Future Farmers is built largely around the needs of the individuals in the chapter, the community needs, and the training desired, but it should also include those things which will assist in putting across the state and national programs formulated annually.

The Future Farmers have established relations with the national American Farm Bureau Convention, and other farm meetings. The leaders of these organizations are keenly interested in

[8] *Annual Report of the Superintendent of Public Instruction of Virginia for 1933-34*, p. 73.

the Future Farmers and its success, and give it their good will and hearty backing.

"Since the Future Farmers of America is now in its seventh year it has a valuable fund of information on the efficiency of the training the organization gives to its members in the records of former students who have participated in its activities and are now 'on their own.'" The follow-up of former members and students is an activity which is being seriously considered. Effort is being made to organize a so-called alumni association for the Future Farmers which should promote this end.

State associations are now devoting themselves to increasing their membership and organizing new chapters. They will not be satisfied until they have 100 per cent participation in all the agricultural schools. Mr. Maltby says "I feel confident that no other organization of a similar kind has shown the progress that the Future Farmers of America have shown since 1928. They are building a place for themselves in this country and their influence is extending into other countries. By keeping a straight course with the ideals of the F. F. A. in mind the organization can and will become the most dynamic factor for the improvement of agriculture and the rural home which has thus far been devised in this country." [9]

TYPES OF TRADE AND INDUSTRIAL EDUCATION

Instruction in trade and industrial education aims to prepare persons who are employed, or expect to be employed, in the mechanical trades with a general education and the technical preparation which will help them most. These courses are best organized in connection with the existing high schools in the cities and villages. Several kinds of classes are provided.

1. Trade schools are organized in the high schools for boys and girls who go into industrial pursuits. They meet during the daytime and emphasis is placed on acquisition of trade skills and trade information. At least one-fourth of the day is devoted to the pursuit of general academic subjects. Shops are common in junior and senior high schools, the objectives of which are not to give specific technical training but to enable the students to acquire manual skill and technical information. They enable the boys to give expression to any mechanical or scientific in-

[9] Maltby, *op. cit.*

terest they may possess, and tend to give pupils who have limited intellectual ability an opportunity to prepare themselves for useful work.

2. Evening vocational classes are provided for persons who are employed during the day in shops and factories. Instruction in this case is supplementary to the kind of work these persons are doing.

3. Continuation part-time classes are organized for the benefit of workers in offices, stores, and industries who will thereby increase their skill and knowledge of the vocation they are following or complete their academic education. Anything is taught in these classes which will help the workers.

4. Technical part-time classes are provided to increase the skill of persons who are employed a half-day in some industrial pursuit. Unemployed persons are also taught new trades or given that instruction which will make them more proficient in those they formerly pursued.

The organization of trade and industrial education in Virginia, where all the courses are given in the regular schools, offers an excellent pattern for this kind of instruction. Six thousand, six hundred and ninety-seven students received instruction in 1934 in the several different kinds of courses in the state, and 4,398 were enrolled in general industrial classes. The per capita cost of evening classes was only $2.95 ; for part-time trade extension classes, $22.89 ; for general continuation classes, $20.03 ; and for all-day trade classes, $31.69. Instructor-training, including foremanship training and local supervision of vocational courses, instruction in summer school extension courses, and individual instruction, costs $51.27 per instructor. The federal government and the state together provided $52,961.45, and the local communities provided $125,606.92 for this instruction in Virginia. It seems a moderate investment for so large and efficient a program.

The depression has created in women and in school girls a new interest in all courses of home economics. The problem of maintaining the health and happiness of the family on a more limited income has led to an effort to help women and girls to use to the best advantage the small means they have. Teachers report that interest in gardening has increased very largely and the amount of canning that is done has grown greatly. Economy in foods ; the proper preparation of the right amounts for the size of the family ; planning ahead ; and preparing the same food in different ways to make it more attractive have been subjects of earnest study. The renovation and making over of old garments, the repairing and refinishing of furniture, the making of rugs, and the use of old sacks in making articles for house furnishings—in general, the study of wise spending in every direction and the development of the importance of using the resources other than money available on the farm have been leading subjects of instruction. The classes in home economics in all the schools have grown in popularity, and evening classes for homemakers are largely attended.

CHAPTER XV

THE RURAL SCHOOLS

The Rural Schools the Foundation of Southern Education

ONE of the most important of the early steps taken by the Southern Education Board was to send out, with the help of the Peabody Fund, a number of supervisors of the rural schools, which were recognized as the foundation of education in the South. When in 1914 the Peabody Board was dissolved, the Southern Board requested the General Board to take up this work and to develop it. This it did in the most thorough way. The first step this board took was to direct a thorough investigation of all the southern states with a view to a more scientific direction of the work for the rural schools. This survey took into consideration the nature of the land, climatic differences, soils, farming population per square mile, and conditions as to ownership and tenancy.

The methods of administration were also carefully studied with regard to the units of direction and control, the administrative power of the county or district boards, school revenues and expenditures, the character and preparation of teachers, the preparation of professional teachers, number of pupils to the school and to the teacher, number of subjects taught, number of recitations per day, average length of recitation periods, and kindred matters. The rural schoolhouses, their location, surroundings, and equipment received special attention. It was a thorough survey of the schools of the South such as had never been made before.

Though some of the towns of the South had grown in recent years, the population by the census of 1900 was still preponderantly rural. The rural population of the entire region ranged from 70 per cent in Louisiana to 88.5 per cent in Mississippi; in seven states the rural population was between 70 and 80 per cent, and in six states, between 80 and 90 per cent of the whole people. Clearly, then, universal public education could never succeed in these states unless the schools in the country were made more effective. This was universally recognized. The southern people were earnestly trying to improve their rural schools, but there were many still in neglected districts and great masses of the people were still sleeping, as it were, in ignorance in 1900. In other districts there was great activity in schools and in some a high degree of enthusiasm and earnest endeavor. The meetings of the Conferences for Education in the South in different cities throughout the country had worked up a greater interest, but it was not yet widely distributed.

The South was beginning to enjoy a degree of prosperity. The farm demonstration work, which had just recently been started, proved that the farmers could make good incomes and pay taxes for better schools when taught to farm correctly. The annual expenditures for schools were already increasing. Of its net state revenue of six and a half millions in Virginia in 1914, one-half was going to education. While North Carolina had paid only about a million dollars towards the support of all her public elementary and secondary schools in 1901, in 1913 she had invested in them $4,300,000, over four times as much.

Whereas South Carolina had spent less than a million in 1901, she spent over two and a half millions for her country schools in 1913, much of which was raised by voluntary taxation in the districts. Tennessee was raising five millions a year for educational purposes, toward which the state in 1913 gave $1,350,000, whereas before 1903, it had given practically nothing at all. And so on through the states. The people were willing to give money for schools if they could make it. The amounts raised were still quite inadequate for complete systems of schools, but the improvements and growth of organizations suggested that the southern people would gradually be able to invest more and more money in their schools and in time might have thoroughly good systems.

But there were also unfavorable conditions and prospects. In many states the educational organization was very poor. Few of them had good laws for raising money. In Alabama, for example, taxation for schools was limited by the constitution to one mill. In none of the states was there proper distribution of authority among state, county, and district officials. In most of them the state superintendent was a political official. In some, like Alabama, the state superintendent could not be reëlected. When two admirable men like Abercrombie and Harman were

secured, good was accomplished by electing one as superintendent for a term, and the other as assistant superintendent; and
the next time electing the assistant superintendent to be the chief
superintendent. In no state was it possible to elect a superintendent from the outside. Too often the county superintendents
were paid miserable salaries, and therefore had to make their
living at something else, giving only a part of their time to their
school duties. In some states a man could not be a county superintendent for more than two terms, and in most of the counties
new men were chosen at each election. In some of the states,
like Alabama and Mississippi, from 60 to 75 per cent of the
country teachers were in their first years, and in some 25 per
cent, in their second. Schoolhouses were still miserable one-room
affairs with very little equipment. A typical country school
was a wooden shack with one untrained girl facing fifty or
sixty pupils of all grades and ages.

In 1904, 75 per cent of the total school enrollment of the
southern states belonged in the rural schools, but the aggregate
attendance on them was less than 45 per cent of the total aggregate attendance in all the schools. Over 30 per cent of all the
instruction given in the country, taking the white and black
schools together, was in wretched one-teacher schoolhouses and
was of very low grade, the work of green young women teachers without experience. As a result the illiteracy of the whites
in the rural South as a whole was still more than twice as great
as in the towns and cities. Of course, among the blacks the
difference was much greater. A study of conditions in twenty-
eight representative counties, for example, in eight southern
states made by the agents of the Southern Education Board
in 1904 showed that these counties contained 1,580 schools for
white children; 1,107 of which were one-teacher schools in small
single-room buildings; 289 of them were in two-teacher buildings; 938 were in old dilapidated buildings, two-thirds of
which were entirely unpainted, 122 unceiled, 485 not even
weather-tight; 455 had only homemade desks, some of them
mere slabs, and twenty-seven had no desks at all, but wooden
benches were used for seats. They were deficient in every
essential.

The Work of the Southern Education Board

A review of this situation showed that the time was ripe for an earnest, systematic effort to arouse the people to build better schools in the country. No such opportunity had ever occurred before, and it was determined, therefore, to enter the field immediately. The Southern Education Board realized that the rural school was the fundamental problem. The rural schools must be greatly improved, or there would be no improvement whatever in the education of the southern people. The problem stated in its simplest terms was, therefore :

1. To provide schools for all the children and to bring the children into them.

2. To make the annual term long enough to give the children real, thorough instruction in the fundamentals of common knowledge.

3. To make the instruction in the schools the practical business of the farm and home—not merely in the making of a living, but in the making of a life. The employment of teachers in sympathy with farm life and the enrichment of the courses by the introduction of nature study subjects, forming the basis of agriculture and home economics.

4. The improvement of the material equipment, the school grounds and gardens by the consolidation of poor little schools into good schools and the establishment of libraries, laboratories, and ample materials for illustration. To make the school the center of the community by bringing to it the farmers and their families.

Rural school supervisors were accordingly established in all of the eleven southern states. In some of the states they were associated with the universities. In the majority of them they were connected with and made a part of the State Department of Education. In 1910 this organization had been completed for all the states as follows :

N. R. Baker was associated with the Department of Education in Montgomery, Alabama ; J. L. Bond, with the Department at Little Rock, Arkansas ; George M. Lynch was connected with the University of Florida at Gainesville but cooperated with the Department of Education closely ; R. H. Powell worked with the Department of Education at Atlanta, Georgia ; T. J. Coates was the supervisor associated with the

Department of Education at Frankfort, Kentucky ; C. J. Brown was with the Department of Education at Baton Rouge, Louisiana ; W. H. Smith, with the Department at Jackson, Mississippi ; L. C. Brogden was connected with the Department of Education at Raleigh, North Carolina ; W. K. Tate was associated with the Department of Education at Columbia, South Carolina ; F. B. Frazier, with the Department of Education at Nashville, Tennessee ; and T. S. Settle was connected with the Department of Education at Richmond, Virginia.

The methods pursued in the different states were adapted to the conditions and needs of those states, but in general the supervisors made the chief aim of their work the introduction of better supervision in the counties, the selection of better teachers for the schools, the promotion of community activities which would develop more civic pride and school spirit, and the establishment of parent-teachers associations to promote better coöperation between the school and the home. Each supervisor commenced by making a thorough survey of his territory, studying the actual conditions, school enrollment and attendance, illiteracy, the opportunities for recreation, the introduction of libraries, better sanitation around the schools, the improvement of the school buildings and the beautification of their grounds, and similar matters.

In doing this work the supervisors sought primarily close coöperation with boards of education and with the state and county superintendents, especially in securing the consolidation of schools, the transportation of pupils, more funds for longer terms, better schoolhouses, larger salaries for teachers, and better supervision. They established teachers' institutes and round tables and conferences, and organized public meetings at appropriate places and times. They endeavored to introduce agricultural and industrial work. The supervisors coöperated in the work with the legislatures for needed improvement in school laws and for the increase of school funds. In their offices, these agents collected and tabulated data about the schools, prepared bulletins on various phases of rural school work, supplied information to the newspapers with regard to improvements to be made, and coöperated with the state normal schools and the universities in their efforts to train rural teachers and county superintendents. The General Education Board provided the salaries and expenses of the agents.

WILLIAM KNOX TATE AND HIS WORK

As it would be impossible to describe the work of each and all of the agents, effort is here made to illustrate it by telling the story of one of them. Among the most accomplished and successful of these agents for rural schools was William Knox Tate, for four years supervisor of rural schools in South Carolina, and for three years professor of rural education in the George Peabody College.[1] He was born September 8, 1870, near Tate Springs, Grainger County, in eastern Tennessee. When the boy was only three years of age the family moved to Benton County, Arkansas, and settled on a small farm near the border of Indian Territory, sixty miles from the nearest railroad station. After attending for a few years a rural school characteristic of the frontier days in Arkansas, the youth entered Siloam Springs Academy, recently founded under the auspices of the Congregational Church in a village which had sprung up near his home. He was such a good student and developed so rapidly both in character and scholarship that at sixteen he was engaged to teach some of the lower classes. At eighteen he was appointed to teach the elementary school at Siloam Springs. Two years later he entered the University of Arkansas for the summer term. Peabody Normal College had announced competitive examinations for state scholarships, which were to be held at the University. There were fifty applicants for three scholarships in Arkansas and Tate secured one of them. In 1890, at twenty years of age, he entered Peabody College. With vigorous, robust health, a good mind, and solid, though limited, preparation, he entered upon college life with great enthusiasm. He took part in all the athletic as well as in the forensic activities of the college and developed rapidly into a popular and successful student. He received his Bachelor of Arts degree in 1892 and immediately determined to devote his life to the teaching profession. Feeling a deep debt of gratitude for the opportunity that had come to him as a country boy, first at the missionary school in Arkansas and then at Peabody College, he determined to devote his life to giving others, situated

[1] Acknowledgment is made to the sketch of Professor Tate by L. E. Pummill, the MS of which is filed in the Library of the George Peabody College, Nashville, Tennessee.

as he had been, the opportunity for the development that he had enjoyed.

On the recommendation of President William H. Payne and his teachers at Peabody, Tate was now appointed a teacher in the high school at Tyler, Texas. After serving there for two years as teacher he was made the principal and immediately went to work to develop the school. He enlarged the course of study in the high school and improved its buildings. He took an active part in the community life of the village. As a prominent worker in teachers' meetings and in church and social organizations, he soon became recognized as a leader. A constant reader and student, his mind was prolific in ideas, which he had the happy faculty of passing on to others. He was a fluent speaker and was much in demand for public meetings of all kinds.

When the principalship of the Memminger Normal School in Charleston, South Carolina, was vacant, Tate was, on the recommendation of Dr. Curry and President Payne, elected to the position. This school, which had been named for Christopher Gustavus Memminger, the father of public schools in Charleston, was now to become the foundation of Tate's work in South Carolina. He began by completely remodeling the buildings, modernizing the courses of study, and inaugurating a system of practice teaching by the pupils in the public schools. He added manual training, domestic science, and arts to the course of study. A building for this department, erected with funds raised by Tate, was named for him after his death. In addition to being principal of the Normal School, Tate was, in 1907, appointed assistant superintendent of the Charleston Schools. In this position he had the supervision of all the elementary schools. Under his administration the grammar school buildings of the city were enlarged and remodeled and a course in industrial education added. He caused to be erected the first Industrial School for Negroes in Charleston.

During this period Tate took an active part in the educational associations in the country. He was secretary of the Superintendents' Department of the National Education Association in 1900 ; member of the Executive Committee of the Southern Education Conference, and state director of the Southern Education Board from 1904 on. Desiring to secure the National Education Association meeting for Charleston, he attended its meetings and advocated his home city until the annual meeting of the Association was secured for it in 1901. He was appointed a member of the state board of education of South Carolina in 1904 and served in this position for a number of years; he became a member of its high school board in 1907 and was president of the State Association of Superintendents in 1908. Tate was an important member and lecturer at the Summer School of the South at Knoxville, Tennessee, from the time of its foundation in 1902 until 1910. When a campaign was put on to secure a permanent and adequate endowment for Peabody College at Nashville between 1903 and 1909, Tate rendered important service to the cause. As the representative of the Peabody Alumni he made many trips through the country, bringing Peabody College to the attention of the different educational funds and the friends of southern education. As a result of this service he was made a member of the new board of the George Peabody College for Teachers when it was organized in 1909.

When in 1910 the General Education Board gave a fund to pay the salary and traveling expenses of a state supervisor of rural schools in South Carolina, Tate was appointed to the position. His office was associated with the University of South Carolina, where he was elected professor of elementary education. Subsequently he was made a member of the faculty of Winthrop College for Women in the same capacity.

Dr. Edwin Mims gives a delightful account of Professor Tate as he found him at work in South Carolina in 1911:

The President, after showing me over the beautiful campus and buildings of that historic institution, pointed to a small building with only two rooms—one on top of the other—which he said was the most valuable building on the campus. It had been used for several years as a junk shop or store room. When Professor Tate was appointed supervisor of rural education in South Carolina, unable to find any other office, he asked that this be turned over to him. . . . There in a little room about eight by ten we found him amidst his few books, kodak pictures, reports, cards, etc. It was almost impossible for him to get into the room or turn around in it. When he began to tell me of his work, all South Carolina seemed to be there. Such a story of consecration, of energy or romance I have scarcely ever heard, and yet he was unconscious of himself as the central figure in the state's development. He was doing the work of three or four men. He was giving a course at the University one day of the week, gathering about him a few choice spirits. He was spending four days in the counties of South Carolina addressing educational meetings, supervising schools, talking to patrons and school officers, learning everything at first hand about economic and social conditions. . . . He had traveled 25,000 miles in one year—a thousand miles in a buggy far away from railroads. . . . Consolidation and coöperation were his watch words. Now he was raging with righteous indignation at the stupidity and selfishness of communities that were permitting such outrages in educational work, as for instance, the community that had built a handsome church and supported a missionary in Mexico, and yet had the worst imaginable school within a radius of five miles. "What are you driving at in all this work?" I asked him. His reply was, "I believe that a school of a new type must be developed, based on the activities of the normal rural child and having as its end a vital relation to the interest of the community." [2]

It was about this time that Professor Tate joined the superintendents who toured the northern states and Canada under the guidance of Dr. A. P. Bourland and under the auspices of Mr. Ogden. He gave a very interesting account of this tour which was published in the Proceedings of the Fourteenth Conference for Education in the South (1911).

In 1912 he established at Winthrop College an experimental school to investigate the rural courses of study and relate them with rural activities. On the appointment of Dr. P. P. Claxton, United States commissioner of education, he became a member of a committee to visit Switzerland, for the purpose of making a study of the Swiss school system. He spent four months in Switzerland and came home filled with new ideas and plans. His report was published in Bulletin 56, 1913, United States Bureau of Education under the title "Suggestive Features of the Swiss System." Throughout the whole of its career Professor Tate was very active in the work of the Conference for Education in the South, contributing valuable reports and addresses to its proceedings.

In 1914 Tate was elected a member of the faculty of George Peabody College, to give courses in Rural Education. These he made very comprehensive, including the following : training a county school ; county school administration and supervision ;

[2] Edwin Mims, *Peabody Alumni News*, Memorial Number, April, 1917.

the community activities of the county school; social and economic phases of rural life; and school problems in the South. While a member of the Peabody faculty he gave two courses in the Religious Education Department of Vanderbilt University. He organized the Country Life Club at Nashville and became its leader.

Tate was the author of many reports and papers on rural education. The most important of these were "Rural School Problems in South Carolina"; "Special Supervision of the Rural Schools in South Carolina"; "Rural School Movements and Ideals in South Carolina"; and "Teachers Manual for Elementary Schools in South Carolina." With Sarah Withers and Hetty S. Brown he prepared a series of readers for the elementary schools under the title *The Child's World*, which had wide use.

Tate was a man of splendid physique, six feet in height, weighing over two hundred and twenty-five pounds. He was endowed with superb health, but even his great constitution could be exhausted by untiring, strenuous work. Unmindful of his own interests he commenced after forty-five to lose his vitality. Working constantly, traveling widely, speaking frequently, and writing between times, he wore himself out. Returning from a trip to Berea College, where he had filled a speaking engagement, he caught a severe cold which resulted in pneumonia. He died on February 7, 1917, at forty-seven years of age.

Dr. Claxton said of him at the memorial meeting at Nashville :

Of the problems of conservative statesmanship in these Southern states during the last decade, the most important and probably the most difficult has been that of the improvement of the rural school and development of the educational life of the open country and rural villages and towns, and through this the improvement of the economic and civil life of these communities. Those who have worked wisely and effectively at this problem have built themselves into the future of this section as no others have or could. By common consent William Knox Tate has stood in the front rank of this group of workers for a decade. If among so many who have worked earnestly and unselfishly in their several ways and places, any one man may be called the leader, few will fail to accord that place to Tate. . . . The improved rural school with its longer term, its better housing and equipment, its readjusted course of study, its more adequately trained teachers, and its firmer grasp on the higher life of the community, is his most appropriate monument.[3]

Although much effort had been expended in South Carolina in behalf of public schools there was really no system until Professor Tate took hold of them. The chief trouble was that there had been no general supervision of the schools. In some communities local leadership had developed fairly good schools, but in others, where such leadership was lacking, the schools were comparatively worthless. Without official supervision there can be no system of good schools. The first thing that Tate did, therefore, was to urge a scheme of supervision.

For the training of teachers he recommended and secured all year courses and summer schools in connection with Winthrop College and the University. Supervisors of methods were appointed who visited the schools, observed the work, and assisted the teachers in organizing and classifying their pupils, and in the adoption of correct methods of teaching. Tate was finally successful in having these county school supervisors put in twenty-nine counties of the state.

Tate constantly preached consolidation with the result that in 1934 there were only 350 one-teacher schools left in the state. Transportation which began in connection with consolidation has been extended over almost the whole state.

Beginning early in his career, Tate urged the adoption of a compulsory attendance law. This was difficult to secure and more difficult to enforce, but it is now believed that South Carolina has one of the most effective compulsory attendance laws in the South. Tate was sponsor for several important financial measures for school support which have been finally adopted, some of them since his death. South Carolina schools are now supported from state taxation, county taxation, and local taxation. State taxation is provided for in the Constitution. The county element is embodied in the Constitution in the form of a mill tax. State aid under the Extension Act is conditioned on the vote of at least the two-mill special tax in the district. Increase in the number of districts voting special levy for additional support of their schools has been steady. South

[3] P. P. Claxton, United States Commissioner of Education, *Peabody Alumni News*, Memorial Number, April, 1917.

Carolina's system of raising money for the schools appears thus to be quite adequate.[4]

The Consolidated Rural Schools

The efforts of the rural school supervisors to secure consolidated schools has already been mentioned repeatedly, and, without question, the most important way of improving rural education was, and is, through consolidating the little isolated country schools into larger and more effective units. This plan is today being carried on in the South to a large extent, but it is well to state the necessity for it again, since many poor weak schools still remain. Some of the reasons for consolidating schools are as follows : First, the lack of school population sufficient to maintain the life and enthusiasm which would render the school an effective intellectual and social center. Second, the lack of sufficient taxable areas, that is, of taxable property, to provide funds to conduct a school to meet the needs of modern life. Consolidated school districts must usually be about twenty square miles. Third, the lack of permanency. These schools are too often migratory in character, depending for location upon the shifting centers of population or upon the wishes of the influential neighbors. Fourth, the want of efficient school officers. A small adult population rarely supplies enough competent men to serve the school as directors or committee men. A small adult population means a small school population, a smaller enrollment and smaller attendance, more limited social contacts, and the want of wholesome incentive and emulation between the children. Social coöperation, which it is so important to teach children on the playground, in the school garden, in the classroom, and in their contests, remains impossible in the small school. Fifth, the lack of teachers to divide up the work according to their ability and tastes. When one teacher has to teach seven grades every day, as is the custom in the small country school, allowing from twenty-five to thirty classes, she has an impossible task. Sixth, the lack of efficient trained professional teachers. Thirty or forty per cent of the

[4] General reference to W. K. Tate, "Rural School Problem in South Carolina," *University of South Carolina Bulletin No. 24*, Part 2 (Jan., 1911) ; W. K. Tate, "Country School Movements and Ideals in South Carolina," *University of South Carolina Bulletin No. 36*, Part 2 (Jan., 1914).

teachers in the small unconsolidated schools are always raw recruits, having no experience. As soon as a teacher gets experience, the desire for association with other teachers and for advancement to larger schools takes her away. We can never have trained teachers as long as we have small isolated schools. Professional teachers will not, as a rule, take them. Teaching in them is regarded as a makeshift occupation, a temporary employment preparatory to marriage or some other engagement. Seventh, the impossibility of thorough classification and gradation of pupils in the small school. If a teacher has, as said, from seven to eight grades and some twenty-five to thirty daily recitations of twelve minutes each, classification and gradation are absolutely impossible. In such classes the bright and ambitious children are held back by the stupid and lazy ones and have no incentive to attend school promptly and no interest in their studies. This is one reason why so many drop out at the end of the fifth grade. Eighth, with all this work, it is impossible for the teacher to do anything but to teach the regular twenty-five or thirty recitations; she cannot enrich her course or bring in any new studies such as manual training, gardening, sewing, or cooking. Ninth, such a multitude of small schools cannot have adequate supervision. With one-teacher schools scattered over from three hundred to a thousand square miles, efficient supervision is impossible, even for the best superintendents.

Finally, a most serious trouble is the great cost of these small schools. A small school population, small daily attendance, renders inevitable an exceedingly high per capita cost per pupil. In the average southern state in 1910 the monthly cost per pupil in daily attendance, where there were up to twenty pupils only, was $2.10 as against $1.33 per month per pupil in daily attendance in the elementary department of representative city schools and less than that amount in consolidated country schools. One should mention in addition the inevitable lack of high school privileges in such cases. It is necessary to send young children away from home to distant towns or else deny them the advantages of high school instruction.

The most important aim of the consolidated school is to provide the country child with additional opportunities, approximating those enjoyed by the children of the cities; to provide the child with a well organized, well conducted school, with large, comfortable, sanitary, attractive and well equipped school buildings, with playgrounds, gardens, and shops which shall make the work vital and interesting. With six or more professionally trained teachers representing different lines of work, the school can be made far more effective and interesting and the teachers can have fewer recitations with a longer time for each, making possible an enriched course, a study full of the things of the home and country life. And there should be a library of good books, not only for the use of the children, but for the use of the community.

Now let us notice some of the advantages of the consolidated school. In the first place, let us understand that the consolidated school is not just the union of two or more adjacent one-teacher schools. The term is used to describe only schools having as a minimum at least six rooms, six teachers, two or more acres of ground for a school garden, a cooking laboratory, work benches, and employing one or two busses for free transportation of pupils.

There is no equal to a consolidated school to build up a powerful public spirit in the community ; coöperation in public schools on this plan does almost as much good to the parents as to the children. The consolidated school is the great permanent unifying center of social and intellectual life for the people.

In the old days the country church was the center of the people. The social, educational, and religious life centered around it. The protracted meetings were great social events. Practically all social developments (including the weddings) had their source in the church and the Sunday school. Now all this is changed. The church is losing its hold on the life of the country people. It is true that eight-tenths of the teachers and preachers are reared in the country, but we put our best preachers and teachers in the cities, and yet we still look to the country to feed the city with its best brain and heart. From the country's sources of spiritual, physical, and moral sustenance we draw constantly, but we do little to renew this fountain of the nation's life. Some think that we can restore this community service through lyceums, granges, or other agricultural organizations. They have largely failed also. The solemn fact is that no church can undertake all the coöperative work needed in the country because it is interested in only one phase of life, the spiritual life, while the whole community is equally interested in the public school. The school is the natural, the organic center of country life and it should be large and representative.

The proportion of agricultural to city population is steadily decreasing, with the result that the farm people are more and more separated and so more and more individualistic, while the people of the cities are becoming more and more collective and coöperative as is necessary in our modern civilization. The consolidated school is the best method of promoting coöperation in a rural community.

CHAPTER XVI

WALTER HINES PAGE ON PUBLIC EDUCATION

"The Training of an American"

THE story of the services of Walter Hines Page to the American people has been well and completely told by Hendrick,[1] but no narrative of the progress of public education in the South would be complete without an account of his labors for this cause.

Possessing a keen, strong, well trained mind, Page had many intellectual interests. He was an accomplished classical scholar and was well versed also in English and American literature. The political history of the Anglo-Saxon race was his lifelong study. Though never a politician, he was an earnest student of the political history of his country and took a deep interest in all national questions. His political, economic, and social philosophy he learned from Thomas Jefferson. When still a young student he read Randall's *Life of Jefferson,* and annotated it copiously. Page revered Jefferson as both the architect and the master workman of democratic society. From Jefferson he learned to believe in the worth and dignity of the individual man. Jefferson was the first emancipationist, and naturally the young student considered slavery the curse of his land. Like Jefferson, Page believed in common folks. The democracy he considered that order in which every man everywhere, of every race or land, rich or poor, black or white, was to have an opportunity to make the most of himself; and the great interest of his life was to give all men a chance to complete their lives.

Believing with Jefferson in local government in local affairs, Page believed in the unity of our American system. Jefferson had said, "I can scarcely contemplate a more incalculable evil than the breaking of the Union." Like Jefferson, Page was a convinced nationalist.

Page's reasonings and activities started from these principles. Like Thornwell, Minor, Curry, and other followers of Jeffer-

[1] Burton J. Hendrick, *The Life and Letters of Walter H. Page; idem, The Training of an American.*

234

son, he realized that schools for all the people were the only safeguard of the republic.

To the ordinary southern politician, the democracy of Jefferson had ceased to be anything more than a mere theory, to be blatantly proclaimed on platforms and at anniversary dinners. Page would make it a practical method of building up civilization through education. He strove to democratize the point of view of an old aristocratic society, to revolutionize its operations, to stimulate community effort for public ends, and to train a succession of capable leaders to carry on the genuine Jeffersonian program for training a people.

Page was a broad, true American, free from sectional prejudices. His interests were as wide as humanity ; yet through all of his life, from youth to age, his dearest interest was in the southern people and in the rebuilding of their institutions. North Carolina, his native state, came first, and then the South —these were the objects of his lifelong devotion. "I have not," he said, "as some old wanderers are said to have done, carried with me wherever I have gone a pot of my native earth, but I have carried with me always what the pot of earth would stand for." [2] Wherever he lived, whether at Raleigh, Boston, New York, or London, whatever his daily task, the welfare of his "Old Land," as he always affectionately called it, was constantly in his mind and heart. With his clear insight into their economic, educational, and social needs and with complete unselfishness, friendliness, patience, and courage, Page worked his whole life long for the improvement of his people.

WORK IN THE SOUTH

When a mere youth of twenty-three, Page wrote articles in a North Carolina paper, pleading for schools for southern children. About the same time an article written by him, descriptive of the life in an "Old Southern Borough," was published in *The Atlantic Monthly*, of which he was one day to be the editor. The closing paragraph shows that the narrowness and bigotry of the southern people, which he had to contend with for many years, was already concerning his thought. He said : "The new South cannot build up its possible civiliza-

[2] Speech at Greensboro, N. C., June, 1897, "The Forgotten Man," published in Walter Hines Page, *The Rebuilding of Old Commonwealths*, p. 1.

tion merely by looking backward and sighing, nor yet by simply pressing blindly forward in the new paths that are now open. With a reverential respect for the past, which unhappily certain communities are too rapidly losing, and by a vigorous work for the future, which many more communities neglect, it has through poverty a chance for greatness that is almost unparalleled in history." [3]

As soon as Page had learned his trade, he went to Raleigh and took over an almost defunct weekly paper called *The State Chronicle*. He then commenced with deliberate purpose an effort to promote reform movements in North Carolina, which would develop the educational and economic interests of the state and of the South. The development of the natural resources of the South, of its ores and building materials, of its water power, of its forests and fisheries, but chiefly of its agriculture, was his constant interest. But, as he always declared, the greatest resource of the state was its people. The education, the training of the people, as he preferred to express it, was his chief theme whenever he wrote and wherever he spoke.

He took an active part in the organization of the Watauga Club, an association of young men to advance those causes, the story of which has already been told. [4]

Page was a ready and forceful speaker, clear, direct, and virile. His addresses showed earnest thinking and deep conviction. He was also an attractive teacher. His pupils never forgot him. Among his students at the summer school in Chapel Hill, where he taught when he was only twenty-three years of age, were Alderman, McIver, and Aycock. These men became his fast friends, and he their faithful adviser, throughout their whole careers. His friends wished him to be a university professor. But he was too much a man of action to be contented in a professor's chair. "Action and only action clears the vision," [5] he declared, and this his life illustrated.

Page's zeal was so great, his passion so intense, that he sometimes scolded and ridiculed the southern people for narrowness and conservatism. He urged them to cease living in the past and to strive for the development of their land and its children. He made sport of the men who thought and talked of nothing

[3] *The Atlantic Monthly*, XLVII (May, 1881), 658.
[4] See Vol. I, Chap. IX.
[5] Nicholas Worth [W. H. Page], *The Southerner*, p. 414.

but "before-the-War" things and called them "mummies." The old ladies who spent their time writing poetry and organizing societies to build monuments to Confederate heroes he called "The little sisters of the dead." Although he was roundly abused and called a "traitor" to his section, his criticisms were always in the spirit of a devoted son. In later years he took a more philosophical view of the attacks made upon him and faced the abuse of his southern critics with patient humor. In due time he won them over.

After a struggle of several years in Raleigh, Page left North Carolina and turned his paper over to Josephus Daniels. The times were not ripe for his advanced program of educational and economic reform. The people were not yet prepared to support the movement. But this temporary discouragement did not deter him.

As a Journalist in the North

A facile writer and an accomplished journalist, Page won in the North a high place in his profession. He was a most successful editor of magazines and had remarkable skill in finding people who could write and in helping them to develop their powers. His catholic interest drew out the best in everybody— an outstanding gift actuated by a noble generosity, wide knowledge, and keen curiosity. Instantly he appreciated the gift of each person and encouraged him into expression. Many aspiring southern writers attained success through his friendly aid.

As editor of a review of the world's progress, he became an earnest student of international affairs. As a member of the General Education Board and the International Health Board, he studied the interests of many foreign peoples. When, therefore, the call came, he was prepared to be an able ambassador at the greatest court in the world. His services during his five years at the court of St. James, which included the period of the World War, were extended to many people besides his own. By the English he was greatly beloved. He became "The Friend of Britain in Her Sorest Need." [6]

[6] Inscription on the tablet to Walter Hines Page in Westminster Abbey. See Burton J. Hendrick, *Life and Letters of Walter H. Page*, III, 431.

"THE FORGOTTEN MAN"

To get a true conception of Page's service to the southern people one must first understand his teachings and then his accomplishments. For he was a teacher as well as a wise worker and leader.

Page has left his economic and political philosophy in the form of many essays and addresses.

"The Forgotten Man," the so-called "white trash," and the neglected man of the hills and the mountains, formed the theme of Page's address at the North Carolina State College for Teachers in June, 1897. This speech became the gospel of the campaign that followed. He said in part : "In making an estimate of a civilization it is the neglected and forgotten man more than any other that must be taken into account. . . . In considering the level of the life of any community, you must not give undue value to any class of men. A community is not rich because it contains a few rich men, it is not healthful because it contains a few strong men, it is not intelligent because it contains a few men of learning, nor is it of good morals because it contains good women—if the rest of the population also be not well-to-do, or healthful, or intelligent, or of good morals."

In the days of our fathers . . . the mass of the people were common people; they lived directly out of the soil and they had the manners and the virtues and the limitations of a simple agricultural population, which was much the same in the early part of the century in all countries where a livelihood was easily obtained. . . . The dominant idea of education was that it was a luxury for the rich, or a privilege of the well-born—if a necessity at all, a necessity only for the ruling class. . . .

In the old days when education was dominated by the aristocratic idea, the chief influences that shaped opinion were the stump and the pulpit. . . .

Now let us see what these two powers . . . did for the education of the masses. . . . The first conception of education was the aristocratic conception, and the first system of teaching was controlled by those who held political power; it was the old system of class education. It did not touch the masses. They had no part in it. They grew up with the idea that education was a special privilege; they did not aspire to it, did not believe that it was attainable, and at last they came to believe that it was not desirable, certainly that it was not necessary. They remained illiterate, neglected, forgotten.

Later than the aristocratic system of education and overlapping it, came the ecclesiastical system. In establishing and developing this, the preachers did valiant service.... Still they [the schools] were class institutions....

The forgotten man remained forgotten.... The general level of education was almost as low as it had ever been.... What have the aristocratic system and the ecclesiastical system of education to show for themselves?

First, what did they do for their own favoured classes? North Carolina is one of the old thirteen States. The aristocratic system had free play here for nearly a hundred years, and the ecclesiastical system has had free play for at least half as long.... By any test that can be made, both these systems of education failed even with the classes that they appealed to. One such test is the test of emigration from the State. In 1890 there were living in other States 293,000 persons who were born in North Carolina. One in eight of every native of the State then living had gone away. When we remember that almost every one of those emigrants went to States where taxes are higher and schools are more numerous and better and where competition is more fierce, and when we remember that they went away from a State that is yet sparsely settled and richer in natural opportunities than most of the States to which they went, the failure of these systems becomes painfully obvious. If a slave brought $1,000. in old times, it ought to be safe to assume that every emigrant from the State has an economic value of $1,000. This emigration therefore had up to 1890 cost us in North Carolina $293,000,000—a fact that goes far to explain why we are poor....

Next, what did these systems of education do for the masses? In 1890, twenty-six per cent of the white persons of the State were unable even to read and write. One in every four was wholly forgotten. But illiteracy was not the worst of it; the worst of it was that the stationary social condition indicated by generations of illiteracy had long been the general condition. The forgotten man was content to be forgotten. He became not only a dead weight, but a definite opponent of social progress....

Now one of the two things is true—either these forgotten men are incapable of development, and belong to a lower order of intelligence than any other people of Anglo-Saxon stock; or our civilization, so far as they are concerned, has been a failure. Of course there is no doubt which of these suppositions is true; for these people are capable of development, capable of unlimited growth and elevation. But, if they be capable of development, then both the aristocratic and the ecclesiastical systems of society have failed to develop them. . . . Since both the politician and the preacher have failed to lift this life after a century of unobstructed opportunities, it is time for a wiser statesmanship and a more certain means of grace. . . .

A public school system generously supported by public sentiment, and generously maintained by both State and local taxation, is the only effective means to develop the forgotten man, and even more surely the only means to develop the forgotten woman.[7]

Belief in "the Democratic Quality of Southern Character"

In a little book entitled *The Rebuilding of Old Commonwealths*, now out of print, are preserved several notable addresses by Page to southern audiences. In one of these, after speaking of "the baffling facts of a sparse population and of a self-satisfied life that lingers past its day," he continues :

Do they give reason for despair? Not at all ; but they do give reason for patience. The problem is the most important that has been presented in our national life. It is not the education of a few millions of neglected persons ; it is not the modernizing of a few picturesque institutions ; least of all is it the task of imposing on these people the civilization that has been developed elsewhere. . . . But the larger question is this :—

Since democracy means constant social growth and social mobility, is Southern life becoming democratic or is it remaining stable, or going back to an essentially aristocratic structure? Are forces inside it asserting themselves that give promise of shaping this life in line with democratic growth? Or are the native forces reactionary? Is democracy there at last to be a failure? Is it equal to the task of assimilating the master race and the freed race? . . .

There is no undemocratic trait in the Southern people that is not directly accounted for by slavery and by the results of slavery. The most conspicuous institutional results were the political machines that were built on race differences first by one political party and then by the other, and the ecclesiastical machines that are the direct result of popular ignorance and isolation. The country people that I have described are men of good mettle, men to make free commonwealths of. The very strongest impulse they have is patriotic and democratic. The contrary tendencies are clearly survivals of a deflection of their development. So strongly have I been

[7] *The Rebuilding of Old Commonwealths*, pp. 2-35.

impressed with the democratic quality of Southern character that I believe if a democracy existed nowhere in the world, Southern life would now evolve one, perhaps even of a radical type. . . .

The leaders of the best Southern opinion have come to recognize . . . that the schools must do something more than teach the three R's, for a people without diversified occupations and without training do not care for the three R's, nor do the three R's profit them greatly. An idle and unproductive man is no less useless because he can read and write. . . .

It would be interesting to speculate on the effects of Jefferson's plan for public education if it had been carried out. Would the public schools not have prevented the growth of slavery? True, public schools and slavery, as well as most other human institutions, are the results of economic forces; but, if the masses of the Southern population had been educated, or trained to work . . . a stronger economic impetus might have been given to diversified pursuits than cotton-culture gave to slavery, and the whole course of our history might have been changed. But, whatever may have been the results of Jefferson's educational policy if it had been worked out, . . . the development of Southern life in the next hundred years will be determined by the success with which it shall now be worked out. The nature of the problem is clear. The work will be slow and the recovery from these last effects of slavery may require as long a time as it required to abolish slavery; but of the ultimate result no man who can distinguish dominant from incidental forces can have a doubt. . . .

I have purposely not written of the Negro as a separate part of the population, for in the building up of the commonwealth he will yield to the same kind of training. The Negro, at once the beneficiary and the victim of slavery, yet holds the white man, who was its victim and not its beneficiary, in economic bondage ; and he is himself also in economic bondage and in bondage likewise to the white man's race-feeling. Training that brings economic independence sets the strongest and most natural forces of life at play. I long doubted whether a democracy could absorb two different races thus living together and yet apart. But the practical results of right training, both on the white man and on the Negro, have left no room for doubt. . . .

Without right training, you have such a problem as men nowhere else in our country have. It will yield little to reason. Argument will not solve it. Time alone will bring slow change. . . . The white man has held the Negro back, the Negro has held the white man back; and dead men have ruled them both. Training to economic independence is the only true emancipation.[8]

[8] *Ibid.*, pp. 124-26.

NECESSITY FOR "THE RIGHT TRAINING OF ALL THE PEOPLE"

At the Birmingham Conference, Page made a powerful address on universal education for the South from an economic standpoint. He showed the economic errors of the Southern people in the past and with warm fervor pleaded for the training of both the Negro and the white man as the only way to advance the whole country.

Among other things he said :

The right training of all the people would come pretty near to ending all our troubles—to removing our difficulties, economic, political, and ethnological. For instance, you have seldom known a well-trained white man and a well-trained negro ... —both men of economic worth—to have difficulty because one is white and the other is black.... But one untrained worthless white man or one untrained worthless negro may cause trouble throughout a whole county. For this reason it is important to train the child of every hill-billy, ... of every negro.... In every case it is an economic reason, not a merely personal reason, not a race reason, not a class reason.... Clear thinking brings us home to this truth. A knowledge of our own history brings us home to the same truth. The one great structural error made in our past was an economic error. We shall correct it only by economic correction....

But it is not enough to regard the subject from a bald economic view only. We have other reasons for training all the people than the sheer profit of it, though that is reason enough.

There is one high reason that includes all others. It is necessary for our freedom of opinion that all the people be trained....

Public opinion is not always the thought of educated men in the community, but the blind push of untrained men. Thoughtful men are often not free because of the mass of unthinking men about them. Always an untrained mob will control thought if the people be not trained. In an untrained democracy low minds will lead; and an organized howl will lift demagogues to power.

After speaking of the many physical and other changes in the South which called for educated men, Page concluded with this remarkable prophecy :

A time is coming, men of the South, and it is coming before we die, when other and even greater economic problems will press on our national life for solution. They press already. They are new problems and no government has yet met them. When we grapple with them in earnest, we shall need leadership of a quality that is got only from a hardly won victory. The men who have passed resolutely through one struggle for economic truth and free opinion will have had the best training for other struggles for economic truths and for free opinion.... A democracy in its days of trial calls its leaders from those who struggled last. When we win this battle here—over ourselves and over inherited error—the nation may have need of us.[9]

The "Creed of Democracy"

Early in the campaign of the Southern Education Conference, Page gave the people of the South his "Creed of Democracy" :

I believe in the free public training of both the hands and the mind of every child born of woman.

I believe that by the right training of men we add to the wealth of the world. All wealth is the creation of man, and he creates it only in proportion to the trained uses of the community; and, the more men we train, the more wealth everyone may create.

I believe in the perpetual regeneration of society, in the immortality of democracy, and in growth everlasting.[10]

Lifelong Worker for the South

To summarize, throughout his whole career, Page wrote and spoke for the cause of real progress. As has been told, he was one of the organizers and the chief spirit in the Watauga Club, which started the campaign in North Carolina. A friend of Ogden and of Frissell, he was one of the promoters of the Conference for Education in the South and one of the originators of the Southern Education Board, out of which grew other boards. His counsel weighed heavily in these bodies. He was a member of the first General Education Board, of the first Sanitary Commission, and of the International Health Board. He was also a member of the Slater Board and of the first Jeanes Fund Board.

[9] *Proceedings of the Seventh Conference for Education in the South, Birmingham, Ala., 1904,* pp. 103-9.

[10] Walter H. Page, "The School that Built a Town," address at the State Normal School at Athens, Ga., 1901, published in *The Rebuilding of Old Commonwealths,* p. 102.

As editor of the *World's Work,* he did his best to advance the cause of southern education. To the people of the country at large, he preached the doctrine of universal education as the only way to abate prejudice between the sections and to solve the race problem. After spending two months and a half touring the whole South, he published in June, 1907, a special southern number, of which thousands of copies were distributed. He describes his journey through the southern states and writes an editorial on "The Arisen South." "The present industrial awakening in the Southern States," he asserts, "is the most important economical event in our history since the settlement of the West.... There is nothing in our contemporaneous life more interesting or more important than the rise of these people in these States, eager to the task of their own development and of the development of this richest region of the Union.... The most important change that has taken place is not the development of the wealth—great as that is—but the development of the people, who until now have been isolated, side-tracked, held back, kept out of the highways of life."

As long as he controlled this magazine, he kept up this policy of explaining to the world every phase of southern development. Scarcely a number appeared without some article on the consolidation of rural schools, the improvement of sanitation, the methods of farm demonstration work, the development of the water powers and the industries in the South, or some related subject.

Page was a member of President Roosevelt's Country Life Commission through which he accomplished much for the improvement of the agricultural classes. In the course of his travels with this commission he first met Dr. Charles Wardell Stiles, who explained to him the evils of the hookworm and interested him in sanitation as a means of improving the people. In another place, we shall tell the story of how he called the attention of the Southern Board, and through it, of John D. Rockefeller to this subject and helped to organize the Sanitary Commission, which grew into the International Health Board. From this contact a world-wide campaign against malaria, yellow fever, tuberculosis, and other diseases resulted. With Buttrick he introduced Knapp, the great "Farm Demonstrator," to the United States Department of Agriculture and thus helped to start the greatest plan ever organized for giving the farmers of the country practical education in agriculture. To the end of his life he was devoted to every cause that made for the development of his "Old Land." He lived to see the fulfillment of many of his hopes. The thirteen years since his death have proved the wisdom of every measure he advocated.

The capacity of a country to produce strong and brave men to fight its moral battles is the highest test of its vitality. Page was of the blood and bone of North Carolina. That the old state gave birth to such a man was proof that she still had this potency.

At first communities fail to recognize their great sons. So it was with North Carolina and the South—they at first did not appreciate Walter Hines Page, but time has already revealed him as one of the ablest, wisest and noblest of their sons. We have no Westminster Abbey on whose walls to write Page's name, but his life is written in the hearts of a people he taught and served.

Though the requirements of his profession made it necessary for him to reside elsewhere, he belonged to the soil of the Old North State. This he himself felt and proudly declared. It was his wish to return to North Carolina to live. There indeed he built a home for his old age and thither in obedience to his command, when exhausted in the service of his fellowman, his sons bore him—to die and to be buried in the soil of the "Old Land" he loved so dearly.

CHAPTER XVII

EDUCATION IN SANITATION AND HEALTH [1]

THE RELATION OF THE CAMPAIGN AGAINST HOOKWORM TO EDUCATION

WE have seen how Walter Hines Page, when in North Carolina in 1883-1884, gave an impulse to the movement for educating the "forgotten man"; and how he helped to start the Southern Education Board in 1901, and two years later the General Education Board. Now he was to call attention to another great need of the southern people and to help start another campaign to meet that need. It is another illustration of his keen perception, sound judgment, and forceful and effective action.

The Sanitary Commission, which did such great work in controlling hookworm and in improving sanitation in the South, was in the beginning a part of the educational movement. Measures designed first to cure people of the disease immediately gave rise to an educational campaign for sanitation, which was carried out chiefly through the schools. Begun to remove the source of the hookworm disease, the campaign was extended later to include the fight against malaria, typhoid, tuberculosis, pellagra, and yellow fever; and thus the Sanitary Commission, projected first for the southern states of North America, grew into the great International Sanitary Commission, which was extended finally to the other Americas, the countries of Europe, and the East. Beginning with an appropriation of $1,000,000 for the southern states, Mr. John D. Rockefeller has promoted, through this Sanitary Commission and the several other boards

[1] The work against hookworm described in this chapter originated in a meeting of the Southern Education Board. It was absolutely necessary to clean up the hookworm before children could make much progress in the schools. It was, therefore, as much an educational work as any ever done. Its methods were all educational, and were carried on chiefly through the superintendents, principals, and teachers of the schools. This work was as much a part of the great campaign for the improvement of public schools as was the work to increase taxation or build better school houses. The work for improved sanitation and the work against malaria were done for a similar reason and by similar methods.

and commissions formed under the Rockefeller Foundation, the greatest plan ever undertaken in the world for the education of people in the principles of sanitation and healthful living. This world-wide campaign for disease prevention, sanitation, and public health commenced with a fight against the comparatively insignificant and unknown little hookworm. First, then, what is this worm whose pursuit gave rise to so great an enterprise?

The hookworm is an intestinal parasite, less than one-half of an inch long when fully grown, of the genus *uncinaria*. It enters the body most often through the skin, where the feet come in contact with polluted soil, though it may be taken in through the mouth. The females in the intestines produce a vast number of eggs, which hatch when deposited in the soil. The worms frequently cause an itch on the feet and legs, commonly called "ground itch" or "dew itch"; thence they work their way into the blood and so into the intestines. When once they get lodgment there, they may persist for many years, causing an anemia which debilitates the person, making him permanently feeble, lazy, and stupid. In children it frequently dwarfs their growth. Because of this characteristic of the patients, the hookworm has been called the "germ of laziness." Rarely fatal itself, the disease prepares the victim for other diseases, especially typhoid and tuberculosis. The soil of the earth between 36° North latitude and 30° South, when presenting the right temperature and moisture, is favorable for the development of the larvae. All countries between these latitudes are liable to be polluted.

The worms like loose, sandy soil in which they can find protection, moisture, and warmth. In a tight clay soil they cannot thrive. The method of control becomes thus somewhat a question of geology. The health officer directs the campaign against the worm in accordance with the difference in soil, moisture, and temperature. In the sand-lands he expects to find serious and extensive infestation; in the clay-lands, only local and less infestation. The sandy soils of the South Atlantic states have been found especially subject to hookworm infestation, and it is in them that the most strenuous work has been, and must continue to be done.

There is a significant relation also between the economic condition of the people and the prevalence of the hookworm disease. The actual amount· of infestation has been found to vary with the wealth and poverty of the people as shown by the per capita tax valuation. In well fed, modern communities, where the people wear shoes, there is always less trouble with this disease.

For unknown centuries the hookworm disease has been spreading around the world throughout this zone, unrecognized and unrestrained. Millions and millions of people through the years have been the unconscious hosts of these small, life-sucking parasites, which lowered their vitality, reduced their strength, and inhibited their intellectual as well as their physical growth. When one member of the family became infected, he generally gave it indirectly to all the others. In the course of a few years a healthy, happy, and prosperous family would become weak, worthless, and miserable, fall into debt, and be reduced to poverty by a disease which is easily curable and preventable.

Children healthy, bright, and doing well in their classes at school, lost their mental alertness and energy, and, falling behind their classmates, became discouraged and dropped out of school. The school records showed that infected pupils, though apparently not ill, averaged lower in their studies than those free from the disease. Teachers everywhere reported great improvement in zeal and intelligence, as well as in weight and physical appearance, of such children immediately following the removal of the parasites.[2]

An old Dutch doctor, John Brickell, in his book on the *Natural History of North Carolina*, published first in Dublin in 1737 and in several later editions, describes the diseases he studied in North Carolina.[3] One description matches perfectly what we know of the hookworm disease.

CHARLES WARDELL STILES

An Italian zoölogist found the first hookworm in a human being in 1838. Charles Wardell Stiles, a young American student, learned about it in the course of his studies at the Uni-

---

[2] Condensed from the *United States Bureau of Education Bulletin No. 20, 1914*, pp. 14-15.
[3] John Brickell, *The Natural History of North Carolina*, pp. 395 ff. This book is in the Library of the University of North Carolina.

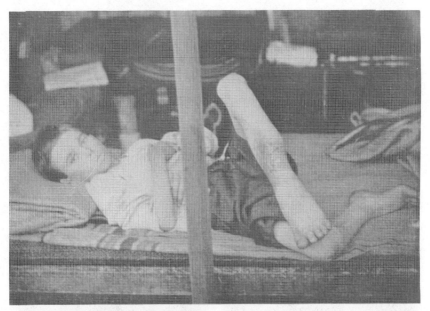

Upper, a boy suffering from hookworm disease, with a severely infected leg. Lower left, the same boy after treatment. Lower right, two brothers showing the dwarfing effect of hookworm disease. The taller, uninfected, is seventeen years old and weighs 126 pounds. The other, infected, is twenty-one years old and weighs sixty-six pounds

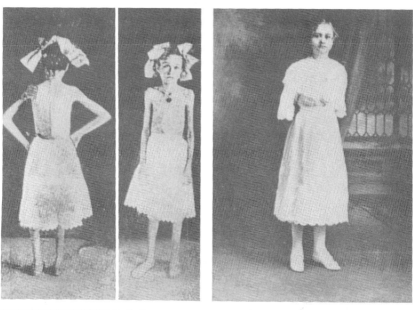

Upper left, a girl of sixteen before treatment for hookworm disease. Upper right, the same girl after treatment. Lower, a "hookworm family," all infected

versity of Leipzig in 1888. A book, containing references to the hookworm found in France, Italy, and Southern Germany, after describing the appearance of persons afflicted with it, stated that it probably existed in the American states bordering on the Gulf. This arrested Stiles's attention, so that when he returned to the United States in 1891 and was appointed zoölogist in the Bureau of Animal Industry of the Department of Agriculture in Washington and custodian of the National Museum in charge of the collection of parasites, he commenced to look for hookworms in this country. Failing to find any specimen of the species of hookworm that infects man, he searched the medical literature. In this he found no reference to an endemic hookworm disease in America. Recognizing the conditions as favorable to this disease he asserted it must exist. It was not, however, until 1902 that he had opportunity to prove its presence and widespread distribution in the southern states.

A disease variously described as "chronic anemia" or "continuous malaria" was endemic in many parts of the South. The people having the disease were frequently described as "dirt eaters" or "clay eaters" because of their morbid diet habit. The disease was supposed to be limited to the people described as "poor white trash" or "crackers," who were noted for their laziness and general worthlessness. Stiles knew, however, that dirt eating was a symptom and not a cause, and he therefore commenced at once to look for the disease among this class of people. Believing that it would be found, and seeking the coöperation of southern physicians who had never reported it, Stiles presented the matter to a meeting of medical men at the Johns Hopkins University and told them he believed that hookworm was the cause of the disease they had been calling "anemia." Polite skepticism and even positive disbelief met him. Dr. William Osler said he thought it would have been recognized by the physicians of the South, if it had existed there, and rebuked Stiles for reflecting upon them. Stiles's reply was : "Wait and see." [4]

Stiles continued to use every opportunity to declare his conviction that the hookworm was widely endemic in the South, and to interest physicians in looking for it. To his classes in medical zoölogy at Johns Hopkins, Georgetown University,

[4] Mark Sullivan, *Our Times, Pre-War America*, p. 306. Confirmed to the author by Charles Wardell Stiles.

and the Army Medical School, he would say : "Gentlemen, if you are ever in the tropics and find a case of anemia that you cannot explain, see if it is not due to hookworms."

HOOKWORM IN THE SOUTHERN STATES

Young Lieutenant Bailey K. Ashford, who had been a pupil of Stiles at Georgetown University, while serving as assistant surgeon in Porto Rico in 1898-99, found that fully two-thirds of his patients, natives and American soldiers, were afflicted with a persistent anemia. After trying without effect every known tonic, he examined these patients' feces and there found myriads of the eggs of the hookworm. Beyond the possibility of a doubt the blight that had lain upon the natives of rural Porto Rico for many years and had caused people to consider them a degenerate race, was simply hookworm. With the usual remedies, he worked a marvelous change in this people. The disease-burdened peasants were given new life with new strength and ambition. When Ashford went to Porto Rico, twelve thousand people annually had been dying from diseases traceable to this "anemia." Within a half dozen years he reduced this yearly toll to less than a thousand.[5] On hearing of Ashford's discovery, Stiles sent him a letter of congratulation, and when Ashford returned he brought a collection of hookworms to Washington, which Stiles examined. These Porto Rican specimens were soon recognized as identical with a new kind of hookworm which Stiles, through coöperation with colleagues (Allen J. Smith and others) had recently located in Virginia, Florida, and Texas. This specimen he named *Necator americanus*, "American Murderer." This confirmed Stiles in his belief that the anemic people of the South were hookworm sufferers, but his duties at the time prevented him from personally investigating the southern field as he so much desired to do.

When the question arose in 1902 as to whether the American soldiers who returned from Porto Rico and Cuba might not spread the disease throughout the country, Stiles asserted it was already present in the South, and it was then that Surgeon General Wyman gave him the opportunity to prove his theory. During a trip through the southern states he succeeded in thoroughly establishing this claim.

[5] *Ibid.*, pp. 308-10. Confirmed by Charles Wardell Stiles.

Stiles established the first clinic in the country at Columbia, South Carolina, with the aid of two local physicians. After eight years of personal work, during which he had amply confirmed his theory that the hookworm was the cause of much of the "anemia" and so-called "pernicious malaria" which had previously been charged to climate, Stiles realized that he must get either the government or some organization to back him up before he could make an effective campaign against the disease. Congress had for many years been making large appropriations to investigate the causes of cholera in hogs and to kill insects that injured crops, but it was less generous to human beings. He found thus that he must seek the assistance of private wealth. The story of how a man was found to finance the campaign is a dramatic one.

THE SANITARY COMMISSION ORGANIZED

Walter Hines Page had been appointed by Roosevelt as a member of the Country Life Commission to prepare a report on the agricultural, economic, and sanitary conditions of the farmers and their families throughout the country. At the request of the Commission, Stiles was appointed to accompany it as consulting sanitarian. Page and Henry Wallace, editor of *Wallace's Farmer* and a member of the Commission, accompanied by Stiles, were on a journey of investigation through North Carolina when some cases of hookworm disease were brought to their attention. Here let Stiles tell the story :

One morning we got up very early in Goldsboro, North Carolina, and took a train before daylight for Raleigh. As daylight began to break, Mr. Page, Mr. Wallace and I were in the smoking room ... when the train stopped at a country station. A typical "dirt-eater" was on the platform. . . . Mr. Wallace looked at him in surprise ... and asked what the matter was with this man. Page immediately replied that he was a typical extreme example of the poor tenant whites of the South. Wallace asked, "Is that the type that is called the poor 'white trash'?" Page replied in the affirmative, but added that it was better not to use that expression, "white trash," south of the Potomac. At this point, I entered the conversation and remarked that this was a typical example of an extreme case of hookworm disease. Page had heard of hookworm disease, but had never before seen a case to recognize it. He looked at me in surprise, and asked me whether that man's condition was actually due to hookworm. I replied it was and that he had a very severe ... infection, doubtless of long standing. He asked me whether the man could be cured. I replied that he could be for about fifty cents worth of drugs. Immediately Page became very much interested. ... During the discussion before a meeting of the Commission with local people at Raleigh, an incident occurred which intensified his interest. ... The chairman asked a physician who was testifying whether there was much hookworm disease in North Carolina. This physician replied that he had never seen a case. Hereupon the chairman turned to me with an amused, inquiring look, ... and I replied to his unworded question immediately, by stating that there were four well marked cases of hookworm disease in the room at that moment. This remark produced quite a sensation, and we entered into a discussion of hookworm disease, typhoid fever and sanitation. ... The next day the Governor of the State came out with a sharp criticism of the incident, and of the Commission and myself in particular, for the statement I had made. He called upon the State Board of Health to declare the facts. ... One of its officers immediately came out with the statement that the assertions which I had made ... were exceedingly conservative and ... below the statistics of the State Board of Health. This made Page's interest in hookworm disease still more decided, and he and I spent a number of hours discussing the problem during the next few days.[6]

When they came to consider the methods of curing and preventing the disease, Stiles told Page about a gentleman who had planned to finance a campaign against it and had suddenly died. Page, already deeply concerned about this phase of the problem, remained quiet for a few moments and then remarked : "Well, don't get discouraged. Perhaps we can get some money from some other source." [7]

Now events leading to the starting of the work follow rapidly. Page took the first opportunity to talk with Wallace Buttrick of the General Education Board and immediately won his interest. Buttrick brought the matter to Dr. Gates's attention, who took under consideration the question of presenting it to Mr. Rockefeller. Governed by his usual conservatism Gates wished first, however, to gain the reaction of southern men to the proposal and selected the Southern Education Board as an ideal group for this purpose. At the time of the meeting

[6] Condensed from a letter from Charles Wardell Stiles to Burton J. Hendrick, dated May 22, 1922, given to the author by Arthur W. Page.
[7] *Ibid.*

of the Southern Education Board at Abenia on Lake George in August, 1909, George Foster Peabody invited Gates and Stiles to meet with the members there and arranged an evening for Stiles to give the company a lecture on the life history of the hookworm and its potential relations to the educational work the Board was doing. The gentlemen present expressed a deep interest in his statement, none more than Gates. For that night Gates took Stiles aside and said to him: "Mr. Rockefeller's office is going to support the hookworm work." After a conference in New York between Gates and Stiles as to the program of the campaign and the amount of money required to carry it out, Mr. Rockefeller sent a letter to the commission formed to carry on the work, which read as follows: "If you deem it wise to undertake this commission [the hookworm work] I shall be glad to be permitted to work with you to that end and you may call upon me from time to time for such sums as may be needed during the next five years for carrying on an aggressive campaign, up to a total of one million dollars ($1,000,000)." [8]

It appeared necessary now to have a special organization to do this work. The Sanitary Commission for the Eradication of the Hookworm Disease was, therefore, formed in October, 1909. It was organized with Wickliffe Rose, at this time agent of the Peabody Board and executive secretary of the Southern Education Board, as administrative secretary, and Charles Wardell Stiles, of the United States Health Institute, with permission of the Surgeon General of the Army, as scientific secretary. The members were Dr. Frederick T. Gates; Dr. William H. Welch, of the Johns Hopkins Medical School, and Dr. Simon Flexner, of the Rockefeller Institute, representing medical science; John D. Rockefeller, Jr., and Starr J. Murphy, representing Mr. Rockefeller, Sr.; and Walter H. Page, P. P. Claxton, H. B. Frissell, J. Y. Joyner, E. A. Alderman, and D. F. Houston. The undertaking was proposed by Page. Rose, the administrative secretary, and five members were members of the Southern Board. This Commission was thus an outgrowth of the Southern Board.

This gift of a million dollars by Mr. Rockefeller for the study of hookworm disease was unique in the history of preven-

[8] Quoted in the *Fifth Annual Report of the Rockefeller Sanitary Commission, 1914*, pp. 8-9.

tive medicine. It was the first time private funds were ever given in such an amount for the promotion of public health. It was not only a great gift to the people of the South; it was a great gift to the world of science; for it was the beginning of a service to civilization that was to be world-wide.

The day the Commission was organized, October 26, 1909, Page writes in his diary: "Today this organization was made, with a gift of a million dollars by John D. Rockefeller.... The one greatest single cause of anaemia and stagnation in the South will by this fund be ultimately removed and two million inefficient people be made well. This result came about from the work of the Country Life Commission appointed by President Roosevelt, and from my bringing Dr. Stiles within the range of Dr. Buttrick's and Mr. Gates' knowledge and interest. It is the largest single benefit that could be done to the people of the South. This is one of the inheritances of slavery, the disease having been brought from Africa by the negroes.... A big day's work for the old land!" [9]

THE CAMPAIGN AGAINST HOOKWORM

The Commission defined its primary task in the study of hookworm in the southern states as threefold: To determine the geographic distribution of the infection; to estimate the degree of the infection in each area and to cure the present sufferers; and to remove the sources of the infection by introducing sanitary measures to put a stop to soil pollution.

Serious difficulties had to be met. The announcement of the wide prevalence of the African disease among the whites as well as blacks aroused angry denial and resentment. Among some prejudiced people, Stiles with his northern backing "appeared in the light, not of a deliverer but of another damn Yankee bent upon holding the South up to ridicule." [10] The *Macon Telegraph* asked "where was this hookworm or lazy disease when it took five Yankee soldiers to whip one Southerner?" [11] The most violent attack came from a southern state whose people Stiles had described as having the "hookworm

[9] Hendrick, *The Training of an American*, pp. 372-73.
[10] Gerald W. Johnson, *Baltimore Sun*, 1927, quoted by Sullivan, *op. cit.*, p. 327.
[11] Sullivan, *op. cit.*, p. 327.

complexion." The editor of the local paper in a certain town in this state threatened Stiles in an editorial with lynching if he ever set foot in the place. Stiles packed his apparatus and left at once for the place, went to the hotel, and registered under his own name. After spending a week in investigating the school children and the people generally, and making the microscopic examinations which yielded him ample evidence of the disease, he wrote to the editor, telling him what he had been doing and the results of his investigations, and added : "The lynching may begin when you are ready." The editor called on Stiles and dined with him, spent half the night talking hookworm, and became a convert. The next day his paper published a generous retraction.[12] The facts produced, especially the wonderful results in curing people, soon stopped all this opposition. Stiles, though requested by the Board of the Sanitary Commission to continue with it permanently as scientific secretary, returned after five years to the United States Health Institute, which he has served with ability ever since. He had started this great campaign of education in health and sanitation and left it in efficient hands to be carried into many lands.

As in the case of all the work done under Mr. Rockefeller's direction, the plan of the campaign was based on coöperation with the existing agencies of the states and counties. It was recognized that no outside agency could accomplish the ends aimed at. The Commission could only aid the local governments in organizing, educating, and bringing into activity their own forces. Moreover, it was regarded as necessary both for economy and for efficiency that the work be done through the existing medical organizations, boards of health, the public press, and especially the officers and teachers of the public schools. These and many other organizations were used effectively in teaching the people, first, the curative measures, and then the methods of sanitation which, when thoroughly carried out, would stamp out the disease entirely.

Rose established his office for the general and administrative work at Washington, D. C. Stiles had his headquarters for the scientific work at Wilmington, North Carolina. Rose's task was to form an organization to determine the distribution and the effects of the hookworm disease and its treatment and pre-

12 *Ibid.*, p. 328.

vention. This he did on a new plan that showed remarkable sagacity.

All the field work was done in coöperation with the health boards of the states and counties. The states were organized by units under state directors with field directors in the counties, all selected by the state departments of health. The Rockefeller Commission appropriated about one-half of the funds required to carry on the field work, the local authorities the remainder. The Commission also supplied the general administration and scientific direction and aided in selecting the microscopists and in providing the scientific apparatus for the field work.

The first thing was to educate the people about the plague and the methods of preventing it. The plan was :

1. To demonstrate to the people that the hookworm disease was a reality ; that it was a serious and persistent handicap, because of the feebleness and bad health induced ; and that it was curable and preventable.

2. To make surveys to show the degree of infection in each county for the purpose of education and to ascertain the conditions of soil pollution responsible for the presence and spread of the infection.

3. To teach the people through the schools and by means of lectures, visits, clinics, and demonstrations the importance of having all the children, and, as far as possible, the whole population, examined and thus find the infected persons, and have them treated ; showing them how the examination was made, how simply and economically the disease could be treated and cured, how the infection was spread, and how it could be prevented by using proper sanitary arrangements.

4. To show the physicians how to diagnose and treat the disease and the importance of making the examinations for the parasite a part of their routine, and to enlist the coöperation of the hospitals and visiting nurses.

5. To get the press to help in informing the people about these things and to enlist the coöperation of all the managers of mills, factories, mines, and other industries, and of all farmers' associations, chambers of commerce, women's clubs, and every type of association.

6. To make the teaching of the dangers of soil pollution and of how to prevent it, a regular part of the instruction in

Above, a county dispensary for the free treatment of hookworm disease. Below, a free dispensary for the treatment of colored victims of the disease

Above, a group illustrating the effect of coöperation on the part of the treated patient. Three generations are represented. The father (standing by the door), after being cured, got thirty-seven of his family connection and many of his other neighbors treated. The boy holding the dog gained twenty-one pounds in four weeks after one treatment. Below, a cotton-mill school, in which nearly all of the children have hookworm disease, some of them very severe cases

the public schools. The superintendents, principals, and teachers were the chief agents of this most important phase of the work.

7. To arrange and exhibit approved sanitary toilets or privies suitable for the country and to show the people how a community could by proper methods control the disease.

"Unhooking the Hookworm" was the title of a motion picture film which was used by the Sanitary Commission in its campaign. The hatching of the hookworm, its methods of entering the human body, its progress through the blood to the intestines, and its propagation were set forth vividly by microphotographs and diagrams. The methods of soil pollution, the need of sanitary precautions, the methods of treatment, and the results of the cure were illustrated in successive scenes. The film was successful in impressing the people with the danger of infection and with the possibilities of both cure and prevention.

The infection in the sand-lands being vastly greater than in the clay-lands or mountains, the survey alternated irregularly between these zones in order not to produce a panic in any one zone and depreciate property. This method resulted in more general education on sanitation.

Finally, by these measures it was sought to lay the foundations of complete county and community self-services, which would not only prevent hookworm, but all other diseases due to food, water, or soil pollution ; and, in general, to show the people how to organize permanent control of all health conditions.

During the first four years of the campaign 496,000 school children of 488 counties in eleven southern states were examined and 40 per cent were found to be infected. Of the 892,000 persons of all ages taken at random in this same territory, 34 per cent were found to be suffering from this disease. It was difficult to get some people to take the remedies given them, but vast numbers were apparently completely cured.[13]

By these methods of coöperative study and education, a new conception was developed among the people of their individual and group responsibility in the control of all preventable diseases and the general promotion of public health. It was a campaign at first to prevent a particular disease, but the finest result was that it taught the people to organize systems of

[13] *United States Bureau of Education Bulletin No. 20, 1914*, p. 14.

public health education and service and give them their support. States and counties were induced to make increased appropriations. All welfare agencies, in fact, were imbued with a keen sense of their responsibility for the public health, and went at the work with increased vigor and initiative, which were bound to produce marked results.

So successful was the public health work in overcoming prejudice that fifteen years later an eminent sanitarian in the South said: "The South was fortunate in some respects in having the hookworm infection, for hookworm disease has been the means of stimulating rural health work as nothing else could have done." [14]

The finest result of the work of this hookworm campaign was in the education of the people about the source of diseases and how to abate their danger by proper and right living. The former popular idea was that the climate was the cause of the diseases peculiar to the South and that the lowlands were especially unfit for white residents. The lean, clayey-faced, shiftless people of these lands were supposed to be the victims of the heat, the humidity, or "miasma"—whatever that was. It is true that in areas of heavy rainfall and warm winters, of sandy soils polluted with excreta, children running with bare feet picked up the larvae of hookworm more frequently. It was not the climate but hookworm that was primarily responsible for the disease.

So it was learned that it was not the heat, the humidity, or the imaginary "miasma" of the swamps, that caused chills and fevers, but the mosquitoes bred in them that carried the germs of malaria. We know now that when these lands are drained and the mosquitoes destroyed, sanitation established, and the hookworm eradicated, the desolate sand-flats, coastal swamps, and river deltas of the South become as healthy as any part of the country.

In like manner, it was supposed at first that pellagra was a climatic disease, but now we know that it is the constant diet of fats and carbohydrates, usually corn meal, fat bacon, and molasses, without fresh fruits or vegetables, that causes this disease.

[14] Quoted by Dr. W. H. Welch in "Address on The Services of Wickliffe Rose to Public Health," in pamphlet, *Wickliffe Rose, 1862-1931*, p. 6.

THE CAMPAIGN AGAINST MALARIA

Beginning in 1914 the Sanitary Commission, now merged into the International Health Board, started a similar campaign, which lasted for a number of years, against the mosquitoes carrying malaria. In the summer of 1920 it joined with the United States Public Health Service in concerted demonstrations in fifty-two towns in ten southern states. The possibility of ridding small communities of malarial infection at a cost within their resources was demonstrated in towns in Arkansas and in a country district in Mississippi. It was found that the infection could be reduced 75 to 95 per cent at an annual per capita cost of from forty-five cents to one dollar. The state boards of health and local authorities did their customary part in these undertakings, contributing funds and personnel, which led, as in the case of the hookworm disease, to the establishment of more or less permanent sanitary measures.

As a result of this work in Mississippi, for example, great improvement has been made in the Delta section, where the people had always been subject to chills and fever. Glenn W. Herrick, a professor in the Agricultural College of Mississippi, writing in the *Popular Science Monthly* for April, 1903, said : "The Delta region of Mississippi is the second-best farming land in the world, being inferior only to the Valley of the Nile. In 1903, however, much of the land could be bought for from $10 to $20 an acre. The reason...was...chills and fever." Compare this statement with another one twenty-four years later. R. W. Harned in an address before the Association of Economic Entomologists in 1927 said that "whereas the hospital at the Mississippi Agricultural and Mechanical College twenty years before would be crowded with students from the Delta section...suffering from malaria, in 1927 there was not a single case. The mosquitoes and malaria are being reduced from year to year. Where a generation ago they went unchecked, a new agricultural empire is developing in a region with soil as fertile as any on the continent, and where health conditions are now above the average and are improving constantly." [15]

The malaria was definitely reduced in all the communities where the work was done, but the finest result was the increase of community pride in popular education and in interest in

[15] L. O. Howard, *The Insect Menace*, pp. 186-88.

health problems. The results of this work against mosquitoes in the southern states were so convincing that the methods thus demonstrated were extended to many foreign lands. Guayaquil, Ecuador, for example, the most plague-infected town in the world, was cleaned up by the Commission. It had been from the earliest days the breeding place of yellow fever, typhoid, small pox, and the bubonic plague, as well as malaria, "with the result that our fine young men in the diplomatic and consular service were losing their lives there. At the time of the revolution in 1912, we sent our ship, the *Yorktown*, in there to help them. The *Yorktown* sailed up the Guayas River and the men landed to help bury their dead. The *Yorktown's* captain and a number of our young men were stricken with the plague before they got away. Being near Panama it endangered the whole Canal Zone, which we had cleaned up." [16]

RESULTS OF THE CAMPAIGN

After a survey of the southern states made in 1931, Stiles gave us his conclusions as to the progress made in these states since the inauguration of the campaign against the hookworm in 1909.[17] "Prior to 1910," he says, "a person could stand on a street corner of practically any city or town in the sand lands of the South and in an afternoon ... see from five to twenty, so-called, 'dirt eaters.'" Now it would take several days to find one. During the trip in 1931, he found less than forty among 18,649 school children inspected. The hookworm disease is still widespread, but "lighter in form." As for yellow fever : he continues, "The epoch-making demonstration of mosquito transmission of yellow fever has revolutionized the 'shotgun methods' of quarantine." It is hoped and believed that it will never have a chance to appear in the United States again. With regard to malaria : "The screening of houses is better and more common than ... thirty years ago. The good accomplished by drainage projects is distinctly evident. ... The evidence of malaria is still found, however, and these measures should be prosecuted."

With regard to typhoid fever : "There has been an enormous reduction in the typhoid death rate ... from 1900 to 1920 ... due to several factors (anti-typhoid inoculation, im-

[16] Editorial, "A Menace to Panama," *World's Work*, June, 1912, pp. 131-32.
[17] Charles Wardell Stiles, manuscript report, copy given the author.

proved hospital and nursing facilities, improved diagnosis, . . . and improved sanitation). It is difficult to evaluate the proportionate effect of these different elements. The important thing is that typhoid fever has decreased despite the dual race problem which is so favorable to the spread of the disease. . . . Any locality with a dual race problem labors under a serious public health handicap . . . —a handicap for both races. The South is no exception to this rule and to permit sentimentality to blind us to the disadvantages and dangers is an unkindness to both races." [18]

But the greatest improvement that Stiles found was in the schools. This was notable in the improved schoolhouses and especially in their sanitation. "No school seen in 1931 compared as a disease center with the majority of the rural schools in 1902 (when they were all surrounded by polluted soil). This is a marvelous advance." It should be recalled, however, that "many rural children still live in homes where there are no outhouses. . . . This training cannot be done in a day—or in a generation."

"The correlation between good roads and the consolidation of schools is . . . very marked." Good roads have had great influence in educating the people about sanitation. "There is a saying that 'the paint brush follows the asphalt.' People living along improved highways take a greater pride in their homes." Although these conditions do not manifest themselves at all the homes, they appear to affect a sufficient number to set an example of improved sanitary conditions. Conditions in filling stations along the road, in boarding houses, hotels, and barber shops have been considerably improved.

With regard to country churches Stiles says : "One is impressed by the fact that numerous rural churches still fail to observe the principles contained in the injunction in Deuteronomy XXIII, 12-13. They have not kept pace with the schools. Many of them . . . represent the same potentialities for soil pollution and the spread of disease that they did in 1902. . . . In my experience, as a rule, ministers are true friends of the health departments especially during an epidemic . . . and back up the health officer." [19]

The cotton mills have exerted an excellent influence in

[18] *Ibid.*   [19] *Ibid.*

improving conditions in their villages and on the tenant farms from which the operatives come.

A marked improvement has been in the development of interest in public health work. In 1902 eleven southern states expended only $230,496 for public health work, two states, Arkansas and South Carolina, making no appropriations whatever. In 1930 thirteen states, including these two, expended a total of $4,217,997. County health officers have been multiplied to a gratifying degree. In 1902 whole-time county health officers were all but unknown. In 1931 there were 339 whole-time health officers in these thirteen southern states. Where a single county is unable to have one, adjoining counties have united in employing a health officer, though some still remain without local health supervision. The coöperative county health work has been of very great value, but "we still need 'medical missionaries' in some exceptional . . . localities of the United States about as bad as China does." [20]

Medical inspection of school children did not exist in 1902. Now it is more or less widespread in counties having full-time officers and occasionally in other counties, where progressive school principals have organized medical inspection by volunteers from the local medical and dental professions.

Up to the beginning of this campaign against hookworm the masses had a very vague idea about germs as the causes of disease. They had heard of them but had never seen them. Many still did not believe in them. They were disposed, therefore, not to pay much attention to the principles of sanitation based on the germ theory of disease. But here was a germ half an inch long which they could see. They could see also how it could be killed and the results in the improved health of people. It was a demonstration of the truth of the germ theory such as was never seen before and was convincing evidence of the necessity of using methods which would prevent the pollution of the soil. When once convinced of the cause of disease, people were prepared to believe in the germ theory of typhoid, of tuberculosis, of malaria, and of other such diseases.

As Rose developed the campaign against hookworm so as to make it the basis for a large scheme for public health work, so he used the campaigns against typhoid, malaria, pellagra, yellow fever, and other infectious diseases to introduce meth-

[20] *Ibid.*

ods of sanitation against all diseases. The experience and influence gained by this work prepared the way for a wider and greater service to scientific institutions in many parts of the world.

Awakened by the Rockefeller Sanitary Commission, the public health officials of the South have achieved a remarkable triumph in preventive medicine by teaching the people how to eliminate malaria, as well as hookworm. Sparsely settled areas in the lowlands are still subject to malaria, but all communities willing to pay the price and to do the work, may now drain, clean up, and guard their environs to secure freedom from the malaria-bearing Anopheles. The health problem of the South is now comparatively simple. Drain the swamps and sinks, empty the old barrels and cans, screen the houses, and put shoes on the children, build sanitary toilets, and teach the people correct habits of eating and living, and the Southland will smile all over with health.

It is not within the scope of this book to tell of all the work of the International Health Board against yellow fever, tuberculosis, and other contagious diseases or of the aid rendered to public health and medical institutions in many other lands. But a few facts will show its immense importance.

Out of this Sanitary Commission grew the greatest health movement the world has ever known. Take one year's work, for example. During 1926 aid was extended by the Rockefeller Foundation to fourteen medical schools in ten countries ; to the medical school and hospital in Peking ; to fifteen institutions for public health in twelve countries ; to nurse-training schools in Brazil, France, Poland, Yugoslavia, China, Japan, and Siam ; to the help of twenty-one governments in their fight against the hookworm ; to the organization of health service in two hundred and forty-four counties in the United States and thirty-four districts in twelve other countries ; to health services in sixteen countries ; to Brazil to help control the yellow fever in ten states ; to yellow fever surveys in Nigeria and the Gold Coast ; to the showing of methods of controlling malaria in nine North American states and in Nicaragua, Salvador, Argentina, Italy, Spain, Poland, Palestine, and the Philippine Islands ; to the furnishing of books and laboratory apparatus to medical institutions in twenty impoverished European countries ; and to the Health Committee of the League of Nations. The Foundation spent $9,741,474 in one year for these causes.[21] Work similar to this done in 1926 has been carried on under the auspices of the International Health Board for twenty years. This vast world-wide service to science and health grew out of the first Rockefeller Sanitary Commission.

No one rejoiced more in the stupendous success of this health movement than Walter Hines Page, who had been largely responsible for starting it. In *The Life and Letters*, Hendrick tells us of an incident which will fitly close this chapter : "Dr. Wickliffe Rose, the head of the International Health Board, came to London to discuss the possibility of beginning hookworm work in the British Empire, especially in Egypt and India. Page, as Ambassador, arranged a dinner at the Marlborough Club, attended by the leading medical scientists of the kingdom and several members of the Cabinet. Dr. Rose's description of his work made a deep impression. He was informed that the British Government was only too ready to coöperate with the Health Board. When the discussion was ended the Right Honorable Lewis Harcourt, the Secretary of State for the Colonies, concluded an eloquent address with these words : " 'The time will come when we shall look back on this evening as the beginning of a new era in British colonial administration.' " [22]

[21] Rockefeller Foundation, *A Review for 1926*, pp. 7-10.
[22] Burton J. Hendrick, *The Life and Letters of Walter H. Page*, I, 101.

CHAPTER XVIII

WICKLIFFE ROSE AND HIS WORK [1]

ORIGIN AND EARLY PREPARATION

WHEN we consider the diversity and extent of the services of Wickliffe Rose in the causes of education, science, and health to the people of many lands, his career appears one of the most notable of his generation. From a country schoolmaster in Tennessee, he became in fifty years president of the General Education Board and of the International Education Board and director-general of the International Health Board. In this time he had much variety of experience as student at normal school, college, and university ; as instructor, professor, and dean of a college ; as administrator of educational funds ; as investigator and director of field work for sanitation and health ; and finally as the trusted agent of Mr. Rockefeller in the investment of vast funds in the advancement of science, education, and public health in many parts of the world. Successful in all these positions, "he ascended from one place to the next as naturally as the vine that climbs the wall in the sunshine." He had the ability and he had the character.

The origin of this man and his early preparation for his remarkable career are instructive and inspiring. He was born on November 19, 1862, on a farm near Saulsbury, Hardeman County, Tennessee, the second son in the family of six sons and one daughter of Kinchen Langston Rose and Jeannette C. Cherry. The family was of Scotch descent via Virginia and

[1] As a southern man, born and bred and educated in Tennessee and trained at Peabody College and the University of Tennessee, and as an officer of the Bureau of Investigation and Information of the Southern Board, the work of Wickliffe Rose clearly belongs to the history of the Southern Board. The fact that he was an officer of and did tremendous work for the General Board and the Rockefeller Foundation, and helped the International Health Commission and the International Education Commission, does not obliterate his first great work. In fact, he was working for southern schools more or less all his life. We claim him, therefore, as a large factor in our campaign, and he is entitled to a place in this history. The description of his talents, his character, his methods, and his accomplishments will be a valuable lesson to southern youth, and it is included for the inspiration it will give to all who wish to serve their region. The South claims him as her own.

North Carolina. They came from North Carolina to Tennessee in 1853 in what is still spoken of as The Great Migration.

Wickliffe Rose received his early training under his father, who was a farmer and respected minister in the Church of the Disciples, and a mother of sterling character, who though having had limited education was, her son said, "one of the best thinkers he ever knew." The boy had a great love for books and developed early an intense love of nature. He was fond of tramping in the fields or by woodland streams into the mountains, hunting the hiding places of the wild flowers and birds. Later in life he became an enthusiastic fly fisherman, an art which he pursued in many parts of the world as opportunity offered. For refreshment and renewal of spirit he sought always a return to nature.

While still a lad Rose taught a two months' country school in the neighborhood. Having an earnest desire for more education, he at sixteen entered an academy taught by a Dr. Wines, a minister of the Church of the Disciples, at Saulsbury. Wines was one of those rare teachers who inspire their pupils with a desire for learning, and two years under him laid the foundation for high scholarship. After teaching a private school for two years at Orange Springs, Alabama, Rose went in 1886 to the University of Nashville, Tennessee. A. P. Bourland, at that time a professor there, tells how he discovered young Rose at a teachers' institute he held at Bolivar, Tennessee, and, attracted by the boy's great earnestness and apparent talent, encouraged him to go to college. At Nashville he was a brilliant and successful student from the beginning. One of his fellow students writes of him : "He had the finest intelligence and personality and the most gracious spirit of any student I ever knew there or anywhere." [2] He was active in all student enterprises and a regular speaker in the literary society. Rose took his Bachelor of Arts degree at the University of Nashville in 1889 and Master of Arts in 1890, and was immediately appointed an instructor and taught there for eleven years. His student experiences and professional duties developed in him a deep attachment to the institution and a faith in its future, which led him later to labor to reëstablish the institution as a university for the training of teachers and leaders for the South. In his vacations between 1897 and 1902 he studied at the University of

[2] Professor J. R. Moseley in letter to the author of Oct. 31, 1932.

Chicago under Dewey, Tufts, and others, making a specialty of education, philosophy, logic, and ethics. His studies in philosophy ranged from Aristotle and Plato to Herbert Spencer and Huxley and they shaped for life his thought and methods of work.

Before he finished his course for his Ph.D. at Chicago in 1902, which would have been completed at the end of the year, Rose was called to the professorship of the history and philosophy of education at the University of Tennessee. He here first came in contact with the movement represented by the Southern Conference, the Southern Education Board, and the Summer School of the South, of which he was secretary and in which he also taught for two years. He now grew and broadened rapidly and got his vision of service as a builder of scientific and educational institutions. Rose was destined by nature to be a great teacher and administrator ; but it was in this movement that he found the opportunity to try his wings. Here he came in contact with the men who first organized the movement. It at once fastened his attention and fascinated his imagination. He made a study of it and joined enthusiastically in it, and was the first to interpret it to the public in print.[3]

Rose was an able and attractive teacher. A great student himself, he inspired others to study. One of his pupils at the University of Tennessee, who has since become a professor of education himself, says, "he was preëminently one of the best teachers and thinkers in the philosophical aspects of education that I have known." His colleagues and students in this field have always expressed regret that he left the professor's chair to become an administrator, believing that he would have been recognized as one of the great philosophers of our day. As it was, they claim he was one of the three ablest educational thinkers of his time in America.

HIS THEORY OF PUBLIC EDUCATION

His theory of public education he stated briefly in an address before the Conference for Southern Education at the Memphis meeting in April, 1908, on compulsion in education. "Educa-

---

[3] See "The Educational Movement in the South," *Report of the United States Commissioner of Education, 1903*, I, 359-90.

tion . . . ," said he, "is concerned with the evolution of life. The
evolution of life is a bipolar fact, manifesting itself on the one
side in individual development and on the other in social progress. The individual life and social life, individual growth and
social progress, individual interest and social welfare, are but
two sides of one fact, each existing because of its organic relation to the other. It is only when we conceive the individual
as a social outcome, society as made up of free individuals, and
both as organically related as inseparable factors in the development of life that we shall discern the real meaning of compulsion
in education."

If the State is fundamentally interested in social progress . . . it
must establish and maintain systems of schools. . . . All social progress has its beginning in the life and efforts of the individual. Every
step that society makes forward is a step that is first made by some
individual. It is the new thought, the new invention, the new tool,
the new social form, the new feeling, the new aspiration of some
individual which society takes over and adopts as its own. The
progress of a society is thus conditioned upon the inventive, the
constructive capacity of its individual members. Each member is a
potential factor in group development. The degree of individual
efficiency is the measure of social advancement. If social development be the chief concern of the State, then its most valuable asset
is the educated citizen. Every neglected class represents a waste of
assets; every individual left in ignorance is a possibility thrown
away. The State will inevitably reap the results of such neglect in
the form of arrested social development.
   But assume that the prime purpose of the State is to promote
the development of the individual citizen, or, if you will, of any
particular class of citizens. The State must at once face the fact of
social solidarity by which each contributes to the life of all and all
contribute to the life of each. The individual life while contributing
to social progress is in turn a social outcome, and derives its content
from the milieu from which it springs. If the State would elevate
and enrich the life of the citizen, it must elevate and enrich the
social environment in which he lives and moves and has his being.
The neglected individual or the neglected group in any society is
the dead body to which the favored individual is tied and from
which there is no escape.
   From this fact of social solidarity ; from this organic relation
and interaction of the individual and society in the development of
life springs the necessity of *universal education*. So far we have

found no means of making education universal save through ... the enforcement of compulsory education law.[4]

After two and a half years at the University of Tennessee, Rose became, in 1904, dean of the Peabody College and the University of Nashville. What the South now needed, he declared, was leaders in all lines of thought, especially in educational work. He was given a free hand here to accomplish what he had in mind, which was the building of a superior college for teachers and educational leaders in the South to be a memorial for George Peabody. To this task he devoted ten years of arduous work.

His Work for the Training of Teachers

Rose held that the training of teachers was the first thing to be accomplished in this movement and that this could be done only by a unified system of schools—high schools, normal colleges, and universities. In an address before the Sixth Conference for Education in the South at Richmond in 1903, he said :

The strategic point, therefore, in all our educational endeavor is in the equipment of teachers....

Since the vital factor in the elementary school is the teacher, and since the teacher, to be vital, must come to his work from a higher plane, it is evident that any efficient system of elementary education is conditioned on the maintenance of a system of adequately equipped high schools and normal schools. But these high schools and normal schools must in like manner draw their life blood from the college and university.... The teacher in a school of given grade should be educated in a school of higher grade ; the university alone, by training the independent scholar capable of directing his own advancement, being in position to supply its own instructors. The university stands at the head of the system, supplying inspiration, vitality, directive power to the whole.

The system is an organic unity, and any part of it depends for its vitality upon its articulation with the organic whole.... Certain failure awaits any scheme of reform that would undertake to build up the elementary rural school as an independent institution. Any permanent advance at this point will come as a phase of the evolu-

[4] *Proceedings of the Eleventh Conference for Education in the South,* Memphis, Tenn., 1908, pp. 150-51.

tion of the system as a whole. Until we frankly recognize that the building of a great university is a part of the program for the maintenance of efficient elementary rural schools, we shall be wasting our energies in a misguided endeavor.[5]

The idea of the organic unity of the entire system from elementary school to university has now become central in southern universities, as in all the western state universities.

In 1907 Rose accepted the position of general agent of the Peabody Education Fund. The appointed time for closing up the affairs of that Fund and establishing the permanent Peabody College had come, and for this his services were sought by the Board. In 1910 he became administrative secretary of the Rockefeller Sanitary Commission for the Eradication of the Hookworm and moved to Washington, but all the time he kept up the work for the cause of a great central teacher-training university at Nashville, founded on the Peabody Fund, and made a long fight for it. After he secured endowments from the State of Tennessee and the City of Nashville, to add to the principal of the Peabody Fund, the George Peabody College for Teachers, as told previously, was finally established in 1914.

When Rose was offered the presidency of this new college, he declined, to the great disappointment of his old pupils and friends, because he did not wish people to think that he had been working for himself, or run the risk of perpetuating the opposition which the contest had aroused. He never sought a position in his life and declined many. When offered the secretaryship of the Sanitary Commission he first declined it, saying he was unfit. Asked to consider it for twenty-four hours, he decided finally to accept the position because of its relations to the schools of the South, in which he was so much interested. In the meantime he was busy with many other things.

IDEAS AND METHODS OF WORK

Rose was a member of the Southern Education Board from 1909 until its dissolution in 1914 and was its executive secretary from 1909 to 1913. He was a trustee of the John F. Slater Fund for Negro Education from 1909 to 1923, a member of

[5] *Proceedings of the Sixth Conference for Education in the South, Richmond, Virginia, 1903*, pp. 188-89.

the General Education Board from 1910 to 1923 and its president from 1923 to 1928. He was general director of the International Health Board from 1914 to 1923 and became president of the International Education Board in 1923. It is amazing the amount of work he accomplished in these many positions. In all of them he labored whole-heartedly in the service of health, science, and education until his retirement in 1928.

It is impossible here to describe Rose's accomplishments in these many fields. But it will be instructive to consider some of his ideas and methods of work.

The application of private philanthropy to the problems of public health and preventive medicine was a new problem in the world. Rose was a pioneer in devising methods for doing this among many different people in different countries. That his methods were sound is proved by the results, which were almost uniformly successful.

His first principle was to enter a field only on the invitation of the government authorities, national, state, or municipal, and to coöperate with them as an integral part of the constituted health agencies. The appearance of meddling was thus avoided, and the existing official agencies were rendered more efficient and important.

A second principle was that the local authorities must contribute a part of the expense—one-half or more.

A preliminary survey of conditions in the territory to be served was always insisted upon. The Commission, as an outside agency, could help only as it aided the state to organize and develop the activity of its own forces. The interest of the local medical profession was, therefore, enlisted and local men trained to do the technical work. Through the schools and the press the people were educated to use the proper methods of sanitation and prevention. He believed in teaching the people through demonstrations.

Convinced that the promotion of the physical well-being of man is dependent upon the advancement of scientific knowledge, Rose advocated the founding of hygiene and public health departments in universities and the building of research laboratories and centers for training workers. He urged, as absolutely essential, the organization of state, city, and county boards of public health independent of politics and with adequate scientific staffs and equipment.

Rose recognized, moreover, that this plan would promote the advancement of scientific knowledge in the widest sense. He saw that sanitary work would open the way for scientific investigation in many fields and in many countries. He entered next, therefore, with great enthusiasm upon the work of the International Health Board. Writing to Robert C. Ogden on June 11, 1913, he says : "It is distinctly understood by the Commission that this work in foreign countries is to be taken up as the entering wedge to all other things that may follow later looking toward the improvement of human civilization."

SERVICE IN FOREIGN LANDS

This sanitary work proved, in fact, the "entering wedge" for a vast scientific and educational service for the Board to many foreign people. Following Page's introduction of Rose to the British authorities,[6] the Health Board met with cordial coöperation in British sanitary undertakings all the way from London to Hongkong. From the British Isles radiate cultural, educational, and scientific influences to every quarter of the globe. With the development of the new spirit of coöperation between the different dominions, dependencies, and Crown colonies, the home government has been able to promote in an increased measure public health and medical education in them. Hence the importance of developing in London the best form of training for health service.

It was Rose's business to direct the investigations of institutions or countries requesting aid in the development of science, education, or sanitation, to decide what should be done and what appropriations should be made, and then to coöperate with the local authorities in carrying out the plans agreed upon. In the performance of this task he traveled widely and resided in foreign countries for long periods. Everywhere he made fast friends and won the confidence of the government representatives.

Out of the International Health Board grew the International Education Board, founded in 1923 with Rose as president. As all material human progress depends on research in the pure sciences, the results of scientific discovery made in any country are to be shared freely with science workers in all countries.

[6] See above, p. 140.

As a means of promoting scientific research and international comity in the use of the discoveries, Rose planned to provide : First, assistance in raising capital sums to provide centers of scientific study at convenient places where they would be supported from national resources ; second, assistance in rehabilitating institutes of research formerly supported by international coöperation ; and third, fellowships for foreign study. "The migration of students in the interest of the advancement and dissemination of scientific knowledge." Carefully selected young scientists were given the opportunity to collaborate with workers in the same field in foreign countries and grants were made to help the institutes where they were received. Under this plan some fifty scientists were aided in their work and ten laboratories provided with equipment before 1930.

SCIENTIFIC INTERESTS

Rose was a marvelously versatile man. This characteristic is well illustrated by two great interests, beside his immediate educational interest—his plan for the establishment of an Oceanographic Institution to study the depths of the ocean and his plan to build a great new telescope to explore the universe above us.

By inquiries in Europe and Canada, he had developed the opinion that economic values of great importance were available in the ocean and that these problems, in which so many governmental agencies are concerned, rested upon a better knowledge of the sciences of the seas. He accordingly asked Dr. Frank Lillie of the University of Chicago to organize a committee of the National Academy of Sciences to deal with oceanography and to investigate the part that the United States of America should play in the development of a world-wide program. He secured funds for the work of this committee which he followed with interest.

Just before his retirement, he presented the plans to his Board with estimates of the expense of establishing an American institution of oceanography adequately equipped for work on the high seas. The result was the establishment of the Woods Hole, Massachusetts, Oceanographic Institution with building and endowment funds totaling three million dollars. Dr. Lillie became the director, and it began operations in the summer of 1931. Its vessel, the *Atlantis*, has already made several important explorations.

From this terrestrial subject Rose turned immediately to a celestial one. At the same time that he was investigating an institution to study the ocean he was studying the needs of the Wilson Observatory and the California Institute of Technology, which were to study the heavens. Dr. Robert A. Millikan, the president of the Institute, and Dr. George E. Hale, the director of the Observatory, tell us that Rose grasped at once the advantages of the coöperation they had organized between the Institute and the Observatory, realizing that the study of the enormous masses, temperatures, pressures, and velocities of celestial objects was as essential to the progress of physics and chemistry as the knowledge discovered by these sciences in the laboratory is to the interpretation of astronomical phenomena. He therefore gave hearty support to the proposition to establish a department under Dr. Thomas H. Morgan, to develop the various phases of mathematics, physics, chemistry, biology, and geology in accordance with a scheme involving close coöperation among all these sciences. Rose therefore approved also the proposal of the director and staff of the Observatory and the trustees of the Institute to form a coöperative scheme to carry out these investigations and immediately proposed the establishment for the further study of such problems, of a new Observatory under the auspices of the Institute, with a much larger instrument than the Hooker one-hundred-inch telescope on Mount Wilson. Says Dr. Millikan of the Institute :

Dr. Rose early saw the greatness of the opportunity which was here afforded, and, from the time of our first interview, . . . he exerted his influence in most constructive ways. His most remarkable quality was the boldness with which he grasped a great opportunity, and the energy with which he threw himself into the task of finding ways to get things done which he saw ought to be done. He has been one of the most potent influences . . . at work shaping the development of the California Institute of Technology. In making this statement I am not referring merely, nor primarily, to the securing of the needed funds. His judgment as to the direction in which it was best to move in order to meet the need and to realize the opportunity was just as important as his direct assistance in enabling us to obtain the necessary funds. He has undoubtedly been one of the most constructive forces in the development of the graduate and research institutions of the United States.[7]

The surprising proposal for both a new telescope and a greater laboratory was cordially approved by the president and executive committee of the Carnegie Institution of Washington, of which the Mount Wilson Observatory is a development. On the recommendation of Dr. Rose, who originated this plan for a greater telescope, the necessary funds to construct the instruments and build the Observatory were appropriated by the Rockefeller International Education Board on condition that the Institute provide the necessary endowment to carry on the work. The result is the erection of the new Observatory building in connection with the Institute and the construction of the unparalleled equipment for it.

CLOSING YEARS

To the regret of all his colleagues and friends throughout the world and to the great loss of the Rockefeller organizations, Wickliffe Rose retired on June 30, 1928. When, soon after the announcement of his purpose, the writer visited him and, finding him apparently well, protested against his giving up just at the time when he seemed to have reached the acme of his usefulness, his reply was, "I have reached the age when our rule requires that I should retire and I must obey the rule I helped to make." When asked then what he was going to do, he said : "I am going fishing. I have never had enough fishing in my life." He was going back to nature to rest for good. The summer of 1929 he spent fishing for salmon in Norway and Finland and the winter following in Southern France.

Deeply interested in the problem of world peace, he during his residence abroad took up the study of international economics in Paris and Berlin. He thought the fair adjustments of the economics of the nations would be the best foundation for peace. The winters he spent with his wife on the Riviera, in the Canary Islands, Morocco, Algiers, and Sicily. He was never idle, but wherever he was he continued to observe, to interview government officials, and to collect documents and information

[7] Letter of Dr. Robert A. Millikan, president of the California Institute of Technology, to the author, Feb. 1, 1932.

on the subjects in which he was interested. At the time of his death he was engaged in writing in French a series of papers on these problems.

While on a fishing trip on Vancouver Island in British Columbia with his old friend and associate, Dr. L. D. Fricks, medical director of the United States Public Health Service, on September 5, 1931, he died suddenly of heart disease. He knew of his weakness, but had told no one except his son. His end was peaceful and beautiful, just such an end, no doubt, as he desired.

Rose was a man of great native talent. He had remarkable powers of acquiring knowledge, of analyzing and classifying the facts learned, and of drawing conclusions. He was a rare combination of the scholar, investigator, philosopher, and administrator. Though not a technical scientist, for he had received very little practical training in laboratories, he thought in a scientific way and had no difficulty in dealing with scientific men in their own fields. He had a penetrating intelligence, which was able to extract from conflicting feelings and opinions sound principles of action.

In his administrative work, Rose had a calm faith in good causes, and tireless energy and devotion in working them out. When a certain course was decided upon, he would carry it through with courage and tenacity. His approach to every problem was scientific and he never entered on any new enterprise without having studied it fully. These methods, followed first in his work against hookworm disease, he applied later in making great plans for research in biology, chemistry, physics, and astronomy.

Dr. Hale gives us this characterization of Wickliffe Rose and his method of studying problems and advancing the sciences :

In my experience I have met very few men who comprehended as clearly as Dr. Rose did the interdependence of the various branches of knowledge and the consequent importance of cultivating them in close coöperation. His enthusiasm for our project and his willingness to do everything possible to assure its accomplishment were truly extraordinary.... I shall never forget his wholehearted sympathy ... and the cordial manner in which it was expressed. Such support as this is rarely experienced by men of science, who can therefore appreciate it to the full.... Dr. Rose felt

that the greatest need of the world is not more institutions. He preferred to concentrate his attention on the accomplishment of a comparatively few exceptional results rather than a large number of
lesser ones. This was through no lack of sympathy with the average
problems of everyday life. The solution of these problems, if I
correctly interpret his view, can be best accomplished by the establishment and development of exceptional institutions, out of which
leaders of thought and of action may be expected to come.[8]

Rose was a modest man, self-effacing and magnanimous in
giving others credit for good results and in taking blame upon
himself for failure. He was all kindness and consideration and
had a sympathetic understanding of the difficulties of others.
He had great constructive genius. He was a remarkable judge
of men and a good organizer. He had a large list of friends in
many lands and through them exerted extraordinary influence.
He helped in large measure to make the Rockefeller agencies
what they are, the most remarkable and successful organizations
for the advancement of education, science, and health that the
world has ever known.

Rose's services to education as teacher, and as trainer of
teachers, as agent of the Peabody Fund and real founder of the
George Peabody College, have been told. The scope and value
of his services to science, public health, and medicine cannot
be appraised yet, but that he laid the foundations for great
advance in knowledge is evident. His work will surely live after
him. As Mr. John D. Rockefeller, Jr., wrote to Mrs. Rose:
"Because of his modesty and self-effacement, the world will
never begin to know the importance and extent of the service
he has rendered humanity. Richly and usefully has he lived,
beautifully and gloriously did he die. His memory will ever
be a joy and an inspiration to those who were privileged to
know him."

[8] Letter of Dr. George E. Hale, of the Mount Wilson Observatory, to the
author, Jan. 27, 1932.

CHAPTER XIX

CONFERENCES AND EXCURSIONS

THE SEVENTH CONFERENCE, BIRMINGHAM, ALABAMA, 1904

THE annual meeting of the Conference for Education in the 'South was held in Birmingham on April 26-28, 1904. We may take Mr. Ogden's excursion to this meeting as an illustration of his methods. He brought from the North a company of eighty-four, which grew as he proceeded from place to place through the South. Stops were made at Hampton, Winthrop Normal College in Rock Hill, South Carolina, the Alabama Polytechnic Institute at Auburn, the Normal School at Troy, Tuskegee Institute, Montgomery, the Calhoun School, the University of Alabama, and the Girls' Industrial School at Montevallo.

Receptions were tendered to the party by the heads of the institutions and the citizens of the communities at each of these places, and brief meetings were held and addresses made by the visitors and their hosts. Following these meetings opportunity was provided for the men and women from the North and the South to mingle in conversation, which proved enlightening for the visitors and led to many enduring friendships. Friends of the institutions by the score met the company with their vehicles at the stations, and great cordiality and frequently hilarity characterized the meetings. At Calhoun a wagon with a great ox-team waited with the other vehicles. Ogden and a few favored friends rode to the hall behind the four big steers amidst the cheers of the assembled population. An old-fashioned, low-swung carriage, drawn by two mules, was assigned to the Right Reverend W. N. McVickar, Bishop of Rhode Island. When he entered it and stood up, the floor broke through. The mules started off, dragging the good bishop along in a very undignified position. He was promptly rescued and enjoyed the ludicrous situation with the others.

Samuel Crothers, the great preacher and essayist, here entertained an audience, almost solidly black, with inimitable humor. At the University of Alabama the company was welcomed by

President Abercrombie and a company of ladies. The addresses at the University were made by DeWitt Hyde of Bowdoin College, Maine, and Charles W. Dabney of the University of Tennessee. The *New York Tribune* report said : "Men from the North and the South spoke freely their opinions. They had by no means been in entire agreement heretofore, but their discussions have brought them to a closer understanding, and all were united in support of the fundamental doctrines of education for all men and equal justice for all men. The outspoken analysis of Southern conditions by Southern men and their readiness to face disagreeable facts was particularly noteworthy. President Dabney, ... son of a Confederate soldier, aroused enthusiasm when he urged Southern young men to emulate their fathers' virtues and heroism by devotion under the new conditions to the up-building of the South through the education of its people." [1]

At Birmingham the company, which had been increased by the presidents and principals of the various institutions visited en route, was welcomed by John Herbert Phillips and a committee on arrangements. The session of the Conference was called to order in the Jefferson Theatre at 8:00 P.M. on the 26th, before the largest audience that had ever assembled there. The Honorable T. G. Bush, representing the mayor of Birmingham, welcomed the members.

Mr. Ogden in his opening address appealed to the business men of the South to take more interest in public education, as the business men of Birmingham were doing, stating that it was most encouraging that in Birmingham, the great industrial center of the New South, business men were aiding largely in building up schools.

The meeting was saddened by the announcement of the death of Joseph B. Graham, the zealous and efficient agent of the Southern Board, who by his attractive personality and unselfish devotion had endeared himself to all the people and had given a great impulse to the movement.

Walter Hines Page spoke on "The Unfulfilled Ambition of the South." [2] His address was a frank discussion of the economic and educational errors of the southern states.

The chief topic of discussion at this meeting was the need of local taxation for schools in Alabama.

[1] May 3, 1904.   [2] See above, p. 242.

Professor H. O. Murfee, of Marion, Alabama, made a philosophical argument for local taxation. He took exception to the customary statement that the situation of public education in the South was due to slavery and aristocracy, and contended that the chief cause of this depression of public education was in the lack of a system of support and control. "Supported and controlled by the remote power of the State," he said, "public schools have come to be regarded as eleemosynary institutions, ... which are never held in high esteem among a free and independent people.... The low esteem in which public schools have been held in the South is not due to a spirit of arrogant aristocracy. It is due to the belief that the education of our children should never be delegated to an authority too obscure and a power too remote. When public education is entrusted to the people, when the people perceive that they possess the sovereign power of support and the saving grace of control, then will public education become each citizen's private concern and each Christian's religious obligation." [3]

Bishop Charles B. Galloway of Mississippi made an address on the Negro question, which was published in the *Proceedings*.[4]

THE EIGHTH CONFERENCE, COLUMBIA, SOUTH CAROLINA, 1905

At the Columbia Conference for Education in the South, April 26-28, 1905, Mr. Ogden and his speakers made a point of meeting some of the misunderstandings which had been expressed in the newspapers regarding the purposes and plans of the work of the Conference.

South Carolina had been the source from which most of the misunderstandings of the movement had been disseminated. The addresses at Columbia were therefore planned in part to remove these misunderstandings as far as possible. In his opening address, Mr. Ogden explained again the origin and purposes of the Conference and of the organization of the Southern Board. "With the fourth year at Winston-Salem," he said, "the Conference found itself. The ringing words of Curry, Dabney, Dickerman, Aycock, McIver, and others, presented a panorama of appealing conditions that kindled a flame of earnestness

[3] *Proceedings of the Seventh Conference for Education in the South, Birmingham, Ala., 1904*, pp. 114-17.
[4] *Ibid.*, pp. 27-38.

which burns with more warmth and brilliance each passing
year.... In November of 1901 the Southern Education Board
was created under most interesting circumstances. Six of the
eight original members were Southern men by birth or residence. By simple and forceful methods a systematic campaign
for education was inaugurated that stretched from the Potomac
to beyond the Mississippi, and from the Ohio to the seaboard.
... It is simply the evangel of the public school, carrying forward persistently a campaign for popular education, striving to
awaken in the minds, especially of rural communities, a knowledge of educational needs, a longing for improved conditions
and a willingness to pay by contribution, taxation, or both, for
the advantages which are the right of American childhood. In
this appeal no voice other than that of the Southern men has
been heard....

"This movement came...at the psychological moment.
Throughout this Southland ... many ... well-informed and soli-
tary souls were brooding over the needy conditions of certain
localities with which experience had made them painfully
familiar. And with the perception of need was associated a conscious helplessness and vague, indefinite hopefulness.

"Nor was this condition of mind solely confined to the
isolated.... Men of large public affairs, women socially prominent, were both equally anxious...to help. Here a voice had
been raised, there a little local effort had started, and beyond
this the prophets were beginning both persuasion and prevision.
Then followed an awakening of the earnest and anxious thinkers. A strength of association was promptly created. Symptoms
of many sorts indicated the educational epiphany that has
commanded the admiration and respect of educators throughout
the land." [5]

President George H. Denny made an address aimed at removing misconceptions which had led to the opposition. He
first recalled the fact that his predecessor, President William L.
Wilson, of Washington and Lee University, formerly congressman and member of the cabinet of President Cleveland—and
there was no more devoted southerner in the South—had been
one of the leaders in founding the Conference and had given
"freely the sympathy of his great heart and the thought of his

[5] *Proceedings of the Eighth Conference for Education in the South*,
Columbia, S. C., 1905, pp. 9-11.

great mind to the men and women who through the Conference are endeavoring to serve their country, until he was laid to rest ... almost under the shadow of the spot where the Conference was born," at Capon Springs, West Virginia.[6] An abstract of this address is given above.[6a]

THE RAILROAD ACCIDENT

Miss Emily K. Herron, of Hampton Institute, who was on the train, tells of the accident to Mr. Ogden's party following the Columbia Conference. Mr. Ogden's train left Columbia about midnight bound for Biltmore, North Carolina, to visit the estate of Mr. George Vanderbilt. About eight o'clock in the morning, as this special train was nearing Greenville, there came a crash. The train had collided with a switching freight train.

Dr. Julius D. Dreher says he was sitting by Mrs. Thorpe (the daughter of Longfellow) in the dining-car when they found themselves dropping through the car to the ground. He gave her his arm and escorted her to a seat on a pile of ties where the company had gathered. Mr. St. Clair McKelway, editor of the *Brooklyn Eagle*, who had been an almost constant attendant upon the Conferences and a devoted supporter of its work, though seriously injured, crept from under the wreck and a moment later was sitting on a trunk writing a telegram to his paper. For the majority of the party it was an almost miraculous escape. The baggage car was smashed to flinders and the trunks thrown hither and thither. Five railroad men were badly injured. Immediately after the wreck the splintered cars caught fire and the baggage and parlor cars, the smoker and two dining-cars were completely destroyed. All the baggage was ruined.

Mr. Ogden, who was overwhelmed with solicitation for his guests, came forward immediately and checked off the list of his passengers, to see if they were all safe. Amid the scene which distressed him more than any one else, he showed the same superb ability which characterized him on all occasions. He immediately made note of the damage done to the baggage, took the business up with the railroad officials, and saw that every one was paid for the losses incurred. The people of

[6] *Ibid.*, p. 15.   [6a] See p. 49.

Greenville efficiently succored the injured company. The plans for an extended trip were immediately abandoned, and before evening Mr. Ogden had a complete new train ready to take his company back North.

THE NINTH CONFERENCE, LEXINGTON, KENTUCKY, 1906

The next Conference was at Lexington, Kentucky, May 2-4, 1906. Mr. Ogden brought with him again a large delegation of ladies and gentlemen from the North, and there were hundreds of school officials and citizens from all over the South. They were most hospitably received and entertained by the people of Lexington, so noted for their kindness and social grace.

An amusing editorial in the local paper did not reflect the real spirit of the people. The races were on during the same days as the Conference. It is well known how Kentucky people love horses and how long they have been educated in this popular sport. For two days out of three the races had occupied the attention of the citizens. An editorial headed "The Educational Conference" starts out by saying : "The race meeting was successful from every standpoint, the sport good, the weather perfect. . . . The people of the Blue Grass showed by their attendance at the race meeting that the love of a horse race is still potent in Central Kentucky." Following this in the same column was a notice of the Conference meeting.

There was a meeting of the state superintendents, with reports from the different states and a discussion of compulsory school attendance. The chief feature of the meeting was the discussion of education for rural life, which was led by Dr. James W. Robertson, of Canada, known in his country as the "Agricultural Wizard of the North." "The rural schools should be brought into touch with rural life," he said. "They should not be wholly apart from the home, a place for books only, but they should be for training also by means of tangible objects. . . . Education is a series of experiences leading up to the possession of certain powers. It leads from helplessness of body into ability of body, and therefore it should include bodily training" and all kinds of real work. A child should be trained to be useful to the community. He is "a coming citizen, . . . one unit in the eternal procession of the human race out of the depths of animalism, and the degradation of ignorance, ... into the glory of a perfect civilization." [7]

An interesting event of the meeting was an address by Miss Martha Berry of the Berry School, of Rome, Georgia. Knowing her reputation for eloquence, Mr. Ogden, after introducing her in his usual gracious manner, gave her a gentle hint that the time was limited and that she must use only ten minutes. Miss Berry commenced her address by giving an account of the history of her school; how she first collected at a place called "Possum Trot" a few children in a log cabin for a Sunday School and taught them to read, and how the great school grew out of it, step by step, until it became the big institution it is today for the education of mountain boys and girls and their training to work. Thus she became known as the "Sunday Lady from Possum Trot." The audience gave her rapt attention and manifested its delight by frequent applause. When Miss Berry continued past the time limit and the chairman gave her a delicate hint, her hearers protested vociferously, calling on her to go on. After she had been speaking somewhat longer a terrible rain-storm descended upon the roof of the wooden building, making such a noise that she could scarcely be heard. Still she continued and finally conquered the rain-storm also. It was a delightful experience for her hearers who became the friends of the "Lady of Possum Trot" and her school.

THE TENTH CONFERENCE, PINEHURST, NORTH CAROLINA, 1907

The Tenth session was held at Pinehurst, North Carolina, beginning April 9, 1907.

On account of ill health, the great leader, Mr. Ogden, could not be present. It was the first Conference that he did not attend with a company. To Dr. Samuel C. Mitchell, the vice-president, he wrote: "It is a painful and unwelcome task to give you official notice that it will be impossible for me to attend the Tenth Conference for Education in the South, which will assemble at Pinehurst, North Carolina, on Tuesday, the 9th inst.... My personal disappointment ... is proportionate to my faith and hope in what will be accomplished on the present occasion. The extraordinary progress in many directions is full

[7] *Proceedings of the Ninth Conference for Education in the South, Lexington, Ky., 1906,* p. 106.

of inspiration. The great undone margin is a challenge to self-sacrifice and lofty endeavor." In conclusion of his letter Mr. Ogden requested to be permitted to retire from the office of president which, of course, the members declined to concur in.

Dr. Mitchell opened the discussion with an address on "The Task of the Neighborhood." Dr. Edgar Gardner Murphy, the executive secretary, presented a valuable history of the Conferences for the past ten years.

A session was chiefly devoted to the subject of the high schools. President James H. Kirkland spoke of "The High School and the University." Mr. W. H. Hand told of the work for secondary education in South Carolina, and Dr. Bruce R. Payne of high school progress in Virginia.

At a business meeting resolutions were adopted in appreciation of the life and services of Dr. Charles Duncan McIver, one of the earliest and greatest workers in the cause, who had passed away since the last meeting. Chivalrous in his respect for womanhood, and convinced that "no State which will educate its mothers need have any fear about future illiteracy," his first great accomplishment was "the creation of a college for the training of teachers and the higher education of women, an enduring monument erected at public expense and consecrated by his devotion to the public service of his native state. ... Other states eagerly sought his assistance. And every appeal for help, whether from his own beloved South, or from the North, or from the West, was answered to the limit of his strength." [8]

Another session was devoted to the education of the farmer and was addressed by Dr. Knapp and Dr. Liberty Hyde Bailey of Cornell. Mr. T. O. Sandy reported on "Farm Improvement in Virginia." Honorable Josephus Daniels of North Carolina concluded the session with an earnest plea for more and better public schools.

Dr. Knapp's paper has been noted above.[9] Dr. Bailey's paper discussed the organization of the affairs of rural life. The city, he said, has developed greatly because of the improvement of communication and the effectiveness of the education and entertainment provided. The country people are, therefore,

[8] *Proceedings of the Tenth Conference for Education in the South, Pinehurst, N. C., 1907*, pp. 160-61.

[9] See p. 000.

looking to the city more and more for these things and "I am wondering whether the time will not come when we shall endeavor to improve and redirect the common schools and provide some of the good old country entertainments and games. . . . The rural school needs fundamental re-direction." This does not mean a new curriculum but it means that all subjects should be taught in the terms of the environment. Illustrating this he said :

Geography is the surface of the earth. It may well concern itself with the school grounds, the highways, the fields and what grow in them, the forests, hills and streams, the hamlet, the people and their affairs. When I began to study geography, it was a ballooning process. I began up in the air somewhere off in the universe and gradually dropped down to the solar system until I reached the earth. When I landed on the earth it was in South America and Asia. I learned about the anacondas and boa constrictors of South America and the lions and tigers of the old world jungles. I never learned anything about the pigs and chickens on our farms. . . . All this, of course, is rapidly changing. We are now interesting the child in the earth on which he stands, and as his mind grows we take him out to the larger view. A good part of geography in a rural community should be agriculture, whether so-called or not. Geography can be so re-organized and so re-directed as in ten years to revolutionize the agriculture of any State. . . .

So we . . . need a re-direction in rural government, . . . a more active and compact government, . . . and to give more attention to the rural churches. They consist chiefly of a preaching room and a vestibule. They have changed very little within two generations. Concerned in too many cases with technical religion, formal piety . . . empty social duties, the country church lacks the activity and real connection with life to appeal to . . . the strong personalities in its community.[10]

The business of the Conference had become very extensive and complicated. The meeting heard reports from the field directors of the Southern Education Board on citizens organizations, schoolhouses, school libraries, consolidation, rural high schools, industrial education, supervision, compulsory laws, the school as an educational center, and work for Negroes. There was a wide and long discussion. Attendance at the meetings

[10] *Ibid.*, pp. 202-5, 207.

numbered 347, besides nine members of the Southern Education Board and many teachers and visitors who did not register.

The Eleventh Conference, Memphis, Tennessee, 1908

In Memphis on April 22, 1908, the Eleventh Conference was welcomed by General Luke E. Wright, one time governor of the Philippines, who spoke of the absolute importance of universal education, judging from his experience. "The grave problems which tremendously affect our political, economic and social life ... can only be solved through the intelligent, educated judgment of our people.... Fortunately they are coming to understand as never before, that through wise legislation and the united efforts of all citizens ... there should be a steady evolution in our system of schools."

The session was happy to greet its great president, Mr. Ogden, again. He was deeply moved by the cordial welcome given him.

The state superintendents' meeting was an important one. Superintendent Joseph D. Eggleston discussed high school; Mr. O. B. Martin spoke of school funds; and Professor J. J. Doyne discussed supervision; Professor J. S. Stewart presented a paper on teacher training.

The Honorable J. B. Aswell, state superintendent of Louisiana, discussed county supervision: "The school system," he said, "is an organism, not a dead thing into which the child must fit. It is an organism that breathes and feels and lives and thinks and loves. It is composed of school boards and people and children and schoolhouses and benches and other things; but it is a living organism that has a head and a brain. The question ... is, Who will be this professional head of the school systems of this country? ... In some places the school board is the head,—or thinks it is—a deformed head ... of from five to nine members, each disjointed from the other.... Mark Twain, you remember, said that the Lord, in His infinite wisdom, ... first created fools; He did that for practice, and He then created school boards.... Do not misunderstand me. The school board is an important factor ...; but ... it is not and cannot be the initiative force; it cannot do the things professionally that must be done for the schools." But conditions are changing. We are gradually getting professional school superintendents and supervisors. The tax payers are turning to trained school men and women for the supervision of their schools.

A discussion of compulsory education was led by Dr. Wickliffe Rose. The argument for compulsory education, he said, may be presented either from the philosophic point of view or from the practical. Differences of opinion about it arise from our different conceptions of the rights of individuals and the meaning of education. If we set up the abstract that the individual is entitled to a life divorced from society we have no right to educate him. On the other hand, if we conceive of a man as by nature a part of the human organism we call society, we have the right to educate him. As a matter of fact, no individual is or can be divorced from the social organism from which he springs and in which he lives.[11]

Others who discussed the subject of compulsory education were Edwin Craighead, editor of the Mobile, Alabama, *Register*, Honorable Clarence Poe of North Carolina, Professor W. H. Hand of South Carolina, and Dr. J. H. Phillips of the Birmingham schools. Dr. Henry S. Pritchett discussed the subject of "Industrial Education" to the great enlightenment of the members.

The Conference felt greatly honored by the presence of Honorable James Bryce, the ambassador of Great Britain. Mr. Ogden in introducing him said : "We cannot help thinking of the author of *The American Commonwealth* as, in a sense, an American himself, although he represents officially our great sister country." Ambassador Bryce surprised his audience by saying that he had been reading the records of these Conferences and was much interested in them. His address was on "Popular Education and National Efficiency." "We in England, when in 1870 we passed an act providing schools all over the kingdom, hoped at first to avoid the necessity of having to apply compulsion by law, but after the experience of several years, we were convinced that it was necessary to apply that compulsion. . . . Accordingly, we passed a compulsory act, and we appointed school attendance committees, . . . to see that the act was enforced. . . . We have succeeded . . . on the whole very satisfactorily. The only difficulty is with . . . the waifs and stray population of the cities. . . . Nevertheless, . . . we are stead-

[11] An extract from this speech appears in the preceding chapter.

ily reducing the proportion of non-attendance, and we have now brought down illiteracy . . . to a very small percentage." He explained the sources from which the schools are supported in England, namely, partly out of local taxation levied on the parish and partly out of the revenue of the state paid from the public exchequer. It was found that this plan had two advantages, just as we had found in America : It enlists the local interest and it gives the state authority for supervision and interference, if necessary. The state lays down certain conditions to which every school must conform if it is to receive its share of the state grant. Supervision is by a central authority and its power of keeping the schools up to the mark is a valuable feature. The schools are controlled by a school committee, an elective body, which imposes the local taxation and appoints the teachers. In the case of city schools, "we have a body of persons called managers"—a small number, five to seven residents of the neighborhood, who are appointed to look after the daily working of the schools. They receive no salary. Women are usually the most useful members of these bodies. In the country, there are two sets of schools, the primary or elementary schools, which give instruction up to the age of twelve or thirteen, and the high schools or secondary schools for children between the ages of fifteen and sixteen. The British, he said, were comparatively backward with high schools but were developing more of them as they recognized their enormous importance in the educational system of the country. "Our secondary schools . . . are not universally free, as yours are. . . . There are fees to these schools. If there is a child of superior intelligence and diligence and . . . its parents are too poor to . . . pay the fees of the secondary school, . . . we arrange to give it . . . a scholarship."

There has been a great awakening, he said, in Britain on the subject of teachers and their preparation. The idea of giving teachers a certain amount of preparation and professional training did not come to us as early as to you. "I have no doubt that special preparation is valuable, but I want to remind you . . . that special preparation will not be enough to make a good teacher unless the good teacher has had a superior fundamental education himself." He must have had a great deal more than to be somewhat ahead of his pupils.

"Democracies need leaders just as much as, perhaps more

than, any other government does. The larger number there are of people who vote, the greater is the need that the leader ... shall be a wise man, a man in whom the voters may put their trust. ... I venture to say, therefore, that there is no country in which high schools—schools that give men the best kind of education and fit them for the world of public life ... —there is no country in which such men and schools ... are more needed than in a free country like yours or like England." [12]

THE TWELFTH CONFERENCE, ATLANTA, GEORGIA, 1909

The Twelfth meeting of the Conference was held at Atlanta, April 14-16, 1909. It was decided to make the keynote of the Conference, the improvement of conditions in the open country, and addresses were fortunately obtained from President Van Hise, of the University of Wisconsin, and from Dr. John Lee Coulter of the University of Minnesota. Mr. Ogden conducted his usual excursion of northern gentlemen and ladies to the Atlanta meeting. They were welcomed by Governor Hoke Smith before a large and enthusiastic audience. Mr. Ogden made an unusually happy address in which he described some of the progress made during the year. Dr. Samuel C. Mitchell made the opening address on "The American Spirit in Education"—public in support, civic in motive, scientific in method, and national in scope, social in its effects and moral in its ideals. It promotes reverence for the law, enriches the heart, vitalizes the will and makes the conscience responsive to duty.

The Conference was honored by the presence of Dr. Elmer Ellsworth Brown, United States commissioner of education, who discussed the national program of education of his Bureau. He gave a historical survey of the educational activity of the Federal government; of its policy in making grants in annual installments to encourage certain forms of education in the states. He stressed the need for the coöperation of the states and the nation in making educational systems which shall be strong enough to meet the demands that modern society makes upon the schools.

The state of Texas, which was never visited by the Conference, organized a conference for education of its own, and

[12] *Proceedings of the Eleventh Conference for Education in the South,* Memphis, Tenn., 1908, pp. 93-103.

Mr. Clarence Ousley, of the *Fort Worth Record*, president of the Conference for Education in Texas, made an interesting report of its work, which, following along the lines of the General Southern Conference, was going far ahead of it in many directions.

Professor Charles L. Coon, of North Carolina, presented at this meeting his paper on "Public Taxation and the Negro Schools," the result of investigations commenced while at the Bureau of Investigation and Information of the Southern Education Board at the University of Tennessee and completed in the Department of Education of North Carolina. His conclusions were interesting and new to all. The first one was that "upon a fair division of the present school funds [of that time] of the three States under consideration [1909, North Carolina, Georgia, Virginia], the negro would likely fare as well as he does at present. In the absence of such division I am confident, whether my figures are absolutely accurate or not, that any one who takes the pains to ascertain the present sources of the public school funds of these States and then tries to make a fair division of them between the races will come to the conclusion that the negro school is not very much of a white man's burden in at least three States.... And, in view of the facts set for these three States, will the white man be able to maintain successfully that he pays nearly all the cost of the negro public schools in these States?" Professor Coon thought that these conclusions were probably true of all the other southern states. Another interesting conclusion was that if all the Negro children of these states were white, it would cost just about five times as much to give them the same amount of education they were then getting. With regard to the economic importance of the Negro he showed that whereas in 1891 the Negroes of North Carolina listed only $8,000,000 of property for taxation; in 1908 they listed nearly $22,000,000, an increase of 170 per cent in seventeen years. The property listed by whites in the same period increased only about 90 per cent. In other words, Negro property increased nearly twice as much as white property during these seventeen years. He found that about the same was true of Georgia, where the ratio of increase for Negro property maintained a rate more than twice that of white property. "Such facts give us glimpses of the economic importance of the negro and justify us in hoping that the senseless race prejudice which has for its object the intellectual enslavement of negro children will soon pass away. I do not believe that any superior race can hope for the blessing of heaven on its own children while it begrudges more light and efficiency for those of an inferior race." [13]

The betterment of the conditions of rural life was an interesting subject of discussion by Honorable Gifford Pinchot, chief of the Bureau of Forestry of the United States, who explained how the national government may coöperate with the states. Dr. Coulter of the University of Minnesota discussed the reorganization of rural life. He urged farmers to deal with the "product of a year's labor as a stock of goods which can be converted into a visible supply at will.... In order that this may be done, intelligent sorting,...grading and storing are essential."

At a great reception given by the local committees of Atlanta Mr. Ogden was presented with a loving cup by Mr. J. K. Orr, chairman of the Executive Committee. Among other things, he said : "When the history of the last two decades is written, Mr. Ogden will be counted among its great statesmen. No scheme for helping a people in time of need was ever more generously devised or executed with greater delicacy of feeling ...for all concerned than he has carried out."

THE THIRTEENTH CONFERENCE, LITTLE ROCK, ARKANSAS, 1910

The Conference crossed the Mississippi River for the first, and only time, when it went to Little Rock, Arkansas, to hold its thirteenth meeting April 6-8, 1910. This Conference included the members of the various coöperative associations, of the School Improvement Leagues, and of the Association of Southern State Superintendents, which had been separately organized for several years in the past. It was, therefore, one of the largest conferences held. The total number of persons registered was 1,518. The central theme of the Conference meetings was again "The Rural School and Its Work" and "Agricultural, Home Economics and Health Education in the Elementary Schools, High Schools and Normal Schools."

In his opening address, Mr. Ogden, in explaining the pur-

---

[13] *Proceedings of the Twelfth Conference for Education in the South, Atlanta, Ga., 1909,* pp. 157-67.

poses and plans of the Southern Education Board, called attention to the fact that it had been in operation nearly ten years and gave some general facts about the results of its work during these years. Current expenses for public education in the southern states had increased, since 1900, 150 per cent; the value of school property, 200 per cent; expenditures on normal schools and other means of professional education, 200 per cent; appropriations for state universities and other institutions of higher education, 100 per cent; high school facilities in cities and towns, 100 per cent, and in villages and rural districts, 400 per cent. The average length of the school term had increased from 20 to 25 per cent in the whole South. Since there was little or no increase in the term in the cities, this meant an increase of 30 per cent in the rural districts. In some states the term of the rural schools had increased from 40 to 50 per cent. The average monthly salaries of teachers increased from 30 to 50 per cent and the annual salaries about 70 per cent. The salaries of county superintendents had been doubled. Much progress had been made in adapting the courses of study to the needs of the people through instruction in agriculture, industrial arts, and domestic science. More than half of the states had reorganized their courses for the elementary schools. Georgia had established eleven; Arkansas, four; Virginia, several county agricultural schools; and Alabama had doubled the appropriations for her nine agricultural schools. Summer schools at the universities had been multiplied and extended. Kentucky, Virginia, and Tennessee had educational commissions making surveys and plans for the better organization and coördination of their schools. With the help of the Southern Education Board and the Peabody Fund, several states had employed agents for the rural schools. The organizations of women for school improvement had multiplied greatly and were doing much toward making better and more attractive schoolhouses and grounds. The literature on public education put out in the states had increased vastly and was having great influence in developing public opinion in favor of public schools.

The discussions at the meeting were devoted to the rural schools and the methods to be used in teaching agriculture and home economics.

The Little Rock Conference was a significant one. It revealed great progress both in public sentiment favorable to universal public education and in the development of institutions putting it into effect. Dr. St. Clair McKelway, vice-president of the University of the State of New York, who had attended these Conferences for ten years, in an editorial in the *Brooklyn Eagle* (April 24, 1910) described this change in public opinion in the South :

The South is proving itself to be the prophetic force of the nation and is becoming its conservative bulwark—the prophetic force, because it is finding in education of the people, on lines that are marked by a relation to usefulness, a solution of what we of the North call economic or psychological "issues" or "problems." . . .

The South has passed from speculation to conduct ; from the discussion of "State rights" to the consideration of state needs. It is now not "arguing" the constitutional question of "powers." It is regarding the impact of duties. It is recognizing the right way of meeting and doing them. The time when every lawyer was a statesman, every clergyman a moral dictator and every doctor an oracle has been exchanged for a better time. "The schoolmaster is abroad" and is everywhere in evidence. He is a very practical schoolmaster. He is instructing the Negro in thrift, home making, soil tilling and soil ownership. He is instructing the whites, especially the young of their number, in the art and need of trades, organizations and systems.

. . . Realization of the reciprocal needs of the two races has come. The humble and weak cannot be the only injured. That fact of itself will pull down the stronger as well as the weaker. Neither race stands or falls by itself or of itself alone. The black man and the white man cannot be separated from responsibility for and need of one another. Distinct like the billows, yet one like the sea, the two constitute and comprise the collective South. While each man, white or black, must bear his own burden, he must also do what he can to lighten the load of the other.

This is the doctrine Robert C. Ogden spoke to the conference at Little Rock. With this the press of the South fills its columns of counsel, today. With this, the more than one thousand educators, official and unofficial, state, county, city and rural, women and men, from every part of the South and massed in Little Rock, filled and thrilled their wise words at the Conference. . . . It was not a revival or a renaissance. It was a new creation with the strength of a new faith and with the heat and heart of a new fire. The progress it attests, the steps it vindicates, the results it assures and will certainly conserve and augment supply reasons from which to take courage and for which to thank God.

THE FOURTEENTH CONFERENCE, JACKSONVILLE, FLORIDA, 1911

The Fourteenth Conference for Education in the South was held at Jacksonville in April, 1911. Mr. Robert C. Ogden, permanent president since its beginning, presided. The interests of the rural population were the chief themes and the meeting gave further impulse to the movement for better rural schools. The Conference heard valuable papers from Count Carl Moltke, minister to the United States from Denmark, who discussed the Danish system of People's Schools; from the minister from Switzerland, Dr. Paul Ritter, on education in Switzerland; and from Mr. John Christian Bay on the unique and interesting "Folk High Schools of the Scandinavian Countries."

Dr. H. B. Frissell spoke of Sir Horace Plunkett's work in Ireland. Professor E. C. Branson read a paper on "Our Country Life Problem," in which he discussed the menaces and the remedies—farm tenancy, landless and migratory folk, their poverty and its causes. As defenses and cures he pleaded for schools better adapted to country life, for churches that take more interest in agricultural life, for improved highways, for coöperative enterprises, all based on farm ownership.[14]

THE FIFTEENTH CONFERENCE, NASHVILLE, TENNESSEE, 1912

The Fifteenth Annual Conference was one of the most powerful ever held. It met on the third, fourth and fifth days of April, 1912, at Nashville, Tennessee. Mr. Ogden made a statement of the financial results of the campaign in the past ten years. He said: "I apologize for venturing upon this drowsy subject. It is a question of taxes. How much taxation can you stand? Patience is the tax which the ungodly collect from the godly, and I will put your godliness to the test by a brief statement of a few facts relating to the accomplishments of the Southern Education Board in getting people to tax themselves during these last six years. . . . The territory is the eleven former Confederate states from Virginia to Louisiana. . . . The total sum . . . is an increase in the taxation and appropriation for education during the period of 1904-1910 of $51,500,000. . . . Each year adds to this annual increase. The increase last year was $18,-

14 *Proceedings of the Fourteenth Conference for Education in the South, Jacksonville, Florida, 1911.*

ooo,ooo.... The plans of the Board did not raise all this money, but nothing is included that the ... labor of the Board did not either originate or make possible.... But what are the people getting out of this increased expenditure? For the last two years the ... most interesting activity of the ... Board has been the supervision of the rural elementary schools. Capable school men ... have been employed in all the states to carry instruction and encouragement to the lonely teachers in the country districts.... These supervisors are organized and they are here for conference.... You will hear from them.... Let me illustrate by one state. Mr. T. J. Coates, supervisor of Kentucky, ... 'in the year 1910 the State of Kentucky expended $3,000,000 upon her rural public schools, and one third of it was paid to young teachers without experience or previous training.' This is monumental folly, or would be, if better teachers could be had." Coates made plans for the reform of this.

Continuing, Mr. Ogden showed that there was a marvellous uplift in this rural school work. The supervisors were all enthusiasts ; and their influence was revealed in the increased enrollment and attendance. While the aggregate showed an increase in the schools, there was a falling off in the rural schools because the towns were drawing continually on the country.

He told how the service of the women of the School Improvement Leagues had been fine also. Their beneficence moved quietly, but as surely as the forces of nature. The Coöperative Education Association of Virginia, of which Mrs. B. B. Munford was president and Mrs. L. R. Dashiell director of Citizens' Leagues, included "the regeneration and beautifying of the schoolhouse and grounds, ... cultivating vegetables, ... and even the creation of tennis courts and ball grounds. Included in this reform are the giving up ... of one-room schoolhouses, consolidation of schools, transportation of school children ..., building of new and better schoolhouses by ... popular subscriptions ..., voluntary voting of taxes and issuing of bonds. In all this pulsating harmony comes ... the refrain concerning the lack of teachers properly trained for the great trust of educating young Americans as citizens of our great national experiment in democracy....

"I am asked about the sources of the funds for this work." These educational associations and leagues raise a large part of their money and spend it themselves. For a number of years the Board has supplied means for crusades in different states on behalf of the local tax. Every man voting for it becomes thus a contributor to these local state taxes which have increased to $1,200,000 in North Carolina. In other states the taxes are levied by counties and the amounts are not known. Voluntary gifts to schools have been very numerous. Three years ago in Virginia the sum was $28,000, of which $16,000 was given by Negroes. Last year one state reported $33,000, another $65,000, another over $11,000, all raised at home for home uses.

"Eleven years ago at the Winston-Salem Conference, Dr. Charles William Dabney, then President of the University of Tennessee, now the honored President of the University of Cincinnati, made a powerful presentation of the real conditions of illiteracy in these eleven Southern States. He told the plain truth and was soundly abused for his honesty. . . . The work of eleven years has somewhat modified, but has not entirely changed the facts he gave. On the objective side the story would read like a wondrous fairy tale ; on the subjective side pitiful and sad and yet full of encouragement and hope. . . . One of the hopeful items is the personal uplift that has come to great numbers of people through association with others of similar aspirations concerning the lack of proper educational facilities for the plain people. Thus they entered into the conscious fellowship of the great spiritual democracy. The fellowship that is above and beyond all creeds and confessions, includes Jew and Gentile, Protestant and Catholic, Heathen and Christian ; that cannot find any dark spot on this earth so dark that it does not contain an element of human sympathy, a fellowship including all who . . . have an earnest desire to assist some fellow beings toward a better and happier life.

"We are here in the interest of our common country and our common humanity by the command of the little child. The humbler and more needy the child the more absolute is the command. We are here in obedience to the spirit of holy service that marks the noblest religious expression of the expanding period. If we bring our best and most mature attainment to the service of the child, we will create the highest blessings for which this Conference stands." [15]

[15] *Proceedings of the Fifteenth Conference for Education in the South, Nashville, Tenn., 1912*, pp. 13-26.

This was Mr. Ogden's last utterance at the last Conference he attended.

President Edwin A. Alderman, of the University of Virginia, spoke on the university and the public schools. He named the steps to be realized. Education must be made universal in a genuine sense ; it must be made compulsory in a just and genuine sense ; it must be made vocational to the extent that the 98 per cent of human beings who must live by the work of their hands shall do so with skill and intelligence ; it must be made coöperative, so that perfect understanding and articulation shall exist between all its parts ; and lastly, in order that this may be done, all universities should systematically undertake university extension work in order to discover the state as a field of service and to reveal themselves as the servants of the state.

Dr. Walter Hines Page told of a scheme for farmers' credit. He took a country neighborhood adjacent to a small town in one of our southern states and made an inquiry for the purpose of finding out the economic condition of every human unit in it—that is, of every family. The inquiry showed that there were only eleven who had bank accounts in the adjacent town, two who were supposed to have bank accounts in the city near by, and forty who could borrow small sums on their land from money-lenders or from a bank. And this accounted for only about half the people. Still this is a prosperous farming community. How about the other 50 per cent who have no credit, no way to borrow money? They are below the credit line. When one is below the credit line he must borrow at an unreasonable rate of interest. More than half had not capital enough to do their work passably well. These men organized credit associations so as to make every one of them responsible for the debts of every other one. "Why do these men become good creditors when they are bound together? Because every one is interested in every other one's success. . . . The land and the men—these are the bases of life. God has made the land more capable than we ever dreamed of. . . . It yields riches in proportion to the character and skill of the men who cultivate it. . . . The sand-hills of the South . . . were given away for a fraction of a dollar an acre for taxes. I have seen that country yield sixty bushels of corn and one and one-half bales of cotton to the acre by fertilization and culture. We want the right kind of man on the soil and some capital to help him. The financial organization of our society is based ... on privileges, on class distinction and advantage. Though a poor man I can borrow ... because I have a certain respectability. Many men my equals in capacity for labor cannot borrow a dollar, because they lack that quality.... What we call democracy, we have not yet applied to our economic life. So far it means chiefly equality of opportunity in politics, in the ... conduct of government, and ... opportunity for education. *It does not mean an equal economic chance.*"

Now to apply these remarks. "We believe that the extension of opportunity, the spread of democracy, the willingness to give other men the same chance you have yourself, is the most important truth for social and economic progress. To you, therefore, educators and scientific men, I make an appeal to direct your thought to the application of democracy to the economic condition of our country.... We believe in giving the utmost opportunity that can be given to every man without exception.... If you believe this, your labor will bring to pass not only a living country school and a living country church, but a living country man. If any of these things seem radical to you today, be sure they will be conservative tomorrow." [16]

Chancellor David F. Houston of Washington University, St. Louis, discussed the "Rural School a National Failure." Though in the last thirty years, he said, the wealth of this nation has reached a figure which the mind cannot grasp and the South has made great strides in the expenditures in town and city schools, the citizen of the country is prohibited from spending as much for the education of his children as the citizen of the town spends. Does any rational person fear that any body of people anywhere will tax itself too much for education? Is it not time to wipe from our statutes and constitutions many absurd restrictions against progressive measures? "I concur heartily in the declaration of a distinguished North Carolinian that the ... constitution is the most ingenious instrument ever designed for obstructing human progress.... Three things constitute a source of wonder to me—first, why ... rural teachers continue to teach ; second, why communities continue to employ them on any terms ; and third, why a man who has any

[16] *Proceedings of the Fifteenth Conference for Education in the South, Nashville, Tenn., 1912,* pp. 97-101. Page made this address in the year 1912. Has not his prophecy been fulfilled?

regard for the future of his children will remain in the rural district, as it exists today, if he can possibly get out. . . . It is the paramount duty of the state to see that there is provided, . . . an elementary school, . . . in reach of every child, of every color, . . . and . . . an efficient high school, with transportation facilities, so that every child in each community may continue his training and look to the higher reaches of intellectual life and service. And the state must do other things. It must take the schools out of politics from top to bottom, and . . . devise administrative machinery, in the hands of capable experts, which shall intimately reach every part of the educational system and administer it with the greatest possible efficiency. Democracy commits no greater crime than . . . dealing with . . . its great educational . . . interests on a personal or political basis. . . . Education is the most important business of the state." [17]

President Charles W. Dabney, of the University of Cincinnati, spoke on "The Rural School as the Center of Country Life." "We know," he said, "what a steady drift there is from the agricultural states to the cities. In Tennessee, for example, whose urban population had increased by the last census (1910) 31 per cent, the rural population had increased none. This is the most ominous menace of our time. As Mr. James J. Hill put it : 'Land without population is a wilderness, and population without land is a mob.' This change is not explained by the falling off of agricultural production. The farmer is doing his work. The resources of soil and climate are limitless. It was our proud boast formerly that the American farmer occupied the highest position of independence of all our citizens, but he is now becoming completely submerged. He, who should be the foundation, is now being rammed down below the surface and made a mere mud-sill. Land values decrease, farmers move away, young people drift to the cities, dwellings become vacant, schools and churches dwindle, until finally all country life drops into decay. . . .

"How shall these things be prevented? One great need of the South is schools ; another is to make the school a social center of life.

Schools should be related to the economic life of the people and prepare them to work under the conditions in which they must earn their livelihood. . . .

[17] *Ibid.*, pp. 130-41.

If the rural school is to accomplish what we expect of it, it must then not be a thing apart from the life of the people, as the old school was. We must take the life and the work of the people into the school and carry the teaching and influence of the school into the life of the people. The practical work of the farm and the home must go into the school, and the thought and knowledge of the school must go on to the farm and into the home. . . .

The only hope of success in American self-government is the revival of a meeting in the schoolhouse similar to the old New England meeting. Nothing has ever equalled the town meeting for the development of civic responsibility and the spirit of coöperation in the citizen. We must learn to use the schoolhouse also as a place for public discussion, as a place where candidates of the various parties can speak before election, and where representatives who have been elected can report to the community what they have done ; a place where the citizens can discuss problems of the community, of the country, of the state, and of the nation, and thrash them out in the light of the common interest. We would thus remove the whole political machine from the atmosphere of the saloon, the country store, or even the court house, the citadel of the local "gang." We would shift the scene of political activity from a selfish atmosphere to an atmosphere that is helpful and invigorating. In making the school the political forum as well as the social center of the people, lies, we believe, the chief hope of perpetuating the democracy and perfecting all its institutions.[18]

Writing of this Nashville meeting *The Outlook* of April 20, 1912, says in an article by a staff correspondent :

To how many will it seem an indulgence in extravagant language to say that the Northern visitors who had the privilege of attending this Conference came back with the conviction that the American public school is being made by the people of the Southern States, and may be made in the rest of the country, the center of one of the greatest missionary movements that the United States has ever seen. Northern States may have to call upon the Southern States for missionaries to show us of the North how the work of vitalizing common school education may be extended to our own rural and city public schools.

Excursions of State Superintendents of Public Instruction

We have told of Mr. Ogden's many excursions of northern men and women to visit the southern schools and attend the

[18] *Ibid.*, pp. 142-52.

Conferences. His faith in the value of travel led him next to turn his excursions in the opposite direction and to take southern school officials into the North and Northwest to give them an opportunity to observe the educational institutions there. He arranged three tours of this kind, the first one to the North, the second to rural schools in Iowa, and the third into Ohio and Indiana and Canada.

In October, 1908, he invited all the southern state superintendents of public instruction to meet at a hotel in New York and go with him as the guests of the Southern Education Board to inspect the schools of that city, of Boston, and the State Department of Education at Albany. The superintendents were organized and led by Dr. J. Y. Joyner, superintendent of schools of North Carolina. With one exception in the case of a superintendent who was ill, all of the southern states were represented. Wickliffe Rose of the Peabody Board at the time and P. P. Claxton, chairman of the Campaign Committee of the Southern Board, accompanied them. Mr. Ogden himself accompanied the party throughout the whole itinerary. The company were the guests in New York of Mr. Ogden and in Boston of Mr. James J. Storrow, overseer of Harvard and president of the Boston School Board.

October 12 was devoted to visits to Teachers College, Columbia University, under the guidance of President Butler, and to the Horace Mann School, with a luncheon as the guests of Dr. Russell, and a visit to the College of the City of New York, with President John H. Finley as host. On October 13 visits were made to the Girls' Normal School in Brooklyn and the Commercial High School under the guidance of Superintendent W. H. Maxwell. The morning of Wednesday, the 14th, the company visited the schools in the East Side district of Manhattan. In the afternoon they proceeded to Boston, where the company gathered at a hotel on Copley Square, facing Trinity Church, the new Old South with its historic traditions, and the Public Library, where, from the windows of their rooms could be read the motto cut in stone : "The Commonwealth requires the education of the people as the safeguard of liberty and order." The visit in Boston taught them how thoroughly Massachusetts was endeavoring to carry this out.

October 15 was richly filled with a visit to Harvard University. On the 16th visits were made to the public schools of all grades including the Commercial High School and the Girls' Normal School. In the evening the party proceeded to Albany. The entire day of the 17th was devoted to an examination of the records of the New York State Department of Education. The Commissioner, Dr. Draper, had prepared a careful analysis of the department's work and furnished a copy to each member.

A mere statement of the program can convey no idea of the intellectual and spiritual importance of each step of the tour. Dr. Joyner, president of the Association, wrote: "Since... I have had time to review our itinerary and reflect upon what we observed and learned, it is my deliberate conviction and that of all of the superintendents... that this opportunity to inspect the best in two of the greatest public school systems in this country, and to look into the organization of the best organized State system in the United States, will result in more practical help in the development of the school systems in their respective States, and be more far reaching in its influence upon the future educational progress of those States than any other opportunity that has yet been afforded them through the kindness and generosity of the Southern Education Board."

The next excursion for the state superintendents was a visit to the rural schools in Page County, Iowa, and to investigate the rural coöperative activities such as creameries, elevators, and coöperative stores in the country around Minneapolis. It was also proposed to visit two types of agricultural schools, the district school at St. Paul and the famous county agricultural schools at Menomonie and Oshkosh, Wisconsin; and the agricultural coöperative work of the great University of Wisconsin, the university that claims the whole state for its campus. This party was under the direct charge of Mr. Ogden and Dr. Wickliffe Rose, and every southern state except Oklahoma was represented. The gentlemen met at St. Louis and travelled from there to Page County. Professor Stearnes, of Virginia, in his report says that the county superintendent of Page County was Miss Jessie Field. Her education and training fitted her especially for supervisory work and leadership in rural education. She had the courage of high ideals, untiring energy, and great tact in getting along with teachers and children. All of her time was devoted to her school work. She knew every child by name and it was beautiful to see their faces light up in response to the call of their leader. The teachers chosen by her were personal friends. Many had declined places in town schools in order to work in these rural schools. The agricultural and industrial work and instruction were connected with the regular school studies. The grammar school instruction was shaped to do much for the shop, for the farm, and for every-day life as well as for the highest home life.

These schools and their teachers command the coöperation and respect of the community by constantly challenging them to pass upon the results. In one letter to the parents the teachers said : "If the writing is not good, condemn us ; if the reading or spelling is not better, withhold your support ; if our farm arithmetic does not make good mathematicians, do not spare our feelings . . . ; if the work in basket-making, the milk testing, school gardening, or that with hammer and saw, does not provide general, as well as special, training, tell us so and we will do away with it. If, on the other hand, you believe that we are giving that training of heart, head and hand that will fit the children for sober, useful and contented lives in their home environment, then give us your financial support and your hearty interest in such a way that the school levies may no longer be regarded as a tax but as a coöperative effort to give the children what they deserve, namely, the best possible chance in life." "The lesson that we got from the two days spent in Miss Field's schools," says Professor Stearnes, "was the effectiveness of systematic, sustained effort along simple and practical lines. . . . There is no county in Virginia that cannot duplicate the work of Page County, but among our county superintendents, how many are there of the Field clan?" [19]

Professor J. N. Powers, superintendent of education of Mississippi, tells what they found at Menomonie : "One of the most interesting departments was the creamery. . . . We also saw a class working in the black-smith shop, looked in upon the boys and girls busy with hammer and saw in . . . agricultural engineering, and inspected with interest the domestic-science department where girls are taught that it is just as dignified to cook and . . . to cut and fit garments as it is to demonstrate a proposition in mathematics. What do these schools mean to the farmers? Answer, Just this : they are a means of educating their children,

[19] *Proceedings of the Thirteenth Conference for Education in the South, Little Rock, Ark., 1910,* pp. 291-98.

developing their agriculture, and improving their homes. The intelligent and logical system of education is that which carries the best advantages to all the people." [20]

Mr. Ogden gave the southern superintendents a third "excursion into ennobling experiences," this time into the northwestern states.[21] A group of southern state superintendents and rural school supervisors met at Indianapolis and were taken in hand by Dr. A. P. Bourland, representing the Southern Education Board. The itinerary included the study of consolidated schools in Indiana and of the University of Toronto, and attendance upon important meetings of the Ontario Horticulture Association; a visit to the Ontario Agricultural College at Guelph and a study of the methods of agricultural education in the Province of Ontario; a visit to consolidated schools in Ohio; a study of the work of the Agricultural High School at Philopolis, Maryland; and a visit to Hampton Institute. The main purpose was to study school administration and supervision, consolidated schools, transportation of pupils, the work of the Agricultural College of Ontario, and special methods of agricultural education in the public schools.

The state superintendents passed resolutions expressing their appreciation of Mr. Ogden's generosity in making these trips possible and thanked Dr. Wickliffe Rose, as manager of the excursions, for his untiring interest and many courtesies.

[20] *Ibid.*, pp. 298-301. Harry C. Gunnells, Superintendent of Alabama, made a report on the Boys' Corn Clubs; Professor George B. Cook, of Arkansas, made a report on industrial coöperation as illustrated by creameries and federated coöperative stores in Minnesota. Professor J. C. Crabbe, superintendent of Kentucky, made a report on the University of Wisconsin and its experiment station, illustrating it by the work done in seed selection and cross-fertilization. The reader must be referred to these interesting reports for details. See *Proceedings of the Thirteenth Conference for Education in the South, Little Rock, Ark., 1910.*

[21] Professor W. K. Tate's full account of this tour is available in the *Proceedings of the Fourteenth Conference for Education in the South, Jacksonville, Florida, 1911.*

CHAPTER XX

THE END OF THE "OGDEN MOVEMENT"

THE SIXTEENTH CONFERENCE, RICHMOND, VIRGINIA, 1913

THE Sixteenth Conference for Education in the South was held on April 15-18, 1913, and was called in Richmond, Virginia, ten years after the previous conference there. Mr. Ogden was ill and could not attend. He had been not only the creator and director of them all, but their inspiration and their very life. His absence, therefore, foreshadowed the ending of these Conferences; and though a strong effort was made to continue them, many of us felt that their end was near.

In view of Mr. Ogden's feebleness and his expected absence from the meeting, the work of organizing the new Conference fell to Professor A. P. Bourland, the executive secretary. He planned a combination of many conferences on different subjects; there were six pertaining to rural life, a separate conference for farmers, one of business men, another of rural churches, and another of women interested in rural problems; there was a special conference on taxation and a conference on Negro education; there was a conference of the Association of Colleges and Preparatory Schools of the Southern States, and another conference of the League of Southern Women Writers. The tenth session of the Southern Association of College Women and a session of Southern Editors were held in connection with the meeting. With others not mentioned, these made a total of seventeen major and nine minor meetings to be held in the space of four days.

More limited meetings were proposed for district supervisors, state high school inspectors, teachers of agriculture in schools and colleges, agents for boys' and girls' demonstration work, presidents of state normal colleges and of state agricultural colleges, workers for the education of teachers, such as deans and professors in the schools of education in colleges and departments of universities. There was a college conference of presidents and members of faculties of universities, as well as a meeting of state superintendents of public instruction. An exhibit of all the activities working for rural progress in the South was arranged to be held in the high school building, covering health agencies, farm demonstrations, and rural school progress. There were exhibits from several states, including Florida, Kentucky, West Virginia, and Tennessee.

The secretary, Professor Bourland, had issued circulars for all of these many conferences and meetings and had scattered them by the thousands. He had carried on a campaign of publicity through the newspapers, and had been assisted by the railroads. In addition to this he had issued "A Call of the Country," an appeal signed by the governor of Virginia, asking the governors of the other southern states to name delegates from their states. Persons so named from the states were sent letters by their governors, appointing them as delegates.

The parent Conference for Education in the South was allowed only three evening meetings—April 16, 17, and 18. It was a great mistake to undertake so many conferences. The secretary, in seeking to get a great crowd together, smothered the original Conference for Education in the South almost completely. So many conferences divided the membership and killed the interest.

In a letter of June 24, 1913, the secretary, Professor Bourland, reported to Mr. Ogden that he never got all the delegates to the various conferences registered, but he says that there were more than two thousand names on the register, which he analyzed by occupation, as far as reported : farmers, 310 ; business men, 194 ; school workers of various ranks, 990 ; professional men, 37 ; ministers, 88 ; congressmen, 3 : miscellaneous, 426—a total of 2,048. All of the states east of the Rockies were represented and the District of Columbia and Canada. There were 1,388 from Virginia, 163 from North Carolina, 60 from Kentucky, 44 from New York, 41 from Georgia, and so on.

Many valuable papers were presented and published in a volume of 325 pages entitled Proceedings of the *Sixteenth Conference for Education in the South*. But we must restrict our notice to the papers presented at the meetings of the original Conference for Education in the South. As has been stated, this had three sessions. In the absence of Mr. Ogden, Walter Hines Page presided. Mr. Ogden from his home in New York sent the Conference this message through the secretary :

At the approach of the time for holding the Sixteenth Annual Conference for Education in the South, it becomes a painful necessity for me to inform you that I cannot be present nor fulfil any of the duties incumbent upon the presidency.... Yet, I am confident that no detriment to the cause for which the Conference has stood during the fifteen years of its completed life will result from my absence ;... Under such guidance the cause cannot fail to progress ; and the absence of one who has been left behind ... will not produce the smallest ripple of disturbance....

I beg of you to urge that the Conference drop my name from any further official consideration.... I desire through you to express to the Conference my sense of obligation for the continued confidence expressed by my continuous re-election to the presidency during the years from 1903 to the present. I esteem this honor one of the most precious possessions of memory.[1]

In opening the Conference, Page said :

There will, of course, on account of Mr. Ogden's absence, be no annual address of the president.... In these sixteen years since this Conference began,... our country has come a long way.... Sixteen years ago I dare say that most men thought of education as something that was done to children in a house.... We still do things to children in houses, but the idea of education has extended beyond the child, ... taking in the adult. It has extended far beyond the house and it reaches the utmost limits of human activity and we have come to realize that every man and woman of us never finishes our education.... Consequently it has seemed fit to the Committee who had charge of making the program ... to lay special emphasis upon the building up of country life.[2]

Mr. O. B. Martin presented at the Conference an interesting account of how the Boys' Clubs were organized, and he introduced a boy, Frank Brockman of Amherst, Virginia, to tell his story of how he raised 167 bushels of shelled corn on one acre of Virginia land and how he had made $150 upon that acre, thereby breaking the corn-growing record of the state.

One of the distinct impressions derived from the meeting was that many people in the South had come to realize that a Negro population more intelligent would be a great gain in the economic, sanitary, and moral condition of the country. A

[1] *Proceedings of the Sixteenth Conference for Education in the South, Richmond, Virginia, 1913*, pp. 231-32.
[2] *Ibid.*, p. 232.

man from one of the Gulf states, who acknowledged that he had always before been opposed to Negro education, remarked significantly : "I realize now that the Negroes in my state are a burden. We must change them into an asset."

In closing the meeting Walter Hines Page gave a brief summary of the accomplishments of this Conference : "Never ... have so many thoughtful ... people come together from so many regions of the South. ... The largest problem that faces American civilization lies in building up its country life. ... We have passed through a period of organization of the machinery of the modern world—making the city and the railroad, the mills and the factories—but we have left the country out. ... We must build it up. ... In the coming centuries, as in the past, we all know that the ... vision of American life will come from the soil. ... In the early days our characteristic ... was individualism. Great as this was for the cause of democracy, it rested upon a false economic basis. ... A larger vision and a larger liberty and a larger opportunity ... create for us a larger task. ... We must organize the country. ... The historian of the progress of democracy could not write a more thrilling chapter than the events of the past ... fifteen years, taking as his cue the record of the Conference for Education in the South. We begin with the school and the child, and we end with the school and the child ; but every step has been toward a widening democratic ideal, nothing less. ...

"Our great prophet, Dr. Knapp, let a flood of light on all this problem. I am not sure but that he was the greatest schoolmaster of the age. ... To till the soil, to train the children, to make the home, ... I count as ... the greatest privilege that can fall to man. We have worked in this Conference on a program to bring to pass the dream of the fathers, that our republic shall be and remain the hope of the world. With that thought, and with infinite gratitude ... , and with a growing hope, I declare the Conference for Education in the South adjourned."

THE SEVENTEENTH CONFERENCE, LOUISVILLE, KENTUCKY, 1914

The seventeenth meeting of the Conference, so called, held at Louisville, Kentucky, April 7-10, 1914, can hardly be called a meeting of the original body. It was swallowed up in the Southern Educational Association. The executive secretary, encouraged by the large crowd he had gotten together at the Richmond Conference the year previous, planned to have a similar large series of meetings. The Southern Educational Association, composed of school officials, was called to meet at the same time in various sections and occupied most of the time. This association, of which the Honorable J. Y. Joyner, superintendent of schools from North Carolina, was the president and Professor R. A. Clayton of Birmingham, Alabama, was secretary, had a very large membership. A plan, which originated at the Richmond meeting, was to combine the Southern Conference, created by Mr. Ogden, of which he had been the head for thirteen years, with this Southern Education Association. This was done nominally, but in reality the Ogden movement soon died. The Southern Conference for Education used totally different methods from those of the Southern Educational Association. From the beginning, the Ogden Conference had but one object, to bring together the people of the North and the people of the South in mutual understanding and fellowship in helping the people of the South in their task of universal education. Its methods were thus purely informational, spiritual, and inspirational. It did not do any executive or administrative work beyond its own field. As fast as it developed an opportunity for such work, the Southern Education Board, the executive agent of the Conference, turned it over to the General Education Board.

The new leaders of the Southern Educational and Industrial Association, as it was now called, departed entirely from the original purpose and ideals of the Southern Conference when they attempted to combine the old and inspirational Conference with the multitude of new meetings for deliberative purposes on educational, economic, and industrial questions.

Mr. Bourland wrote early in May, 1913, to Mr. Ogden, submitting his plan for the Louisville meeting and asking his counsel. But Mr. Ogden, after saying that his activities were at an end and that he could not give him any advice, replied: "In the plans for the next Conference I venture to suggest that the meetings be arranged so that the spiritual note of previous years be continued." Probably without the experienced and revered leader this was impossible, but it was a fatal mistake to fill the program with a multitude of other meetings and to try to merge the Conference into another association.

The program for the combined meeting in Louisville was similar to that of the Richmond meeting, with conferences and sectional meetings on every conceivable subject connected with the social and economic interests of the South. There were the general meeting of the Southern Educational Association; meetings of various sections and departments; special meetings on normal schools, on teacher training, kindergarten education, elementary education, and secondary education; a department for the university, and a separate department for colleges; a meeting on libraries; a conference on the education of the Negro; the annual session of the Southern Association of College Women; the meeting of the League of Southern Writers; and a business men's meeting. The business men's conference was the largest one of all and discussed every subject from training for rural life to railroads. A committee on the state system of public schools made an excellent report.[3] There was also a country women's conference; a conference on the country church, led by Dr. Warren H. Wilson, of the Presbyterian Board of Missions, which developed many new subjects; a farmers' conference, and others. The farmers' conference discussed agricultural finances in all its phases, the essentials of marketing organizations, coöperative buying, and many other subjects. A conference of country doctors considered community aspects of the health problem, some of the topics of discussion being rural nurses, treatment and administration of remedies, and the doctor's bills!

Dr. William Goodell Frost, president of Berea College, made an earnest plea for the long neglected mountain people of the South:

To some people rural life means automobiles and sunken gardens—city luxuries transplanted to the country. But the typical rural life is that shown in Whittier's "Snowbound," and Mrs. Stowe's "Old Town Folks." The characteristic of the rural condition is the intense family life, and the intimate but limited acquaintance with surrounding households. The farmer in a western State knows everybody within a radius of a half day's travel, and his thought, influence and activities are largely limited to this circle. The super-rural condition in the mountains is the same thing intensified. In-

[3] Published in the *Proceedings of the Seventeenth Conference for Education in the South and Twenty-fifth Annual Meeting of the Southern Educational Association, Louisville, Kentucky, 1914.*

stead of having an acquaintance throughout a circle of twenty miles in diameter, the mountain man has acquaintance only ten miles up stream and ten miles down stream in a narrow valley.

This life of isolation is a life of deprivation. . . . When we come to know the mountaineer intimately, we find that his peculiarities are almost never of the nature of degradation. They are honest survivals. The mountain people are living as all good people lived in earlier times. . . . George Washington and Martha, his wife, would be much at home today in the primitive conditions of our southern mountains. The very fighting qualities which are so often brought up against the mountaineer are only an honest survival of old Saxon temper. . . .

Why, if our mountain friends are so capable and promising, have they settled in the mountains? The answer is simple. Everybody went west after the Revolutionary War. No man at that time could foresee the coming of the railroads. The northern pioneer was helped out by the Erie Canal. For in those earlier times ideas traveled by water. This Erie Canal probably did more for civilization than the Panama Canal can ever do. . . . Thus the northern pioneer was kept in touch with civilization until the railway overtook him.

The southern mountaineer is, as I have said a thousand times, *our contemporary ancestor.* And it is our business to provide for this vast region the special educational adaptations which will make it as strong in America as Scotland is in Great Britain.[4]

Mrs. Desha Breckinridge gave at this meeting a thrilling description of her social work in Kentucky. Superintendent Coates told of his methods of improving rural schools through demonstration schools ; Professor Baker of Alabama spoke of the improvement of rural schools through consolidation ; Mr. J. H. Binford of Virginia, of rural improvement through community activities ; and Mr. Jackson Davis of Virginia, of the improvement of rural schools through industrial supervisors. There were addresses by the United States commissioner of education, Honorable P. P. Claxton, and Dr. J. H. Dillard, secretary of the Slater Board. The department of industrial education heard addresses from R. B. Daniel about the famous schools of Columbus, Georgia, which have been described be-

[4] *Ibid.,* pp. 62-63.

John Fox said that the southern migrants all started west, but when the axle of the wagon broke in the mountains they had to stop and found the scenery so entrancing, the soil of the valleys so inviting, and the game so abundant that they just settled there, where their descendants are today.

fore, and from J. A. Baldwin, of Charlotte, North Carolina, on educational conditions in southern cotton mill communities. There were 1,939 members in attendance at the combined meetings.

MEMORIALS OF ROBERT CURTIS OGDEN

This was the end of what had been known for thirteen years as the Ogden or Southern Education Movement. The beloved leader was gone. Mr. Ogden, the creator, the father, patron, and inspirer of the movement, had died on the 6th of August, 1913, about three months after the Richmond Conference. The projection of this vitalizing personality into the work, the beauty of his simplicity, the strength of his gentleness, and the wisdom of his righteousness were irresistible. Misunderstandings and prejudices, once piled high between the North and the South, were rolled away and the knowledge of each other which led to fellowship and unity gave increased strength for the great national task. Without his beautiful and lovable character, without his commanding genius, the Movement could not last.

At the meeting there was a memorial service for Mr. Ogden at which the Honorable P. P. Claxton, national commissioner of education, made the principal address. After giving a brief description of Mr. Ogden's splendid talents and superb leadership, he concluded by saying : "The heart and soul of the Conference and under God above all others the leader and inspirer of the movement, has been a simple, honest, lovable, great man, Robert Curtis Ogden. His annual addresses as president of the Conference have inspired us all to better things. His tactful, masterful and inimitable method of presiding, his wit and good cheer, his patience, his constant self-sacrifice, ... can never be forgotten. His benediction rests on this Conference and all its work. Whatever impressions members had, whatever attitudes they took towards the Conference and its work, all who knew Mr. Ogden loved him. His memory will long be cherished by thousands of the people of the South, and the lives of millions who may never hear his name spoken will be better, richer and fuller because he lived."[5]

[5] *Proceedings of the Seventeenth Conference for Education in the South and the Twenty-fifth Annual Meeting of the Southern Educational Association, Louisville, Kentucky, 1914*, p. 10.

The conference adopted this resolution : "Since the last meeting of this Conference, its beloved President, generous benefactor, wise guide, Robert C. Ogden, has fallen on sleep and has left in our work a vacant place that can never be filled, in our lives an uplifting influence that shall never cease, in our hearts a sorrow and sense of loss that must be left unexpressed because inexpressible." [6]

FRANK ROSS CHAMBERS

On October 25, 1913, Mr. Frank Ross Chambers was elected president of the Southern Education Board to succeed Mr. Ogden. Mr. Chambers, born in Mobile, Alabama, in 1850, left an orphan at eleven, and having no formal schooling of any kind thereafter, educated himself by reading and private study and became a cultivated man and an excellent writer and speaker. His first job, at twelve years of age, was that of messenger boy in the Confederate Arsenal in Montgomery. At fourteen he was an assistant in a bank. At sixteen he made his way to New York. The only man he knew there found him a position. After several years, he entered a mercantile organization with which he has been connected ever since, advancing finally to be its president. Throughout his whole career Chambers, who had no opportunity to go to college himself, has been the generous helper of scores of young men and women struggling for an education. He shaped the government and organized the schools of his home village of Bronxville, New York, to which he also gave land and equipment. Interested especially in progressive education, he provided equipment for the Bronxville schools for teaching industrial arts and home economics and helped them to develop until they have become known throughout the country as models of their kind. His ability in educational matters and his lifelong interest in southern schools and colleges, many of which he aided, caused him to be made a member of the Southern Education Board. Desiring to introduce the methods of this Board into his college, the first Dean Russell of Teachers College of Columbia University invited Chambers and Walter Hines Page to become trustees of that institution. After a few years, Chambers was made chairman of its executive board. At the time of his election to the

[6] *Ibid.*, p. 12.

presidency of the Southern Education Board Mr. Chambers had been its valuable and active supporter for a number of years and was intimately acquainted with its affairs.

After the death of Mr. Ogden, resolutions were adopted merging the Southern Conference for Education with the Southern Educational Association. The Southern Education Board proceeded to provide for the continuance of the work of the various agencies in the South for a year, to pay all its obligations and to settle all its business, and so prepare to dissolve at the end of a year. All of these agents were notified that the responsibility of this Board for their salaries would cease after July 1, 1914.

At the meeting of the Southern Education Board on May 29, 1914, it was resolved to transfer the work of supervision of rural schools and all the other work of the Board in the South supported from the contributions of the General Education Board to the latter Board. Honorable J. Y. Joyner, president of the new Southern Conference for Education and Industry, was elected a member of the Southern Education Board, and Professor A. P. Bourland was elected secretary of that Board without salary until the next session of the new Conference to assist in the closing out of the Conference for Education in the South and the Southern Education Board. It was resolved that the terms of office of all the officers and members of the Board cease with the next, the final, meeting of the Conference for Education in the South without resignation.

By these measures the Conference for Education in the South was merged into the new Conference of Education and Industry in the South, and the original Southern Education Board dissolved. The Board before adjournment expressed its best wishes for the new organization and urged that every effort be made to bring together the representatives of the South and of the North in the future conferences as had been done in the past.

"A Master of Men"

Memorial services for Mr. Ogden were held in many places. One was held in Philadelphia, where he was born, another in New York on October 26, and another in Brooklyn, on November 9, 1913. Addresses were delivered by Dr. William Adams Brown, president of Union Theological Seminary, where Mr.

Ogden had served as trustee for many years ; by Dr. Francis G. Peabody, of Harvard, vice-president of the Board of Trustees of Hampton Institute, of which Mr. Ogden had been president for many years ; by Dr. Samuel C. Mitchell of Richmond, Virginia ; by Dr. L. Mason Clarke, pastor of the First Presbyterian Church, Brooklyn ; by the Honorable J. E. Hedges of New York ; and by ex-President William Howard Taft, of Yale University. These addresses were published with a biographical sketch in a pamphlet entitled *A Life Well Lived*. Mr. Henry E. Fries and his southern friends also published a volume in his memory.[7] In the latter volume are also a biographical sketch by his beloved friend, Hollis Burke Frissell ; an address of appreciation made at the Ogden memorial meeting at Richmond on November 26, 1915, under the auspices of the Coöperative Education Association of Virginia, by President Edwin A. Alderman of the University of Virginia. Walter Hines Page wrote : "Mr. Ogden opened long vistas and disclosed large visions to his faithful followers. He stimulated Southern thought ; built up Southern character ; and fired Southern men to the most patriotic endeavor." Mr. George Foster Peabody, who was the first to name him as "an Unofficial Statesman,"—a remarkably happy name,—wrote : "It is undoubtedly true that no man has done so much . . . in bringing about an interweaving of minds and intermingling of hearts of men and women of the North and . . . of the South as this believer in all men, who had faith in the unification of the whole country and in the sure result of patience in well doing. All hail to this true statesman!"

Dr. Wallace Buttrick under the title, "A Master of Men," said : "I think his chief contribution lay in the fact that he brought men of like mind and purpose together, and enabled them to know and understand one another." Mr. Henry E. Fries wrote four poems about Ogden as a patriot, as a statesman, as a Christian gentleman, and as a man.

The following resolutions were adopted at the meeting of the Southern Education Board on May 29, 1914, and directed to be engrossed and copies sent to the members of Mr. Ogden's family :

"The Southern Education Board approaches with hesitation

[7] There is a copy of each of these publications—*A Life Well Lived* and *In Memory of Robert Curtis Ogden*—in the Library of the University of North Carolina.

and with reverence the duty of placing on its records a tribute to the memory of Robert C. Ogden. No words can fittingly express the sentiments of respect and regard felt toward him by the members of this body, or their estimate of his value as a man and as a citizen. To an extent unusual in any organization he incarnated the whole Board. He was its organizer and its only President during the years of his life. It was his high conception of duty and privilege that held the Board to its task and rendered the results of its labors so remarkably successful. He mapped the course, he led the way, he inspirited each follower, and by his life and death he consecrated the work.

"A review of the years passed shows that the activities of this Board have been directed to various ends—to educational campaigns that have aroused one state after another, to needed changes in educational legislation, to general improvement in rural schools, and to the elevation of rural life. Rarely has any work so far-reaching been originated and carried through with so small an outlay of material resources. The wisdom of those who have directed these activities has been justified by wonderful results. Mr. Ogden was responsible for the selection of these workers. His insight recognized the tasks and chose the agents best suited for their accomplishment. By the power of his personal influence he held the Southern Board together, and directed the energies of busy men to the unselfish duties which he assumed. That same wonderful personality impressed itself upon the nation at large. Through the Conference for Education in the South he touched the great hearts of the North and the South, and put upon the nation's conscience a universal need. All this was done so quietly, so simply, that we wonder still at the results. Not by persuasion, not by fanatical insistence, but by the contagion of his own personal devotion, he rallied men from every section, from every walk or station in life, rich and poor, high and lowly, white and black, to the cause which he advocated.

"The South owes him a peculiar debt. He understood the temper and temperament of its people. He admired its strength, and was kind in his judgment of weaknesses. He understood its problems and sought a rational solution of them. Not by patronizing aloofness and cold counsel, but by personal aid and warm sympathy, he made his contributions to the uplift of a whole nation.

"Through his efforts our national life has been strengthened, brothers once estranged have become united, service feebly performed has been rendered efficient, and racial coöperation has taken the place of racial conflicts.

"Robert C. Ogden was a man of high ideals and far-reaching vision. To great purposes he consecrated his life with a devotion unsurpassed. By the compelling power of personal friendship he lifted others to the high plane on which he lived, and joined other hands to his in noblest service.

"Therefore, we, the members of the Southern Education Board, dedicate to him these pages in our records. The written words but feebly attest our love and our loss. The record of his life is the best part of our institutional history. His memory is an inspiration, the consciousness of his continued love and friendship our comfort still, his work the foundation on which we must forever build. Who seeks his monument will find it both in national achievement and in the consecration of many hearts.

"To the God of the nations, we render thanks for the life and for the memory of Robert C. Ogden.

Edwin A. Alderman	Henry E. Fries
A. P. Bourland	Hollis B. Frissell
Sidney J. Bowie	John M. Glenn
Wallace Buttrick	David F. Houston
Frank R. Chambers	J. H. Kirkland
Philander P. Claxton	S. C. Mitchell
Charles W. Dabney	Walter H. Page
George S. Dickerman	George Foster Peabody
J. H. Dillard	Wickliffe Rose
	Albert Shaw"

A memorial tablet was erected in the Chapel of Salem College at Winston-Salem, North Carolina, in which the Fourth Conference was held, where the active work was first organized under the Southern Education Board appointed by Mr. Ogden. The tablet reads:

In this chapel was held
THE FOURTH CONFERENCE FOR EDUCATION IN THE SOUTH
April 18, 19, 20, 1901
All former conferences were held at Capon Springs, W. Va.

————

President

Robert C. Ogden, New York

Vice-Presidents

Walter H. Page, New York, Rt. Rev. Edward Rondthaler,
North Carolina, Eugene C. Branson, Georgia

Secretary and Treasurer

Rev. A. B. Hunter, Raleigh, N. C.

Auditor

Wm. J. Schieffelin, New York.

————

Committee on Platform and Resolutions

Charles D. McIver, Albert Shaw, Charles W. Dabney,
John Graham Brooks, Rt. Rev. Edward Rondthaler,
G. R. Glenn, Henry St. George Tucker, W. H. Baldwin, Jr.,
Walter H. Page, J. L. M. Curry

This place, where Ogden stood on the platform in front of the bust of Comenius and made his ever-to-be-remembered address, will always be a shrine for southern people.

CHAPTER XXI

THE CAMPAIGN IN VIRGINIA

A Perfect Political Machine

ONE of the first states in which the Southern Education Board started systematic work was Virginia. This was begun in 1902. The work done in this state during the next ten years by the constitutional convention, the legislature, the new board of education, and the new superintendent constituted a revolution in the administration of the schools, laying the foundation for great progress in them.

Though there had been some improvement in public sentiment with regard to public schools under Dr. Ruffner, Virginians had never been completely converted to universal free education for both blacks and whites. There were still many who were doubtful about the practicability of public schools under the changed conditions following the Civil War. From the time Dr. Ruffner was put out,[1] the administration of the schools had fallen more and more under the influence of the politicians, until it had now become a machine operated largely in their interests. To provide more jobs and to accommodate the local people, the schools had been split up and multiplied in the country districts, the terms kept down, and the salaries of the teachers held at so low a figure that the schools were of little use. Dr. Frazer tells of one community in a good county which had six poor little one-room schools in a district six miles across. The schoolhouses were wretched and the equipment negligible. Favoritism and nepotism in the appointment of teachers helped to destroy the efficiency of the instruction. The result of these conditions was that many citizens, who had been inclined to favor the new public schools, became antagonistic to them. While such conditions prevailed, the people naturally did not like to pay increased taxes for the schools.

The chief obstacles to the development of public schools in the South were poverty, prejudice, and politics. The causes of the desperate poverty of this people following the Civil

[1] See above, p. ooo.

War and Reconstruction are thoroughly understood. Their prejudice against all schools introduced from the North by the Freedmen's Bureau and by religious and benevolent associations is understandable. We had a good illustration of the way politics can ruin the schools.

The State Board of Education in Virginia before the constitutional convention of 1902 consisted of the governor and the attorney-general, elected by the people, and the state superintendent, elected by the legislature—all political officers. These three appointed every county superintendent in the state. A board, called the electoral board, consisting of the county superintendent, the Commonwealth's attorney, and one citizen appointed by the judge of the county court, all political appointees, named the trustees of the school district. The state superintendent was supposed to be an educator, but, as a matter of fact, he was usually a tool in the hands of these politicians. The teachers fell in line, following their superiors. It was a perfect political machine from bottom to top, used to further the interests of the party in power in national, as well as in state and county elections. The result was a general demoralization of the whole system.

LEGISLATIVE REFORM SECURED

It was fortunate that the constitutional convention was called at the time the Conference for Education in the South was just starting its work in Virginia. "This programme of propaganda for popular education," started at the Winston-Salem Conference in 1901, "was the motive power that touched the social conscience in every rural community in Virginia and over the entire South, and resulted in an era of wonderful achievement for popular education," says Heatwole.[2]

After conferring with friends in the state, the Southern Education Board engaged the Honorable Henry St. George Tucker, professor of law at Washington and Lee University and for many years congressman from Virginia, who had been one of the organizers of the Conference at Capon Springs, and Dr. Robert Frazer, president of the Virginia State Normal School, to act as field agents for the state. They went to work immediately to make a canvass of all parts of the state, and put them-

[2] Cornelius J. Heatwole, *A History of Education in Virginia*, p. 309.

selves in touch with the members of the convention about to assemble.[3]

It was fortunate that the Reverend Richard McIlwaine, D.D., president of Hampden-Sydney College, was chairman of the committee on education of the constitutional convention. Like all of his predecessors in the presidency of the college since Jonathan P. Cushing, who organized its first Institute of Education, he was a strong believer in and worker for state public schools. In a notable address before the convention, he advocated a complete system of schools for both blacks and whites directed by educators.

The result of the combined efforts of these gentlemen was the adoption of provisions in the constitution which revolutionized the school administration. It was provided that the state superintendent of public instruction should be an experienced educator elected by the people for a term of four years. He was to be ex-officio member of a state board of education, composed of the governor, the attorney-general, and three experienced educators elected by the state Senate out of nominations made by the faculties of the leading educational institutions of the state. These six now elected two superintendents, one from a county and one from a city, to be additional members.

The State Board of Education divided the state into school divisions and appointed a superintendent for each division for a term of four years, subject to the approval of the Senate. It had full charge of the investment, care, and distribution of the state school funds under the law. All school funds should be distributed on the basis of the school population, including all persons between the ages of seven and twenty. The annual property tax should be not less than one, or more than five, mills on the dollar, and each county, town, city, and school district might levy a tax of not over five mills, to be appropriated by the local school authorities. Each magisterial district constituted a separate school district with three trustees selected in accordance with the law.[4] The board made all needful rules for the management and conduct of the schools, which should have the approval of the legislature and have the force of law.

---

[3] H. B. Frissell, *Proceedings of the Sixth Conference for Education in the South, Richmond, Virginia, 1903,* p. 51.

[4] For details of the school laws, see *Constitutional Provisions,* Secs. 129-42 inclusive ; and *Virginia School Laws, 1930,* Secs. 653-786 inclusive.

The board appointed the directors for the management of the state library and elected the librarian. The constitution also gave power to the General Assembly to establish agricultural, normal, and technical schools, to legislate for compulsory education and to supply textbooks for the children. Some of these provisions have been modified and improved in recent years, but these provisions gave the schools of Virginia an opportunity to make a new start.

THE COÖPERATIVE EDUCATION ASSOCIATION ORGANIZED

Governor Montague called a meeting of a few friends of the movement to confer on plans for starting a campaign in Virginia and to discuss what might be done under the new constitution and to discover a way to get in line with the Conference for Education in the South, which was to meet in Richmond the following April. Present at a conference on January 29, 1903, besides Governor Montague, were Frissell ; Joseph D. Eggleston, at that time superintendent of schools of Prince Edward County ; Samuel C. Mitchell, of Richmond College ; and Robert Frazer, of Warrenton. It was decided at this meeting to perfect an organization to carry forward a campaign to induce the people of Virginia to see the necessity of better schools. The meeting of the Conference for Education in the South was the beginning of this general campaign, which was now carried forward with great energy by these gentlemen, assisted by Dr. Frazer and Mr. Tucker, the field agents of the Southern Education Board.

In the spring of 1904 Governor Montague requested a number of the leading citizens of the state to meet in Richmond to consider the educational, economic and civic interests of the Commonwealth. These citizens were in session for two days at the Capitol and resolved to form an association and to strive to provide the following : A nine months' school for every child each year ; a high school within reasonable distance of every child ; better trained teachers ; agricultural and industrial training ; better supervision ; the promotion of school libraries ; and special schools for the defective and dependent. The association adopted as its motto, "Progress through coöperation," and its plan was "To help people to help themselves." On the proposal of Dr. Mitchell, the association was called "The Cooperative Education Association" and its plan was to coöperate with the Southern Education Board in its educational propaganda and to unite all friends of education in societies and leagues. For this work the Southern Board made an appropriation for a number of years.

The constitution of the association provided that its board of directors should be made up of the governor of the state, the superintendent of public instruction, the commissioner of agriculture, the state librarian and fifty citizens who were elected annually by the association. The commissioners of health, highways and welfare and the directors of farm and home demonstrations were added when these departments were created. Community school improvement leagues for adults and junior leagues for young people were formed. The movement spread rapidly. With the school as the center, these local organizations were kept at work on well planned programs, which included every interest of the school. Some of their aims were : To bring parents and teachers into better understanding in working together ; to help to secure the best teaching force and equipment ; to study the physical needs of the children, to coöperate with health workers in discovering and correcting the physical defects of the pre-school children as well as of the school children, and to make the health conditions of the school and the community the best possible ; to bring the community to accept its responsibility for promoting proper social, recreational, and civic conditions ; to coöperate with the agricultural leaders in encouraging unity of effort in gardening, farming and marketing ; to coöperate with the home economic and other leaders in promoting better homes ; to study the needs, ways, and means of securing the best highways ; to coöperate with the judge of the Juvenile Court, the Board of Public Welfare, and the churches in looking after neglected and delinquent children, and in promoting general social welfare work. By the end of 1905 over three hundred community leagues had been formed. The junior league work was started in 1911. The leaders in the county and the city community leagues were usually citizens not connected with the schools. The junior leagues were under the supervision of the principals and teachers with students as their officers. The executive director and the secretaries were much in the field, directing and aiding the various voluntary agencies. It will be interesting to note in passing the recent status of this movement. In 1933 the state was divided into seventeen districts with a district organization in charge of each. There were forty-five county federations and six city federations. The number of community leagues was 722 and the membership was 23,445. The number of Junior Leagues in the county and city schools was 1,072 with a membership of 58,529. The total membership in both classes of leagues was over 81,000. Three hundred and sixty-three community leagues and 471 junior leagues made contributions to the expenses of the work to the amount of $35,473, by the junior leagues, and $73,229 by the community leagues, a total of $108,702. It is a most remarkable coöperative organization and is a splendid illustration of what can be done by the people when they get together with a high purpose. It is notable that many of the distinguished men and women who started this movement in Virginia have continued in the service of the cause throughout the thirty years.

The May Campaign

At the meeting of the Coöperative Association in Norfolk in November, 1904, a resolution was adopted requesting Governor Montague and President Alderman, of the University, to lead in a campaign in the state in the month of May following, planned to interest the people in a more thorough system of public education. This became known as the "May Campaign" for schools. The executive committee of the Coöperative Association, consisting of Alderman, Mitchell, Frissell, Mrs. Munford, Frazer, Payne, and Mrs. Dashiell, directed the campaign. Professor Bruce Payne, at that time at William and Mary, Mr. Carter Glass, of Lynchburg, since United States senator, and Mr. Copeland, of the *Times-Dispatch* of Richmond, were the committee having charge of the speakers and of publicity. "The plan was to solicit speakers from among educators, ministers, state officers, and citizens—every type of man or woman who would work for the cause. . . . Eight points were definitely stated for discussion around which all addresses were made : The consolidation of schools ; vocational education ; primary instruction ; improved schoolhouses ; the lengthening of the school term ; the increase of local taxation ; thorough supervision and the creation of a secondary school system." [5] Outlines

[5] Bruce R. Payne, memorandum to the author, Jan. 23, 1933.

for addresses on these subjects were prepared and sent to the speakers, and articles were sent to the press. A hundred or more men and women traveled over the state, addressing large audiences, mostly in the country districts. Numerous local speakers aided in these meetings. Governor Montague and President Alderman addressed many of the largest meetings with great effect.

Says Heatwole: "Never was a state so bombarded in the interest of any cause. Men spoke in the remotest communities. ... Preachers found a fresh application of the principles of religion. Editors gave their editorial and news columns for the dissemination of knowledge and the inspiration of the people. College presidents and professors in the state and private institutions found new fields for useful labor.... Two hundred thousand pages of educational literature were issued, and fifty citizen school associations were organized. All this was done in thirty days." [6]

Payne describes a meeting at Blackstone: "The speaking was in a tobacco warehouse, and the seats were slabs laid on little wooden blocks. It was a very large audience—several thousand—including several hundred girls from a school in the town. Some of the speakers wished me to come first, but I demurred on the ground of their seniority and distinction. Then the lieutenant-governor began to speak. Very soon the logs fell, and the girls squealed. The president told them to sit down on the floor, which they did. Then the remainder of the seats began to come down by sections, perhaps two hundred people at a time and two hundred squeals each time. Finally the entire audience was sitting on the floor. As the lieutenant-governor sat down, I remarked to him that I had heard of the house being 'brought down' by eloquence before, but I had never actually seen it. But by that time the audience was in very good shape for the message I had to deliver....

"We had a State convention of the Coöperative Education Association at Lynchburg that fall (1905), and I tried to get as many people to come to it as possible. In a mountain county in the southwest I found a big red-headed Scotch-Irishman who bossed the neighborhood. I asked him to bring all his people to this meeting. When I got to Lynchburg, ... he met

[6] Heatwole, *A History of Education in Virginia*, pp. 315-16.

me at the door of the hall and said, 'Here we are. We have all come.' " [7] And they had.

At the time of the May Campaign, the political forces of Virginia were engaged in a campaign for the election of a United States senator, a governor, and other officials. Eggleston contributes this description of it : "Some of the politicians rather resented the idea of their campaign being interfered with, and coolly stated that the people of Virginia would take no interest in a campaign for public education, when so much stirred up over the political campaign. But the politicians did not know the real heart-hunger of the people for better schools. . . . In a week after our campaign started, the people were flocking to our meetings, and neglecting the political meetings. . . . The politicians now came on the run, begging that they might be permitted to take part in our meetings and make speeches in behalf of public education. They now became fervid in behalf of schools. I think that most of them believed that the interest would soon die down and that things would settle back in the old rut. . . . They did not realize what forces had been turned loose by the new Constitution, and how, with them, the State Board of Education had the power to unify and set going great new agencies for education." [8]

The May Campaign was a prodigious success. It was described in the papers as "a tidal wave" for education. It proved epoch-making in that it secured the enactment of laws for the betterment and extension of the schools authorized under the new constitution, which marked the beginning of a new era in public education in Virginia.

The time had now arrived when under the constitution a new superintendent must be elected by the people. After conference with many leaders, the friends of the cause agreed unanimously upon Joseph Dupuy Eggleston as the man for the office. He was a native Virginian, a graduate of Hampden-Sydney College, a school man of rich experience. He had worked with Alderman and Claxton in North Carolina. He had been identified with the southern education movement from the beginning and had been associated with Dabney in the Southern Board's Bureau of Information. Eggleston had spoken throughout the state in the May Campaign, devoting himself entirely to

[7] Bruce R. Payne, memorandum to the author, Jan. 23, 1933.
[8] Joseph D. Eggleston, memorandum to the author, Oct. 17, 1933.

the issues presented by the Coöperative Association. He was nominated and duly elected and entered upon his duties in January, 1906. He went into office with hands free of political ties.

IMPROVED SECONDARY SCHOOLS

Care had been taken to elect men to the legislature who were committed to the program for better schools. One of the points stressed in the campaign had been the need of secondary schools. The deplorable condition of these schools was described, and what would be required to make them efficient was explained. Outlines of the arguments were supplied to the candidates of both political parties, who used them and pledged themselves to support plans for high schools. Payne says: "Afraid they might forget their pledges to the people..., I subscribed to a paper in each county; and great was my delight to find that every man had used our copy as a part of his speech. I cut these speeches out and carried them with me to Richmond when the legislature met in January, 1906. Running true to form, nearly all these men... had forgotten what they had said in their campaigns; and even some of those who had spoken... in favor of a secondary school system... turned against it. Therefore, the state superintendent, Mr. Eggleston, and I went before the committee to bring our bill out on the floor. The patron of the bill did not speak, as was expected, but, without notice to us, said that we wished to speak. We pulled their pledges out of our pockets and told them that if they did not report the bill we would republish them in their home papers. Although I shall always believe that they had the power and the desire... to destroy the bill creating the secondary schools, they did not dare do it after that." [9]

SUMMER SCHOOLS FOR TEACHERS

A summer school for teachers was established at this time at the University of Virginia, which has since developed into a regular term. Professor Payne had now been appointed professor of psychology and secondary education in the University and this school was put under his charge. Summer schools had heretofore been conducted as chautauquas for popular instruction

[9] Bruce R. Payne, memorandum to the author, Jan. 23, 1933.

and entertainment rather than as schools for real study. There was, therefore, strong opposition at first to recognizing for credits in the University the work done in this school. Payne made this summer school a real educational one, recognized as a part of the permanent program of instruction in the University. A fine faculty of teachers and lecturers was organized and the plans for the school extensively advertised in the state, with the result that 750 students appeared the first session. They were earnest students, and the professors of the regular faculty were soon convinced that these common-school teachers were able to learn even faster than their regular students. "Many of them," says Payne, "never had talked with women teachers in their lives and couldn't understand that women could be as smart as men." And he adds : "I regard the summer schools for teachers with credit work as the greatest service ever rendered to public education in America. They have ... brought learning of a valuable sort to the teachers and the teachers ... have taken it to the schools. At that time the University of Virginia had only eight students from public high schools. The state had only a few high schools which could prepare them for entrance to its University." As a result of the success of this school, four other summer schools were established in different parts of the state for the benefit of the teachers who could not afford to go to the University. They did good service.[10] The quality of the instruction of the teachers improved ; the high schools multiplied and became accredited to the University, and the attendance from them grew rapidly.

CONSTRUCTIVE LEGISLATION

The May Campaign gave a great impulse to carrying out the provisions of the new constitution. When the legislature met in January, 1906, the people of the state were prepared for constructive work. Realizing that the hour had struck for a great educational development, Superintendent Eggleston now presented to the people the program of improvements in the school system which had been advocated by the Coöperative Association. The Department of Public Instruction was reorganized in accordance with the constitution. The board laid off the state into five divisions and appointed an inspector for each whose

[10] *Ibid.*

duty should be to examine and certify teachers and to organize a system of supervision. It was the duty of these inspectors to make plans for the training of teachers ; to promote the consolidation of the scattered one- and two-room schools into larger central schools, including high school departments, with schoolhouses built according to modern sanitary plans on larger school grounds ; to establish methods of transportation by school wagons ; to coöperate with district and county officials in securing funds for buildings and increasing the pay of teachers ; to educate the people through public meetings to make the schools the community centers ; and to show the possibilities of extension work through the schools. These measures were made possible by constructive legislation enacted in January and February, 1906, at the instance of Superintendent Eggleston. He threw down the challenge to the legislature that, if $50,000 was appropriated by the General Assembly, to be used by the State Board of Education for the promotion of rural schools, he would guarantee that the local communities through increased local taxation and private subscription would raise an aggregate of $750,000 additional for them. When the next legislature met in 1908, the aggregate increase had reached $1,000,000. On the strength of this, the annual appropriation for the encouragement of consolidated high schools was increased to $100,000.

Further to stimulate the closing up of the small schools through the consolidation into large central ones, a Loan Fund bill was passed in 1908. This provided for the lending of money from the Literary Fund to be used in erecting buildings on plans approved by the department. This money was loaned at the rate of 4 per cent and was to be repaid in ten installments. By this measure the Department of Education secured the direction of the improvement of the school buildings throughout the state. Adequate floor space, proper ventilation, heating, lighting, and sanitation, were secured by this measure in all the school buildings.

Other provisions of the acts of 1908 were the establishment of normal training schools in connection with high schools designated by the board and of agricultural and home economic instruction and extension work in one high school in each congressional district.

In 1906 there were only seventy-five so-called high schools, but only ten of these gave free instruction in a four-year course.

Under the stimulus of these provisions, the high schools increased by 1910 to 360 ; 143 of them giving a two-year course ; 81, a three-year course ; and 83, a full four-year course. The enrollment of the pupils in these schools increased from 3,400 in 1906 to 15,300 in 1910. The value of the school property increased during this period from $463,000 to $2,574,000.

Another bill of importance passed in 1908 permitted two or more small counties to unite and combine the funds available for the purpose of getting expert whole-time superintendents. As these officials were to be selected by the state board, this measure caused a storm of opposition from the politicians, who saw that this was a crisis for them. Superintendent Eggleston says of this, "Of all the fights we had this was the most terrific. While the State Board was not able, for the want of material, to go as far as it desired, it broke the back of this opposition, ... and from that time on, there was a steady growth of public opinion in favor of expert supervision through experienced superintendents. It was fortunate that we had as a member of the State Board of Education a Governor—Governor Claude A. Swanson—who was a wise and powerful man. His wisdom and experience moderated hasty action, but he stood by us to the finish." [11]

FARM DEMONSTRATIONS AND BOYS' AND GIRLS' CLUBS

Farm demonstrations, beginning with adult farmers, were introduced in Virginia by Dr. Seaman A. Knapp at the request of Superintendent Eggleston in 1907. Boys' corn clubs were started the following year. When the agricultural department of the Virginia Polytechnic Institute declined to forward the enterprise, Eggleston got Dr. Knapp to come to Richmond to explain the purposes and methods of his scheme to a number of persons whom he had invited to meet him. Dr. Knapp agreed to start the work in Virginia on condition that an effort would be made to secure an appropriation for its extension from the next legislature. Mr. T. O. Sandy was appointed demonstration agent and began his work in three counties. In 1908 the girls' canning and poultry work was organized and Miss Ella G. Agnew put in charge. In that same year the legislature made a small appropriation for the work. The farm demonstrations and

[11] Joseph D. Eggleston, memorandum to the author, Oct. 17, 1933.

boys' and girls' clubs aroused great interest, and the demand for them extended rapidly. County fairs to exhibit the work of the young people, at which prizes were offered, were inaugurated and attracted universal interest and enthusiastic approval. In 1914, after Superintendent Eggleston had become president of the Virginia Polytechnic Institute, the administration of this work was transferred to that institution. The demonstrations and clubs had now become general throughout the states and the business of conducting them was turned over to the agricultural colleges and has since been supported by appropriations of the national government and the states. Since a national system of farm demonstrations and "4-H Clubs" has been developed, this Virginia organization has been merged into it.

RESULTS OF DR. EGGLESTON'S ADMINISTRATION

Dr. Eggleston was superintendent of public instruction for nearly eight years, when he was elected president of the Virginia Polytechnic Institute. Heatwole sums up the accomplishments of this period as follows :

"The provision for public education in the new constitution of 1902 was one of the results . . . of the work of the Capon Springs Conference and the Southern Education Board. . . . The people of Virginia were stirred to the point of action by organized efforts of the leaders working through the Coöperative Education Association. . . . It was an opportune time for a man of ideas and action. Superintendent Eggleston realized that this enthusiasm must be conserved and utilized for great educational achievements. He . . . laid down a programme of procedure which resulted in the remarkable series of accomplishments which characterized his administration.

"The following are some of the outstanding features of his work : (1) the State Department of Education was systemized . . . and made effective as an educational force in the state ; (2) the various educational activities of the state were unified . . . into one great educational effort, directed toward the goal of popular education ; (3) a series of . . . legislative acts, providing for, (a) a state system of high schools, (b) a plan under which the trustees in the counties might borrow money from the Literary Fund for the purpose of erecting school buildings, (c) the control by the state Board of Education of the systems of heating, lighting, and ventilating of school buildings, (d) a scheme by which the division superintendents' salaries could be increased so as to secure expert supervision of the schools, (e) an appropriation to encourage the consolidation of one-room schools into two- or three-room schools, (f) the establishing and maintaining of normal training high schools and agricultural high schools, (g) a modified form of compulsory education, (h) a retirement fund for teachers, (i) establishment of three state normal schools for women, (j) the control of the sanitary and health conditions about the schools, (k) a system of medical inspection of the school children; (4) a system of demonstration and extension work by which agriculture and kindred subjects could be taught through ... boys' corn clubs and girls' canning and poultry clubs." [12] On this broad, strong foundation the present public school system of Virginia was built.

THE COLLEGE OF WILLIAM AND MARY

Of special interest in the field of public education in Virginia within recent years has been the work of the College of William and Mary.[13] Ecclesiastical and aristocratic in its origins, and long adhering to the traditions and beliefs of the Virginia planters whom it mainly served, it did not become a state institution until 1906.

The great Dr. James Blair, Commissary of the Bishop of London, with the sanction of the clergy and the Virginia Assembly, obtained from King William and Queen Mary in 1693 the charter of the College of William and Mary. It was the second college chartered in America. Harvard was the first. The college building was erected after plans of Christopher Wren. It was governed by a private Board of Visitors.

In the eighty years preceding the Revolution, it trained many of the men who formed the Republic, including Thomas Jefferson, George Washington (licensed as a surveyor by the College), John Marshall, and the author of the Monroe Doc-

12 Heatwole, *op. cit.*, pp. 346-48.

13 When Dr. Blair applied to Attorney-general Seymour with the royal command for his charter, it is said that Seymour objected on the ground that the country could not afford the expense to plant a college in Virginia, and when Blair urged the necessity of training ministers of the Gospel to save the souls of the people, Seymour replied, "Souls! Damn your souls! Make tobacco!"

trine. When Jefferson succeeded Patrick Henry as governor of Virginia in 1779, he proposed a plan for broadening the College to adapt it to the needs of the new country, and this plan was adopted by the Visitors. Divinity was dropped and the College divided into schools of philosophy, mathematics, including natural sciences, medicine, law, and modern languages. The Law School had been started by George Wythe, signer of the Declaration. The School of Medicine was preceded only by the one in Philadelphia. The elective system and the honor system were introduced for the first time. These changes gave character to American higher education in the years following. Jefferson proposed also at the same time that the College be turned over to the state and made the University of Virginia, but the Assembly, regarding it as the institution of the Established Church, refused to do so. It therefore continued, under the Board of Visitors, to represent the Church and the aristocracy, training members of Congress, governors, judges, legislators, and planters, who maintained the ideals of the Old Dominion and opposed public free schools. Lucian Minor, professor of law, was the only man at William and Mary who is recorded as having worked for public schools.[14]

Suspended in 1861 and its buildings occupied by Federal soldiers, the College burned in 1862. Though incompletely restored in 1865, it languished for years, suspending operations again in 1881. But the noble Dr. Benjamin S. Ewell, who had been president since 1854, rang the college bell regularly himself to show that William and Mary was still alive.

President Lyon Gardiner Tyler, elected in 1888, reorganized the institution as a college of liberal arts, and having secured the approval of the General Assembly in 1888 established a normal school in connection with it. Finally, an act approved on March 7, 1906, transferred the ownership of the College to the state and continued it with a normal school.[15]

Dr. Julian Alvin Carroll Chandler was elected president on July 1, 1919, and did a great and comprehensive work. He secured increased appropriations from the state and erected a fine new plant of buildings, including a model library. Mr. John D. Rockefeller, Jr., restored the old College building after the orig-

---

[14] See extract from his address at the Hampden-Sydney Institute of Education in 1835 in Vol. I of this work, pp. 72-73.

[15] College of William and Mary Bulletin, VI (No. 13, Jan., 1913), 41-42.

inal plan of Christopher Wren as the first feature in the restoration of the town of Williamsburg. Chandler reorganized and developed the College and advanced the standards of admission and of graduation. He made it a first-class college to prepare students for technical and professional schools and for public and social service. He built a great school for teachers. To do this work a large and highly competent faculty was formed. Dr. Chandler died in 1934. His monument is the new College of William and Mary, now a part of the state system and performing active service in the work of public education.

CHAPTER XXII

THE REVIVAL IN NORTH CAROLINA

CONDITIONS AT THE TURN OF THE CENTURY

THE story of the struggle for public schools in North Carolina continues to be interesting and instructive. In a former chapter the early struggles down to the beginning of the new century were told. The law passed by the legislature of 1897 failed. It sought to make local taxation the basis of public school support and ordered a vote to be held in every district in the state. But only eleven districts in the entire state voted for the tax. The people were not yet prepared to support their schools.

The census of 1900 showed that out of 286,800 native white voters 54,300, or nearly 19 per cent, were still illiterate. There were still forty-three counties in North Carolina in which one-fifth of the native white voters were illiterate. The illiteracy of the native white population of North Carolina ten years of age and over was 19.5 per cent, the largest of all the states in the Union. The North Carolina school census of 1901-1902 showed that there were 10,678 male white children and 10,246 male Negro children between twelve and twenty-one who could not read and write. Under the "Grandfather Clause" of 1908 no North Carolina man, black or white, twenty-one years of age, could vote unless he could read and write. This situation only spurred the people on to make more strenuous efforts to educate the entire population.

The new campaign in North Carolina in coöperation with the Southern Education Board commenced in 1902. Governor Aycock authorized Dr. McIver, chairman of the campaign committee of the Southern Education Board, to call a conference of the educators of the state to meet in the Capitol at Raleigh on February 13, 1902. Aycock himself presided. It was attended by some forty educational workers in the state, representing all the institutions of higher education, normal schools, and country school systems, who proceeded to organize a systematic educational campaign. As Connor says: "There was but one man in

336

the State who could have brought together all these warring factions and accomplished this purpose—him all, whatever their differences may have been, were willing to follow." [1]

As has been told before, Charles B. Aycock had been elected governor and pledged himself in his inaugural address, to the development of schools. His administration thus became one long fight for education. The situation offered the Southern Education Board a great opportunity, which the Board did not fail to use. Fortunately McIver, who, with Alderman, had made the campaign for better schools in the nineties, became chief field director of the Southern Board and organizer of the campaign in this state, where he had already done such fine work.

James Yadkin Joyner, professor in the State Normal and Industrial College at Greensboro, had recently been appointed superintendent of schools. He was most admirably qualified by training and experience for service in the proposed campaign and for leadership in shaping a new school system. After the death of McIver he carried on the campaign until 1919. The growth of all the schools which followed was in large part due to his wise and able leadership.

Aside from the awakened interest in the people as represented by their brilliant new governor, the devoted president of their Normal College and this strong superintendent, there was but small foundation to build upon. The situation with regard to local taxation was very unpromising. Only thirty districts in the entire state, all of them in towns and cities, had levied a local tax for the support of schools. The office of county superintendent was either a political job given to some attorney as reward for party service or a charity used to help some old teacher or preacher to support his family. The average salary of public school teachers was only $91.25 for a term of seventy-three days in each year, and that of the county superintendents was less than a dollar a day. There were few professional teachers in the public schools. Little interest had been taken in the erection and equipment of suitable school houses. Nine hundred and fifty public school districts had no school houses. The children were taught in poorly ventilated rented buildings, while those in 1,132 districts sat on rough pine boards in log cabins chinked with clay. Connor and Poe say : "Perhaps

[1] R. D. W. Connor and Clarence Poe, *The Life and Speeches of Charles B. Aycock*, p. 119.

under all these circumstances it was well enough that the schools were kept open only seventy-three days in the year, and that less than one-third of the children of school age attended them. ... To complicate a situation already sufficiently difficult, the race issue injected its poison into the very vitals of the problem.[2] Such was the situation when Governor Aycock and Dr. McIver started the new campaign with the help of the Southern Education Board. It was a well organized effort and it created a great revival of interest in schools in North Carolina ; as shall be shown later, it accomplished great results.

THE DUTY OF LOCAL TAXATION FOR SCHOOLS

The main objective of the campaign was the education of the people as to their duty to support the schools through local taxation. Down to this time the people of the South had not recognized this duty. Everything in the past history of their school finances had tended to make the people rely upon the state for the support of such schools as they had.

It is customary to attribute the wretched condition of public education in the South to slavery and the landed aristocracy. These had great influence in producing the educational situation, but the low esteem in which public schools were held in the South was not due entirely to the slaveholding aristocracy. It was due in part to the fact that the people had been educated to look to the state for all funds for the support of the schools. All the states had established their "Literary Funds" collected from miscellaneous sources such as fines, forfeitures, licenses, sale of public lands, etc., and had parceled meagre sums out to the counties for schools. This practice had been carried to such an extent that the people had no conception of their own duty.

This failure of local taxation for schools was the chief cause of the dearth of public revenue and the general apathy of public opinion in regard to universal education. A comparison between the revenues of schools in Massachusetts and in North Carolina as given in the report of the United States commissioner of education for 1902 shows that the total revenue in Massachusetts for the previous year was $14,192,760, while that in North Carolina was only $1,484,921, and that Massachusetts raised 97.2

2 Connor and Poe, *op. cit.*, p. 115.

per cent of this revenue by local taxation, while North Carolina raised by local taxation only 12.5 per cent.[3] Comparisons of western states, which had universally adopted the plan of local taxation, with southern states show the same thing. Wherever local taxation has been used it has been a source of ample revenue. Dearth of revenue for schools and apathy in public opinion about them go together. When public education is entrusted to the people for support and when the people know they have power to control it, then the schools become every citizen's private concern, and then the schools are certain to progress as the people progress in earning power.

"Declaration Against Illiteracy"

This movement for local taxation was the beginning of the great revival which brought in the new era in North Carolina educational history. The Conference at Raleigh adopted a "Declaration Against Illiteracy." The Declaration based its argument on the great illiteracy in the state and the pitifully small expenditures then being made to remove it. The Report of the United States Commissioner of Education for 1899-1900 had shown that, for every man, woman, and child of its population, the country at large was spending $2.83 for the education of its children while the people of North Carolina were spending barely $.67 ; that while the country at large was spending on an average $20.29 for every pupil in its public schools, North Carolina was spending only $3.00 or $4.00—the smallest amount expended by any state—and, finally, that while the amount spent for each child of school age in the United States was approximately $9.50 in 1900, in North Carolina it was only $1.78.[4]

Taking these facts as the basis of its argument, the Declaration continues :

"These facts should arouse our pride and our patriotism, and lead us to inquire whether the future will not hold this generation responsible for the perpetuation of conditions that have resulted in the multiplicity of small school districts, inferior school houses, poorly paid teachers, and necessarily poor

[3] *Report of the United States Commissioner of Education, 1902*, I, lxxxiii-lxxxiv.

[4] *Report of the United States Commissioner of Education, 1899-1900*, I, lxxvi-lxxix.

teaching ; that have resulted in twenty white illiterates out of every hundred white population over ten years of age . . . and, finally, in that educational indifference which is the chief cause of the small average daily attendance of only one-half the children enrolled in our public schools.

"We believe the future will hold us responsible for the perpetuation of these unfavorable conditions, and, therefore, we conceive it to be the patriotic, moral, and religious duty of this generation of North Carolinians to set about in earnest to find the means by which all our children can receive that education which will give them equal opportunities with the children of other sections of our common country.

"Viewing our educational problems and conditions in the light of educational history and experience, we declare it to be our firm conviction that the next step forward for North Carolina, in education, is to provide more money for her country public schools, making possible the consolidation of small school districts, the professional teacher, and skilled supervision of the expenditure of all school funds and of the teaching done in the schools.

"The adoption of the principle of local self help by thirty-five graded school towns . . . must surely be an inspiration and an example to every . . . rural community. . . . In adopting this principle of local taxation, they have secured . . . adequate school funds, . . . competent supervision, and . . . skilled teachers. . . .

"Remembering that in the last year thirty communities in North Carolina, some of them rural, have adopted . . . local taxation, we think this time most auspicious to urge a general movement of . . . all patriotic . . . men and women . . . to band themselves together under the leadership of our 'Educational Governor' and State Superintendent, . . . aided by the Southern Board, to carry forward the work of local taxation, and better schools." [5]

THE CAMPAIGN FOR BETTER SCHOOLS

The campaign was organized by forming an Association for the Promotion of Public Education in North Carolina. This Association arranged local conferences in all the different districts in the State. The first one of these was held in Greensboro,

[5] This campaign was financed by the Southern Board until the General Education Board was organized and endowed by Mr. Rockefeller.

in Guilford County, which was largely attended and addressed by Governor Aycock, Dr. McIver, and Superintendent Joyner. Dr. Wallace Buttrick, representing the General and Southern Education boards, offered to provide $4,000, to be used in encouraging the local districts to tax themselves, on condition that each school district should first levy a special local tax for free public schools. By private subscription $4,000 additional was raised at this Conference. The Greensboro people added $1,500, making the total fund $9,500. This resulted in raising, by a special tax in the districts, a fund of over $10,000.

The question of local taxation was the chief one presented to the people in all the conferences now held in the counties of the state. Governor Aycock, Thomas J. Jarvis, Dr. McIver, Dr. Joyner, and Dr. E. C. Brooks spoke at all these conferences. At each place local speakers helped to make the meetings successful.

Another Association which aided greatly in this improvement was the Woman's Association for the Betterment of Public School Houses. This was formed at a meeting at the State Normal and Industrial College in Greensboro, and included not only the officers and students of that institution but representative women, teachers, and citizens in various sections. Branches of this Association were formed in nearly all of the counties. The purposes of the Association were to prepare estimates for building new schoolhouses and remodelling old ones, for equipping them and improving the school grounds; to start libraries in the schools and to prepare lists of books for them; to decorate the school buildings with pictures, to prepare programs for entertainments, both social and literary, and to look after the sanitation and health in the schools, and the health of pre-school children. The Federation of Women's Clubs of the state and the North Carolina Teachers' Assembly coöperated with this Association with the result that it was soon in successful operation throughout the whole state.

The legislature in 1901 had made a small appropriation of $5,000 to encourage the starting of libraries in the rural schools. When friends had raised $10, the county board of education provided $10 more, which, added to the $10 from the state, made $30 to start a little library in each rural school.

By act of the legislature of 1903, the sum of $200,000, already accumulated from the sale of swamp lands belonging to the State Board of Education, with all moneys thereafter derived from the same, was made a separate fund to be used as a loan fund for building and improving public schoolhouses. From this fund loans were made to the county boards of education, payable in ten annual installments and bearing 4 per cent interest. Preference was to be given to the schools of rural districts and small towns, where the need was greatest, and they were required to supplement the amount thus loaned them. All buildings and improvements were to be made in accordance with plans and specifications approved by the superintendent, who supplied them. Since the establishment of this loan fund, sums amounting in the aggregate to more than one million dollars have been lent to communities in practically every county for building new or improving old schoolhouses. During the biennial period closing June 30, 1914, seventy-nine counties were aided by the fund, and the total value of houses built or improved during that time was nearly $800,000.[6] The legislature began in 1899 to make annual appropriations, to be distributed to the counties of the state, to lengthen the school term. The first was $100,000. From 1901 to 1908, $200,000 was appropriated annually. From that time this appropriation has been gradually increased until in 1916 it amounted to $250,000 annually.[7] In 1903 the salary of the state superintendent was increased and a secretary was given him for the first time. This was the only salary of a state officer increased in twenty years. An appropriation was also made for his office and expenses, and authority was given him to issue at public expense bulletins on educational topics such as local taxation, consolidation of schools, improvement of schoolhouses, and like subjects. The press of the state was of incalculable service in this campaign. McIver showed great talent as a publicity man and his numerous scrapbooks, containing clippings with regard to the different meetings and the progress of the work from all the newspapers, show how active he and his colleagues were.

YEARS OF PROGRESS

From the official report of the state superintendent of public instruction we get the following summary of the progress made

[6] Edgar W. Knight, *Public School Education in North Carolina*, p. 338.
[7] *Ibid.*, p. 337.

in the rural public schools for the decade 1901-1910, when this campaign was carried on under these auspices and with the support of the Southern or the General Education Board :

1. Expenditures for the elementary rural schools increased from $1,018,000 to more than $2,126,000.
2. The average term increased nearly a school month.
3. The value of rural school property increased from $1,146,000 to $3,094,000.
4. More than 3,450 new schoolhouses were built.
5. Expenditures for teachers' salaries doubled.
6. Enrollment increased 22 per cent.
7. Average daily attendance increased 41 per cent.
8. Average salaries of county superintendents increased from $243 to $796.
9. The number of local tax districts increased from 18 to 1,167.
10. The number of rural teachers increased from 7,971 to 9,440, and schools having more than one teacher increased from now on.
11. The number of rural libraries increased from 472 to 2,272.
12. Illiteracy among the white population above ten years of age was reduced from 19.4 to 12.3, and among the Negroes from 47.6 to 31.9.
13. The number of towns and cities establishing schools between 1901 and 1910 increased from 42 to 118 and in 1910 city school property was double the value of the total State school property ten years before.[8]

During the next decade, 1910-1920, several pieces of legislation of great importance were enacted. A state-wide property tax of five cents was levied for an equalizing fund. This fund was intended to lengthen the school term to six months. The legislature of 1913 required counties to show that they had provided funds for a four months' term for schools before they received any part of this equalizing fund.

The same legislature passed a rather mild and conservative act for compulsory attendance which required all children between eight and twelve years of age to attend school at least four months in the year. Another law of great importance passed in 1913 was one prohibiting children under twelve years of age from working in factories. The same year the state-wide law

[8] *State School Facts*, Vol. V (Nov. 1, 1928), No. 4; E. W. Knight, *Public School Education in North Carolina*, p. 341.

providing for the teaching of agriculture and domestic science in schools was passed. Another act permitted counties to issue bonds on approval by vote of the people to provide funds for building schoolhouses.

A State Association of County Superintendents was authorized by the legislature in 1905, and the counties were required to pay the expenses of the superintendents while in attendance. The seven normal schools for Negro teachers were consolidated as five and much improved under the direction of Charles L. Coon, one of the ablest school men in the state.

In 1907 rural high schools were authorized, and $45,000 was annually appropriated for their aid. This was increased to $50,-000 in 1909 and to $75,000 annually in 1911. This was the beginning of secondary education in North Carolina.

A professor of secondary education provided at the University by the General Education Board acted as supervisor of the high schools. Between 1907 and 1911 over two hundred rural high schools were started in ninety-three counties supported by state appropriation, special local taxes, county school funds, and private subscriptions.

First the Peabody Board and then the General Education Board provided the salary and expenses for a supervisor of rural elementary schools who assisted the county superintendents and teachers in the improvement of these schools. A supervisor of teacher-training was also appointed to direct county institutes and teachers' associations. By these measures the professional training of the teachers in the rural schools was much improved. There was a great improvement in the institutes and normal schools, and a corresponding improvement in the instruction in the rural as well as the city high schools during this and the next decade.

Two additional normal schools were established, one in the western section of the state in Boone known as the Appalachian Normal School (now the Appalachian State Teachers College), and another at Greenville in the eastern section known as the East Carolina Teachers Training School (now East Carolina Teachers College). The teachers' institutes were also increased and strengthened. The Normal and Industrial School, established and presided over by Dr. McIver, has been in operation since 1892 and has since become the Women's College of the University of North Carolina. The women educated in this college have been the builders of North Carolina schools and the promoters of social advancement in all departments of the life of the state.

CHARLES BRANTLEY AYCOCK

The great momentum given to education in North Carolina during this period was due to Aycock and his tireless and devoted workers, McIver, Joyner, Walker, Brooks, and the faculties and alumni of the universities and colleges. It was said of Aycock that he was "the leader of the State of North Carolina which was the leader of the entire South." His brilliant work gave him a wide reputation throughout the country and his services as an educational campaigner were called for from Maine to Alabama and from North Carolina to Oklahoma.[9]

The creed of these men was Universal Education—as Aycock put it, "educating everybody . . . and educating everything." Though concurring in the disfranchisement of the black man until he could qualify himself for intelligent action in public affairs, Aycock was the most conspicuous advocate for Negro education in the South in his time. He led in the fight to prevent an amendment to the Constitution to divide the school taxes to each race in proportion to the amounts paid by each. Such an amendment, he affirmed, was both unjust and dangerous and a gross violation of a solemn pledge that all the people of both races should be given equal educational facilities to prepare themselves for intelligent citizenship. The labors of Aycock and his fellow workers will ever continue a blessing to the future generations of the people of North Carolina as they were an inspiration to the people of the entire South.

EUGENE CUNNINGHAM BRANSON

When President Edward Kidder Graham called Dr. Branson to the University of North Carolina in 1914 to establish there a department of Rural Social Economics similar to the one he had started at the Georgia Normal College,[10] he told him that his duty would be to "Sell North Carolina to North Carolinians—and not the North Carolina of day-before-yesterday but the North Carolina of day-after-tomorrow." The de-

[9] Knight, *Public School Education in North Carolina*, p. 342.
[10] For Branson's early history see Vol. I.

partment organized by Branson had a four-fold purpose, each represented by a separate agency.

First, it should teach students the economics and sociology of the rural populations and train them to be investigators and practical workers.

Second, it should conduct field studies of the county governments and social conditions in the rural regions.

Third, it was to create a seminar library of books and sources of information, including bulletins, journals and clippings, and

Fourth, it was to develop a bureau of information to answer all calls for help.

All courses of instruction were elective for juniors, seniors, and graduate students. Courses were given also in the summer school and through the Extension Department. Approximately five thousand students were in attendance in the various courses during the eighteen years.

As a method of collecting data and training workers a "North Carolina Club" was formed of faculty members and students, which met fortnightly to plan the county investigations and study the economic, social, and civic situations and problems thus revealed.

During the last ten years sixty-five rural counties in North Carolina and twelve in other states have been reviewed by the field workers, usually students from the counties, studying county government, taxation, budgets, and other affairs in the courthouses. When desired by the people and paid for by them, these social economic surveys have been published ; otherwise copies are supplied to officials for their use. The North Carolina Club has published sixteen Year Books containing reports of its investigations.

The chief conditions attacked in these reports have been illiteracy and farm tenancy. When the North Carolina General Assembly met in January, 1923, the members found on their desks a report of 200 pages giving them the facts about the economic and educational conditions of farm tenants, which had been collected by Branson's men. There were 63,487 white farm tenants in the state, who with their families numbered 318,000 souls, or one-fifth of the population of the state. Sixteen per cent of the adults were illiterate. How to change these people into home-owning, educated, industrious, civic-minded citizens, is the problem North Carolina is now striving to solve.

The department originated for the benefit of the people at large, a Know-Your-Home-State-Movement. South Carolina, Arkansas, and Mississippi have established similar departments and started like movements.

The members of Dr. Branson's staff have published many volumes of economic and social investigations ; and forty-three research studies of counties have been published. The library now contains a volume of organized information about the home state, which is being used as the foundation of the improvement of the schools and other institutions of the people. All sound economic and social progress must rest on a basis of facts. This department has greatly advanced the knowledge of the people of North Carolina about themselves and their state. It has unquestionably contributed to create the progressive spirit which has so characterized that state in recent years.

Dr. Branson died at his post on March 13, 1933, after serving the people of North Carolina and Georgia devotedly for nearly fifty years. His work was original, fundamental, scientific, and epoch-making. Branson was not only a philosopher ; he was also a pathfinder. The future development of education and of all social progress in the South must be based on similar studies of the actual conditions in these states.

CHAPTER XXIII

THE CAMPAIGN IN KENTUCKY

JOHN GRANT CRABBE

THE campaign to educate the people of Kentucky about the needs of their public schools was projected by Superintendent Crabbe, whose term extended over two years and gave public education a fresh start in that state.

John Grant Crabbe was a professionally trained teacher and superintendent. After being graduated from a Kentucky high school, he took first the literary course in the Ohio Wesleyan University and then the teachers' course in the Ohio State University, from which he was graduated in 1897 with the degree of Master of Pedagogy. He taught for a number of years in the Flint (Michigan) Normal College, where he gained valuable experience. After serving as superintendent of the city schools at Ashland, Kentucky, for eighteen years, he was elected, in 1907, superintendent for the state. He resigned in 1910 to become president of the Eastern Kentucky State Normal School, where he has done a fine piece of work.

"A WHIRLWIND CAMPAIGN" AND ITS RESULTS

A definite plan to inform the people of Kentucky about the condition of their schools and their needs was carefully arranged by Superintendent Crabbe. Speakers were engaged, the press of the state was supplied with information, and what was called "A Whirlwind Campaign" was conducted for nine days in the fall of 1908. Thirty speakers, chosen for the purpose, addressed three hundred public meetings attended by sixty thousand people. Only three counties failed to coöperate and to make the necessary arrangements for these meetings.

The success of the first year's work was so great that a second campaign was organized in 1909. A hundred speakers were kept in the field for eight days, from June 27 to July 4 inclusive. The meetings were extensively advertised from the superintendent's office and by the local committees in each county.

Special efforts were made to carry the campaign into the rural districts. Rally days, all-day, open-air meetings, were planned for the country, with special programs, bands of music, and processions, which were attended by hundreds and thousands of people in some counties, where the people remember them to this day as the greatest events in their history. The speakers were some of the most prominent men and women in the business, social, and educational life of the state. The newspapers of the state were helpful. Leading in this work was the *Lexington Herald*, of which Mr. Desha Breckinridge, a grandson of the great Dr. Breckinridge, was president.

MADELINE McDOWELL BRECKINRIDGE

A powerful worker in this campaign was Mrs. Desha Breckinridge who had previously become a great leader in the social work in Kentucky. This remarkable woman was now to do a great work in the development of education, as well as of other social institutions of this and other states. She was a splendid example of what a talented brave woman can do for the betterment of our American life.

Madeline McDowell Breckinridge inherited some of the best blood and traditions of Kentucky. Her mother was Anne Clay, a daughter of Colonel Henry Clay, Jr., son of Henry Clay. Her father was a descendant of the Scotch-Irish Presbyterian pioneer, Samuel McDowell, who, after serving in the French and Indian wars, was awarded a tract of land in Kentucky and moved thence from Virginia. Samuel McDowell's fourth son, known as Judge Samuel McDowell of Mercer County, was appointed in Jefferson's administration as the first United States marshal of Kentucky. Another son was Ephraim McDowell, the great pioneer in the field of surgery. Educated at Edinburgh, he was the first man in the world to risk the operation of ovariotomy, the forerunner of many other abdominal operations. Madeline's grandfather, Dr. William Adair McDowell, was also a distinguished physician and published one of the earliest books on the possibility of the recovery from tuberculosis. Madeline's father, Major Henry Clay McDowell, the son of Samuel of Mercer, after studying law and practising it for some time, entered the Union Army, in which he served as an aide to General McCook. He was from 1862 to 1864 United

States marshal for Kentucky. Madeline McDowell, great-granddaughter of the "Great Commoner" and these Kentucky pioneers, married Desha Breckenridge, a grandson of Robert Jefferson Breckinridge, member of another pioneer family, whose life and distinguished services are told in an earlier chapter. As her biographer, Sophonisba Preston Breckinridge, says : "There was no Kentucky of which she was not a part." [1]

By birth inheritor of the best of Kentucky, endowed by nature with a brilliant intellect, indomitable energy, and a spirit on fire with love for humanity, Madeline McDowell Breckinridge devoted her splendid powers throughout her short life to the service of the people of her state and her country. The amount of work she accomplished is marvelous.

Beginning work as a journalist in association with her husband, the editor of the *Lexington Herald*, she aided in organizing in 1894 the State Federation of Women's Clubs and in 1898 the Women's Suffrage Association of Kentucky, of which she was made president. She later became vice-president of the National American Suffrage Association. She was next the active worker and propagandist in developing the Civic League of Kentucky for social service. Through this League, of which she was president, she was instrumental in making many social reforms and improvements. Her influence was soon felt throughout the nation, and she became an officer of the National Conference on Social Work, of the National Child Labor Committee, and of many other educational and social organizations of the country.

It is impossible to enumerate all the services of this good woman to various causes. It is her service to the children of Kentucky and their schools which interests us particularly. One of the most important pieces of work undertaken by the Civic League under her direction was the reform and improvement of the elementary schools of Lexington and of the state. This found an early expression in the Lincoln School of Lexington, which became a model institution for the whole state.

Mrs. Breckinridge was instrumental also in creating boards of education for all cities of the second-class in Kentucky ; the Kentucky Tuberculosis Association and the Blue Grass Sanatorium at Lexington ; a State Public Health Nursing Associa-

[1] The author is indebted to *The Life of Madeline McDowell Breckinridge : A Leader in the New South*, by Sophonisba Preston Breckinridge.

Upper left, Eugene C. Branson, pioneer in investigating the problems of rural life, founder of clubs for such study, organizer of the Department of Rural Social Economics at the University of North Carolina. Upper right, William H. Hand, for many years state high school inspector of the schools of South Carolina, professor of secondary education in the University of South Carolina, and superintendent of the city schools of Columbia. Lower left, William Knox Tate, one of the Southern Education Board's agents for rural schools, whose work for the schools of South Carolina was most distinctive. Lower right, James Yadkin Joyner, professor in the State Normal and Industrial College at Greensboro, North Carolina, later state superintendent of public instruction, and member of the Southern Education Board

Upper left, Madeline McDowell Breckinridge, a leader in social and educational work in Kentucky and a powerful worker in the "Whirlwind Campaign" of 1908 and 1909. Upper right, Henry Hardin Cherry, first president of the Kentucky Education Association and president of the Western Kentucky State Teachers College. Lower, Library of the Western Kentucky State Teachers College

tion ; and a system of associated charities in Lexington, which became a model system of relief and social welfare work.

Mrs. Breckinridge took an active interest in the work of the Southern Education Board and its representatives in Kentucky and had a part in several meetings of the Conference. She was an effective speaker and mingled wit and sarcasm in her eloquent appeals. At the meeting of the Fifteenth Conference at Nashville, Tennessee, April 3-5, 1912, she made an address on the "Public Schools and Southern Development," in which she said : "We have been passing through the 'Valley of the shadow' for some years now since our attention was first . . . called to the facts and figures contained in the United States census. We have dwelt in the depths of humility. For we were told that in certain tables of illiteracy of 50 states and territories there were none below us but Louisiana, with her overwhelming negro population, North Carolina, with her onus both of negroes and mountain whites, and New Mexico, with her hybrid Spanish and Indian population." (It is said that when she made this statement in an address to Kentucky women, some vehement person ejaculated, "Thank heaven for New Mexico!") She continued :

When we tried to lay the blame on our negro population, we found that it took the negroes to bring us up in the scale of illiteracy. When we tried to lay it on our mountain white population, we were told that in 10 Blue Grass counties there were but 92 fewer white illiterates than in the whole state of Maine, nearly twice as many as in the whole state of Massachusetts, and nearly twice as many as in the whole state of Nebraska. Now that made club women from the Blue Grass feel even more illiterate than when we were told we stood 47th in the scale of 50. . . .

But we are feeling better now because we have done something. We women of the Federated Clubs have at least made a beginning in what must be the long struggle against illiteracy in our state, and though it is but a beginning we like to tell about it. The educational conscience, the attention of the Federation was first aroused by the conditions of isolation and ignorance in the Eastern Appalachian Mountain region of our state.[2]

She then proceeded to tell about the settlement schools in the mountains of eastern Kentucky and of the traveling library

[2] *Proceedings of the Fifteenth Conference for Education in the South, Nashville, Tenn., 1912*, pp. 221-22.

work among them. This "library work found its culmination when the Kentucky Legislature of 1910 passed a bill put in by the Federation of Women's Clubs creating a State Library Commission."

In 1906 the Federation decided upon a definite effort to improve the condition of schools in Kentucky, and chose as its instrument the formation of the school improvement league.... An organizer was brought from North Carolina to show us the way, and the members of the education committee threw themselves...into the breach,...went to little country towns on and off the railroads, making school improvement league speeches, urging tired and unpaid teachers at teachers' institutes, on hot afternoons of July and August, to become inspired, and to go home and inspire the mothers and fathers of the school children.... Sometimes even we got the fathers and mothers to hear us.... At the end of a year and a half the *chairman of the Education Committee* reported that school improvement leagues were started in 110 counties. They began in the little humble ways that you all know : Washing school house windows—where there were windows ;—(in some of our log cabin school houses there are none)—polishing the stoves ; painting the school houses ; grubbing up the stumps in the school yard ; or what not. These leagues raised thousands of dollars from private sources for the schools. They furnished books and maps, book cases, teachers' desks, and desks for the pupils sometimes, school organs, and manual training tools.... The conscious object of the Federation was accomplished. There has begun to be a new school sentiment in Kentucky. It has already begun to show in better school laws and better enforcement of them, and in higher local taxation....

In the meantime a member of the Federation was working on the committee that drew the new county school board law for 1908. It is a very defective law ;...we had to make it defective because we were afraid to change too much at once. But it established a principle of county taxation that meant a great step forward. Following that the Federation was represented by order of the Legislature on the State Educational Commission. They drew a body of laws for the session of 1910...only it did not pass them. The Federation women have worked for the new small school board laws which will govern five of our cities next fall. The law for first-class cities was obtained in 1910, the law for second-class cities in 1912. Under these three laws political parties are eliminated from school affairs. Nomination is by petition of citizens. The ballot has at its head "School Ticket" and no party emblem is allowed, so that a virtual educational qualification is established. . . .

We feel that the capstone has been set to the work of our school improvement leagues by the establishment of a permanent organizer of school improvement leagues in the office of the Superintendent of Public Instruction. . . .[3]

Mrs. Breckinridge's address was described by the editor of the *New York Evening Post* as "the most brilliant utterance of the entire Conference."

THE "EDUCATIONAL LEGISLATURE"

Professor P. P. Claxton of Tennessee, representing the Southern Education Board, a speaker in the campaign, says that Mrs. Desha Breckinridge "was one of the fire-brands setting off the conflagration." This campaign had a fine effect in bringing the gospel of universal education nearer the hearts of the people.

The results of the "whirlwind campaign" appear in the legislation and in the increased taxation which followed. The legislature of 1908 passed the new county school district law, calling for the complete reorganization of the school system and the establishment within two years of a high school in every county. It passed a law regulating child labor. It made liberal appropriations to the State College and to the normal schools. It made the State College the State University and enlarged the scope of its usefulness. It changed the name of Kentucky University, a private institution, back to its old name of Transylvania University. It appropriated funds for the Kentucky Normal School for Negroes at Lexington. It passed a compulsory attendance and truancy law for cities of the first, second, third, and fourth class. It authorized an Educational Commission to make a thorough investigation of the whole system and report to the next General Assembly. This session of the legislature of 1908 has been called ever since the "Educational Legislature." It deserved the name. Dr. George J. Ramsey, professor of education in Central University, the secretary of the Educational Commission, prepared for it an elaborate report, considering every section of the law and comparing the usages of Kentucky with those of the other states. A new tentative code of laws was submitted. This code, which was based on the

[3] *Ibid.*, pp. 223-29.

existing laws and customs, so as to be evolutionary rather than revolutionary in character, provided for the gradual development through progressive legislation, of a greater and richer educational life in Kentucky.

It was not adopted by the legislature, but many of its recommendations became laws in later years. Under the new county school district law adopted, the local taxes in counties and districts were increased from $180,000 in 1907-08 to $1,000,000 the year after the first campaign.

The Kentucky Federation of Women's Clubs, under the leadership of Mrs. Breckinridge, now took up the matter of public education as its chief business, and, uniting with the State Library Association, established ninety-four traveling libraries containing six thousand volumes, which were circulated in 1909 in twenty-nine mountain counties. Forty school improvement leagues were organized by Mrs. Charles P. Weaver of Louisville, alone.

The Kentucky Education Association

The Kentucky Education Association was organized in 1902. Its purposes as stated by its first president, Dr. H. H. Cherry, were :

1. To bring together all the educational agencies in the State into a system organized in the interest of economy and efficiency.

2. To devise and get enacted a body of revenue laws which will provide for all educational purposes funds adequate in amount and stable in character.

3. To bring the State's educational business under an effective system of administration.

These three tasks are so intimately related that the working out of any satisfactory plan for financing the business will involve the working out of a scheme for its organization and administration....[4]

In a campaign document Dr. Cherry said :

The most serious indictment that can be justly registered against Kentucky is her failure to organize the educational agencies of the State in the interest of economy and efficiency, and to bring the State's educational business under an effective system of administration.... Kentucky for many years made the monstrous

[4] H. H. Cherry, *A Greater Kentucky*, p. 11.

error of turning over to incompetent hands millions of dollars from the treasury without exacting an educational standard or without offering a plan for an effective administration of the fund. As a result the millions of dollars were wasted on incompetent teachers, poor schoolhouses, inadequate and antiquated equipment, and a small, vacillating, and uncertain attendance. The present tax system of Kentucky is one of the greatest barriers in the way of development. . . . But the people do not need money so much as vision, moral and intellectual stimulation and direction, not only concerning things spiritual, but things material. The development of our State depends more upon the possession of information and constructive ideals and an appreciation of opportunities than upon the possession of dollars. . . . I believe in an educational "policy that will reach the homes of the land, improve the productive capacity on the farm, in the factory and elsewhere, and make the State rich in material things; but I would make the motive that prompts the effort love, service, and moral enthusiasm that will stamp each dollar with integrity and give it a conscience that will transmute it back into life, into ideals, into freedom, into human efficiency." . . . The State has no higher function than to take advantage of these great opportunities.[5]

On this platform the Kentucky Education Association went to work. Dr. Cherry tells us in an address made in 1931 what had been accomplished in the twenty-five years since the first campaign.

Twenty-five years ago—the school term was six months. Now, nowhere less than seven months and in many counties eight or nine. Then, the State per capita for education was $3.30; now, $9.00.

Then, the average salary of the rural teachers was $39.00 per month; now, $80.00.

Then, no consolidated schools; now, 403.

Then, only 41 four-year high schools; now, 631 fully accredited four-year high schools.

Then, fewer than 8,000 pupils in the high schools; now, 64,369.

Then, no provision for school supervisors; now, supervisors for special lines of educational work in the elementary and the secondary schools.

Then, teachers' certificates were issued carelessly and renewed on the basis of examination; now, high school plus college credits form the basis and renewals are made only upon the completion of accredited and professional work.

[5] *Ibid.*, pp. 10-19.

Then, the old trustee system of three members; now, each county has a board of education of five non-political members.

Then, the superintendents were elected on a partisan ticket and must come from their own counties; now, elected by the county board on the basis of training and experience irrespective of residence. They must be college educated.

Then, there was no provision for teaching music or agriculture; now, these are provided.

Then, physical education and sanitation were taught in only a few of the cities; now they are taught in all of the secondary schools.

Then, home economics was not recognized as a high school subject; now, it is given in many of the high schools.

These are some of the manifestations of the educational advancement in Kentucky since the Educational Association went to work.[6]

This was a truly splendid achievement.

HENRY HARDIN CHERRY

Henry Hardin Cherry holds the record of having taught forty years in Bowling Green in his native county—fourteen years as president of a private institution and twenty-six years as president of the Western Kentucky State Teachers College, which grew out of the private institution. During his administration over fifty thousand students have attended the regular sessions of the Teachers College and many more have studied under the Extension Department, in the training school, or in the model rural school. Cherry was a member of the executive committee of a commission for the campaign organized by Superintendent Crabbe in 1905 and one of the speakers. He was the leader in the campaign for the establishment of the normal schools. This committee secured from the General Assembly in 1908 more constructive educational legislation than had ever been enacted before. He was a member of the Illiteracy Commission, appointed by Governor McCreary in 1914, which became the model for the whole country. With J. B. McFerran he started the Farmers' Chautauqua movement, to give the country people recreation and culture—a movement which has been very popular and helpful and has spread into other states. And most important of all, he started the movement which

[6] H. H. Cherry, Address, *Teachers College Heights, Bulletin of the Western Kentucky State College,* January, 1932, p. 37.

culminated in the passage of a law in 1930 to equalize the distribution of the school per capita among the counties of the state.

Cora Wilson Stewart and the "Moonlight Schools"

The great movement of 1930 for the elimination of adult illiteracy throughout the country was started in a remote mountain county in eastern Kentucky. The people in this region had never had any but the poorest and crudest schools. In 1910 over twenty out of every hundred of the native born whites ten years of age and over in the mountain counties were illiterate. In 1911, after studying these conditions in Rowan County carefully and finding that the census showed 1,152 illiterates in its population, Mrs. Cora Wilson Stewart, at that time superintendent of schools of the county, decided to try the experiment of night schools for adults in the public schoolhouses. It was an original and bold undertaking. After making a canvass of the homes and explaining the plan to the people on Labor Day, September 4, Mrs. Stewart and her volunteer county teachers opened the schools the next evening. The roads were bad, the trails through the mountains were stony, and the bridges, consisting of only a single log, were dangerous. For these reasons the schools were to be held only on moonlight nights ; so they were called "Moonlight Schools."

The teachers waiting in their lonesome schoolhouses on that memorable September night expected only a very few to come ; but as Mrs. Stewart has told us in her delightful book, over the hills and out of the hollows there came that first night to the different schools twelve hundred people,[7] some of them to improve their imperfect education acquired in their childhood, but four hundred of them to receive their first lessons in reading and writing. Among them were not only illiterate young men and young women, but illiterate farmers and their illiterate wives, illiterate storekeepers, postmasters, and even illiterate ministers. There were storekeepers who knew only a few figures and kept their accounts on shingles ; postmasters who relied upon a boy or a girl who had been in school to keep their accounts ; and preachers who had to have the Bible read

[7] Cora W. Stewart, *Moonlight Schools*, pp. 16 ff.

to them. The first week the ages ran from eighteen to eighty-six.

The work of the first year was so successful that it was decided to continue it on a larger scale. So Mrs. Stewart organized in the following summer a Moonlight School Institute to train the teachers, prepare texts, and make other provisions for improving the teaching. As the grown-ups did not like to use the readers and spellers of young children, a broadside newspaper was printed called, *The Rowan County School Messenger*, which contained the neighborhood news, arranged so as to make reading and arithmetic lessons adapted to adults. The idea of being able to read a newspaper was fascinating to these people.

The second year one thousand six hundred pupils attended the night schools, of whom three hundred could not read or write when they came ; three hundred were students of the former year, and one thousand were men and women of meager education. The opportunities afforded were greatly appreciated and well improved by a majority of students. Competitions between the different classes and the different school districts were started and prizes awarded to those districts which succeeded in bringing in all their illiterates and teaching them to read. An enthusiastic man who had learned to read would bring his neighbor, and children would bring their parents to the schools. In this way the illiterates in the county were reduced in five years to twenty-three, of whom all were invalids or imbeciles except four obdurate or ashamed individuals.

Such enthusiasm was aroused in Rowan that the movement spread quickly to other counties. By 1913 twenty-five counties in the state had Moonlight Schools and Mrs. Stewart requested Governor James B. McCreary to appoint an Illiteracy Commission for the state. He commended Mrs. Stewart heartily for what she had done and announced on September 21, 1914, the Kentucky Illiteracy Commission, consisting of Mrs. Stewart, president J. G. Crabbe of the Eastern Kentucky State Normal School, President H. H. Cherry of the Western Kentucky State Normal School, and Miss Ella Lewis, superintendent of the Grayson County schools. Upon their call a thousand teachers offered their services and went to work immediately. This was the first commission of the kind ever appointed. Since that time similar commissions have been organized in most of the states.

They have awakened a deep interest and have reached people never reached before.

The Moonlight Schools did not undertake a complete educational regeneration. Their chief aim was to redeem the illiterates. But another purpose was to afford an opportunity to the "near illiterates" and the "half educated." The by-products have been very important. Chief of these have been the increased attendance on the regular day schools; increased interest and support for all the schools; the support of progressive legislation; and increased taxation for the schools. In 1910 there was no law on the statute books of any of the states referring to adult illiteracy. In 1931 there were laws in all the states providing for the teaching of adult illiterates; for the training of teachers for these schools; and for salaries for them. In some states there are laws compelling illiterate operatives to learn and providing for their instruction in the factories, mills or mines. Henry Ford, for example, enforces this in his factories and declares that it has resulted in a reduction of 54 per cent in accidents and losses.

Another purpose is the more complete utilization of the school plant. Think of it! There are 8,760 hours in the year and the schoolhouses open less than 1,000 in most districts where only six-months schools are conducted. What a tremendous waste in the plant and what an opportunity for the education of the grown-ups! For years the American people have been working to get a school in every community. From a doubtful experiment the local night school for illiterates has become an established institution. Why not night schools in every community in the same schoolhouses for more adult education, for more general culture, for vocational training, and for the promotion of community organization and coöperation? [8]

Though illiteracy in the southern states has been greatly reduced in the last thirty years, there is still much to do. These states still have the highest illiteracy in the country, only two other states, Arizona and New Mexico, comparing with them. They come at the bottom of the list of the states with from 5 to 15 per cent of illiteracy. Kentucky, for example, still has 6.6 per cent and South Carolina 15 per cent of illiteracy.

The methods used in the Moonlight Schools were followed

[8] *Illiteracy in the United States and an Experiment for its Elimination, United States Bureau of Education Bulletin No. 20, 1913.*

in the World War in educating illiterate soldiers in the army and in the rehabilitation work after the war. The National Education Association of the United States, the greatest educational society in the world, accepted the idea, proclaimed the emancipation of illiterates as the "second emancipation," and has made the removal of illiteracy the first purpose in its education program. The National Council of Education, the General Federation of Women's Clubs, and many other organizations have appointed committees to coöperate with it. In 1920 the eradication of illiteracy within a definite time was written into the platform of one of the major parties and was urged by both of the candidates as one of the tasks to which the nation should apply itself. There is now a National Illiteracy Commission connected with the Office of Education of the Interior Department with Mrs. Stewart chairman of its executive committee. Out of this movement has grown a still larger and broader movement for adult education.

Kentucky, the state so long backward in public education, has now an admirable system of public schools. And a Kentucky woman by inventing the "Moonlight Schools" gave the world the most effective plan ever proposed for removing illiteracy.

Mrs. Stewart, who invented, organized, and started the movement, had a knowledge of the needs, the intellectual ability to make a plan to meet them, a love of mankind, and the energy to do what no one else had thought of doing. She will go down in history as one of the great pioneers in universal education.

CHAPTER XXIV

THE REVIVAL IN TENNESSEE

CAUSES OF THE REVIVAL

SEVERAL causes contributed to the revival of interest in the schools in Tennessee, which began in 1902. The Peabody Normal College had been in operation in Nashville since 1875 and had trained many teachers who had now attained positions of commanding influence in the southern states. Its influence was beginning to be felt in Tennessee. The University of Tennessee had started a summer school for teachers in 1901, which with the aid of the Southern Education Board was enlarged into the Summer School of the South in 1902. A Department of Education was established in the fall of 1902, and Dr. P. P. Claxton was called to be its head. It was the largest faculty in education at that time of all the universities in the country except the University of Chicago and Teachers College of Columbia University. Among its members were Wickliffe Rose, who, after service in the Southern Education Board and the Peabody Board, became president of the General Education Board and the International Education Board ; Burtis B. Breese, afterwards professor of Psychology at the University of Cincinnati ; Emilie W. McVea, afterwards dean of women at the University of Cincinnati and president of Sweet Briar College ; Lilian Wycoff Johnson, afterwards president of the Western College for Women, Ohio ; Anna M. Gilchrist, afterwards director of home economics in India and New Zealand ; and Amanda Stoltzfus, later of the University of Texas Extension Department. The present College of Education in the University is the outgrowth and continuation of this department. The Bureau of the Southern Education Board had been established at Knoxville and, as has been told, was collecting information about the condition of the schools in the South for use in the campaign. The whole South was now awakening to a sense of its duty to education, and all the friends of the schools were preparing to start campaigns for their improvement. Tennessee was one of the first states to start this movement, and its University and Summer School were centers of propaganda for better schools.

THE WORK OF GOVERNOR FRAZIER

In November, 1902, James B. Frazier was elected governor. He was a graduate of the University of Tennessee, had attended the Conference for Education in the South, and had visited and lectured before the Summer School of the South in 1902. His message in January, 1903, voiced the Jeffersonian doctrine.

Universal education is the only safeguard for universal suffrage. It is the very bed rock of our civilization as well as of our prosperity; it raises the standard of citizenship, while it decreases crime and cheapens government; it increases the productive energy of the people and it augments the wealth of the State; it encourages healthful immigration and adds desirable citizens to the Commonwealth. It has come to be universally conceded in all the American Commonwealths that public education is a function of the State.[1]

He called attention to the large degree of illiteracy and the sad condition of the schools and said: "Our first and imperative need to improve the public schools of the State is more money." As a first measure he recommended that the surplus left in the treasury at the end of each year be added to the school fund and distributed; secondly, that the counties be empowered to raise their rate of taxation for school purposes to such a figure as would produce an amount sufficient to maintain the public schools for not less than six months in the year. He urged a reasonable and practical consolidation of the weak schools and the making of the school districts coextensive with the civil districts. He recommended an appropriation for county institutes, the continuance of the appropriation to the Peabody College, and the giving to the State University of "such aid as its necessities demand." It was the first message from any governor of Tennessee making such recommendations.

One of the first acts of Governor Frazier was to appoint Seymour A. Mynders, a graduate of the University of Tennessee, to the office of superintendent of public instruction. He was the best professionally trained man who had occupied the office since Eaton.

[1] *Message of Governor James B. Frazier to the Fifty-third General Assembly, State of Tennessee, January 23, 1903*, p. 5.

The first money paid by the State of Tennessee for public education other than the interest on the school fund or the certificate issued to represent the fund "lost" during the war, was the appropriation made by the legislature of 1903 on the recommendation of Governor Frazier. The act for this was drawn by Mynders and Dabney. It provided that any balance in the treasury at the end of the year after paying all the state's obligations, including the interest and sinking fund obligations and the interest on the school certificate, should be distributed to the counties for their public schools on the basis of their school population. The members of the legislature evidently thought that there would be no balance, or a very small one. But behold! At the end of 1903 there was a balance of about $250,000, which was distributed according to the law. At the end of 1904 this balance for distribution was over $375,000. When the legislature met in January, 1905, the members hastened to introduce a bill forbidding the distribution of this balance until further legislation could be enacted; but the comptroller, who was a friend of the schools, had already seen to it that the warrants for the money were sent out promptly and they could not be recalled. In 1905, however, the legislature annulled this act and made a definite appropriation for the elementary schools and provided a special fund for the weak schools in poor counties. These funds were both increased in 1907 and it was provided that to share in the special fund a county must first levy a school tax of four mills on the property and one dollar on the poll in addition to the dollar already required by the constitution. After 1909 these items were taken care of by the percentage of the funds created by the General Education Act.

THE BEGINNING OF THE HIGH SCHOOL MOVEMENT

As stated before, only one county high school had been established in the state under the law of 1899. There were high schools in the cities and larger towns and a number of private academies, but there were no adequate high schools for country boys and girls. One of the first things, therefore, that the University undertook, after it had established the Department of Education, was to promote the establishment of county high schools. The people had no conception of what a county high school should be. With the help of the General Education Board a county high school was established in 1904 near the University in Knox County, which it was hoped would serve as a model for others. It was named the Farragut High School for the great Admiral who was born near the place. It became a complete county high school. An elementary department was conducted in connection with it. With twelve acres of land, used for a garden and test plots, and with its teachers' home, barn, and poultry house, it demonstrated what a country school could be and should do. As a result, six other high schools were established in different sections. The Farragut School continued its work for many years and served an admirable purpose.

In 1905, by the help of the General Education Board, the University established a professorship of secondary education and combined with it the position of high school inspector. The duties of this position were added to those of Professor Claxton. From this the high school movement had its beginning in Tennessee. A few years later the legislature passed a law requiring every county to maintain at least one regular four-year high school. In 1931 there were, including high schools in the cities, 694 high schools in Tennessee and approximately 394 of them were regular accredited four-year high schools. The establishment of these high schools has promoted the interest of the people in education more than any other one thing that was done in these years.

CAMPAIGNS FOR BETTER SCHOOLS

In 1904 Superintendent Mynders and Professor Claxton organized a systematic campaign for better schools in Tennessee, which, aided by the General Education Board, continued through the year 1906. When Mynders went out, Claxton became manager of the Campaign in 1907 and continued to direct it until the summer of 1911. Advantage was taken of every opportunity to reach the people at commencements, religious meetings, meetings of farmers, and even picnics. Ministers were asked to speak on education and editors to write about it. Women's clubs put educational topics in their programs, and labor unions heard these speakers. The purposes of the campaign were discussed in teachers' meetings and institutes. Later the campaigners arranged their own meetings. Educational rallies, addressed by Mynders and Claxton were held in thirty-six counties in East Tennessee alone in the summer of 1905. Before the wrtier is a poster issued by the superintendent giving the dates of sixty-four educational rallies in Middle and West Tennessee, between July 30 and October 12, 1906. In this year rallies and mass meetings were held in all the counties of the state. Claxton writes :

Usually these rallies lasted all day with picnic-dinners. The best of them had wagon loads of water melons.... At these we spoke to more than 100,000 people during the year. In some counties half the voters were out. In many places the attendance ran up to two, three or four thousand and once to six thousand. It was a political campaign year and ... candidates were ... out for the legislature, governorship and United States senatorship. But we had much larger attendance at our educational meetings than the political speakers had.[2]

Besides Mynders and Claxton, "some fifty persons" spoke at these meetings. Seven distinct purposes were put before the people for action : More money for elementary schools with per capita distribution ; special help for weak schools in poor counties ; school libraries ; state appropriation to supplement salaries of county superintendents ; state appropriation for county high schools ; three normal schools for the preparation of white teachers and one for Negro teachers ; and a larger appropriation to the University of Tennessee.

These purposes were printed in the form of resolutions for adoption by the meetings and were presented to the county courts, boards of trade, boards of education, chapters of the Junior Order of United American Mechanics and other labor unions, patriotic associations, and women's clubs, which were frequently addressed by representatives of the campaign. Every one of these meetings adopted the resolutions unanimously except one, and at this meeting there was only one vote against them.

When the legislature met in 1907 the resolutions were submitted with a petition signed by a hundred thousand citizens urging action. A number of separate bills, carrying out the program outlined above, were prepared and submitted. Addi-

2 P. P. Claxton, memorandum to author, Sept. 18, 1931.

tional money for distribution to elementary schools and to weak schools was obtained at this session, but the other bills failed.

A Coöperative Education Association was organized to carry on systematic work for the improvement of schoolhouses and grounds, for the increase of the school tax, and for the creation of public sentiment which would result in the needed legislation.

The General Education Bill

In 1908 Claxton and his corps, with the coöperation of R. L. Jones, then state superintendent, conducted another campaign. Speaking teams were sent out and all the counties reached. Experience with the previous legislature had shown that it was wiser to put all the desired educational provisions into one bill. Resolutions, asking for the passage of a General Education bill and giving a summary of its purposes, were read, explained, and adopted at all these meetings. They were also adopted by the labor unions, women's clubs, farmers' institutes, boards of education, and some of the county courts. The bill met with great opposition at first, but after a long debate in both houses and a hard struggle it was passed by a good majority. This act appropriated 25 per cent of the gross income of the state to a General Education Fund and apportioned the Fund to the several purposes on a percentage basis.

This was the real beginning of educational progress in Tennessee, which has since proved steady and permanent. All parts of the system of public education were aided by this act; all were treated as essential parts of one school system with one heart and one life—not separate parts antagonistic to each other. The principles of this act had marked influence on the educational planning and legislation in other southern states. A prominent professor of education in Teachers College of Columbia University pronounced it "the most statesmanlike education measure ever pased by any legislative body in America." In a modified form this act is still the law in the State of Tennessee.

The Work and Influence of Philander P. Claxton

Claxton in 1909 wrote and secured the passage of a compulsory attendance bill, adopted first for twenty-eight counties and afterwards extended to the whole state. As chairman of a Committee of the State School Officers' Association he prepared a revision and code of the school laws of the state, which, though not adopted as a whole at the time, has since been enacted into the law in many of its features.

When Claxton came to Tennessee in 1902, the total income for all the public schools was about $1,800,000, or $2.36 per capita of school population; when he left in 1911 it was $5,537,029.90 or $7.31 per capita of school population. The school term had increased over 23 per cent; the value of the school property, about 75 per cent; the annual salaries of teachers, 82 per cent; the number of public high schools in towns and villages had more than doubled, and the number of public county high schools increased from one in 1902 to fifty; the largest appropriation made to the University before Claxton's time was $15,000. The General Assembly in 1911 appropriated to the University and the Agricultural Experiment Station $67,236 per annum; the appropriation to the Normal Schools which had been established was $156,281.

Claxton was a member of the Southern Education Board from 1906 to the close of its work and was secretary of the Conference for Education in the South from 1910 to 1912 and director of its Campaign Commitee in 1908-09. He was a member of the Rockefeller Sanitary Commission during the entire period of its existence. He was appointed commissioner of the United States Bureau of Education on July 1, 1911, and served ten years. He was provost of the University of Alabama, 1921-23; and superintendent of the city schools of Tulsa, Oklahoma, 1923-29.

In the campaign for the improvement of the southern schools, conducted by the Southern Education Board and the General Education Board, Claxton was one of the most active and efficient workers. While United States commissioner of education he extended his activities to the entire nation with great effectiveness. Though the work of shaping legislation and getting appropriations for education in the southern states has been Claxton's chief task, he has always been a student of the content of the school courses and of methods of teaching. He has broadened the courses in all the schools with which he has been connected, introducing music, drawing, manual training, and home economics in the lower schools, and science and philosophy in the higher ones. He has been a successful administrator of every type of public institution from the village school to the department of education of the University, the normal college, and the Bureau of Education of the United States. His long service to the cause of universal education has ever been distinguished for its wisdom, zeal, and devotion.

Though invited at different times by large universities to become their president, Dr. Claxton has adhered all his life to the task which he has considered most important for the country—the development of the rural schools. He is now president of the Austin Peay Normal School at Clarksville, Tennessee, an institution devoted exclusively to training teachers for the rural schools and the working out of plans for their courses of study, organization, and support. The rural school is the biggest problem left to be solved, and the work of this school will be watched with interest by public school men everywhere.

CHAPTER XXV

THE WHOLE SOUTH AWAKENING

THE REVIVAL IN LOUISIANA

THE soil had been broken and good seed sown in Louisiana when the Southern Education Board offered its assistance in developing public opinion for the schools. President Edwin Anderson Alderman, who had been elected to succeed President Johnston at Tulane University in 1900, was the director of the campaign work of this Board and was effectively assisted by Professor James H. Dillard of Tulane University, Professor R. L. Himes of the Louisiana State University, President B. C. Caldwell of the Louisiana State Normal College, Mr. James B. Aswell, and especially by President Thomas D. Boyd of the Louisiana State University.

Now came the great awakening in public education. J. B. Aswell was elected to the office of state superintendent in 1904. He was a graduate of the Peabody College, had been a teacher in the State Normal School and an institute conductor, and had developed marked ability in organizing as well in instructing people. He brought to Louisiana from the Peabody College many persons for parish superintendents, regardless of their previous locations. These professional superintendents stimulated the whole personnel. His administration of four years (1904-1908) was filled with notable accomplishments.

Upon the recommendation of Governor N. C. Blanchard in his inaugural address in 1904, a constitutional amendment providing for a state bond issue of $1,000,000 for purchasing sites and erecting school buildings, was submitted to the voters. The proposal was defeated at the polls, but the fact that such a proposal was submitted by the legislature was encouraging. The amount proposed was entirely too small, and it was decided wisely that the local authorities should raise the money for school buildings rather than depend upon the state. Later history showed fully the wisdom of this, for, a few years after, a single city, the city of Alexandria, voted a bond issue of $1,250,000 for three school buildings. Most of the parishes and many of the towns and cities have since provided liberally for housing and equipping their schools. Other important legislation secured in 1904 was a law giving the state superintendent authority to issue state certificates to teachers, and to require parish superintendents to pass examinations and secure professional certificates before they were appointed. An act was passed requiring parish school boards to add to the fund for schools and to purchase library books. In a few years working libraries were found in all the better schools.

With the hearty support of Governor Blanchard, the president, and the members of the State Board of Education, the state superintendent now succeeded in getting competent and energetic superintendents in the parishes. Following the example of the State Board, only competent and qualified persons were appointed on the parish boards. These changes enabled the superintendent to put all the teachers and officials upon a professional basis, lifted the public schools out of politics, and infused the entire corps with a high purpose.

The institute work was turned over to the State Department of Education at this time, and an institute conductor was engaged for his full time. The position was filled first by J. E. Keeny, and upon his resignation to become president of the Louisiana Industrial Institute, it was taken over by L. J. Alleman. Distinguished men, such as Charles and Frank McMurry, of Teachers College, Columbia University, L. D. Harvey, president of Stout Institute, Wisconsin, and Superintendent Stetson of Maine, were brought to give instruction in these institutes, which now became an important part of the school machinery, inspiring the teachers with ambition to improve themselves and developing professional spirit.

The General Education Board for a number of years paid the salary and expenses of an elementary school inspector and still pays the salaries of a librarian and a secretary for the library extension division of the department.

Up to 1890 there were practically no public high schools in Louisiana except in the City of New Orleans. Joseph A. Breaux, superintendent of schools in 1888, recommended the establishment of high schools in each parish, as a part of the system, but nothing was done to put them in the country until with the aid of the General Education Board, Dr. S. E. Weber, a graduate of the University of Pennsylvania and an experienced high school teacher, was secured in 1907 as high school inspector. As a result of his work, the legislature of 1908 made an appropriation of $26,500 for the purpose of stimulating the development of high schools in accordance with the standards prescribed by the State Board of Education. Weber's admirable work in laying out courses of study and planning high school buildings and equipments, has borne fruit in the establishment of many high schools in the rural districts. After some years the state took over the expense of this work, and there were three men and a secretary engaged in it in 1930.

Special levies of taxes for schools now became more and more common. When the people of a community desired a better school, they secured it by providing funds through special taxes. The boundaries of a district would be defined by the police jury and an election ordered for so many mills for so many years. These elections were required to carry both in the number of votes and in the value of the property voted. For these elections warm campaigns were carried on, and during the years the public school system was in the making the battles were numerous and hard. The voters had to be convinced that it was wise to spend more money on the schools. Public meetings were held and the voters were canvassed from house to house. The success of the schools in one district would lead the people of an adjacent one to seek equal privileges for their children. The good work spread in this way from district to district and parish to parish, until in 1920 most of the parishes had voted special taxes for new school buildings and for longer terms and better salaries for more competent teachers. In some parishes the enthusiasm for schools became so great that a special tax as high as fifty mills would be voted. It was at first impossible to raise adequate school funds in the large areas. In the small areas the people could be educated to give their money for schools because they there saw the benefits from them. The right of local taxation was given thus to the smallest units first. This plan resulted in unequal school facilities. The people of the well-to-do districts would tax themselves to establish excellent schools, while those in the poor districts were neglected. Thus it was gradually realized that larger taxing units should be used in raising school funds. For school buildings and equipments special taxes should be assessed locally, but for current expenses and for supervision the taxes should be voted on the whole parish. Every state should have a general school fund to aid the weak districts, at least in starting their schools.

Hundreds of new school buildings were erected during this period, many of them for consolidated schools. The business of consolidation was extended as fast as improved public highways permitted. So popular was the movement, in fact, that many children were hauled over mud roads in horse-drawn wagons. Road building was difficult and expensive in southern Louisiana, but the schools promoted the building of roads, and better roads made better schools.

The administration of Superintendent Aswell was characterized thus by a great school awakening. Ground was broken and seed planted by him which has been growing ever since. Aswell's accomplishments are summarized by his successor, Superintendent Harris, in his *Story of Public Education in Louisiana*, as follows : the crystalizing of public sentiment in favor of tax-supported schools ; the large increasing of school revenues in the form of special school taxes ; the building of hundreds of schoolhouses ; the placing of the institutes on a better basis ; the stimulating of the consolidation of country schools ; and the inaugurating of a high school system. "As State Superintendent of Public Education, he placed the entire State very greatly in his debt." [1]

Louisiana has been most fortunate in having Thomas H. Harris serve it as state superintendent of schools since 1908, a term unequaled in the country. When taken in connection with his service as principal of the Opelousas and the Baton Rouge high schools for the ten years previous, it is a record to be acclaimed. "His was a very difficult task, but with clear vision and quiet courage he has worked at it persistently and conservatively, and considering the difficulties he encountered . . . , he has done one of the best pieces of work in the South." [2]

As a result of the work of the high school agent, the number of high school teachers in Louisiana has increased from some 100 in 1900 (it was difficult to define a high school at that time) to 2,479 in 1930, and the number of high school pupils enrolled, from 2,215 in 1900 to 51,541 in 1930.

The total revenues for schools, reported by the superinten-

[1] Thomas H. Harris, *The Story of Public Education in Louisiana*, p. 95.
[2] From a letter to the author from former United States Commissioner of Education P. P. Claxton, dated Jan. 5, 1932.

dent in 1897, were only $1,052,420. For the session 1930-31, they were $20,902,363, or twenty times as much.[3]

Most encouraging is the progress made in eliminating illiteracy, as shown by the succeeding censuses. The total illiterates ten years of age and over in the total population in Louisiana, whites and Negroes, in 1880 were 49 per cent ; in 1890, 45.8 per cent ; in 1900, 38.5 per cent ; in 1930, 13.5 per cent. Of the total white population ten years of age and over in Louisiana in 1900, 17.3 per cent were illiterate ; by 1930 this was reduced to 7.3 per cent. Of the Negro population of the same ages in 1900, 61 per cent were illiterate ; by 1930 this was reduced to 23.3 per cent.

These figures give evidence of great progress, but more encouraging are the statistics showing the advance among the white males over twenty-one years of age, whom we must still recognize as the chief factors in the development of a really efficient democratic state. The percentage of illiteracy in this group was 16.9 per cent in 1900 ; 11.6 per cent in 1920 ; and 9.7 per cent in 1930. When we recall the difficulties that had to be overcome in Louisiana—the polyglot population with different customs and traditions, burdened with a great mass of untrained Africans, and the suffering under war and reconstruction—we are justified in rejoicing in the progress made by these people and in confidently hoping that enlightened and good government will soon be established in this great state.

PROGRESS IN FLORIDA

Considering the heterogeneous character of the population and the way it was scattered in small groups over a vast territory, Florida had made a good beginning by 1890. In the next twenty years there was a great growth in population and wealth, with a corresponding growth in the interest in free schools. The total population, which was less than 400,000 in 1890, increased by 1910 to 750,000, and by 1920 to nearly a million, three-fifths of whom were whites. One-third of the inhabitants of the state were born in the other South Atlantic states or in the northern or midwestern states. They came with

[3] *Report of the State Superintendent of Public Education of Louisiana, 1930-31*, pp. 22, 39.

ideals about schools and had great influence in advancing education.

The state now entered on an era of great material development. Lumber and cattle, which had been the chief industries, were replaced more and more by the fruit and vegetable industries. The railroads were extended and highways were being built. Florida was becoming a great pleasure ground and winter resort ; the old towns were extending their boundaries and new ones were being laid out almost monthly. The towns engaged in rivalry with each other in creating inducements for settlers, and good schools were made one of the attractions.

Summing up the financial situation of the schools in 1910, we find that there was a one-mill tax distributed to the counties in proportion to the average attendance. The county commissioners had the authority to levy a seven-mill tax and actually levied from three mills to the maximum. A three-mill school district tax was also authorized. In addition, there was the interest of the state school fund derived from the lands given by the United States, one-fourth of the sale of state lands, and the proceeds of escheated property. There were no direct appropriations by the legislature for the schools, for the constitution did not permit it. Superintendent Holloway made a strong effort to have this changed. He said :

Florida is the only State whose legislature, by constitutional inhibition, is prevented from appropriating money to the public schools.... It may appropriate money for the erection of monuments to our heroic and distinguished dead, but it cannot appropriate money for the live boys and girls. It may appropriate a million dollars for ... the State institutions of higher learning, with an aggregate attendance of less than one thousand students, but it cannot appropriate a cent towards even a common school education for two hundred fifty thousand boys and girls who are the sons and daughters of the taxpayers ... of this Commonwealth. A county may bond for a million dollars for good roads, or for the erection of a court house, or for any other public purpose, but it cannot bond for a cent for school purposes.... Any municipality may bond for the improvement of streets or for the erection of any public building of any character whatsoever, except that it cannot bond for the erection of a public school building.[4]

[4] Proceedings of the Fourteenth Conference for Education in the South, Jacksonville, Florida, 1911, p. 17.

This powerful plea accomplished nothing at the time.

Superintendent Holloway now led in forming a Florida Conference for Education. It was a volunteer association of the friends of education whose purposes were to awaken the people to a sense of their duty to the elementary schools and the high schools and to make the school the center of community life. Its platform was as follows : at least one high school for each county ; trained teachers, longer terms and better supervision ; the introduction of industrial and domestic arts, agriculture and business ; a laboratory for elementary science and a library. One of the results of this move was the organization of one hundred and eighty school improvement associations with twelve thousand members. These associations secured many enlarged campuses and improved buildings and libraries for the schools. Many counties increased their mill taxes, and personal contributions for school buildings and improvements reached an unprecedented amount. The conference had the hearty support of all the town chambers of commerce, and, what was remarkable for this time, it had the backing of the Farmers' Union, with its thirty thousand members, for compulsory education, the county high school, and the constitutional amendment for the additional one-mill tax. Directly and indirectly, the campaign of these associations "was the means of raising $425,000 for school purposes." [5]

The progress in high schools during this period was great. The standard of the high schools was much advanced and they were classified as standard junior, intermediate, and senior high schools. They were now real high schools with separate buildings and trained and adequate staffs. The senior high schools were later accepted by the Association of Colleges and Accredited Schools of the Southern States. In 1920 there were fifteen junior, nine intermediate, and thirty-eight senior high schools, a total of sixty-two with an enrollment of seven thousand. It is claimed that the advantages offered in Florida for high school education are not surpassed in the South.

These admirable standards were possible only through the improvement of the teaching body. This had increased proportionately in numbers, qualifications, and experience through better agencies for preparing prospective teachers and for training those in service, through a better system of examining and

[5] *Ibid.*, pp. 109-11.

certifying them, and especially through the offering of better salaries.

For the training of teachers in service special appropriations were made for summer training schools. Later provision was made for summer training schools at the University and the State College for Women. Similar provisions were made for the preparation of Negro teachers and their training in summer schools and in the State Normal and Agricultural and Mechanical College at Tallahassee.

For such a rapidly growing system of schools, largely increased revenues were required. To this demand the people of Forida have in recent years responded liberally. To summarize : Three constitutional amendments increased the school taxes. First, in 1904, the maximum rate required to be assessed in each county was raised from five to seven mills ; the next amendment in 1912 allowed an additional tax of five mills to be collected annually in any district where a majority of the electors voted for the issuance of bonds for the use of the schools of the district ; and a third amendment raised the maximum county school tax to ten instead of seven mills on the dollar. The people of Florida have at least shown their willingness to provide for the education of the white children of the state.

The condition of the schools for the Negroes has remained far from satisfactory. Though Negro children of school age constituted 40 per cent of the total school population, they had only 900 schools out of 2,600. Of the school population only 50 per cent were enrolled in all the Negro elementary and secondary schools and only 35 per cent were in daily attendance. The average school term in Negro schools was only 102 days as against 130 days for whites, and the average number of days attended by each Negro child was only 36. The number of Negro teachers employed was 1,300 out of a total of some 6,000, and one-half of these held only third-grade certificates, or less than eighth-grade preparation. The value of Negro school property was only $800,000, or less than 7.5 per cent of the total, and the amount spent for Negro education was less than $500,000, about 5 per cent of the total expenditure, or $3.65 for each Negro child of school age. The average annual salary paid teachers was only about $185. It is evident that there is much still to be done before it can be said that even the elements of an education have been provided for this people who form nearly half of the population of Florida.

The federal government has made large appropriations for the improvement of education in Florida, as in other states ; since 1892 the state has received nearly a million dollars for the maintenance of its Agricultural and Mechanical College. During 1914-19 it received $236,000 for agricultural extension work, and since 1917 it was given approximately $90,000 for the promotion of vocational education. These appropriations were duplicated by the state and have aided greatly in the advancement of rural education.

Florida had by 1920 a continuous school system from elementary schools through the high schools to the College for Women and the University.

In her commendable effort to provide facilities for higher education in the different parts of her widely extended territory, Florida had made the mistake of trying to maintain too many institutions, more than her wealth and population would justify. In addition to the State Normal School for white students at the De Funiak Springs and the State Normal School for Negroes at Tallahassee, there were the East Florida Seminary ; the West Florida Seminary, known as the State College after 1901 ; the Florida Agricultural College, known as the University of Florida after 1903 ; and the South Florida Military College at Bartow ; and the State Normal and Industrial School at St. Petersburg. The state had tried to differentiate the work of these institutions from that of high schools and from each other, but found it impossible. After this plan had been tried for some years, the leaders recognized that these institutions should be concentrated as well as differentiated. The legislature accordingly passed an act, known as the "Buckman Act," merging all the institutions for higher education for white students into two : One, the University of the State of Florida for men, located at Gainesville ; and the other, a college for women, the present Florida State College for Women, located at Tallahassee. The Agricultural and Mechanical College and Normal School for Negroes was continued at Tallahassee and provides both literary and industrial education and normal training for Negro men and women.

The University was opened in the fall of 1905 in the buildings of the former university at Lake City, where it remained until suitable buildings could be erected for its accommodation at Gainesville. It was removed to the new site of five hundred acres the following year. Since that time, a fine outfit of new well equipped buildings has been progressively erected. The object was to do better work, to save money, and to eliminate forever politics and local rivalries from the management of the institutions of higher learning. These institutions, forming an integral and vital part of the public education system, were therefore placed under one State Board of Control, coöperating with the State Board of Education.

One of the leading men in securing the Buckman Act was Dr. Albert Alexander Murphree, then president of the Florida State College at Tallahassee. Murphree is a fine example of the product of the Peabody College for Teachers. He was born at Walnut Grove, Alabama, of Scotch-Irish parentage ; received his early education at the local junior college and commenced teaching when fifteen years of age. After a competitive examination, he secured a scholarship at Peabody College. Upon the completion of two years there and two years in the University of Nashville, he was granted an A.B. degree in 1894. The degree of Master of Arts was conferred upon him in 1902. He became superintendent of schools in Cullman, Alabama, in 1894 and later principal of the Summit Institute in the same state. Murphree was next principal of the high school at Cleburne, Texas, where he remained until elected to the chair of mathematics in the Florida State College. In 1905, upon the passage of the Buckman bill, he became president of the State College for Women.

The new organization for the University of Florida went forward slowly. In 1909 Doctor Murphree was elected unanimously by the Board of Control and the Board of Education to the office of president of the University of Florida. He at first declined the appointment, desiring to continue with the State College for Women, where he was greatly honored and beloved. But after the call of the boards to the University was loudly echoed from all over the state, he decided that it was his duty to undertake the great task.

Under Murphree's guiding hand, the University of Florida grew from a small institution of a dozen instructors and forty-seven students in 1909 to one employing 400 professors and instructors and attended by 2,200 students in 1929. The physical plant was greatly enlarged. He made the institution a true state university, with a college of arts and science, a college of agriculture, a college of engineering, a college of law, and a graduate school leading to the degrees of masters of arts and science. The normal instruction was reorganized, and a higher teachers' college and normal school, with a summer school to which women are admitted, was established. When the Smith-Hughes Act for training teachers of agriculture, trades, and industries was passed, this department was named as the one to do the work. An agricultural experiment station, coöperative agricultural demonstration work, and a university extension bureau were established later.

But buildings and the number of the students and faculty do not measure the influence or success of President Murphree. A fine scholar and a devoted Christian gentleman, his influence over the students, faculty, and alumni was great. His vision of the University was the culmination of a life of earnest study and rich experience. He died too soon, but left a great monument to his devotion and wisdom.

President Murphree was succeeded by Dr. John J. Tigert, former United States Commissioner of Education. The most important development in the Department of Education in the University during President Tigert's administration has been the erection of the P. K. Yonge Laboratory School. The very complete and handsome plant for this school was erected with funds from the state's general revenue supplemented by a grant from the General Education Board. The buildings, which are models of their kind, contain typical school rooms, laboratories, shops, library, lecture and conference rooms, auditorium and gymnasium. There is a department of fine arts, an agricultural unit, laboratories of domestic science, and a cafeteria.

The school covers all the work from the kindergarten through the elementary schools and the high school—twelve grades in all. It was organized under the direction of Dean James W. Norman, of the College of Education and is directed by Dr. A. R. Mead.

The primary objective of the school is that of improving the education of children by the development of knowledge and efficiency through the investigation of problems of education. The preparation of teachers—their selection, instruction, training, guidance, placement, and follow-up in service—is the first purpose. The school provides many courses for graduate students as well as persons preparing to teach. It has a summer school open to both men and women, which is largely attended. This school is not only a noble addition to Florida's plant for the training of her teachers, but is a valuable acquisition to national resources for educational research.

Mississippi and Her Consolidated Schools

The system of education in Mississippi, as shown in the code of 1906 and the amendatory statutes, may be summarized as follows : There is a state superintendent elected by the people. A board of education is composed of the superintendent, the secretary of state and the attorney general, and has the management and investment of the school funds. There is a state board of examiners, appointed by the superintendent, which prepares the examination questions and grades the papers of candidates for positions as teachers. A textbook commission, appointed by the governor, selects and adopts a uniform series of textbooks for use in all the public schools for a period of five years. An illiteracy commission was created in 1916 after the pattern of the Kentucky commission.

In 1908 the county school board was empowered to establish an agricultural high school, one for white youths and another for colored youths exclusively in each county, in which instruction in the various high school branches and in agriculture and domestic science must be given. Twenty acres of land with buildings, including dormitory facilites, must be provided for each one. When these were established it was mandatory on the board of supervisors to levy a tax not to exceed two mills, for them. State support, varying from $1,500 to $4,000 annually, was also provided. By 1917 agricultural high schools had been established in forty-four of the eighty-two counties.

Consolidated schools were introduced in 1910 in sixty-seven counties, and the new consolidated school was entitled to all the funds received by the schools from which it was formed. The people might levy an additional tax for them. This has resulted in great improvement in the instruction given.

Mississippi claims to "lead the nation in the number of Consolidated Schools." The Survey Commission headed by Dr. O'Shea says : "There is a question whether any State in the

Nation has moved more rapidly for the organization and building of rural school plants than has Mississippi during the last decade and a half." Between 1910 and 1928 the white consolidated schools increased from 2 with 205 pupils and one teachers' home, the plants costing $8,000, to 969 with 168,523 pupils, 405 teachers' homes, costing $15,825,000. The homes are free of rent, and enable the teachers to take an effective part in the community life. The vocational—the Smith-Hughes—schools are the most effective of these consolidated schools. There were 350 of them in 1928—159 having agricultural classes, 78 mechanical shops, and 113 of them home economics classes.[6]

The high schools for whites in Mississippi have increased from 155 in 1920 to 427 in 1929. In addition, Mississippi has twenty-two agricultural high schools which enrolled in 1933-1934, four thousand students. They are all accredited high schools. Eleven of these schools have junior college work with three thousand college students enrolled. The plants are valued at over three million dollars. All these schools have dormitories with board as low as ten dollars a month. Also, each has a farm in connection with the school, which furnishes food for the dining-room and at the same time provides work for many students. In this way many students are enabled to work their way through high school and junior college.

Thirty-five consolidated schools and fifty teachers' homes for Negroes have been established in Mississippi since 1909 with the aid and coöperation of the General Education Board and the Rosenwald Fund. Five hundred and fifty-seven Rosenwald schoolhouses had been erected in Mississippi up to 1932.

The additional school plants for Negroes in the state are classified as follows: colleges, fourteen ; agricultural high schools, one ; County Teacher Training Schools, thirty-three ; Smith-Hughes Schools, seventy-nine. Fifteen summer schools are attended by over four thousand Negro teachers annually. Thirty-four different counties have Jeanes supervisors through the coöperation of the Anna T. Jeanes Fund.

The experience of Mississippi with transportation of pupils may be taken as representing the average in the southern states.[7]

---

[6] All data are from *Education in Mississippi* by W. F. Bond, state superintendent of education, 1930.

[7] Data from "Transportation Survey Mississippi Public Schools," in MS Bulletin No. 78, 1934.

Mississippi has fewer paved roads than the other states. Some think this accounts for the fewer collisions and accidents from other cars.

The total number of school routes in Mississippi	4,779
Combined mileage is	38,812
Average length of roads, in miles	8.1
Miles of paved roads	1,280
Miles of gravel roads of different grades	24,091
Miles of dirt roads of different grades	14,314
Total cost of all vehicles—4,312 busses, 449 horse-drawn	$3,109,514
Daily average number of pupils transported	136,001
Daily pupil miles transportation	1,309,503
Daily cost of transportation in state	$11,068
Annual cost of transportation in state for 1933-34	$1,770,914
Cost per pupil-mile	8½ mills

It will be noted that the cost of transportation is very low compared with other methods of travel—less than 1 cent per mile. The number of accidents compares very favorably with other kinds of automobile accidents. Mississippi had more accidents with ordinary passenger automobiles in two weeks in 1932 than the school busses had in a year. If, as is claimed, the safest method of travel is on a railway train, then the next safest is in a school bus.

After a long struggle under the most difficult conditions, in the face of a gigantic race problem ; through indifference and incompetence among its own people ; through war, Reconstruction, and poverty, Mississippi at last established a system of public schools. It is still incomplete and imperfect, especially in the provisions for the training of the Negroes ; but the fact that such progress has been made under these stupendous difficulties is ground for the faith that Mississippi will succeed ultimately in establishing a system "in which," as her first "Educational Governor" said, "every poor child in the country may secure free of charge the advantages of an education."

THE REVIVAL IN TEXAS

The Conference for Education in the South had begun its work for education in the southern states in 1902, but it did not reach Texas. It is probable its officers thought that Texas with her tremendous wealth was amply able to take care of her own affairs, but doubtless the movement of the Conference in other states stimulated Texas to independent action. The leading citizens and educators got together and organized a Conference for Education in 1907, which started a campaign in the state similar to that being conducted by the other southern states. Popular meetings were held each year for the discussion of educational conditions, and information was scattered throughout the state explaining the condition of the schools and their needs. The Conference continued this work for six years and achieved some valuable results, chiefly two constitutional amendments adopted by popular vote in 1908 and 1909.[8]

It will be recalled that under the Constitution of 1883 the property-tax-paying voters of a school district could, by vote of two-thirds majority, levy a local tax of twenty cents on the $100. It was frequently impossible to get a two-thirds majority to make this levy, which was totally inadequate in many places. Through the leadership of the Conference a campaign was carried on for some months, and in November, 1908, an amendment was carried by a majority of nearly three to one, which made a number of important changes. School funds derived from taxation might be used for the equipment of buildings as well as for their erection; the two-thirds rule was abolished, and a majority of the tax-paying voters could carry the tax. The limit of taxation was raised also from twenty cents to fifty cents on the $100. The next year, 1909, another amendment was approved by popular vote, permitting the formation of school districts lying in several counties. This rendered it possible to organize for better schools in very sparsely settled sections.

These constitutional amendments of 1908 and 1909, led to a large increase in local taxation. In the rural districts, where it had increased 7 per cent between 1904 and 1906, it increased under the new amendment 35 per cent. In the five-year period between 1905 and 1910 the increase in local taxation in common school districts was 153 per cent. Common school districts in 1905 were granted the privilege of voting bonds for building schoolhouses, for the first time. When it was found difficult to sell these bonds, the problem was solved by a law passed in

[8] Eby, *Development of Education in Texas*, pp. 220-22.

1909 permitting the State Board of Education to invest the permanent school fund in these district school bonds, as had been done for the bonds of the towns and cities heretofore. This solved the problem of financing schoolhouse construction.

The movement for the consolidation of small schools in country districts had been started also. Between 1910 and 1914, 148 consolidations were made in 123 counties. But due to "bad roads, community feuds, local prejudices, excessive cost of transportation, rivalry in re-locating schools, opposition of absentee landlords, sparseness of settlement ... distance to the consolidated schools, and the jealousy of local boards," [9] the effort at consolidation was largely a failure.

Another effort of the Conference for Education, in which it was aided by Parent-Teachers Associations, the State Teachers' Association, and other organizations, was to secure a compulsory school law. A number of bills were introduced, and the subject was thoroughly discussed throughout the state. The people were told that Texas enjoyed the distinction of being one of the five most backward states which had failed to enact a compulsory measure. As a consequence of this discussion, the legislature passed in 1915 a compulsory attendance act requiring all students from eight to fourteen to attend school for a minimum of sixty days. It went into effect in the fall of 1916. The next year the attendance was raised to eighty days and thereafter to one hundred days. Children might, however, be excused under certain conditions, and provisions for enforcing the law were weak, with the result that there was much laxity in its enforcement in the first few years after its enactment. But the people in the school offices became gradually more in sympathy with it, so that in 1918-1919 the school enrollment was 87.4 per cent of the school census, and in 1921-1922 it had reached 93.4 per cent, a most significant improvement.

Sam Houston Normal Institute founded in 1879 was such a success that all the other sections of the State wanted similar institutions. They were greatly needed for the training of teachers and have done a most useful work in Texas. Counting the Sam Houston Institute and the School of Industrial Arts for girls at Denton, Texas has eight teachers' colleges, as they are now called, in different sections of the state.

⁹ *Ibid.*, p. 229.

It was always in the mind of the people of Texas to establish a second educational institute in the far West. The people there clamored for it for years until in 1923 the legislature established the Texas Technological College at Lubbock in the extreme northwestern corner of the state. It is an institution for the practical training of youth in the arts and sciences.

It was not until 1911, sixty-six years after the entrance of Texas into the Union, that the state could be said to have completed its system of common schools. It was in that year that the privileges of secondary education were first extended to children of the rural districts. The opinion prevailed for a long time in Texas that the common schools should be limited to the elementary education that would fit the child for intelligent citizenship, and that the primary school was supposed to give him sufficient training for this. As late as 1884 Benjamin M. Baker, the state superintendent, declared that this was sufficient education "to enable him to participate in the privileges of a citizen and discharge the duties incumbent upon him as a member of society.... Is the high school necessary to mould the character of citizenship mentioned? I believe not." [10]

The church people favoring the academies opposed the high schools at first. William Carey Crane, president of Baylor University, one of the finest scholars in Texas, and Dr. Robert L. Dabney, professor in the University, opposed state public schools as late as 1886.

The towns and cities established their high schools in the early days, but it was a hard struggle for the counties to get any secondary schools. The private and church academies provided secondary education for many of the young people. The public funds were insufficient to provide high school instruction in the country. There was no adequate provision for secondary education for the poor boys and girls of the rural districts.

Governor Roberts, Secretary Hollingsworth of the Board of Education, Dr. Baldwin, principal of the Sam Houston Normal Institute, and Mr. Oscar H. Cooper, a Yale graduate who succeeded Mr. Baker as state superintendent, took up the matter of high schools for the towns and villages, and many were established by 1880. Rural high schools were not generally

[10] Quoted in *ibid.*, p. 248.

established until after 1910. Before that date conditions had not ripened sufficiently.

State Superintendent F. M. Bralley declared in 1911 : "The cold hard fact, ... is that, ... ninety-nine out of every hundred of the brightest and best of our farmer boys and girls will never have even a chance to enter a high school. No intelligent citizen, no statesman interested in the public welfare, no farmer with genuine concern for the future of his children ... can doubt for a moment the righteousness, the wisdom and the necessity of providing high schools ... for the farmer boys and girls of the commonwealth." [11]

It was the thirty-second legislature of the State of Texas in 1911 that took up the matter in a small way. It passed a law creating county boards of education and authorizing them to classify the county schools as primary, intermediate and high schools ; to establish rural high schools, arranging for free tuition in them ; and to consolidate school districts, "thereby giving high school privileges and opportunities ... to all children of scholastic age residing in the rural districts."

The small sum of $50,000 was appropriated for each of two years to help the districts to introduce agriculture, manual training, and domestic economy in these public high schools, and forty-five high schools were started the first year and seventy-four the second. The University of Texas gave the high schools an impulse when it established a list of accredited schools to train students for its classes. The Texas Teachers' Association urged their establishment and they gradually multiplied until in 1925 there were over two thousand five hundred high schools in the rural districts in Texas.

Thus was completed in outline the system of public schools that had been dreamed of by the fathers who founded the republic one hundred years before.

DEVELOPMENT OF THE ARKANSAS SCHOOLS AND THEIR LATER FINANCIAL HISTORY

John H. Hinemon, who succeeded J. J. Doyne as superintendent in Arkansas in 1902, was an aggressive man. He claimed that as the public school system was already established, it should be adequately supported. To accomplish this, the consti-

[11] Quoted in *ibid.*, p. 260.

tutional tax limit in the state should be raised from two mills to five and the district maximum should be raised from five mills to ten. The people eagerly voted the highest taxes permitted, which however were wholly inadequate. A committee of the State Teachers Association made a strong report in which they urged a larger taxing unit, extension of the constitutional limit of taxation, and consolidation of schools and transportation. Action was secured at last. The legislature in 1905 submitted to the vote of the people a constitutional amendment, and it was carried. It raised the limit from two to three mills for general taxation and from five to seven mills in the districts.

J. J. Doyne succeeded Hinemon in 1906 and carried on the work. By an act of 1907 an appropriation of $15,000 was made in order to start the much needed state normal school. This was located at Conway, and Doyne, who had been urging it for years, was elected president. The school received $10,000 from the Peabody Fund for an agricultural department and farm. It opened in September, 1908, with eight teachers and 105 students.

Doyne resigned from the presidency of the college on account of his health in 1917 and was succeeded by Dr. Burr W. Torreyson, who had been professor of education in the University and supervisor of high schools. For some years Professor Doyne has been superintendent of schools at Lonoke, Arkansas, where he began his teaching career fifty-five years ago, and is greatly honored and beloved. Doyne was one of the chief builders of the Arkansas public schools.

Another important act of the 1907 legislature was the permission to elect county superintendents. Eight counties elected superintendents the next year. Twelve years passed, one county after another electing a superintendent; then, in 1919, a law was passed requiring all counties to have superintendents appointed by the county boards.

George B. Cook was elected superintendent in 1908. He was also an aggressive officer and made a campaign to educate the people by publishing statistics and graphs showing how poor the Arkansas schools were as compared with those of other states. In 1906-1907 Arkansas ranked near the bottom of the columns in most things. The devotion of the teachers and the friends of the schools, who had been agitating for better things, and the work of Superintendents Hinemon, Doyne, and Cook, now began to bear fruit in legislation. The legislature of 1909 will go down in history as the one which started the real development of Arkansas schools. A compulsory attendance act was passed requiring children between eight and sixteen years of age in thirty-one counties to attend school not less than half the term. It was a weak, poor law, and forty-three counties were exempted from this act, but it prepared the minds of the people for a better law. Other acts of the 1909 legislature required the teaching of agriculture in the schools and appropriated $160,000 for four schools to train teachers of agriculture.

The legislature of 1911 continued this progressive work and passed acts permitting consolidation wherever two or more districts voted it, and endowing the consolidated districts with the powers of the special districts to borrow money, where so voted, and to provide transportation. A better compulsory act was enacted, a state board of education was created, and three-fourths of a fund received from the federal government on account of the forest reserves in Arkansas was given for the use of the county schools. Arkansas now began to have a real system of rural schools.

By 1915 all the public schools, which had now multiplied far beyond the means available for their support, were in great financial difficulties and were resorting to all kinds of expedients to keep open. There were too many small schools. Some communities raised special funds; some schools collected tuition from their pupils. The high schools suffered first and most. Their terms were shortened, salaries cut, teaching forces reduced, classes enlarged, standards ignored, and supervision abandoned in many schools. The limit of development for both elementary and high schools, under existing laws and with existing funds, had been reached and educational growth had ceased.[12]

[12] A series of twelve bulletins, published in 1926 under the administration of Superintendent A. B. Hill for the education of the people of Arkansas, about the history, progress, condition, and needs of their public schools, supply interesting information. These bulletins are models of publications intended for the instruction of the people. From them and from the biennial reports of the later superintendents, the facts used were gathered. These bulletins were published under the general title, *Four Years with the Public Schools of Arkansas, 1923-1927,* by A. B. Hill, State Superintendent, State Department of Education, Little Rock. Some of the titles are : *From the Beginning,* fifty years of growth ; *A Solid Foundation,* what the child studies ; *From Six to Twenty-One,* enrollment and attendance ; *Who Is Your*

Fortunately Dr. C. H. Brough, formerly professor of economics in the University, was elected governor in 1916. He advocated a tax amendment to the constitution and a liberal policy for the support and development of the state's educational institutions. The amendment to the constitution which was now adopted permitted local school districts on a majority vote of the electors to levy a tax up to twelve mills.

The twelve mill tax amendment, passed under Governor Brough, resulted in the increase of local revenue for school districts from $1,891,334 in 1910 to $5,450,856 in 1920. The next act passed on the recommendation of Governor Terral in 1925 permitted the districts to vote 18 mills school taxes. This act increased the local revenues from $6,491,820 in 1926 to $9,900,-000 in 1930. These measures enabled the people to maintain their schools in increasingly better shape. Governor McRae, following the recommendation of the school authorities, secured measures which increased the per capita apportionment fund from $1,730,234 in 1922 to $3,636,104 in 1926, a per capita increase per child of from $2.49 to $5.92. These additional funds were obtained largely from the severance tax and the cigar and cigarette tax. In 1929 these taxes amounted to $5.17 per enrolled child.

The most important legislation was the Equalization Fund law passed during the administration of Governor Martineau, and the Revolving Loan Fund law, which provided for the payment by the state of the money borrowed from the permanent school fund to take care of deficits since 1899. On account of the failure of the 1927 Assembly to provide revenue for the Equalization Fund, it remained for Governor Parnell and the Assembly of 1929 to do it. Parnell was the first public official to champion the Equalization and Revolving Loan funds publicly. Through his effort also the income tax law was enacted and the cigar and cigarette law amended. From these two sources $824,000 was received during 1929 for the Equalization Fund. The tobacco tax more than doubled by 1929.

The progress in the use of these laws is interesting. In 1927

Teacher, numbers, training, etc.; *A High School in Reach of Every Boy and Girl*; *A Place to Play and a Place to Work*; *A Library in the Reach of All*; *Me Too*, what is done for the Negro child; *Bigger Units—Better Schools*; *Agriculture and Home Economics*, and a study of the *Financial Support of Education in Arkansas*, sources of funds, ability of the state and deficiencies.

only 36 per cent of the districts voted the eighteen mill tax; in 1928 only 48 per cent; in 1929, however, following the provision for the Equalization Fund, 62 per cent of the districts, representing 80 per cent of the total assessed property values of the state, voted an eighteen mill tax. In 1930, 65 per cent of all the districts, representing 88 per cent of the total property values of the state, voted for the eighteen mill tax. Ninety per cent of all the children in the state now lived in districts voting eighteen mill school taxes. State aid encouraged the people to make the maximum effort to provide better schools for their children.

Consolidation was increasing rapidly in 1930. In 1929-1930 a total of $779,000 was distributed from the Equalization Fund in 392 consolidated districts in sixty-seven counties. As a result, nearly one hundred new consolidated school buildings in sixty counties were erected. The Revolving Loan Fund had distributed $586,000 to ninety-six consolidated schools in forty-five counties. It is noteworthy that, at the same time these funds were distributed, the per capita apportionment from the common school fund increased seven cents per child.[13]

The elimination of small school districts tells the story of consolidation. The peak in the number of small districts was reached in 1920 when there were 5,118 in the state. The state funds have caused their reduction to 3,478 in 1930. Calling attention to this, Superintendent Hirst quoted a Michigan bulletin as saying, "The place for the little red schoolhouse ... is in the Smithsonian Institution along with the flail and the ox-cart."

Consolidation brought about by the general application of the Equalization and Revolving funds has also increased the enrollment and advanced the standards in the high schools just as it has improved the elementary schools. The teachers in all the schools are improving. One-half of them, Negro as well as white, were in attendance on summer schools in 1930.

The Department of Education of Arkansas was organized in 1932 in divisions of teacher training and certification, elementary schools, high schools, research and information (including finance), Negro schools, vocational education (agriculture, home economics, trade and industries), and the Revolving and

[13] From the Biennial Report of the State Superintendent of Public Instruction (C. M. Hirst) for 1928-1930, p. 9 ff.

Equalization funds. Adult education (including civilian rehabilitation), sponsored by the federal government, was initiated in 1934. The General Education Board supplied funds for a director of teacher training (white) and a supervisor of teachers for Negroes, in addition to the agents for high schools and for rural schools previously mentioned.

The recent educational experiences of Arkansas are full of encouragement for states seeking Equalization funds.

CHAPTER XXVI

THE CAMPAIGN FOR LOCAL TAXATION IN ALABAMA

THE WORK OF JOHN WILLIAM ABERCROMBIE

JOHN WILLIAM ABERCROMBIE, who was elected state superintendent of education of Alabama in 1898, was an educator by profession and already had a rich and varied experience. He understood the fundamental needs of the schools and had the courage to tell the whole truth about them and the ability as both a writer and a speaker to put the facts and arguments in a way to stir the consciences of the people. As Dr. Weeks says, with perfect justification: "With the administration of Mr. Abercrombie begins the modern era of public education in Alabama." [1]

The greatest accomplishments of Abercrombie's first year as superintendent were acts of the Assembly which added $100,000 by direct appropriation, increased the amount available as interest on the sixteenth-section land funds, and levied a state tax of one mill for the exclusive use of the schools. These increased appropriations were apportioned in 1900 and raised the per capita distribution for that year from 73 cents to $1.05 and the next year to nearly $1.50. The total school fund now amounted to over a million dollars.

Abercrombie next called attention to the fact that the maximum limit of taxation in the state authorized by the constitution had been reached, so that no more could be obtained from the state as a state. In an appeal for local taxation, he said :

If our funds are not sufficiently large what shall we do? Shall we fold our arms and wait until Alabama doubles in wealth? If so, is it not likely also to double in population?... What we should do —what other states have done—what we must do, if we would properly qualify our people for citizenship, is to give to counties, townships, districts, and municipalities the power of taxation for educational purposes. ... The right of local self-government is a principle for which the southern people, and especially the people of Ala-

[1] Stephen B. Weeks, *History of Public School Education in Alabama*, p. 135.

bama, have always contended ;... yet, in the matter of providing for the education of our boys and girls, it is a right which the fundamental law of the State denies to us.... There should be no limit, constitutional or statutory, general or local, to the power of the people who own property to tax themselves for the purpose of fitting the children of the State for intelligent and patriotic citizenship.[2]

For this principle a fight was made in the constitutional convention of 1901, which was only partially successful at first. The new constitution of 1901 made it imperative that a state-wide tax of thirty cents on the hundred dollars should be levied by the legislature for public schools. It thus increased and made constitutional a tax, which, while already in the law, was of questionable legality under the court decisions of 1875. By making imperative this thirty cents, it changed the lump-sum appropriation, which had to be fought for at each session, into a perpetual one, which increased automatically with the wealth of the state. The lump-sum, together with the ten-cent tax of 1898-99, produced only $831,000. This new constitutional provision caused this total sum to increase steadily, until by 1914 it was $1,734,000 ; and it has been growing steadily ever since.

The new constitution also granted to counties the power to levy a total tax of fifty cents on the hundred, of which ten cents might be levied for school purposes.

In the cities and towns the tax limit was fixed by the new constitution, as it had been under the old, at fifty cents on the hundred, but to Montgomery, Birmingham, and some other cities was given the power to levy a special tax for public schools and other public improvements.

The constitution of Alabama of 1901 made another provision which was to have great influence on universal education. It established an educational qualification for voting. According to the census, 59.5 per cent of the male Negroes and 14 per cent of the male whites of voting age were illiterate. While the object of this law as drawn was frankly to eliminate in large part the Negro vote, it was recognized that the law would work for the elimination of illiteracy among both whites and blacks. After a limited period, if adequate educational facilities were provided for both races, it should develop a practical equality

[2] *Ibid.,* pp. 135-36.

in the right of suffrage. In the long run, therefore, the franchise laws adopted in most of the southern states at this time must be viewed as calculated to advance universal education and so to be an advantage to both races. But it should be impressed upon all that these laws created a new and greater obligation to provide proper schools for blacks as well as whites. The state, which after making such laws fails to provide facilities for its citizens to meet those laws, perpetrates an outrage upon them. This obligation is generally recognized by the southern people, although their purposes are still far from being fully accomplished.

In these respects the constitution of 1901 was an improvement on the former one, but it did not touch the most important matter, namely, the question of direct taxation for schools in the local units and in the towns and cities. These amendments, though good as far as they went, came so far from meeting the needs of the situation and the demands of the champions of the schools that Superintendent Abercrombie commenced immediately an agitation for another amendment. In his report of 1902 he says: "An amendment to the constitution should be submitted allowing school districts to levy a local tax for school purposes whenever the people of the district desire it. The schools of Alabama can never rank with the schools of other States until provision is made for local taxation." [3]

THE CAMPAIGN FOR LOCAL TAXATION

Edgar Gardner Murphy, executive secretary of the Southern Education Board, had been actively at work in the state and had enlisted the interest of many of its people in the new educational movement. Some of the men who had attended the meeting of the Southern Education Conference at Athens, Georgia, in April, called a meeting for May 29, 1902, at Montgomery, which was attended by a large delegation of college presidents and superintendents and principals of schools of the state. State Superintendent of Education Abercrombie presided and introduced Dr. Wallace Buttrick, secretary of the General Education Board, who stated the purposes and plans of the General Board in its coöperation with the people of the different states. This meeting inaugurated a new campaign for support for the

[3] *Ibid.*, p. 142.

Upper left, Braxton Bragg Comer, "educational governor" of Alabama. Upper right, John Herbert Phillips, builder of the schools in Birmingham, Alabama. Lower left, John W. Abercrombie, president of the University of Alabama, who, as state superintendent of education, began "the modern era of public education in Alabama" (copyright by Harris & Ewing). Lower right, Burr Walter Torreyson, president of the State Teachers College, Conway, Arkansas, and superintendent of public instruction in Arkansas

Above, the P. K. Yonge Laboratory School at the University of Florida. Below, the Administration Building of the Florida State College for Women at Tallahassee

schools. Murphy represented the Southern Board and announced that Joseph B. Graham, an attorney-at-law of Talladega, had been appointed field agent for Alabama. Graham had been a school teacher and county and city superintendent in Alabama for many years. He was chairman of the committee on education in the state constitutional convention of 1901.

The first object of the campaign now started was to secure an amendment to the constitution to allow counties and districts to levy local taxes, which the school men of the state had favored for longer than a decade. Murphy got out a pamphlet entitled, *Alabama's First Question*, containing arguments for local taxation by a number of leading school men.

The Alabama Educational Association joined in the movement, and local associations were formed in various parts of the state. Teachers, ministers, and citizens helped generally. The newspapers supported the movement actively. It was a campaign of education for the education of the people in the new plan of supporting the schools.

After having been reëlected in 1900, Abercrombie resigned on July 1, 1902, to accept the presidency of the University of Alabama, and his unexpired term was filled out by Harry C. Gunnels, who renewed the recommendations of his predecessor and carried on ably the work started. The constitution of 1901 had unfortunately provided that no state superintendent should be eligible to succeed himself. After serving his term, Gunnels was succeeded by Isaac William Hill, an educator of long experience. During his term the agricultural schools were reorganized and a state textbook commission was created.

The most important act of the legislature during Hill's administration was that of 1903 for "redistricting the public schools of the State and for the management and control of the same." [4] It will be recalled that from 1876 separate or special school districts had been created in increasing numbers. These districts could not, under the old constitution, levy a school tax, but it was now possible to arrange them topographically, making them much more convenient for administration than the old township lines laid out by surveyors in rectangles. County boards of education were authorized to lay out the counties into school districts in accordance with the topography of the country and the location of the people, so that every child

[4] *Ibid.*, p. 142.

would be if possible within two and a half miles of a schoolhouse, and no school would contain fewer than fifteen children. Districts which provided graded schools for not less than eight months duration could elect five district trustees instead of three and "assume entire control of the public schools, ... reporting only to the county authorities." The act did not apply to any county previously districted. Cities and towns which had been made separate school districts before continued as they were. The county was thus made the basis of administration instead of the township. In this way for the first time the whole state was reorganized into districts on the basis of topography, population, towns and cities—a result of immense importance as the foundation for future development. Hill was succeeded in 1906 by Harry C. Gunnels, who now served a full term of four years.

GOVERNOR B. B. COMER

Governor B. B. Comer, elected in 1906, got behind the educational campaigners and urged the legislature to enact the laws necessary to make the Alabama schools what they should be. He demanded a more liberal policy toward educational and charitable institutions and more careful attention to the other responsibilities of the state. He urged the necessary legislation and liberal appropriations for a complete educational system, including common schools for both races, rural schools, and normal schools. County high schools and the girls' technical institute were also established. Buildings were erected at the University, at the Polytechnic Institute, and at the Woman's College at Montevallo. When the people protested against the increased appropriations, he declared "that he was considering future citizenship as well as the contemporary taxpayers ; with more training in how to think and how to work, posterity would have a proportionately greater earning capacity and he would rest his case with posterity who would help to pay the debt." [5]

Comer was the leading cotton manufacturer in Alabama employing native laborers from the country around his mill. Placed thus within the reach of schools and the awakening influence of community life, the people rapidly advanced in effi-

[5] Thomas M. Owen, *History of Alabama and Dictionary of Alabama Biography*, III, 388.

ciency and usefulness and earned an increasing wage which enabled them to live better. He caused to be passed a child labor law, restricting the age to twelve years, and a compulsory education law requiring the mill children under sixteen to attend school at least eight weeks in the school term. This age limit was afterwards advanced to fourteen years. His mills showed excellent provisions for the health, education, and living conditions of his employes and led to distinct progress in these respects in all the mills in Alabama. He was said to have been the "most audacious executive who ever ruled Alabama"; but he was a fighter who protected and built up and did not destroy. He was called by a grateful people the "Educational Governor."

HENRY JONES WILLINGHAM

Gunnels gave place as superintendent in 1910 to Henry Jones Willingham. Willingham published a series of excellent brochures on the subject of local taxation and compulsory education, which were designed to educate the people about school conditions and needs. He showed that "even after the children are enrolled in the schools of Alabama . . . they attend only an average of 73 days." In a report he said, "Alabamians are willing to admit that their children are the best and the brightest of any in the world, but it is complimenting them rather too highly to expect them to compete in life's battles on 73 days' schooling with other children who attend twice as long." In another place, in referring to school conditions in 1914, he said : "School attendance is required throughout the civilized world today, except in Russia, Spain, Turkey, and six of the Southern States. How much longer shall we . . . in Alabama be willing to say 'Here we rest'?" [6]

Willingham became president of the State Normal School at Florence in 1913 and was followed by William F. Feagin, who was elected for a term of four years in 1914.

WILLIAM F. FEAGIN

The agitation over this question of local taxation had continued for fifteen years. Action had been urged by all the meet-

[6] *Educational Exchange*, February, 1914.

ings of the educational associations and by every superintendent during the interval.

The United States commissioner of education had placed Alabama at the bottom of all the states in the Union in educational efficiency. Owing to lack of educational facilities, the rural communities of Alabama were shown to be among the most unproductive in the South. These arguments opened the minds and hearts of the people, with the result that the campaign became a kind of educational revival.

In his report for 1913-1914 Feagin pointed out that one out of every twelve white persons, and one out of every four Negroes, between ten and twenty could not read or write. At the rate of decrease in illiteracy which had prevailed during the ten years past, he calculated that it would take sixty-five years to educate all the people of the state to read and write. He showed that in 1914 the percentage of enrollment in average attendance in the elementary schools was 61.6, while the percentage of the school population in attendance was only 37.2. The time was ripe now for great educational reform and improvement.

By way of illustration, it was shown by an educational survey made in 1914 of three typical counties that one man in a rural community with a low-priced automobile had more invested in it and spent more for its upkeep than a single community spent for maintaining its school, including the teacher's salary.

Superintendent William F. Feagin proved the man for the hour, and it was due to his leadership and work that fifteen laws, constituting a fairly complete school system, were passed in 1915 by the legislature. The most important of these laws was one authorizing the submission to the vote of the people of the state the question of a local school tax amendment. Other laws provided for better school supervision, a system of certification of teachers, teachers' institutes, a board of trustees for the control of the normal schools, and the establishment of an Alabama Illiteracy Commission, which should devise means for removing, as far as possible, adult illiteracy. Superintendent Feagin secured the passage of a law providing for a county system of supervision similar to that in the towns ; an elective county board of education with authority to control and regulate the schools and to elect and direct a county superintendent who must be professionally competent and devote all of his time to the work of supervision.

The most important act of this legislature of 1915 was that which submitted to the vote of the people an amendment to the constitution, authorizing the counties and school districts each to levy and collect a school tax not to exceed three mills. For more than fifteen years all of the state educational officials and teachers associations had been urging the necessity for such a local tax. Superintendent Feagin organized with great skill and carried out with great energy a campaign for this amendment. Through public addresses, through the press, and by the use of circulars, the people were informed about the conditions of the backward counties and the necessity for this measure. Finally after a hard contest the amendment was ratified by a vote of the electors of the state in November, 1916. Thus was established in Alabama at last the principle of local taxation for schools.

Next to the law permitting local taxation in all local units, the provision for compulsory education was the most important educational legislation enacted during Feagin's administration. The chief points of this law are as follows : The attendance of all children between the ages of eight and fifteen for a minimum period of eighty days in the year was required. County boards had authority to reduce this to sixty days in the farming districts when necessary. The only children to be exempted under the law were those who had finished the seventh grade ; those who lived more than two and a half miles from schools, unless transportation was furnished ; those who were physically or mentally incompetent ; those attending private or church schools ; and those unable to attend on account of poverty. Attendance officers were provided to investigate cases and report them to the teachers and to enforce attendance. Habitual truants might be put into state institutions and their guardians fined or imprisoned. This was an extremely difficult law to enforce among a people who had always believed in select schools and the right to control the education of their own children as they pleased, but it was a great step in progress. It was as strong as conditions in Alabama would permit at the time. The necessity of using the country children on the farm late in the fall and again early in the spring had to be recognized. But the chief cause of the lax enforcement of the compulsory law was that the school facilities were not sufficient to accommodate all the children even if they could be forced to attend.

THE TRAINING OF TEACHERS

The training of teachers for the public schools has always been and is still, next to the question of adequate funds, the greatest problem in all the southern states, and Alabama was no exception. Tutwiler had urged the necessity for better teachers and trained many of them for the private schools and academies. Perry, the first state superintendent, had discussed the necessity of schools for training teachers, but there were no normal schools or other agencies for this purpose until the Reconstruction period. The State Board of Education, established by the Reconstruction assembly, made provision (1868) in the academies of each of the cities for teacher-training classes. Pupils were admitted to these normal classes upon the recommendations of their teachers and upon promising in writing that they would teach in the schools of Alabama, when properly prepared, for at least two years.

It is said that in 1869 there were three hundred pupils in nine normal classes in the city schools of the state. At the last session of this Board of Education in 1871, provision was made for four normal schools for training Negro teachers of both sexes in as many towns, for which $4,750 a year was appropriated ; and for four normal schools for white teachers in four other places for which the sum of $4,500 was appropriated. Another act provided for a normal school for white women and set aside $5,000 for its use. Still another act established a Central Normal School for white teachers in the State University.

After the abolition of the Board of Education some of these acts were suspended. One act, which survived Reconstruction and was made a law in 1877, provided "A school of education for white ... teachers" in the building of Wesleyan University at Florence. A similar school was established in the Lincoln School in Marion for Negro teachers. As these acts were merely reënactments of the legislation of the Board of Education of the Reconstructionists, we must give that board the credit for making the first provision for training teachers in Alabama. In 1913-1914 there were six normal schools in the state devoted to the education of white teachers and three for Negro teachers. In addition to the contribution made by the state to their support, they received important gifts from the Peabody and Slater funds and, in the case of Tuskegee, from many other sources. In 1913-1914 the total contributions of the State of Alabama to all these normal schools was $114,500. This has since been largely increased.

Agricultural Schools

The district agricultural schools had their beginning in 1888 when one was established in each congressional district. Their purpose was to train the youth of the country for work in practical agriculture and horticulture. But the people, who naturally wanted their children to get a general education before giving them vocational training, made most of these schools into ordinary secondary schools. Thus these so-called agricultural schools were combined with the local public schools to make institutes, covering everything from primary to collegiate branches.

The law in 1903 attempted to restore these schools to their original purpose by putting them under a state board of control. They have since been put back upon their original plan and developed into real agricultural schools. In 1913-1914 there were nine of these schools, with a total attendance of 1,449, only 367 of whom were in the preparatory department and 1,082 in the high school course. Approximately one thousand students were studying agriculture.[7]

The Foundations Laid

Governor O'Neal in his message of January, 1915, pointed out the necessity for the next reform, which was to give equality of opportunity for elementary education to every child in Alabama. An apportionment of the school funds to the counties on the basis of school population was "manifestly unjust and inequitable," and he urged the distribution on the basis of attendance. To accomplish these purposes an attendance fund was created by the legislature of 1927 to be apportioned to the several counties according to the aggregate attendance therein during the preceding year.

In 1920 Abercrombie again became state superintendent of

[7] Weeks, *op. cit.*, pp. 178-81.

education by the appointment of the governor to fill out an unexpired term of two and one-half years. In 1922 he was reëlected for a term of four years. The recommendations in his reports were in accordance with the best educational ideals of the time. He succeeded in having some of them embodied into law ; many of them have become laws since. During his several administrations he reorganized the State Department of Education and the public school system. He raised the minimum qualifications of county superintendents to one year of collegiate study above normal school graduation or three years of college. He organized civilian rehabilitation in accordance with the provisions of the federal acts after the World War and arranged a service for crippled children in the division of vocational education in the State Department of Education. His success in defeating in the legislature measures which would have destroyed the county unit system of school administration and thrown it back into politics, was almost as important as his constructive work.

By these acts Alabama laid the foundations for her present system of schools and progress has been steady ever since, or until the economic depression which began in 1929.

JOHN HERBERT PHILLIPS AND THE BIRMINGHAM SCHOOLS

John Herbert Phillips, the builder of the system of schools in Birmingham, Alabama, was born December 12, 1853, in Covington, Kentucky, of Welsh parents, who had come to the United States in 1849. The boy grew up on a farm in Gallia County, Ohio, and attended the common schools and the county academy. After teaching in rural schools for several years, he took his A. M. degree at Marietta College in 1883. He studied at the Universities of Chicago and Edinburgh, and at thirty years of age he had made a reputation as a scholar, teacher, and principal. By his addresses at educational meetings, he attracted the attention of the profession, with the result that in 1883 he was called to organize and superintend the public schools of Birmingham. Here he labored continuously for thirty-eight years and built from the foundation one of the best systems of schools in the country. He died at his post on July 21, 1921, the most beloved citizen of his city and one of the most respected public school men of the country.

Birmingham in 1883 was a small new town, producing coal,

iron, and steel. It had a population of between four and five thousand, nearly half Negroes. As a majority of the whites were of the native stock, having the old southern ideas about schools, they preferred private and church institutions. There was, however, an element of northern and western people and enough progressive southerners to decide in favor of free public schools.

Phillips was an ideal man for the position. He had the social outlook and the breadth of view that fitted him for work in this growing southern city. He took immediate root and grew rapidly in sympathy with the community and influence in it. His first move was to start a normal school, which he taught himself. In this school he trained many of the men and women forming the excellent body of assistants and teachers, who helped him to build his system of schools. Tested merit was the basis of all appointments and promotions. Continuity in service under such conditions gave the teachers experience and developed in them *esprit de corps* and devotion to their leader and to their work for the children.

Such a body of teachers attracted more and more pupils, whose parents soon came to believe heartily in the public schools. As the attendance increased, surveys were made to ascertain the trend of the population ; the needs were explained to the people, who then voted bonds for sites, buildings and equipment ; and a school plant of admirable structures was progressively erected. Beautiful school gardens and ample playgrounds were constructed.

With great sagacity and foresight, Dr. Phillips secured from the legislature at the beginning laws for the organization of the city government and of the board of education, which were new in the country at the time, but have proved most wise and advantageous. A commission form of government was constituted. This commission, made up of leading citizens, appointed a board of education of five members, one member being appointed every year to serve for five years. This plan has produced a fine board of the best qualified citizens. The members have thus been able to keep the schools free from the influence of politics and all special interests—the bane of many public schools. One significant result of the plan has been the continuity in service for long terms of the administrative officers of the board and of the schools. A staff of experts has served the board for years. In fifty years there have been only two superintendents, Dr. Phillips and his able successor, Dr. Charles B. Glenn, who had long been associated with him and was elected immediately after his death. Carrying out the admirable policy of promotion of trained and experienced men, Principal Charles A. Brown, of the Central High School was made associate superintendent in charge of high schools and Principal L. Frazier Banks, of the Martin School, was made assistant superintendent in charge of the elementary schools. The board has been a remarkably permanent one also. For example, the board in 1932, consisting of five, had two members who had served for ten years and one who had served nine.

The laws Phillips secured for providing funds for the system were unique in school history and have proved most satisfactory. A three-mill levy for the schools, to be raised annually until 1952, was first authorized by the legislature. When the schools grew, an additional levy of two mills was approved to run until 1941. More recently a special levy of one and one-half mills was authorized to be raised each year until 1934. All moneys so raised are set aside in the treasury for the use of the schools and may be used for no other purpose. This plan gives regular, permanent funds for the support and upbuilding of the schools. They can grow thus with the increase in wealth of the city. New sites, buildings, and equipment are provided from bond issues. The wisdom and advantage of this plan of financing the system of schools are evident. The plan of mill levies is used in some states to provide funds for the support of their universities, but it has not become general for schools. It is commended to all cities. School funds should be adjusted to the school population and permanently provided and should not depend on changing political currents. If economic conditions change, school funds should be the last thing to be changed.

The school revenues of Birmingham are received from two principal funds :

1. The Board of Education Fund, derived chiefly from the tax levies distributed to the school districts of Jefferson County, of which Birmingham is one, on the basis of daily attendance. This forms about 40 per cent of the total revenues.

2. From city tax levies, about 51 per cent of the total.

3. Other revenues from state and other sources about 9 per cent.

The total operating cost of the schools in 1920-21, the last year of Phillips's administration, was $1,230,023.

The per capita cost per pupil, white and Negro together, was $43.74 per annum.

The total operating cost in 1929-30 was $2,932,562.

The per capita cost was $65.15.

The average per capita cost in 52 cities in the United States in this year was $112.89, or nearly double the Birmingham cost.

But Birmingham spends for schools about 10 per cent more of its total operating costs than the average city in the United States and it ranks fourth in the country in its proportional expenditure for schools—a practical proof of the appreciation of the people of their schools.[8]

The growth of the schools is the best evidence of their appreciation by the people. In the past ten years (1921 to 1931), the total school enrollment increased 57 per cent, while the school census enumeration increased only 21 per cent. During the same period the high school enrollment has increased 159 per cent and the night school enrollment 215 per cent. In 1930 Birmingham ranked ninth among eighty-one cities in the United States of 100,000 population in the percentage of its total population in the schools.

Phillips introduced many features into the Birmingham schools, which were new in the South at the time. The department of child health made inspections of the children at entrance each fall and regular examinations to locate defects and note progress in their development during the year. It made sanitary inspections of every part of all the schools. It taught health in the elementary schools and gave health lessons once each week in the auditorium of every school.

Music was taught individually and collectively through singing lessons, instruction in music appreciation, rhythm bands, glee clubs, choirs, bands, and an orchestra. Art was taught, not merely through "drawing," but by study of fine examples. Self-expression in art was developed through working out problems in decoration and design and in art clubs. A department of home economics trained for home-making in all its interests. There was a credit system for home and outside work in music, art, and home economics. There was a department of vocational training and a corps of the R.O.T.C.

[8] From statistical circulars of the United States Office of Education.

Religious education included daily Bible readings in each group, as required by state law. Coöperation with the Sunday schools and credits for Sunday school work were arranged. In 1920-1921 certificates of credits on Sunday schools were issued to 25 per cent of the average membership in the public schools. Religious schools in connection with some of the high and elementary schools were conducted by the city Sunday School Council, and pupils were permitted to attend twice a week for thirty minutes. Teachers paid by the churches joined in this work. The religious instruction in the schools is now carried on under a regular supervision. The Kiwanis Club erected a building near one of the high schools and an elementary school for this purpose. The system of religious instruction in the public schools of Birmingham has become a model for the country.

A separate system of schools for the Negroes, with ample buildings and an excellent corps of teachers, was developed at the same time. The system includes a full list of elementary schools, a high school and an industrial school. In the Negro schools the same general plans are followed as in the white schools. In the elementary schools the courses of study are modified to meet the needs of the Negro boys and girls. More industrial work is introduced, such as cooking, laundering, tailoring, gardening, and handicrafts generally. The same records of enrollment and attendance are kept and the same methods of organization and supervision are followed by the assistant superintendent in charge. The same emphasis is put on health and character education and right living.

The Negro schools have shared in the benefits of the large building plans. Small schools for primary grades have been multiplied in the Negro districts and ample shop facilities provided in the larger ones.

The Industrial High School for Negroes, started in 1899, is now the largest in the South. In 1921 the enrollment was 615 pupils with 19 teachers. In 1931 it had 2,794 pupils and 72 teachers. The present building covers a whole city block and contains various shops and laboratories. The course, which is academic and industrial, is designed to give the boys and girls the best preparation for the work of life. One-third of the time of every student is devoted to two industrial arts, such as mechanical drawing, carpentry, and gardening, for boys; and sewing, cooking, and laundering, for girls. In the advanced classes such trades as printing, auto-mechanics, upholstering, millinery, nursing, and household management, are taken up. The musical talent, so characteristic of the race, is cultivated individually and collectively. The athletic activities are organized in baseball, football, and basketball teams. Community sings and athletic events are greatly enjoyed by the people. As a result of the work of this excellent school, there are more Negro high school and industrial school graduates in Birmingham than in any other city in the South. An excellent library in a separate building is maintained for the Negro people.

This statement would not be complete without a reference to the influence of the character, life, and services of Dr. Phillips's wife, Minnie Holman, a teacher of unusual ability and charm in the schools of Birmingham. Equipped with first-hand knowledge of educational matters, a cultural background, and innate qualities of leadership, during twenty-three years of happy married life Minnie Holman aided Dr. Phillips in all his progressive work for the benefit of the children of Birmingham. She died on July 11, 1921.

Immediately after this ideal companionship was broken, Dr. Phillips seemed to loosen his grasp on the things of this earth. In ten days, on July 21, 1921, he yielded to the ravages of pneumonia. Birmingham lost two of her most valued citizens within a month.

The John Herbert Phillips High School and the Minnie Holman Elementary School were erected by the people of Birmingham as memorials to these esteemed benefactors of the community.

It is, of course, impossible to discriminate between the influence of the different social institutions, such as the churches and the schools, but the enlightened attitude of the people to public questions, the advanced standards of social and civic righteousness distinctly notable in Birmingham in late years, are certainly to be attributed in part, at least, to the schools. The two generations trained in the schools Phillips built have made Birmingham one of the most substantial and progressive southern cities. The same notable results have followed in a greater or a less degree in all the cities in the South where good schools have been developed.

CHAPTER XXVII

PROGRESS IN HIGH SCHOOLS

The Low Estate of Secondary Education

THE situation of the high schools in the southern states, at the time the campaign of the Southern Board commenced, was perfectly chaotic. In the reports of the state departments and of the Bureau of Education many high schools were enumerated, but upon investigation the statistics given for them were found almost entirely erroneous. Apparently the people of the South did not know what a real high school was. There were real high schools in some of the cities ; but, in most of the other cases, what was enumerated as a high school was only the addition of two or three grades to an elementary school. Frequently these grades were taught by the same teachers in the same rooms. Sometimes they had separate rooms and separate teachers, but they were not high schools.

For example, at the time the Board's work commenced there were in Virginia outside the cities some thirty or forty schools which claimed to offer three extra grades of high school work. In North Carolina there were probably thirty-five outside the towns which could set up a claim of this kind, but in most cases the high schools reported were mere myths. They had no separate teachers and no regularly organized courses of study or classes, and there was little differentiation of subject matter from that of the elementary school. It was merely a continuation, and a poor one at that, of the elementary school. Of libraries and laboratories for scientific work there were generally none whatever. In Alabama there were, in 1902, 409 schools reported as teaching high school branches, but nothing was said about the branches taught. They were probably just higher grades in the elementary schools. At best, the pupils were studying, under most unfavorable conditions, a few subjects not ordinarily included in the elementary course. Outside of Nashville, Birmingham, and a few other cities in the South, the high school of this period was nothing more than an addition of a few miscellaneous courses to the common school.

Twenty years ago very few schools offered courses of sufficient length to call them high schools.

How, then, were the boys and girls prepared for college? The answer is by private schools and academies, usually having a poor equipment and a temporary existence. A college graduate would settle in a near-by town or village and open a school in some private building. He would take the children from the elementary schools and teach them Latin, Greek, and mathematics very well; and after a few years they would enter the university. North Carolina had some famous academies, like the Bingham School and the Horner School, which were continued for years and which trained many fine men. Georgia had some excellent academies, like the Richmond Academy at Augusta. The majority of these schools were temporary, however, and they gave only classical or college preparatory training. Neither the constitution nor the state by-laws recognized them as a part of the system, except by exempting them from taxation. These private schools were, however, good enough and numerous enough to prevent the establishment of public schools for some time.

In Tennessee the legislature, before this period, had authorized the county courts to establish and maintain one or more county high schools in each county by levying special taxes for their support. Several towns took action under this law, but in 1904, when the campaign commenced, there was in all only one county high school in Tennessee. When the author went to Tennessee as president of the University in 1887 there were only four public high schools which were recognized as competent to prepare students for the institution. These were in the cities. Fortunately there were a number of admirable private schools and church academies, else the University of Tennessee would have had no students above the preparatory department, abolished at that time.

In Mississippi the school trustees had been authorized in previous years to establish, in the so-called "graded schools," high school courses of four years or less and to fix the fees which should be paid for the same. This was made optional and no provision was made for any support, direction, or supervision. In Virginia a proposition to create state sustained high schools had been presented in the legislature but no action was taken.

THE DEVELOPMENT OF HIGH SCHOOLS IN GEORGIA

The State of Georgia furnishes us the best illustration of the condition existing in the South with regard to high schools and of the manner in which they developed under the influence of the new movement. They will, therefore, be used as an illustration.

The Constitution of Georgia, made in 1877, had provided for a common school system "in the elements of an English education only," and forbade taxation in counties for schools except for "instruction in elements of an English education only." This provision did not apply, however, to incorporated towns. It also permitted aid to the state University but unfortunately not to the counties. As a result Georgia had a common school system, so-called, at the bottom, and the University at the top, but no connecting schools between except a few city and town schools. By a system of accredited schools, passed upon after examination and found to have approved courses of study, suitable laboratories and libraries, and properly prepared teachers, the effort was made to arrange a system of high schools, some public-supported and some private, which would prepare students for the University. Many of the western states, like Minnesota and Wisconsin, had such systems of accredited schools which seemed to work well. For instance, Minnesota had given in 1894 just $400 to each high school which came up to its required standard for an accredited high school in its courses of study, equipment, and teachers. The effect on the school was favorable, as it brought in boarding students from the surrounding territory and enabled thousands to extend their studies beyond the elementary school and enter the University. Minnesota had taught over twelve thousand students in these high schools, and it was the universal verdict that the system worked to the advantage of the schools and colleges and to the general cause of education. Still this was only a sort of half-way system of state secondary schools.

With these examples of the western states before him, Chancellor Walter B. Hill tackled the problem of preparing students for the University of Georgia. This University had never had a preparatory department like most of the other universities and colleges in the South, with the result that its attendance had always been limited. The first idea of Chancellor Hill, therefore, was to develop a strong list of accredited schools to prepare students for the University. To accomplish this it was necessary to have a special agent in the University. Therefore, in 1903, the Board of Trustees authorized the appointment of Dr. Joseph S. Stewart to be the University's high school agent. Mr. George Foster Peabody of New York generously agreed to pay one-half of the salary and expenses of this officer for two years. Dr. Stewart was also made professor of secondary education in the University. He went to work immediately. The first thing he did was to study the educational conditions in the several counties in Georgia. He traveled through the state, met the school authorities, encouraged the establishment of high schools by local support, relating them to the elementary schools below and the colleges and universities above, so as to knit both the existing and the new schools together in a system.

A system of accredited schools to prepare students for the colleges and universities was distinctly the first aim of this move, which was broadened out later into a system of high schools to prepare boys and girls for life. For it was recognized that the real public high school is a training school for life and work and not merely for entrance to a university. Such a high school does not appear to have been in the minds of the university faculties at first but Stewart later brought them to understand this truth and broadened out the courses of high schools so as to include agriculture, manual training, and home economics.

Stewart commenced by cultivating better relations between the existing academies and high schools and the University of Georgia with particular reference to preparation for college. He won thus the support of all educational workers of Georgia and secured their coöperation.

After a study of the educational conditions in the state and the prospects for developing this plan, Professor Stewart recommended to the faculty of the University the adoption of a regular accredited system such as that in operation in the northwestern states. It was adopted in 1904. The University made rules governing the accrediting of high schools in the state and issued application blanks to the principals of all high schools, public, semi-public, and private. The requirements were low, but they proved too high at that time. They required that there should be two teachers in the so-called high school, one of whom might be the principal. Thirteen units were required as the standard for admission to the University, and conditions were allowed in three of these. Ten recitations a day of thirty minutes' length should be the maximum required of any high school teacher, and five prepared lessons a day the maximum for any high school student.

The University of Georgia was the first of the southern states to appoint a special professor for the purpose of organizing accredited high schools and to adopt an accredited system with unit values given to high school subjects. A manual was issued in 1904 for high school teachers, with chapters on the aims of a high school, its organized course of study, selection of high school libraries, means of support, and related subjects. This pamphlet argued that a system of accredited high schools gave the state a standing for efficiency and enabled communities to build up schools of recognized standing; that it was a pull upward which should inspire all pupils and teachers and school patrons to greater educational activities.

Fifteen years of experience proved that this was true. Only seven four-year public high schools and four private four-year high schools were accredited in 1904-1905; thirty-nine three-year public high schools were accredited the same year, making a total of fifty announced in the first list in 1904-1905. These schools had an enrollment of 1,600 boys and 1,900 girls, and they graduated the second year from the full four-year high schools 54 boys and 40 girls and from the three-year high schools 161 boys and 277 girls. The fifty schools had a total of 150 teachers. But these schools were not sufficient. Only the first step had been taken towards a complete system of public high schools.

A bulletin published in 1906 showed clearly that the common schools in communities that did not have accredited high schools suffered very much, first, through lack of teachers; second, from lack of incentive among the pupils to go on in the course; and third, through overcrowding of the elementary schools with pupils hanging on, never to get any more education.

It was shown further that the colleges still suffered from the lack of high schools to prepare country boys and girls. The higher institutions were therefore compelled to resort to all kinds of expedients to secure even a few prepared students.

In 1914, according to the official reports on secondary schools by the government, there were only 279 pupils prepared for college in the graduating classes in all the high schools of Georgia, so that the dozen or more colleges of the state had a very small body from which to draw each year. There was, no doubt, a vast body of young people looking wistfully towards the college but finding no means of securing the four years' preparation necessary to enter its doors. Compare Georgia's figures in 1914 with the number of college preparatory students in Ohio, 6,000; in Indiana 2,400; in Illinois 3,900; in Michigan 2,700 ; in Iowa 2,500 ; in Massachusetts 9,000 ; and we see at once why their colleges were crowded and ours were not. Minnesota, which had begun encouraging high schools fifteen years before Georgia, had 18,000 pupils in these schools, and the attendance at the University had grown during these years (1903-1914) from 280 to 3,800.

Coming back to Georgia, it is interesting to note now that, whereas, in 1904-1905 only 215 boys graduated from three- and four-year accredited schools and only 50 entered the freshman class of the University from all the schools, including the private ones, there were, in 1910-1911, 950 boys in the graduating classes, of whom the University admitted 146 the following September ; in 1915-1916 there were 1,300 boys in the graduating classes in the schools and the University admitted 197 of them ; in 1918, 1,500 boys were in the graduating classes and the University admitted 269. Here we have absolute proof that public high schools are necessary to feed a university. Similar reports came from all the other colleges in the state. As a result, the six best colleges abolished their preparatory departments. In addition, the professional schools of law, medicine, and dentistry were enabled for the first time to require graduation from a four-year high school for admission.

By 1919 the report of the Department of Secondary Education showed 142 four-year public high schools and 24 private schools, or a total of 166 high schools accredited to the University. In addition, there were 40 three-year high schools partially accredited, and 8,698 boys and 11,162 girls, or 19,860 pupils, enrolled in the four-year public high schools, with 2,493 enrolled in the four-year private schools, making a total of 22,353 four-year pupils in all the accredited schools of the University. There were 3,391 pupils graduated that year (1919) from the four-year public high schools, 361 from the private four-year schools, a total of 3,752 graduates, more than had been enrolled in all the schools capable of being accredited when the work began. The number of teachers had increased to 1,200, of whom 736 held university degrees.

Following the example of the University, all the colleges of the State of Georgia adopted the accredited system, and all the other southern states have adopted it since. Meanwhile, the Southern and North Central College associations' minimum standards of accrediting were fixed and have been increased from time to time during the last eighteen years. Over 90 per cent of the students who entered college in 1920 in the states represented in the Southern and North Central associations did so on certificates from regular four-year high schools. The example of Georgia has thus borne great fruit.

It remains to note the legislation passed in Georgia during this time for the support of the accredited high school system. First, there was a constitutional amendment in 1905 abolishing the antiquated prohibition of high schools in Georgia and allowing counties and districts to levy taxes for them; second, in 1906 there was an act establishing district agricultural schools; third, in 1910 a constitutional amendment was adopted striking out the words limiting the county to taxes for the "elements of English education only"; fourth, in 1912 another amendment struck out these same words in the educational section of the constitution, thus making the high school for the first time a legal part of the public school system; fifth, there was an act requiring a state license for high school teachers; sixth, in 1919 an act setting aside a part of the state fund as an aid in the establishment of four-year standard high schools. Another act in 1919 required every county to levy a local tax for school purposes up to five mills and permitting local areas to levy from one to five mills in addition for their schools, including high schools—a remarkable series of progressive legislation as a result of this splendid work for high schools. Provision was made for ample support both in elementary and secondary schools in every county of the state.

The final and greatest act of legislation in Georgia was one passed in 1919 which required that one-half of the total revenue of the state must be set aside sacredly for the maintenance of the public schools. The Smith-Hughes Act which went into operation first in 1917 helped very much as a stimulus for vocational education in the high schools. The state appropriated an amount equal to one-half of that given by the federal government. For example, in 1919-1920, $80,000 of federal money and $40,000 state money were expended in Georgia for vocational education in high schools. After a long hard struggle Georgia secured by 1924-1925 public high schools and professional high schools within riding distance of the youth of the whole state. For aid in accomplishing this work Stewart, in his report of 1919, expressed his thanks to the General Education Board for the aid it had given in the movement.

Stewart's work proved so successful that the General Education Board decided to extend the same plan to other southern states. Following the Columbia meeting of the Conference for Education in 1905, where the results in Georgia were discussed, the General Education Board offered to appropriate to each of the southern states the funds necessary to pay the salary and expenses of professors of secondary education whose chief work should be to promote the development of a system of public high schools. This marked the beginning of a new epoch in secondary education in the South. This act of the General Board has ever since been considered as one of the wisest and most fruitful it ever undertook.

Professors of secondary education who should be agents for high schools were appointed in the fall of 1905 in the several states. Bruce R. Payne became the professor of secondary education in the University of Virginia and high school agent. N. W. Walker was appointed to a similar position in North Carolina ; Philander P. Claxton, already connected with the University of Tennessee, was made agent for the high schools in that state. Joel C. DuBose was appointed for Alabama and was soon succeeded by James J. Doster. South Carolina was given a similar professor and agent in 1906 ; Florida and Louisiana received high school agents in 1907 ; Arkansas and Mississippi, in 1908 ; and Kentucky, in 1910. In making appropriations for the salaries of these professors of secondary education the General Education Board provided not only for their traveling expenses in their respective states but also authorized them to attend the meetings of the state superintendents of public instruction, the Conferences for Education in the South, and any other meetings that might be necessary. This enabled them to learn much from each other and to promote the development of high schools throughout the South.

The campaign for high schools in the other southern states, carried out by the professors and supervisors, supported at state universities by the General Education Board, was generally less arduous than that described in Georgia. But the example of Georgia, especially the work of Professor Stewart, was an inspiration to them all.

Joseph Spencer Stewart, the pioneer in high school development in the South, was born in Oxford, Georgia, September 23, 1863, and died at Athens, Georgia, March 25, 1934. He received his academic education at Emory College, where he was graduated with the A.B. degree in 1883, and began his educational career as principal of Cherokee Institute at Cave Springs, Georgia, where he served six years. He was then president of Harwood Seminary at Marietta for two years. His school work there was so successful that it attracted the attention of public authorities, who made him superintendent of the Marietta public schools. These schools he reorganized in excellent shape. He next became president of the North Georgia Agricultural College at Dahlonega, where he remained until 1903, when he was called to the University of Georgia to undertake this new work for high schools. Here he labored until his death.

Stewart's influence extended far beyond his state. He was the first to suggest the organization of the National Association of High School Supervisors. When the Commission for the reorganization of secondary education of the National Education Association set up its reviewing committee, Stewart was chosen as the southern representative. His knowledge and ability won him recognition throughout the nation as a leader in secondary school work.

In 1906 Stewart presented a paper before the Southern Educational Association on "The High School Population of the South and a Plan for Correlating High Schools and Higher Institutions." This paper foreshadowed the need for a commission to direct a general standardization of high schools. In 1911 Stewart presented a report to the Southern Association on regulating and improving the administration of the certificating system. After considerable discussion the recommendation of the report that a commission on secondary schools be established was adopted. This commission was organized April 4, 1912, in

Nashville, Tennessee. Its first annual meeting was held in Spartanburg, South Carolina, in November, 1912, when Stewart was elected chairman and N. W. Walker secretary. Stewart continued to serve as chairman until the fifth annual meeting in 1916, when R. E. Blackwell was elected chairman. Stewart had been thus not only the pioneer in high school development in Georgia but he was the father of the Commission of Secondary Schools for Southern States and its guiding genius during all its early years. He was the leader in secondary education in the South. His work was well done and will endure.[1]

THE DEVELOPMENT OF HIGH SCHOOLS IN SOUTH CAROLINA UNDER WILLIAM H. HAND

The story of the development of high schools in South Carolina is typical of that of all the southern states. The movement for the establishment of these schools dated from the annual report of O. B. Martin, state superintendent (1902–1908), to the General Assembly in December, 1905. In this report Superintendent Martin presented an able argument for high schools as a part of the public school system. The absence of high schools marked a gap in the educational system which should be supplied. He pointed out that the growth of higher education was impossible without preparatory schools. It is poor policy, he said, for a state to spend a quarter of a million dollars on colleges, as South Carolina was doing, and make absolutely no provision for high schools. "We have been attacking the problem of education in two independent separated parts —the common schools and the colleges, omitting almost entirely the secondary schools. Growing up under separate control these several parts have not been thought of by the public as essential parts of the whole. Often the friends of one part have been antagonistic to the others. It is time that we should think of these parts not as wholes in themselves but as essential parts of a system. Until this unity and coöperation are secured the educational interests of these states cannot be developed so as to secure the best results for all parts."

[1] See "Joseph Spencer Stewart of Georgia : An Appreciation," by N. W. Walker, professor of secondary education in the University of North Carolina, being an address before the Commission on Secondary Schools of the Southern Association of Colleges and Secondary Schools, Atlanta, Georgia, December 4, 1934, in The High School Journal, XVIII (January, 1935), No. 1.

Moreover, he continued, without high schools the common schools suffer through lack of teachers. Two-thirds of the white teachers in the schools at the time had little education beyond that of the common schools. The majority had never attended any school higher than that in which they were attempting to teach. As a result, one-fourth of these teachers dropped out each year. The common school suffers further through lack of incentive for the pupils to complete their course and reach up to a higher one. The high school becomes the goal of the ambitious youth who never dreamed of seeking a higher education before. The lengthened course lifts the educational standards of the entire community.

Without high schools, he said further, the colleges formerly had to resort to all kinds of expedients to secure a few prepared students. In 1904 there were only 253 pupils prepared for college in all the high schools of South Carolina, and only 606 in all the private schools. There were many young people in all our southern states who wished to go to college, but who found no means of preparing themselves to reach it. The colleges can never do their full duty to the state until provision is made at home to prepare these students for entrance into the higher institution. These conditions have a demoralizing effect upon education in general. The evil effects of poor preparation follow the young students throughout their college course. Many become discouraged and drop out, who would be successful if they had had better preparation. From whatever angle the work is viewed, the colleges suffer where the high schools are few and poor, and they prosper only where the secondary schools are sufficient in number and thorough in their work. Yet preparation for college is not the chief purpose of the high school. The high school trains the citizens for life work and service. The Canadians, for example, have given agricultural subjects a prominent place in the curriculum of their high schools, with the result that after six years farm exports have more than doubled, meat exports trebled, and dairy products increased more than fifty times over. Every industry, profession, and condition in life will feel the effect of the higher training, culture, and skill of the constantly increasing number of youth coming out of these schools.

In conclusion Superintendent Martin proposed a plan for promoting the development of high schools in the state similar to that established in Georgia, already described. This plan was endorsed and adopted at a meeting of the City and County Superintendents' Association in December, 1905, and at a meeting of the South Carolina Teachers' Association in July, 1906. The latter Association appointed a committee to draft a bill which was presented to the legislature and enacted in a bill approved February 19, 1907. This bill appropriated the sum of $50,000 to be used in encouraging the development of high schools. It provided that any county, township, or aggregation of townships or school districts, or any incorporated town or city, might hold elections to decide the establishment of high schools and to authorize and levy a tax for their support not exceeding two mills on the dollar in addition to the levy already allowed by law. It provided for three grades of high schools, one grade teaching a four-year course, a second grade teaching a three-year course, and a third grade having a two-year course beyond the common school grades. It provided that each one of these schools should include "instruction in manual training and in agriculture and domestic science." It constituted the state board of education a board to erect, inspect, and classify the high schools under this act.

In 1906 the General Education Board proposed to the trustees of the University of South Carolina to appropriate a sum of money annually to pay the salary of a professor of secondary education, to be a member of the faculty to teach the principles of secondary education, and, in addition, to devote such time as he could to the study and inspection of the high schools of the state. This offer was gladly accepted, and the trustees appointed William H. Hand, superintendent of the Chester public schools, to the position. Mr. Hand accepted the position and began work July 1, 1906. This was the beginning of a distinguished and successful career.

As high school inspector and professor of secondary education in the University, Hand now confronted a new problem. When he entered upon this work the term "high school" had no definite meaning in the state. His first task was to diagnose the secondary school situation, as presented by private as well as public schools, and form a plan of operation to establish a system. His second task was to get the approval of the people of the state to secure the necessary legislation and appropriations both from the state and the people of the counties. These tasks required a thorough knowledge of educational principles, tact and skill as a campaigner, and great courage and persistence. Hand was well prepared both by study and by experience and soon rose to the occasion. His success was unqualified. It is the consensus of educational authorities in the South that Hand was the father of the present system of public high schools in the state.

At the beginning of this movement every school district with any probability of qualifying for state aid applied for a share of the money appropriated. So-called high schools sprang up all over the state and every possible plea was made to secure a portion of the funds. Between 1907 and 1917 fifty-eight districts undertook to maintain high schools which they had afterwards to give up. Under the population limitation, no aid was given to towns of more than a thousand population. There was great opposition to the plan and confusion of ideas about its proper execution, and Hand issued a Bulletin explaining "The Way to Secure a High School" and "How to Maintain a High School." [2]

The General Assembly in 1908 amended the law by increasing the population limit from a thousand to twenty-five hundred, and with the census of 1910 twenty-five of the largest high schools were debarred from participation in the state fund. Year after year the legislature was urged to repeal this clause but without success until 1916, when a new law was made under which the population limit was entirely removed. The high school must have at least two teachers and twenty-five pupils. The district must levy at least four mills local tax before receiving state aid. High school pupils could, without tuition, attend any state high school in his county or the adjoining county. The state appropriation was increased to $75,000 annually. An important improvement was the authorization of as many as five teacher-training courses in connection with approved high schools.

The colleges now established entrance examinations and petitioned the State Board of Education to authorize a system of accredited public high schools which would prepare students in accordance with their requirements, which was done. The State High School Board offered a diploma to any pupil of any high school approved by the state inspector and accredited with

[2] *Bulletin of the University of South Carolina,* XIII (April, 1908).

fourteen standard units, and these diplomas were accepted by the colleges for entrance. In 1910 seventy-two high school diplomas were issued from eight high schools. This number greatly increased until in 1915 three hundred were issued.

Hand's chief labor now was to advance the standard of high school teachers. Teacher-training courses were established in the University and in Winthrop College. A high school manual was prepared by Professor Hand to help the high school teachers. With the same end in view Hand was instrumental in establishing the first summer school for high school teachers held in the state. This was conducted at the University from June 23 to July 17, 1914. The enrollment the first year was seventy-six, which was increased to 530 in 1929.

A synopsis of the growth of these high schools between 1906, when Hand started the movement and 1918, when he resigned, would be too lengthy to give here. Only the following facts are selected : In 1906-1907 there were only ninety-five so-called public and private high schools in the state with 235 teachers and 4,812 students. Many of these were not real high schools. In 1917 there are 142 public high schools of the several classes with 368 full-time teachers and 10,627 pupils. Of these teachers, one-half were men and a large majority of both the men and women had received a college education and some professional training.

In August, 1918, Professor Hand became superintendent of schools of the city of Columbia, succeeding Professor E. S. Dreher. In his first report to the Board of School Commissioners he presented a careful survey of the city field, recounting all the conditions. He first made a strong plea for better schoolhouses, better equipped with libraries and laboratories. He reported that a manual training shop had been installed in the high school; and a domestic science department provided instruction for the girls. Laboratories for chemistry and physics had been established.

Professor Hand devoted his chief attention, however, to the development of the teaching force. His statements on this subject deserve to be quoted :

So far as the schools are concerned, the type of manhood and womanhood produced in any community, depends upon the quality of the teaching of the teaching force employed. Here, too, are found varying standards in the popular mind. Popular standards for teachers are often very crude and very erroneous. People do not discriminate between social popularity and teaching efficiency, or between the so-called brilliant young man or woman and one who can grip the lives of boys and girls. . . . The qualifications which go toward making a good teacher are too varied and numerous to be possessed by any one person. Perhaps they may be summarized under personality, scholarship and professional skill. It is utterly hopeless to make a teacher of a man or a woman weak in personality. There is nothing on which to build. . . . Some excellent scholars are total failures as teachers, simply because they can not attract pupils. Pupils must be caught before they can be taught. . . .

The teacher who never meets his pupils outside the classroom, on terms of companionship, rarely ever succeeds in entering their inner lives, their holy of holies. In order to make a companion of a pupil the teacher must meet him on his own plane. . . . The teacher must learn the pupil's tastes, his hopes, his aspirations, his difficulties, his discouragements. He must find these out indirectly. They are too sacred to be discussed in the class room, and the average pupil can not be lured into discussing them seriously among his fellows. The following are from Tom Brown's School Days : "The object of all schools is not to ram Latin and Greek into boys but to make them good English boys, good future citizens ; and by far the most important part of that work must be done, or not done, out of school hours. . . . Were I a private schoolmaster, I would say, 'Let who will hear the boys their lessons, but let me live with them, when they are at play and rest.' "

In successful teaching there is no substitute for sound scholarship. The mastery of anything worth while begets confidence with pupils. . . . No teacher can teach what he does not know thoroughly. Few sights in the schoolroom are more pathetic than a teacher with his eyes glued upon the page. . . .

Just as accurate scholarship inspires confidence, so does professional skill enable the teacher to utilize his scholarship to the best advantage. The real teacher never ceases to be a student. Too many teachers cease to be students after they have taught a few years and rely upon their experience and it is exceedingly difficult to convince them that they have ceased to grow. If a mummy could speak, no doubt it would deny being dead. So with the teacher who has ceased to grow ; he may be ripe, and dead.[3]

Two of the cardinal aims of a school system should be to improve or develop the teachers already in the system, and to retain as long as possible those who continue to grow. Every teacher . . . has a right to expect the opportunity and the incentive to grow. . . .

[3] *Annual Report to the Board of School Commissioners, 1919.*

A superintendent has the responsibility of developing his teachers as well as his pupils. The two should grow together.[4]

Mr. Hand favored a plan whereby teachers of ability and success should be rewarded in a financial manner, As a result, a graduated salary schedule for teachers of the Columbia system went into force in 1924-1925. He said, "Our principals, supervisors, and teachers have been at work for more than a year readjusting our program. Every white teacher in the system has made some contribution to this work out of her own experience and each deserves her reward." [5]

Another progressive step was the organization of special classes for retarded pupils with supervised study under the immediate eye of special teachers. In response to the earnest plea of Professor Hand, bonds were issued in 1926 for one-half million dollars to be used in carrying out a four-year building program for high schools in Columbia.

Another of Hand's progressive steps was the establishment of a special school for the overgrown pupils, the habitual repeaters and the very dull ones. A hundred such pupils were put under six teachers for special training. Each was given a Simon-Binet test and an effort was made to find why he was unable to keep up with his class. Since it proved impossible to hold the group together permanently, the special school was divided into groups which corresponded to the special needs of the individual student. This school, which had four teachers especially trained for the work and an average of fifty pupils, cost four times as much as that for normal children. A manual training shop was set up in connection with the school, free lunches were served to the pupils, and a bus carried those living at a distance to the school.

A building for the industrial department of the Negro school was erected and provision was made for woodwork, mechanical drawing, and brick and cement work for the boys, and cooking, sewing, and laundering for the girls.

Mr. Hand favored athletics for all, provided the sports were kept clean and controlled absolutely by the school, which should subordinate them to the development of character and the fos-

[4] *Triennial Report of the Public Schools, Columbia, S. C., for the years 1922-1925 inclusive*, p. 21.
[5] *Ibid.*, pp. 19, 53.

tering of sound scholarship. In the matter of medals and prizes Hand took a high position. Where there can be but one successful winner in a given class, he said, they are particularly objectionable. The pupil who enters life with the notion that material reward should follow effort enters it with the wrong idea.

In September, 1926, Professor Hand recommended to his Board the establishment of a junior high school in Columbia. The crowded condition of the high school made it necessary that some step should be taken. The junior high school was dedicated on November 27, 1927, and opened with a corps of thirty teachers and an enrollment of 688. It was his last active development of the school system of Columbia and it is noteworthy to hear him say with regard to it : "I have faith in our experiment and I am satisfied that we have made no mistake." Had he lived until September, 1930, he would have seen his dream fully realized, for the great junior high school which bears his name was completed and opened to the pupils of the city.

In the ten years of Professor Hand's administration of the public schools of Columbia the enrollment increased 33 per cent; the teaching force 50 per cent; and the physical equipment was more than doubled.

The *Columbia State* said of his administration : "Dr. Hand had his own ideas of how things should be done and his advanced line of thought has been adopted in many other cities. He insisted that a day's work be done ; that distractions be cut to the bone." [6]

A memorial sketch prepared by Miss Mary Elizabeth Peay says : "His constant thought was the welfare of the school children of Columbia and of the improvement of the school system. Nothing was allowed to take precedence over that. . . . The outstanding position the Columbia schools now occupy in the educational world is largely due to the untiring efforts, the intelligent investigation and the close study of Mr. Hand. He never recommended a change in school administration or teaching methods without thorough investigation and study. He always had reasons for his recommendations and, again, these reasons went back to the question, 'What is best for the child.' "

Hand had spent forty years moulding the life of the children of South Carolina. He commenced as teacher of elementary

[6] *Columbia State*, August 8, 1928.

schools, and became principal, superintendent of schools, state high school inspector, and professor of secondary education in the University. He left his mark upon every part of the state system. He built his greatest monument as superintendent of city schools of Columbia. He did much in addition to convince the people of the state of the necessity for sufficient funds to maintain a complete system of education. In a large degree the whole present system of schools of South Carolina is the result of his influence and labors.

The Organization of High Schools in Alabama

The campaign for an organized system of tax-supported high schools in Alabama was the result of the work of Dr. John W. Abercrombie of the University. To aid in this movement Dr. Abercrombie secured the coöperation of the General Education Board, to pay the salary and expenses of a professor of secondary education whose duty it should be to cultivate a sentiment for the establishment and support of high schools. The first agent employed in this work was Dr. Joel C. DuBose, a fine classical scholar, who had been a successful teacher of boys. He canvassed the state in advocacy of a law establishing county high schools, with the result that the legislature of 1907 passed an act providing for a high school in each county on condition that the people of the county should acquire five acres of land and erect and equip a building. This done, the state provided a fund for the employment of teachers. Thirty-one county high schools, located in towns averaging about twelve hundred in population, were established during the first year, and approximately a half million dollars was pledged for their buildings and equipment. Professor DuBose was succeeded by Dr. James J. Doster, an Alabamian, who had received his early training at the Troy Normal School and then had taken a course at Teachers College of Columbia University, and had taught in all grades of state schools.

Realizing that he could not succeed in building up a system of high schools without regard to the elementary schools below and the colleges above, Doster undertook first to teach the people that a proper educational organization for the state was one of unity and complete coördination of all its parts. With this end in view he visited every part of the state, addressing the teachers and the people, using a chart in the form of a ladder with three sections representing the elementary schools, the high schools, and the colleges united to form a complete state system of schools. To the elementary and high school teachers he expounded their relations to colleges above them, urging them to stimulate their students to climb the scale as far as they could. To college people he presented his ladder to show them the necessity of building elementary schools and high schools as the foundation for their work.

The absolute necessity of a sound elementary school system as a foundation led Dr. Doster to concern himself first with this problem. He labored, therefore, for proper financial support for these schools, for a uniform course of study of seven grades, and for efficient supervision. With Professor Henry J. Willingham, of the State Department of Education, he prepared a course of study for the elementary schools which was approved and sent out by State Superintendent Gunnels in 1908. This was the first step towards the improvement of the work of the common schools in Alabama and its articulation with the high schools. Doster next prepared a manual for elementary schools which established the line of demarkation between them and the high schools.

After planning the foundation of elementary schools, Doster took up the problem of the modern high school. He urged the towns to expand their high schools into four-year schools and eliminate the elementary work they had been doing. He advocated the introduction of the sciences, agricultural and industrial education, and home economics. He encouraged the formation of boys' and girls' clubs in connection with the county high schools. After two years of experience and conference with college and high school teachers, he prepared a high school manual for a four-year course of study based upon the seven years of the elementary schools.

In the absence of proper high schools to prepare students for them, the colleges of Alabama had preparatory departments. These had first to be cleared out. Doster urged that the colleges maintain full college standards of admission and vacate entirely the high school field. The University of Alabama led in this movement, and in 1908 Dr. Abercrombie established the Alabama Association of Colleges for the purpose of elevating collegiate standards, of securing uniform standards of admission and graduation, and of articulating thoroughly the high schools and colleges. Dr. Doster organized the Alabama High School Association, which then coöperated with the College Association in separating definitely the realms of collegiate and secondary education and properly articulating the two.

In 1909 the colleges joined the Southern Association of Colleges and Accredited Schools, which had been previously organized, and raised the entrance requirements to fourteen units, providing at the same time for uniform enforcement of the arrangement between high schools and colleges. This action, which left the field of secondary education to the high schools, greatly stimulated the movement for them. High schools that did not give the four years of standard work were soon overhauled and expanded so as to prepare their students for admission to the colleges under this system.

This great development of both high schools and colleges soon created a demand for more and better teachers for both. Dr. Doster, as professor of secondary education and inspector of the high schools, led now in the movement for the establishment of normal schools for the training of elementary school teachers. A six weeks' summer course at the University for all the teachers who could not attend the regular college sessions was established and a School of Education at the University was started in 1909. This school offered a two-year professional course based on at least two years of college work. The degree of Bachelor of Science in Education and a certificate of fitness to teach in the high schools was granted at the completion of this course. The normal schools for teachers of both races were aided by state appropriations, gifts from educational boards, and local subscriptions. Teachers' institutes, which had for sometime been supported by contributions from the Peabody Fund, were endowed by the state in 1911 and attendance was made compulsory for those who had not received professional training in the normal schools or higher institutions.

The Educational Association of Alabama now became a powerful influence in uniting and coördinating educational forces and in promoting the professional spirit and viewpoint.

One of the most effective organizations was the School Improvement Association started in 1905, an organization of women whose main purpose was the erection of better school buildings and the improvement of school grounds. This group also assisted in organizing school libraries and lyceums, encouraged club movements for boys and girls, and promoted in every way the establishment of schools as socialized centers for rural community life. The rural library law of 1911, which provided for a joint annual contribution of ten dollars from the district, county, and state for a library in each rural school, was a factor in the advancement of rural communities. A Teachers' Reading Circle, organized in 1909, promoted the general improvement of all grades of teachers. The law of 1911 for rural libraries aided in this. Great improvement in teacher-training agencies and in the scholarship of teachers of all grades had been made by 1914. The work done by Superintendent Feagin, Dr. Abercrombie, and Dr. Doster in the development of the high school system, the grading and improving of the elementary schools, the training of better teachers, and the systematic organization and articulation of all the elements of the school system between 1900 and 1914 constituted a real educational renaissance. The improvement in the organization was accompanied by an improvement in buildings and equipment, and in increase of funds for all the schools. Several towns issued bonds to improve old buildings or build new ones. But there was practically no improvement in the schoolhouses until 1907, when the state made provision through special taxes for the repair and erection of rural schoolhouses. School districts which raised funds up to $200 were entitled to a part of the special county funds. Stimulated by this aid, hundreds of communities improved their elementary school buildings. Towns and villages and rural communities vied with each other in this work and in that of securing better teachers and improving their schools in every way. It is said that between 1910 and 1912, 2,686 communities received aid from the state for improving their schoolhouses.

Great progress was now made in school supervision also. By 1911 the duties and powers of the county superintendents were increased. By the aid of the Peabody Fund a rural county supervisor was secured for the white elementary schools, and through the generosity of the General Education Board a similar inspector for Negro rural schools was put in the field in 1913. Sixteen Jeanes' school supervisors were employed to assist the county superintendents in improving the schools for Negroes. Fine results came out of both of these movements.

The total expenditures for education thus increased considerably between 1900 and 1914. The total from the special tax of thirty cents for public schools increased from $250,000 to nearly $1,750,000. The city and county appropriations increased from $663,000 in 1907-1908 to $3,363,000 in 1914. The total available funds for schools increased between 1900 and 1914 from $1,180,000 to $4,446,000; and the value of school property, from $934,000 to $8,417,000. The per capita from state funds increased from $1.27 in 1904 to $2.75 in 1914. The total salaries for teachers increased from $920,000 to $3,046,000 and the number of teachers employed, from 4,682 to 7,753.

Alabama had made great improvements, but it must be recalled that it had begun at a very low level and there was still a great deal more to be done. Notwithstanding these increases, the public school fund of 1914 was still inadequate. The average rural school term was still limited to five months, and the funds available were barely able to pay a third-grade teacher for that time. The average annual pay for rural teachers was still less than the state received from the hire of an able-bodied convict. Private subscriptions were necessary to run even a fairly satisfactory school, and it was fully recognized that the situation could not be improved until the country, town, and school districts were given power to levy special school taxes. The survey made in 1914 of three typical counties showed that the average annual pay of teachers was only $353 or $27.75 a month for twelve months.

The Development of High Schools in Arkansas

The Conference for Education in the South, held in Little Rock in 1910, awoke the people of Arkansas to make more earnest efforts for the improvement of their schools. The General Education Board made an appropriation for the salary of a professor of secondary education in the University of Arkansas, who would at the same time be an agent for the schools. Professor Burr W. Torreyson was appointed to the position. Torreyson had been educated at the National Normal University at Lebanon, Ohio. From 1888 to 1893 he was principal of the high school at Mexico, Missouri, and from 1893 to 1903 he held the same position at Fort Smith, Arkansas; from 1903 to 1905 he was superintendent of schools at Forth Smith; from 1905 to 1909 he was superintendent of schools at Little Rock.

From 1909 to 1917 he was professor of secondary education at the University of Arkansas ; from 1917 to 1931 he was president of the Arkansas State Teachers College at Conway and president emeritus until his death on May 29, 1932. He served the schools of Arkansas ably for thirty-nine years.

Before 1911 high schools might be established by the local school boards, but there was no appropriation for them. There was no supervision from the outside and no reports from the county or state officials in regard to them. Reports collected by Torreyson in 1910 showed that, while there were about one hundred schools claiming secondary rank with an enrollment of nearly five thousand pupils, only thirty-one were four-year schools. Only a dozen could be rated at fourteen or more units; in all the other schools, the grades of study pursued were irregular, the recitation periods short, the teaching force inadequate, and the school terms less than nine months. The existing high schools were all located in towns; there were none in the country. The result was that high school privileges were denied to the vast majority of the children. The first thing to do was to standardize the existing schools with respect to these matters.

This state of affairs was the first thing to attract the attention of the Education Commission. Torreyson was made secretary and instructed to study the high schools of the state and gather the experiences of other states. A vigorous report was published : "The public high school is essential to the life of the school system. . . . It is the college of the people. . . . It multiplies the productive power of the people. . . . It prepares for citizenship." The high school vitalized the elementary schools by putting before the pupils an opportunity for a higher career and by preparing better teachers.[7] The result was a law in 1911 which provided a state high school board consisting of the president of the University, the state superintendent, and a city superintendent selected by the governor. This board was instructed to classify the high schools and to establish normal instruction in those having four-year courses. The state fund was granted only where local districts raised an equal amount and was to be paid to the teachers. Towns with over 3,500 population must support their own high schools without state aid.

[7] Arkansas Education Commission, *State Aid to High Schools*, Bulletin No. 2.

The first appropriation was $40,000 for high schools and $10,000 additional for normal instruction in them. Torreyson went to work now to standardize the existing schools. Regulations were made with regard to courses of study, teaching force, length of term and of recitations, number of classes per teacher, and material equipment. Schools in towns must include at least twenty-five pupils and in the country fifteen in order to get state aid. Under these regulations ninety-three high schools were organized in 1910-1911. Among these were eleven normal training schools, nineteen four-year, twenty-six three-year, and thirty-seven two-year high schools. There were fifty schools in towns and new buildings were erected to the amount of $1,052,-000. The teachers must have had two years of college work and normal school diplomas, or three years of successful teaching experience. In the normal departments the course included fourteen units of academic work and three of professional work. Licenses to teach were given to the graduates in sixty-five of the state aid high schools. There were 1,700 students out of a total of 6,638 who took the courses in agriculture. Manual training and home economics were taught in only eight schools. In 1911-1912 the number of high schools had increased to 146 and the pupils enrolled to 9,622. In teacher training in these schools there were 327 students. The high school system was now on the way and progress was good from this time on.

CHAPTER XXVIII

FOUR GREAT FUNDS AND THEIR WORK FOR NEGRO EDUCATION

A Story of Coöperation

NOTHING has occurred in the history of public education surpassing in interest the work of certain public foundations for the promotion of the education of the Negroes. The story of their varied activities, as told in the following pages, presents many interesting features and valuable lessons for the guidance of those proposing plans for the development of public education. In the first place, all of the donors have left to their trustees or boards almost complete responsibility for the disposition of the funds donated. This has made it possible to go from one field of service to another as opportunity offered, stimulating different institutions, and securing thus the greatest results from a small amount of money. The policy of all the boards has been one of encouragement in the development of independence and self-reliance. In most cases the donors have given their trustees the right to use both capital and income with either a suggestion, as George Peabody did, or a definite limitation upon the operation of the fund, as Mr. Rosenwald did. Many of these boards have commenced by aiding elementary schools, extending their help to training classes, high schools, colleges, and universities as general education was developed. Private and church schools have received a large proportion of aid, especially in the field of the education of Negroes. In the case of whites, the proportion of funds devoted to private and church institutions has decreased in favor of assistance to public institutions.

The most interesting result of the whole movement has been the coöperation of the different philanthropic foundations in their mutual endeavor. Without any suggestion of combination, the boards have been concentrating their efforts and funds in helping each other. This has been especially true in the work done for Negro education in the southern states. There is nothing finer in the history of education than this story of the cooperation of the Rockefeller funds, the Jeanes Fund, the Slater Fund, the Phelps-Stokes Fund, and the Rosenwald Fund in their work for the Negroes.

THE SLATER FUND

Under the inspiration of the gift of Mr. George Peabody, Mr. John F. Slater, of Connecticut, made over to a board of ten trustees, to be incorporated in New York, the sum of $1,-000,000, the "income of which was to be used to assist in the education of the Negro people of the South." After authorizing the incorporation and giving the trustees some business instructions he said : "The general object which I desire ... is the uplifting of the lately emancipated population of the Southern States, and their posterity, by conferring on them the blessings of Christian education. ... But it is not only for their own sake, but also for the safety of our common country, in which they have been invested with equal political rights, that I am desirous to aid in providing them with the means of such education as shall tend to make them good men and good citizens." He expressed the wish that the Fund be administered "in no partisan, sectional or sectarian spirit, but in the interest of a generous patriotism and an enlightened Christian faith." And in conclusion he said : "I am encouraged ... in this charitable foundation of a long-cherished purpose, by the eminent wisdom and success that has marked the conduct of the Peabody Education Fund. ... I shall commit it to your hands ... and humbly hope that the administration of it may be so guided by divine wisdom, as to be ... an encouragement to philanthropic enterprise on the part of others, and an enduring means of good to our beloved country and to our fellow men."

Mr. Slater invited a distinguished group of men to become the first trustees of his Fund, namely ex-President Rutherford B. Hayes of Ohio, Chief Justice Waite of the Supreme Court, William E. Dodge of New York, Bishop Phillips Brooks of Massachusetts, President Daniel C. Gilman of the Johns Hopkins University, Mr. John A. Stewart of New York, former Governor Alfred H. Colquitt of Georgia, Morris K. Jesup of New York, and the Reverend James P. Boyce of Kentucky. No more eminent men could have been found in the country.

They represented both the North and the South. The trustees have always been men of this type.

Dr. Atticus Green Haygood of Atlanta, Georgia, was elected the first director of the Slater Fund in 1882. He was a true southerner of old southern stock. Born on November 19, 1839, he was old enough to have seen some of the slave ships and the auctions of their captives. He never forgot the horrors he witnessed and from his youth had sought to find some solution of slavery.

Haygood was educated in Emory College, Oxford, Georgia, had studied theology, and was elected president of Emory College in 1875. From 1878 to 1882 he edited the Wesleyan Christian Advocate, a church paper. During this period he commenced the discussion of the Negro problem and wrote articles in his paper which were later published in a book entitled *"Our Brother in Black : His Freedom and His Future.* He taught that the Negro was not an inferior but a depressed being who must be a citizen in every sense of the word and could be made a good citizen only by training. In a later work entitled *Pleas for Progress* he urged the southern people to join earnestly with their northern neighbors in an effort to uplift this people and make them good citizens of the republic. He took a moderate and hopeful view of the situation between the races and did much to develop a better feeling between the whites and the Negroes of the South. His books had a great influence among the thinking people of the South though they offended some of the extremists.

Elected bishop in 1882, Dr. Haygood declined the position to become the agent of the John F. Slater Fund for Negro Education. He resigned as president of Emory College in 1884 to devote himself wholly to the task of promoting better race relations and Negro education. When elected bishop the second time in 1890 at a General Conference of the church of which he was not a member, he resigned the position as director of the Slater Fund, accepted the bishopric, and moved to California.

Simple, clear, and earnest of speech, Haygood was powerful in argument. He opposed the bloody shirt legislation, strove to promote good will between the North and the South, and favored federal aid for the Negro. He died January 19, 1896, greatly loved by people of all sections of the country.

The second agent of the Slater Fund was Dr. J. L. M. Curry

JULIUS ROSENWALD

Upper left, James Hardy Dillard, president and director of the Jeanes Foundation, director of the Slater Fund, member of the Southern Education Board
and of the General Education Board, vice president of the Phelps-Stokes Fund,
and Rector of the Board of Visitors of the College of William and Mary
(Champlain Studios, N. Y.). Upper right, Thomas Jesse Jones, president of
the Phelps-Stokes Fund and authority on the education of primitive peoples
(Buckstone Studios, N. Y.). Lower left, James Longstreet Sibley, inspired and
trained under the influence of the Southern Education Board, who gave his
life to the cause of Negro education in Africa. Lower right, William Burns
Paterson, founder and builder of the Alabama State Normal School for Negroes
at Montgomery

of Alabama, whose service to southern education has been told fully in Volume I.[1] He was elected in 1891 and served until his death in 1903. For twelve years he traveled over the South, teaching the people that the advancement of the Negroes was a necessary part of the advancement of the South; that there was no process by which the South could advance its white people economically and educationally which did not also advance the Negroes; that there was no way to save the Negroes except as a part of the whole South. Owing to the influence of Reconstruction the South was not at the time in a mood to undertake the education of the whole Negro race. At the same time it was evident that the North could not educate the Negro without the coöperation of the South. From the beginning, therefore, the Slater Board, under Dr. Curry's guidance, stuck to the principle that the South must not only coöperate but must lead in the development of Negro education. The task must be done by the best of the North and the best of the South working together. The Board thus approved Dr. Curry's plan for general coöperation between the North and the South in the development of education which has been the principle followed by all of the other Boards later organized. These principles finally won the leaders of the South, who from this time on coöperated with the Boards in trying to improve the condition of the Negro population.[2]

The next director of the Slater Fund was Dr. Wallace Buttrick, a member of the Southern Education Board and of the General Education Board. Dr. Buttrick's service has already been described;[3] but it should be said here that with his common sense, his wisdom, his understanding, his sympathy, his patience, and his unwavering faith in good men and righteous causes, he made a great contribution, not only to the solution of the problem of Negro education but to the advancement of the economic and cultural life of the whole South. Dr. Buttrick rendered a great service to the cause of Negro education by bringing the philanthropic funds together in one coöperative enterprise—a plan of coöperation which was afterwards extended to include the state departments and local agencies in the service of all the schools of the South. Dr. Buttrick served

[1] See Vol. I, Chap. VII.
[2] See his *Nunc Dimittis* in the Introduction to this volume.
[3] See above, p. 8 and Appendix II.

only a few years, resigning in 1910, but he did a fine act in bringing James H. Dillard, W. T. B. Williams, and B. C. Caldwell into the service of the Slater Fund.

Dr. George S. Dickerman of New Haven, Connecticut, who had been studying the conditions of the schools of the South for a number of years as representative of a philanthropic society in the North and had assisted in the work of the Conference for Education in the South, served the Slater Board with great devotion as field agent between 1907 and 1910. He was succeeded by B. C. Caldwell, who until his resignation in 1931 rendered fine service to the cause. Dillard became the next director and Williams a field agent of the Fund.

The first plan of the Slater Board was to use the fund for the training of teachers for Negro people in suitable institutions of higher learning. During the twenty-eight years from 1882 to 1910 the appropriations were made chiefly to private and church institutions, mostly to those which had been established by the northern church societies for training teachers, and to public schools doing similar work. The largest donations were to private and denominational schools. Those given for public schools were mainly for industrial and vocational training. In the first year, 1883, the Board made total appropriations of $16,250 to twelve institutions.

Dr. James H. Dillard, president of the Jeanes Fund, also modified and greatly extended the service of the Slater Fund.[4] This Fund now began lending assistance to a few counties for the establishment of county training schools for Negroes. These were vocational schools which gave teacher-training in addition to the elementary and high school courses. Such was the success of the first experiments with them that Dr. Dillard called the attention of all state superintendents of education to this new plan of coöperation. He proposed that the Slater Board coöperate with the county boards in the effort to improve the character and quality of teaching through the establishment of training schools wherever the public authorities would join in. The matter was received favorably.[5]

The plan was that the property of the training school should belong to the county, state, or district, and the school should

<hr>

[4] See below, p. 445.
[5] The John F. Slater Fund, *Occasional Papers, No. 14, County Teacher Training Schools for Negroes; Proceedings and Reports, 1929*, pp. 11-14.

be a part of the public school system. There should be an appropriation for salaries of not less than $750 from state, county, or district. The term should be at least eight months, and the teaching should extend through the eighth year, with the intention of adding two more years as soon as possible. By 1914-1915 seventeen schools were in operation in the South. The purpose of these county training schools was, first, the cultivation of efficient citizens among the rural Negroes; and second, the training of teachers right at home for the rural schools.[6] The work grew rapidly, and the Slater Fund had to ask for, and received, the coöperation of other foundations in developing these schools.

The Slater Board expended $166,000 in this work up to 1920, but it continued to supply the private and church schools with the largest part of its annual income down to 1919-1920. Though these training schools became popular after 1912, they were not the only or the largest of the Board's work prior to 1921. While it gave $22,000 to training schools, it gave $41,600 to private and church schools.[7] The Slater Board in 1914 received the sum of $350,000 in the final distribution of the Peabody Fund. The Carnegie Foundation entrusted funds to it from time to time also, and the General Education Board, beginning in 1915-1916, gave increasing sums for the support of the county training schools.[8] The Fund has also received gifts from the Julius Rosenwald Fund. These amounts, together with the amounts designated from the Slater Fund each year, totaled between 1920 and 1929, $811,200. The largest contribution to the Fund during this period was $288,000.[9]

Of this coöperation of the various agencies in the work of the county training schools, Dr. Dillard says in his report for 1929:

Coöperation has become a great word in our day. In really effective coöperation in the field of education the County Training Schools furnish the most striking example that I know of. Let me give one instance of one of the schools which I recently visited. This school had received help from seven sources: the State, the

[6] The Slater Fund, *Proceedings and Reports*, *1915*, p. 16; *ibid.*, *1920*, pp. 12-13.

[7] Ullin Whitney Leavell, *Philanthropy in Negro Education*, pp. 98, 174.

[8] General Education Board, *Reports*, *1914-1915*, p. 37; *ibid.*, *1927-1928*, pp. 22-23; *ibid.*, *1931-1932*, p. 42; *ibid.*, *1932-1933*, p. 22.

[9] Leavell, *op. cit.*, p. 122.

county, the contributions of the people themselves, the Slater Fund, the General Education Board, the Rosenwald Fund and the Federal Fund, known as Smith-Hughes. This last was supplying the salary of a teacher in agriculture and shop work.... Besides all these agencies the Carnegie Corporation made through the Slater Board liberal contributions to County Training Schools in the critical middle period of their development.[10]

The Slater Board has maintained the policy that its assistance should be continued until the training school has reached the full four-year high school grade. There has been a consistent increase in the number of these schools which have become four-year high schools. The total number of training schools in 1924-1925 was 233, of which forty were full high schools ; in 1927-1928 the full number had increased to 328, of which 104 were four-year high schools.[11]

Another line of work of the Slater Board has been that of assisting public high schools to maintain industrial teachers. An appropriation of from $50 to $250 per school is granted with the understanding that an equal amount be given from public funds. This plan has stimulated to a great degree industrial instruction in urban schools. From 1921 to 1929 the Board maintained its policy of support to denominational institutions of college grade. Prior to 1926 its donations went to colleges to pay salaries of industrial, agricultural, and normal teachers. Whereas in 1921 in the institutions aided there were only thirteen hundred college students, in 1926 there were five thousand students in these colleges. This condition raised the question whether it would not be wise for the Board, after caring for training schools, to devote the remainder of its income to help Negro colleges in securing competent professors. Not being able to do all of this itself, the Board called the attention of other boards to the large need here and succeeded in getting additional assistance for paying professors of English and science in certain colleges. No state or public institutions received aid in this period. The total number of colleges aided in this way has increased from twenty-three in 1920-1921 to thirty in 1928-1929, and the donations have increased from $16,500 in 1883 to $42,000 in 1928-1929. The number of students in these

[10] The Slater Fund, *Proceedings and Reports, 1929*, p. 14.
[11] *Ibid., 1925*, pp. 10-12 ; *ibid., 1928*, p. 9.

colleges, as noted above, increased from one thousand three hundred to five thousand.[12]

A complete statement of the Board's activities since its founding in 1882 down to 1929 shows that out of a total of about $3,252,000 granted to all causes of Negro education, the sum of $2,244,000, or about 70 per cent, has been granted to private and church institutions. The total amount granted by the Slater Board to various types of institutions from 1921 to 1929 was $1,057,000. Of this the appropriations to public education totaled about $728,000, or 69 per cent of all the grants, while private education received about $329,000 or 31 per cent. From this it clearly appears that the Slater Board has distinctly stimulated the public to a larger support of county training schools and of colleges for Negroes.[13]

The work of the Slater Fund has attracted a great deal of favorable attention and has encouraged other agencies interested in the education of the Negro in the rural South. Though its appropriation seems modest in comparison with the large amounts that have been invested in this cause by Mr. Rockefeller, Mr. Rosenwald and others, the Fund has really accomplished a vast amount of good in helping schools for Negro teachers. The coöperation between the Slater Fund and the Jeanes is described in the account of the Jeanes Fund following.

William Burns Paterson and the State Normal School at Montgomery, Alabama

One of the schools which the Slater Fund has aided most effectively is the Alabama State Normal School at Montgomery, whose story is one of the most interesting of all the schools for Negroes in the South. Founded by a poor young man for the benefit of his Negro laborers with no help and little encouragement at first, it grew in forty years from a small private school to be the largest school for Negro teachers in this country, and, as far as known, in the world. The founder and builder of the school was a young Scotchman, William Burns Paterson, who was born on February 9, 1850, at Tullibody, Clackmannanshire, Scotland. He was a lineal descendant of John, brother of the poet, Robert Burns. After only three years in the elementary schools of Scotland, he was employed as a boy on the

[12] Leavell, *op. cit.*, pp. 124-26.   [13] *Ibid.*, pp. 128-29.

estate of Lord Abercrombie, located near his home, and it was here that he acquired his great love for flowers and learned the art of rose-culture which played so important a part in his life. From early youth he was filled with the missionary spirit, and the story of Livingston in Africa created in him the earnest desire to go to Africa to work among the Negroes. When he was unable to raise the money to go to Africa, he came in 1869 to America, landing in New York.

After working as a common laborer in various places in the North and Middle West, he drifted south to work on a railroad being built near Selma, Alabama. Here he became very much interested in the Negroes, and in 1870 he started a class for them in the vicinity of Greensboro, Alabama. From 1871 to 1879 he conducted a school for Negroes there which he called the Tullibody Academy for his old home in Scotland. In 1879 he removed to Marion, Alabama. Paterson was much misunderstood and suffered many hardships, but finally he overcame opposition and prejudice and won the esteem of all good people, with the result that he was called to be president of the Lincoln Normal University at Marion, Alabama, which had been established by act of the legislature in 1873. It was the first and for many years the only school of the kind in the southern states. Paterson travelled extensively, visiting the Negro churches and communities throughout the state, lecturing in the interest of the school and collecting money for it. In this way the school became well advertised and he succeeded in building up a regular attendance of students, adding to its list of supporters many substantial friends among the whites as well as among the Negro people. The school soon became a beacon light for the Negroes of that section of the state.

The physical plant of the Normal University at Marion consisted in 1885 of one main building with eight classrooms, an auditorium, and a small shop for carpentry. There was a small dormitory for forty young men; eighteen Negro girls lived in the principal's home and others in families in the neighborhood, making a total of about one hundred boarders who with the day students made up a total of three hundred students.

In 1887 the school was removed from Marion to Montgomery, and the name was changed to the State Normal School for Colored Students. When Montgomery was selected as the new location, great opposition was voiced by many of the white people of that city. But Paterson went ahead with his work, and, after conferring with some of the more liberal-minded citizens, called a mass meeting in a Negro church known as the "Old Ship." He told the people that if they would buy the land the state would erect upon it buildings for the school. The fund for the purchase of the land was raised by Negroes assisted by a few of their white friends. Being desirous of opening the school at once, Paterson sought a temporary location and was offered the use of the Beulah Baptist Church. On the opening day four hundred children, together with their parents and friends, gathered in the basement of this church for registration. Seven residences on adjoining streets and two buildings which had been used as stores located in the neighborhood were secured for classrooms. The first faculty consisted of nine teachers. Mrs. Paterson, a graduate of Oberlin College and a helpmate indeed for her brave husband, was one of them. Tuition of one dollar a month was charged at first, so that the teachers all labored at great sacrifice, receiving little or no salary. After two years in Beulah Church the school was moved to its present location, the state having erected two buildings on the land purchased by the Negroes and their friends. The school has been in successful operation here for forty-five years.

Paterson trained his pupils to be industrious and prepared them for various lines of labor and service as well as teaching. He acquired land in the neighborhood of the school and established the Rosemont Gardens, where he grew flowers, specializing in roses, for which he became famous. He opened a flower store in Montgomery, where he sold his products. He and the students did all the work. When asked by a visitor how he got so much work done so economically, he said that the students did most of it in working out their demerits—his discipline was strict—and he added quaintly, "In the spring and summer when there is much work to be done, I am *very* strict!"

In connection with the normal and industrial departments Paterson had a model elementary school, a kindergarten, shops for teaching carpentry, wheelwrighting, and blacksmithing for boys, and cooking and sewing rooms for the girls.

Bishop Haygood, the agent of the Slater Fund, and afterwards Dr. Curry, his successor, visited the school and recommended an appropriation for it. In the report to the Slater Board for 1904-1905 it is said that the school had property

consisting of land, $18,000, and buildings, $27,000, all belonging
to the state. The annual income from the state was $8,500,
from the Slater Fund $3,500, from the Peabody Fund $1,400,
and from tuition $1,500, making a total of $15,000 a year. In
that year there were five white instructors, six Negro men and
seventeen Negro women, a total of twenty-eight teachers. The
students numbered 1,058 and were classified as follows : agriculture, 85 ; carpentry, 81 ; blacksmithing, 43 ; wagon-making,
51 ; sewing, 403 ; bookkeeping, 36 ; mechanical drawing, clay
modeling, and other arts, 298. The majority of the men teachers
in industrial arts were drawn from Tuskegee. The teacher of
art was a graduate of Pratt Institute in New York.

The main building of the school, a very poor one, erected
when it had very little means, was destroyed by fire in 1904.
Paterson wrote : "Our disaster revealed an interest in our work
and the existence of more friends than we had dreamed of."
Donations were made of money, lumber, and various other materials, and by January 1, 1905, the Industrial Department had
made additions to other buildings, giving six recitation rooms in
addition to the carpenter shop and the blacksmith shop.

The influence of this school on the community became more
and more noticeable every year. Paterson himself was a living
example to his students. He taught them, worked with them,
and best of all he lived as an illustration of what a gentleman
and a teacher should be. He was throughout his whole career an
unfailing servant of the public, helping wherever he could. To
a gentleman who left a package in his greenhouse to be taken
to his hotel, and who proposed to pay a messenger to do this,
he said : "Do not say a word. There was a time when I hadn't
a thing in the world that I could not carry in my hand. I will
bring it to you."

Paterson's report to the Slater Fund for the year 1911-1912
says that he had thirty-five instructors in the school, thirty-one
of whom had taught two or more years previous to that year ;
of the 1,163 students, 367 were male and 796 female ; 377
boarded in the institution.

Paterson's pupils went out into the world to do the work
for which they were prepared. Hundreds became teachers and
others worked at the various industrial arts. In 1907 he compiled
a list of 973 former students in and around Montgomery and
found that 195 were teachers ; 59, farmers ; 8, ministers ; 9,

doctors; 62, carpenters; 42, brickmasons; 31, blacksmiths; 23, painters; 21, railroad porters; and the others were distributed through various industrial professions including seven office clerks, eleven railroad mail clerks, and sixteen mail carriers. A majority of the women had become homemakers, but there were fifty-one dressmakers, eleven milliners, nine trained nurses and twelve professional cooks. Twenty-one of the list were taking professional or advanced courses in other colleges. Of all the students who had attended the school during this period there were only three who had been convicted of crime.

William Burns Paterson died during the session of 1914-1915 and was succeeded by John W. Beverly, who had been one of his pupils at Greensboro and had been graduated from the Lincoln Normal University in 1882. When the school was moved to Montgomery he went there with it. In 1890 Beverly went to Brown University, Rhode Island, where he was graduated in 1894. Returning then to Montgomery he became professor and secretary of the State Normal School, which he served with great efficiency. Upon the death of President Paterson he served as president of the State Normal School from 1915 to 1920. He is at the present time a professor of English and history at the Prairie View Normal and Industrial College in Texas.

The school was made a standard normal school by the addition of the Junior College department in 1920. This comprises two years beyond the high school, and it has since been recognized by the State Board of Education as a Class A normal school, carrying all the privileges and advantages of schools of this class. It is the only such school in Alabama for Negro people.

In 1920, upon the resignation of President Beverly, George Washington Trenholm was appointed president. He served from 1920 to 1925 and was succeeded by his son, H. Councill Trenholm, an A.M. graduate from the University of Chicago, who is still president of the College. In 1929 the institution was expanded into a four-year Teachers College as part of the program of development inaugurated by the State Board of Education for all the two-year Class A normal schools. The third-year work was begun in September, 1929, and the fourth year added for 1929-1930, so that the first college graduates were awarded their Bachelor of Science degrees in June, 1930.

The school has grown steadily in numbers and importance. In 1930-1931 there were 430 students in the college, 574 in the high schools, and 157 in the various elementary grades of the laboratory schools used for training. These cover all the grades from the nursery to the ninth grade.[13a]

This school has been a pioneer in the field of extension instruction and of regular summer school work consisting of sixty days—ten weeks—six days per week during the summer. In 1930-1931 this College had an enrollment of 2,369 in its summer school at Montgomery and an enrollment of 1,219 in its extension division. This is the largest enrollment of summer schools and extension work for Negroes in the country. During the year 1930-1931, therefore, the total number of students instructed in the college, high school, laboratory schools, elementary schools, summer schools, and extension courses, was 4,749.

WILLIAM TAYLOR B. WILLIAMS

Dean Williams of Tuskegee has been the efficient field agent of the Slater and Jeanes funds for almost his whole working life. He was born in Stonebridge, Virginia, in 1869 and was graduated from Hampton Institute in 1888. He later completed courses at Phillips Academy, Andover, Massachusetts, and at Harvard University. After serving for a time as principal of a school in the Middle West, he was appointed field agent for the Jeanes and Slater funds. In this service his work has been brought into direct contact with the Negro schools of the South and he has probably visited more of these and understands their needs better than any other man in the country. He is, therefore, able to recommend to those in charge of the Jeanes and Slater funds where their money can best be spent. He is now not only field agent for the Jeanes and Slater funds but also dean of the College at Tuskegee. A man of fine scholarship and culture, an admirable executive, he has made a great success of every task he has undertaken, and he has accomplished much for southern schools.

[13a] State Teachers College, *1931 Yearbook: Catalogue of Faculty and Students for 1930-31, Alumni Register, Bulletin of 1931 Summer Quarter, Announcements for 1931-32*, Montgomery, Alabama, 1931, pp. 14, 101.

THE JEANES FUND AND ITS WORK

Miss Anna T. Jeanes, a Quaker lady who had made many gifts of various kinds to institutions in Philadelphia, was induced by Mr. George Foster Peabody, treasurer of the General Education Board, to make the first gift to Negro education in 1905. To this Board she sent a check for $200,000 "for the assistance of Negro 'Rural Schools' in the South," designating at the same time that the fund should be expended under the direction of Dr. Frissell of Hampton and Booker T. Washington of Tuskegee. The following year Dr. Frissell received from Miss Jeanes a donation of $10,000 for Hampton and a similar amount for Tuskegee. At this time she said : "I should like to help the little country schools for Negroes." Following out this idea, in 1907 she gave a deed of trust to a board of trustees for an endowment fund of $1,000,000. After signing the papers, she said to Dr. Frissell : "Dost thee remember when thee came I gave thee $10,000 for Negro schools. And then I gave thee $200,000 more. I am now giving all for the little schools. This is a great privilege. I am just a poor woman, and I gave it not to save my soul, but just because I wanted to." [14] Miss Jeanes directed that her fund be invested in government bonds. When the trustees asked her to change this, she quietly but firmly refused. It has proved wise that she did.

Among the first trustees of the Jeanes Fund were President Taft, Andrew Carnegie, George Foster Peabody, Robert C. Ogden, Walter H. Page, Hollis Burke Frissell, James H. Dillard, Samuel C. Mitchell, Booker T. Washington, Robert R. Moton, and Robert L. Smith, a Negro banker of Texas. President Taft took a great interest in the needs of the Negroes of the country, and this Board met several times in the Cabinet room of the White House. Dr. James H. Dillard was elected president and director of the Fund and continued in charge until 1931.

The purpose of the Fund was to encourage and to coöperate with other established educational agencies without relieving them of the responsibility which they should rightly bear in improving the Negro rural schools. The trustees commenced at once on a plan of coöperation, first with the Southern Edu-

[14] *The Negro Rural School Fund, Inc. (Anna T. Jeanes Foundation)*, *1907-1933*, pp. 7-9.

cation Board, and then with the Peabody Board and the General Education Board, a plan which has accomplished great results. The origin of this useful coöperation forms an interesting story.

This Fund given by Miss Jeanes was the first one to be strictly confined to the public education of the Negro rural schools in the South. It has had great success in developing common schools for Negro children, in encouraging rural teachers of these schools, and in promoting a healthy pride in the school work of the children in the communities where such schools are located.

Mr. Jackson Davis was, between 1906 and 1910, the active and efficient superintendent of schools of Henrico County, Virginia, and had charge of both the Negro and white schools. In going over this county, Davis found a Negro school, taught by a teacher named Virginia Randolph, which was distinctly superior in every way. She was a simple woman, but she knew the common industrial and domestic arts. Her school was in perfect order, windows washed, floor scoured, yard cleaned. In the back of the schoolroom was a cookstove, well polished, where the children cooked vegetables and meat for a hot lunch. Davis became very much interested and noted that every time he went to see that particular school something a little better was being done. On one of his visits Virginia Randolph asked permission to visit some of the other school teachers and help them to improve their schoolhouses and to start industrial training. Davis secured a supply teacher to take her place, so that she could go on Friday of each week to visit the teachers in the other schools in the neighborhood and help them. Thus Virginia Randolph began a visitation of the schools of the county which resulted in their complete transformation. She was not attempting to do a new or a big thing, but just to go among the schools and to show the teachers how they might teach the children to make better homes. This was done the year the Jeanes Fund was established. It was the beginning of a valuable plan of improving these schools.

When Davis told Dr. Dillard about Virginia Randolph's method and her remarkable success, Dillard decided to try the plan on a moderate scale at first. A part of the Jeanes Fund was appropriated for the purpose. The plan soon proved such an excellent one that it was made permanent and extended to

Upper left, Miss Anna T. Jeanes, donator of the fund for Negro elementary rural schools. Upper right, Virginia Randolph, whose work started the system of "Jeanes supervisors" of Negro rural schools. Below, farm and home-makers' clubs receiving instruction, Jefferson County, Florida, 1919

Above, the five-thousandth Rosenwald School, a six-teacher rural school in Elizabeth City County, Virginia, costing $20,000, of which the Negroes contributed $1,000, the Julius Rosenwald Fund $2,600, and the public funds amounted to $16,400. Below, agricultural students harvesting sweet potato crops at Hampton Institute

all the Negro elementary schools in the county. When other superintendents visited the county and saw Virginia Randolph's work, they asked for similar teachers. Dillard paid the salaries of the teachers from the Jeanes Fund and similar work was next started in seven counties in Virginia. The movement spread from Henrico County down to Norfolk and then into North Carolina. Hampton Institute assisted at first in paying the expenses of these additional supervisors.

Sixty-five such teachers were supplied on this plan in 1908-1909 by the Jeanes Board, at a total cost of $13,600. The plan proved so successful that the next year the number increased to 129 teachers working in as many counties at a cost of $44,250. In 1912-1913 the counties were asked to assist in paying the salaries of these teachers, and the plan of conditional support was undertaken. The response was gratifying and the sum of $3,400 was paid in that year to help the work. County support from this beginning increased to $44,500 in 1920, or 88 per cent of the total cost. The assistance of the Jeanes Board in this work was soon in such great demand throughout the South that the income proved insufficient. Later the Phelps-Stokes Fund, the General Education Board, and the Rosenwald Fund came to the assistance of the Jeanes Fund, so as to increase the support of the supervising teachers. The total of this outside support has amounted to over $921,000.

So it happened that the aged Quaker lady in Philadelphia and the humble Negro teacher in a rural district in Virginia, contributed each in her own way to one of the most fruitful undertakings that has touched the life of the blacks in the South. The Jeanes Board simply adopted Virginia Randolph's plan by placing supervising teachers similar to her throughout the South and so brought the schools to bear upon the life of the communities in a practical way.

State Agents for Negro Schools

Jackson Davis's excellent work in Henrico County attracted the attention also of the officers of the Southern Board, who induced the Peabody Board to make a contribution to enable Davis to go about the state representing the Department of Education and conferring with the county superintendents and local school boards in the interest of better school facilities for the children of the blacks. Davis thus brought about better co-operation between the races and created a better public opinion on the subject of training the Negroes in economic proficiency and useful citizenship. In the space of two years he accomplished results in this direction which exceeded anything which had been done elsewhere.

This demonstration of what could be done in winning support for Negro schools led the General Education Board to extend this service to other states. In 1914, therefore, when the operations of the Peabody Fund and of the Southern Education Board had come to an end, provision for the appointment of agents for Negro schools in all the southern states was made by the General Education Board. This became part of a general plan for the improvement of the rural schools for both races. The Board offered to coöperate with the state departments of education in providing funds to pay the salaries and expenses of state agents for Negro public schools to be appointed by them.

These rural agents for Negro schools were accepted by the twelve southern states—Alabama, Arkansas, Georgia, Kentucky, Louisiana, Maryland, Mississippi, North and South Carolina, Tennessee, Texas, and Virginia, and the expenditures for this work amounted, between 1915 and 1920, to $246,500.

These state agents for Negro schools were attached to the departments of education of the states, so that their function became practically that of assistant state superintendents of Negro schools. They have exercised a great influence in determining the policies for Negro schools and have helped the authorities in the states to centralize the administration of these schools on a state basis. Their activities had fine influence in stimulating local efforts for consolidated schools, erecting new buildings, improving courses, organizing clubs, and increasing generally the expenditures in the counties for Negro education.

As the Negro race had no representatives in these states upon the boards and the councils of education which fixed the expenditures for Negro schools, there still remains, among some boards of education and superintendents of schools, a lack of proper feeling and responsibility for the Negro schools under their supervision. There are some boards and superintendents who consider the Negro schools as secondary. In counties where these superintendents are elected by the patrons of the white schools they naturally consider their first duty to the white children. The state supervisors of Negro schools have been able largely to overcome this condition.

At the same time that the state agents were appointed, the Jeanes Fund came forward and offered to provide a certain number of county supervisors to do throughout these states work similar to that done by Virginia Randolph in Henrico County. This combination of the resources of the General Board and the Jeanes Fund completed the establishment of most important agencies for the improvement of elementary Negro schools.

Probably no single agency in the South has done more important work than this of the state agents for Negro schools operating in connection with the various state departments of education in directing and supervising the Negro schools. They were the pioneers in the advance of Negro education. Born and reared in the South, in sympathy with its ideals and familiar with its schools, these agents were made possible by the generous aid of the men in control of, first, the Peabody Fund, then of the Southern Education Board, and finally of the General Education Board. The work of such men as N. C. Newbold, who has been in charge of this service in North Carolina since 1914, of J. S. Lambert, for thirty years state agent in Alabama, of D. E. Williams of Florida, Leo M. Favrot of Louisiana, and C. T. Bloodworth of Texas, all of whom have served for long periods, and of the other men in this service, will go down in the history of education in the South as epoch-making.

COÖPERATION OF THE GENERAL EDUCATION BOARD WITH THE SLATER AND JEANES BOARDS

The General Education Board has coöperated with the Slater and Jeanes funds in all their work. From 1902, when the General Education Board commenced its work, down to 1920, the chief agencies used by this Board were state agents for Negro schools; county training schools, schools with normal and industrial departments in advance of the primary school; coöperation with the Jeanes Rural School Fund and grants to the Slater and Jeanes Funds; summer schools for Negro teachers; and numerous scholarships for teachers seeking advanced training in colleges. The largest grants from the Board since 1914 have been for the promotion of Negro public schools by paying the expenses of state agents for them.

The General Education Board also assisted in the construction of school buildings and the equipment of rural schools. Between 1914 and 1920 it assisted the Jeanes Fund in forming "Home Makers' Clubs," under the direction of the industrial teachers or supervisors. These teachers organized the women and children of the communities into clubs for instruction in gardening, cooking, canning, sewing, home sanitation and other practical household activities. The United States Government took over this work in 1920.

In 1916 the Board formed summer schools for Negro teachers in thirty-five institutions in nine states. Over three thousand Negro teachers attended these schools. The following year the number of schools increased to forty-eight, with an enrollment of over six thousand. The terms of these schools ranged from four to six weeks, and the courses were designed to strengthen the teachers in every way in their preparation for giving both literary and industrial instruction. The schools were located in state agricultural and mechanical colleges, normal schools, and public high schools, as well as in private colleges and secondary schools. The Board also made donations to pay the expenses of students attending these schools.

These are only a few of the different activities of the General Education Board in coöperation with other boards for the advancement of public schools and for the preparation of teachers. For these purposes between 1915 and 1920 the Board expended approximately $675,000.[15] In addition, between 1902 and 1920 this Board granted a total of $1,770,264 to Negro schools and colleges. Thanks to the great bequest by Mr. Rockefeller, most of this work is still going on.

In the year 1919 the General Education Board commenced the policy of paying the salary of one teacher in each of several church colleges "for the purpose of improving the facilities of teacher training." This work, which was put under the supervision of the Slater Fund, has proved one of the best schemes thus far undertaken. During the years 1925 to 1929 over two thousand students were enrolled in the teacher-training courses

[15] General Education Board, *Reports, 1914-1915,* to *Reports, 1919-1920;* Leavell, *op. cit.,* pp. 105, 175.

and over one thousand graduated. They were promptly employed in the public schools of the states and became fine examples to the other teachers. A number of institutions aided by this fund in the beginning are now actively supporting teacher training from their own funds.

The appropriation of the General Education Board for the period from 1923 to 1929 shows a total of $13,742,500 for all causes of Negro education, of which 70 per cent was apportioned to private and denominational colleges. At the same time this Board has added to the Jeanes Fund the amount of $507,-150, and to the Slater Board the amount of $366,525.[16] Hampton and Tuskegee Institutes received from the Board $30,000 while the teachers in denominational schools were supported at a cost of $89,250. The General Education Board, while co-operating with other foundations in support of their work, is putting its emphasis upon the training of teachers for the schools and upon education in higher private and church colleges.

JAMES HARDY DILLARD

No man of the day in the South represents more perfectly the best old southern ideals and traditions of what a scholar can do in the South in the era since the Civil War than does James Hardy Dillard. It was, therefore, eminently fitting that Dillard should be selected to take up the cause of Negro education and better race relations. James Hardy Dillard was born on October 24, 1856, in Nansemond County in the extreme southeastern corner of Virginia, in the Tidewater section, where Virginia civilization started, of the best old Virginia stock. His father, Major James Dillard, was a Princeton graduate and a liberal-minded man who had always held serious views on slavery. His mother was Sarah Brownrigg Cross, of similar stock, a woman of most unusual ability and initiative. The boy grew up on a large plantation with 350 slaves, and like other southern boys played with Negro boys, to some of whom he early became attached.

When the war came and all the men went into the service everything was changed, but the strong mother directed the affairs of the estate with ability and reared her son to be a real

[16] General Education Board, *Reports, 1923-1924*, to *Reports, 1928-1929*; Leavell, *op. cit.*, pp. 135, 180.

man. At the close of the terrible contest which had raged all around them, the estate was completely wrecked and the father left in ill health. The boy, now ten years old, was sent to a teacher in the neighborhood, under whom he remained two years and got a good start in Latin forms. At twelve he was sent to live with an aunt in Norfolk, Virginia, where he could be under a famous classical teacher, Professor William R. Galt.[17] Galt was a perfect master of Latin, Greek, French, German, and Anglo-Saxon, all of which he taught with skill and thoroughness. The boy who was under him for some five or six years made great progress in the classics and developed into a manly fellow. Dillard has written a description of this old school which is a gem of literature and should be read by every student of the history of education of this period.[18]

Washington College was in 1875 an institution which attracted southern boys above all others. General Lee was dead, but his son, G. W. Custis Lee, had succeeded him and maintained there the same standards of culture, honor, and chivalry. After being graduated with the A.B. and A.M. degrees Dillard studied and took the degree in law for the purpose of entering upon that profession, but his father was so broken in health that he had to give up this ambition and take a position as teacher in Norfolk, Virginia, where he could earn a moderate salary. Here he was president of the public library. The father died, and there followed years of hard work and severe discipline. He now taught for fifteen years in the Sauveur Summer School of Languages, which held its sessions in different colleges in the North. This was one of the first summer schools in the country, and Dillard undoubtedly got, not only added experience, but some of his ideas of practical education while working in it. He was called next to be principal of Mary Institute, the woman's department of Washington University of St. Louis. Here, though still a young man for such a position, he was a success both as administrator and as teacher.

His old friend and teacher at Washington College, Colonel William Preston Johnston, called him next, to be professor of Latin in Tulane University, which he had just reorganized. What we now call university extension was one of Johnston's

---

[17] Acknowledgment is made to *Doctor Dillard of the Jeanes Fund*, by Benjamin Brawley.
[18] *Sewanee Review*, Vol. XXIX (October, 1921), 410-16.

plans for improving the culture of the town, and Dillard gave many public lectures in the city which attracted interested audiences. In time he became a general public servant, helping in every way to promote the education and the culture of the city. He was president of the city library board and a member of the state board of education, and he took much interest in developing the public high schools of the state. He was a trustee of a number of colleges. After his resignation he became a member of the Board of Administrators of Tulane University.

The reader will recall that this period (the early nineties) was one of bad feeling towards the Negro race, especially in Mississippi and Louisiana. In the year 1892 there were 255 known cases of lynching in the country, almost all of Negroes in the South, and in February, 1893, the average was nearly one a day. For example, in Jackson, Louisiana, where there was a Negro church meeting, a crowd of white men fired revolvers into the Negroes as they passed to and fro. About the same time a Negro girl of fifteen was taken from jail and hanged. These crimes stirred Dillard greatly, and he made up his mind that something must be done.

Realizing that nothing permanent could be accomplished without a change of public opinion, he went to work in a quiet way to create a better state of mind among the white people. The public library of which he was president did not admit Negro citizens. Andrew Carnegie had given money for a new library building. Dillard saw to it that one branch was built and set aside for the Negroes. Meeting incidentally a group of white teachers of Negro colleges in Louisiana, who had always been ostracized by the whites, he shook hands and talked with them. One of them said : "I have lived here twenty years and you are the first southern white man who ever spoke to me voluntarily." He went on quietly and by his work and example influenced many of the liberally minded people of New Orleans to take a kindlier view of the Negro. He was made trustee of four Negro colleges in Louisiana. When friends remonstrated with him about his course, he went ahead calmly, maintaining his stand for justice and righteousness.

When in 1907 the trustees of the Anna T. Jeanes Foundation offered to him the position of president and director he declined at first. The classical work in which he was engaged and his social service in New Orleans attracted him very much, and it seemed to be his duty to remain there. A friend who had watched his course told him, referring to his association with Negro education: "You are the only man in Louisiana who could 'get by' with this." To Dillard's surprise many of the leading citizens there advised him to take the position with the Jeanes Fund. He accepted with deep interest and some anxiety, and on the first of January, 1908, took charge of the Negro Rural School Fund established by Miss Jeanes and re-signed his position in New Orleans. He left a distinguished and delightful post and entered upon a new, untried, and difficult service. In 1910 Dillard accepted the directorship of the Slater Fund for the education of the Negroes and united this service with that of the Jeanes Fund in a wise plan of work which proved very effective in advancing the common cause. Dr. Dillard was a member of the Southern Education Board, and of the General Education Board. He is still vice-president of the Phelps-Stokes Fund and rector of the board of the College of William and Mary. In recognition of his work for Negro education and out of their great esteem for the man, the trustees of two colleges for Negroes in New Orleans recently united them into one institution and named it Dillard University. It is a worthy monument to a great scholar, a great educator, and a great public servant. Dr. Dillard resigned as president and director of the Jeanes Fund in 1931. He was succeeded by Dr. Arthur D. Wright.

Arthur D. Wright

Born in Boston, Dr. Wright received his early education at the McGuire School in Richmond, Virginia, a typical south-ern private school of the highest class; and after being gradu-ated from the old College of William and Mary, took his Mas-ter's Degree in education at Harvard. He taught in the high school at Hampton, Virginia, and was then principal of the Baker School, a Negro public school, of Richmond. He was superintendent of schools first at Fredericksburg and then of Henrico County, Virginia, getting thus complete experience in both town and country schools. He was next state supervisor of Negro Education of Virginia from 1915 to 1920. For a time he was professor of education at Dartmouth. During this period he was a member of the survey staff of the Virginia State

School Survey of 1919, and in 1928 he was on the staff of the Florida State School Survey. No man could have been better trained to become the president of the Jeanes and the Slater funds or to be the successor to Dr. Dillard.

THE PHELPS-STOKES FUND

Miss Caroline Phelps Stokes, the founder of the Phelps-Stokes Fund, came of a family distinguished on both sides for its religious enthusiasm and humanitarianism. Her grandfather, Thomas Stokes, who came to America in 1789, was one of the founders of the American Bible Society, the American Tract Society, and the New York Peace Society. Her grandfather on her mother's side, Anson Greene Phelps, was president of the New York Colonization Society, one of the founders of the American Board of Commissioners for Foreign Missions (the A.B.C.F.M.), president of the New York Blind Asylum, and intimately associated with Thomas Stokes in the American Bible and American Tract societies. It was said at the time of his death that Anson Greene Phelps left more money for religious and humanitarian purposes than any man had previously bequeathed to such causes in the State of New York. Miss Stokes's mother was one of the board of directors of the New York Negro Orphan Asylum, an active worker for temperance, and an abolitionist without being violent. There was hardly a character-building institution in New York that Miss Stokes's ancestors were not connected with in some way, either by gift or by active work.[19] Devotion to religion, the desire to relieve human suffering in every form, and sensitiveness to every human need were characteristics of both the Phelps and Stokes families to a degree which made them conspicuous illustrations of the truth that righteousness and the love of fellow man is an inherited trait.

Caroline Phelps Stokes was interested from early girlhood in the education of the Negro race in America and other similar enterprises. When as a school girl she spent a winter in Asheville, North Carolina, she became deeply interested in the needs of the white people of the mountain districts. Her gifts

[19] *Educational Adaptations: Report of Ten Years' Work of the Phelps-Stokes Fund, 1910-1920;* and *Twenty-Year Report of the Phelps-Stokes Fund, 1911-1931.*

to establish benevolent enterprises in New York were numerous and constant.

On the death of Miss Stokes in 1909 it was found that by her will she had directed that the interest and net income of her residuary estate should be devoted to "the erection or improvement of tenement house dwellings in New York City . . . and for educational purposes in the education of negroes both in Africa and the United States, North American Indians, and . . . deserving white students." As trustees she named the Protestant Episcopal Bishop of New York, for the time being, the Chancellor of the University of the City of New York, for the time being, Reverend Dr. Lyman Abbott, her sister, and several of her nephews and nieces with power to elect additional members. The board was incorporated in May, 1911, by the legislature of the State of New York with her sister, Miss Olivia, as a member. The Reverend Anson Phelps Stokes, D.D., at one time secretary of Yale University and more recently canon of the Washington Cathedral, is the present chairman. The estate was found at first to be about $1,000,000.

The Board announced that though Negro education was not the exclusive interest to which the Fund was devoted, its policy was to dispense its philanthropy as far as possible through existing institutions ; that the coöperation of the best white citizens of the South was of prime importance ; and that it would use a liberal amount in investigations and reports on educational institutions of Negroes and connected problems. One of the first things that the Board did was to have a study made of the education of the Negroes of the United States with the coöperation of the Government Bureau of Education. This work was placed under the direction of Dr. P. P. Claxton, commissioner of education of the United States, and put in charge of Dr. Thomas Jesse Jones, who became afterwards the educational director of the Fund. The report of Dr. Jones, called *Negro Education*, was published by the Bureau of Education in two volumes.[20]

One of the first appropriations made was $2,500 to add to salaries of Jeanes supervisors of Negro schools in the South, and the next action was to establish fellowships for the study of the Negro question at the University of Virginia and the University of Georgia. The next thing done was to employ a

[20] *Bureau of Education Bulletins, Nos. 38 and 39, 1916.*

permanent agent, as he was called at first, to make a field study of Negro education and advise the Board with regard to the plan of work. Dr. Thomas Jesse Jones, who had been a statistician in the United States Census Bureau and had charge of the first report, was made this agent. He has since become, and is now, the educational director of the Phelps-Stokes Fund. Dr. Jones's studies and other activities have made him an important factor in the development of plans for Negro education in this country and in Africa.

THOMAS JESSE JONES AND HIS PHILOSOPHY OF EDUCATION

Thomas Jesse Jones came with his parents to America as a young boy in 1884 from the mountains of Wales. He grew up in an Ohio mining town, where he early acquired a strong sympathy with the working class. After attending Washington and Lee University and Marietta College, he entered Union Theological Seminary in New York to study for the ministry. The socialized study of religion appealed to him most, and he attended classes in Columbia University under the great Dr. Giddings, who gave him the foundation for his future studies in sociology.[21]

During his student days Dr. Jones devoted much of his time to service under the Church Federation in New York tenements and made them the subject of his dissertation for his doctor's degree at Columbia. In intervals of his university and seminary career he was headmaster of a school. All of his training and experience led him in the direction of social service ; so he decided to devote his life to the study of education in its sociological relations. Called by Dr. Frissell of Hampton to be chaplain of the Institute in 1902, he took charge of the social work of that institution and became the director of its research department.

Dr. Jones remained in Hampton from 1902 to 1909 and then went to the Census Bureau as a specialist in statistics of the American Negroes, remaining there two years. In 1911 he was called by the United States Bureau of Education, to

---

21 Columbia University conferred on Dr. Jones a prize for original investigations of a sociological character carried on for five years. These reports on Negro education are of great value for reference by students of education and race relations.

make the report for the Phelps-Stokes Fund, and remained there until 1919. Between 1917 and 1919 Jones also did war work in connection with the Division of Morale of the War Department. In 1919-1922 he made studies in West, Central, and South Africa. "The Educational Commission on Africa" was sent out under the auspices of the Phelps-Stokes Fund with Jones as director. The result of the Commission's investigation was published in England in a volume entitled, *Education in Africa*. Of this report the British Under-Secretary of State said in the House of Commons on July 25, 1923: "We want to explore the experience of the world as to what is the best and most helpful form of education we can give to the Africans, for the purpose of giving light to new Africa. With this in view we formed a permanent committee.... We were led to this largely as result of a most extraordinarily interesting report issued by Dr. Jesse Jones who has travelled not only through the British Colonies, but through French Africa, the Belgian Congo and the Portuguese Colonies. He has made a most helpful contribution to the subject of African education from the point of view of the natives." His Excellency Brigadier-General Guggisberg, governor and commander-in-chief of the Gold Coast Colony, said of this book: "One of the most important events that has occurred in the history of the progress of the African people is the publication of the Report of the African Education Commission which recently visited this country under the auspices of the Phelps-Stokes Fund. *Education in Africa* is the book of the century, a combination of sound idealism and practical common sense."

Friends of Africa had realized by this time that that continent was bound to have in the future a great influence in world affairs. The missionary societies had become convinced that the educational work they were doing there needed a complete overhauling to adapt it to the Negro people. A combination of different missionary societies was therefore formed for this purpose, and this organization invited the Phelps-Stokes Trustees to undertake a survey of the work being done. Dr. Jones selected Dr. James E. K. Aggrey as a member of the Commission. Aggrey's African origin, his knowledge of the country and the people, his broad training, common sense, and sensible attitude toward the problem of race relations made him a valuable man for this work. Jones has continued his studies in

Africa, his last trip having been to Liberia for the purpose of studying the conditions of peonage and slavery which had grown up in recent years. He has also made a number of tours for study of conditions in the Near East. On a recent visit to Greece, for example, he had a conference with Venizelos, who told him that he wished to introduce agricultural instruction in Greece in accordance with our American plan, as developed by Dr. Knapp. He quoted the fact that Xenophon chided the Athenians of his day for not raising enough wheat to keep the people alive and said that this has been true ever since. Venizelos thereupon recommended to the Greek government to confer upon Dr. Jones, the "Gold Cross of the Savior" for his contribution to education. Jones says that in all the countries of the world where he has been, a great revolution in education and social science is growing out of the better consciousness of the community.[22]

As a result of his studies in the Census Bureau and the Bureau of Education and of the investigations made during his visitations to Africa, Jones has become the chief authority in the world on the education of primitive peoples. He has also made the best analysis known to the writer of the essentials of education.[23] Believing his analysis of the new education is correct and that it is the education we need, it will be described here.

Jones begins by asking: "What is the school for?" All educators agree that the key to education is preparation for life. Upon that everything else should depend. What, then, is preparation for life? The answer Jones gives is that the larger preparation for life must depend upon a "consciousness of the community" as well as upon the training of the individual. But how is consciousness of the community to be expressed? He illustrates with the physicist, pondering over the mysteries of matter. The physicist begins his thinking with the atom and the electron, out of which are built up all the complex bodies of nature. Similarly in defining the claims of the community,

[22] For an outline of Jones's teaching on this subject see Chapter I of his book, *Essentials of Civilization*, pp. 6 to 34 (see next note). What follows is a condensation.

[23] This work was first published in a small book entitled, *Four Essentials of Education*, and later in a larger one entitled, *The Essentials of Civilization*, in the American Social Science Series, under the editorship of Howard W. Odum of the School of Social Science and Public Welfare in the University of North Carolina.

Jones, basing his theory on his observation of life in its simplest forms in an African village, found there what he calls the "four simples" or "four essentials" or "universals" on which all education must be based. In the most highly developed community, as in the most primitive village, these are the four essentials which are based upon the consciousness of the community. These "simples" are, first, health and sanitation; second, the appreciation and use of the environment, both material and human; third, the home, the unit of society, and the household; and fourth, re-creation and culture. If it is a success, says Jones, education, however limited in a narrow range, must provide for these four assets. Unless it provides them, however large its program, its staff and equipment, the school has failed.

By "consciousness of the community" Jones does not mean simply a course in civics or even in social service in the neighborhood, but that the whole course of study should be dominated and humanized by teachers who have a knowledge of community life. All school subjects and activities should be rated according to their contribution to personality and citizenship. The multiplication of educational aims, too often unrelated and sometimes conflicting, must be simplified. The objective by which all aims should be tested should be the true career of men and women as members of the human family.

Jones disapproves the modern over-emphasis on psychology and administration. Without underestimating their importance, and recognizing that psychology has laid bare many processes of the mind previously unknown, and that schools and colleges need better systems of administration, he declares that neither psychology nor administration has solved the problem that now confronts school and college. These factors are not enough. There must be consciousness of the community pervading all school instruction and activities.

Next, what does Dr. Jones mean by "simples?" The first is health. All the material resources of the country, all its accumulated tradition, history, science, are useless unless the people themselves are both eager and energetic. All achievement in letters, music, sculpture, painting, poetry, and the other arts is retarded by ill health. Full appreciation of the arts is only possible to people well in body, mind, and soul. No statistics are so vital as the vital statistics of the nation—what does it mean that the death rate in New Zealand is less than 9 while that in the United States is about 12, in England and Wales about 13, in France 17.5, in Spain nearly 22, and in Chile nearly 30 (statistics of 1922)? Many factors, such as climate and food habits, explain these variations, which are, in Jones's opinion, the best general barometers of civilization.

The work of curing diseases has in recent years been followed by work for its prevention. Education should pass beyond these two aims in order to build up the greatest reserve of health and physical vigor, both in the individual and in the community. Such a reserve is essential to the higher activities of the entire mentality and the soul. Jones's second "simple," therefore, appreciation of the environment, human and material, has been often described as social and civic responsibilities. But how superficially and artificially these aims have influenced the school program and activities! Until recently there were few examples of socialized education in rural America. How greatly the South needs still to realize this responsibility, where the freedman needs an education based on both individual and community conditions. "To put the matter in a nut-shell," says Jones: "A boy when he leaves college should be able to answer two questions: first, 'How am I to earn my living?' and, second, 'How am I to serve my neighbor.' For girls also, whether they marry or not, these questions are vital to true success."

The school should, therefore, present the pupil a picture of the world as a whole, civic, national, and international; the use of the land for the production of food; the manufacturing of commodities; application of science to the service of man; the operations of trade; the methods of government; the meaning of politics; the responsibility of the voter—whatever else is or is not taught, these matters should never be left to chance. The choice of a vocation should be considered carefully and the pupil shown that the main object is not money or property, but full preparation for these tasks in life, earning a living and serving a neighbor.

Third, says Jones, is the claim of the family in the home— the claim not on houses, churches, colleges, hotels, sky-scrapers, but on the social unit on which depends everything in the life of the nation. The family should be presented in all its relations. The great increase in divorce in America is said to be due largely to the juvenile marriage of persons morally or socially unprepared. The ambition for large expensive homes, for luxuries and pleasures, is held before young people. Happiness is not in these things. Home-building ought to be held before young people as of most importance, the most beautiful and thrilling of all human enterprises—to get the most out of their incomes, in the rearing of healthy and happy children, in establishing the relations between husband and wife, between children and parents, between the rising generation and the grandparents and all their kinsfolk. All this, says Jones, is not a task merely but a call. To accomplish this there should be close attention in the school to the home life of every child. Training in domestic arts for girls should be compulsory. The use of the hands in all industrial arts should be given the boys. All should be fully instructed in what are the essentials of the home, the value of the garden, pride in the house—how to build, furnish, and preserve it—and especially to honor it. Finally, the home must ever be the training ground of youth for the responsibilities of life.

Jones's fourth "simple" is re-creation. This, he says, completes the round of human interests. The play of primitive people expressing the universal play instincts of adults as well as children are games of all kinds. The healthful amusements and diversions of modern society, museums of art, academies of music and especially the inspiration of religion—these are also means of re-creation. With the barbarian re-creation is the desire to break away from the mere struggle for physical existence, for food and drink, to feel the freedom of play, the joy of the realization of power, grandeur or beauty. The same instinct in civilized man impels him to spend great sums of money, energy, and thought on various forms of re-creation, physical, mental and spiritual. No education that ignores the spiritual can ever succeed. In our schools and colleges at present there is little if any teaching of organized religion. The Bible is little taught in the modern home and the Sunday school gives only scrappy lessons from it. "The calling of the teacher, whatever his subject, is a spiritual calling. To inspire reverence for the good and beautiful ... should be his main object. The question is not how much the pupil reads at school but how much he will read when school is over. An ear for music, an eye for pictures, a mind for books, a zest for games, a hobby, these are the assets that make for happiness." Lectures, exhibits, imposed instruction are not enough. The worth of a man is not in what he has learned but what reserves he has in his being to help him in this re-creation which is ever to be renewed.

Finally, Jones would urge the responsibility of the teacher "to apply the consciousness of the community to every subject, to every project, to every administrative provision, from the lowest school grade through the activities of the colleges and universities." The "project method" of teaching, now extensively used, increases the possibilities of relating school activities and subjects to the four essentials. The consciousness of the community enables the teacher to direct the expansions of the project into the various phases of society with the assurance that the pupil will acquire a comprehensive understanding of the subject.

In conclusion, Jones "taking the three great departments of education in order finds that the elementary grades offer the most general opportunity to relate education to the essentials of the community. The three R's ... are susceptible of health lessons of very great value. They merge naturally with the home life from which the children come. The exchanges of school and home can be most intimate and real, with great advantage to both. The essentials of re-creation and environment may color all the elementary school processes." Similarly in the "secondary schools every subject and activity may be adapted in some of its phases to impart an appreciation of health, home, material resources, human elements and recreations. . . . Social studies, including civics and history and the records of public and private organizations for welfare, are fruitful sources of information concerning health. . . . The mathematics and physical sciences . . . are so directly related to medical and sanitary science as to be easily adapted to the teaching of health. . . . The social functions of the home, adjustments of the household to changing conditions . . . may be discussed in connection with history, social science, economics, or physical science." Jones would apply the same principles in the work of the colleges and universities. The four elements of community are entitled to serious consideration in the selection of the major research of the student. As in the case of the project in the elementary and secondary schools, so in the expansion of the major study in the university the four elemental "simples" should be in constant use in determining lines of study and investigation.

One of the results of the consciousness of the community will be the recognition of the educational importance of agriculture. Urban as well as rural schools should help to counteract the indifference or opposition to country life. They should endeavor to carry on thus the realities of education as they were organized by the pioneers of our country in their struggle with nature.

Another result of community consciousness would be larger adoption of industrial training and the processes of physical science. "Education has been so long associated with books and the art of expression as to seem strange when presented in the form of 'learning by doing.' . . . The increase of industrial and technical schools is . . . inspired by the broad conception of the intimate relation of industrial activities to the mental, moral and social progress of humanity."

Jones has presented in his book an admirable analysis of what we call the new education. His rich experience, following his close study and thorough training and his wide observation of both civilized and primitive people, entitle him to be called our modern philosopher of education.[24]

THE ROSENWALD FUND

A most interesting event was the dedication on November 21, 1930, of the five-thousandth Rosenwald school at Greenbrier, Elizabeth City County, Virginia. This school building was a milestone in the educational development of the county and, in fact, of the entire South. It was here on this soil that Captain John Smith landed before sailing up the river to Jamestown. Here he says he was kindly received by the Indians. Not far from the spot where the Rosenwald school now stands was founded the first free school in America, the Symms School, which was first endowed by Benjamin Symms in his will of February 12, 1634. The story of this school has been told in Volume I.[25]

Near the old Symms School Mr. Julius Rosenwald, with the whites and the blacks of the neighborhood coöperating in raising the money, erected his five-thousandth school for Negro

[24] Acknowledgment is made to Dr. Jones's books and to a summary of his theory of education in the *New York Times*, January 3, 1926.
[25] See Vol. I, Chap. III.

children. The building is a handsome one-story structure containing six classrooms, offices, and modern equipment for domestic and industrial arts. The school grounds and the school garden make the surroundings attractive. The cost of the building was $15,997, of which patrons and friends contributed $875.64 and Hampton Institute $600.

This building, under the Rosenwald bequest, illustrates a great new plan for improving the Negro schools of the South, devised by Mr. Rosenwald.[26] Mr. Rosenwald was a trustee of Tuskegee Institute. While visiting that institution in 1911 he inspected a number of small rural school buildings which the Institute had erected in its neighborhood to take the place of wretched shacks. The sight of these school buildings gave Mr. Rosenwald his suggestion. After a preliminary consultation with Booker T. Washington, a conference was held with President Taft, Andrew Carnegie, and other friends of the cause, which resulted in the adoption of the plan for building better schoolhouses for Negroes in all the southern states.

On his fiftieth birthday, August 12, 1912, Mr. Rosenwald announced his purpose to try the experiment first with $25,000 to be divided among such schools as Booker T. Washington selected. The erection of a few schools in Macon County near Tuskegee brought Dr. Washington into active coöperation with Mr. James L. Sibley, state agent for Negro Rural Schools for Alabama, a man of remarkable initiative and magnetism. Dr. Washington and Mr. Sibley took Mr. Rosenwald to see the new schools recently erected. As a result of this demonstration in Macon County, Mr. Rosenwald extended the offer of assistance to the whole state of Alabama. Under the energetic efforts of Mr. Sibley, the school officials of the state soon became interested, and they aroused the people of many communities to definite coöperative action. Within a short time forty-two modern rural schools had been built in the state.

The plan of operation of the Rosenwald Fund was simple. Mr. Rosenwald offered to aid in building Negro schools whenever the state, local Negroes, and the white constituency would

26 It is said that Mr. Rosenwald's interest in the Negroes was first awakened by reading the biography of William H. Baldwin, Jr., vice president of the Southern Railway and one of the first members of the Southern Education Board and the first president of the General Education Board, written by John Graham Brooks. How Baldwin became a member of the board of trustees of Tuskegee Institute is told above, p. 150.

contribute towards the necessary funds for a school of modern type for Negro children. For example, the first school erected was in Lee County, Alabama. The total cost of the building was $942, of which $150 was raised from the local people and labor was volunteered to the amount of $133. Negro and white citizens donated a sum of $360 in cash, and Mr. Rosenwald's share was $300. Mr. Rosenwald agreed in 1914 to continue his aid to the Negro school buildings for five years, to the extent of $300 each, until one hundred buildings had been erected. His plan was to have an agent in charge of the fund in each state who should work through the county officials. A few favorable counties should be made the unit of operation at first. The work should include the building of schoolhouses, the provision of equipment for industrial education, and a garden or a small farm ; the extension of the school terms ; and increase of teachers' salaries. The people of the vicinity and the Negroes themselves should be required to contribute to the improvements as much as they were able. Care was taken that the people did not rely upon the fund but that each county was stimulated to do more than it had ever done before. Ninety-two schoolhouses were erected under this plan during the following fifteen months. The next year, 1916, one hundred and eighty-four school units met the qualifications of the Rosenwald aid.

Like a wise man Mr. Rosenwald continued to make experiments for a while longer. By the end of 1916 he had expended a total of $61,784 for this work, about $50,000 for construction and $11,000 for promotion. The average cost per building to Mr. Rosenwald was only $275. By the end of another year the quota of buildings was taken up by various other localities in the southern states.

Feeling now that the period of experimentation was passed, Mr. Rosenwald called a meeting of the state rural school agents from the states where his schoolhouses had been built and, after conferences, decided to make the plan permanent. So on October 30, 1917, "The Julius Rosenwald Fund" was incorporated under the laws of the State of Illinois. The Fund was most successful, during the eight-year period from 1912 to 1920, in stimulating the public and the Negroes to construct better buildings. Eleven states tried the experiment and six hundred and forty schoolhouses were contracted for by July 1, 1920, four hundred of which were completed by that date. An expert

employed to examine the schoolhouses reported that they were
far better than those which they had superseded, though he
found room for improvement. He was called upon to make
standard specifications, which were followed thereafter in the
constructions of buildings.

So interesting had the work now become that Mr. Rosenwald called a conference of friends of the cause in May and
June, 1920, to consider the advisability of establishing an independent office for the administration of the Fund. The conclusions reached were published in a letter sent to all superintendents of public instruction in the South. It was entitled, "Plan
for the Distribution of Aid from the Julius Rosenwald Fund
for Building Rural Schoolhouses in the South," and contained,
among others, the following items : The Fund will coöperate
with public school authorities in the effort to provide and equip
better schoolhouses for the Negroes of the Southern states ;
sites and buildings shall be the property of the public school
authorities. The trustees of the Fund and the state department
of education must agree as to the number of buildings. The
site must include ample space for playgrounds and for farm
work. The site and plan for the building must be approved
by a representative of the Fund. It is a condition precedent to
receiving aid from the Fund that the people of the communities shall secure from other sources, such as public school funds
or private contributions, an amount equal to or greater than
that given by the Fund. Land, labor, and material may be
counted as cash at market values. The money of the Fund will
be available only when the amount otherwise raised and given
is sufficient to complete, equip, and furnish the building. The
Fund will deposit with the state the sum of $5,000 to begin with
from which to make disbursements as required. The state department will report at the end of every month. Thereupon the
Fund will replenish its deposit. The amount appropriated for a
school by the Fund shall not exceed $500 for a one-teacher
school, $800 for a two-teacher school, and $1,000 for a three-
teacher school. Every community must agree to complete,
equip, and furnish its building in twelve months after it has
met these terms. A teachers' home should be provided in the
vicinity of the school. The Fund will coöperate in erecting such
homes in a limited number of selected localities at first. The
Fund reserves the right to discontinue its operations after rea-

sonable notice to the state departments. The foregoing provisions became operative on July 1, 1920.

The state superintendents of public instruction of all the southern states accepted these conditions. Mr. S. L. Smith, state agent for Negro Rural Schools of Tennessee, was appointed general field agent, and the work was transferred from Tuskegee to Nashville, Tennessee. Mr. Smith had studied schoolhouse construction under Dr. Dressler at Peabody College and had been remarkably successful in the erection of schoolhouses in his state. The Fund also gave assistance to consolidated and county training schools, allowing $1,200 for four-teacher schools, $1,400 for five-teacher schools, and $1,600 for six-teacher schools. The communities later were given assistance for teachers' homes to a maximum of $1,000 on the basis of equal expenditure.

The constitution of the Rosenwald Fund provides that the entire fund in the hands of the board, both principal and income, shall be expended within twenty-five years after the founder's death—a novel and very wise provision. In 1928 an additional grant was made to the fund by Mr. Rosenwald, bringing it up to $22,000,000. In making this magnificent bequest Mr. Rosenwald wrote: "I am not in sympathy with this policy of perpetuating endowments and believe that more good can be accomplished by expending funds as Trustees find opportunities for constructive work than by storing up large sums of money for long periods of time. By ... this policy ..., we may avoid those tendencies toward bureaucracy and ... perfunctory attitude toward the work which almost inevitably develop in organizations which prolong their existence indefinitely. The coming generations can be relied upon to provide for their own needs as they arise." [27]

Since closing the general building plan, the Rosenwald Fund has extended its work in several new directions. The limit of high schools was finally extended in 1928 to buildings of the ten-teacher type at a maximum of $2,100 for one building. In order to stimulate construction of buildings of brick, $50 additional was added per room, this continuous effort being made to increase the number of well equipped high schools until they are comparable to the high schools for whites throughout the South. As the schools grew, it became necessary to add

[27] Julius Rosenwald Fund, *A Review to June 30, 1928*, p. 4.

another feature to the building program. Funds were designated for aid in constructing additional rooms to Rosenwald schoolhouses already completed. These additions commenced in 1921. The following year, seventy-two additions were made. A new room always provides for a new class or for increased attendance resulting from consolidation and the enlargement of the service of the school to the community. For these additions the public has borne a large part of the cost, giving about 62 per cent of the cost of additions to the buildings, of which amount the Negroes have donated about 20 per cent. The total given to these additions by the Rosenwald Fund down to 1929 was $80,700 or about 13 per cent of the total cost. The next new building enterprise was the construction of separate vocational buildings or industrial shops in connection with the Rosenwald schools. This was made necessary by the consolidated schools and the introduction of vocational instruction. In 1927-1928 the Board offered to assist in the erection and equipment of shops or vocational buildings of different sizes from one-room to six-room structures. The work done for industrial teachers by the Jeanes Board and the Slater Board made this necessary, and the buildings erected under the usual plan for these purposes have proved a great help. Out of a total of $206,400 which the vocational buildings have cost, the public has paid about $72,000, or 35 per cent; the Negroes gave about $48,000, or 23 per cent; while the Rosenwald Fund contributed only $31,400, or about 15 per cent toward these buildings. These figures show how remarkably the Rosenwald Board has been able to stimulate improvement of schoolhouses and vocational buildings. This stimulation of construction has caused the public in these states to contribute $20,000,000 to be dispensed for modern, sanitary, well constructed houses for the benefit of the Negro children in about four thousand communities. The increase in demand for assistance in the construction of high school buildings speaks volumes for the future of the educational opportunities for the Negroes, since public funds have borne an increasing proportion of the expense of these schools.

Two hundred and sixty additions were made to buildings, and 183 teachers' homes and eighty-two special vocational buildings were erected through the coöperation of the public,

the Negroes, their white neighbors, and the Rosenwald Fund.
A most encouraging record.

The people of the South, of course, appreciate the work of
Mr. Rosenwald in the highest degree. The Rosenwald Day for
celebrating his work in improving the schools was held in
Louisiana in 1927-1928. Patrons and friends met· at the school
where a program was rendered and topics important to the
improvement of the community were discussed. All the expenses were, of course, paid by the local people. This plan has
been tried in all the states since and has been found to be of
great value in stimulating the efforts for the improvement of
Negro schools. The latest thing the fund has done was to offer
to assist any county or school unit to extend the term of its
schools. Assistance is offered for three years on a diminishing
scale to bring the term of the Negro schools up to that of white
schools. The Fund supplies one-half of the total expense for
salaries the first year, one-third for the second, one-fourth for
for the third, with the understanding that the expenses after the
third year shall be borne by the public or the local community.
Such is the admirable plan now in operation.

At the celebration of the opening of the five-thousandth
school in 1930, the secretary of the Fund, Mr. Embree, stated
that $25,000,000 had been invested in better buildings for Negro
schools since the plan started, and of this Mr. Rosenwald had
contributed up to that time $4,000,000. The Negroes themselves
had contributed $4,500,000, and their white friends about
$1,000,000.

It is impossible to tell the whole story of the results of
this interesting movement. Some of the results are given by
Mr. Smith, the general agent, in his report for November,
1928. At that time, out of every five Negro schools in the
South, one was a Rosenwald school. One-third of all the Negro
children enrolled and teachers employed in the rural Negro
schools in that year were in Rosenwald school buildings. Of
all the elementary pupils enrolled in the southern states in 1925-
1926, 28 per cent were in the Rosenwald schools.

Seventy per cent of all the Negro children of school age in
the southern states in 1927 were country children. The Rosenwald schools have a capacity sufficient to accommodate 23.5
per cent of all of them.

It is interesting to find that while the average enrollment

for all rural Negro schools in the South was only 65, the average total capacity of the Rosenwald schools in 1928 was 124, or double the size of the average country schools. There were about 32,000 Negro teachers employed in the rural public schools in the southern states for 1927, or an average of one for every 45 pupils. The capacity of the Rosenwald schools is 35 per cent of all Negro teachers thus employed.

The most hopeful sign of development in these rural Negro schools is in the increase of school terms. The average terms of the fourteen southern states for 1914-1915, the year Mr. Rosenwald started the business in Alabama, varied from three to six months in one or two states, an average of four and a half months. The reports for 1926-1927 show that the average term has increased to six and a half months.

The county training schools and high schools have been stimulated by the Fund in allowing aid to pay salaries as well as to erect buildings. One hundred and sixty-six high school buildings were erected between 1926 and 1928. The Fund increased its allotment from a six-teacher maximum to a ten-teacher maximum, and its maximum amount of aid from $1,600 to $2,100. This increase in high school progress has been due, of course, to the development of better rural schools from which more students were graduated, and also to the assistance of the Slater Fund and the General Education Board in helping county training schools. Better-trained teachers held the children in the schools longer, and Negroes everywhere through the South are developing a stronger desire to give their children the best possible education.

There are still many counties in the South without Rosenwald schools. The total number of counties in which they were located up to July 1, 1928, was 778, leaving 144 counties with about 10 per cent Negro population which have no Rosenwald schools. This is not the fault of the management of the Fund but the result of extreme poverty in the districts, causing lack of interest among the Negroes as well as the whites.

Now with regard to the value of rural school property created by this Fund for Negro elementary schools. Compiling the values from the United States Census Report, Bureau of Education *Bulletin* (1928), No. 12, we find that the property of all the rural Negro schools in twelve southern states in 1926-1927 was about $25,600,000, while the value of the Rosenwald schools developed under this Fund amounted to about $17,-600,000, or about 58 per cent of the total value of all Negro schools in the South. Note that this was in 1927. The amount has increased very much since then.

The president of the Rosenwald Fund gives us the latest results in his *Review* for 1931-1933. The Fund has now completed its building program which has been going on for twenty years and has helped to build 5,357 schools in 883 counties in fifteen southern states. All these schools are regular public schools and all the buildings were erected with public funds or funds raised locally with small aid from the Rosenwald Fund. The schools are all maintained now by public money. The maintenance cost has been increased with the development of the schools. School bus transportation has been promoted also, and in 1931, nine thousand Negro pupils were being transported to consolidated high schools, the major part of the expense being borne by the state or local public school authorities.

"It was decided that this project of building schoolhouses had served its purpose and should be concluded, lest it become a crutch instead of a stimulus." The Fund, however, is not ceasing its appropriations but has shifted its work from the buildings to aid the better preparation of teachers and the improvement of equipment and better textbooks. For example, in 1928 an offer was made to Negro colleges to aid them in the purchase of books for their libraries. Within a two-year period twenty-four colleges qualified for aid ranging from $500 to $2,500 by the Fund, the cost of the books purchased amounting to $100,000. The Fund has also furnished school libraries of one hundred volumes each to about two thousand Rosenwald schools and has coöperated with eleven southern counties in county-wide library demonstration programs, sending out trucks with library books to borrowers in their farm homes. The health work for Negroes is still being carried on. A plan has been started for reducing the cost of medical care for poor people.

Nothing has done more to stimulate improvement in the South for Negro schools than the work of the Rosenwald Fund in aiding the people, especially those in the rural districts, to provide attractive school buildings with gardens and shops and to give them different kinds of social service like that of the Y.M.C.A. The results of this movement have exceeded all expectations. "Not only has it stimulated Negroes in their efforts toward improvements but it has provided ground for active co-operation between the races in the solution of one of the most serious phases of race adjustment in our country, at the same time giving direct stimulus to education for whites as an indirect but positive result." Where Negroes and their friends have erected better schoolhouses the whites have soon done so also.

JULIUS ROSENWALD

Mr. Rosenwald was born in Springfield, Illinois, August 12, 1862. His life extended thus from the period of the Civil War through the great development of American industry following it, and through the Great War down to the recent period of the depression. Young Rosenwald grew up in the town of Abraham Lincoln's home. Debates on human slavery and the federal union as opposed to states' rights and secession were still echoing there, and his mind and heart were no doubt captivated by the ideal of a unified nation and the extension of the rights of citizenship to all men regardless of race. The principles thus early imbibed seem to have inspired his whole career. After he became wealthy his chief philanthropies were given to help the ignorant and the oppressed. He gave without racial or religious bias, his grants covering a wide field of Catholic and Protestant as well as Jewish agencies. For Negro education and welfare he is said to have expended $4,000,000, leaving many millions more in the foundation he established. To Jewish charities and Jewish institutions in Europe and Russia, he gave $10,000,000 ; to war work and war relief, $2,000,000 ; to arts and crafts and industrial museums, $5,000,000 ; to hospitals and health agencies $3,000,000 ; to general education and scientific research, $3,000,000 ; and to other causes, including the family trust created to carry out his charitable interests after his death, $10,000,000.[28] But these figures do not give a complete picture of his benevolences, which flowed in small amounts in a steady stream to many institutions and many societies such as Tuskegee in the South ; Beirut in Syria ; Fisk University, Harvard University, Wellesley College, and the University of Chicago. He

[28] Julius Rosenwald Fund, *Review for the Two-Year Period, 1931-1933,* pp. 7-9.

was interested in all kinds of social activities; in fact, in every activity that promised any social betterment anywhere.

Rosenwald was a great civic servant. Chiefly concerned for the righteousness of his city, he was one of the few public men who stood steadfast in the fight, risking business, when rackets crept into the highest places of the City of Chicago. He gave himself as he gave his funds, helping the boards and agencies personally. He was an active worker as well as a large contributor. He had the courage of his convictions in his giving as well as in his public life. For example, he refused to contribute to the Zionist movement, which swept the race with such emotion, because he did not believe in it. He always stuck by his convictions in matters where it would have been much easier to float with the tide.

Julius Rosenwald died on January 6, 1932. His career was that of the ordinary, honest, industrious American citizen. He had only a limited education. Like many other Americans, he made his fortune with his own hands and brains. Many men starting with just as little as he did made fortunes just as great, but how few have used them so well!

Some Conditions in Negro Schools

On the whole the improvement in the education of Negro children in the southern town and city public schools in the last twenty years is encouraging. In the country districts the schools remain very poor and inadequate. In the densely settled Negro districts, such as those in Mississippi and Alabama, where there are no compulsory laws, the enrollment will average fifty and the attendance twenty-three; 30 per cent of the school population never enter a school; 65 per cent of the children in the rural elementary schools will usually be in the first three grades, and 85 per cent leave the school before the seventh grade.

The relative length of the school terms of white and Negro schools gives us a measure of the work accomplished in the schools. The United States Bureau of Education gives us the following facts. In 1920 the sessions of white schools were only 145 days, of Negro schools 120 days. In 1928 the school sessions of white schools had increased to 161 days, that of Negro schools to only 131 days. In 1920 the white schools in North

Carolina held for 137 days and the Negro schools for 127 days; in 1928 the white schools in this state had increased their terms to 154 days and the Negro to 138 days. These figures show a substantial improvement in facilities for Negro education over that of twenty years ago, but the fact remains that the elementary schools for Negroes in the southern states are still far below those for the whites.[29]

McCuistion in his paper, *The South's Negro Teaching Force*, gives us this summary description of the Negro rural school teacher in 1930: "From facts and estimates given in this study it appears that the typical rural Negro teacher of the South is a woman... about twenty-seven years of age. She has completed high school and had ten weeks in summer schools. She teaches forty-seven children through six grades for a term of six months, remaining about two years in the same school. Her annual salary is $360,"—say, one dollar a day, and she teaches in different places for about five years.[30]

A special investigation recently made of three hundred Alabama Negro teachers showed that over 80 per cent of those reported to have had high school education had ability in reading and arithmetic equal only to that expected of eighth-grade pupils. Making all allowance for progress, it is still certain that more than half of the teachers in Negro elementary schools have much less training than the minimum now required for white teachers of elementary schools. This is to be expected, but the difference should not be so great as it is.

Since the organization of the state systems there are very few white teachers in the schools for Negroes. In some states, as in Florida, whites are forbidden by law to teach in schools for Negroes, under a penalty of $500 or six months' imprisonment.[31] These laws were promoted by the Negroes to prevent competition in this field. It is questioned whether this is a wise provision at the time when the Negro public school teachers needed the help of the white teachers especially in their normal schools and as principals.

[29] Condensed from *Twenty-Year Report of the Phelps-Stokes Fund, 1911-1931*, pp. 36-37.
[30] Fred McCuistion, *The South's Negro Teaching Force*, p. 10.
[31] *Compilation of the School Laws of the State of Florida*, Sec. 23 (5870), p. 15.

HIGH SCHOOLS FOR NEGROES

Little information was available with regard to the provision for secondary education for Negroes in the public schools until recently. In many town and city schools classes of secondary education were attached to elementary schools, but of separate public high schools there were few until after 1912. In 1910, according to the Slater Fund report, there were in all the South, county and city, fewer than fifty public schools for Negroes offering any secondary work.[32] In 1911, therefore, the Slater Fund offered one school for Negro secondary grades, to each of four counties in the South. The purpose of this was to encourage the development of such schools in these and other counties by public funds. These first four Slater aided schools were located in Sabine and Tangipahoa parishes, in Louisiana, Hempstead County, Arkansas, and Newton County, Mississippi.

The results were sufficiently encouraging to cause the Slater Fund to expend during the following twenty-two years the sum of $1,216,475 in stimulating the establishment and development of other such schools. This Fund has aided to date 612 schools located in as many different counties in the southern states.

For the purpose of ascertaining what developments have taken place in high schools for Negroes, the trustees of the Slater Fund in April, 1933, authorized Mr. Edward E. Redcay to make a study and report on the subject. The enrollment figures are for the end of the school year 1932-33. The superintendents of city, town, and county schools in all the southern states where separate schools for Negroes are maintained were asked as to name, location, teaching staff, and enrollment of each school within his jurisdiction, giving any secondary work whatever for Negroes. The information obtained from each state is published in this report. Only a brief summary of the facts obtained can be given here. Data were collected for the states of Delaware, Maryland, Virginia, North Carolina, South Carolina, Georgia, Florida, Mississippi, Louisiana, Arkansas, Tennessee, Kentucky, Alabama, Oklahoma, Missouri, Texas,

---

[32] Data given in the following paragraphs are from the *Public Secondary Schools for Negroes in the Southern States of the United States.* Published by the Trustees of the John F. Slater Fund, as *Occasional Papers No. 29.*

West Virginia, and the District of Columbia. No attempt was made to separate the figures here but the summaries are interesting. The age-group of fifteen to nineteen years constitutes approximately 11 per cent of the total Negro population in a given state.

The total number of counties in these states having some provision for public secondary education is 1,501. There are 373 counties having fewer than fifty Negro youth between fifteen and nineteen years of age, which have made no provision for secondary education. There were only 4,717 Negroes between these ages living within these 373 counties, or one-half of 1 per cent of the total number of Negroes of potential high school age (fifteen to nineteen) living in the seventeen states investigated. Counties without any facilities for secondary education numbered 186.

The kind of secondary education provided varies greatly. Some of the schools give only one year, others two years, some three, and a good many four years of secondary education. There are 70 counties that give only one year of secondary work in connection with the elementary school, 154 counties give two years, 118 counties give three years only, and 600 counties give four years of secondary education.

The data in regard to the number of schools, the teachers, and the enrollment are also interesting. The total Negro population (fifteen to nineteen years) in these seventeen states was 1,073,500.[33] The number of secondary rural schools was 1,391 ; of city secondary schools, 631—a total of 2,022 secondary schools in these states. Of the 631 city schools, 62 offered only one year of secondary work, 89 offered two years, 61 offered three years, and 419 gave four years of secondary work.

The enrollment in these schools was as follows : in the rural schools 47,750, in urban schools 101,104, or a total of only 148,854 secondary pupils of all grades in the southern states.

The teachers engaged in these schools were classified as follows : part-time teachers 1,478, most of whom gave the rest of their time to elementary classes ; full-time teachers, giving all their time to high school work, 5,298.

The county training schools and the parish training schools, as they are called in Louisiana, are included in this statement.

[33] United States Census, 1930.

These schools and many of the other schools give some regular teacher-training and are authorized to certify their graduates for positions as teachers in the public schools. There are a large number of such certified training schools in Virginia, Kentucky, and North Carolina, but there are far too few of them in the other southern states. Much still remains to be done for secondary education and especially in the training of teachers for the Negro elementary and other schools.

At the beginning of the century few of the Negro teachers in elementary schools had had any professional training beyond the elementary school. In 1915 the available statistics showed that 70 per cent of the Negro teachers were found to have had less than six elementary grades of education. McCuistion tells us that, in 1930, 38 per cent, or 18,000, of the Negro teachers still had less than high school training; 9,400, or 20 per cent, had more than high school training but less than two years of college; while only 15,000 had two years of college or the equivalent,—a remarkable improvement in fifteen years.[34]

For a time there were no state schools for the training of Negro teachers. Now there are twenty-three in the South for this definite purpose, North Carolina having five such colleges, and Georgia three. Having been established under the Morrill Act appropriating additional money from the land-grant colleges for teaching agriculture and the industries, they are generally called Morrill state schools. The law appropriating this fund specified that the benefits must include Negro students as well as whites; that is, that Negroes must have an equitable share in proportion to their population. This meant that all the southern states must have separate schools to get the benefits of this fund. In most of the states there was no such school for some years. But now all the states in the South have established agricultural and mechanical colleges with normal departments for Negroes. Where the Negro population exceeded the whites, as in South Carolina and Mississippi, the Negroes were entitled to more than half of the fund annually appropriated. At first these schools were very poor, but recently they have been improved and separated from the private institutions to which the fund was attached at first.

[34] *Op. cit.*, p. 20.

Fisk University

Though not a public institution, Fisk University in Nashville, Tennessee, should be mentioned as a great power in the advancement of Negro education in all fields. Founded in 1865 by the American Missionary Association and the Freedmen's Aid Commission aided by the Freedmen's Bureau of Tennessee, the institution continued under their control until 1912, when it was turned over to a private board of trustees. Fisk University comprises a college of liberal arts, a music department, and a graduate school accredited by the Southern Association of Colleges and the New York State Board of Regents. The University has been accorded national recognition by the Association of American Universities. With the affiliated Meharry Medical College it makes Nashville the center of higher and professional education for Negroes in the South. Through its leadership in these ways and through its work in training teachers, Fisk has aided greatly in improving public schools for Negroes. Its music department has done notable work in training musicians. Its famous Jubilee Singers, by concerts given on a series of tours in this country, raised a fund for a hall on their campus and have rescued from oblivion and have popularized the interesting and beautiful spirituals of their race.

Interracial Relations

The Interracial Committee has become a powerful agency for promoting good will between the races, and fairness and justice in the treatment of the Negro. The origin of this Committee is most interesting. At the close of the World War there was fear in the minds of some that the returning Negro soldiers might cause trouble between the races and that some steps should be taken to prevent it. This fear proved to be entirely groundless. But in some sections of the so-called "black belt" of the South the interracial conditions were still very primitive and most deplorable. In certain remote counties in the Southwest it was found, for example, that thousands of Negroes were being held on the farms in a state of practical peonage. By keeping them in debt for rents and supplies the law was used to prevent their leaving the farms. In some cases they were forcibly brought back when they attempted to leave.

These conditions had naturally created some bad feeling which it was feared might lead to violence.

There had been in Atlanta for several years a small group of southern leaders earnestly seeking to promote interracial relations. A leader among them was Dr. C. B. Wilmer, formerly professor in the University of the South and at the time a minister in an Episcopal Church of Atlanta. Dr. Wilmer had worked for many years among the Negroes and held their affectionate regard which they had testified by presenting him with a loving cup inscribed :

"A pioneer in Interracial Goodwill.
"He practiced Truth and his Neighbor is all Mankind."

Others in this group were Dr. M. Ashby Jones, Baptist minister ; Mr. John J. Eagan, a devoted churchman ; Dr. Plato Durham, of Emory University, Dr. W. D. Weatherford, and Mr. R. H. King, officers of the Young Men's Christian Association, Dr. W. W. Alexander, of the War Works Council in charge of the returning Negro troops, Dr. James H. Dillard, president of the John F. Slater and the Jeanes Funds, and Mr. Jackson Davis, representative of the General Education Board in the South. These men had the counsel and support of Dr. John R. Mott, Dr. Wallace Buttrick òf the General Education Board, and Dr. Thomas Jesse Jones of the Phelps-Stokes Fund, in shaping an organization. While they were forming plans, a representative group of Negro leaders met at Tuskegee for the same purpose. Among these were Dr. Robert Russa Moton, Bishop Robert E. Jones, Mrs. Booker T. Washington and Dr. John Hope.

The purposes of the two meetings were the same, namely, the promotion of good will and interracial justice. Inspired by this faith the two groups met in Atlanta a few weeks later and formed what was first called the Commission on Interracial Coöperation. It at once went to work in organizing committees in the entire South through which understanding between the races might be created. Membership in the committees was composed chiefly of educators, ministers, business men, and professional men. Later it included many women social workers.

The motto of the Commission was "Justice through Conference and Coöperation." The movement did not seek "to solve the race problem" but to take the next practical step in the "direction of justice and good-will." It did not assume to dictate to any state or community what it ought to do, but left it to the leaders of each community to find their own problems and to seek honestly to solve them. It undertook only to set up the necessary machinery and to find the facts and to suggest remedial measures. The experience of ten years of work of the Commission, which is now called "The Interracial Committee," has proved that its principles are sound and its methods effective. The Committee has now won the full confidence and the support of the most intelligent leadership in both races. Dr. W. W. Alexander is its head with offices in Atlanta.

The Commission carried on a continuous campaign to create public opinion against lynching. Prosecutions of lynchings were conducted leading to conviction and long prison terms as never before. A booklet entitled "Mississippi and the Mob" was prepared by the Mississippi State Bar Association and had great influence in preventing lynchings. Since the founding of the Commission, lynchings have decreased from 83 in 1919 to 10 in 1929. Special laws for the control of mobs have been secured in South Carolina, Virginia, Tennessee, Kentucky, and several other states through the influence of the Interracial Committee.

The Committee has endeavored to reach the churches of all denominations, the colleges, and the schools in behalf of better feeling. A press service reaches thousands of newspapers and magazines in many sections, North as well as South. The editors are universally sympathetic and coöperative, and there has been great improvement in the handling of stories of crime. Inflammatory news is tabooed and all the facts of Negro achievement and advancement are given prominent place.

Colleges and high schools have been reached through the organization of junior committees in them and through the giving of courses and the offering of prizes for essays on the subjects connected with the Committee's work. An annual one-theme competition has enlisted several hundred college students, representing over a hundred institutions in the South. A monograph on "The Negro's Part in American History" has been prepared and supplied to teachers and students. A study of race relations based on this book has met with fine results in the high schools. From the church press, from the pulpit, and by conferences the Committee has, with the aid of many religious leaders of the country, reached churches, Sunday schools, young people's societies, conferences, and conventions.

A commission of one hundred white women, all leaders in social work, met in Memphis in October, 1920, with representative Negro women, to form an auxiliary commission. Out of the meeting came a statement expressing "a deep sense of responsibility to the womanhood and childhood of the Negro race, and an earnest desire for the settlement of the problems that overshadow the homes of both races in accordance with Christian principles." Strong state committees of women have since been set up for the purpose especially of urging protection for Negro women and children. Such statements from prominent white women have gone far towards the creation of a new public conscience on these questions.

The Committee sought also to deal with the conditions in the schools and secure a fair distribution of funds and better buildings for Negro schools. It has also sought to improve in every way the Negro's economic status. The Negroes cannot protect their economic gains and opportunities for work and are frequently helpless victims of unscrupulous physical action. From all parts of the country, North as well as South, reports were coming in that Negroes were being supplanted by white people in many kinds of work. Even in the South, where the positions of barber and waiter were formerly filled by Negroes, they were being supplanted by white people. Whatever the cause, this condition is regarded as very serious and the Commission has made a special study of it in the hope of finding a way of safeguarding the economic future of the race. It is hoped that a way may be found by which justice may be accorded, and the rights and duties of citizenship, irrespective of race, be protected without sacrificing either the integrity of the ballot or the liberty of the individual.

A "Stabilization Fund" committee, with a very large membership of leading men of the country, raises funds for the advancement of this work. Principal Moton is chairman and Mr. George Foster Peabody, treasurer.

An effort is also being made to give the Negro a fairer hearing and a better position in the current literature of the country. The current novels and magazines and newspaper articles rarely depict the Negro at his best. They give his poetry and songs, his spirituals, and they describe his musical and artistic talent, his fancies, foibles, and frailties, but they never discuss his substantial characteristics of mind or soul, or his loyalty, devotion, gratitude, and integrity. There is abundant evidence of the latter qualities, but one rarely hears them described except in a sensational way in connection with his position as slave. It was a noble instinct which led Moton to resent the treatment of the Negro as a buffoon. There has been far too much of this not only in our amusement halls, but in our literature, our histories, and especially in our halls of legislation. The Negro is a citizen of America, a representative of a strong race, and should always be thought of and treated as such. The American people need to learn to think of the Negro as a very man, with intelligence, heart, and soul, to realize that it is their duty to give him a chance to become the best man that he can. When this is done the Negro may contribute his share toward making America a better country.

CHAPTER XXIX

TENANCY AND EDUCATION

THE EXTENT OF FARM TENANCY

IN a previous chapter we have quoted Dr. Seaman A. Knapp's explanation of the necessity of teaching tenants how to farm profitably as the first step toward land ownership. He says : "Whether this country is going to be a democracy or a plutocracy will be decided in the next ten years and ...decided largely along these lines :

"As to whether or not the ordinary man makes the soil prosper, whether he wins the ownership of the land and then the proper understanding of how to cultivate it and get his share of the profits of the country." [1]

All social and economic improvement among a people depends upon the conditions of land and home tenure. People must have settled homes before they can become efficient and useful citizens. This is especially true of farm land tenure. Under the present system of land ownership in the South the tenant family on the plantations, both white and black, is usually exploited for profit. Even when schools are provided for them, the children have a poor opportunity for getting an education and the parents a poor chance of ever earning a home. This is true for the whites as well as for the Negroes. The white tenant exerts little influence in schools or in other public affairs ; the Negro, none. The proprietor of the land controls these matters as he does most other things in the countryside.

Tenancy has thus a distinct relation to general education. Tenancy prevents education, while education is the only means of preventing tenancy. It concerns us seriously, therefore, to ascertain the condition of home and land ownership in the South. The United States Census gives us the number of families, the percentage of owners, the percentage of tenants for both town and country, and the average size of the family in each state. In the twelve southern states of Virginia, Kentucky,

---

[1] Quoted by Dr. H. B. Frissell in Memorial address on Dr. Knapp.

Tennessee, North Carolina, South Carolina, Georgia, Alabama, Florida, Mississippi, Louisiana, Arkansas, and Texas, the average per cent of tenants in the entire population is 58.4[2] The per cent of tenants is found to be largest where the Negro population is largest. It is 64 per cent in Alabama, 66 per cent in Mississippi, and 67 per cent in South Carolina and Georgia. There are more tenants in these southern states in proportion than in any other part of the country. But the ominous fact is that there are in the whole South more white than Negro tenants and that the white tenants are increasing.

Wisconsin has the largest percentage of families living in homes of their own—sixty-two out of every hundred families in that state own the homes in which they live. Georgia ranks lowest of all the states—less than 30 per cent of the families own their homes—and this is closely followed by South Carolina, Mississippi, Alabama, and Louisiana.[3]

According to the Census, farm tenancy, as distinguished from town and village tenancy, has increased decidedly in the whole United States in the decade from 1920 to 1930, while the tenancy ratio in the cities and towns is decidedly on the decrease. In the southern states, farm tenancy has increased during the last decade. Taking as an illustration North Carolina, the state having one of the best school systems in the South for all classes, we find that of all the families in the towns and country 54.3 per cent are tenants. But while home ownership is on the increase in the United States, it is on the decrease in North Carolina. This is almost wholly due to the large increase in farm tenancy. In 1930 there were in North Carolina, 210,455 white rural families of whom 57.3 per cent owned their farms. There were 85,455 Negro rural families of whom only 23.8 per cent owned the land they worked. In this connection it is interesting to note also that of all the states North Carolina has the largest families—4.85 persons per family as compared with 4.01 persons per family for the rest of the country. It is to the credit of North Carolina that it ranks highest of all the states in the per cent of the total population enrolled in the schools. North Carolina has also more school children in proportion to the number of tax payers than any of the other

[2] The statistics used are from the *News Letter* of the Extension Division of the University of North Carolina, Vol. XIX, Nos. 11 to 25.

[3] United States Census, 1930.

states ; and South Carolina and most of the other southern states have a high percentage of school children in proportion to the tax payers. The average family in the United States numbers 4.01 ; in the southern states the average family is 4.333. Having one-twelfth more children to the family the burden on the southern people for education is thus one-twelfth heavier than that of the other states of the Union.

The regions in the South where farm tenancy is the greatest are the southeastern sections of Virginia, where the crops are cotton, tobacco, and peanuts ; the eastern portions of North Carolina and South Carolina, where the chief crops are cotton and tobacco ; and the cotton-growing sections of Georgia, Alabama, Mississippi, Louisiana, Arkansas, and Texas. In the states from South Carolina to Texas it is the white and Negro tenancy that constitutes the chief problem of education.

Taking North Carolina as an illustration, we find that the percentage of Negro owners is 23.8 while that of the whites is 57.3. Only 50 per cent of all the white farmers in the states just mentioned are full owners of their farms ; 10 per cent of them are part owners, while nearly 40 per cent are full tenants.

Conditions Among White Farmers and Tenant-Farmers

Let us now see what these farmers and tenant-farmers earn. The condition of the small white farmers is not much better than that of the tenants.

Here is the report for one county in eastern Alabama which is typical of the kind of county populated by small white farmers in the cotton states.

The landowning farmers in the county are estimated as 38 per cent, the "croppers," or tenants, as 62 per cent. All reported are whites. The landowners are divided as follows : one-plow farm owners, 25 per cent ; two-plow farm owners, 13 per cent. The yearly gross income of a one-plow farm owner is as follows : cotton, average 2½ bales, $150 ; chickens, eggs, and miscellaneous, $25 ; 80 to 100 bushels corn consumed, and the gardens, yielding sweet potatoes and cane for syrup, etc., supply some food. The total cash was thus $175. Yearly costs were : Fertilizers, $20 ; seed, $5 ; ginning cotton, $8 ; taxes, $10. Total, $43. The average net income of the one-plow farm owner for year was $132. A two-plow farmer will earn in the same way on the average $260.

Now how about the tenants? A tenant working on shares divides the crop equally with the landowner who pays half the cost of fertilizers and ginning. He will net an income of from $70 to $80 on the average.

To sum up, the average yearly net cash income of a tenant is $70 to $80 ; of a one-plow farm owner is $132 ; of a two-plow farm owner is $260. Out of this must come the groceries, clothing, and general expenses (including doctor and dentist bills and church contributions) for an average family of four and one-third persons.

Conditions Among Negro Tenants

The worst conditions are among the Negro tenants on the great cotton plantations. Here there are fewer farm owners and more tenants, and their earnings are less than in the cases described above. We find these people accordingly living under the most wretched conditions. Such tenants are usually allotted from ten to twenty-five acres of land, with a poor shack for a house. They are supplied with the larger implements, with fertilizers, seed, and other necessities by the landowner, who "carries them," as the expression is, through the season ; that is, he supplies them with meal, bacon, and other groceries, and the simple necessities of clothing. At the end of the year the crop is sold and a settlement is made with the proprietor which usually leaves little or nothing for the tenant. Many are left in debt to the proprietor and so become practically peons if they do not sneak away between suns. In these cases the proprietor may go after them and haul them back, if there is any chance to exploit them further. Such people move frequently from place to place.

There is nothing sadder than the sight of one of these poor wanderers, with his miserable furniture and hand tools loaded upon a little wagon drawn by a mule or by a horse and an ox, traveling from one place to another seeking a shack and a plot of ground. He rarely possesses a cow or pigs, though sometimes he has a few chickens. His wife and the younger children sit on top of the load while he and the older ones walk. A couple of hounds usually trail behind. These wanderings ordinarily begin in late autumn or early winter and may continue for weeks.

The average cropper works on one piece of land only four years. Many move because of dissatisfaction and in the hope of improving their condition. Some are forced to move. And these are American fellow-citizens of the twentieth century!

It must not be inferred that there are no patient and generous proprietors. The relation is feudalistic. In bad years or in other times of misfortune the landowner will feed and support his tenants for long periods at his own loss. In almost all cases the relation is a friendly one. Many of the ignorant prefer not to own land and to follow this system.

The Negro population of the South during the last forty years has changed considerably from a rural to an urban one. Between 1890 and 1930 the percentage of Negroes living in the country districts decreased from 84.07 to 68.03 of the total Negro population. The movement to the cities was largest during the last two census decades. In 1930, however, there were still left on southern farms 6,395,252 Negroes (more than half of the total Negro population of the country), of whom the great majority were laborers working for small wages. Out of this number there were 882,850 farmers, of whom only 181,016 were owners of the land which they worked. The Negro tenants numbered 700,911, nearly four times as many as the land-owners.[4]

Although the progress of Negroes in acquiring farm lands was large for the first few decades following their emancipation, and although the doctrine of land ownership, earnestly preached by Booker Washington, was promoted through land ownership in those portions of the South where his pupils settled, their purchases were unfortunately not of the rich bottom lands but of the cheaper pine lands, and were frequently lost. The richer alluvial areas have been held strongly by the whites, and it is in these regions that the great masses of the Negroes are still hanging on as tenants, and are falling more and more into the most abject class of croppers to be found in the country —into a condition equivalent to peonage.

The condition of the tenants and croppers in these regions became much worse during the period of the depression and many of them had to be put "on relief." This is due to the fact that they made but one money crop, the prices of which were much reduced. Never having been taught to grow a

[4] Census of 1930.

variety of crops and to keep cows, pigs, or poultry, these people were left without food. Land is cheap and they could and ought to raise all these things and produce nearly all their food. The boll-weevil has taught some of them this lesson but most of them need still to learn it.

What will happen to these cotton-growing tenants, black and white, when the cultivation and harvesting of cotton is entirely mechanized, is serious to contemplate. A cotton-picking machine will undoubtedly be perfected, if, indeed, this has not already been done, and it will drive all small growers completely out of the business. For cotton will then be produced only on the large plantations with their broad level fields where seeding and cultivating machines as well as cotton harvesters will do all the work. Cotton tenants should all be taught now to grow food crops and to keep cows, pigs, and poultry, and so be prepared for this approaching revolution.

It is evident from the facts here presented that the problem of tenancy in the South, both of whites and of blacks, is not going to be solved simply by putting these people on land of their own. They must first be taught how to use the land. They must cease to be merely cotton or tobacco farmers and learn to be subsistence farmers, that is, to grow food crops in gardens and fields for their families and their animals. The farm demonstration agents and the home economics agents must train them to do this. Certainly the tenant or the cropper who sticks to his old methods will never pay for his land.[5]

VOCATIONAL EDUCATION THE REMEDY

More schools, better schools, and vocational schools will require much larger revenues. The crucial question is, Have the southern states now, or can they be expected to have at any early time, the financial ability to educate and train the children of poor tenants, black and white, as they should be, as they must be, if the next generation is to be any better off than their parents? Fortunately for the present study, the facts on this subject have been freshly prepared for us. The Research Division of the National Education Association, the Directors of Research of the Peabody College Conference, and the Committee on Finance of the National Conference on the Education

[5] J. C. Lambert, for thirty years agent for Negro schools in Alabama.

of the Negro, called by the Office of Education of the United States Department of the Interior, have published in the last four years studies based on the Census, on other government reports, and on the reports of the state and city departments of education. These studies give us the data from which to draw reliable conclusions.[6]

THE BURDEN OF THE NEGRO SCHOOLS

The fact that the southern states have to maintain a separate set of schools for Negroes adds greatly to their burden. The separate school plants and separate staffs of teachers for the Negroes give rise to great additional expense. The dual system of schools is an established thing in the South. Mixed schools are not an open question. Separate schools are accepted as a necessary part of the South's system which must be adequately provided for. Our first point, therefore, is to see how the southern schools are taking care of Negro children. What is the South really doing to meet this necessity and, if she is not meeting it, has she the ability to do so?

What is the size of the burden? The Census of the United States for 1930 tells us that there were 2,182,507 Negro children enrolled in the schools in twelve southern states (Texas included). The number in attendance averages about 75 per cent.[7] The proportion of these children in attendance in the elementary schools has increased slightly in the last ten years, but it has not kept up with the increase in population. In contrast with the 3½ per cent of white children out of school, the 25 per cent of Negro children not in attendance creates a serious problem. Compulsory attendance laws, where they exist, are ineffective in the case of the Negro children. This is due in part to the inadequacy of the provision made for the Negro schools.

[6] The titles of the reports used are : Can the State Afford to Educate Their Children? ; Research Bulletin of the National Education Association, Vol. VII, No. 1 (January, 1929) ; Fred McCuistion, Financing Schools in the South (1930) ; Twenty-Year Report of the Phelps-Stokes Fund, 1911-1931; Fred McCuistion, The South's Negro Teaching Force, published by the Rosenwald Fund, 1931 ; Fred McCuistion, School Money in Black and White, a bulletin published in 1934 by the Rosenwald Fund.

Statistics assembled by the Extension Division of the University of North Carolina and published in the News Letter have also been helpful.

[7] Census of 1930.

Now how is this situation being met? First, let us consider some of the more comprehensive facts. The Negro public schools in eleven southern states spent in 1930 a total of $23,461,000, and the same year these eleven states spent $216,718,000 for the white pupils. In other words, expenditures for Negro schools were about forty millions of dollars short of what was necessary to bring the expenditure per pupil in the Negro schools up to the average of the white schools in those eleven states. To bring the expenditures for both white and Negro children in these eleven states up to the average of the nation would require an additional annual expenditure of 430 millions of dollars. Of course it is not implied here that a correspondingly large proportion of the public money could be wisely expended on the Negro schools at present. A new type of school, adapted to the needs of Negro children, will have first to be gradually developed, and that will take time.

THE ABILITY OF THE SOUTH TO SUPPORT SCHOOLS

The crucial question now is, Can the South carry this burden alone? Before we decide, let us investigate thoroughly the ability of the people of the South to support all their schools.

1. What does the Census tell us of the ability of the South to carry out the great task of educating all its children? There are several ways of measuring this. The first is to ascertain the per capita wealth of the people. The Census of 1930 tells us that for the southern states the average per capita wealth was $1,785 as compared with $3,609 for the other states. Only eleven states in the Union have a total per capita wealth less than $2,000 and all of those are in the South. If the South spends far less money for schools than the average of the other states it is because she has not the money to spend. The southern states are poor compared with all the other states. The differences in wealth of the different states are graphically shown in Chart I. But we shall find that the effort of the southern states is great compared with their means.[8]

8.The charts here used are copied by permission from *School Money in Black and White,* published by the Rosenwald Fund, Fred McCuistion, editor. The figures used in these charts are for the eleven southern States of Virginia, North Carolina, South Carolina, Kentucky, Tennessee, Georgia, Florida, Alabama, Mississippi, Arkansas, and Louisiana. West Virginia as a part of Virginia, and Maryland and Texas as former slave states are sometimes mentioned in comparisons.

2. A better measure of the ability of a community to support education is the total wealth per school child (five to

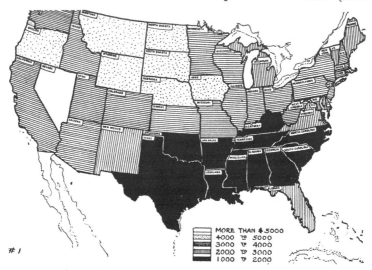

CHART I. WEALTH PER CAPITA, NORTH AND SOUTH

seventeen years). The national average is $10,200 per child.
In thirteen southern states the average is $4,900, or less than
half the national average. In Mississippi it is $3,600, or about
one-third the national average. Chart II shows the states having

CHART II. TOTAL WEALTH PER SCHOOL CHILD

less than the national average. Again the entire South is black compared with the remainder of the country.

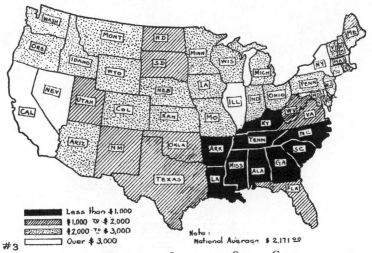

CHART III. ANNUAL INCOME PER SCHOOL CHILD

3. Another and perhaps the best way of measuring the financial ability of a people to support schools is their total annual income per school child. The national average income per inhabitant of school age (five to seventeen years) is $2,171.

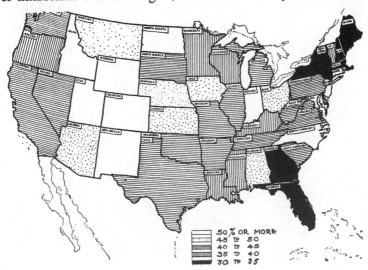

CHART IV. PER CENT OF ALL TAXES SPENT FOR SCHOOLS

In the southern states the average income of each inhabitant of school age is $872. In Mississippi it is only $512 per school

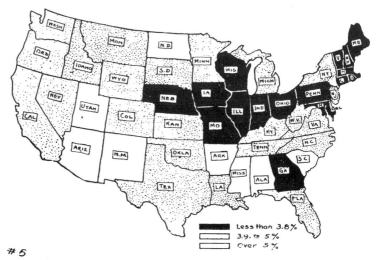

5

CHART V. PER CENT OF TOTAL INCOME SPENT FOR SCHOOLS

child. One reason is that the South, as stated above, has more children per family than the other states. In Chart III, the black sections show nine states with average annual income less than $1,000 per school child.

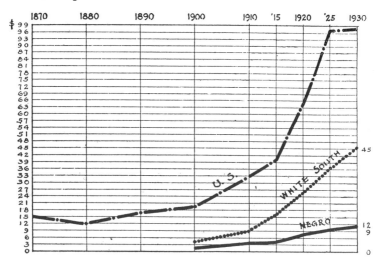

CHART VI. AVERAGE YEARLY EXPENDITURE PER PUPIL

4. The situation appears more favorable for the South when we consider her effort in relation to her ability, for although poor, the South spends a larger proportion of her funds on schools than do the other sections. The average state in the Union spends for schools 40.2 per cent of all tax collections. The average for fourteen southern states is 41.3 per cent. Of the seven states spending less than 35 per cent of all tax collections for education, only two are in the South. The South is making a good effort to support her schools. North Carolina is one of the eight states of the Union which spend more than half of their taxes for schools. She gives them 52.6 per cent. See Chart IV. It is notable that New York and some of the New England states devote less than 35 per cent of their taxes to the schools. This is because of their great wealth's producing a large volume of taxes, while Georgia and Florida use less than 35 per cent for their schools for the opposite reason, their relative poverty.

5. Still another and a very practical way of looking at the problem is to see the per cent of the total annual income expended on the public schools. The national average is 3.8 per cent of the total annual income of all the people. Georgia again is the only southern state spending less than this. The remaining southern states spend 4.4 per cent of the total annual income from all sources for education. Again their effort is shown to be greater in proportion to their means than that of other states. Chart V shows this very forcibly. The other states using the smaller proportion of their income for schools are in the North and the Central West.

How are these expenditures divided between the whites and the Negroes? It is not the purpose here to assess blame against any state or people. But it is well to look squarely at the facts. The average expenditure for every pupil in the nation in 1930 was $99. For white children in the South it was $44.31. For Negro children, it was, in 1930, $12.57 or only about one-fourth of that of southern white children and one-eighth that of the average of the nation. In the Black Belt the discrimination is still greater. Georgia spends an average of $35.42 for each white pupil and only $6.38 for each Negro. Mississippi spends for its white children $45.34 but only $5.45 for the Negro children. In other words, two million enrolled Negro children in the South received less than one-fifteenth the opportunity for education of average American children. Chart VI shows how slowly the average expenditure per pupil for the children of the South has increased in comparison with the expenditures in the whole country and how little that for the Negroes has relatively increased since 1900.

The salaries paid both white and Negro teachers in the southern states are extremely small as compared with those paid in the other states. It is encouraging, however, to find that they have increased somewhat since the southern school movement commenced. In 1900 the average annual salary of white teachers in elementary schools in the South, of three to five months' terms, was $162 and that of Negro teachers was $106—65 per cent. By 1930 the school terms had lengthened and all the conditions in the schools, both town and country, had improved materially. But while the average annual salary of the white teachers had increased to $901, the average of the Negro teachers was only $423 or 47 per cent of the white teacher's salary. In some of the rural counties in the Black Belt the difference is much greater.

Finally the figures for the yearly amount per pupil paid white and Negro teachers in the deep South is significant. In 1931 the figures were $28 per pupil annually to white teachers and $4 per pupil to Negro teachers, or one-seventh.[9] Remember that this is for the darkest part of our southern "Darkest Africa." But it describes the conditions of the schools in a region of some million Negroes. If we believe in educational opportunity for all children, in giving them the chance to learn to live and make a living, it appears that we expend seven times as much in training a white child as we do in training a Negro child. The scientific educational expert might think it should be just the other way—that it might well cost more to train the child of a primitive race, than one from a white American family.

In June, 1904, I made a trip with representatives of the Southern Education Board through some of the districts in the South most thickly populated with Negroes, including what is called the "Black Belt" of Alabama and Mississippi. Our purpose was to find the best method of training the Negroes of this region to become effective workers and good citizens. It is unnecessary to describe at length now the conditions on the large plantations as they were then. With the

[9] McCuistion, *School Money in Black and White*, p. 21.

exception of those in villages and those who had been house servants, these people were found to be almost totally ignorant. Many were unable to speak more than a few sentences of English. Trained only to do the simplest work on the plantations, they were but slightly advanced from the savage condition in which their parents arrived in this country.

After a review of the field, it was decided that the best thing to do was to back up Principal Booker Washington of Tuskegee in his plan of training these people in character and habits of work. Washington was therefore made the field director for this task and was given full powers and the necessary assistance. We have learned in previous chapters how this plan was carried out with the aid of the General Education Board, the Slater Fund, the Phelps-Stokes Fund, and the Jeanes Fund. These boards have expended some twenty-three millions during the last twenty-five years chiefly in training leaders and teachers. In more recent years the Julius Rosenwald Fund has expended $4,364,869 in building over five thousand model rural public schools for Negroes in 883 counties of fifteen southern states.

In December, 1934, I went over a part of this field again for the purpose of seeing what had been accomplished during the intervening years. I wished to learn by personal observation what improvements had been made in the social and economic condition of these people on the plantations. In the course of the tour I consulted principals, teachers, plantation owners, cotton factors, bankers, preachers, and physicians in contact with the Negroes. Negro schools and churches were visited. The families were visited in their homes. Their premises, their gardens and plots were inspected. Everywhere I was received kindly and told freely about their work, their earnings, their desires, their privations, and the many trials and troubles which formed the chief part of their story.

In the towns and villages there had been considerable improvement over their condition thirty years ago. The Negroes were working more regularly and living better; and many homes showed evidences of industry and thrift. But on the plantations conditions were still quite miserable. The wretched shacks, the filthy premises, were still in evidence. The men, women, and children dressed and looked about as they did thirty years before. A system of elementary schools had indeed been introduced throughout the country, but they were taught by poorly trained Negro women, half of whom had never had any education beyond that of the elementary schools, living on pitiful salaries ($25 to $30 a month) for only four to five months in the year, and little had been accomplished to improve this population intellectually, morally, or economically. It is true that illiteracy had been reduced among these people from 95 to about 40 per cent, but the little learning they had acquired seemed of slight use to them. With no, or uninforced, compulsory laws, only seventy out of a hundred ever attended school at all. Sixty per cent of all the children in the schools were in the first three grades. Many who were sixteen to twenty years old were enrolled in the elementary grades. Eighty-five per cent of all those attending school left before the end of the sixth grade. Exceptions to these conditions were the training schools of the Slater Fund, Rosenwald schools with trained teachers, and schools having Tuskegee teachers, or schools with Jeanes' supervisors going about from school to school teaching cleanliness, order, and simple domestic arts. The communities where they served were bright spots on the dark map.

One result of the schooling of this population during the last thirty years has been to prepare the best and most intelligent individuals to go North. Those who had learned something and how to do something, struggled to get out of their environment. Most of the men and women who should have been leaders and teachers of their people had emigrated. The majority of the Negroes left on the large plantations were living in much the same condition of poverty and squalor in which I had found them thirty years ago. The industrious men were receiving fifty cents a day as farm or road laborers for twelve or fourteen days a month, making the total cash income of a family six or seven dollars. It seems perfectly clear that these men have not been given the right kind of education. The first thing to do with such people is to teach them how to live decently and how to make a living out of the soil. Farming is the natural occupation for them, and there is plenty of cheap land. With proper training and with financial assistance many could become small farm owners. They are multiplying rapidly, so that emigration does not reduce the population left on the plantations. This great, ugly problem of these masses of ignorant croppers and laborers on the southern plantations remains to be solved.

Industrial and agricultural education after the plan of Booker Washington still seems the only hopeful solution.

Many intelligent white citizens throughout the South are still firmly of the opinion that the schools for the Negroes have done no good and so condemn them totally. This was the general opinion of the cotton planters in the districts visited. In a sense they are justified in this view. They should not, however, condemn all the schools but rather the type of training that the majority of the Negroes have received. Wherever the Negro children had received vocational training, as in the county training schools, I found that the white citizens were changing their opinions. The people who know the pupils of Tuskegee and the other vocational schools in the South agree that they have been greatly benefited. My belief is that if vocational education were given generally in the elementary schools for Negroes, the southern planters and other whites would soon become more favorable to Negro schools and give them more encouragement and assistance than they do now.

What Shall Be Done?

To sum up some of the facts we have learned. We have here learned that there are over 1,000,000 white and 700,000 Negro tenant farmers in the southern states. The Census showed that between 1920 and 1930, 200,000 more whites became tenant-farmers through the loss of their land by foreclosure. Nearly 60 per cent of the farms in the cotton states are worked by tenants and half the tobacco farms are worked by croppers. This is a most unhealthy condition. Are a half of our farmers to become peasants? Are they not peasants already—poor, ignorant, and impoverished peasants, as compared with those in the enlightened European countries? Is not this the greatest economic and social problem before the American people? In the West the immigrants from Europe have been given land and schools and many have become independent citizens. Our nation paid the Indians for their land and gave them schools. In the South we have neglected the Negroes who were brought here and made our slaves.

In the North, Negro children are presumed to have equal opportunities with the other pupils with the chance of getting the training they need. In the southern states, two entirely separate school systems must be maintained. Four-fifths of the American Negroes live in these southern states, forming one-third of the total population of the South. Of the three million Negro children of school age in the South, only two million were enrolled in 1930, an excessively large per cent of whom are in the elementary grades. In 1930 there were only 107,000 in real high schools and 19,000 in teachers' colleges and university classes. These three million physically and mentally undeveloped Negro children, and the other millions who preceded and will follow them, constitute one of the chief factors in the nation's greatest social problem, the training of the black man and the forgotten white man.

The Nation owes the Negro a special debt. The fathers of these people were liberated seventy years ago and set adrift in the Republic without any preparation for citizenship or for making a living. The Freedmen's Bureau, the churches, and certain societies attempted to educate them but devoted their attention chiefly to training teachers, preachers, and professional men. The great masses of the Negroes have not yet been reached. Is it not time that our nation should make amends for the gross injustice done these people? The people of the South, impoverished by war, their manhood decimated and their economic system destroyed, could not in 1865, and cannot in 1935, undertake unaided the task of training this great body of primitive people for American citizenship. We have shown that the people of the South cannot yet do for their own children what they want to do.

Special schools should have been provided by the Nation for training the people it freed. These schools should have been chiefly vocational. But this work of vocational education was left entirely to a few philanthropic people led by General Armstrong of Hampton. Wherever his plans have been carried out, there has been great improvement in the Negro population. Tuskegee, the child of Hampton, was built by Booker Washington, who had been trained entirely at Hampton by Armstrong. It is instructive to recall that he and the other efficient leaders of the race commenced their careers by doing manual labor. Neither Washington nor Moton ever studied Latin or Greek. It has been shown in these last years that Armstrong's and Washington's plans are the best ones for training primitive people everywhere. Their methods of education are now being used to train such people in all parts of the world. Then shall not our nation extend these plans to all the poor and ignorant populations here at home?

Only by these measures may Southern cotton farmers hope to realize the prediction that the great Henry W. Grady made fifty years ago. Grady said: "When every farmer in the South shall eat bread from his own fields and meat from his own pastures, and disturbed by no creditor and enslaved by no debt, shall sit among his teeming orchards, gardens, barnyards and dairies, pitching his own crops in his own wisdom and growing them in independence, making cotton his clean surplus and selling it in his own time on his own chosen market and not at a master's bidding—getting his pay in cash and not a receipted mortgage that discharges his debt, but does not restore his freedom, then shall be breaking the fullness of our day."

THE NEED OF A NATIONAL EQUALIZATION FUND

We have shown that this great work of educating the poor whites and the Negroes of the South cannot be done by the southern people unaided. As it is impossible for a single locality to meet more than a small part of the expense of the school, making it necessary for the state to help, so it has come about that the state cannot bear all the expense of its schools, making it necessary for the federal government to help. The training of these neglected people is not merely a state task; it is a national task—a national duty.

The government should set up a National Equalization Fund, to be distributed to all the states, not for schools in general, but in proportion to their needs as shown by the conditions of poverty, tenancy, and ignorance. These funds should be used exclusively for elementary schools, with emphasis on vocational work, and for training teachers for rural elementary schools. The federal government should underwrite this educational work in the states and see that it is well done. Only in this way can the neglected people of the nation be given the vocational education they need to make them respectable self-supporting citizens.

This question of national aid to education was discussed widely and warmly thirty to forty years ago, and the plan was finally repudiated by southern statesmen chiefly on the theory that the government should not interfere with education in the states. Since then, the government has provided funds for the agricultural colleges and experiment stations, for Smith-Hughes and other schools throughout the states. It has recently given about one hundred and fifty million to save the schools in some of the states from the results of the depression. Departments of education, colleges, and universities are earnestly soliciting their share of these funds. It is evident, therefore, that the Southern people have changed their minds on this subject.

The funds appropriated from the national treasury for this purpose should be administered on an agreed plan, through the established educational agencies of the states under the direction of national authorities. The departments and boards of education in the South are now well organized, and the educational administrators, including all the superintendents and principals of schools are far superior to what they were thirty years ago. The universities, the George Peabody College, and the many normal colleges have supplied a noble corps of professionally trained men and women to serve the schools of the South. Systems of schools are already well organized and their administration is ably provided for. No revolution in southern systems is proposed, only the development and expansion of the present schools and the provision of more complete and thorough vocational training in the elementary rural schools.

The wealth in all the states is inevitably concentrated in certain states in stocks, bonds, and other securities. Drawn from all the states, some of this wealth should go back to them. The federal government, moreover, is taking in these days more and more of these modern forms of wealth for revenue, leaving fewer sources of income to the states. Taxable intangibles have a way of dodging from state to state with great facility. The result of these conditions is that the agricultural, non-industrial, and non-commercial states have not had and probably never will have the wealth to produce sufficient funds to support their schools as they should be supported. These considerations make it absolutely necessary for the federal government to assist the states to provide adequate support for standard schools for all the people. This is not a socialistic but a democratic proposal. It is necessary to insure the intelligence, the morality, and the economic efficiency of the men and women who are to maintain the solidarity and permanence of the Republic.

CHAPTER XXX

SUMMARY AND RESULTS

A Long Brave Fight

I HAVE in this book endeavored to tell the story of the century-long struggle for free public schools in the southern states, and to tell it, not in the terms of laws and statistics, but in the deeds of men and women, who, following Jefferson, saw that the Republic could not exist without an educated constituency. It was a long, brave fight that the men of the western hills and the mountains, the Scotch-Irish, the Germans, and the other non-slaveholding classes in other sections made for the schools in the early days. Witness the prolonged struggle in Virginia under the leadership of Henry Ruffner and Alexander Campbell, and in North Carolina under that of Murphey and Wiley. They failed largely at the time, but they prepared the way.

After the way was cleared by the emancipation of the slaves, the contest was renewed with persistence and intelligence. No cultural movement was ever founded on a higher purpose or planned with greater wisdom or carried on with more courage, patience, and intelligence than this struggle of the people of the South since 1870 to establish universal education. This movement since 1902, popularly known as the Southern Education Movement, marshaled by the patriotic Ogden and officered by southern men and women, is one of the most notable in the history of the country.

George Peabody had, as we have told, come into the South with his noble largess, to help prepare the way for schools. It thus appears to the writer that his meeting with General Lee at White Sulphur Springs [1] may be considered the starting point of the great new movement. Mr. Peabody's patriotic gift [2] and the act of General Lee in taking up the work of a poor college in the South appear to have been the inspiration. We may, therefore, take the conference of these great men at White Sulphur Springs, where Sears and Curry, the future

[1] See Vol. I, Chap. VII. [2] *Ibid.*

leaders, and many of the leading men of the South were present, as the beginning of the movement. The meeting of these men to greet and confer with Mr. Peabody about the use of his fund was the first act in this great movement.

The Southern Conference and Board were indirectly at least the children of the George Peabody Fund, which had prepared the way and set the example. The great work of Sears and Curry in the South suggested the plan, and men like McIver and Alderman of North Carolina, Claxton and Dabney in Tennessee, Abercrombie in Alabama, Preston in Mississippi, and many others had already worked with Dr. Curry. They had been aided also by such generous friends as George Foster Peabody. George S. Dickerman, who had been studying the southern schools for the American Missionary Association, and A. D. Mayo, who had been for several years visiting them, investigating their condition and writing their history for the United States Bureau of Education, had helped to prepare the way for a systematic campaign.

The time was opportune for the organization of a general southern movement. These men had done enough to show the great need and how the problem was to be met. It was exactly the moment for organization. The men and women drawn together by Mr. Ogden at Winston-Salem were thus united for the first time in a common effort. They felt that their first task was to build up out of the old individualistic, conservative, and aristocratic form of society, oppressed with unjust debts and embittered by wrongs, real and unreal, a new public spirit which would support a movement for the solution of their problems. A sound public opinion was the first thing to be created.

It was natural and proper, therefore, that Dr. J. L. M. Curry, the director of this new vital agency, should place his mantle on the new leader, Mr. Ogden. This task the Board took up with consecration and enthusiasm. It accomplished an amazing total of results in the space of thirteen years.

The Conference for Education, which met at Winston-Salem, North Carolina, in 1901, and the Southern Board organized by it there, were absolutely unique as educational bodies. There was never before anything like them. The Conference was a purely voluntary meeting of governors, bishops, business men, industrialists, farmers, lawyers, ministers, leaders in women's clubs—men and women with no other claim to recognition than their deep interest in education in the South. It was in no sense a professional society, and in this respect it differed from all other educational societies that had ever existed. To meet these people Mr. Ogden annually brought trainloads of men and women from the North who were interested in the same subject ; and many other interested people came voluntarily. The Conference had no fixed membership and no fees.

Except for the initial gift of Mr. George Foster Peabody to support its work for the first two years, the Board had no large funds and never had any endowment. No body of men ever accomplished with so small means so much of tremendous value. Its means were used to make it possible for earnest men of the South interested in education to induce their people to do their duty to their own schools. It realized from the first that no amount of endowments could support the southern schools as they ought to be supported, but that the people had to support their schools themselves, and had to be taught first how to produce from the soil the necessary funds.

Each annual Conference organized itself for the year following. and every time it elected Mr. Ogden president. He, with an executive committee, had entire direction. Mr. Ogden was head and soul of the Conference for thirteen years. The Conference was thus the least organized body ever projected. This was a great element of its strength and influence. The Southern Education Board, authorized by the Fourth Conference and appointed by Mr. Ogden to carry out its plans, was its only agency.

We have told of the meetings in the different places in the South, but we have not told of the actions at the various meetings of the Southern Education Board. They were expressed in the work done. At the conferences of the Southern Education Board in New York, at Mr. Ogden's dinners, at the meetings at Abenia, the summer home of Mr. George Foster Peabody on Lake George, and with Mr. Walter Hines Page in Garden City, the members of the Board met with many representatives of large national interests to listen to reports and discuss the work. The subjects covered a wide range of questions relating to education.

The general results have been a nobler, broader, clearer conception of our government and its functions, and especially a better understanding by the men and women of the North and the South as to their duty to educate all the people, blacks as well as whites, for the preservation of democracy.

So extensive have been its operations, so varied its work, so large its development, and so numerous the societies that have grown out of it, so wide has been its influence over the states, legislatures, and boards, that it is most difficult to sum up the results of the Conference for Education in the South and its executive agency, the Southern Education Board. Only some of the main results can be named here.

The annual sessions of the Conference for Education in the South were generally held in April, and their unique interest as educational gatherings played a most important part in the advancement of the cause. Some of them were great mass meetings, as at Richmond in 1903 and at Lexington in 1906. Some were smaller assemblies for intensive and intimate discussions, as at Pinehurst in 1907. Some have combined both features, their programs providing for the larger mass meetings and for the smaller conferences of different classes of members, as at Little Rock in 1910 and at the Richmond meeting in 1913. But all were deeply interesting.

These Conferences introduced an entirely new kind of educational discussion. The scheduled addresses were not limited to professional teachers, but the programs contained the names of men of all callings and interests—all who had a message were gladly heard. The subjects of discussion were not the ordinary ones discussed at teachers' meetings and educational associations, such as courses of study, discipline, and methods, but took in a very wide range including legislation, taxation, organization, administration, community life, agriculture, better homes, better health, and coöperation. The aim of all the meetings, consciously or unconsciously, was—to help the people to attain a fuller life, a truly abundant life. Another result of such discussions was the destruction of misunderstandings, the breaking down of prejudices through the bringing together in intimate relations the men and women of the North and the South, developing a new, truer, more direct and deeper feeling of sympathy and coöperation.

At each annual meeting a set of resolutions was passed to crystallize the results of the discussions. These resolutions often

Frank R. Chambers, life-long friend of southern schools, member of the
Southern Education Board and its final president

The Southern Education Board at Garden City, New York

repeated the same thoughts, but it will be well briefly to summarize the principles agreed upon.

1. It was resolved that the benefits of the public schools should be open to all regardless of class or race, provided only that the children of the black race should be taught in separate schools, adequately officered and furnished in accordance with their needs and advancement.

2. It was resolved that it was an economic error and a sin to neglect the education of any of the children. Every child had the right to an opportunity for the full development of his God-given powers, be he black or white. It was an economic necessity of the first magnitude to train the productive power and potential intelligence of every child. Therefore, an education was the right of every child—not an act of private benevolence or simply of public prudence.

3. It was resolved that in the system of democratic education class distinction should not enter into the course of study or influence the methods or the discipline. The rich and the poor should all have the same opportunity and the same treatment.

4. It was resolved that the proposal to divide the school funds raised by taxation between the two races on the basis of the amount contributed by each was unjust and undemocratic.

5. It was resolved that the training of the country child must be of a character to make country life better and happier, to remove its isolation and loneliness by good roads, by telephones, by libraries, and thus place the future generations in touch with the great outside world. In order to accomplish this it was agreed that the South must hereafter emphasize individualism less and community effort more.

6. It was resolved, in order that every child might have the benefits of the best education in a large group of his fellows, that the pitiful little country schools must be consolidated into larger schools, with better teachers, better buildings, better grounds.

7. It had already been agreed that there was to be a real university practically free in every state which should train the ablest sons and daughters of the state for the higher positions, as teachers, professional men and leaders in all public affairs.

8. It was resolved that agricultural and industrial education

should be provided in all grades of schools from the bottom to the top as a means of giving the children a knowledge of nature, training in the use of their hands and in the disciplinary work which will give every citizen the habit of economic support. Vocational education, training in how to live and make a living, should be extended down into the elementary schools, where a majority of the country children get their only education.

9. It was resolved that girls and women should have equal opportunities for education and training in accordance with their natural functions and duties.

10. It was resolved that such complete systems of education should be supported by taxation distributed over the states as wholes, the counties, and the districts as the people themselves should decide.

11. And it was resolved finally that the administration and improvement of the schools should be divided between the state boards or superintendents and the county and district officers as seemed best and that thorough supervision must be provided.

It was to establish these principles and to accomplish these ends that the Conference and its Board and coöperating agencies labored.

As has been said, the chief function of the Southern Education Board was propaganda in favor of a better understanding of the need and duty of the southern people—the creation of better public opinion. For doing this work the Board had directors or agents in each one of the states, chief of whom at first was Dr. Curry, who was afterwards succeeded by Dr. McIver, with Principal Booker T. Washington in charge of the general work for Negro schools. The people of the different states were encouraged to form their own agencies and societies. The most popular and successful of these were the coöperative education associations and the improvement leagues of the women, such as those in Virginia.

Aided by small appropriations from the Board, which were largely supplemented by other funds, the various school workers in the southern states organized many local leagues for the improvement of schoolhouses, grounds, gardens, sanitation; for school libraries; and for a variety of other desirable objects. One of the finest effects of these coöperative and improvement leagues has been the development of more intelligent interest in school affairs and community work.

Dr. Knapp's system of farm demonstration work was first taken up by the Southern Board and afterwards introduced and supported by the General Board, in coöperation with the Department of Agriculture of the United States. Undoubtedly no other one educational agency has done so much for the development of agricutural interests and the general economic welfare of the rural communities of the South as has this demonstration plan. Related to it was the work of the corn clubs for boys and the canning clubs for girls, which have now been organized under the Extension Department of the United States Department of Agriculture and which have been extended over the whole country under the name of "Four H Clubs"—meaning "Head, Heart, Hand and Health Clubs."

Mr. Ogden's excursions had a marvelous influence in promoting personal friendships, like-mindedness, and interest between the people of the North and those of the South. Northerners learned to know the South as they never had before. The excursions of state superintendents of schools and other officials into the North, conducted personally by Mr. Ogden, had a great and happy influence in promoting sympathetic insight and coöperation. The leading teachers of North and South came to know each other. The southern officials learned a vast deal which they have since been trying to apply in their own work.

As a result of these excursions and Conferences the South was drawn from its isolation into the full stream of national life. Millions who had formerly been hidden away in remote places in the South commenced to learn for the first time that they were citizens of a great republic. This movement helped to prepare the people of the South for the noble participation they took in the World War.

The southern people, being, like other Americans, intensely individualistic, had been in the habit of acting independently in most things. The tendency to separatism prevailed in almost every movement for social development. This had gone on until it had almost paralyzed their educational, social, and religious service. Churches were split up into independent sects until they were losing their hold on the people. Every denomination had its educational boards, schools, orphan asylums, hospitals, and so on. Social service organizations were multiplied until they got in each other's way. If the Southern Conference and its associated boards had done nothing else, it was worth while to have taught the southern people how to work together and coöperate in organizing and supporting their schools. The example of the Conference certainly had a fine influence in this way. Coöperative educational associations uniting the teachers, parents, the school improvement associations, and the citizens generally, and even some of the church societies, have been most useful in developing the schools. They have developed a fine spirit of coöperation in many other ways. Coöperation is becoming more and more the method of doing things in the South, and separatism is giving way to united effort.

Only a few statistics of the remarkable progress made during the period of the existence of the Southern Education Board, 1901-1914, will be given.[3]

Illiteracy among the white children of the fourteen southern states between the ages of ten and twenty was reduced on an average from 9.5 in 1900 to 5.5 in 1910 and 4.00 in 1914. The illiteracy of the states where this campaign was most active, such as North Carolina, was reduced from 15.6 in 1900 to 4.2 in 1914; in Georgia from 9.5 in 1900 to 3.8 in 1914; in Tennessee from 10.8 in 1900 to 4.5 in 1914. In other words, the illiteracy among the white children of these states was less than one-half of what it was fourteen years ago. These figures are eloquent of persistent and effective endeavor. The figures for the reduction of illiteracy among the colored children for these ages is even more remarkable.

The number of days in the annual school term in these states is still too small, but the increase in the average for all these states from 1900 to 1912 was from 105 days to 130 days in the year. In some states where the campaign was most active, as in North Carolina, the increase in days in the annual school term was from 71 days to 109 days; in Georgia, from 112 days to 142 days; in Alabama, from 78 days to 132 days; in Tennessee, from 96 days to 128 days.

The United States Department of Education reports that the expenditure for public schools in these states during the

[3] *Proceedings of the Seventeenth Conference for Education in the South, and the Twenty-fifth Annual Meeting of the Southern Educational Association, Louisville, Kentucky, 1914*, pp. 3-4.

period from 1900 to 1914 (a large part of this period being before the beginning of Mr. Rosenwald's work), was from $23,000,000 to $82,000,000, an increase of $59,000,000, or 256 per cent. From the same source we learn that during this period the expenditure per capita of the whole population has increased from $1.10 in 1900 to $2.75 in 1914. During the same period the value of school property has increased from a total of $40,000,000 to $175,000,000, or 337 per cent. The character of the schoolhouses has been greatly improved. The women's clubs and school improvement leagues have accomplished much also in beautifying the grounds, in sanitary provisions, and in providing gardens.

In 1915, when the active campaign of the Southern Board was concluded, the Rosenwald Fund was carrying on most active and successful work in improving Negro schools which had been lamentably poor before, and it had reached in 1930 its five-thousandth school. The method of drawing in the Negroes and the whites of the community to help in this work has stimulated many other communities, which the fund could not aid, to improve their Negro schools and grounds.

The most notable progress in public education in these states in the last fourteen years has been in the high school. There were comparatively few public high schools in the South outside of the cities when the Board started its work. The number of these schools has now increased very greatly and their attendance has been doubled and doubled again. Many of the high schools in the country were merely attachments to the elementary schools, and very few of them were high schools proper. Their standards have now been greatly raised, and they are taking their rightful place as the center of the public school system. The high schools in the towns and cities have also extended their courses from two to three years, as they were thirty years ago, to standard four-year high schools. Many of them have industrial and technical departments. Hundreds of good high schools have also been opened to the boys and girls of the villages and open country. The influence of these schools, especially in preparing for the normal schools students who will ultimately become teachers in their home localities, has been felt throughout the entire system and has greatly influenced the life of the communities in which they live.

All the states now have numerous state normal schools.

Some of the states have five or six each. Several of them, like Tennessee, Kentucky, Mississippi, and Arkansas, established their first normal schools during this period—1900-1914—and have largely increased the appropriations for their support and equipment. Tennessee has led the way in establishing a college exclusively for rural school teachers. This is under the presidency of Dr. Philander P. Claxton, former commissioner of education of the United States, and constitutes one of the most important and significant steps in the history of southern education.

Beginning with the work of the Southern Board in the Summer School of the South in 1902, there was a remarkable increase in the number and importance of high grade summer schools for teachers all over the South. In these, the teachers met for higher instruction and inspiration under the guidance of the best professors from all over the country.

Most interesting is the fact that all grades and kinds of schools have modified and enriched their curricula and courses of study to meet the demands of modern life in the country or in the town. They are all seeking, not merely to teach the three R's or to prepare their students for college, as was the old idea, or to prepare them to make a living, but to train them for life and for service to their communities as their talents and abilities will permit.

No less remarkable was the progress during this period in higher education, built as it was upon the work of the elementary and high schools. The colleges and universities and the technical schools of the South have developed enormously, not only in attendance, but in equipment, in appropriations and expenditures, and best of all in efficiency. Standards have been raised in all of them. Proprietary medical schools have been converted into state and university medical schools, and technical schools and schools of all classes have been advanced to standards equal to the best. Only the law schools seem to have lagged behind. But they show signs of early and great improvement. There are still many proprietary law schools.

In 1914, at the closing of the work of the Southern Education Board, it was evident to all that a new era in education had begun in the South, and in the last twenty years this has been, in great measure, realized.

The Southland which so long had wandered in the wilderness of poverty, following the destruction of war and Reconstruction, was at last coming into its own. The most remarkable thing in this era was the change of public opinion. People, who were indifferent and antagonistic toward public education at public cost, have now come to look upon the education of all the children as the first duty of the people and the highest function of the democratic state.

THE SOUTHERN EDUCATION BOARD AND THE BOARDS WHICH GREW OUT OF IT OR WERE PARALLEL TO IT

Out of the Southern Education Board and the opportunity for service have grown a number of other boards and foundations, formed to help in the southern educational work and in similar causes throughout the country. Some of these grew directly out of the Southern Board. Some were suggested by it and grew parallel with it as auxiliaries. Other agencies have grown up, which, after studying the work in America, have applied the same principles in foreign countries.

The first of the agencies to grow directly out of the Southern Education Board was the General Education Board. After one year's operation of the Southern Board, Mr. Rockefeller was so pleased with its work that he proposed to a group of gentlemen to incorporate a General Education Board, which should do a broader work in the whole country. The group consisted of seven out of the twelve members of the Southern Education Board. Six of them were northern residents, with Dr. Curry as a citizen at large ; four were elected from Mr. Rockefeller's former advisers, one of whom was his son. These gentlemen organized the General Education Board, which was duly incorporated in January, 1903.

William H. Baldwin, Jr., a member of the Southern Education Board, was president of the General Education Board for the first three years, and Robert C. Ogden, the fourth and fifth years. George Foster Peabody, one of the founders of the Southern Education Board, was the treasurer of the General Board until 1909. No greater compliment could have been paid to the men who organized the Southern Board than this—to have their work copied and extended as it was in this tremendous new enterprise, one which was destined in the next thirty years to do a world-wide service to humanity.

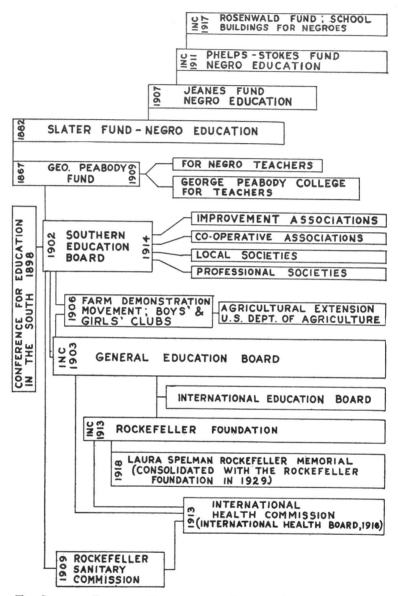

THE SOUTHERN EDUCATION BOARD AND THE AGENCIES GROWING OUT OF IT
OR COLLATERAL WITH IT

The next organization was the Rockefeller Foundation, established in 1913 by Mr. Rockefeller as a financial holding and executive board, to handle funds which he wished to set aside for different educational and benevolent purposes. To this new foundation, including $50,000 given by Mrs. Laura Spelman Rockefeller and the Laura Spelman Rockefeller Memorial, which he had previously established with $73,875,457 and which was consolidated in 1929 with the Rockefeller Foundation, Mr. Rockefeller and his son had given, up to March, 1932, $256,667,081.[4]

To the General Education Board Mr. Rockefeller gave, up to March, 1932, $129,209,167.10.[5]

The Rockefeller Sanitary Commission, which grew directly out of the Southern Board, was organized in October, 1909, and, as has been told, was designed originally to fight the hookworm in the South. Its first administrative secretary was Dr. Wickliffe Rose, member of the Southern Board, formerly professor in Peabody College and in the University of Tennessee, and a member of the Bureau of Investigation and Information of the Southern Board. Its scientific secretary was Dr. Charles Wardell Stiles, of the United States Health Service. This Commission later extended its work to fight malaria and yellow fever and to give instruction to the people of the South in better sanitation. It was afterwards enlarged into the International Health Commission, subsequently in 1916 called the International Health Board, as an integral part of the work of the Rockefeller Foundation. To this work, which was continued by the International Health Commission, Mr. Rockefeller gave one million dollars.[6]

The China Medical Board, which in fact resulted from the work of the International Health Commission in China, was a related but an entirely separate enterprise. Besides health work in China this Board acquired the Union Medical College at Peking (Peiping), which Mr. Rockefeller endowed then with $12,000,000.[7] To the International Education Board formed for the purpose of promoting scientific investigation in foreign, chiefly European countries, and aiding institutions crippled by the World War, Mr. John D. Rockefeller, Jr., gave $21,116,-

[4] From a statement furnished the author by the Secretary of the General Education Board. See Appendix IX.
[5] *Ibid.*   [6] *Ibid.*   [7] *Ibid.*

785.[8] All of these items are not a part of southern history, but it is interesting to note that for education and science and medicine up to March, 1932, and not including their former gifts to various institutions, Mr. Rockefeller and his son have given to the General Education Board, to the Rockefeller Foundation, the Sanitary Commission and to the international Boards, a total of nearly $408,000,000.[9]

It has been impossible to ascertain the exact amount of the expenditures of the Southern Education Board. This Board secured very large sums of money for different educational institutions or agencies in the South which were paid directly to them. Of these we have unfortunately no complete record. The expenditures of the Southern Education Board for its own purposes and its officers were very small in view of the tremendous results accomplished.

The treasurer of the Board, Mr. George Foster Peabody, in a letter to the author estimates them at from $30,000 to $40,000 per annum.[10] These sums were contributed by Mr. Peabody, who underwrote the expenditures of the Board for the first two years, by Robert C. Ogden, the chairman for twelve years, by Frank R. Chambers, who succeeded Mr. Ogden, by Andrew Carnegie, Morris K. Jesup, and John D. Rockefeller through the General Education Board. William H. Baldwin himself contributed and was largely instrumental in securing contributions from others. The General Education Board contributed a total of $97,126 to the Southern Education Board.[11]

Miss Anna T. Jeanes, of Philadelphia, gave $200,000 to the General Education Board to be expended for rural schools in the South before she created her own separate fund. It cannot be questioned that Mr. Rosenwald was influenced in establishing his great fund for building better schoolhouses and promoting Y.M.C.A.'s for Negroes in the South by the example of these great donors and by the work of the Southern Education and the General Education boards.

The multiplication of foundations for scientific and other purposes in this country since George Peabody, John F. Slater,

---

[8] *Ibid.*   [9] *Ibid.*

[10] Letter of June 6, 1934, of George Foster Peabody to Charles Wm. Dabney.

[11] From the statement of the Secretary of the General Education Board.

and especially John D. Rockefeller set the example has been phenomenal. The Twentieth Century Fund, Inc., an association formed for the purpose of studying American foundations and their fields of work, reported in 1932 that there were 129 foundations in this country for educational, scientific, and benevolent purposes of different kinds. These foundations vary in the amount of total grants from a few thousand dollars to the millions given by the Rockefellers and others. The purposes for which they are given vary in a most interesting way. This report shows that the amounts donated for the two years 1930 and 1931 only, may be rated in this order : Medicine and Public Health—the largest amount, General Education—the next largest, Social Science, Physical Science, Social Welfare, Child Welfare, Aesthetics, Government, Economics, International Relations, Humanities, Religion, Agriculture and Forestry, City Planning and Housing, Race Relations, Engineering, Labor.

INFLUENCE OF SOUTHERN SCHOOLS IN FOREIGN COUNTRIES

An important but little realized result of the long struggle for universal education in the South is the use in certain foreign countries of the educational methods worked out in the southern states. The principles of education for life—for making a living in agriculture and in industries, for improving sanitation and other living conditions, based on the general ideas developed by Armstrong in this country for educating primitive people, and on the methods of Knapp in farm demonstrations, in boys' and girls' clubs supported by the Smith-Lever and Smith-Hughes plans for agriculture and extension work, and in the training of teachers in agriculture and domestic science—these principles are now being utilized in the education departments of several foreign governments. The colonial administrations of Great Britain and Africa, for example, are using them.[12] In Mexico Dr. Saens, commissioner of education, has translated Jones's *Four Essentials of Education* into Spanish and has distributed it in Central and South America as a basis of education. Uruguay and Paraguay are also introducing southern methods.

Most impressive in this connection are the extensions of the methods of the various boards in institutional work and in the

[12] *Journal of Over-seas Education*, Vol. I. Published by the Advisory Commission of Education in London.

work of the churches' missionary schools as developed in the plans of the Near East Foundation. This Foundation proposes now to stop, as far as possible, the work of administering to those suffering as a result of the war, a work which is now fairly well completed, and devote its resources and energies to teaching the people in the Near East how to live, through better farming and improved industries, and to maintain health through sanitation. This they will undertake to do by means of elementary education, following the plans developed in the South, which will take the place of the old dead academic education that their teachers and missionaries gave them in the past.[13] We can here give only some suggestions to the student who wishes to follow up the influence of the southern schools in these new fields. The Commission to Africa and the Near East, of which Dr. Dillard was a member, was instrumental in introducing Jeanes teachers in Kenya. Sir Edward Denham, governor of the British Guiana, in a letter of November 20, 1930, to Dr. Dillard says "There is a big opening for Jeanes school teachers amongst the negro population." "Education is suffering from the lack of policy and the lack of funds," and he begs Dillard to help him introduce the Jeanes school system. There are plenty of schools, he says, and the material is quite good, but sadly needs improvement in methods, general conduct, and character-building, especially in the direction of the organization of school life in which the Jeanes school system is so very valuable. Hundreds of African visitors have visited our Southern states during the last few years to study their methods.

In the book, *The Near East and American Philanthropy*, prepared at the instance of the different organizations working in the Near East under the direction of a Survey Committee of which Dr. John R. Mott, Dr. John H. Finley, Mr. Cleveland Dodge, and Dr. James I. Vance were members, and Dr. O. W. Caldwell was chairman, the plan of survey made by Thomas Jesse Jones is explained. This plan calls for, first, a study of the economic and sociological backgrounds of the Near East countries ; second, a study of the educational activities maintained by these countries in the Near East and by foreign agencies. All of this work looks to the introduction of the new southern methods in those countries. Methods of teaching agriculture and

[13] Ross, Fry, and Sibley, *The Near East and American Philanthropy*, pp. 7-9.

the adoption of the Smith-Lever country farm type of work are beginning to function in Armenia, Turkey, Palestine, Greece, and Bulgaria.[14] Secondary agricultural education is already under way in all of them save Syria and Trans-Jordania. Agricultural elementary education is making promising beginnings in Armenia, Palestine, Greece, and Bulgaria. The International Education Board, the outgrowth of the General Education Board, endowed by John D. Rockefeller, Jr., is coöperating with Bulgaria in building a national college of agriculture at Sofia on the American plan. Messrs. Rosenwald and Rockefeller and others have been helping the Jewish Agricultural Corporation for modern agricultural training to start some similar projects in Russia. Americans are aiding by starting American-directed and native-staffed agricultural schools.[15]

At a conference held at Constantinople in September, 1927, the resolutions adopted recommended that "agriculture is the most important basis of national life" and suggested its teaching in the schools after the southern plan.[16] This all shows the influence of the southern schools and their methods.

One illustration only of the influence of the southern educational methods upon a particular foreign school may be mentioned.

A few miles from the city of Thessalonica where St. Paul in pursuance of his youthful training worked as a tent-maker, and not far away from the place where Aristotle taught Alexander the Great, there is an agricultural school today modeled after the southern schools. It is the Thessalonica Agricultural and Industrial Institute at Salonica, Greece. The president of the school is the Reverend John Henry House, D.D., father of Miss Grace House, one of the principals of the Penn School, in South Carolina, described in this book. The Thessalonica Institute was begun about thirty years ago. Among its trustees are Dr. Kenyon L. Butterfield, formerly president of the Massachusetts Agricultural College, Dr. John H. Finley, of the *New York Times*, Dr. Thomas Jesse Jones, of the Phelps-Stokes Fund, and Mr. Ray Stannard Baker, the well known writer. In a letter of February 15, 1927, Mr. Baker says of the work of Dr. House :

[14] *Ibid.*, pp. 275-80.
[15] *Ibid.*, pp. 277-79.
[16] *Ibid.*, pp. 281-84, 289-90.

I was greatly impressed by the rare combination of idealism and common sense which he applied to the difficult situation in which he was placed. As his experience ripened he began to see that the traditional missionary methods were not effective in meeting the new problems which were confronting the world. He saw how much his neighbors needed to know of new agricultural and industrial methods, and he believed the various elements in that mixed population could be brought together and made to understand one another through the natural contacts of the industrial school better than through the older method of religious teaching. He organized the Thessalonica Agricultural and Industrial Institute in the outskirts of Salonica. Here he has brought together many races, trained young men for leadership in agriculture and industry, and at the same time given them the true spirit that lies within and back of the Christian religion.

In the *New York Times* of Sunday, September 13, 1925, Dr. House, the principal, describes the work of the school. "The work-day is divided between the classroom and the farm. The academic study is always carried into the practical field ; students learn to add and to subtract in the barn-yard, and become familiar with the square foot in measuring the size of a field. I personally supervise the agricultural work, instructing the lads myself in the principles of farming, taking them right into the fields to make demonstration." As correct methods of sewage disposal are unknown in the country, the boys are taught them and go back to their villages to put decent methods into practice with great benefit to the health of their people. This school has been called the child of the Penn School, South Carolina. The Penn School, we know, was the child of Hampton, Virginia. The school is appreciated by the Greek government, which has arranged to send twenty-five students at the expense of the government each year, the students being selected from different parts of Greece. It is hoped they will become leaders in agricultural development in their native villages. Premier Venizelos has shown great interest in it.[17] The Greek Government has conferred upon Dr. John Henry House the Cross of the Chevalier of the Order of the Saviour, which is equivalent to knighting him.

The southern schools are also attracting the attention of the

[17] Interview with Dr. John H. House, "Farm Boys of Balkans Trained by Americans," *New York Times*, September 13, 1925.

superintendents, directors, and teachers of schools in various other foreign countries. The Penn School, South Carolina, has been visited by many foreign teachers and has become a model for them. Here is one testimonal : Mr. H. S. Keigwin, Director of Native Development of Salisbury, South Rhodesia, says : "Everywhere I am asked what place in the South impressed me most, and every time the answer darts instantly, 'Penn School' " (on St. Helena Island, South Carolina).

Here is the story of one young man who was inspired and trained under the influences of the Southern Board and gave his life for the cause in a foreign country. At the Conference for Education in the South at Athens, Georgia, in April, 1902, a young student sat in the audience and listened to the addresses of Mr. Ogden, Governor Aycock, Dr. Buttrick, and the others, with keen interest. He was greatly impressed, and after meeting and talking with Mr. George Foster Peabody and the other gentlemen in attendance on the meeting, he there resolved to devote his life to the cause of public education. He taught for a short period in the public schools of Georgia and, becoming filled with the missionary spirit, accepted a position as teacher in the Philippines in the United States government service. This young man was James Longstreet Sibley, born in Juniper, Georgia, June, 1883, of a distinguished family related to General Longstreet of the Confederate army. After three years in the Philippines, young Sibley returned by way of the East Indies, India, and Europe, studying, as he traveled, the social conditions of the people. He learned a great deal and the experience confirmed him in his purpose to devote himself to education. He next took a position as teacher in the State Normal School at Jacksonville, Alabama, where he came under the influence of Honorable Henry J. Willingham, the state superintendent of education (1910-1913).[18] Willingham had become deeply interested in the education of the Negro children of his state and frequently talked to Sibley about the problem. The young man had developed such broad views on the subject of the training of primitive peoples by this time that Mr. Willingham offered him the position of state agent for Negro rural schools in Alabama, an office which the General Education Board had authorized him to establish.

Sibley began this work for the Negroes in 1913 and soon

[18] Now president of the State Teachers College at Florence, Alabama.

became one of the most useful and popular members of the state educational staff. Endowed with great common sense and a fine sense of humor, important equipments for any man in executive work, he knew how to discuss all the difficulties between the whites and the blacks and to overcome their prejudices and differences. He gradually led the public opinion among the whites in the direction of more liberal treatment of the Negroes. His attractive manner and his spirit of helpfulness made him welcome everywhere. Traveling over the state he made himself the friend, counsellor, and assistant of all the county superintendents, principals, and teachers.

Sibley was a friend of Principal Washington and a frequent visitor at Tuskegee, where he learned a great deal from Washington and from his successor, Principal Moton. After his observations in the East and in Alabama, he was prepared to take up with enthusiasm Washington's method of education as a method for building up a rural civilization. Coming in contact with the Jeanes teachers, he worked with them, helping them to adapt their school program to the home life of the people. About this time he met Mr. Julius Rosenwald, who was just beginning his work of building better schoolhouses for Negroes and helped to build the first ones in Alabama.

In 1918 Sibley resigned this position to help in war work and was put in charge of the Veterans' Rehabilitation Bureau in New Orleans. His sympathy and common sense served him well in this position, in which he continued until the needs of the returning soldiers had been met.

The University of Georgia called Sibley next to organize its extension work in social welfare. Here he came in contact with Dr. Branson, from whom he learned a great deal about social service. When Dr. Knapp's demonstrations and club work were started in Alabama, Sibley went to Auburn to take charge of the boys' agricultural club work, which he organized successfully.

After these remarkable and varied experiences it was not surprising that in July, 1925, Sibley was called by a group of mission boards to become educational adviser for them in Liberia. Arriving there in December, 1925, he traveled widely over the country, making friends with the government officials and missionaries, and studying the social condition of the people and the possibilities of agriculture, industry, and commerce. He put to good use his extensive experience in the Philippines and with the Negroes in the South. The next year he returned to America to make his report to the boards. He expressed great faith in the possibilities of the natives and especially in Mr. Firestone's scheme to produce rubber and so build a civilization upon a better economic foundation. He held a Conference on Liberia at Hampton in 1926, and in 1927 with the aid of Dr. Moton and Bishop Clair of the Methodist Church Board made plans for a school in Liberia modeled after Tuskegee. With Dr. Diedrich H. Westermann, head of the Institute of the African Languages of London, he coöperated in writing a book entitled *Liberia Old and New,* said to be the best one ever published on the subject. The report to his boards was received with hearty approval and he now set to work upon a definite program. One of the first things he did was to get out a set of simple textbooks which Colonel George A. Plimpton of Ginn & Company kindly published for him. These were based entirely upon African conditions and were promptly adopted by the Liberian government. They have since proved an important contribution to education in Africa and have been used in many other parts of the country. The next thing he did was to organize a staff consisting of Miss Mitchell, as trainer of teachers, and Mr. Harold R. Bare to take charge of the agricultural work for the boys. Mr. Bare is now principal of the Booker Washington Institute.

In 1927 Sibley, with the coöperation of Dr. Dillard of the Slater Fund and other American leaders, organized the Association of American Jeanes Teachers for Liberia. Virginia Randolph of Virginia was honorary president, Dr. W. T. B. Williams of Tuskegee was treasurer, and Mrs. A. W. Holland of North Carolina was secretary. The object was to train and raise money to support Jeanes Teachers in Liberia. Miss Rebecca Davis, a Jeanes teacher of long experience, went to Liberia in 1928 and organized a class for training teachers. She traveled in different parts of Liberia and introduced the system in many schools. Unfortunately the death of Sibley in 1929 temporarily disrupted the work of this association. It has been resumed recently, however, with renewed energy.

Basing its recommendation on the experience with Negro schools in the southern states, the Commission of the Phelps-Stokes Fund, which in 1920-21 had visited and studied the

schools in West and South Africa, urged the educational authorities of these states to introduce the Jeanes plan of supervision.
This they did in the schools in Kenya. Dr. C. T. Loram, authority on African education, who some years before had visited
Hampton and studied the methods used there, has since declared
that the use of Jeanes Teachers is the best measure ever tried for
the improvement of Negro schools in Africa. The editor of
Oversea Education gives the following description of the work,
based upon a report from a Jeanes teacher in Kenya:

A Jeanes School is one maintained for the training of selected
village school teachers, with a view to their eventual supervision
and improvement of groups of schools. Such schools derive their
name from an American lady who saw the potential value of such
a scheme in the foundation of an educational system and left
money for its furtherance. Each teacher, after training, travels
around his district to bring each school into closer touch with
village life by showing what improvement it can effect in such
life and to convince each village of the communal advantages of
the schools.... Such schools have been established by the Government of Kenya, Nyasaland, and Northern Rhodesia.[19]

The same methods are being used with marked success in
the Belgian Congo and in Portuguese Africa. They are also
being introduced in British Guiana, the Virgin Islands, Jamaica,
the Fiji Islands, South America, and Asia. "It is not possible,"
says Dr. Jones, "to enumerate the widespread influences of the
Jeanes plan throughout the world.[20] Such is the reach of the
plan endowed by Miss Jeanes, the Quaker lady of Philadelphia,
and designed by Virginia Randolph, the Negro teacher in Henrico County, Virginia.

Sibley was the originator of the idea of establishing a Booker
Washington Institute in Africa, and succeeded in getting the
government to approve it.

Miss Olivia Phelps Stokes agreed to give $25,000 toward
the endowment of the school, provided the Methodist Board
gave a like amount, which it did. From these beginnings the
Booker Washington Agricultural and Industrial Institute was

[19] *Oversea Education*, Vol. I, No. 1 (Oct., 1929).
[20] *Report of the Negro Rural School Fund, Inc., The Anna T. Jeanes
Foundation, 1907-1933*, pp. 155-67.

developed. The Liberian government granted a charter in 1928, one thousand acres of land, and $5,000 annually for ten years. In her will Miss Stokes gave $50,000 additional for education in Liberia. With these funds Sibley proceeded to organize the Institute. It was founded on March 17, 1929, and dedicated at Kakata, a village forty-five miles inland from Monrovia. With the help of Mr. R. R. Taylor, vice-principal of Tuskegee Institute, he made all the plans for construction and the program of instruction for the Institute, which then was definitely launched. Mr. Henry L. West, for many years head of the American Colonization Society, was elected the first president of the board of trustees, and other members were Dr. Moton of Tuskegee, Canon Anson Phelps Stokes, the president of the Phelps-Stokes Fund, and Dr. Thomas Jesse Jones of the same fund.

A staff, consisting of a principal and heads for agricultural and industrial work, was elected, and several native teachers were engaged to teach the elementary subjects. The necessary buildings were constructed and native buildings utilized. The Institute began by giving both boys and girls an elementary education and teaching them how to live and earn their living in agriculture, trades, and industries. Rules of health, home-making, and community and national life were stressed. One hundred native boys and girls were enrolled at the beginning in 1931. They are instructed on the part-time plan, going to school one day and working the next, in accordance with their interests. On work days the boys interested in agriculture go to the fields where they dig the soil and plant tropical crops; boys interested in carpentry, brick-making, tailoring, or basketry, find ample opportunity to learn these trades. The girls are taught the household arts in a similar way. Their teachers report that they are apt and become skilled in a short time because of their tribal gifts for such work.

Sibley had completed four years in the country and was very happy with the prospects. He had settled down in Monrovia for the rainy season and was making plans for a summer school for training more Jeanes teachers when he was suddenly stricken at his post with yellow fever and died on June 28, 1929. On his deathbed he directed that his body should be buried at Kakata, the site of the Booker Washington Institute, the establishment of which had been the result of his efforts, and that $5,000 of his estate should be given to it.

Sibley was at first interested in education and was trained for his very successful work in the course of his experience in southern schools. He was a devoted follower of Dr. Branson, Superintendent Willingham, Principals Washington and Moton, and Dr. Knapp; and the methods of the Jeanes Board as developed by Jackson Davis and Dr. Dillard were accepted and applied by him with great success.

Sibley was more than a school teacher, he was a diplomat who understood thoroughly the relations between the United States and Liberia. He sought to impress his fellow men with a sense of their obligation to bring to bear upon the problems of Africa the very best in American educational methods, economic development, and idealism. He sought to build in the dark continent a Christian civilization based upon a sound economic foundation. He taught that this could be done for the African only through education in agricultural and industrial arts. Upon his fellow Americans he urged fairness, patience, and coöperation. His life was an honor to his country, and in his death Africa and his native land both suffered a great loss.

In view of the need of instruction in agricultural and industrial arts among primitive peoples, an Agricultural Missions Foundation was organized in 1930 in the United States to coöperate with the various mission boards of the churches in extending these new methods to all countries where rural training is needed. Dr. John R. Mott is chairman and Dr. Thomas Jesse Jones is a leading member of the board, which is composed of directors of agricultural stations, presidents of colleges, and lay citizens. Considering that the peoples among whom missionaries labor are 90 per cent rural and ignorant of the simplest principles of sanitation and health conservation, as well as of the method of making a living, it is believed that all missions should pay more attention to these subjects.

This rural outlook in world-wide missionary enterprises is an outstanding development in recent decades, and the boards directing them are now looking more and more to America and especially to the institutions of the southern states for guidance in this work. Their agents and teachers come to Hampton, to Tuskegee, and to our agricultural colleges to study the methods of teaching practical agriculture and domestic economy. Dr. Knapp's demonstration methods and the plans of the boys' and girls' clubs and the Jeanes visiting teachers are being introduced in several foreign lands.

Finally, in regard to the influence of southern schools in foreign countries there is no finer testimony than that of Dean William F. Russell of Teachers College, Columbia University, given in his report for 1928-1929, in which he says : "To many of our foreign students the most illuminating and most inform-ing part in all our history of education is the relatively recent development of education in the southern states. Many coun-tries in the world today curiously resemble the South of a generation ago. There is the same spiritual discouragement re-sulting from unsuccessful warfare ; the same economic depres-sion . . . ; the same inability to forge ahead, due to the unpro-ductivity, the wastefulness and ill-health that are consequent upon lack of schooling ; and the same pride and self-reliance that refuse to ask for aid and scorn it when offered. Our foreign students follow with keen interest the way in which Dr. Knapp and his associates, by means of demonstration agents, corn, pig, and canning clubs, taught the children, and through them the elders, how to produce and conserve ; and thus developed an economic base upon which schools and other social agencies could be built. They watch the development of agricultural and home demonstration work. . . . In their imaginations they joined the party of travelers with Robert C. Ogden and learn how men and women of the North became interested in the problem. ". . . They watch the development of a system of schools in the South and see that this is followed by further increase of pro-duction, decrease of waste, and improved health, which in turn provide better education ; so that at the present time the South affords the North and the West examples of the best that is found in American education. . . . Thus our foreign students learn that the educational rehabilitation of the South was a result neither of schools and colleges supported by the North, of educational missionaries, nor of acts of Congress . . . ; but that the development came from the sequence of four factors : the presence of men of vision, the development of an economic base, the training of leaders, and the encouragement of their work of promotion at home. This is a significant lesson, possibly the most important to be learned from the history of ... the United States." No better analysis than this has been made of the methods, influence and results of the Southern Education Movement.

APPENDICES

APPENDIX I

MEMBERS OF THE FIRST CAPON SPRINGS CONFERENCE
June 29-July 3, 1898 [1]

W. P. Thirkield, Atlanta, Ga.; A. D. Mayo, Boston, Mass.; R. E. Lee Dinwiddie, Greenwood, Va.; John Wilkes, Charlotte, N. C.; Jane R. Wilkes, Charlotte, N. C.; E. S. Dreher, Columbia, S. C.; Geo. T. Fairchild, Berea, Ky.; Julius D. Dreher, Roanoke College, Va.; Thomas Lawrence, Asheville, N. C.; H. M. White, Winchester, Va.; Jas. A. Quarles, Lexington, Va.; John Eaton, Washington, D. C.; L. Y. Graham, Philadelphia, Pa.; Chas. F. Meserve, Raleigh, N. C.; James E. Gilbert, Washington, D. C.; Sarah J. Gilbert, Washington, D. C.; D. J. Satterfield; Edward Abbott, Cambridge, Mass.; Katharine K. Abbott, Cambridge, Mass.; T. J. Morgan ; Caroline S. Morgan, New York; Sarah L. Hunter ; Sister Ella, Morganton, N. C.; Nellie C. Satterfield, Scotia Seminary, Concord, N. C.; Kate B. Conrad, Winchester, Va.; T. U. Dudley, Bishop of Kentucky ; A. B. Hunter, Raleigh, N. C.; H. B. Frissell, Hampton, Va.; Edwd. C. Mitchell, New Orleans, La.; Marcia Savage Mitchell, New Orleans, La.; Alice S. Eaton, Washington, D. C.; May E. Kintzing, Brooklyn, N. Y.; Mary B. Landell, Philadelphia, Pa.; Helen Landell, Philadelphia, Pa.

APPENDIX II

EDUCATION IN THE SOUTHERN STATES

By Dr. J. L. M. Curry

Address at the Second Capon Springs Conference, 1899

I have been requested, said Curry, to present a survey of the educational field of the South. ... The starting-point is the War between the States, which resulted in the most gigantic revolution of modern times—the emancipation of slaves ; the disorganization of the entire labor system of the South ; the reversal of traditions, habits, and institutions ; the impoverishment of the South ; and the addition to the voting population of a large mass of people who, recently in bondage, were suddenly transformed by act of the United States into a body of citizens having the highest privileges and prerogatives. Few people can realize—no one outside the limits

[1] From the Minute Book, Capon Springs Conference (in manuscript), p. F.

of the Confederate States—how utterly transformed everything was; what an upheaval, overthrow, of cherished convictions, of habits of life, of social and political environments, and destruction of property. When the surrender of the armies under Lee and Johnston occurred there came the necessary duty of rehabilitation, of setting houses, churches, schools, and government in order for the new and the strange life. During the war, through the Freedmen's Bureau and a few religious organizations, efforts, partial and local, were begun toward giving some education to those who were within the Union lines. This... proper effort was often in the hands of fanatical men and women ignorant of negro peculiarities, inexperienced as to methods of teaching, full of self-conceit, and possessed of a fatal facility of rubbing the fur the wrong way.

It must be borne in mind that under the ancient régime no public-school system providing universal education existed at the South. There was no system adequate even to the education at public expense of the white youth. Our peculiar social system forbade the education of the negroes.... In the course of a few years systems for both races were established. The difficulties were very great. Population was sparse, roads were bad, school-houses did not exist, there was an absolute want of acquaintance with the machinery of public schools,... few competent teachers were to be had, and weighing down all spirit of hopeful progress was the dreary poverty of the taxpayer. It is impossible for those living north of Mason and Dixon's line to realize how universal and crushing was the bankruptcy of the South after Appomattox. In 1861 the real and personal property of Georgia was valued at $661,000,000. At the close of the war $121,000,000 were left. *Ex uno disce omnes.* Superadd the horrors of reconstruction, its robberies, insults, corruptions, incompetency of officials, and the deliberate attempt to put the white people in subjection to the negroes.

Despite the environments and the hopelessness of the outlook, there were a few men who felt that the salvation of the South, the recovery of its lost prestige, depended on universal education. They felt that no better service could be rendered to the country and the great problems which embarrassed or darkened action than a scheme of applying systems, tried and known elsewhere, to the renaissance of the South. Therefore, with hope and courage amid the gloom of disappointment and poverty and despair, the pressure of adverse circumstances, and the struggle for subsistence, they advocated and secured the incorporation into organic law of general education as the only measure which promised to lift up the lately servile race and restore the white people to their former prosperity. They persevered in their efforts until now, in view of the magnificent results achieved, we can set up our Ebenezers. Every State in the South has now State-established, State-controlled, State-supported schools for both races without legal discrimination as to benefits conferred. About $100,000,000, drawn very largely from the taxation of the white people, have been given for negro education, and 1,250,000 negro children are enrolled in the schools. Nothing in the history of civilization is comparable to this sublime self-denial and this work of enlarged patriotism.

When the Government emancipated the negroes there was an imperative resulting obligation to prepare them for citizenship and freedom, but the Government has persistently and cruelly refused to give one cent of aid to this indispensable work. Along with what the States have done, Northern religious societies and some benevolent men and women have given liberally for the education of the negroes, and such institutions as Hampton, Tuskegee, Spellman, Tougaloo, Claflin, Shaw, St. Augustine, and others have done most valuable service in preparing the negroes for their changed conditions. These schools, however valuable the work done by them, reach not more than 30,000 pupils ; and, if all these turned out well, what are they among so many? Every Southern man and woman is profoundly grateful for what Northern people have done for the education of the negroes ; for making coequal citizenship of the two races in the same territory an endurable possibility. The public free schools are the colleges of the people ; they are the nurseries of freedom ; their establishment and efficiency are the paramount duty of a republic. The education of children is the most legitimate object of taxation. Eighty-five or ninety per cent of the children will never know any education as given by schools except what they obtain in free State schools. It is not, therefore, a question of relative worth of different methods, but of education at all. . . .

It need hardly be said that our institutions of learning shared in the universal poverty which swept over our land. The colleges in some cases were used as barracks and hospitals for the soldiers. Libraries and apparatus were removed or destroyed, and in some instances there has been a weary waiting for compensation after proof clear and full, leaving no loop to hang a doubt upon. Buildings for dormitories and science halls, very much needed to meet pressing demands, are not finished for want of funds. Professors, faithful and scholarly, are poorly paid. Most pathetic calls from young men and young women, hungry for education, are heard, and yet they must be turned away in the absence of scholarships and endowments. Some single colored schools have a larger annual income and expend more for running expenses than any university except Johns Hopkins, and as much as the combined outlay of four or five white colleges. . . . Is there any wonder that Southern colleges cannot compare or compete with Harvard, Yale, Cornell, Princeton, or Chicago, with their plethoric millions? . . .

I shall not stultify myself by any fresh argument in favor of negro education, but I must be pardoned for emphasizing the fact that there is greater need for the education of the other race. The white people are to be the leaders, to take the initiative, to have the directive control in all matters pertaining to civilization and the highest interests of our beloved land. History demonstrates that the Caucasian will rule. He ought to rule. He made our Constitution; he achieved our independence; he is identified with all true progress, all high civilization; and, if true to his mission, while developing his own capabilities, he will lead out and on other races as far and as fast as their good and their possibilities will justify. This white supremacy does not mean hostility to the negro, but friendship for him. On the intelligent and more refined class of the white people the negroes have been compelled to rely heretofore for the educational advantages which they possess, and on them in the future they must depend to prevent a widening of the breach between the races and to bring about their higher advancement. It is hopeless to think of the small number of educated negroes protecting themselves against wrongs unless there be men and women, cultured, courageous, broad-minded, to correct, elevate, and lead public opinion. . . .[2]

Much has been said—too much cannot be said—of the negro problem. It does not "down" at any man's bidding. It is a living, ever-present, all-pervasive, apparently irremovable fact. Its solution

[2] That the whites of the South would have to be educated before much progress could be made with the education of the Negroes was the accepted view of the wisest thinkers of the North as well as of the South. In an address before the Senate in advocacy of his bill for federal aid, Senator Henry W. Blair, after quoting Dr. Curry where he said that the southern people had paid out, up to that time, for the education of the Negroes $50,000,000, and General Armstrong where he said that the southern tax-payers were doing more than any others at that time for the Negroes by maintaining 16,000 free schools for them at an annual cost of $3,000,000 and that of every $100 of this $91.50 was paid by the white people, added: "If I were undertaking to do the best possible thing for the negro child, I would give every dollar to the education of the whites, so as to dissipate the ignorance in the white community, for, as you remove ignorance, you remove prejudice, and as you increase intelligence, you render more comfortable the situation of the colored man and his child. . . . There is nothing we can do which will be an ultimate and permanent remedy of the evils we complain of at the South, so far as the colored man and his suffrage are concerned, until the whole community is transformed by the magic power of education, and we must begin with the white child, and if we get money enough, help both."

baffles statesmanship and philanthropy. Education—moral, intellectual, industrial, civic—should be persistently, generously furnished; but, if universal, it is slow in its results; and, while immensely beneficial, does not settle irreconcilable racial antagonisms, and it leaves two heterogeneous, unassimilable peoples as coequal citizens with growing cleavage in the same territory. Preachers, sociologists, humanitarians, with their altruistic speculations, may from a safe distance pooh-pooh the problem, but there it is and there it will remain.

Recent tragic occurrences at the South are not the gravamen of the problem. They are horrifying, but are incidents. . . . It needs no argument that the more debased, the less self-reliant, the more unskilled, the more thriftless and unemployed the race or any portion of it is, the more dangerous it will be, the less desirable as inhabitant, as laborer, as citizen, as voter. Plato said a man not sufficiently or properly trained is the most savage animal on earth. Nothing can be more illogical, more indefensible, more unjust, more cruel, more harmful to both races than to hold the negroes responsible for the outrages of a few of their race. . . .

It is sometimes said that we must rely on the universities to furnish the means of meeting social and civil questions, and for leading a community or nation out of darkness into light, out of bondage into freedom. Such is not my reading of history. Art grew out of handicraft. The revival of real art came from a new beginning among humble craftsmen and hard-working artisans. Political reforms for amelioration of the condition of the masses have been achieved with unrelenting opposition of those in power and in high places who are on the catalogues of universities. It is an interesting fact, says President Harper, that all the great religious truths were worked out in the popular mind before they were formulated by the thinkers. Nearly every step in throwing off the tyrannies of church establishments and winning freedom of worship has been taken with the bitter, insulting, unforgiving hostility of those who boasted of their social and intellectual superiority. Exceptions honorable there have been, but the truth remains that not all of the advancements of the race have been due to those who have had the advantages of highest instruction. It is upon the condition of the great masses of the people, and not upon the elevation and welfare of a limited and privileged class, that we must mainly rely for the stability of our free institutions and for the permanent maintenance of public order.

Far be it from me to underrate the utility of these institutions, which are monuments to the dignity and worth of the human mind; exert a conservative influence on society; furnish, through the vigilance of the wise, safeguards of freedom, and are essential to our safety and well-being at home and to our honor abroad. . . . My contention is that our main dependence as a republic is on the capacity and integrity of our general citizenship, and the importance of the trust demands the use and improvement of every educational agency from kindergarten to university. Ours is a federal, democratic, constitutional, representative republic, and individual liberty is greater and can be safely intrusted in proportion as people rise in the scale of virtue, intelligence, patriotism, and in acquaintance with the nature and ends of free government. When a people are ignorant, superstitious, debased, corrupt, purchasable, the prey of demagogues and adventurers, the slaves of prejudice and passion, individual liberty is less and less, until it becomes extinct and despotism is a necessity. Our American republic, which we love, is the guardian of the holiest trust ever committed to a people. . . .

These representative institutions must not perish nor be set aside as vain experiments, nor replaced by forms or realities which deny popular sovereignty and the blessings of a written constitution. We must all feel that in us and in our republic the highest life of man is vitally and inseparably associated. Our country is the glory of earth, the hope of the oppressed of all lands, the realization of the dignity of man, . . . the fulfillment of the dreams of all who have built their hopes on human capabilities and human liberty, and nothing can surpass the duty to omit no exertion of transmitting unimpaired all these blessings and hopes to those who are to come after us, and this can only be done by an educated citizenship.[3]

APPENDIX III

LIST OF GUESTS OF MR. ROBERT C. OGDEN TO THE CONFERENCE FOR EDUCATION IN THE SOUTH

Winston-Salem, N. C., April 18-20, 1901

Rev. Lyman Abbott, D.D., and Mrs. Abbott, New York City ; Robert Admanson, the *New York World*, New York City ; Mrs. S. C. Armstrong, Hampton Institute, Hampton, Va.; President Truman J. Backus, Packer Institute, Brooklyn, N. Y. ; Mr. and Mrs. William H. Baldwin, Jr., New York City ; Mr. and Mrs. W. D. Barbour ; George Gray Barnard, New York City ; Mr. and Mrs. Charles E. Bigelow ; Dr. David Bovaird ; Dr. and Mrs. John Graham Brooks,

[3] *Proceedings of the Second Capon Springs Conference for Education in the South, Capon Springs, W. Va., 1899*, pp. 25-32.

Cambridge, Mass. ; John Crosby Brown, New York City ; Reverend L. T. Chamberlain, D.D., New York City ; Reverend and Mrs. Henry E. Cobb, New York City ; Dr. J. L. M. Curry, Washington, D. C.; H. Y. Darnall ; Miss Jane E. Davis, Hampton Institute, Hampton, Va. ; Reverend G. S. Dickerman, D.D., New Haven, Conn. ; Miss Dickerman, New Haven, Conn. ; Right Reverend William C. Doane, Bishop of Albany, and Mrs. Doane, Albany, N. Y. ; Mr. and Mrs. Frank Nelson Doubleday, New York City ; Rev. Albert Erdman, D.D., and Mrs. Erdman ; A. S. Frissell, New York City ; Dr. H. B. Frissell, Principal of Hampton Institute, Hampton, Va. ; Henry Wilder Foote, Boston, Mass. ; James T. Gardiner, New York City ; Doane Gardiner, New York City ; Julian Hawthorne, New York City ; Mrs. Charles W. Ide, Brooklyn, N. Y. ; President James MacAlister, Drexel Institute, Philadelphia, Pa. ; Right Reverend W. N. McVickar, Bishop of Rhode Island, Providence, R. I. ; V. Everit Macy, New York City ; Miss Ellen F. Mason ; Dr. and Mrs. John Meigs ; Reverend George E. Moore, Providence, R. I. ; Miss Belle Noyes ; Mrs. Robert C. Ogden, New York City ; Robert M. Ogden, New York City ; Dr. and Mrs. Walter Hines Page, New York City ; Reverend Charles H. Parkhurst, D.D., New York City ; Reverend Francis G. Peabody, D.D., and Mrs. Peabody, Cambridge, Mass. ; George Foster Peabody, New York City; Alexander Purves, Treasurer of Hampton Institute, Hampton, Va., and Mrs. Purves, Hampton Institute, Hampton, Va. ; Mr. and Mrs. William Howell Reed ; John D. Rockefeller, Jr., New York City ; Dean James E. Russell, Teachers College, Columbia University, and Mrs. Russell, New York City ; Dr. William Jay Schieffelin, New York City ; Dr. Albert Shaw, Editor of the *Review of Reviews*, New York City ; Miss Florence Sibley ; Miss Mary Lamar Turpin, Washington, D. C. ; Mrs. William Potter Wilson, Philadelphia, Pa. ; Mrs. Joseph Yeoman, New York City.

APPENDIX IV

SOCIETY FOR EDUCATION IN THE SOUTH [4]

to be developed out of the ("Capon Springs") Conference for Education in the South at the next meeting.

OBJECT : The promotion of public education in the South, especially "free public schools for all the people, black and white alike."

[4] Submitted by Charles W. Dabney at the meeting in Mr. Ogden's office in June, 1901.

MEMBERS : Those enrolled at the Salem meeting. Form hereafter a fixed membership by election ; fee small.

OFFICERS : Mr. Robert C. Ogden, President, &c., as at present.

EXECUTIVE BOARD : Of the President and seven members as at present, authorized to be appointed by the President ; two or three from the North, and four or five from the South.

OBJECT : To take charge of the propaganda work of the Society (see Resolution). A Campaign of Education in the South to be carried on for at least five years.

METHODS : (1) A literary bureau. Work through newspapers, serial publications (using second class rates), leaflets, &c.

(2) Bureau of information and advice on school legislation and organization, addressing meetings, institutions, &c.

OFFICERS : A chief executive officer, chairman or secretary, writers, field agents, clerks, &c.

HEADQUARTERS : In some centrally located Southern city, having requisite facilities, preferably an educational centre, having libraries, &c.

FUNDS : Try to raise at least $25,000 for first year, increasing to $50,000, for five years.

EXPENSES : Printing, folding, mailing ; salaries, travelling expenses, office rents, &c.

APPENDIX V

A BRIEF STATEMENT

CONCERNING THE ORIGIN AND ORGANIZATION OF THE

SOUTHERN EDUCATION BOARD

THE EXECUTIVE BOARD OF THE CONFERENCE
FOR EDUCATION IN THE SOUTH

———

The fourth annual assembly of the Conference was held at Winston-Salem, N. C., in April, 1901. In the course of the proceedings the following platform, preamble and resolutions were unanimously adopted.

The Conference for Education in the South, on occasion of its fourth annual meeting, held at Winston-Salem, April 18, 19, and 20, 1901, reaffirmed its conviction that the overshadowing and supreme public need of our time, as we pass the threshold of a new century, is the education of the children of all the people. We declare such education to be the foremost task of our statesmanship, and the most worthy object of philanthropy. With the expansion of our population and the growth of industry and economic resources, we recognize in a fitting and universal education and training for the home, for the farm and the workshop, and for the exercise of the duties of citizenship, the only salvation for our American standards of family and social life and the only hope for the perpetuity of our institutions, founded by our forefathers on the four corner-stones of intelligence, virtue, economic efficiency and capacity for political self-control. We recognize the value of efforts hitherto made to solve our educational problems, both as respects the methods to be used, and also as regards the sheer quantity of the work to be done. But we also find in the facts as presented at the sessions of this Conference the imperative need of renewed efforts on a larger scale; and we also find in the improved financial outlook of the country and in the advancing state of public opinion better hopes than ever before of a larger response to this greater need. As the first great need of our people is adequate elementary instruction, and as this instruction must come to children so largely through mothers and women teachers in their homes and primary schools, we desire to emphasize our belief in the wisdom of making the most liberal investments possible in the education of girls and women.

WHEREAS, therefore, the conditions existing in the Southern States seem now fully ripe for the large development as well as further improvement of the schools; and,

WHEREAS, This Conference desires to associate itself actively with the work of organizing better school systems and extending their advantages to all the people,

Resolved, That this Conference proceed to organize by the appointment of an Executive Board of seven, who shall be fully authorized and empowered to conduct:

1. A campaign of education for free schools for all the people, by supplying literature to the newspaper and periodical press, by participation in educational meetings and by general correspondence; and,

2. To conduct a Bureau of Information and Advice on Legislation and School Organization.

For these purposes this board is authorized to raise funds and disburse them, to employ a secretary or agent, and to do whatever may be necessary to carry out effectively these measures and others that may from time to time be found feasible and desirable.

Under this direction of the Conference, the President named the following members of the Board.

Hon J. L. M. Curry, Agent of the Peabody and Slater Boards, Washington, D. C.

Dr. Charles W. Dabney, President of the University of Tennessee, Knoxville, Tenn.

Dr. E. A. Alderman, President of Tulane University, New Orleans, La.

Dr. C. D.. McIver, President North Carolina State Normal and Industrial College for Women, Greensboro, N. C.

Dr. H. B. Frissell, Principal Hampton Institute, Hampton, Va.

Rev. Wallace Buttrick, D.D., Albany, N. Y.

George Foster Peabody, New York.

The Board held its first meeting in the City of New York in the week beginning November 3d, 1901. It then added to its membership :

William H. Baldwin, Jr., New York.

Dr. Albert Shaw, New York.

Dr. Walter H. Page, New York.

Hon. H. H. Hanna, Indianapolis, Ind.

By special action of the Conference, its President, *Robert C. Ogden* was created a member of the Board.

The Board was organized by the election of

Robert C. Ogden, President.

Charles D. McIver, Secretary.

George Foster Peabody, Treasurer.

Under the instructions of the preamble and resolutions the Board has decided that no portion of the fixed sum of money it hopes to secure for current expenses shall be applied "to the assistance of any institution or school, but that it shall be expended exclusively for the purpose of stimulating public sentiment in favor of more liberal provision for universal education in the public schools."

The practical work of the Board is in the form of a popular propaganda, through its own printed issues, the public press and more especially public speech—the living epistle.

The plan of organization includes the following :

Supervising Director, Hon. J. L. M. Curry, Washington, D. C.

Director of Bureau of Information and Investigation, Dr. Charles W. Dabney, Knoxville, Tenn.

District Directors, Dr. C. D. McIver, Greensboro, N. C. ; Dr. E. A. Alderman, New Orleans, La. ; Dr. H. B. Frissell, Hampton, Va.

Campaign Committee, Hon. J. L. M. Curry, Chairman ; Dr. Charles W. Dabney, Dr. C. D. McIver, Dr. E. A. Alderman, Dr. H. B. Frissell.

Field Agents, Dr. G. S. Dickerman, New Haven, Conn.; Dr. Booker T. Washington, Tuskegee, Ala.

Executive Secretary Associated with the President, Rev. Edgar Gardner Murphy, Montgomery, Ala.

By the operation of the plan indicated in the foregoing the Board will call into its service other prominent men who cannot yet be named.

Contributions may be sent to George Foster Peabody, Treasurer, No. 27 Pine Street, New York.

General correspondence may be addressed to Rev. Edgar Gardner Murphy, Montgomery, Ala.

APPENDIX VI

PUBLICATIONS OF
THE BUREAU OF THE SOUTHERN EDUCATION BOARD
March 10, 1902, to December 21, 1903

CIRCULARS

No. 1, April, 1902, *Southern Education Board : Its Origin and Purpose.*

No. 2, May, 1902, *Thomas Jefferson on Public Education.*

No. 3, June, 1902, *A Statement Concerning the Southern Education Board.*

No. 4, October, 1902, *Progress within the Year.*

BULLETINS

May, 1902, *Educational Conditions in the Southern Appalachians.*

December, 1902, *Educational Conditions in Tennessee.* Continued as a series under the title of *Southern Education :*

No. 1, March 12, 1903, Local Taxation ; Better School Houses ; Consolidation of Schools ; School Libraries.

No. 2, March 19, 1903, Trained Teachers and Expert Supervision.

No. 3, March 26, 1903, Value of Education ; Preparation of Teachers.

No. 4, April 2, 1903, School Houses ; Local Taxation ; A Teachers' College.

No. 5, April 9, 1903, The German High School Teacher ; Local Taxation ; Southern Education Board ; Horace Mann on Necessity of Training for Teaching.

No. 6, April 16, 1903, The Tennessee Campaign ; Local Taxation.

No. 7, April 23, 1903, Some Supervision Data ; The Race Question ; Illiteracy Statistics ; The South Carolina Campaign ; Comparative Church and School House Values ; School House Improvement Recommendations.

Nos. 8 and 9, May 7, 1903, *The Richmond Conference ;* The Negro at Richmond.

No. 10, May 14, 1903, *North Carolina Edition :* County Supervision ; Educational Waste ; Local Taxation ; Illiteracy ; School Houses ; Rural Libraries ; Teachers and Salaries.

Nos. 11 and 12, May 28, 1903, *Rural Libraries ;* A Rural Graded School Described.

Nos. 13 and 14, June 11, 1903, *Louisiana Edition :* Local Taxation ; Money Value of Education ; Louisiana Constitution and Schools ; Digest of School Laws ; Illiteracy ; Supervision and Consolidation.

Nos. 15 and 16, July 10, 1903, *Mississippi Edition :* Rural Schools ; Local Taxation ; Consolidation ; Population and Illiteracy.

No. 17, October 1, 1903, *South Carolina Edition :* Consolidation ; County Superintendents ; Woman's Work ; Population and Illiteracy ; School Libraries ; Local Taxation.

No. 18, November 2, 1903, *Rural Libraries :* Libraries and the Public Schools ; A Rural School Library Described ; Rural Libraries in the South ; Public Libraries.

No. 19, December 1, 1903, *Woman's Edition :* North Carolina Woman's Association for the Betterment of School Houses ; Work of the Federation of Women's Clubs in the Southern States ; Norfolk Kindergarten Association.

No. 20, December 21, 1903, *Education of the Negro :* Comparison of White and Negro Illiteracy ; Kind of Education the Negro Needs ; The Negro as an Economic Factor in Southern Life ; Division of Public School Funds ; Outpost Work of Tuskegee Institute ; The Negro Common School ; Negro Schools before the War ; Compulsory School Attendance.

Southern Education Notes

A Bi-Weekly Series of educational notes in convenient form for use by newspaper editors, 26 numbers.

APPENDIX VII

DECLARATION OF PRINCIPLES
1902

We, the 1,700 teachers attending the Summer School of the South, representing every Southern State, do, on this the day of our national independence, unanimously adopt the following declaration of educational policy :

1. We bear grateful testimony to the great sacrifices made in behalf of education by the people of the South, who in their desolation and poverty have taxed themselves hundreds of millions of dollars to educate two races.

2. Notwithstanding these efforts, we are confronted with the appalling fact that the large majority of the 3,500,000 white children and 2,500,000 black children of the South are not provided with good schools. In 1900 ten Southern States having twenty-five per cent of the school population of this country owned only four per cent of the public school property and expended only six and a half per cent of the public school moneys. We must recognize these conditions and frankly face them. We therefore declare ourselves in favor of a public school system, State supported and State directed, in which every child may have the open door of opportunity.

3. Conscious of our dependence upon the God of our fathers, and believing that the highest and truest civilization can be attained only by following the precepts of the great teacher, Jesus Christ, we favor the recognition of the Bible in our public schools.

4. We regard local taxation as the foundation upon which a public school system should be built, and therefore favor an agitation in behalf of such taxation in every community.

5. If an increased expenditure of money is to be of lasting value, a more intelligent public interest must be brought to bear upon our schools. But even greater than the need of money and interest is the need of intelligent direction.

6. A mere extension of the present school term with the present course of study will not meet the needs of the children. The lines of development in the South must be both agricultural and mechanical. Our people must bring a trained brain and a trained hand to the daily labor. Education should be a means not of escaping labor, but of making it more effective.

The school should be the social center of the community, and should actively and sympathetically touch all the social and economic interests of the people. In addition to the usual academic studies, therefore, our courses should include manual training, nature study and agriculture.

7. To secure more efficient supervision, to encourage grading and to broaden the social life of the children, we favor the consolidation of weak schools into strong central schools. It is better in every way to carry the child to the school than to carry the school to the child. We indorse the movements recently made by the women of the South for model schools, built with due regard to sanitation, ventilation and beauty.

8. Teaching should be a profession, and not a stepping-stone to something else. We therefore stand for the highest training of teachers and urge the school authorities of every State to encourage those who wish to make the educating of children a life profession. We call upon the people to banish forever politics and nepotism from the public schools, and to establish a system in which, from the humblest teacher to the office of state superintendent, merit shall be the touchstone.

9. We express our hearty appreciation of the work of the Southern and General Education Boards, which by their earnest sympathy and generous means have made possible this great Summer School of the South and in numerous other ways are strengthening the patriotic efforts of the Southern people to improve their educational conditions.

10. With gratitude to our fathers for the heritage of a noble past, with thankfulness to God for the many blessings bestowed upon our people, with due recognition of our present problems and their deep importance, we face the future with a faith which we shall endeavor to make good by our works, to the lasting glory of our Republic.

(Signed)

Alabama, Edgar Gardner Murphy ; Arkansas, A. H. Abbott ; Florida, Arthur Williams ; Georgia, Joseph D. Smith ; Kentucky, J. T. Gaines ; Louisiana, Edwin A. Alderman ; Mississippi, D. H. Hill ; North Carolina, Collier Cobb ; South Carolina, Ernest Wiggins ; Tennessee, Wickliffe Rose ; Texas, A. L. Malone ; Virginia, B. R. Smith.

CHARLES D. McIVER,   CHARLES W. DABNEY,
        Secretary   *Chairman*

APPENDIX VIII

PURPOSES AND METHODS OF THE SOUTHERN EDUCATION CONFERENCE

EXCERPTS FROM ROBERT C. OGDEN'S OPENING ADDRESS AT THE
RICHMOND CONFERENCE IN 1903

The inquiry is legitimate: "What is the theory of this Conference?" The reply is clear: ... "The Conference exists for the advancement and promotion of the education of all the people." ... This Conference has created nothing, but has merely brought together influences that have been growing for many years in separate places.... We are happy to find here in ... Richmond, as we found in every place where we have been privileged to meet, hosts of earnest souls filled with the desires which move this Conference.... All are perfectly familiar with the sovereign demands—material, intellectual, spiritual—of educational interests. Executive combinations of many sorts—land, buildings, taxation, legislation, systems, methods—are under requisition for the service. Its infinite details increasingly enlist the ... toil of hundreds of thousands of painstaking teachers, men and women, representing every grade of instruction from the simplest to the most abstruse.

For the moment, in the center and foreground of this vast perspective, stands this Conference—a composite aggregation of men and women.... Some are profoundly ignorant of the technicalities of education, quite unfamiliar ... with recitation rooms or the methods of ... the school. Others belong to the ... fraternity of teachers, ... representatives of every rank in the profession. Still others are charged with the official responsibility of educational management on behalf of the state or corporate bodies. All are here with one accord in one place—officials and citizens, professionals and laity—by reason of a common belief in the beneficent power of education.... So much for the personnel of the Conference.

. . . . .

From the foundation of our government until now, ringing out ... with clarion voice, rising ... distinct above the clamor of politics—above the loud barking of the dogs of war, above the harsh controversies concerning the nature of the national federation, above the debates upon the ethics of domestic institutions—the note of democracy ... has ever resounded dominant and universal.... In a very special way, our political institutions unfold an inspired mission that deeply concerns the moral progress of the world. . . . But a true democracy can only exist through the fidelity of its citizens. Individualism—cynical, selfish, cold and indifferent—cries out: "Am I my brother's keeper?" "Who is my neighbor?" A true democracy answers quickly: "Thy brother is he that hath need of thee." . . . There is a divinity in democracy; in society as in the individual there is personal and organic spiritual life. Witness the restless longing for social service that marks the serious side of present-day life in America. So much for the patriotic inspiration of the Conference.

And thus it has come about that this varied collection of men and women, moved by ethical and patriotic incentives, have come from many remote localities that they may be mutually instructed and inspired in a conference based upon the common belief that the general education of all the people is essential to the salvation of society; that without general education, progress in the arts, in the diffusion of happiness, in the things that make for the good character, family peace, clean living, human brotherhood, civic righteousness and national justice is impossible. In this atmosphere of a common human sympathy the Conference for Education in the South lives and moves and has its being. . . .

The program presented to the Conference, . . . demands no explanation. It speaks for itself. . . . Within the limitation of this orderly program this Conference is an open forum. . . . Its function is inspiration by discussion rather than decision. Resolutions have never been its vogue. Its conclusions have been enshrined in individual thought and not expressed in the vote of a majority. . . . The intrusion of disagreement into a domain of thought and sentiment . . . so sacred has seemed to all to be sacrilege. Thus the life of the Conference has been that of unity and agreement. The standing ground of common need is so broad, the vital point . . . so eminent; points of difference are so . . . inconsequent that perfect accord in those aims has been natural—any other condition would be contradictory to the spirit of the men and women here assembled. . . . If this description of the theory and practice of the Conference meets with approval, let the resolve be to add another year of rich experience to . . . its previous useful record. . . ."

[Referring to the recent death of the great southern leader who had inspired the movement Mr. Ogden said]

The appeal for personal service in this cause of popular education comes with largely added force from the fact, so painfully impressed upon us today, that we meet with ranks sadly broken. The Nestor of this Conference, Dr. J. L. M. Curry . . . has paid the debt to nature. . . . The solemnity with which we face the question of the personal call to duty is made more profound by his inspiring example. . . . The intense personal force of his nature was dedicated with uncompromising devotion to the work of universal education. The moulding power of his constructive mind will ever remain permanently impressed upon the educational systems of our Southern states. . . . His example is a call to duty, his legacy to us is a bequest of labor for the cause he loved. As the standard has fallen from his hand, let us raise and carry it floating skyward until we in turn surrender it to other hands. And then may it be ours to leave the same impress of a noble task well performed as a benediction to our world and a challenge to others." [5]

APPENDIX IX

The following statement of the total sums contributed by Mr. Rockefeller and his son to the various Boards up to March, 1932, was furnished by the Foundation:

Gifts of Mr. John D. Rockefeller and son:

To the General Education Board	$129,209,167.10
To the Rockefeller Foundation, including $50,000 given by Mrs. Laura Spelman Rockefeller	182,791,624.00
To the Laura Spelman Rockefeller Memorial, consolidated in 1929 with the Rockefeller Foundation	73,875,457.37
To the Rockefeller Sanitary Commission, the work of which was continued by the International Health Commission as an integral part of the work of the Rockefeller Foundation . .	1,000,000.00
Gifts of Mr. John D. Rockefeller, Jr.:	
To the International Education Board	21,116,785.78
	$407,993,034.25

No money was given by Mr. Rockefeller direct either to the International Health Commission, subsequently the International Health Board and then the International Health Division of the Rockefeller Foundation, or to the China Medical Board which likewise was an administrative organ of the Rockefeller Foundation until incorporation in 1929 of a China Medical Board with independent self-perpetuating Trustees. At that time a sum of $12,-

[5] *Proceedings of the Sixth Conference for Education in the South*, Richmond, 1903, pp. 18-31.

000,000 was set aside by the Rockefeller Foundation for the China Medical Board.

The total gifts of the General Education Board to the Southern Education Board amounted to $97,126.23.

BIBLIOGRAPHY

A. PRIMARY SOURCES

I. LETTERS AND OTHER MANUSCRIPTS

(All the manuscripts, letters, and pamphlets collected by the author and remaining his property, have been deposited in the Southern Historical Collection of the Library of the University of North Carolina.)

Alderman, Edwin A. Letter to Charles Wm. Dabney, Dec. 31, 1929.

Branson, Eugene C. Letter to Charles Wm. Dabney, Oct. 27, 1902.

Buttrick, Wallace. Letter to George S. Dickerman, Jan. 21, 1903.

Chambers, Frank Ross. Recollections of Robert C. Ogden. MS in collection of papers of Robert C. Ogden in the Library of Congress.

Chambers, Kate W. (Mrs. Frank R.). Recollections of Miss Julia Tutwiler, Oct., 1932.

Claxton, P. P. Letter to Charles Wm. Dabney, Sept. 8, 1929.

—— Letter to Charles Wm. Dabney, Jan. 5, 1932.

—— Manuscript reports of the fourth (June 20 to July 28, 1905) to the tenth (June 20 to July 28, 1911) sessions, inclusive, of the Summer School of the South, Knoxville, Tenn.

—— Memorandum for Charles Wm. Dabney, Sept. 18, 1931.

Curry, J. L. M. Papers of, deposited in the Library of Congress.

Dabney, Charles Wm. Manuscript report on the first Summer School of the South, June 19 to July 31, 1902, Knoxville, Tenn., to the Peabody Education Board and the Southern Education Board.

Dickerman, George S. (Associate Secretary of the Southern Education Board). Papers of, including letter books and scrapbooks. Donated for use in writing the history of the Southern Education Board. Deposited in the Southern Historical Collection of the Library of the University of North Carolina, Chapel Hill, N. C.

Dreher, Julius D. A Short Account of the First Conference for Christian Education in the South, Capon Springs, West Virginia, June 29 to July 2, 1898; *and also* The Fourth Conference, at Winston-Salem, 1901. (Written for Charles Wm. Dabney.)

Eggleston, Joseph D. Letter to Charles Wm. Dabney, Aug. 25, 1931.

—— Memorandum for Charles Wm. Dabney, Oct. 17, 1933.

Frissell, Hollis Burke. Copies of letters and publications of Hampton Institute. Donated for use in writing the history of the Southern Education Board. Deposited in the Southern Historical Collection of the Library of the University of North Carolina.

Hale, George E. Letters to Charles Wm. Dabney, Jan. 27 and March 23, 1932.

Harllee, Col. William Curry. Letter to Charles Wm. Dabney, Nov. 25, 1933.

Hunter, A. B. Letter to Charles Wm. Dabney, July 8, 1931.

Jarvis, Thomas J. Letter to Charles Wm. Dabney, July 3, 1902.

Johnson, D. B. Letter to Dr. G. S. Dickerman, June 28, 1901.

Joyner, James Yadkin (State Superintendent of Public Instruction of North Carolina, 1902-1918). Papers of, letters and reports. Donated for writing the history of the Southern Education Movement. Deposited in the Southern Historical Collection of the Library of the University of North Carolina.

Lambert, J. S. Letter to Charles Wm. Dabney, Apr. 5, 1935.

Lillie, Frank R. Letter to Charles Wm. Dabney, Feb. 17, 1932.

McIver, Charles Duncan. Papers of. In the possession of the Woman's College of the University of North Carolina, Greensboro, N. C.

Millikan, Robert A. Letter to Charles Wm. Dabney, Feb. 1, 1932.

Minor, John B. Letter to William H. Ruffner, May 28, 1870. In the collection of papers of Dr. Ruffner in the Historical Foundation of the Presbyterian and Reformed Churches, Montreat, N. C.

Moseley, J. R. Letter to Charles Wm. Dabney, Oct. 31, 1932.

Ogden, Robert Curtis. Papers of. Deposited in the Library of Congress. Used through the courtesy of his daughter, Mrs. Alexander Purves of Hampton Institute, Va., and New York City.

Page, Walter Hines. Papers from his files in the possession of his son, Arthur W. Page, New York City.

Payne, Bruce R. Memorandum for Charles Wm. Dabney, Jan. 23, 1933.

Peabody, George Foster. Letter to Charles Wm. Dabney, June 6, 1934.

Pummill, L. E. Biographical Sketch of William Knox Tate. Manuscript filed in the Library of the George Peabody College, Nashville, Tenn.

Rose, Wickliffe. Letter to Robert C. Ogden, June 11, 1913.

Ruffner, William H. Diary, March 2, 1870, to August 24, 1907. Among the Papers of William Henry Ruffner, deposited in the Historical Foundation of the Presbyterian and Reformed Churches, Montreat, N. C.

——— An Educated Negro Preacher of a Century Ago, John Chavis. MS among the Papers of William Henry Ruffner, deposited in the Historical Foundation of the Presbyterian and Reformed Churches, Montreat, N. C.

—— Letter to J. A. McGilvray, Jan. 31, 1902.

—— Letter to A. D. Mayo, Jan., 1900.

The Southern Education Board. Files of the Executive Secretaries, Wickliffe Rose and A. P. Bourland. Deposited in the Southern Historical Collection of the Library of the University of North Carolina.

Stiles, Charles W. Certain Factors Operative in Public Health Advancement in the South since 1900. MS report on progress in combating the hookworm. 1931.

—— Letter to Burton J. Hendrick, May 22, 1922. (Copy to the author through the courtesy of Mr. Arthur W. Page.)

Wallace, D. D. Letter to Dr. Patterson Wardlaw, June 17, 1931.

Wright, J. C. Letter to Charles Wm. Dabney, Apr. 23, 1935.

II. OFFICIAL PUBLICATIONS

1. General

Buttrick, Wallace. The Beginning and Aims of the General Education Board. Journal of Proceedings and Addresses of the Forty-second Annual Meeting of the National Educational Association, Boston, Mass., 1903. Winona, Minn., published by the Association, 1903.

Capon Springs Conferences for Education in the South, Proceedings of, 1898 to 1900. (The original Minute Book as well as the printed proceedings.)

Commission on Industrial Relations. Final Report and Testimony, Vol. IX. Washington, 1916.

Conference for Education in the South, Proceedings of, 1901-1914.

Congressional Record, Feb. 3—March 7, 1890, Vol. XXI, Part II.

Curry, Jabez Lamar Monroe (General Agent). Reports to the Trustees of the John F. Slater Fund, 1891-1902. Proceedings of the Trustees of the John F. Slater Fund, 1892-1902.

—— (General Agent). Reports to the Trustees of the Peabody Education Fund, 1881-1902. Proceedings of the Trustees of the Peabody Education Fund, Vols. III-VI. Cambridge, John Wilson and Son, 1888-1916.

Dickerman, George S. The Conference for Education in the South and the Southern Education Board. Report of the U. S. Commissioner of Education, 1907, Vol. I. Washington, 1908.

Federal Board for Vocational Education, Bull. No. 167. (The Earning Ability of Farmers who have Received Vocational Training. By Walter S. Newman.) Washington, June, 1933. Reprinted as a pamphlet.

General Education Board. An Account of Its Activities, 1902-1914. New York, 1915.

—— Annual Reports, 1914-1915 to 1932-1933.

High School Quarterly, Vol. XVIII, No. 4 (July, 1930). Official Organ of the Southern Commission on Accredited Schools of the Georgia High School and National High School Inspectors Association. Athens, Ga.

John F. Slater Fund. Occasional Papers, No. 14. County Teacher Training Schools for Negroes. 1913.

—— Occasional Papers, No. 1. Documents Relating to the Origin and Work of the Slater Trustees, 1882 to 1894. 1894.

—— Occasional Papers, No. 23. A Study of County Training Schools for Negroes in the South, by Leo Mortimer Favrot. 1923.

—— Proceedings and Reports, 1903-1904 to 1920; 1925; 1928; 1929.

—— Proceedings of the Trustees, 1892-1934.

Jones, Thomas Jesse. Negro Education. United States Bureau of Education, Bull. No. 38, Vol. I, 1916; Bull. No. 39, Vol. II, 1916.

Julius Rosenwald Fund. A Review to June 30, 1928. Chicago, 1928.

—— Review for the Two-Year Period, 1931-1933. Chicago, 1933.

Knapp, S. A. The Farmers' Coöperative Demonstration Work. United States Department of Agriculture Year Book for 1909.

Negro Rural School Fund, Inc. (Anna T. Jeanes Foundation) 1907-1933. Washington, published by the Negro Rural School Fund, Inc., 1933.

Negro Year Book: An Annual Encyclopaedia of the Negro. Monroe N. Work, ed. Tuskegee Institute, Alabama.

Peabody Education Fund. Memorial of the Trustees, with the Report of their Committee on the subject of the Education of the Colored Population of the Southern States, February 19, 1880. Cambridge University Press: John Wilson and Son, 1880. Published also in the Proceedings of the Trustees listed immediately below.

—— Proceedings of the Trustees. 6 vols. Boston and Cambridge, John Wilson and Son, 1875-1916.

Phelps-Stokes Fund. Educational Adaptations, Report of Ten Years' Work, 1910-1920. New York, Phelps-Stokes Fund.

—— Twenty-Year Report, 1911-1931. New York, Phelps-Stokes Fund, 1932.

Rockefeller Foundation. Annual Reports, 1913-1914 to 1933.

—— A Review for 1920. New York, 1921.

—— A Review for 1926. New York, 1927.

Rockefeller Sanitary Commission for the Eradication of Hookworm Disease. Reports for 1910-1914. Washington, Offices of the Commission, 1910-1915.

Rose, Wickliffe. The Educational Movement in the South. Report of the United States Commissioner of Education, 1903, Vol. I. Washington, 1905.

Sears, Barnas (General Agent). Reports to the Trustees of the Peabody Education Fund, 1868-1880. Proceedings of the Trustees of the Peabody Education Fund, Vols. I-II. Boston, John Wilson and Son, 1875-1881.

Slater Fund. See John F. Slater Fund.

Southern Education Board, Minutes of, 1901-1914.

Southern Society for the Promotion of the Study of Race Conditions and Problems in the South. Proceedings of the First Annual Conference at Montgomery, Alabama, 1900. Richmond, Va., B. F. Johnson Publishing Company, 1900.

Summer School of the South. Announcement, 1902. University of Tennessee Index, Ser. 3, No. 2 (March, 1902).

—— Announcement and Courses of Study, 1903. University of Tennessee Record, Vol. VI, No. 4 (April, 1903).

—— Announcement and Courses of Study, 1904. University of Tennessee Record, Vol. VII, No. 4 (April, 1904).

Territory South of the Ohio River, Acts and Ordinances of the Governors and Judges of the, Chap. XVIII, 1794.

True, Alfred Charles. A History of Agricultural Extension Work in the United States, 1785-1923. United States Department of Agriculture Miscellaneous Publication No. 15, October, 1928. Washington, 1928.

Tuskegee Normal and Industrial Institute. Principal's Annual Report, 1924-25 (R. R. Moton). Tuskegee Institute Bulletin.

United States Bureau of the Census. Seventh Census, 1850; Ninth Census, 1870; Tenth Census, 1880; Eleventh Census, 1890; Fifteenth Census, 1930.

United States Commissioner of Education. Report for 1884-1885. Washington, 1886.

—— Report for 1899-1900, Vol. I. Washington, 1901.

—— Report for 1900-1901, Vol. I. Washington, 1902.

—— Report for 1903, Vol. I. Washington, 1905.

—— Report for 1904, Vol. I. (The Work and Influence of Hampton. Proceedings of a meeting held in New York City, Feb. 12, 1904, under the direction of the Armstrong Association. Letter from Grover Cleveland, addresses by Andrew Carnegie, Charles W. Eliot, H. B. Frissell, and Booker T. Washington). Washington, 1906.

United States Congress, Acts of March 3, 1845. United States Statutes at Large, Vol. V, Chap. LXXV, Sec. I.

—— American State Papers, Election of the Delegate from the Southwestern Territory. Miscellaneous, Vol. I, No. 55.

United States Department of Agriculture. Status and Results of Extension Work in the Southern States, 1903-1921. Department Circular 248 (November, 1922).

United States Office of Education, Division of Vocational Education. Digest of Annual Reports of State Boards for Vocational Education to the Office of Education, Division of Vocational Education, for the Fiscal Year ended June 30, 1934.

—— Report of Federal Agent on Problems in Connection with Southern Regional Program of Work. By Robert D. Maltby. January 28, 1935. (Mimeographed)

Virginia Company of London. The Records of The Court Book, From the Manuscript in the Library of Congress. 2 vols. Ed. by Susan Myra Kingsbury. Washington, 1906.

2. Alabama

Alabama State Teachers College Catalogue, 1930. Florence, Alabama.

—— 1931 Yearbook: Catalogue of Faculty and Students for 1930-31; Alumni Register; Bulletin of 1931 Summer Quarter; Announcements for 1931-32. Montgomery, Alabama.

Birmingham Board of Education. Report of Progress, Birmingham Public Schools, 1921 to 1931. Birmingham, Alabama.

United States Bureau of Education, Bulletin, 1919, No. 41. An Educational Study of Alabama. Washington, 1919.

See also under Secondary Sources below.

3. Arkansas

Arkansas Education Commission. State Aid to High Schools. Bull. No. 2, Little Rock, 1910.

Arkansas House Journal, 1860.

Arkansas Senate Journal, 1868.

Dawson, Howard A., and Little, Harry A. Financial and Administrative Needs of the Public Schools of Arkansas. Issued by C. M. Hirst, State Superintendent of Public Instruction. Little Rock, Nov., 1930.

State Superintendent of Public Instruction (A. B. Hill). Four Years with the Public Schools in Arkansas, 1923-1927. A series of 16 bulletins. Little Rock, State Department of Education.

State Superintendent of Public Instruction (C. M. Hirst). Biennial Report, State of Arkansas, 1928-1929, 1929-1930.

State Commissioner of Education (W. E. Phipps). Biennial Report, State of Arkansas, 1932-1933, 1933-1934.
Treasurer. Report for 1899-1900; Report of September 5, 1910.
Superintendent of Public Instruction (Josiah H. Shinn). Biennial Report for the Years 1893 and 1894.
United States Bureau of Education, Bulletin, 1923, Nos. 10 and 11. The Public School System of Arkansas: Report of a Survey made under the Direction of the United States Commissioner of Education at the Request of the Arkansas State Educational Commission.
See also under Secondary Sources below.

4. Florida

Florida House Journal, 1846-47.
Florida, Laws of, 1839; 1848-49, Chap. 230; 1866.
Florida, School Laws of the State of, Sec. 23 (5870). Compiled from the Revised General Statutes and the Acts of the Legislature up to and Including Laws of 1929, by W. S. Cawthon, Superintendent of Public Instruction, Tallahassee, Florida.
Superintendent of Public Instruction. Report for 1870; Report for 1873-74.
Superintendent of Public Instruction (William N. Sheats). Biennial Report for the Two Years ending June 30, 1894.
University of Florida, Board of Control. Record of the Proceedings in the Matter of Charges against Ludwig W. Buchholz, Professor of Psychology and Pedagogy at the University of Florida, held by the Board of Control at Tampa, Florida, on November 11, 1918, in the Municipal Court Room of the City Hall.
See also under Secondary Sources below.

5. Georgia

Branson, Eugene C. The Georgia Club at the State Normal School, Athens, Ga., for the Study of Rural Sociology. United States Bureau of Education, Bulletin, 1913, No. 23. Washington, 1913.
See also under Secondary Sources below.

6. Louisiana

State Superintendent of Public Education, Report for 1930-31. Eighty-second Annual Report for the Session 1930-31, Bulletin 220, December, 1931.
See also under Secondary Sources below.

7. *Mississippi*

Mississippi Constitution of 1868, Art. VIII, Sec. 6.
Mississippi Constitution of 1890, Art. VIII, Sec. 207.
Mississippi, Revised Code of 1871, Chap. 39, Art. 1, Sec. 1994.
State Rural School Supervisor (J. T. Calhoun). Consolidated Schools in Mississippi. Bull. No. 34, Session 1922-23. Issued by W. F. Bond, State Superintendent of Education.
State Superintendent of Public Education (J. R. Preston). Report of 1886; Biennial Report, 1889-1890 and 1890-1891; Biennial Report, 1891-92, 1892-93.
State Superintendent of Education (W. F. Bond). Education in Mississippi, 1930.
Transportation Survey Public Schools of Mississippi, 1933-34. Bull. No. 78, 1934. Issued by W. F. Bond.
See also under Secondary Sources below.

8. *North Carolina*

North Carolina Baptist State Convention, Minutes of, Nov., 1880.
North Carolina, Constitution of, 1776, Art. XLI.
North Carolina House Journal, March 1, 1887. H. B. 591.
North Carolina, Laws of, 1789, Chap. 3; 1885, Chap. 308; 1887, Chap. 410.
Superintendent of Public Instruction (C. H. Mebane). Biennial Report, 1896-97 and 1897-98.
The Watauga Club of Raleigh, N. C. The Need of an Industrial School in North Carolina, together with the Estimates of the Cost of Establishing and Maintaining It. A Memorial to the General Assembly. Raleigh, N. C., Daily Chronicle Office, 1885.
See also under Secondary Sources below.

9. *South Carolina*

Columbia (S. C.) Board of School Commissioners. Annual Report to, 1919.
——— Triennial Report of the Public Schools, 1922-23, 1923-24, 1924-25. Columbia, S. C., 1926.
State Superintendent of Education. Sixty-third Annual Report, 1931.
Tate, William Knox. Country School Movements and Ideals in South Carolina. University of South Carolina Bull. No. 36, Part II. Jan., 1914.

—— Rural School Problem in South Carolina. University of South Carolina Bull. No. 24, Part II. Jan., 1911.

Thornwell, James H. Letter to His Excellency Governor Manning on Public Instruction in South Carolina. Columbia, S. C., R. W. Gibbes and Company, 1853. Republished in the editions of the Charleston News and Courier, July, 1885, by the City Council of Charleston. Issued in pamphlet form by a Committee of Citizens, Charleston, S. C., the News and Courier Book Presses, 1885. Printed in the Report of the U. S. Commissioner of Education, 1899-1900, Vol. I. Washington, 1901.

See also under Secondary Sources below.

10. *Tennessee*

Acts of Tennessee, 1796, Chap. 4.

Acts of the State of Tennessee, 1853-54, Chap. LXXI; 1899, Chap. 279.

Journal of the Constitutional Convention, 1834.

Merriam, Lucius Salisbury. Higher Education in Tennessee. U. S. Bureau of Education, Circular of Information No. 5, 1893. Washington, 1893.

Senate Journal, 1853-54.

Superintendent of Public Instruction (John Eaton, Jr.). First Report, 1869.

See also under Secondary Sources below.

11. *Texas*

Eby, Frederick (comp.). Education in Texas: Source Materials. University of Texas Bull. No. 1824. April 25, 1918.

Governors' Messages: Coke to Ross (Inclusive), 1874-1883. (Oran Milo Roberts, 1879-1883). Austin, Archive and History Department of the Texas State Library, 1916.

See also under Secondary Sources below.

12. *Virginia*

Campbell, Alexander. An Address on the subject of primary or common schools, Clarksburg Educational Convention, 1841. Virginia House Journal, 1841-42, Doc. 7.

Code of 1849, Chap. 198, Sec. 31.

Constitutional Provisions, 1902, Secs. 129-142.

Documents and Messages, 1861-62, No. 7.

Educational Association of Virginia, Minutes of, July 16-19, 1867. Lynchburg, Va.

Educational Journal of Virginia, Aug., 1870. Report of a commit-
    tee of the Educational Association of Virginia on the Merits
    and Defects of the Prevailing Schemes of Common School
    Education in the United States. (Organ of the Educational
    Association, Nov., 1869, through Dec., 1891.)
—— Minutes of, July 13, 1869. Lexington, Va.
Journal of the House of Delegates, Oct. 11, 1776; 1816; 1838,
    Doc. No. 4; 1841-42, Doc. No. 35 (Proceedings of Educational
    Conventions).
Literary Fund. Sundry Documents on the Subject of a System of
    Public Education, for the State of Virginia. Published by the
    President and Directors of the Literary Fund, in obedience to a
    resolution of the General Assembly, Richmond, 1817. (Con-
    tains A Bill for the More General Diffusion of Knowledge,
    proposed by the Committee of Revisors of the Laws of Vir-
    ginia, 1776; Letter of Thomas Jefferson to Peter Carr, Sept. 7,
    1814, and other important documents.)
Proceedings and Debates of the State Constitutional Convention of
    1829-30; 1867-68.
Ruffner, Henry. Proposed Plan for the Organization and Support
    of Common Schools in Virginia. Lexington Educational Con-
    vention, 1841. Virginia House Journal, 1841-42, Docs. No. 7
    and No. 35. Also in the Report of the U. S. Commissioner of
    Education, 1899-1900, Vol. I.
School Laws, 1930, Secs. 653-786.
Smith, Benjamin Mosby. Report on The Prussian Primary School
    System, with Suggestions on the Application of the System of
    Primary Schools to Virginia. Journal of the House of Dele-
    gates of Virginia, Jan.-Apr., 1839, Doc. 26.
Superintendent of Public Instruction (William H. Ruffner). First
    Annual Report, Virginia School Report, 1871.
—— Report for 1878.
Superintendent of Public Instruction, Annual Report for the School
    Year 1833-34. Bull., State Board of Education, Vol. XVII,
    No. 3 (Sept., 1934). Richmond, Va.
Washington College Catalogue, 1867-68; 1868-69; 1869-70. Lexing-
    ton, Va.
See also Secondary Sources below.

III. NEWSPAPERS

Atlanta Journal, Nov. 4, 1902 (Solons Addressed by Dr. Buttrick).
Columbia State, Apr. 28, 1905; Aug. 8, 1928.
News Letter, Vol. XIX, Nos. 11-25 (1933). University of North
    Carolina, Extension Division.

New York Times, Nov. 9, 1901; May 4, 1902 (Edward Cary); Sept. 13, 1925 (Interview, John R. House, "Farm Boys of Balkans Trained by Americans"); Jan. 3, 1926.

New York Tribune, May 3, 1904.

Richmond Dispatch, Apr. 5, 8, 12, 13, 1876 (articles by W. H. Ruffner); Apr. 22, 26, May 4, 1876 (articles by Robert L. Dabney).

Richmond Enquirer, Apr. 20, 22, 26, May 4, 1876 (articles by Robert L. Dabney).

Winston-Salem Sentinel, Apr. 20, 1901.

B. SECONDARY SOURCES

Abbott, Lyman. Silhouettes of My Contemporaries. Garden City, N. Y., Doubleday, Page and Company, 1922.

Adams, Henry. History of the United States of America. 9 vols. Vol. I. New York, Charles Scribner's Sons, 1891-92.

Adams, Herbert Baxter. Thomas Jefferson and the University of Virginia. United States Bureau of Education, Circular of Information, No. 1, 1888. Washington, Government Printing Office, 1888.

Alderman, Edwin A. Charles Brantley Aycock, An Appreciation, The North Carolina Historical Review, I (July, 1924), 243-50.

——— Service. Published in The Function of the State University, being Proceedings of the Inauguration of Edward Kidder Graham as President of the University of North Carolina, pp. 51-52. Chapel Hill, N. C., The University of North Carolina Press, 1915.

——— Woodrow Wilson: Memorial Address, delivered before the joint meeting of the two Houses of Congress as a tribute of respect to the Late President of the United States. Hall of the House of Representatives, December 15, 1924. Washington, D. C., 1925.

——— and Gordon, Armistead C. J. L. M. Curry: A Biography. New York, The Macmillan Company, 1911.

Alexander, James Waddel. The Life of Archibald Alexander, D. D., First Professor in the Theological Seminary, at Princeton, New Jersey. New York, Charles Scribner, 1854.

Alexander, Will W. The Slater and Jeanes Funds, An Educator's Approach to a Difficult Problem. The John F. Slater Fund, Occasional Papers No. 28.

Allan, William. Life and Work of John McDonogh. Baltimore, the Trustees of the McDonogh School, 1886.

Ambler, Charles Henry. Sectionalism in Virginia, 1776 to 1861. Chicago, The University of Chicago Press, 1910.

American Academy of Political and Social Science. The Annals, XXII (July, 1903—Dec., 1903), 245-329.

—— The American Negro, The Annals, CXXX (Nov., 1928).

American Annals of Education and Instruction. (13 vols., 1826-38) I (May, 1831), 225; II (Jan. 15, 1832), 94-96; II (Apr. 1, 1832), 239.

American Foundations and Their Fields. Edition of 1932 (Covering activities of the year 1931). New York, Twentieth Century Fund, Inc., 1932.

Armstrong, Samuel C. Lessons from the Hawaiian Islands. Journal of Christian Philosophy, Jan., 1884.

—— Twenty-two Years' Work of Hampton Institute. Hampton, Va., Normal School Press, 1893.

—— and Ludlow, Helen W. From the Beginning. Reprinted from articles in Twenty-two Years' Work of Hampton Institute.

Armstrong's Ideas on Education for Life. Hampton, Va., Hampton Normal and Agricultural Institute, 1926. (Pamphlet)

Arrowood, Charles Flinn. Thomas Jefferson and Education in a Republic. New York and London, McGraw-Hill Book Company, Inc., 1930.

Ashe, Samuel A'Court. History of North Carolina. 2 vols. Vol. I, Greensboro, N. C., Charles L. Van Noppen, 1908; Vol. II, Raleigh, N. C., Edwards and Broughton, 1925.

Ashmore, Otis. Chatham Academy in Savannah, Georgia. The High School Quarterly, XVIII (July, 1930), 173-77.

Aycock, Charles B. Southern Education, I (Dec. 21, 1903), 418.

Baker, William M. The Life and Labours of the Rev. Daniel Baker, D. D., Pastor and Evangelist. Philadelphia, William S. & Alfred Martien, 1858.

Baptist Encyclopedia, William Cathcart, ed. Philadelphia, Louis H. Everts, 1881.

Barker, Eugene C. The Life of Stephen F. Austin, Founder of Texas, 1793-1836. Nashville and Dallas, Cokesbury Press, 1925.

Barnard, Frederick A. P. A Letter to the Honorable, the Board of Trustees of the University of Mississippi. Oxford, Miss., The University of Mississippi, 1858.

Barnard, Henry, ed. American Journal of Education (32 vols.), XIX, 338.

Battle, Kemp P. History of the University of North Carolina. 2 vols. Raleigh, N. C., Edwards and Broughton Printing Company, 1907-12.

Bell, Sadie. The Church, the State, and Education in Virginia. Philadelphia, Science Press Printing Company, 1930.

Beverley, Robert. The History of Virginia, in Four Parts. London, printed for F. Fayram, J. Clarke, and T. Bickerton, 1722. "The Second Edition revis'd and enlarg'd by the Author."

Boaz, Franz. The Mind of Primitive Man. New York, The Macmillan Company, 1911.

Bond, Christiana. Memories of General Robert E. Lee. Baltimore, The Norman, Remington Company, 1926.

Bowers, Claude G. The Tragic Era: The Revolution after Lincoln. Cambridge, Mass., Houghton Mifflin Company, 1929.

Branson, Eugene C. Farm Tenancy in the Cotton Belt: How Farm Tenants Live, The Journal of Social Forces, I (March, 1923), 213-21.

—— Farm Tenancy in the South, The Journal of Social Forces, I (May, 1923), 450-57.

Brawley, Benjamin. Doctor Dillard of the Jeanes Fund. New York and Chicago, Fleming H. Revell Company, 1930.

Breckinridge, Robert J. Memoranda of Foreign Travel: Containing notices of a Pilgrimage through Some of the Principal States of Western Europe. 2 vols. Baltimore, D. Owen and Son, 1845.

Breckinridge, Sophonisba Preston. Madeline McDowell Breckinridge: A Leader in the New South. Chicago, The University of Chicago Press, 1921.

Brickell, John. The Natural History of North-Carolina. With an Account of the Trade, Manners, and Customs of the Christian and Indian Inhabitants. Dublin, James Carson, 1737.

Brooks, John Graham. An American Citizen: The Life of William Henry Baldwin, Jr. Boston and New York, Houghton Mifflin Company, 1910.

Brown, Alexander. The Cabells and Their Kin. Boston and New York, Houghton Mifflin and Company, 1895.

Bruce, Philip Alexander. History of the University of Virginia, 1819-1919; the Lengthened Shadow of One Man. 5 vols. New York, The Macmillan Company, 1920-22.

—— Institutional History of Virginia in the Seventeenth Century. 2 vols. New York and London, G. P. Putnam's Sons, 1910.

—— Robert E. Lee. Philadelphia, George W. Jacobs and Company, 1907.

Buttrick, Wallace. What is Education?, Peabody Journal of Education, III (Nov., 1925). Reprinted as a pamphlet.

Butts, Alfred B. Public Administration in Mississippi. Jackson, Miss., Mississippi Historical Society, 1919.

Cabell, Nathaniel Francis (ed.). Early History of the University of Virginia as Contained in the Letters of Thomas Jefferson and Joseph C. Cabell. Richmond, Va., J. W. Randolph, 1856.

Campbell, Alexander. Popular Lectures and Addresses. Philadelphia, James Challen and Son, 1866.

Capers, Henry D. The Life and Times of C. G. Memminger. Richmond, Va., Everett Waddy Company, Publishers, 1893.

Caruthers, E. W. A Sketch of the Life and Character of the Rev. David Caldwell, D. D. "Near Sixty Years Pastor of the Churches of Buffalo and Alamance." Greensborough, N. C., Printed by Swaim and Sherwood, 1842.

Cherry, Henry Hardin. A Greater Kentucky. Frankfort, Ky., Department of Education of Kentucky, 1913. (Pamphlet)

—— The Spirit and Achievements of Western Kentucky State Teachers College during a Quarter of a Century. Teachers College Heights, Bulletin of the Western Kentucky State Teachers College, XIII (Jan., 1932), 37.

Chinard, Gilbert. Thomas Jefferson: The Apostle of Americanism. Boston, Little, Brown and Company, 1929.

Claxton, P. P. Address at the Robert C. Ogden Memorial Meeting. Proceedings of the Seventeenth Conference for Education in the South, Louisville, Ky., 1914. Reprinted as a pamphlet (The Work of the Conference for Education in the South: A Record of Progress through Sixteen Years).

—— Peabody Alumni News, Memorial Number, Apr., 1917.

Cochran, Thomas Everette. History of Public School Education in Florida. State Department of Education, Bulletin, 1921, No. 1.

Collins, Lewis. History of Kentucky. 2 vols. Covington, Ky., Collins and Company, 1874; Louisville, Ky., John P. Morton and Company, Inc., 1924.

Condorcet, Marie Jean Antoine Nicolas Caritat, Marquis de. Outlines of an Historical View of the Progress of the Human Mind: Being a Posthumous Work. Translated from the French. London, printed for J. Johnson, 1795.

—— Rapport et projet de décret sur l'organisation générale de l'instruction publique. Présentés à l'Assemblée nationale, au nom du Comité d'instruction publique, les 20 et 21 avril, 1792. Œuvres de Condorcet (12 vols., 1847-49), Tome Septième. Paris, Firmin Didot Frères, Librairies, 1847.

Connor, R. D. W. Ante-Bellum Builders of North Carolina. Greensboro, N. C., North Carolina College for Women, 1923. First published in 1914 as the North Carolina State Normal and Industrial College Historical Publications No. 3.

—— Walter Hines Page, published in Southern Pioneers, ed. by Howard W. Odum. Chapel Hill, N. C., The University of North Carolina Press, 1925.

—— and Poe, Clarence. The Life and Speeches of Charles Brantley Aycock. Garden City, N. Y., Doubleday, Page and Company, 1912.

Cook, Harvey Toliver. The Life and Legacy of David Rogerson Williams. New York, 1916.

Cooke, John Esten. Virginia: A History of the People. Boston, Houghton, Mifflin and Company, 1884.

Cooley, Rossa B. School Acres: An Adventure in Rural Education. New Haven, Yale University Press, 1930.

Coon, Charles L. The Beginnings of Public Education in North Carolina. 2 vols. Raleigh, N. C., North Carolina Historical Commission, 1908.

—— Charles Duncan McIver and His Educational Services, 1886-1906. In the Report of the U. S. Commissioner of Education, 1907, Vol. I. Washington, Government Printing Office, 1908.

—— Facts about Southern Educational Progress: A Study in Public School Maintenance for Those Who Look Forward. Durham, N. C., Campaign Committee of the Southern Education Board, June, 1905.

Coulter, E. Merton. College Life in the Old South. New York, The Macmillan Company, 1928.

Cubberley, Ellwood P. The History of Education. Boston and New York, Houghton Mifflin Company, 1920.

—— School Funds and Their Apportionment. New York, Teachers College, Columbia University, 1906.

Curry, Jabez Lamar Monroe. Address before the Association of Confederate Veterans, Richmond, Va., July 1, 1896. Richmond, B. F. Johnson Publishing Company, 1896.

—— A Brief Sketch of George Peabody (1795-1869) and a History of the Peabody Education Board through Thirty Years. Cambridge, Mass., University Press: John Wilson and Son, 1898.

—— Civil History of the Government of the Confederate States with Some Personal Reminiscences. Richmond, Va., B. F. Johnson Publishing Company, 1901.

—— Education in the Southern States. Printed in the Proceedings of the Second Capon Springs Conference for Education in the South, 1899.

—— The Southern States of the American Union Considered in their Relations to the Constitution of the United States and to the Resulting Union. New York and London, G. P. Putnam's Sons, 1895.

Dabney, Charles Wm. Jefferson, the Seer: His Vision of a System of Public Education. Address before the Conference for Education in the South in session at the University of Virginia on April 25, 1903.

—— The Living Waters of Singing Spring, The Outlook, CI (June 8, 1912), 313-16.

—— A World Wide Law: Ratio of Education to Production, University of Tennessee Index, Ser. II, No. 10 (Jan., 1901).

Dabney, Robert L. Article in Southern Planter and Farmer, April, 1876.

—— Discussions. 4 vols. Mexico, Mo., Crescent Book House, 1897.

—— Secularized Education, Libbey's Princeton Review, Sept., 1879, 55th year (N. S. 4), pp. 377-400.

Daniels, Frank A. Address at the Presentation and Unveiling of the Memorial Tablet to Charles Brantley Aycock, Goldsboro, N. C., Nov. 1, 1929.

Daniels, Josephus. Charles Brantley Aycock—Historical Address, North Carolina Historical Review, I (July, 1924), 251-76.

Dawson, Howard Athalone. Satisfactory Local School Units: Functions and Principles of Formation, Organization, and Administration. Nashville, Tenn., Division of Surveys and Field Studies (Field Study No. 7). George Peabody College for Teachers, 1934.

Denison, John H. Samuel Chapman Armstrong, The Atlantic Monthly, LXXIII (Jan., 1894), 90-98.

Derrick, S. M. Education in South Carolina before the Revolution, University Weekly News, May 12, 1926. Columbia, S. C.

Destutt de Tracy, Antoine Louis Claude, Comte. Observations sur Le Système Actuel D'instruction Publique. Contained in Élmens D'Ideologie, Troisième partie, Tome deuxième, De La Logique, Paris, 1825.

Dexter, Edwin Grant. History of Education in the United States. New York, The Macmillan Company, 1904.

Dillard, James H. A School of the Past, The Sewanee Review, XXIX (Oct., 1921), 410-16.

Du Bois, W. E. Burghardt. The Suppression of the African Slave-Trade to the United States of America, 1638-1870. New York, Longmans, Green and Company, 1896.

Du Pont de Nemours, Pierre Samuel. National Education in the United States of America. Translated by Bessie Gardner Du Pont. Newark, Del., University of Delaware Press, 1923.

Dyer, G. W. Democracy in the South before the Civil War. Nashville, Tenn., and Dallas, Tex., Publishing House of Methodist Episcopal Church, South, 1905.

Eby, Frederick. The Development of Education in Texas. New York, The Macmillan Company, 1925.

Educational Exchange, February, 1914. Birmingham, Ala.

Educational Statesman, An, Review of Reviews, LXXV (Jan., 1927), 86.

Edwards, Robert Leigh. The Lighthouse on the Hill. Quoted in editorial in The Southern Workman, LXI (Oct., 1932), 390.

Eggleston, Joseph D. The Attitude of Virginia Leaders toward Slavery and Secession, The Virginia Teacher, XIII (Sept.-Oct., 1932), 1-15.

—— Hollis Burke Frissell, Memorial Address, The Southern Workman, LIII (March, 1924), 102.

—— and Bruère, Robert W. The Work of the Rural School. New York and London, Harper and Brothers, 1913.

Ellard, Roscoe. Robert E. Lee and Journalism, Washington and Lee University Bulletin, XXV (No. 1), 9-10.

Favrot, Leo M. Negro Public Education in the South. Mimeographed copy.

Fay, Edwin Whitfield. The History of Education in Louisiana. U. S. Bureau of Education, Circular of Information, No. 1, 1898. Washington, Government Printing Office, 1898.

Ferrell, John A. (M. D.). The Rural School and Hookworm Disease. U. S. Bureau of Education Bull., 1914, No. 20. Washington, Government Printing Office, 1914.

Fiske, John. The Critical Period of American History, 1783-1789. Boston and New York, Houghton Mifflin and Company, 1888.

—— Old Virginia and Her Neighbors. 2 vols. Boston and New York, Houghton, Mifflin and Company, 1900.

Foote, William Henry. Sketches of North Carolina. New York, Robert Carter, 1846.

—— Sketches of Virginia: Historical and Biographical. 2 vols. Philadelphia, William S. Martien, 1850-55. Vol. II published by J. B. Lippincott and Company.

Foreman, Clark. Environmental Factors in Negro Elementary Education. New York, The Julius Rosenwald Fund, 1932.

Fortier, Alcée. A History of Louisiana. 4 vols. New York, Goupil and Company, of Paris, Manzi, Joyant and Company, successors, 1904.

Frazier, James B. Message to the Fifty-third General Assembly, State of Tennessee, Jan. 23, 1903.

Freeman, Douglas Southall. R. E. Lee: A Biography. 4 vols. New York and London, Charles Scribner's Sons, 1934-35.

Fries, Henry E. In Memory of Robert Curtis Ogden: True Friend, Patriotic Citizen, Unofficial Statesman, Christian Gentleman. Published privately.

Frissell, Hollis B., quoted in A Master Builder by Amelia Josephine Burr. The Bellman, XXIII (Dec. 15, 1917), 658.

Frost, William Goodell. University Extension in the Southern Mountains. [N. Y.?], 1898. Reprinted from The Outlook, Sept. 3, 1898.

Garland, Hugh A. The Life of John Randolph of Roanoke. 2 vols. New York, D. Appleton and Company; Philadelphia, George S. Appleton, 1851.

Gewehr, Wesley M. The Great Awakening in Virginia, 1740-1790. Durham, N. C., Duke University Press, 1930.

Glenn, Thomas Allen. Some Colonial Mansions, Vol. I. Philadelphia, H. T. Coates and Company, 1898. Second Series, Philadelphia, H. T. Coates and Company, 1900.

Grady, Henry W. Address at the Augusta Exposition, November, 1887. Published in Henry W. Grady, His Life, Writings and Speeches, ed. by Joel Chandler Harris. New York, Cassell Publishing Company, 1890.

—— The South and Her Problems. Dallas, Tex., Oct. 26, 1887. Published in Henry W. Grady, His Life, Writings and Speeches, ed. by Joel Chandler Harris. New York, Cassell Publishing Company, 1890.

Graham, Alexander. Events forming Background of Mecklenburg Declaration of Independence, May 20, 1775. Charlotte, N. C., Charlotte Chamber of Commerce, 1924. (Pamphlet)

—— Why North Carolinians Believe in the Mecklenburg Declaration of Independence of May 20th, 1775. Charlotte, N. C., 1895. (Pamphlet)

Green, Fletcher M. Constitutional Development in the South Atlantic States, 1776-1860. Chapel Hill, N. C., The University of North Carolina Press, 1930.

Gregg, Alexander. History of the Old Cheraws. New York, Richardson and Company, 1867.

Grove, Frank L. Julia Tutwiler, the Educator, eulogy at the unveiling of her portrait at the University of Alabama, May 11, 1931, Alabama School Journal, Sept., 1931.

Hamilton, J. G. de Roulhac. North Carolina since 1860. Vol. III of History of North Carolina. 6 vols. Chicago and New York, The Lewis Publishing Company, 1919.

Hamlett, Barksdale. History of Education in Kentucky. Frankfort, Kentucky, Department of Education, 1914.

Hand, William H. (ed.) High School Manual. Bull. of the University of South Carolina, Part XI (Oct., 1907).

—— High School Monograph. Bull. of the University of South Carolina, Part II, No. XIII (Apr., 1908).

Harris, Thomas H. The Story of Public Education in Louisiana. New Orleans, 1924.

Haygood, Atticus G. Our Brother in Black: His Freedom and Future. New York, Phillips and Hunt; Cincinnati, Walden and Stowe, 1881.

Heatwole, Cornelius J. A History of Education in Virginia. New York, The Macmillan Company, 1916.

Heiskell, S. G. Andrew Jackson and Early Tennessee History. Nashville, Tenn., Ambrose Printing Company, 1918. (One-volume edition)

Hendrick, Burton J. The Life and Letters of Walter H. Page. 3 vols. Garden City, N. Y., Doubleday, Page and Company, 1922-1925.

—— The Training of an American: The Earlier Life and Letters of Walter H. Page, 1855-1913. Boston and New York, Houghton Mifflin Company, 1928.

Hening, William Waller. The Statutes at Large: Being a Collection of all the Laws of Virginia, from the First Session of the Legislature in the Year 1619 to 1792. 13 vols. 1819-1823. Vols I and IX.

Henry, William Wirt. Patrick Henry; Life, Correspondence and Speeches. 3 vols. New York, Charles Scribner's Sons, 1891.

Herbert, Hilary A. The Abolition Crusade and its Consequences. New York, Charles Scribner's Sons, 1912.

Herring, Harriet L. Welfare Work in Mill Villages. Chapel Hill, N. C. The University of North Carolina Press, 1929.

Honeywell, Roy J. The Educational Work of Thomas Jefferson. Cambridge, Harvard University Press, 1931.

Howard, L. Q. The Insect Menace. New York and London, The Century Company, 1931.

Hull, A. L. A Historical Sketch of the University of Georgia. Atlanta, The Foote and Davies Company, 1894.

Illiteracy in the United States and an Experiment for its Elimination. U. S. Bureau of Education, Bull., 1913, No. 20.

Jarvis, Thomas J. Inaugural Address, delivered before both Houses of the General Assembly in the House of Representatives, Jan. 18, 1881. (Pamphlet)

Jefferson, Thomas, Autobiography. Ed. by Paul Leicester Ford. New York, G. P. Putnam's Sons, 1914.

—— A Bill for Establishing a System of Public Education. Published in Early History of the University of Virginia as contained in the letters of Thomas Jefferson and Joseph C. Cabell. Richmond, Va., J. W. Randolph, 1856. Also in The Writings of Thomas Jefferson, Library Edition (ed. by Andrew A.

Lipscomb), Vol. XVII. Washington, The Thomas Jefferson Memorial Association, 1903.

———— A Bill for the More General Diffusion of Knowledge. In The Writings of Thomas Jefferson, ed. by Paul Leicester Ford, Vol. II. New York, G. P. Putnam's Sons, 1892-99.

———— Notes on the State of Virginia. Paris, 1784-85; Philadelphia, Prichard and Hall, 1788; also in Writings, Library Edition, Vol. II.

———— The Writings of Thomas Jefferson. 10 vols. Collected and edited by Paul Leicester Ford. New York and London, G. P. Putnam's Sons, 1892-99.

———— The Works of Thomas Jefferson. 12 vols. Collected and edited by Paul Leicester Ford. New York and London, G. P. Putnam's Sons, 1904-5.

———— The Writings of Thomas Jefferson. 20 vols. Edited by Andrew A. Lipscomb. Washington, The Thomas Jefferson Memorial Association, 1907. (Cited as the Library Edition.)

———— The Writings of Thomas Jefferson. 9 vols. Edited by H. A. Washington. New York, John C. Riker and Riker, Thorne and Company, 1853-54. (Cited as the Washington Edition.)

Johnson, Guion Griffis. A Social History of the Sea Islands: With Special Reference to St. Helena Island, South Carolina. Chapel Hill, N. C., The University of North Carolina Press, 1930.

Johnston, William Preston. An Address before the Louisiana State Public School Teachers' Association, December 28, 1893. New Orleans, L. Graham and Son, Ltd., 1894. (Pamphlet)

Jones, Charles C. The Religious Instruction of Negroes in the United States. Savannah, Ga., Thomas Purse, 1842.

Jones, Charles C., Jr. The Dead Towns of Georgia. Savannah, Morning News Steam Printing House, 1878.

Jones, Charles E. Education in Georgia. U. S. Bureau of Education, Circular of Information No. 4, 1888. Washington, Government Printing Office, 1889.

Jones, E. J. National Aid to Education a Continuation of a Policy Already Begun, Andover Review, V, 250. Quoted in Congressional Record, Feb. 3–March 7, 1890.

Jones, James S. Life of Andrew Johnson: Seventeenth President of the United States. Greeneville, Tenn., East Tennessee Publishing Company, 1901.

Jones, Lance G. E. Negro Schools in the Southern States. Oxford, The Clarendon Press, 1928.

Jones, Thomas Jesse. Essentials of Civilization. New York, Henry Holt and Company, 1929.

———— Founder's Day Address. Delivered at Tuskegee Institute, Apr. 8, 1934.

—— Four Essentials of Education. Charles Scribner's Sons, 1926.

—— Frissell of Hampton. Reprinted from The Southern Workman, Vol. LX, No. 1 (Jan., 1931).

Joynes, Edward S. The Origin and Early History of Winthrop College, Bulletin of Winthrop College, VI (Sept., 1912), 55-72.

Keppel, Frederick P. The Foundation: Its Place in American Life. Page-Barbour Lectures, University of Virginia. New York, The Macmillan Company, 1930.

King, Grace. New Orleans: The Place and the People. New York, Macmillan and Company, 1896.

Kneece, Mattie Crouch (Mrs. J. F.) The Contributions of C. C. Memminger to the Cause of Education, Bulletin of the University of South Carolina, No. 177 (Feb. 15, 1926).

Knight, Edgar W. The Academy Movement in the South. Reprinted from The High School Journal, Vol. II, Nos. 7 and 8, and Vol. III, No. 1.

—— Education in the United States. Boston, New York, Ginn and Company, 1929.

—— Public Education in the South. Boston and New York, Ginn and Company, 1922.

—— Public School Education in North Carolina. Boston, New York, Chicago, Houghton Mifflin Company, 1916.

Knight, Lucian Lamar. Reminiscences of Famous Georgians. 2 vols. Vol. I. Atlanta, Franklin-Turner Company, 1907.

La Borde, M. History of the South Carolina College. Columbia, S. C., Peter B. Glass, 1859.

Lane, J. J. History of Education in Texas. U. S. Bureau of Education, Circular of Information No. 2, 1903. Washington, Government Printing Office, 1903.

Latane, John H. Lee's Educational Policies, Lee Centennial Bulletin, Washington and Lee University, New Series, Vol. VI, No. 3 (July, 1907).

Leavell, Ullin Whitney. Philanthropy in Negro Education. Nashville, Tenn., George Peabody College for Teachers, 1930.

Lee, Robert E., Jr. Recollections and Letters of General Robert E. Lee. New York, Doubleday, Page and Company, 1904.

Lewis, Alvin Fayette. History of Higher Education in Kentucky. U. S. Bureau of Education, Circular of Information No. 3, 1899. Washington, Government Printing Office, 1899.

Lewis, Lloyd. Sherman: Fighting Prophet. New York, Harcourt, Brace and Company, 1932.

Life Well Lived, A.: In Memory of Robert Curtis Ogden. Hampton, Va., Hampton Institute, 1914.

Lingle, Walter L. Another Revolutionary Preacher, The Christian Observer, Dec. 16, 1931, Louisville, Ky.

—— A Revolutionary Preacher, The Christian Observer, Nov. 25, 1931, Louisville, Ky.

Littell, William. Statute Law of Kentucky. 5 vols., 1809-19. Vol. II.

Longstreet, Augustus Baldwin. Master William Mitten. Macon, Ga., Burke, Boykin and Company, 1864.

Lucas, T. S. The Background of the History of Darlington County, South Carolina. An Address on Nov. 3, 1933, in the Series of the South Carolina Economic Association.

Lyon, Ralph M. Moses Waddel and the Willington Academy, The North Carolina Historical Review, VIII (July, 1931), 284-99.

McCarthy, Charles H. Lincoln's Plan of Reconstruction. New York, McClure, Phillips and Company, 1901.

MacCorkle, William A. An Address on The Franchise in the South. Published in the Proceedings of the First Annual Conference of the Southern Society for the Promotion of the Study of Race Conditions and Problems in the South, Montgomery, Alabama, 1900. Richmond, Va., B. F. Johnson Publishing Company, 1900.

McCrady, Edward. Education in South Carolina prior to and during the Revolution. Charleston, S. C., Historical Society of South Carolina, 1883.

—— The History of South Carolina under the Proprietary Government, 1670-1719. New York, The Macmillan Company, 1897.

—— The History of South Carolina under the Royal Government, 1719-1776. New York, The Macmillan Company, 1899.

McGee, G. R. A History of Tennessee from 1663 to 1900. New York, Cincinnati, Chicago, American Book Company, 1899.

McIlwaine, Richard. Hampden-Sydney College as an Educational Force from the Revolution to the Civil War. (Pamphlet)

—— Memories of Three Score Years and Ten. New York and Washington, The Neale Publishing Company, 1908.

McCuistion, Fred. Financing Schools in the South. Some Data regarding Sources, Amounts, and Distribution of Public School Revenue in the Southern States, 1930. Issued by State Directors of Educational Research in the Southern States as a Part of the Proceedings of the Conference held at Peabody College, Dec. 5 and 6, 1930.

—— School Money in Black and White. Chicago, Rosenwald Fund, 1934.

—— The South's Negro Teaching Force. Nashville, Tenn., Julius Rosenwald Fund, 1931. (Pamphlet)

Maddox, William A. The Free School Idea in Virginia before the Civil War. New York, Teachers College, Columbia University, 1918.

Martin, Francis Xavier. The History of Louisiana, with a Memoir of the Author by Judge W. W. Howe, to which is appended Annals of Louisiana from the close of Martin's History, 1815, to the commencement of the Civil War, by John F. Condon. New Orleans, James A. Gresham, Publisher and Bookseller, 1882.

Maxwell, William. A Memoir of the Rev. John H. Rice, D. D. Philadelphia, J. Whetham; Richmond, R. I. Smith, 1835.

Mayes, Edward. History of Education in Mississippi. U. S. Bureau of Education, Circular of Information No. 2, 1899. Washington, Government Printing Office, 1899.

Mayo, A. D. Education in Southwestern Virginia. Published in the Report of the U. S. Commissioner of Education, 1890-1901, Vol. II. Washington, Government Printing Office, 1894.

—— The Final Establishment of the American Common School System in West Virginia, Maryland, Virginia, and Delaware, 1863-1900. Published in the Report of the U. S. Commissioner of Education, 1903, Vol. I. Washington, Government Printing Office, 1905.

—— The Organization and Development of the American Common School in the Atlantic and Central States of the South, 1830-1860. Published in the Report of the U. S. Commissioner of Education, 1899, 1900, Vol. I. Washington, Government Printing Office, 1901.

—— Services of Dr. Curry in Connection with the Peabody Fund. Published in the Report of the U. S. Commissioner of Education, 1903, Vol. I. Washington, Government Printing Office, 1905.

Meade, William. Old Churches, Ministers and Families of Virginia. 2 vols. Philadelphia, J. B. Lippincott and Company, 1857.

Menace to Panama, A., editorial in The World's Work, XXIV (June, 1912), 131-32.

Meriwether, Colyer. History of Higher Education in South Carolina. U. S. Bureau of Education, Circular of Information No. 3, 1888. Washington, Government Printing Office, 1889.

Millikan, Robert A. Education and Unemployment, The Atlantic Monthly, CXLVIII (Dec., 1931), 804-10.

Milton, George Fort. The Age of Hate: Andrew Johnson and the Radicals. New York, Coward-McCann, Inc., 1930.

Mims, Edwin. Peabody Alumni News, Memorial Number, April, 1917.

Minor, John B. Institutes of Common and Statute Law. 4 vols. Vol. I. Richmond, Va., printed by the author (Whittet and Shepperson), 1876-79.

Monahan, A. C. The Status of Rural Education in the United States. U. S. Bureau of Education, Bull., 1913, No. 8.

Morrison, Alfred J. The Beginnings of Public Education in Virginia, 1776-1860. Richmond, Va., Davis Bottom, Superintendent of Public Printing, 1917.

—— Six Addresses on the State of Letters and Science in Virginia, 1824-1835. Roanoke, Va., The Stone Printing and Manufacturing Company, 1917. (Pamphlet)

Morton, Richard L. Virginia since 1861. Vol. III of History of Virginia (6 vols). Chicago and New York, The American Historical Society, 1924.

Moton, Robert Russa. Finding a Way Out; An Autobiography. Garden City, N. Y., Doubleday, Page and Company, 1921.

Munford, Beverley B. Virginia's Attitude toward Slavery and Secession. New York, Longmans, Green and Company, 1910.

Murphy, Edgar Gardner. The Basis of Ascendency. New York and London. Longmans, Green and Company, 1909.

—— The Present South. New York, The Macmillan Company, 1904.

National Education Association. Can the States Afford to Educate Their Children?, Research Bulletin, Vol. VII, No. 1 (Jan., 1929).

Noble, M. C. S. A History of the Public Schools of North Carolina. Chapel Hill, N. C., The University of North Carolina Press, 1930.

North Carolina State Normal and Industrial College. Charles Duncan McIver. Memorial Volume prepared under the direction of a committee of the Faculty. Greensboro, N. C., J. J. Stone and Company, Printers, 1907.

Odum, Howard W. (ed.) Southern Pioneers. Chapel Hill, N. C., The University of North Carolina Press, 1925.

Ogden, Robert Curtis. Business Idealism, The Business World, Vol. XXV, No. 6 (June, 1905).

—— Memorial Address. Unveiling of the Memorial Tablet in Memory of William H. Baldwin, Jr., April 4, 1909, Tuskegee Institute, Ala.

Oldham, J. H. Christianity and the Race Problem. New York, George H. Doran Company, n. d.

—— Hollis Burke Frissell and Hampton, The Constructive Quarterly, Vol. VI (Sept., 1918), 575-76.

Outlook, The. Larger Educational Opportunities. Editorial, LXIX (Nov. 23, 1901), 755-56.

—— The Southern Educational Conference. Editorial, LXXI (May 3, 1902), 9-12.

—— The Southern Educational Conference. Editorial, LXXIV (May 2, 1903), 8.

—— The Educational Revival. Editorial, LXXIV (May 9, 1903), 106-9.

—— The Conference for Education in the South. Editorial, LXXX (May 13, 1905), 101-3.

—— Robert C. Ogden. Editorial, LXXXIII (June 23, 1906), 399.

—— Two Leaders in the New Reconstruction. Editorial, LXXXIII (July 28, 1906), 735-38.

—— Education in the South. Editorial, LXXXV (April 27, 1907), 310-11.

—— The Conference for Education in the South. Editorial, XCII (May 1, 1909), 8-9.

—— Uncommon People and the Common Schools. Staff Correspondence of the Outlook, C (Apr. 20, 1912), 856-58.

—— A Great Merchant. Editorial, CIV (Aug. 16, 1913), 842.

—— Memorial to Robert C. Ogden. Editorial, CXI (Oct. 20, 1915), 396-97.

Oversea Education, Vol. I, No. 1 (Oct., 1929). London, British Advisory Committee on Education in the Colonies.

Owen, Thomas McAdory. History of Alabama and Dictionary of Alabama Biography. 4 vols. Chicago, The S. J. Clarke Publishing Company, 1921.

Page, Thomas Nelson. The Old Dominion: Her Making and Her Manners. New York, Charles Scribner's Sons, 1908.

Page, Walter Hines. The Forgotten Man. Published in The Rebuilding of Old Commonwealths. New York, Doubleday, Page and Company, 1902.

—— The School that Built a Town. Published in The Rebuilding of Old Commonwealths. New York, Doubleday, Page and Company, 1902.

—— The Southerner: Being the Autobiography of Nicholas Worth. New York, Doubleday, Page and Company, 1909.

—— Study of an Old Southern Borough, The Atlantic Monthly, XLVII (May, 1881), 658.

Palmer, B. M. The Life and Letters of James Henley Thornwell, D. D., LL. D. Richmond, Va., Whittet and Shepperson, 1875.

Park, Orville A. The Puritan in Georgia, The Georgia Historical Quarterly, XIII (Dec., 1929), 343-71.

Parkinson, B. L. A History of the Administration of the City Public Schools of Columbia, S. C., Bull. of the University of South Carolina, No. 155, Jan. 15, 1925.

Peabody, Francis Greenwood. Education for Life: The Story of Hampton Institute. Garden City, N. Y., Doubleday, Page and Company, 1919.

Pearson, Charles Chilton. The Readjuster Movement in Virginia. New Haven, Yale University Press, 1917.

Peele, W. J. A History of the Agricultural and Mechanical College, The North Carolina Teacher, VI (Sept., 1888), 12-25.

Perry, William F. The Genesis of Public Education in Alabama. Transactions of the Alabama Historical Society, 1897-1898, Vol. II. Tuscaloosa, Ala., 1898.

Phenix, George P. Shaping Courses to Meet Changing Conditions: A Study in Evolution (at Hampton). Published in The Southern Workman, Dec., 1923, pp. 547-79, and Jan., 1924, pp. 24-33. Reprinted as a pamphlet.

Phillips, Ulrich B. American Negro Slavery. New York, London, D. Appleton and Company, 1918.

Poindexter, George. Mississippi Code of 1822. Natchez, 1824.

Prentice, Donald B., and Kunkel, W. B. The Colleges' Contributions to Intellectual Leadership, School and Society, XXXI (Nov. 1, 1930), 594-600.

Prescott, A. T. An Address at the Memorial Exercises for Colonel Thomas Duckett Boyd (1854-1932), The Louisiana State University Alumni News, IX (Dec., 1933), 3-6.

Preston, J. R. Quoted in Rowland's Encyclopedia of Mississippi History, Vol. II.

Ramsay, David. The History of South Carolina. 2 vols. Charleston, S. C., David Longworth, 1809.

Ramsey, J. G. M. The Annals of Tennessee. Reprinted, 1926, with the addition of Fain's Index, for the Judge David Campbell Chapter, D. A. R. Chattanooga, Tenn., by the Kingsport Press, Kingsport, Tenn.

Redcay, Edward E. Public Secondary Schools for Negroes in the Southern States of the United States. The John F. Slater Fund, Occasional Papers, No. 29, 1935.

Reisner, Edward H. Nationalism and Education since 1789. New York, The Macmillan Company, 1922.

Reynolds, John S. Reconstruction in South Carolina. Columbia, S. C. The State Company, publishers, 1905.

Rhodes, James Ford. History of the United States. 8 vols. New York, Harper and Brothers, 1893-1919. (Vols. V-VIII published by The Macmillan Company.) Vol. I used in this study.

Rhyne, Jennings J. Some Southern Cotton Mill Workers and Their Villages. Chapel Hill, N. C., The University of North Carolina Press, 1930.

Rice, John Holt. A Discourse delivered before the Literary and Philosophical Society of Hampden Sydney College, September 24, 1824. Published in The Literary and Evangelical Magazine, Jan. and Feb., 1825, Vol. VIII, Nos. 1 and 2.

—— Memoir of "Uncle Jack," Virginia Literary and Evangelical Magazine, Vol. X, 1826.

Roberts, Ezra C. Tuskegee's Academic Department, The Southern Workman, LIII (Dec., 1924), 537-45.

Rockefeller, John D., Sr. Random Reminiscences of Men and Events. New York, Doubleday, Page and Company, 1909. Published also in The Master Workers' Book. Garden City, N. Y., Doubleday, Page and Company, 1916. Published first in The World's Work, Vols. XVI and XVII, 1908-1909.

Roosevelt, Theodore. The Winning of the West. 4 vols. New York and London, G. P. Putnam's Sons, 1894-1910.

Rose, Wickliffe. School Funds in Ten Southern States. Nashville, Tenn., The Peabody Education Fund, 1909.

—— Southern Education Board: Activities and Results, 1904-1910. Publication No. 7, Southern Education Board, Washington, D. C., 1911.

Rosmer, Joseph. The Development of Secondary Education in the South, Proceedings of the Southern Association of Colleges and Secondary Schools, 1932. Birmingham, Ala., 1932.

Ross, Frank A., Fry, C. Luther, and Sibley, Elbridge. The Near East and American Philanthropy. A Survey conducted under the guidance of the General Committee of the Near East Survey. New York, Columbia University Press, 1929.

Rowland, Dunbar (ed.). Encyclopedia of Mississippi History. 2 vols. Vol. II. Madison, Wis., Selwyn A. Brant, 1907.

—— History of Mississippi, The Heart of the South. 2 vols. Vol. II. Chicago-Jackson, The S. J. Clarke Publishing Company, 1925.

Ruffner, William H. Article in the Educational Journal of Virginia, Aug., 1876.

—— The State Institute for White Teachers, University of Virginia, 1880. United States Bureau of Education, Circulars of Information No. 2, 1885. Washington, Government Printing Office, 1885.

Russell Sage Foundation. American Foundations for Social Welfare. Revised Edition, 1930. Compiled by Russell Sage Foundation Library. New York, 1930.

Sanford, Edward Terry. Blount College and the University of Tennessee. An historical address delivered before the Alumni Association and Members of the University of Tennessee, June 12, 1894. Published by the University of Tennessee.

Scott, Emmett Jay, and Stowe, Lyman Beecher. Booker T. Wash-
ington, Builder of a Civilization. Garden City, N. Y., Double-
day, Page and Company, 1916.
Secondary Education, University of Georgia Bulletin, Vol. XX,
No. 1 (Oct., 1919). Athens, Ga.
Sell, E. S. History of the State Normal School, Athens, Georgia.
Introduction by Henry C. White.
Seward, William H. An Autobiography; From 1801 to 1834. With
a Memoir of his Life, and Selections from his Letters, 1831-
1846. By Frederick W. Seward. New York, Derby and
Miller, 1891.
Shaw, Albert. The Conference on Southern Education, editorial,
Review of Reviews, XXIII (June, 1901), 646.
Sherman, William T. Memoirs of General William T. Sherman by
Himself. 2 vols. New York, D. Appleton and Company,
1875.
Shinn, Josiah H. History of Education in Arkansas. U. S. Bureau
of Education, Circular of Information No. 1, 1900. Washing-
ton, Government Printing Office, 1900.
Slaughter, Philip. The Virginian History of African Colonization.
Richmond, Va., Macfarlane and Ferguson, 1855.
Smith, C. Alphonso. Presbyterians in Educational Work in North
Carolina since 1813. Centennial Addresses, Synod of North
Carolina, Delivered at Alamance Church, Greensboro, N. C.,
October 7, 1913. Greensboro, N. C., Joseph J. Stone and
Company, n.d. (Pamphlet)
Smith, Edwin W. Aggrey of Africa: A Study in Black and White.
New York, Richard R. Smith, Inc., 1930.
Southern Education, No. 1 (March 12, 1903) to No. 20 (Dec. 21,
1903). Bureau of Investigation and Information, Southern
Education Board, Knoxville, Tenn.
Southern Literary Messenger (Aug., 1834, to June, 1864), I, 257;
II, 163. Richmond, Va., 1835-64.
Spears, John R. The American Slave-Trade: An Account of its
Origin, Growth and Suppression. New York, Charles Scrib-
ner's Sons, 1900.
Sprague, William Buell. Annals of the American Pulpit; Or Com-
memorative Notices of Distinguished American Clergymen of
Various Denominations, from the Early Settlement of the Coun-
try to the Close of the Year Eighteen Hundred and Fifty-five
with Historical Introductions. 9 vols. Vol. III. New York,
Robert Carter and Brothers, 1857-69.
State School Facts, Vol. V, No. 4 (Nov. 1, 1928). Raleigh, N. C.,
State Superintendent of Public Instruction.

Stephens, Edwin Lewis. Education in Louisiana in the Closing Decades of the Nineteenth Century. Reprinted from the Louisiana Historical Quarterly, Jan., 1933.

Stevens, William Bacon. Discourse delivered before the Georgia Historical Society at the celebration of their second anniversary, February 12, 1841. Collections of the Georgia Historical Society, Vol. II. Savannah, Ga., 1842.

Stewart, Cora Wilson. Moonlight Schools for the Emancipation of Adult Illiterates. New York, E. P. Dutton and Company, 1922.

Stiles, Charles Wardell. Decrease of Hookworm Disease in the United States. Reprint No. 1398 from the Public Health Reports, Vol. 45, No. 31 (Aug. 1, 1930).

Stoddard, James Alexander. Backgrounds of Secondary Education in South Carolina. University of South Carolina Extension Division, 1924.

Suggested Course for County Training Schools, The John F. Slater Fund, Occasional Papers, No. 18, 1917.

Sullivan, Mark. Our Times: Pre-War America. Vol. III. New York and London, Charles Scribner's Sons, 1930.

Talbot, Edith Armstrong. Samuel Chapman Armstrong: A Biographical Study. New York, Doubleday, Page and Company, 1904.

Taylor, Hoy. An Interpretation of the Early Administration of the Peabody Education Fund. Nashville, Tenn., George Peabody College for Teachers, 1933.

Temple, Oliver P. Notable Men of Tennessee from 1833 to 1875. Compiled by Mary B. Temple. New York, The Cosmopolitan Press, 1912.

Thompson, Ernest Trice. John Holt Rice, Union Seminary Review, XLIII (Jan., 1932), 175 ff.

Thompson, Henry T. The Establishment of the Public School System of South Carolina. Columbia, S. C., The R. L. Bryan Company, 1927. (Pamphlet)

Thorpe, Francis Newton. The Federal and State Constitutions. 7 vols. Washington, Government Printing Office, 1909.

Timberlake, Elsie. Did the Reconstruction Régime Give Mississippi Her Public Schools?, Publications of the Mississippi Historical Society, Vol. XII. University, Miss., 1912.

Trent, William P. English Culture in Virginia. Johns Hopkins University Studies, Seventh Series, Nos. V and VI. Baltimore, The Johns Hopkins Press, 1889.

—— The Influence of the University of Virginia upon Southern Life and Thought. Chap. XI in Herbert B. Adams's Thomas Jefferson and the University of Virginia. U. S. Bureau of

Education, Circular of Information No. 1, 1888. Washington, Government Printing Office, 1888.

Tyler, D. Gardiner, in General Robert E. Lee after Appomattox (ed. by Franklin L. Riley). New York, The Macmillan Company, 1922.

United States Bureau of Education, Circulars of Information, No. 2, 1885.

Waddel, John Newton. Memorials of Academic Life. Richmond, Va., Presbyterian Committee of Publication, 1891.

Waddell, Harrington. Dr. William Henry Ruffner, The Virginia Teacher, V (Oct.-Nov., 1924), 268-274.

Wade, John Donald. Augustus Baldwin Longstreet: A Study of the Development of Culture in the South. New York, The Macmillan Company, 1924.

Walker, N. W. Joseph Spencer Steward of Georgia: An Appreciation, The High School Journal, XVIII (Jan., 1935), 13-23.

Walter Barnard Hill, Chancellor of the University. Bulletin of the University of Georgia, Memorial Number, May, 1906.

Washington, Booker T. Address Delivered at the Opening of the Cotton States and International Exposition, At Atlanta, Ga., September 18, 1895, with a Letter of Congratulation from the President of the United States.

—— The Negro Problem. n. p., n. d.

—— Remarks, Unveiling of the Memorial Tablet in Memory of the Late William H. Baldwin, Jr., April 4, 1909, Tuskegee Institute, Ala.

—— Up From Slavery: An Autobiography. Garden City, N. Y., Doubleday, Page and Company, 1927.

Weatherford, W. D. The Negro from Africa to America. New York, George H. Doran Company, 1924.

Weathersby, William H. A History of Educational Legislation in Mississippi from 1798 to 1860. Chicago, The University of Chicago Press, 1921.

Weeks, Stephen B. History of Public School Education in Alabama. U. S. Bureau of Education, Bull., 1915, No. 12. Washington, Government Printing Office, 1915.

—— History of Public School Education in Arkansas. U. S. Bureau of Education, Bulletin, 1912, No. 27. Washington, Government Printing Office, 1912.

—— Southern Quakers and Slavery. Baltimore, The Johns Hopkins Press, 1896.

Welch, William H. The Services of Wickliffe Rose to Public Health. In memorial pamphlet, Wickliffe Rose, 1862-1931.

Wertenbaker, Thomas J. Patrician and Plebeian in Virginia. Charlottesville, Va., The Michie Company, 1910.

White, Robert Hiram. Development of the Tennessee State Educational Organization, 1796-1929. Kingsport, Tenn., Southern Publishers, Inc., 1929.

White, William S. The African Preacher. Philadelphia, Presbyterian Board of Publication, 1849.

Whitsitt, William H. Life and Times of Judge Caleb Wallace. Filson Club Publications No. 4. Louisville, Ky., 1888.

Williams, Samuel Cole. History of the Lost State of Franklin. Johnson City, Tenn., The Watauga Press, 1924.

Wilson, Henry. History of the Anti-Slavery Measures of the Thirty-Seventh and Thirty-Eighth United-States Congresses, 1861-64. Boston, Walker, Wise and Company, 1864.

Wilson, P. W. An Unofficial Statesman: Robert C. Ogden. Garden City, N. Y., Doubleday, Page and Company, 1924.

Wilson, Samuel Tyndale. A Century of Maryville College, 1819-1919. Maryville, Tenn., The Directors of Maryville College, 1916; 1919.

Wilson, Woodrow. Robert E. Lee: An Interpretation. Chapel Hill, N. C., The University of North Carolina Press, 1924.

Winship, A. E. Men of Achievement; David Bancroft Johnson, Journal of Education, CVI (Dec. 5, 1927), 545.

Winston, Robert W. Aycock: His People's Genius. Founders' Day Address, October 12, 1933, The University of North Carolina. Supplement to The Alumni Review, Vol. XXII, No. 2 (Nov., 1933).

Winthrop, Robert Charles, Jr., A Memoir of Robert C. Winthrop. Boston, Little, Brown and Company, 1897.

Winton, G. B. Sketch of Bishop Atticus G. Haygood. The John F. Slater Fund, Occasional Papers, No. 16, 1915.

Wise, Henry A. Address delivered in 1856 upon his retirement from Congress to accept the position of minister to Brazil. Published in the Report of the U. S. Commissioner of Education, 1899-1900, Vol. I. Washington, Government Printing Office, 1901.

Woodson, Carter Godwin. The Mis-Education of the Negro. Washington, The Associated Publishers, Inc., 1933.

—— The Rural Negro. Washington, The Association for the Study of Negro Life and History, Inc., 1930.

Woody, Thomas. Early Quaker Education in Pennsylvania. Teachers College, Columbia University, Contributions to Education, No. 105. New York, 1920.

Woofter, T. J., Jr., Black Yeomanry: Life on St. Helena Island. New York, Henry Holt and Company, 1930.

INDEX